The gestures of participatory art

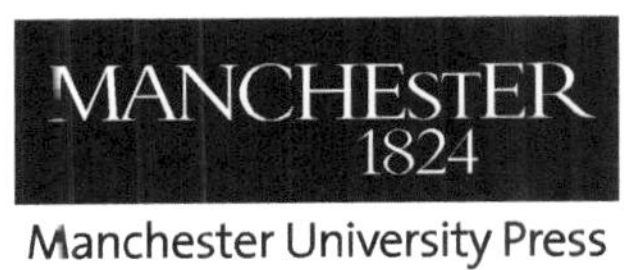

Manchester University Press

The gestures of participatory art

Sruti Bala

Manchester University Press

Published by Manchester University Press
Altrincham Street, Manchester M1 7JA, UK
www.manchesteruniversitypress.co.uk

British Library Cataloguing-in-Publication Data is available

ISBN 978 1 5261 0077 1 hardback
ISBN 978 1 5261 4812 4 paperback

First published by Manchester University Press in hardback 2018

This edition published 2020

Typeset by Servis Filmsetting Ltd, Stockport, Cheshire

To my current and former students,
with much affection

Contents

Acknowledgements

This study is the culmination of ideas, questions and observations that have been growing on me in the course of the last decade, and it would be contrary to the participatory ethos to claim them as entirely my own, although no one other than myself can be held responsible for their limitations.

I am grateful to the International Research Centre 'Interweaving Performance Cultures' at the Freie Universität in Berlin for a fellowship in 2014–15, which permitted me to write the bulk of this study. I thank all the colleagues and scholars at the Centre as well as the 'Aesthetics of Applied Theatre' Research Programme team for stimulating discussions and for their encouragement. I acknowledge the sabbatical leave periods and infrastructural support provided by the Amsterdam School of Cultural Analysis, the Amsterdam Centre for Globalisation Studies, the Netherlands Institute for Cultural Analysis and the Faculty of Humanities of the University of Amsterdam during various stages of research. I am grateful for the sustained support from colleagues at the University of Amsterdam, particularly in the Theatre Studies Department. My very special gratitude to Veronika Zangl for her patient reading and helpful feedback.

I would like to express my sincere appreciation to friends and colleagues from around the world who have helped me with comments, literature and suggestions on various aspects of the study, as well as inviting me to present work in progress: Aristita Albacan, B. Ananthakrishnan, Antônio Araújo, Stephen Barber, Julian Boal, Milena Dragićević Šešić, Erika Fischer-Lichte, Mark Fleishman, Eva Fotiadi, Hjalmar Jorge Joffre-Eichhorn, Richard Gough, Yvette Hutchison, Torsten Jost, Edit Kaldor, Anuradha Kapur, Annina

Klappert, Hanna Korsberg, Sara Matchett, Rabih Mroué, Hudita Mustafa, Nanako Nakajima, Helen Nicholson, Hannah Reich, Kati Röttger, Riku Saastamoinen, Ana Vujanovic, Matthias Warstat, Christel Weiler, the After-Performance Collective and the IFTR Feminist working group.

This study would not have been possible without the generosity and critical support of a number of artists and practitioners, whose work I deeply respect and hold in admiration. I thank Laia America Ribera Cañénguez and other members of Teatro Siluetas, Lina Issa, Aitana Cordero, Rebekka Reich, Oliver Gather, Radha Ramaswamy, Pilvi Takala, Walid Al-Alphy, Annette Krauss and Emily Schaeffer Omer-Man for help with sourcing documents and for their readiness to converse with me. Thanks also to all workshop participants and audience members who shared their personal experiences with me. Arjan Reinders' image of the small fish chasing the big fish aptly captures a participatory ethos for our times.

I am grateful to the peer reviewers at Manchester University Press, whose feedback on my first submission made me rewrite half the study, taking two more years in the process, pushing me to think through its core arguments with greater care.

I thank my parents Shri Devi and S. D. Bala, my aunt Lakshmi, my uncle, the late T. V. Subramanian, Ranganayaki (Paappakka), and my siblings Anand and Sharadha Smrithi for their unconditional affection and humour. Mona Chebbani, Rosemary Kikon, Shad Naved, John Ball, Niti Ranjan Biswas and Ambai have been extraordinarily uplifting friends and teachers. Esther Krop has provided the combination of love, support and unflattering honesty I could no longer imagine life without. Ilja has lightened and brightened life and taught me how one's own story is only ever told by weaving it into another's.

Parts of this study have been published in different earlier stages, although they have been revised substantially for this book: 'The Art of Unsolicited Participation' appeared in Tony Fisher and Eve Katsouraki (eds), *Performing Antagonism: Theatre, Performance, and Radical Democracy* (Basingstoke: Palgrave Macmillan, 2017) pp. 273–287; 'Applied Theatre und die Frage der Institutionskritik' appeared in Matthias Warstat et al. (eds), *Applied Theatre: Rahmen und Positionen* (Berlin: Theater der Zeit, 2017), pp. 274–288; 'Vectors of Participation in Theatre and Performance' appeared in *Theatre Research International* 3 (2012), pp. 236–248; 'What is the impact of theatre and performance?' appears in Maaike Bleeker et al. (eds), *Thinking Through Theatre: A Critical Companion to Performance* (London: Bloomsbury Methuen Drama, forthcoming 2018); and 'Outside and Onstage: Experiences of the lesbian feminist theater collective Teatro Siluetas from Guatemala and El Salvador', an interview with Laia America Ribera Cañénguez, appeared in Ashley Tellis and Sruti Bala (eds), *The Global Trajectories of Queerness: Re-thinking Same-Sex Politics in the Global South* (Leiden: Brill/Rodopi, 2015) pp. 241–262. I acknowledge the kind permission of the publishers.

Introduction

The mode of being of the new intellectual can no longer consist in eloquence, which is an exterior and momentary mover of feelings and passions, but in active participation in practical life, as constructor, organizer, 'permanent persuader' and not just a simple orator. (Gramsci, 1996, p. 10)

The paradox of participation

What does it mean to participate in art beyond the pre-determined roles and options allocated to us? This is the question that the following study grapples with. The issue is at once current and a matter of long-standing debate. Following decades of critical discussion in the field of participatory art, it is not entirely unfair to say that the concept has been found to have reached a point of exhaustion. Yet we are living in times when it is necessary to work towards new concepts, with nothing else to hand but hopelessly inadequate and worn-out ones. Such concepts, seemingly self-evident and clearly defined, strangely become unwieldy when described, confusing when experienced, contradictory when subject to analysis. Their inadequacy may be a consequence of their being co-opted, misused, unmoored or simply unresponsive to the world they are meant to speak to. Yet they cannot be conveniently discarded and replaced with other terms, for the problem is of course neither a matter of terminology alone, nor one of mere inconvenience. There are concepts that insist on being rethought and reconstructed in as much as the discontent with them seems inseparable from the attachment and possibility they offer. Participation is one such concept, at once a source of artistic, social and political hope and simultaneously the vulgar distortion of this hope into a form of profit-oriented governance and subjugation. The study joins the debate around participation at the stage of asking what next: what happens after or beyond the critique of the managerial absorption of participation, when neither grand theory nor the resort to particularism, neither the celebration of its utopian promises nor the criticism of its neoliberal disembowelment, seem to suffice. For even a critique of participation is predicated upon some form of participation, and even non-participation or any other category posited in its place remain equally fallible to the very same charges of critique.

Core to this investigation is the way in which the political premises underlying the call for participation are reimagined aesthetically. The questions that interest me most can be posed in different interconnected ways: first, how do artists and audiences respond to or take part in participatory art in unexpected, unscripted ways; how do the addressees of art take part in and partake of its making beyond the roles and options allocated to them? Second, in what ways does participatory art participate in civic, public life? These questions are interconnected by the vectors of participation. All attempts to answer one inevitably have to deal with the problems of the other. The question of an artwork's participation in public life is partly an expansion of the question of audience participation in art from the micro to the macro scale, since performance practices might, at one level, be viewed as microcosms of a broader social reality. They are not located outside of social reality, in a safely cordoned area marked as an aesthetic space, wherein they may reflect or represent the world outside, undisturbed or untouched by it; rather, these two dimensions are porous, connected by a vector shuttling back and forth between them, not merely transporting ideas from one dimension to the other, but affecting and transforming each of them in the process.

The present study undertakes an examination of participatory practices in contemporary theatre, performance and the visual arts, setting these against the broader social and political horizons of civic participation. It does not attempt to define the field as apparently given, but rather reconsiders the status of participation. My particular stake is in reflecting on participatory art both beyond a judgement of its social qualities as well as beyond the confines of format and devising. I am specifically interested in how participatory art might contribute to delicately altering the terms and conditions of participation, as well as those moments in which the withdrawal or refusal of participation might function as a critical form of participation. I am concerned with the ways in which artistic or cultural thought-practices participate in the social bases they emerge from or respond to, in the unorthodox reformulation of participation.

There is growing interest in the field of participatory art, attested by a vast range of experimental practices in cultural, art, educational and developmental contexts, accompanied by a surge of recent publications on the subject, as well as by its expanding place in university curricula and in the agendas of professional organizations. There is an equally vehement rejection of participatory practices, particularly in relation to their disregard for respected conventions and modes of experience in the arts, but more broadly, in terms of their appropriation and dilution into contemporary models of neoliberal, entrepreneurial governance. The real or attempted transformations in the relations and conventions of interaction between artwork and viewer, between spectators and performers, between authorship and reception, are met with responses ranging from enthusiasm to dismissal. Such responses cannot be explained away as differences in taste or aesthetic judgement, or liberally mediated through mid-way positions, as if it were only a matter of the right dosages of participation; they need to be contextualized and examined across diverse domains. I attempt a cross-disciplinary discussion of participation, bringing together examples from the field of applied and community theatre, performance art and participatory visual arts, investigating points of intersection with existing discussions in the social sciences on participation. Being a contextual question, the appraisal of the category of participatory art, in this wide sense, is accompanied by dangers even in modest generalization. Different disciplines have distinct institutional, epistemological and political stakes in their various conceptions of participation. I use the term participatory art as an umbrella term, yet I do so, not in order to insist on the stability of the category as a genre or defined form, but rather in order to problematize it and dwell on its antinomies, contingencies and contradictory features. I contend with the loaded term 'art', although the disciplinary formations and perspectives guiding my own journey are undeniably located in theatre and performance studies. Despite my repeated desire to expand the field, there are many kinds of participatory practices that I do not discuss at all, from participatory rituals in cultural performances to participation in the virtual electronic sphere. It is easy to offer the disclaimer that these are left out for the sake of providing an achievable framework for the study, but more difficult to retain a peripheral awareness of the ways their inclusion might have complicated its findings and constitutive frames.

The theorization of participation in the arts faces the challenge of transposing a concept with roots in the economic-political arena on to imaginative terrains. The Oxford English Dictionary cites the earliest usages of the term 'participation' in terms of two closely interlocked regimes: commerce and theology. Participation refers to 'commercial involvement in a company enterprise' on the one hand, as well as 'sharing in, or partnership or communion' on the other. 'Taking', 'giving' and 'having' seem to be the crucial connecting verbs here. Participation in the commercial sense became common in the late seventeenth century with reference to a financial involvement in a commercial enterprise. The much older Latin-derived theological use of participation dates back to the twelfth century, referring to being a recipient of or partaking in an act of divinity. In English the term flows between the connotations of taking part in or contributing to something, having a part or a share, in the form of ownership or territorial demarcation, or being (given) a part of or in something larger than what is one's own, staking a claim, pledging alliance. Many languages employ a nominalized form of the verb 'to take part' and distinguish between participation in the sense of 'taking part', which is usually the mere statement or assertion of participation, and 'having a part' or 'acquiring a part', suggesting a more active claim.[1] The term can thus be used descriptively as well as in the form of a demand of an entitlement, or indeed as an assertion of belonging to a greater common social entity. Participation could be a means towards a defined end, or an end in itself. It speaks to the forms and modalities of interaction between individuals and social entities, religious institutions or public goods, sometimes acting as a descriptor of these modalities and at other times placing demands on them.

Translated broadly to the arts, the notion of participation primarily indicates a realignment of the relationship between the makers and the recipients of the arts, whereby the 'recipients', however defined stake a claim to or assume a share in the enterprise of the arts. It is further underwritten by a general assumption that this realignment is beneficial or desirable for the arts and for the wider contexts in which they are located. These points of departure already demonstrate that ideas about participation in the arts remain indebted to its origin in the powerful discourses of shareholding participation in commerce and the provenances of participation in community formation. Just as the idea of shareholder participation marked the transition in ownership from feudalism to a bourgeoisie or a state-led economy, so participatory artistic practices might be regarded as reflecting a transition from the primacy of the artist as creator genius and sole proprietor of an artwork to an economy of redistributing authorship and creative functions in the arts. Just as the idea of participation in a societal sense indicates affiliation to a community or a shared idea, so participation in art might be indicative of a model of shared, dialogical and empathetic artistic practice. Yet the grafting of these discourses on to the artistic terrain is not without its difficulties and contradictions. If participation makes art more democratic, more social, more useful and relational, what remains then of the Kantian 'purposiveness without a purpose', so often regarded as the defining characteristic of the aesthetic realm? If participation in art is benign *a priori*, what remains to be interpreted or critically appreciated? If the terms of participation are already set by such authoritative forces, then doesn't participation in the arts require the greatest vigilance?

Artistic practices seem to have responded to these quandaries with an explosively wide range of different interpretations of participation: devised works involving scripted and stylized audience participation, as in immersive performances[2] or live art;[3] those that manipulate or steer the public or intervene in a situation without the public necessarily realizing that they are participants, as in invisible theatre;[4] delegated performance,[5] where members of the public are specially selected or invited to take part in the artwork or performance;

socially engaged community-based artistic practices; and projects that highlight the collaborative process of interaction and dialogue between artists and the public during various stages of the work, not necessarily only at the stage of its final presentation.[6] They may be short- or long-term, with spectators contributing spontaneously to an ephemeral event, or involve people from neighbourhoods or local communities, as hosts, interview partners, contributors of material, or in playing roles. Live and virtual events involving question-and-answer sessions, direct conversations between artists and audience members, interactive installation-based presentations, performances that involve following instructions on headphones and making dance moves in the street, a museum exhibition inviting visitors to donate items of their own, collective readings, video games that generate scenarios based on images uploaded by players, intermedial storytelling events, do-it-yourself or, for that matter, don't-do-it-yourself artworks, citizen journalism, peoples' juries, crowd-sourced works, community kitchens, flash mobs, audio-tours, bus trips, assemblies, marketplaces, speed-dates, lottery draws, reality shows, visits to the homes of strangers: the list of means of invoking and inviting participation in and through artworks can hardly be exhaustively categorized, as this risks becoming outdated, with new formats emerging in response to distinct circumstances. The category of participatory art is thus by no means confined to the literal fact of audiences taking part in an artwork. It remains pliable and is, as has often been pointed out, invoked for very different ends and in very contradictory ways (Nicholson, 2013, p. 114). 'Participation' can refer to many types of experiences; it is a historical rather than a static concept, implying that participatory art is not unified by formal characteristics, and can be traced to vastly divergent art-historical traditions (Kraynak, 2007, p. 231). It can be a manner of doing, a manner of perceiving, and a manner of perceiving doing.

I do not attempt a systematic or historical analysis of participatory art as a genre, since I am less invested in outlining the possible terms or criteria of genre formation, and more intrigued by the questions that participatory art, when posed as genre, is seen as being able to ask or address: problems related to its institutional affiliations and entanglements, the question of its societal impact, the hierarchies of participation, the relationship between embodied and discursive articulations of participation, the relationship between participation and non-participation. By emphasizing the operations that participatory art practices are used to carry out, I follow the insight of the cultural theorist Raymond Williams, who argued that certain concepts are not understood by way of a genre or terminological discussion, i.e. by analysing and comparing different definitions according to the presence or absence of certain formal traits, but that the meanings of a given concept are 'inextricably bound up with the problems it was being used to discuss' (1983, p. 15). Williams thus questions the assumption that concepts such as culture are expressions of, or indeed determined by, broader economic, social and political forces; instead he proposes culture as a form of material production. In the following I mobilize Williams's proposition as a way of understanding how the operations and vocabularies of participation in the arts are intermeshed with participation in the social and political sense. To do this, it is necessary to closely examine how artistic practices interpret and give life to the concept of participation in historically and contextually specific ways. These might be at the level of formal experimentation, or in the ways in which the artistic practice interacts with or intervenes in a given social environment, or in the mode of navigating the boundaries between the aesthetic and the non-aesthetic, the artistic and the quotidian. In this regard, I do not make a distinction between an active, oppositional, antagonistic participation and a passive, receptive, cohesive (non)-participation, nor do I try to monitor what is or is not a properly participatory form of art (Harpin and Nicholson, 2017). Applause, audience laughter, silence, passing interactions between performers and spectators may all be part of any form of audience participation in the broadest sense. I am interested in moments when such phenomena become foundational to a certain artistic practice, when such seemingly ordinary participatory gestures carry an unexpected potential for realigning the terms of participation.

The question of this study arises from a paradox. The demand for participation intensifies when participation is denied to us. Yet we are inclined to refuse participation when it is demanded of us. If we are only able to participate in ways that are already deemed acceptable or proper, then, sooner or later, our participation becomes an instrument of our own subjugation and pacification rather than a means of freedom. Participation, even in the guise of non-participation, becomes necessary to resist the imperative of participation. The visual cultural philosopher Eyal Weizman elegantly describes the paradox of participation as 'the problem of equally practicing it and avoiding it' (2011, p. 10). Participatory art is by no means exempt from this paradox. In some senses one might claim that the field of participatory art emerges historically from artistic relations to the paradox of equally seeking out and disavowing participation.

Divergent legacies of participatory art

The examples analysed in this study are drawn from three main domains of participatory art: applied or community-based performance, immersive performance and contemporary visual art. These domains each evoke distinct genealogies and modes of conceptualizing participation, and they each have their own milestones as reference points. The question of the histories of participatory artistic practices becomes complicated for several reasons: the diversity of practices, different understandings of concepts, their vastly different disciplinary routes, national and regional differences, as well as distinctive processes of institutionalization. To summarily and ahistorically leave aside these differences and gather any and every artistic or cultural practice in which participation plays a role under the rubric of 'participatory art' can be misleading, risking that the term disintegrates rather than expands as a result of its diversity and ubiquity. Yet the diversity of genealogies of participatory art itself demonstrates that participation in relation to theatre and performance has meant many different things in different historical moments, and that it is a polyvalent category. Participatory practices may be found in all regions and across all historical periods or artistic domains, but this does not mean that participatory art becomes a universal category. The qualities and characteristics associated with participatory art are nevertheless historically bound. This history might be usefully approached not in terms of points of origin but in terms of how participatory practices have been regarded as offering possibilities for realigning the relationship of art to society. This too needs qualification, as the very idea of art being separate from the societal has its own history and geography. What are the specific disciplinary concerns around participation in each of the domains of community-based art, immersive performance and contemporary visual arts? What are the recurring questions to which participatory practices have appeared as offering responses?

Reading across these domains, it is remarkable that scholarship on participation in one sub-field does not necessarily take notice of developments in other sub-fields. Participatory forms of educational theatre tend to be assumed to belong to a different discursive universe from one-to-one experiential performance practices or the participation of visitors in a museum installation. Yet in the process of researching this study, I became aware of a significant number of common concerns between these domains. In terms of their histories, what stands out most are the zigzag currents that run between artistic experimentation and processes of social-political transformation, or, as political philosopher Gerald Raunig has argued, of 'practices emerging in neighbouring zones, in which transitions, overlaps and concatenations of art and revolution become possible for a limited time, but without synthesis and identification' (2007, pp. 17–18). The idea that participatory practices emerge from 'neighbouring zones' or from the thresholds between artistic and social-political concerns is fitting. Their objectives may vary, from a more pragmatic search for alternatives to frontal narrative staging devices to an explicitly political search for ways to alter the grammar of people's relations to issues of significance to the broader society (Katsiaficas, 2004). In some cases, the need for participatory work is motivated by a striking self-consciousness and desire to reflect on artists' positionality and privileges, to call attention to the assumptions underlying certain forms of presentation and representation, possibly through an awareness of feminist, postcolonial and anti-racist critiques and demands for a self-conscious avowal of art's interdependence and inseparability from its external conditions (Jackson, 2008, pp. 143–144). In other cases, the choice of participatory forms may be a trendy mirroring of modes of participation in economic life, characterized by a feverish quest for the new, the innovative, the risky (Raunig, Ray and Wuggenig

2011). The intersections between historical and artistic periods are uneven but not accidental. They make it evident that the meaning of participatory art, or what is defined as participatory, radically changes under different historical circumstances, and that these meanings are usually part of a larger narrative of how art engages with society and politics (Bishop in Barok, 2009).

The grand question of the relationship between art and society and politics can be framed in slightly more modest terms as the relationship between artists or artistic practices and audiences. In the field of applied or community-based theatre and performance, the concern with questions of popular participation and theatrical citizenship in the twentieth century is often traced to Bertolt Brecht. For Brecht, the realignment of the relationship between performers and spectators was simultaneously a reimagining of the relationship of art to society. He envisaged the critical participation of audiences in theatre as a means of transforming the merely entertaining or 'culinary' functions of art. For Brecht, it was less a matter of making audiences get up from their seats and 'do' something and more a question of altering the dramaturgy of theatre in order for audiences to adopt a different attitude (*Haltung*). Similarly, political theatre cultures around the world in the second part of the twentieth century looked for a theatrical language and an aesthetic that could be adequate to the realities of nation formation following the end of colonial rule. Participatory practices often formed the zone of concatenation or overlap between the quest for modernity and the quest to recover lost traditions. The antecedents of participatory performance in the domain of community-based and applied arts can be traced to what Eugene van Erven calls the 'counter-cultural, radical, anti- and post-colonial, educational and liberational theatres of the 1960s and 1970s' (2001, p. 1). This might pertain to both the post-independence political theatres in the Global South as well as to the surge of performance art, happenings and artistic activism in European and North American contexts. They each have their own distinct legacies, but can all be termed participatory in terms of their quest for artistic forms that could accommodate a variety of modes of participation that were not necessarily pre-determined by the makers of the artworks alone.

Similar modes of expanding participation can be found in the transactions between theatre, therapy, education, labour, civil rights or ecological struggles. In the field of educational theatre, for instance, theatrical histories and educational histories converge in specific ways, demonstrating how educational theatre movements in different parts of the world placed audience participation at the centre of theatrical practices, developing 'innovative methodologies that blurred the boundaries between audiences and performers' (Nicholson, 2011, p. 199). In many instances this involved forging long-term alliances with counter-cultural movements, to be able to pursue educational goals even in times of authoritarian rule, travelling and performing widely, conducting workshops, inviting writers in local languages to contribute plays or co-creating works on socially relevant topics (Fernandez, 1996; Roces and Edwards, 2010, p. 45). Participation here is as much about taking theatre to rural or urban-peripheral community life as about inviting young adults to participate in and be exposed to art workshops.

In the terrain of immersive performance, the threshold between artistic and social-political concerns is often to be found in the highlighting of the individual spectator and of the stylized and intimate one-to-one encounter with its visceral, multi-sensorial dimensions (Machon, 2013; White, 2012). In a broader disciplinary genealogy, branching out to cultural anthropology, an immersive experience can be said to refer to a range of cultural practices, involving an intense, engrossed physical and emotional presence of all concerned, often taking place outside of art institutions and spaces (Singer, 1959; Turner, 1975). Each of these understandings of immersive performance points to important distinctions and separate histories. Their contours and their terminology have evolved differently according to region or art-historical tradition. The emphasis on the individual experience of the spectator might, on the one hand, be derived from the post-dramatic and performative turns in the arts, i.e. a shift away from textual, dramatic sources towards embodied performance, to the extent that the turn away from the text is also always a turn towards the audience (Lehmann, 2005, p. 5). In doing away with the authority of the dramatic text and with narrative devices, post-dramatic forms such as immersive performance elicit an alternative dramaturgy of addressing the audience, often deliberately involving spectators in the action on stage, bringing them into close physical contact with the staged environment, or directly evoking 'the real' in the framework of theatrical action. There is no longer any security of the performance being a fictional event in the mode of the 'as-if' (Lehmann, 2005, p. 103). This might be accompanied by a disregard for the solemnity of theatrical conventions, with the spectatorial distance being substituted by a staged environment suggesting a party, rehearsal atmosphere, an intimate setting, or a shared or quasi-ritualistic space into which audiences can enter, as if entering a space of leisure and relaxation (Lehmann, 2005, pp. 122–123).

In what has come to be known as performance art since the 1960s, participation assumes the specific sense of a multi-directional, multi-sensorial and visceral communication between performers and spectators in a highly stylized setting that troubles the boundary between the artistic and the quotidian spheres. In the anthropological genealogies of immersive cultural performances, on the other hand, this boundary crossing has been expressed through the concept of the liminal. Victor Turner (1975) used the architectural notion of the limen, the threshold or sill linking one space to another, as a concept for thinking the process and site of creating a sense of 'communitas' between people, especially in rituals marking rites of passage such as initiation rites or sacred ceremonies and performances. Such liminal events demand a participatory immersion of all concerned for a specific period of time within a dedicated space, allowing for a transition or transformation from one life stage to another.[7]

The border between the space demarcated as aesthetic space and the world it is surrounded by can move in ways that affect the registers of participation. Modes and conventions of performance can, for instance, be brought to bear upon legal and political settings, as a medium for staging political transformations and events of public participation. Examples of this are the profoundly theatrical frames of historical events such as the Truth and Reconciliation Commission in South Africa (Cole, 2009), or the public gatherings and participatory actions in the 1990s of groups such as H.I.J.O.S in Argentina following the years of military dictatorship (Holmes, 2009; Taylor, 2003). Not only is the border between theatrical action and legal-political action called into question in such phenomena, but also the distinct separation of the spheres of production and reception or of performance and spectatorship are troubled.

The legacy of participation in the visual arts reveals yet another kind of entanglement between artistic and social-political spheres. The demand for a radical break with elitist art institutions at the beginning of the twentieth century brought with it a wide range of experiments and programmatic shifts, often deploying participatory practices and attempting to reach out to people in their everyday lives. Tom Finkelpearl argues that the prominence of participatory forms in what he terms public art emerged from a confluence of local political struggles and international influences (2013, p. 49). In the case of the Futurists and Paris Dada, the invocation of the participatory generated what was then a radical break with traditional formats of spectatorship, through performances on the streets or the adoption of popular entertainment forms (Bishop, 2012, p. 47). In Central and South America in the 1960s and 1970s, participatory artistic practices called for an engagement with marginalized social groups and people without a voice in public life. Similarly, in Asian and African contexts, it implied close ties between artists and civil rights and nation-building movements, as well as with feminist and indigenous movements. In Eastern Europe in the 1970s and 1980s, under the conditions of the Cold War, an engagement with participation was a matter of establishing trustworthy publics, who were not allied with the ruling powers (Bishop, 2012, p. 130). In the post-1989 context, under expanding privatization and economic liberalization, the valorization of participatory technologies and formats in the art world can be regarded as complementary to a governmental biopolitics, where participation may not be a staking of a people's claim to ownership or control but a form of government through self-regulation (Lorey, 2012, pp. 52–53). In this context, participation becomes not what people demand from the ruling powers but what is demanded of the people by the ruling powers.

This sketch of the different routes through which the notion of participation is summoned, spanning across the visual arts and theatre and performance, is by no means sufficient to make any comparative historical claims. Yet this much is immediately evident: the antecedents of participatory art in the twentieth century can be read as accounts of how art positions itself in response to societal questions around participation. Instead of looking for overarching commonalities in form and expression in all these instances, one could turn the tables and ask what participatory art sets itself apart from, or to what questions it proposes itself as having answers. To what can the emergence of a participatory aesthetic be seen as responding? Viewed from this angle, the legacies of participatory art do not reflect or mirror their social environments but rather diffract them, at best attempting to offer a critique, intervene in shifting the underlying tenets of the field, and at worst, making the neoliberal socio-economic underpinnings blatantly apparent (Haraway, 2004, p. 70).

The metaphor of diffraction is applicable to a genealogical appraisal of participatory art in so far as the claim to and justification of a certain conception of participation simultaneously marked a distancing or differentiation from existing conventions or understandings. Brecht's participatory learning plays (*Lehrstücke*) were propounded as a move away from what was perceived as the bourgeois convention of segregating spectators and performers, or directors and actors. Similarly, Augusto Boal's concept of the 'spect-actor' – the spectator who intervenes on stage as an actor – was proposed as a system of dissociation from the Aristotelian conception of the theatre. The performative turn that strongly influenced participatory performance art represented a turn away from the primary emphasis on texts and language in humanities scholarship and a turn towards embodied knowledge and practice, thus a reconception of the boundary between the sphere of artistic production and reception, as well as an expansion of the scope of performance outside of institutionalized artistic realms. The happenings and activist performance art of the 1960s marked a significant departure from conventional assumptions of what constitutes an artwork, foregrounding process and ephemeral experience in place of a finished work. A call for non-hierarchical and collective artistic working processes was often born out of the impulse to critically counter institutional frameworks that positioned the artist as creative genius and unique author. An antagonistic, dissenting form of artistic participation often grew out of a rejection of the cynicism of a top-down promotion of participatory citizenship.

Philosophical or political questions thus become diffracted on to the register of the aesthetic. This partly explains why it is difficult to pinpoint the characteristics of participatory art as a genre or in formal terms, for even when issues such as engagement with audiences or spectatorship might appear as a common feature of all participatory artforms, the form of this engagement with spectatorship can vary from the affirmative to the adversarial, or from an assertion of artistic autonomy to a complete rejection of any autonomy.

The gestures of participation

In the process of working on the concept of participation in, through and away from its exhaustion, other concepts unexpectedly emerge as helpful friends. In this study, the notion of the gesture has proven most valuable in comprehending the paradoxes of participation, whereby the demand for it is almost always accompanied by its refusal. I argue that participatory practices are best appreciated in the register of the gestural. As a unit of theatrical or performative action, the gesture is simultaneously an expression of an inner attitude as well as a social habitude. It extends beyond the stage of theatre or performance into the sphere of civic life. It therefore offers a possibility for critically linking the legacies and aesthetic debates on participatory art to larger issues of citizenship, democratic praxis, collective action and social justice. I also propose that the concept of the gesture not only speaks to the contemporary problems and critiques of participation, but also situates these practices in disciplinary terms at the juncture between the visual and performing arts. I envisage this possibility by a reading of the concept of gesture as situated in between image, speech and action, no longer image but not yet act, not strictly within the coordinates of language but also not wholly external to it. I suggest that the concept of gesture might be a rewarding way of theorizing participatory practices at the crossroads of the visual and performing arts. Such a conceptualization can, I hope, avoid two common pitfalls in scholarship on participatory art, namely the problem of explaining participation through assessing and measuring impact on the one hand, or, conversely, the problem of restricting the discussion to formal, aestheticized, medium-specific lines on the other.

The concept of the gesture has proven productive in engaging with the unsolicited, unruly and counter-intuitive aspects of participation that continually intrigue me in this study. As a unit of theatrical or performative action, usually defined as a stance or movement of the body as a whole or a specific body part, it is simultaneously an expression of an emotional condition or an inner attitude, as well as a social habitude. It thus extends beyond the stage of theatre or performance into the sphere of public, civic life. It is a concept derived from aesthetic theory, referring to a central component of the body, language and cultural communication, and simultaneously a concept with social and political ramifications (Mauss, 1973; Wulf and Fischer-Lichte, 2010). A wide array of philosophical reflections on gesture, both in continental European philosophy as well as in several non-Western traditions, support such a multi-layered understanding of the concept as simultaneously embodied and abstract, physical and social, provisional and indicative in its enactment and embodiment, but never fully determined by it. While it would be impossible to offer anything close to a comprehensive review within the framework of this study, I have drawn inspiration from different sources to suggest how participatory art is characterized by gestural qualities. The Brechtian notion of the *Gestus* is one such source, understood as a physical manner of carrying or bearing the body that is equally a social attitude, theorized and sharpened in Walter Benjamin's indispensable companion essay on Brecht's gestures (Benjamin, 1966; Willett, 1974). My mobilization of the concept of gesture is also close to recent approaches to cultural activism, especially scholarship on civic protest. To give one example: in a special issue of *Contemporary Theatre Review* entitled 'Theatre, Performance and Activism: Gestures towards an Equitable World', a number of contributions employ gesture 'as a pivot for examinations of the body in protest' (Hughes and Parry, 2015, p. 302). The editors categorize these into a range of 'gestural repertoires', namely gestures intersecting the public and the private realms, gestures of labour and care work, gestures of mobility and migration, and collective gestures (2015, p. 309). While I do not directly employ such gestural repertoires, they resonate with my reading of participatory art to the extent that they indicate a constant shuttling between art's aesthetic and sociopolitical dimensions, and the intersections between individual and collective forms of embodiment.

While the concept of the gesture speaks to the contemporary problems and critiques of participation, it also crucially situates these practices in disciplinary terms at the juncture between the visual and performing arts. Shannon Jackson keenly observes in her study *Social Works* (2011) that the experiments of crossing the deemed limits of the aesthetic and the social have very different expressions across various domains of the arts. Whereas participatory art in the visual art context seeks out tropes, figures and methods from the performing arts, it can be conversely observed that participatory theatre and performance practices, especially in the institutionalized circuits, increasingly look for inspiration in installation, film, architectural and conceptual art. Jackson rhetorically describes this phenomenon as

> an experimental chiasmus across the arts: a movement toward painting and sculpture underpins post-dramatic theatre, but a movement toward theatre also underpins post-studio art. In such a chiasmus, breaking the traditions of one medium means welcoming the traditions of another. (2011, p. 6)

The rhetorical figure of the chiasmus (literally, 'crosswise arrangement') is characterized by two distinct clauses balanced against each other by a structural reversal. The reference to a chiasmus suggests that the aesthetics of participatory art might be located somewhere at the juncture between the visual arts and the performing arts; or in other words, if one would simplify these domains to their very basic units, at the intersection between the *image* and the *act*. Theatre and performance theory as well as art history have a concept for this intersection: the concept of the gesture. In comparison to the static image or the tableau, the gesture is a dynamic concept: it indicates a transition, often involving a bodily movement, literally a gesticulation, which bears or suggests meaning (from the Latin *gestare*, to carry or bear, German *Gebärde*), and marks a socially recognizable form of conduct (from the Latin *gerere*, to conduct oneself). On the other hand, in comparison to the theatrical unit of the act, gesture can be read as a static concept: it is a condensation or decomposition of an act, close to the term 'gist', i.e. essence. It is no longer an image, but not yet quite an act; it is an act that is condensed into a hint, a suggestion.

By framing participatory art as gestural, as more than an image or a representation, yet not quite an act or action – rather as an indicative, decomposed, interrupted move that extends beyond itself – I suggest that the concept of gesture might be a rewarding way of theorizing participation. Perhaps the force of the participatory lies not in a causal relationship between audience participation in the theatre and people's participation in civic life, but in a relationship of simultaneity, one gesturing (to) the other. The sociologist Marcel Mauss proposed in his 1935 essay entitled 'The Techniques of the Body' that the relationship of physical gestures to the social is not successive but simultaneous (1973, pp. 85–86). An individual bodily technique of walking or making a fist is, he argues, a gesture that is simultaneously corporeal and social-cultural. As I move in this study from broader discussions of institution or social impact to observing concrete moments of delicate participation or categorical refusals of participation, I am interested in how representation and movement, a given form and an imagined form, are interconnected through gesture, how the interdependence between formal and informal gestures of participation is performed and made observable.

The word gesture is also etymologically related to the Latin word *jacēre*, 'to lie', in the sense of ordering or arranging parts of the body, in support of and giving shape to a thought or attitude. In this sense, gestures often have the role of supporting thoughts through bodily movements rather than representing actions on their own. This is most often claimed in relation to the hand or facial gestures that accompany speech. In Giorgio Agamben's reading, gesture has no relationship to causality or utility; it is a means without ends and because it is removed from any use or representational function, it can allow us to see what otherwise becomes invisible when attached to referentiality (Agamben, 1993). Gesture thus involves the disruption or interruption of an action, its breaking down into repeatable and quotable units that conceal as much as they reveal (Benjamin, 1966; Weber, 2008, p. 98). They can range from being codified, ritualized and culturally specific to being expressive, free, emotive and non-formalizable. This oscillation between the formal, codified characteristics of the gesture and its informal, interstitial articulations is repeatedly found in artistic practices that pursue participatory methods or aims. Rather than claiming any absolute subversive potential of participatory practices, I argue for interpreting participation in performance as a provisional and suggestive, but never fully determined element. These gestures of participation in performance, however, indicate possibilities for reconfiguring civic participation in public spaces in unexpected ways, putting less emphasis on direct opposition and instead seeking a variety of modes of resisting co-optation, through unsolicited, vicarious or delicate gestures of participation. Sometimes the performance of a gesture is merely symbolic, at other times gesture may become event (Butler, 2014b).

Outline of this study

How, then, does one study the gestures of participatory art? Where are they to be found and traced? The cases examined in this book are drawn from my own horizon of exposure in the last decade, which can in no way claim to be comprehensive in scope or international outreach, but which nevertheless reflects the privilege of living in and moving between different countries and cultures, from which I have benefited in countless ways. The choice of these cases is most pertinently related to the possibilities available to me, allowing me to become familiar with the projects in some depth, and to gain the trust, support and intellectual camaraderie of those involved, which has proven indispensable to the study.

Chapter 1 begins with the question of institutional critique in relation to participatory art. What is the place of institutional critique in relation to participatory performance? Where might institutional critique be located and how is it practised? I reflect on the challenges and conundrums of institutional critique, exploring the formation of participatory art forms, specifically community-based, applied art, as emergent from the critique of mainstream art institutions. I inquire into modalities of institutional critique which foreground questions of participation or non-participation, and examine their disciplinary configurations within the arts. I compare a number of approaches to institutional critique: the institutional affiliations of a community-based theatre project from Darfur, Sudan, a flash mob performance by an Israeli activist group protesting a Cape Town Opera production in Tel Aviv Opera House, and a breaching experiment by visual artist Pilvi Takala of trying to enter Disneyland dressed as Snow White, among others. Sometimes institutions can be usefully manoeuvred and hijacked to serve progressive causes. At other times they need to be challenged and boycotted. Sometimes the gesture of critique consists in building counter-institutions, and sometimes in fleeing them. Institutional critique, understood as the explicit use of an artistic practice to interrogate, oppose or break out of art institutional frameworks, has very asymmetrical trajectories and conditions across the world and across domains. I argue that they alert us to the changing institutional conditions that allow or restrict participation, exposing not just the rules or norms of a certain institution, but also, or equally, the rules of its specific traditions of institutional critique.

Chapter 2 addresses the relationship between participatory art and the concept of 'impact'. I investigate the assumptions around impact in relation to participatory art, as well as the critical and methodological challenges of thinking the impact of a work of art. Using the 2012 Spanish-language production *Afuera: lesbianas en escena* (*Outside: Lesbians on Stage*) by the theatre collective Teatro Siluetas from Guatemala and El Salvador as a point of departure, the chapter reflects on a number of debates in theatre and performance scholarship pertaining to assessing and evaluating impact in relation to the question of participation. I critically engage with the field of evidence-led impact studies in the arts, particularly those that seek to prove and rationalize the benefits of the arts and demonstrate them as worthy of receiving structural or financial support. I situate the debate on the usefulness or non-utility of participatory art in relation to social science scholarship relating to the ascendancy of 'participation' in the context of international development. I propose that the internal dynamics and modalities of participation cannot be entirely viewed at a remove from their external modes of circulation. I suggest that it is worthwhile to extend the kinds of activities considered as relevant to a participatory aesthetic, to not only analyse performances as distinct works, but to place them in a longer-term aesthetic continuum with workshops, rehearsals, after-talks, meetings with artists, and other para-theatrical events. The chapter grapples with the question of how to discuss impact in relation to participatory art without it being mortgaged into a matter of quantifiable impact alone.

In Chapter 3, I closely examine one workshop setting using the methodological framework of the 'theatre of the oppressed' in the context of a political party-led initiative to run a women's empowerment programme in rural south India, launched in 2013. My analysis focuses on identifying instances and moments of unsolicited participation in a theatrical format explicitly defined as participatory. I question the status of participatory art in the developmental context as forging cohesion and understanding among participants, and instead turn to its ambiguities. The analysis of participation thus seeks to link the macro-dimension of participation in social development with the micro-dimension of community theatre practice. Of particular interest is how participation occurs by way of a nuanced range of reactions, with functions ranging from the disruptive to the ameliorative. The case study calls for methodological attention to ancillary activities that take place at the margins of the theatre event. These phenomena indicate that community participation often assumes unsolicited forms, at times defiant, at times cooperative, at times evasive; it is no straightforward task to classify them as either subversive or subsidiary to the established formats of participation. They are neither interested in offering scholars legible evidence in order to be able to produce a neat account of a certain genre, nor in reassuring theatre practitioners of the efficacy of their methods. I plead for attention to those gestures of participation that may not find their way into discursive iteration, because they may arise out of the very impossibility of such an iteration in language or in formal conventions.

Chapter 4 follows two conceptually inspired performance projects by the Amsterdam-based Lebanese artist Lina Issa, *Where We Are Not* (2009) and *If I Could Take Your Place?* (2010 – ongoing). These works explore the question of what it means to take someone else's place, to participate in someone's life by doing something on their behalf, in their name and in the mode of 'as if'. The commonly held rule of participatory art, which involves audience participation in an already devised or open performance setting, is reversed in Issa's work, either because it is the artist who seeks to participate in a situation that relates to someone else's daily life, or conversely because others are invited to take her place, with audiences witnessing and imagining this process and participating by proxy. By analysing how this vicarious participation unfolds, I foreground the spectatorial parameters of participation, which refer not only to the modes of activating participation, but also deem it the task of participation to make a given situation worthy and deserving of spectators. Here again, the critical theorization of participation calls for an interweaving of the aesthetic with the social or political. Issa's playful performances of standing in for others point to larger questions of what it means to participate in collective processes of imagining and transforming selfhood. I suggest that the solidarity in the gesture of vicarious participation lies not so much in recognizing and finding the so-called 'other' or in respecting and celebrating differences, but rather in being prepared and willing to dispossess oneself of the fixity of one's ideas of the self, a potentially transformative gesture.

Chapter 5 dwells on an installation-based project titled *Nomad City Passage* (2005–09) by the German scenographic and visual artists Rebekka Reich and Oliver Gather, in which visitors are invited to spend one night in a tent in one of several unconventional urban sites, such as the top floor of a high-rise building, a public square in a commercial district or inside a shopping mall. My analysis focuses on how common-sense assumptions around audience participation in theatre and performance theory are called into question by the artwork's foregrounding of sleep as a mode of participation. The delicacy of this is evidenced in the ambivalence of sleep in a scenically prepared setting, oscillating between being an intense, active, dynamic experience on the one hand, and a non-performance, an absence of activity on the other. I suggest that audience participation in the artwork and the artwork's participation in urban spaces differ in significant ways from sociological and political concepts of participation. Where social theory conceives of civic participation in terms of being a part of some larger entity or social unit, the aesthetics of *Nomad City Passage* emphasizes participation in a counter-intuitive way: it becomes possible to participate precisely because of its fleeting and ephemeral conditions, because of its *not* being a part of some shared community ideal.

A feminist impulse is important in one way or another to the selection and analysis of all the artistic practices in this study. Many of the cases discussed prominently involve women, whose choice of participatory methods and approaches to artistic and social engagement is guided by a firm belief in its emancipatory potentials, an emancipation that necessarily and inevitably intersects with questions of gender and gendered power relations. My insistence on the need for the genre of participatory art to remain conceptually open and unfixed is motivated by a feminist critique of genres being not only 'genus' (origin, repository, affiliation), but also 'generative', what Jacques Derrida and Avital Ronell describe as 'a sort of participation without belonging – a taking part in without being part of' (Derrida and Ronell, 1980, p. 59). Affiliation to a given type of participatory practice is thus never far from exceeding those same terms of affiliation: a fundamentally emancipatory gesture, I hope.

Participatory practices pose a number of challenges to existing modes of inquiry in the arts. How should the relation between researcher and researched be realigned, if the researcher is required to participate in an event, obliged to step outside any assumed possible safe outsider position and relate a performance or a certain practice to her own horizon of experience? How can artistic practices from the past be accessed, where there was no possibility of involvement of the researcher as participant observer? Given that participatory works often recalibrate the relationship between process and outcome the question arises as to what should be included or regarded as relevant to the practice; what is the status of a workshop in comparison to a performance in front of an audience, or as opposed to an unexpected intervention in the streets; how should attendant issues such as documentation be taken into account? How should the perlocutionary after-effects of participation be traced, not just on individual participants but also in terms of appraising an artistic practice as social or political praxis? In each of the cases I examine, these questions repeatedly arise, in ways that are inseparable from the central concerns of the study. Methodology is thus not a technical, ancillary task to the main problem of rethinking the concept of participation, but profoundly tied to its theoretical assumptions and axiological visions.

I was involved in several, but not all, of the cases discussed in the study as a participant observer in the workshop or rehearsal process, as a casual passer-by or as a 'regular' audience member with a ticket. In other cases I had to reconstruct a performance and interpret its participatory aesthetics on the basis of documentary evidence, conversations and interviews with other participants, and extensive discussions with the artists. The choice of appropriate methods for collecting and evaluating material was often largely influenced and altered by suggestions and feedback from the artists or other participants. Yet despite the fact that the relations between researcher and researched, or between subject and object of study, had to be repeatedly and necessarily questioned, this is not a practice-led study or a model for participatory action research. A critical and heterodox reflection on the concept of participation and its paradoxes in the arts remains the core objective of this investigation. In the spirit of Antonio Gramsci's quest for intellectual rigour, cited in the epigraph to this introduction, I am in search of ways, however small, to reimagine and reclaim participation at this particular moment of time, not for the sake of eloquence but as a means of collective organizing, constructing, persuading and moving. It is my conviction that participation challenges us to think through this impasse of enabling its potentials beyond the limitations of its administration.

Notes

1 This distinction holds, for instance, for the German terms *Teilnahme* ('taking part in') and *Teilhabe* ('having a part/partaking of'). In my mother tongue Tamil, there are further valences emphasizing a willed action such as *panku perukka* ('to acquire a part') or *paṅkērka* ('to take on a part').

2 The term is used mostly in northern Europe: examples of recent scholarship using the concept of immersive performance are Josephine Machon's *Immersive Theatres* (2013), Gareth White's *Audience Participation in the Theatre* (2013) and Adam Alston's *Beyond Immersive Theatre* (2016), which deal with performances in the UK; Liesbeth Groot-Nibbelink's dissertation 'Nomadic Theatre' (2015), which deals with experiential and immersive performance, though it is not primarily interested in questions of participation, drawing on examples from the Netherlands, Belgium and Germany. In the German-speaking world, no equivalent term exists, with 'Mitmach-Theater' having pejorative connotations of the audience being forced to be interactive, and much recent scholarship being influenced by the term 'everyday experts' introduced by the collective Rimini Protokoll, whose

work sometimes involves audience immersion (Dreysse and Malzacher, 2008).

3   The term 'Live Art' is used mostly in the Anglo-American context; see the three-volume Live Art Almanac series for a selection of found materials on the topic (Brine, 2008; Keidan, Mitchell and Mitchelson, 2010; Keidan and Wright, 2013).

4   The term originates from the Theatre of the Oppressed (Boal, 2000).

5   This refers to certain tasks being delegated to audience members or other lay persons. It is critically appraised by Bishop (2012) and elaborated in Harvie (2013).

6   Collaborative practices inform the discussion of art and its potential for intervention, dialogue or activism in its social contexts in Finkelpearl (2013), Kester (2011) and Thompson (2012).

7   Turner made a problematic distinction between *liminal* events in so-called 'primitive' societies and *liminoid* events in 'technologically advanced', i.e. industrialized, societies, counting the arts and entertainment as belonging to the latter, as they are voluntary and involve a cultural conception of leisure (Turner, 1969). As such a distinction has no purchase in a critical decolonial understanding of the arts and cultures, I use the terms synonymously.

Gestures of institutional critique

We must know what mistake to make with a specific text and must also know how to defend that mistake as the one that will allow us to live. (Spivak, 2012, p. 28)

In the context of contemporary art, the concept of 'institutional critique' refers to the scrutiny of the power of (art) institutions through artistic means. This might include a range of artistic practices: artworks that examine the modus operandi and hidden mechanisms of the institutions they are affiliated to or implicated in, artworks that problematize which persons, subjects and aesthetic modes are allowed to enter the art world and be counted as art. Institutional critique might also refer to the curatorial attempts of art institutions to be self-critical and transparent, for instance by laying bare the motives behind their programming choices. It attempts to account for how institutions ideologically and materially influence the way the history of art is written, determining how its standards must be upheld and when they may be appropriately breached. For a variety of reasons, which have to do with their political economies and the specific relations of artistic domains to institutions, the practice of institutional critique has been far more influential in the visual arts than in theatre and performance. It has a legacy that is often traced to two waves or phases, first in the 1970s and later in the 1990s, both seen as originating in European and North American visual art history (Ray and Raunig, 2009). The first wave of institutional critique can be ascribed to artworks that sought a critique of the authority or authoritarianism of art institutions, thus self-reflexively juxtaposing the ideals to which art institutions normatively pledged allegiance with the material realities and ideological contradictions within which they operate. The aim thereby was to shift viewer perspectives on the claims of art, to reveal the underlying mechanisms at work, to make the structures visible and thus ultimately alterable. A belief in the power to reform, transform and rehabilitate the faults of institutions through artistic practice is prominent in these attempts. The second wave added to this fundamental critique of institutional authority the problem of representation, drawing attention to the classed, gendered and raced dimensions of institutional power and seeking to reassess the relationships between the centre and the periphery and to dismantle the divisions and models of classification that effectively maintained a status quo and allowed privileges to be kept intact. This aspect foregrounds the formation of social, political or cultural subjects and subjectivities through the practices of institutional critique. Institutional critique is therefore not an established form or genre of art with fixed rules and characteristics, but changes continually across different sites and historical circumstances. It combines social critique and self-critique in reflecting on the relationship between institutions and art, and therefore on the relationship between institutions and critique

What is the place of institutional critique in relation to participatory performance? Where might institutional critique be located here and how is it practised? In the following, I reflect on the challenges and conundrums of institutional critique from the vantage point of participatory practices. As a first step I examine the formation of participatory art as a genre, specifically community-based, applied art, as emergent from the critique of mainstream art institutions. In a second step, I inquire into some modalities of institutional critique which foreground questions of participation or non-participation, and examine their disciplinary configurations within the arts.

Participatory art as the critique of institutionalized art

The category of participatory art might be seen to imply that it is a specific kind of art, a genre in its own right. It might suggest that a certain artistic practice is recognizable and classifiable according to whether and how it enables the participation of audiences or the public, usually conceived as non-professionals or non-artists. In an extended sense, it could also refer to the degree and nature of participation of the artistic practice itself in public life. If we use participatory art as an umbrella concept, encompassing what is variously referred to as community arts, arts in development, art in education, art in therapeutic, rehabilitative or restorative processes, it becomes clear that these are by no means neutral, descriptive categories but indicate inheritances of specific operations of demarcation, with their own implicit ideological assumptions. To that extent, viewing participatory art as a genre in its own right primarily has the purpose of setting up the conditions to be able to ask different kinds of questions of the practices: questions that are not necessarily asked when studying proscenium theatre productions or installation-based performance art or any other interactive forms; questions that lead to different kinds of analyses, in terms of how they frame and bring to life the subjects of study vis-à-vis the existing frameworks of the discipline. When posited as a genre, participatory art therefore does not merely register or serve as a repository for a homogeneous community of practices, in the sense of 'genus', but also 'generates' and makes these practices visible in 'general' terms (Derrida and Ronell, 1980, pp. 56–57).

Yet genre also entails problems of exclusion and stratification. Participatory art, especially in theatre and performance studies, is sometimes perceived as synonymous with the applied arts or community arts, and research on this area is rarely discussed on the same platform as studies on, say, scenography or multimedia interactive art, even if the latter may be deeply concerned with issues of participation.[1] The participation of rural women in a so-called theatre for development project in India would thus be deemed as belonging to a different order, when placed alongside the participation of visitors in an interactive performance art installation in a European or US contemporary art museum. The immersive participation of the public in ritual or religious performances is rarely considered on a par with so-called immersive or experiential performance productions, the former largely deemed the metier of cultural anthropologists and the latter that of art historians or theatre and performance scholars. Yet on what assumptions is this difference in aesthetic or medial order based? There seems to be a Bourdieusian 'fine distinction' at work in the scholarly literature on participatory art, where the quest for a taxonomy based on formal criteria is simultaneously accompanied by implicit classificatory schemes that merely serve to keep certain things together and other things apart (Bourdieu, 1984, p. 472). We know from Bourdieu that 'the mode of expression characteristic of a cultural production always depends on the laws of the market in which it is offered' (1984, p. xiii). While this sociological argument may suggest some reasons why a participatory theatre or music workshop with slum-dwellers is rarely (deliberately or otherwise) discussed together with contemporary art projects using a participatory pedagogy in a gallery or exhibition context, it also implicitly demands that this legitimization of differences between these domains through institutions and academic scholarship be questioned and recalibrated from time to time. It cautions against taking the logics governing their separations and divisions for granted, and emphasizes the need to formulate alternative schemes of appraisal and critique, however inconvenient and unwieldy such a task might be (Bourdieu, 1984, p. 7).

If this could be read as a criticism of a problematic segregation of participatory art from broader disciplinary platforms, it is equally a result of the insistence in the scholarship on participatory art on its being distinct from 'conventional' theatre or visual art settings. The relationship of participatory art to institution and institutionalization may be charted in terms of three interrelated moves: a move away from conventional art institutions, a move towards alternative institutions and settings, and a transformative movement within existing institutions (Ray and Raunig, 2009).[2] It is frequently argued, for instance, that the emergence and recognition of participatory theatre as a distinct genre in theatre and performance partly derives from its critique of the canons and regulatory restrictions of high art institutions and its preference for counter-institutions and non-institutionalized spaces of theatrical activity. The critique of the inadequacies of one domain could lead to the formation of another domain, which comes with its own set of institutional entanglements. Participatory theatre is thus viewed as a move away from theatrical forms because of its emphasis on 'ordinary people' and their stories, rather than on professional actors and pre-written scripts, its sustained embeddedness in local contexts, as well as its explicit commitment to combining social and artistic goals (van Erven, 2001). It is seen as emerging from a critical response to the absence of these features in the established national, bourgeois or commercial theatre circuits.

A move away from these institutions implies a search for other institutions, which is characterized by a quest for alternative institutional spaces in cooperation with the people who dwell or work in these spaces on a daily basis, which could take the form of civic institutions such as schools, old age homes, youth clubs, prisons or clinics, or could involve the temporary occupation of common or private spaces such as the street, public squares, rooftops, homes and gardens, inviting the participation of passers-by. The Indian theatre director Safdar Hashmi, founder of *Janam*, or *Jana Natya Manch* [People's Theatre Association], powerfully argued that 'since mainstream theatre is by and large out of tune and touch with the majority of our people, the need remains for a fully developed people's theatre' (1998, p. 32). For Hashmi and his workers' theatre group in the 1980s, the streets were incorporated into the performances of *Janam*, not simply as a backdrop, but as an active and vibrant feature of social life. The move away from the spaces of established theatre institutions is accompanied by a move towards institutions such as labour unions and political parties, whose rallies and public activities often take place in the streets. At the same time, the rejection of established institutions and the embrace of alternative institutions tend also to be accompanied by attempts to transform existing institutions and institutional practices. This could take the form of a call to alter processes of working within the theatre and a questioning of the hierarchical relations between theatre director, actors/actresses, dramaturges, translators, production assistants, stage, lighting and costume designers, such as in the radical experiments of the *creación colectiva* and new theatre movement from Latin America in the 1950s and 1960s. The history of participatory theatre practices across the world testifies to an institutional critique in a combination of gestures of fleeing from, forging new and transforming existing relationships to institutions.

Carefully differentiated critical yardsticks and historical routes are thus required to distinguish different legacies of institutional critique from each other, not in order to retreat into a safe particularism, but rather in order to theorize them from their very finite locales and social and disciplinary bases. What exactly is deemed a 'critical' practice thus differs hugely from one context to another. The following two examples instantiate how a public denunciation of institutional power may be a powerful critical mode in one context, whereas it may be entirely counter-productive in another.

When a support group of the Palestinian Boycott, Divestment and Sanctions movement protested the Tel Aviv staging of Cape Town Opera's performance of George Gershwin's *Porgy and Bess* in 2010 by staging a flash mob in front of the Tel Aviv Opera House on the night of the premiere, the event acutely drew the political context and historical legacy of the performance into the spotlight, and at the same time called attention to what was at stake for audience members who chose to attend it (Dana, 2010). Popular tunes from the musical were deployed by the protesters with altered lyrics: 'Summertime, and the living is easy' became 'Palestine, and the living ain't easy', and 'It Ain't Necessarily So' was rendered with references to the comparability of apartheid in South Africa and the Israeli occupation of Palestine. The flash mob becomes an interesting case for discussing institutional critique only when seen in relation to the specificities of this context. This unsolicited event at the fringe of a performance places the responsibility of art institutions under scrutiny, i.e. how audience participation in such a performance may be a conscious or unconscious endorsement of Israeli government policies and actions, or how the decision of Cape Town Opera to perform in Tel Aviv Opera House may be a manifestation of complicity with a political regime they may not necessarily perceive themselves as having anything to do with. This context is undoubtedly connected to the complex performance history of *Porgy and Bess*, from its emergence in the racially segregated US, to its widespread rejection by the American civil rights movement, to its renewed politicization during the apartheid era in South Africa, with failed attempts to stage performances featuring an all-white cast, to its resurgence and commercially popular reworking in the twenty-first century (Noonan, 2012). The use of a performative flash mob by a group of protestors sought to draw attention to the clout of institutions such as Cape Town Opera in influencing public opinion and taking a stance in support of the Palestinian Boycott, Divestment and Sanctions movement, which is modelled on the South African anti-apartheid boycott movement, by not cooperating with Israeli government-funded institutions.

The very same question of the order of cooperation with hegemonic institutions can take on an entirely different valence in another context. Consider the case of a Sudanese independent theatre production featured at an international theatre festival in Rotterdam in the Netherlands in 2009, with a grant from the Sudanese national government. Given the anti-democratic track record of the Sudanese government, the theatre group might be accused of being co-opted by nationalist agendas in accepting travel grants from a regime it criticizes. Walid Al-Alphy, the theatre director of an independent ensemble from Darfur, Sudan, addressed this point during an after-talk following a performance of *The People of the Cave*. When a member of the audience asked how it was possible to be critical of the ruling powers while simultaneously accepting an award from them in order to present their work abroad, Al-Alphy's response was revealing.[3] Given that Sudanese (not to speak of Darfurian) independent theatre is hardly taken notice of in the rest of the world, and that Sudan is a country often negatively represented in the press, the task of retaining artistic independence inevitably needs to be done from within, and not in an imaginary bubble presumably untouched by the country's messy political environment. Under these circumstances, Al-Alphy pointed out, he perceived it as the responsibility of his theatre group to accept the privilege of showcasing their work abroad, adding that it was not only by authoritarian regimes but also and equally by art circuits and self-appointed guardians of free expression that dissident artists might be co-opted. Refraining from these matters and 'staying in the cave' was not an option, he said, using a metaphor derived from the play. *The People of the Cave*, adapted from an episode in the Quran known as the *Sūrat al-Kahf*, is set in a cave, where five men have fled from a tyrant and fall into a miraculous 300-year-long sleep.[4] When they wake up, they hear radio reports of bombardments, chronic illnesses and attacks on villages. The men fight among themselves about who ought to be the king, and the battle for power results in the new king leaving the cave promising to help the others, though he never returns. One by one, the people of the cave desert each other and look to their survival in the midst of war. The play enunciates a critique of structures of governance that instil fear in people, stultify them and turn them against each other. As a production, it exemplifies theatre as an institution that participates in public debates and takes a stance on current issues. The cave and the world outside were metaphors for the theatre and the world outside. To avoid stepping out of the cave would have been to avoid the possibility of participating in the world. In an interview, Walid Al-Alphy remarked:

> In Sudan, everyone is part of the war. There are perpetrators and victims, but beneath that there is shared responsibility. The new sultans in *People of the Cave* threaten their followers, but the followers themselves are afraid to leave the cave to see the world with their own eyes. They remain in their dormant state. (Heemstra, 2009)

For Al-Alphy's theatre ensemble, the choice to travel abroad with Sudanese government funding, knowing that their work might be misperceived or misrepresented, was an ethical and political choice, explicitly shifting the question of institutional critique from the limited issue of how a theatre company relates to state funding to the broader issue of safeguarding interventionist and activist potentials in terms of theatre's societal responsibility. Institutional critique is thus not a matter that can be resolved once and for all, but needs to be a persistent effort. The very critique of institutional participation is thus predicated upon participation, and the refusal to participate is only one of the ways in which this critique is articulated.

Institutional affiliations and entanglements

I have been arguing thus far that participatory practices have imagined the relationship between 'institution' and 'critique' in terms of their own critical relation to conventional, established theatre institutions. However, this does not resolve the question of how to locate institutional critique within its own terrain. It is worthwhile to examine the institutional affiliations and entanglements of participatory projects, how they operate within or against their supporting institutions in different ways, as well as how institutions invoke or invest in the participatory for various purposes. One could start by distinguishing between at least four kinds of institutional support for participatory applied theatre projects: local or national governments; national or international non-governmental organizations (NGOs); civic institutions such as schools, universities, youth clubs, political parties, hospitals, prisons or community centres; and corporate bodies. Each of these institutional frameworks places its own set of conditions on theatrical or other artistic activities in their environments. At times these conditions become 'conditionalities', i.e. they carry consequences or sanctions for non-compliance (Anderson, 1999). Participatory practices may seek to enter these institutions in order to artfully transform and critique their underlying premises, or because the institutions facilitate their contact with the disenfranchised or marginalized sections of the population who may be perceived as ideal target audiences or participants in their activities. Either way, the involvement with state or non-state apparatuses of power leads to abundant contradictions in artistic practices. The most obvious example of this is prison theatre, which remains bound to the rules of prison institutions, even as it may seek to symbolically or otherwise critique the system of incarceration (Balfour, 2004; Thompson, 1998). Theatre-based workshops for the employees of multinational corporations domesticate and de-politicize methods developed by Brecht or Boal, even as they invoke their anti-capitalist theatrical concepts in pursuit of the goals of increased productivity, improving motivation in the workplace or resolving conflicts that impede efficiency levels (Heinicke et al., 2015).

Another case of the institutional entanglement of participatory art is to be found in the domain known as theatre for development. The deployment of theatre as a tool in developmental initiatives, particularly in participatory rural appraisals, capacity building and mobilization activities, has led to participatory popular theatre forms being adopted by governmental and non-governmental development agencies in many countries of the Global South. While this may be regarded by some as offering new avenues for bridging artistic practices to social transformation, it has also been severely critiqued by others for allowing the instrumentalization of theatre as a tool of soft power over impoverished rural communities. A number of macro-institutional factors have significantly influenced how theatrical practices engage with and critique institutions: the withering of post-independence anti-colonial hopes into authoritarian, corrupt militarized and incompetent regimes; the 'structural adjustment programmes' imposed on many poor, 'developing' countries by heavyweight institutions such as the World Bank and the International Monetary Fund; the subsequent withdrawal of autonomy and financial support from universities and autonomous cultural institutions; as well as a political climate that instrumentalized culture and art while simultaneously censoring dissident expressions.[5] Concepts that grew out of the heady utopian ideals of popular theatre movements, such as grassroots participation and conscientization, mutated into a rhetorical tool of social engineering, promoting the agendas of Western-dominated organizations and maintaining the power bases of local elites (Cohen and Uphoff, 2011).

According to the Bangladeshi theatre scholar Syed Jamil Ahmed, theatre for development, in the way it is practised by some Bangladeshi NGOs, 'identified the central problem not as oppression but as poverty, by converting "dialogue" into "opinion sharing', which is a neutral technique devoid of "politics"' (2002, p. 214). In sub-Saharan Africa, for instance, the area of health education, especially related to HIV/AIDS, is one of the main sources of funding for any theatre work, resulting in a vast number of applied theatre projects in school workshops, teacher training, and in developmental activities. Not only national but also international non-governmental organizational policies thus often indirectly determine what topics ought to be addressed by artists, towards which ends, and even which forms are most appropriate. A politically expedient imperative of utility thus shapes the relation of such institutions to theatre work At worst they take the form of top-down, information-providing edu-tainment, or corporate image repair campaigns camouflaged as developmental programmes (Plastow, 2014, p. 111). If huge breweries promote theatre programmes on sensible drinking, or multinational oil companies support artistic initiatives for participatory citizenship in Nigeria while clamping down on ecological activists elsewhere, the notion of institutional support, as Jane Plastow rightly argues, assumes a downright cynical and dangerous connotation. Plastow's critique could be extended to many other parts of the world, including Europe, where, increasingly, it is 'creativity' or 'social cohesion' that serves as the dispositive, rather than 'development' (Ahmed and Hughes, 2015).

Institutional critique, understood as the explicit use of an artistic practice to interrogate, oppose or break out of institutional frameworks, has very asymmetrical trajectories and conditions across the world and across domains, but these differences have difficulty in finding their way into scholarly assessments. Institutional critique means something else to those operating in established art institutions such as museums, galleries, biennials or theatre festivals in Europe or North America, than it does to those working in countries where such institutions barely exist and where artists are struggling to set them up in the first place (Araeen, 2003). Of contemporary theatre practices in Europe, for instance, it is most commonly expected that they will express some form of institutional critique or self-critique, which demonstrates that they are conscious of how they are both enabled as well as limited by the structures or institutions that host them. The absence of such a self-critical stance is often mistrusted or regarded as an absence of credibility and criticality. While I agree with this in principle, participatory practices, particularly in poorer countries and in precarious sociopolitical environments, do not articulate institutional critiques in terms of anti-institutionality. The absence of an explicit critique of institutions need not always be equated with the absence of a critical attitude.

Shannon Jackson's study *Social Works* invokes the idea that performance cannot take place without an infrastructure, including institutional and intersubjective support systems, and thus calls for an understanding of the artwork as including and extending to social and affective dimensions. She highlights performance concepts such as 'props' (2011, pp. 42ff.), 'supportive roles' and institutional defamiliarization (2011, p. 62) not as mere technical terms, but as bearing important dimensions of sociability and sociality. Jackson further argues that support for institutions and institutionalization need not be at odds with suspicion towards institutions in radical political theory. She questions the assumption that artistic radicalism and progressiveness must be gauged by their degree of anti-institutionality, investigating instances of artworks that sustain, care for and imagine alternative institutions, within the art world as well as outside (Jackson, 2011, pp. 14–15). The question is thus one of expanding the field of institutional critique to be able to take seriously very different ways of relating critique to institutions, including those that may contest the dogmatisms of institutional critique as established by the Western art world.

The institutional operations of participation are not simply restricted to how audience members are integrated into artworks, but also concern the labour and input of experts commissioned to contribute their specialized skills in order to realize the artwork. Jen Harvie examines the participation of technicians, architects, engineers, craftspeople and manual workers or hired extras in the creation of complex installations; for instance, the commissioning of thousands of artisans by Ai Weiwei in China to produce more than one million hand-painted porcelain sunflower seeds, or Anish Kapoor's close collaboration with engineers and architects to realize the large-scale installation *Marsyas* (Harvie, 2013, pp. 33–35). Harvie argues that when assessed on the grounds of labour, these participatory practices may at best cultivate a sense of collective responsibility and pursuit of a shared goal, or at worst replicate or exploit labour trends to the artist's own benefit (2013, p. 41). These differences carry very distinct implications in terms of who are deemed to be the beneficiaries or authors of the participatory process, and who are its invisible domestic hands.

Commercialization and corporate ownership are common conditions of dissemination in the domain of visual art, whereas in many countries, theatre remains either self-funded or directly or indirectly state-supported, and cannot be sold or even circulated as a commodity in a market. In parts of the world, where powerful art institutions are either non-existent or inaccessible to artists, participatory art is found in the frameworks of NGOs and educational institutions. Veronica Baxter identifies a 'tension between the role of the arts as education and social commentary, and their perceived position as part of a "knowledge and creative economy"' (Baxter, 2013, p. 210). At the same time, the restrictions and requirements that result from being institutionally tied to an NGO or to school-based theatre work need not necessarily always mean compromising artistic integrity, but can rather serve as a trigger for fruitful artistic experiments and explorations (Chinyowa, 2015; Dinesh, 2015). It must also be recognized that, in many contexts, international NGO support may be the only avenue available for pursuing artistic work, so any institutional critique tends to take place in tactical and implicit ways (Thompson, Hughes and Balfour, 2009).

In many countries around the world, especially in the initial decades of independence following the end of colonialism, the structure of national sovereignty was established through national institutional frameworks, which were inherited from colonial administrations as well as being attempts at cultural modernization on their own terms (Chatterjee, 1998; Thiong'o, 1998). Historically, it was artists, public intellectuals, educationists, writers and cultural activists who supported the initiation of the institutions of state building, and invested their life energies in shaping these as serious proponents of democratic principles, from cultural and religious associations, libraries, voluntary associations and educational-cultural institutions, to journals and magazines, publishing houses, art venues and public debates. So in the context of post-colonial societies, it was often artists and public intellectuals, the cultural elites, who provided support to the state in various ways to help set up civic cultural institutions, rather than the state supporting artists through institutional means.[6] The very possibility of fostering independent civic cultural institutions was thus in some sense essential to a notion of self-determination and sovereignty. The betrayal of those hopes in the decades of the Cold War and the transition into neoliberal capitalism, what historian David Scott has called the disenchantment of becoming 'conscripts of modernity' (2004), is well known. The relationship to institutional critique in the artistic contexts of formerly colonized countries is thus neither one of romantic progression nor of a nostalgic return to a condition that was, but rather one of living with and working within inadequacies, thwarted hopes and disillusionment. Where nation states have failed to uphold democratic principles, international NGOs or even corporate institutions may offer the only avenue available for pursuing artistic work, so a boycott or outright rejection of their involvement in the arts is often not a constructive option. This does not mean that there is no consciousness of institutional hegemony, but rather that critique might assume indirect forms and dwell in grey areas, it might be expressed beside and at the margins of the institutions rather than within them. I specifically refer to institutions to which participatory projects tend to be attached: on the one hand, the providers of funding, i.e. the charity arms of big corporations, the humanitarian and development aid wings of transnational NGOs and national developmental agencies, educational and cultural foundations; and on the other hand, the so-called beneficiary institutions, community initiatives, schools and small-scale civic organizations. Being institutionally tied need not necessarily mean compromising artistic integrity, for institutions can be politely hijacked for fruitful artistic experiments, or in Gayatri Spivak's felicitous formulation, 'affirmatively sabotaged' (Spivak, 2012, p. 510, n. 3).

Consider, for instance, the situation of a theatre for development presentation in a typical rural setting in the Global South, where villagers are invited to gather in a public square to watch performances on topics such as safe sex, personal hygiene, planned parenthood or electoral rights performed by urban facilitators and actors. Public participation is sought through interactivity on stage, or post-performance discussions with the audience. The resistance of the population to these top-down, heavily didactic performances is commonly expressed by indirect means, as in feigned compliance through offering expected, stock answers to the questions posed by the facilitators. An actor playing a man who insists on sex without a condom turns to the audience to ask if what he did was correct, at which the audience collectively shouts back with an insincere but resounding 'No!' Members of the audience step into roles in forum theatre interventions, but do not follow the instructions of the facilitators, instead using the platform to perform an improvised song and dance on their own. The performance itself sometimes becomes an excuse for an improvised bazaar, with vendors appearing with their stalls to sell food and other items at the margins of the event, and people gathering for conversations, often with complete disregard for what is going on in the theatrical performance (Chinyowa, 2015).

Another intriguing example is the hugely commercially successful prison dance project at the Cebu Provincial Detention and Rehabilitation Centre in the Philippines (Peterson, 2012). With amateur videos that have had millions of views on YouTube, and monthly public shows that have unexpectedly turned the prison into a major attraction for visitors and tourists, the spectacular dance routines involving up to 1500 inmates present at best an ambivalent and oblique critique of the institution, affirmative of incarceration in high-security prisons, even while staging outrage and defiance by dancing to Michael Jackson's hit 'They Don't Really Care about Us'. Yet the Cebu dancing inmates, as they are known, call into question common assumptions about participatory art initiatives with inmates in prison. Their dances are commercial super-hits, very large in scale; they spend absolutely no time on staging confessional, personal narratives and are in no way concerned with the 'us vs. them' problem in much of prison theatre work, confronting the privileges of facilitators with the restrictive circumstances of inmates.

In the Western European context of the visual arts, institutional critique sometimes assumes a conceptual mode. In 2009 the visual artist Pilvi Takala visited Disneyland in France, dressed up as Snow White from the Disney animation film, and documented her failed attempt to gain access in a short video entitled *The Real Snow White*.[7] Takala was certainly aware that seeking entry into Disneyland as Snow White would not be a straightforward enterprise. Many of her works employ breaching experiments as a way of highlighting uncontested social norms.[8] Her intended naivety is met with a heavy-handed response from Disney's gatekeepers, who first refuse her entry on the grounds that she is not allowed to dress up in the costume, since there is a 'real' Snow White inside Disneyland, and later insist that she has to change her clothes in order not to mislead other visitors into believing she is the 'real' Snow White. Yet the seriousness lies in the absurd recourse to law enforcement in order to guard a fiction. It is absurd because 'fiction turns degenerate', in the words of Önder Özengi, its commodity power taking over its fictional power (Özengi, 2010). The 'real' Snow White is the one who has been contracted and employed by Disney, a Snow White sanctioned by corporate law and not by fanciful wit. To mess with that copyrighted fiction is, of course, to be penalized for not being the kind of productive consumer participant for whom the gates of Disneyland are opened. Takala's attempt to be a part of or to take part in the fantasies of Empire puts her at risk – not only the risk of exclusion from Empire, but moreover the risk of being punished for not participating in the right way.

Takala's point was not to protest against Disney or to show her oppositional stance as an artist. Rather, the experiment was about seeing how far it is possible to claim ownership of a fantasy, how far the citation of that fantasy works as its disruption. The video itself follows a fairly conventional format, consciously using a hand-held camera and rough, largely unedited footage, giving the impression of a spontaneous amateur recording. It is the artist who participates or intervenes in a given social setting. She does not follow a script but rather maintains a way of bearing herself, a gesture that makes the terms of her participation as well as the unquestioned rules of that specific social setting noticeable, a kind of invisible theatre if you like, documented and later presented in art gallery contexts. *The Real Snow White* is neither an act of protest against the consumerism of Disneyland, nor an act of opposition to the art world, for that would assume some safe outside from which such an opposition could be launched. It is an act of critical participation through what Slavoj Žižek called, in psychoanalytical terms, 'over-identification', 'an act of taking the system more seriously than it wants you to take it' (BAVO, 2007, p. 29). Yet the work might also be read as a form of institutional critique, if one regards Takala's attempt to enter Disneyland as an allegory of her critique of the commodified art world, with the art world being represented as a kind of Disneyland and the artist over-identifying with its conventions.

Such phenomena are, I would argue, important expressions of critique towards the institutions that turn theatre and performance into a tool of governance, but they crucially adopt a form of critique that is not necessarily oppositional or outwardly showing resistance, and in fact they often do not even bother to directly address the institutions. Rather, they assume informal, para-theatrical modes that ironically seem to resist the very category of institutional critique. What I find most noteworthy is that the critique often comes from the participants and not from the artists or facilitators of the art projects.[9] This makes it difficult to assess them in conventional aesthetic terms. They may not be considered 'artistic', but they are 'artful' acts of criticality, in that they reveal the mechanisms of institutional power that so forcefully shape theatrical practices and the academic discourses that accompany them. Terms such as the 'artwork', the 'production' or 'the artist' prove inadequate when considering that process, experience and encounter, rather than finished, authored works are central to most participatory art forms.

Disciplinary configurations

Institutional affiliations shape and are shaped by the sites of practice. For instance, prison arts programmes, art-in-education and interactive installations in museums may all be driven by participatory pedagogical concepts, but these take on an entirely different significance according to the setting in which they are implemented. Correspondingly, there are many different theoretical positions, which often simply do not take notice of each other or seem incompatible because of their location in disparate settings. Their epistemological routes draw inspiration from very different traditions of theorizing and analysis, which throws open as many questions and contradictions as it provides fruitful points of connection. What would, for instance, Rancière's notion of 'emancipated spectatorship' mean in a prison arts context, where inequality and asymmetry dominate the relations between those who conduct the participatory art projects and those who are meant to be the beneficiaries? How should the 'educational turn' in museum curation practices be compared to or brought to bear upon the 'social turn' of arts in education programmes (Nicholson, 2011; Rogoff, 2008)? Institutional critique, understood as the explicit use of an artistic practice to interrogate, oppose or break out of art institutional frameworks, has very asymmetrical trajectories and conditions across the world and across domains, but these differences have difficulty finding their way into scholarly assessments (Ray and Raunig, 2009, p. xv). Such problems of cross-disciplinary discussion of participatory practices become interesting because they point to the changing institutional conditions that allow or restrict participation. Taken seriously as instances of institutional critique, they expose not just the rules or norms of a certain institution, but also or equally the rules of its specific traditions of institutional critique, thus presenting the possibility of a meta-critical commentary.

Current debates on participation in theatre and performance as well as in installation-based visual art shift between two main and contrasting claims. For the purposes of simplification, these claims may be called the sweet dream and the nightmare of participation.[10] The proponents of participatory art as a sweet dream or a utopian ideal see in participatory methods the potential to overcome what is often regarded as a stultifying barrier between audiences and performers, overcoming the fourth wall, creating real-life, vivid, embodied encounters rather than mere staged representations. It is regarded as being socially progressive, having a relevance beyond the sphere of art alone because of being an experience of relationality and a process rather than a finished product. It is also regarded as a critical response to neoliberal conditions that do not just affect the economy, but financialize all spheres of life. In contrast, the insistence on the participatory, or the involvement of marginalized sections of the population, has been critiqued as concealing inequalities or differences through an apparently inclusive false gesture, an ideal turned into the tyranny of an imperative and absorbed into the mechanisms of neoliberal governance, a form of placation and coercion rather than a means of democratic citizenship, where the responsibility of the artist is outsourced to the audience or to others invited to participate.

On the one hand, it is possible to observe several correspondences between the critique of the neoliberal absorption of participation in social policy, and the deployment of participatory theatre and performance under the aegis of social cohesion or development. Several scholars have argued that it is necessary to be circumspect about celebrating an artwork for its supposed inclusivity and participatory approach. In her study of performance under neoliberal economic conditions in the UK, Jen Harvie notes that 'labour deregulation in art and performance corresponds to the broader deregulation of markets – particularly labour markets – under neoliberal capitalism' (2013, p. 29). This is not only true of large-scale commercial stage productions, but also in the experimental, independent and educational sectors, where volunteers, interns and members of the audience are used in performance settings, a participation that might be rehabilitating in some cases and exploitative in others. Anthony Jackson similarly notes that 'facile assumptions about being able to "make a difference" in people's lives by the very act of engaging them in a participatory drama experience can all too easily lead to patronization, even to a certain kind of oppression' (2007, p. 8). The vocabulary often used to speak about participatory art, terms such as empowerment, collaboration, inclusion, dialogue, creativity, are oftentimes drawn from the public policy discourse that overshadows and hounds NGOs and independent artists and companies in their daily interactions with funding bodies and supporting institutions. This is specifically true of applied or community theatre practices. At one point in theatre and cultural history, especially since the 1970s, these concepts were uttered by anti-establishment thinkers and stood for radical alternatives to authoritarian models of governance, alternatives that were imagined in and through artistic practices. Today they neatly dovetail with the logic of neoliberal thinking (Ahmed and Hughes, 2015).

On the other hand, the ascendancy of participatory forms and approaches in both the visual arts as well as theatre and performance can be interpreted precisely as a critical response to the ever-expanding neoliberal rationality, which frames all spheres of life in market, if not directly monetary, terms. Thus sociality, care, interpersonal communication and affectively grounded interactions become increasingly important as aesthetic values of this 'social turn'. Most often cited in this context are Nicolas Bourriaud's curatorial conceptions of participatory works in the museum context, documented in his study *Relational Aesthetics* (2002). It must be noted that the aesthetics of the relational responds specifically to debates in the visual arts primarily in Europe, and does not address notions of relationality from a theatre and performance perspective. Using scattered references to Marx, Althusser and Debord, Bourriaud propounds the idea of art as a social interstice rather than as a material product (Bourriaud, 2002, p. 14); he suggests using the word 'work' in artwork as a verb rather than as a noun, thus as process and convivial encounter rather than as a finished, unchangeable good (p. 22); and he celebrates social encounters in and through art as proposals of micro-utopias (p. 31).

Tom Finkelpearl's study of what he calls art and social cooperation analyses the history of participatory art in the visual art domain
in the USA through the lens of social justice and counter-cultural
movements, with the 1960s as the historical point of departure.
Finkelpearl delineates the history of participatory practices from the
close ties between artists and the civil rights movement, racial justice struggles as well as the feminist movement (2013, pp. 15–19).
The theoretical influences that Finkelpearl identifies as crucial to the
field are Guy Debord and Paolo Freire. He mentions groups such
as the Diggers in San Francisco and the Yippies in New York, who
experimented with street happenings, set up counter-institutions and
combined artistic and social activities, as well as more institutionally
established artists such as Allan Kaprow and Joseph Beuys, or groups
such as Fluxus, who initiated forms of institutional critique through
participatory practices within and beyond the spaces of art institutions (Finkelpearl, 2013, pp. 13–16). Moving to the late 1970s and
1980s, Finkelpearl charts the rise of socially collaborative public art
projects in relation to urban development and public advocacy, with
prominent figures such as Mierle Laderman Ukeles's 'maintenance
art' in cooperation with municipal sanitation workers, and Suzanne
Lacy's large-scale cooperative performances.

The terminologies of participation operate by way of their disciplinary relationship to other terms. For instance, Bourriaud proposed
the 'relational aesthetic' as a category in distinction from an object-
oriented art (2002). From a theatre studies perspective, such a differentiation may appear irrelevant to a certain extent, as relationality
– the corporeal energy and interaction between human and non-
human presence on and off stage – is always already indispensable to
the medium of theatre and performance, a given prerequisite and not
a special genre. On the other hand, terms such as immersive, invita-
tional or experiential performance indicate foremost their difference
from conventional proscenium stage and arena settings, emphasizing
scenography, the architectural dimension of participation, one-to-one
encounters and the use of installations and stylized environments
(White, 2012). From a contemporary visual art perspective, this distinction may seem outdated or trivial, as spatial considerations and
the institutional circumstances of experiencing, i.e. participating in,

an artwork are perceived as already integral to its aesthetic. Shannon Jackson rhetorically describes these contrasting approaches as an 'experimental chiasmus across the arts: a movement toward painting and sculpture underpins post-dramatic theatre, but a movement toward theatre also underpins post-studio art. In such a chiasmus, breaking the traditions of one medium means welcoming the traditions of another' (Jackson, 2011, p. 6). Jackson's remark that the location of participatory practices is at the crossroads of the visual and performing arts is of critical importance.

Even disciplinary variations of the same term may signal very different practices informed by a distinct set of values. Thus it is arguable that community music, community theatre, community dance and community media have distinct trajectories of scholarship and practice, and need therefore to be referenced with different terms, such that using a broad term such as 'community art' may in fact erase these specific characteristics by lumping them together. A comparability across media is neither self-evident nor necessarily desirable, as questions pertaining to participation in community music, for example, might address musicological issues (Turino, 2008), which are possibly of limited interest to researchers of community theatre, even if both might explicitly deal with how given communities participate in making music or theatre collectively, and even if theatre and music are interrelated performing art forms. Apart from this, competing notions of what 'community' means or how communities are best served obviously shape whether certain participatory artistic practices are nostalgic or confronting, whether they are oriented towards preserving the structures that keep a community together, or towards calling these structures into question. Concepts such as 'play', 'game' or 'playfulness' recur in both the visual arts as well as performance studies in configuring conditions of participation, though referring to very different theoretical frameworks.[11]

Conversely, some terms may carry distinct regional and cultural nuances. The concept of applied theatre, widely used in English-speaking contexts, has commonalities with, but also crucial differences from the German understandings of *angewandtes Theater*. Participation in the former is usually associated with members of an often disadvantaged social grouping who are regarded as beneficiaries, such as homeless people, children, asylum seekers or villagers, whereas the German concept of *angewandtes Theater* is more concerned with delimiting the traditional drama-based conventions of theatre (the root *wenden* indicates a shift or a turn rather than an application), thus extending the term beyond the focus on audience participation or outreach to experimental applications (Matzke, Weiler and Wortelkamp, 2012). Given that such medium-specific criteria variously influence how a certain kind of participatory art is discursively operated, it is less relevant to establish the definition of 'collaborative art' as distinct from 'dialogical art' or 'community art', and more intriguing to explore why a certain term is preferred, to which tradition it is affiliated, in what way it is problematized, and how this choice of terminology tells us something about the underlying or assumed politics of participation.

The disciplinary variations of participatory art demonstrate how nomenclature is a contextual practice. The categorical separation of the aesthetic and the social or political sphere and their institutions risks becoming a form of gatekeeping rather than encouraging an investigation that steps outside of the shelter of canon and discipline. Further, it is important to recognize the turn towards the social as a valid form of critique, a turning away from what might be perceived as the restrictive modes and conditions of the aesthetic sphere, thus an institutional critique (Ray and Raunig, 2009, p. 54). To demand that such a critique must make itself legible to the institutions and existing nomenclatures of art can, under certain circumstances, equally function as a form of confinement and a failure to comprehend the critique. This is particularly so in contexts located outside what belongs to the art world, with reference to the artistic pursuits of peoples far removed from the circuit of the global art market, or unnoticed by interpellating artistic and academic institutions that lend them leverage and legitimacy (Sangari, 2002, pp. 23–24).

Discerning readers may wonder how the above examples might be regarded as 'participatory' if there is no obvious element of audience participation, interactivity and collaboration within the performances or in the process leading up to them. Because of the way that many instances of participatory art exist at the threshold of art and civic institutions or realms, there have been many discussions on how to value and speak about participatory art *as art*, a concern prominently raised by Claire Bishop in her critical appraisal of participatory art (2012, p. 18). I share Bishop's concern to find a suitable vocabulary and frame of analysis that will do justice to the complexity of participatory practices, rather than assessing them with unfitting standards. She proposes a 'transversal aesthetic' in the spirit of Félix Guattari, an agonistic approach inspired by Chantal Mouffe, and 'an aesthetic regime that is constitutively contradictory' in the spirit of Jacques Rancière (Bishop, 2012, p. 278; Rancière, 2002). It is no doubt possible to find convincing examples of artworks where tension, friction, opposition and resistance may well be appropriate markers of critical participation in and through art. Yet I cannot dismiss the concern to intervene in and engage with the social in an ameliorative way as something external to or incompatible with the aesthetic. An agonistic approach, understood in Mouffe's sense of the term (Mouffe, 2013), may well characterize some critical modes of participation. Yet to turn this into an imperative, into the necessary and/or sufficient criterion for deciding the aesthetic autonomy of artistic practices, is to disavow the privileges of a certain class or social position and simultaneously to universalize that position. Artists and activists often have to work out of compromising situations and find ways to break out of the conundrums of oppositional refusal vs. tactical embrace, as the Sudanese example above cautiously demonstrates. To refuse to participate in institutions is, as Eyal Weizman compellingly argues, 'an option only for those who can and otherwise will act' (Weizman, 2011, p. 11).

The category of participatory art can therefore be both generative as well as restrictive. Its position across disciplines and institutions allows for new terms and references to emerge, yet this proliferation of terms is accompanied by the quest to mark participatory art as a distinct class of practices with common, recognizable, exemplary characteristics, as a genre. This suggests a certain unresolvable tension in the political economy of such genre formation, a law of genre that Jacques Derrida and Avital Ronell describe as 'a sort of participation without belonging – a taking part in without being part of' (Derrida and Ronell, 1980, p. 59). Affiliation to a given type of participatory practice is thus never far from exceeding those same terms of affiliation. This becomes evident not only in the process of charting the terminologies and typologies of participation, but also crucially in the way institutions embrace participatory art forms, or conversely in the way participatory art can turn into a gesture of institutional critique.

Notes

1 A comparison of recent journal issues from the fields of applied theatre (e.g. *Research in Drama Education, Applied Theatre Researcher*), contemporary art (e.g. *Third Text, October, e-flux*) and theatre/performance studies (e.g. *Performance Research, Theatre Research International*) reveals several common strands of interest in topics such as participation, artistic activism, art education and pedagogical interventions, or the social impact of art. The theoretical frameworks of reference are, however, largely distinct from each other, with a few prominent exceptions, such as references to the work of Claire Bishop or Nicolas Bourriaud, Chantal Mouffe or Jacques Rancière's philosophical reflections on art and aesthetics

2 Raunig and Ray refer to this in terms of the threefold acts of fleeing from, instituting new and transforming existing institutions (2009, pp. 3–12).

3 The production was initially performed at the Al-Bugaa independent theatre festival in Khartoum, where it won an award in 2008 and was later modified for an international audience. Thanks to Mieke Kolk, one of the curators of the Other Sudan Festival (Rotterdam, 2009), and jury member at the Al-Bugaa Theatre Festival, for bringing me into contact with Walid Al-Alphy.

4 The episode is based on a Christian allegory of the 'Seven Sleepers of Ephesus'.

5 For detailed, historicized discussions, see Thiong'o (1998); Anheier and Isar (2007); García Canclini (2005); Kerr (1991).

6 Chatterjee argues that the associational principles of Western, secular, bourgeois, civic institutions were selectively adopted in countries such as India; however, 'the practices that activate the forms and methods of mobilization and participation in political society are not always consistent with these principles of association', which implied that these practices were both subject to and outside of state control or institutional power (1998, p. 13).

7 Extracts from Takala's film works are available via her website www.pilvitakala.com.

8 The method, also gathered under the term ethnomethodology, is

attributed to the American sociologist Harold Garfinkel as well as to Erving Goffmann, who proposed studying how social reality is constructed by violating its tenets. Stanley Milgram also conducted breaching experiments in public spaces, such as breaking a queue at a ticket counter, or getting into a crowded train and asking people to give up their seats (Holstein and Gubrium, 2011). Takala mentioned in an interview (27 January 2015) that she discovered the existence of breaching experiments only after she conducted the *Real Snow White* project.

9 The journal *Performance Research* has dedicated two special issues to participation (2011). One of these zooms in more specifically on processes of synchronization: how applause and moments of simultaneous reaction in audiences characterize affectively charged though highly coded modes of participation (Brandl-Risi, 2011), or how choirs and call-and-response devices are used in experimental settings to voice dissent, rather than one singular voice (Myers, 2011).

10 I derive this pair from Markus Miessen's study on participation in architecture and urban planning which explicitly uses the term 'nightmare of participation' (2011). Miessen in turn references Slavoj Žižek: 'One of the most disgusting things is when what you secretly dream about is brutally imposed on you from outside. We have a nice name for a realized dream: it is called a nightmare' (cited in Miessen, 2011, p. 2).

11 Eva Fotiadi specifically uses the terms 'participatory' and 'collaborative' synonymously, referring to artistic processes in terms of the metaphors of game and play, and examining the preference for activities in which there is a chain of to-and-fro actions and responses (2009). Harvie invokes the notion of 'fair play' with reference to artistic practices under neoliberal conditions (2013).

2

On the inconvenient means and ends of participation

I am an inconvenient woman
or so my president informed me yesterday
I will never be named ambassador
since ladies' high heels I never wear
and anyway with diplomacy
my many talents just don't match. (Rodriguez, Piercy, and Felipe, 1996)

Participation and impact

'Art is not a mirror held up to reality, but a hammer with which to shape it': this well-known adage captures the complex relationship between theatre and performance practices, the societies from which they emerge and to which they respond. It suggests that art can, indeed ought to, impact upon and transform reality, rather than seeking simply to depict and represent reality in a verifiable manner. It seems to contest the possibility of any simple, mimetic portrayal of reality altogether. For not only are there as many realities as there are ways of perceiving them, but something can only become a reality if we are able to first imagine its possibility. The adage invites us to reflect on who wields this hammer, and how it might be used to impact upon reality. The foundational question of theatre's social, cultural, political or ecological impact continues to productively preoccupy artists, scholars and critics. What are the ways in which we can think through participatory art's impact on the world? The notion of impact in conjunction with the arts remains an imprecise and unwieldy one, yet it seems to command significant power in the way it is repeatedly summoned to justify the necessity of the arts. This can be explained by the way in which the idea of impact has become a core feature in determining the cultural value of the arts by policy makers and public and corporate funding bodies. This chapter investigates the assumptions around impact in relation to participatory art, as well as the critical and methodological challenges of thinking them together. Using the 2012 Spanish-language production *Afuera: lesbianas en escena* (*Outside: Lesbians on Stage*) by the theatre collective Teatro Siluetas from Guatemala and El Salvador as a point of departure, the chapter reflects on a number of debates in theatre and performance scholarship pertaining to assessing and evaluating impact in relation to the question of participation.[1] In closing, the chapter offers a number of points of orientation and aspects to take into consideration when undertaking a study of theatre's impact.

The notion of impact (from the Latin verb *impingere*, i.e. to 'press closely', 'fix firmly' or 'forcibly thrust') suggests that something leaves a perceptible mark or trace on its environment or surroundings. When used in relation to theatre and performance, impact seems to imply that they remain and resonate in some way with the world, that they have a palpable effect on those who partook of their making and presentation, especially after they are over. This is hardly surprising, given the ephemerality of theatre, and the medium-specific difficulty of preserving or reproducing theatrical works. Precisely because theatre seemingly vanishes the moment it is performed in the here and now (unlike a book that can be re-read and stored, or a film that can be copied and distributed, or a piece of music that can be preserved in the form of a recording), it seems to repeatedly prompt the question of impact in manifold ways. In conjunction with the field of participatory art, especially those forms with an explicit social objective, where either specific communities are involved in the performance creation process or audiences are integrated through interactive formats into the concept of the performance, the question of impact recurs with a heightened urgency. Funders are often the first to ask what impact a certain artistic intervention will make or has made on its target audiences. What is usually implied is not impact in a personal, affective sense: lasting (positive or negative) impressions, images, movements, scenes, moments that leave a mark on one's memory, resonating with one's emotions, or triggering visceral responses that may extend well beyond the duration of the performance itself. In relation to participatory art, impact tends not to refer to the cathartic effects of art on the spectator by way of a process of inner cleansing or clarification. Instead, it might refer to what a certain production has achieved by way of contributing to public opinion, or in shaping the discourse around a certain, possibly controversial, topic. What discussions has it triggered, how has it thrown open new ways of addressing or perceiving a certain problem? Impact might further suggest that a performance has a specific target audience who might be treated as beneficiaries, i.e. they will benefit in certain ways from the performance, it will have ripple effects on their lives, attitudes or social relations. To ask the question of impact is thus to inquire into the consequences of an artwork in other spheres of life: how has it contributed to or influenced any level of societal transformation? Impact could equally relate to those who are involved in the creative process, thus implying that the very act of participating in a theatrical production, regardless of the outcome, might serve an educational or other purpose.

The idea of impact is largely, but not necessarily always, positively connoted. This distinguishes it from related concepts such as efficacy, which is regarded as a socially productive function, complementary to the entertainment function of art (Schechner, 2002, pp. 76–77). One might, for instance, speak of the negative impact of a certain performance in its propagation of an aggressive masculinity or its misogynist representations of women. In situations of crisis and violent conflict, theatre may play a part in fortifying cultural stereotypes and thus have a negative impact, serving to polarize rather than de-escalate a latent conflict.[2] However, when we speak of theatre's impact, we tend to assume that there will be (or ought to be) one, and that it will be efficacious, hopefully bringing about some desirable change in our lives. This assumption is fraught with its own contradictions. By emphasizing impact, theatrical practices tend to be valued only in terms of their so-called 'usefulness' in other spheres, and not in their own right. Does it promote social cohesion? Does it raise awareness about problems?

Such a reduction of theatrical art to its benefits for society is a false estimation of its potentials. First, it is extremely difficult to trace any direct or causal link between a certain theatrical practice or event and its positive or negative social outcomes. Indeed, it would be more accurate to claim that no peace accords have been signed or ecological disasters been prevented due to the direct influence of participatory performance. Secondly, and more importantly, the potentials of theatre, like all art forms, are not calculable according to the logic of a benefit analysis. Rather than judging theatre and performance by the same standards of assessment that apply to, say, the impact of drinking water supply on public health, it is the very model of impact which needs to be attuned and realigned to the specific qualities of participatory theatre and performance. We therefore need to think of the impact of art in less quantitative or effect-based and more qualitative and affective terms. As James Thompson points out, in concentrating on output or function, 'we are in danger of losing sight of the art practice. We are becoming target not process orientated' (2000, p. 101). We need to rethink the assessment of impact in order to be able to pay attention to subtle, ambiguous and delicate indicators, which may not make sense in cost–benefit or utilitarian terms. The tools of gauging impact available to theatre and performance scholars ought not to be governed by a narrowly economic or technocratic, evidence-based rationale. Thirdly, and following from this, we can observe that even within the field, different traditions of performance practice entail different understandings of impact, which vary historically and regionally. Classical opera productions and participatory theatre workshops with children with autism operate in vastly different environments and reveal distinct interdependences between artistic and sociopolitical domains. Thus when the question of the impact of a certain theatre practice is asked, it is important to examine the assumptions implicit in the question and its possible claims around usefulness, applicability, causality and measurability, in order to determine a working understanding of impact that is befitting to the practice.

Notwithstanding the various assumptions surrounding the notion of impact in relation to the arts, it continues to be an idea that holds the heady promise of transformation and affective force in the world. The artistic and cultural life of a society is often regarded as the 'barometer' of its well-being, maturity and, indeed, degree of civilization. This widely held orthodoxy tends to assume that the study of impact is therefore about measuring and finding evidence for its existence, rather than interrogating its claims (Belfiore and Bennett, 2008, p. 7). How can we speak about the impact of theatre and performance in the interpretive humanities, without falling prey to the tyranny of evidence and numbers? This is all the more relevant given the growing necessity for artists to demonstrate and quantify the impact of their artistic ideas in order to gain funding. A critical approach to impact could thus serve as a means to respond to funding policies from the grassroots level as well as expanding and shaping the conception of impact in a manner that is adequate to the diversity of the arts.

Outsiders on stage: Teatro Siluetas

The independent performance collective Teatro Siluetas (Spanish: 'silhouettes') was founded in 2011 by four women from Guatemala and El Salvador, self-identified as lesbian feminist activists, with the aim of using theatre as a means to reflect on the experiences of lesbian subjectivities in Central America. The members of the group are affiliated to and involved in various ways with autonomous feminist social justice movements on the continent. Following their participation in the activist initiative 'The Lesbian Feminist School' in Guatemala, they came together with the idea of continuing their activism using the modalities of theatre, with which all four were familiar or in which they were formally trained. To that extent, the formation of the theatre collective itself may be regarded as one indicator of the productive impact of their involvement in the feminist movement. Which is to say that the notion of impact is multi-directional; it is not only about theatre's impact on society but also about the way in which theatre is impacted upon by social developments. Two characteristics of Teatro Siluetas are pertinent in relation to the question of impact and participation: the choice of the organizational form of a collective and the foregrounding of a lesbian subjectivity in the artistic practice. In the following, I examine these aspects in detail in relation to their 2012 production *Afuera: lesbianas en escena* (*Outside: Lesbians on Stage*).

For the members of Siluetas, it was important to organize the day-to-day practices of theatre in a way that questioned and changed the ways in which creative processes tended to be hierarchically organized, with predominantly male directors and playwrights having the voice of authority and actresses merely executing and embodying their ideas. Siluetas therefore collectively wrote and directed and produced a play through a process of experimentation and dialogical interaction, which not only included a horizontal communication between the four members of the collective, but also involved training with renowned artists, including dancers, choreographers and theatre directors such as Jesusa Rodríguez and her singer-songwriter partner Liliana Felipe from Mexico City, with whose input they completed the final version of the play *Afuera* (Cañénguez, 2015). Rodríguez and Felipe are known both for their lesbian-feminist performance activism and for their long-standing engagement with current political themes pertaining to the Latin American continent.

The choice of working as a collective has a well-known heritage in Latin American experimental theatre and performance history. The tradition of autonomous theatre collectives (*creación colectiva*) is often traced to the influence of the new theatre movement in Latin America, some of whose key representatives include Julio Castillo from Mexico, Enrique Buenaventura and Jacqueline Vidal from the Teatro Experimental de Cali in Colombia, founded in 1955, as well as Santiago García and Patricia Ariza from the group La Candelaria, founded in 1966 (Cortés and Barrea-Marlys, 2003; Röttger, 1992). La Candelaria's approach to democratization revolved not only around the selection of appropriate themes for plays and around aesthetic questions, but crucially invoked a form of institutional critique. They called for theatrical institutions and groups to adopt participatory methods not only in their relations to audiences but also in their working processes.[3] La Candelaria's members collectively shared responsibility for all aspects of theatre practice, from artistic direction to staging, lighting, costumes and production work, thus experimenting with alternatives to a playwright- or director-led theatre practice (Weiss, 1980, p. 24). The performances of Teatro Experimental de Cali sought to actively pay attention to audience responses as a means of developing the complexity of a play over time (Taylor and

Townsend, 2008, p. 19). Influential figures such as theatre direc-tor Enrique Buenaventura highlighted the importance of theatre practitioners performing in both urban and rural settings, to a wide range of audiences: 'We are looking for communication basically in the relationship between play and audience. That is why our work and style are not directed solely to workers or peasants, but also to the bourgeoisie and students: colonial deformation concerns us all in different ways' (Buenaventura, 1970, p. 155). Such an approach, envisioning the play and audience as communicating with each other, employs a broader conception of participation than merely the formal element of audience participation during a performance. It seeks a politicization of theatre practice through modalities of establish-ing dialogues with audiences, feedback loops in the dramaturgical process and what is today sometimes referred to as the 'outreach activities' of the arts

The relationship between participation and impact can be further examined through the foregrounding of lesbian subjectivity in the work of Teatro Siluetas. One might regard the launching of a thea-tre group that specifically addresses the needs and lives of subjects regarded as marginalized and under-represented in the mainstream as an identitarian or minoritarian formation, with the purpose of gaining more visibility and acknowledgement in the public sphere. For Siluetas members, however, the motivation in founding a les-bian collective extends beyond an identity-based politics. Rather, the category of 'lesbian' presents for the theatre collective an intersec-tional lens through which all systems of oppression and inequality can be approached (Cañénguez, 2015). Thus it is possible to sharpen one's understanding of racism, ableism, or other forms of social discrimination through paying attention to the mechanisms by which women who are attracted to women are oppressed, for not only are different forms of oppression intertwined, but, conversely, the unique experience of identifying with the figurations of 'lesbian' in a Central American context offers a different perspective on main-stream society, politics and public culture, and sheds light on the construction of categories such as 'homosexual' or 'heterosexual'. The theatrical representation of lesbian lives in *Afuera* can thus be read not as a direct correlate to some authentic reality or indigenous identity, but as a means of unsettling and reimagining the terms of this reality.

The play *Afuera* addresses a range of issues, from lesbophobia, sexual violence and the role of religious institutions in the governance of sexual mores, to the prominent presence of religious conservatism in public affairs, in tandem with the strengthening of neoliberal economic policies put in place after the end of the civil wars in El Salvador and Guatemala in the 1990s. It also examines the lives of lesbians who challenge or try to escape from the binary gender construction with humour and lightness. It speaks of questions of loneliness, the absence of role models and popular cultural points of reference. In dramaturgical terms, it consists of a sequence of short scenes that combine a range of formats, from fragments of daily life experiences, monologues, dialogues, choreographed interludes, to humorous episodes, or elaborate *tableaux vivants*. The scenes sometimes involve conventional role-play, with four actresses playing characters such as a nun or a couple in love, shifting between *femme* and *butch* roles, well-wishers or people who ridicule lesbians. But there are also moments when they step out of their roles and address the audience directly in their own voices as members of the theatre collective and citizens of the society. This makes it difficult to view 'the lesbian' as merely a fictional character on stage, but urges audiences in a non-didactic and non-confessional manner to acknowledge a personally experienced reality on and offstage. Layers of prejudice and unquestioned assumptions about what the idea of sexual orientation implies are gradually peeled off, revealing the vulnerabilities and ambiguities of human existence.

The production *Afuera* toured across Guatemala and was performed not only in theatre venues, but also in schools, universities, community centres and female prisons, covering both urban as well as rural sites. These performances were accompanied by question-and-answer sessions with audiences, and workshops with young adults. The combination of theatre practice with educational, activist and outreach activities is widely found in many women's theatre initiatives in the continent (Underiner, 2004). A documentary film was made in 2013 about the performance *Afuera* with the financial support of the Dutch international development agency HIVOS and in collaboration with

the network of Latin American artists Trasbastidores (Backstage)
All these aspects of a performance's (after)-life are also pertinent to
the assessment of its impact. What counts as impact, under which
conditions? How can impact be evaluated and what are the methods
available to theatre and performance scholars in this quest?

On impact studies

In thinking through the question of impact in the arts, a brief note
on the prominent influence of the domain of social and economic
impact studies is in order. This domain of research gained currency
in the 1980s, at a time when urban regeneration programmes in
Europe, the USA and other industrially developed regions of the
world increasingly looked to arts and culture to fill the gaps that were
emerging from the decline of industries in cities. Artistic and cultural
activities gradually came to be regarded as an 'expanding economic
sector' (Reeves, 2002). This led to the commissioning of studies that
demonstrated how investment in the arts effectively led to greater
economic growth or job creation in other sectors. Such advocacy-
oriented studies started from the premise that the arts are economically beneficial to cities, and looked for evidence of this in order to
advocate public investment in the arts and in cultural activities and
institutions. As Belfiore and Bennett point out, impact studies is
motivated by an evidence-based approach to policy making, whereby
pragmatism and an orientation towards 'whatever brings about the
best results' serves as a guide to policy making, rather than ideals
or principles derived from constitutional or long-standing culturally
rooted grounds (2008, p. 5). The problems of such an evidence-led,
economistic approach to studying impact have been widely criticized
in cultural policy studies. All kinds of claims can be made about
the benefits of the arts, and the search for impact can end up being
based on indicators that are likely to produce the desired findings.
In the logic of viewing the arts as an economic sector, the study
of impact often becomes a matter of arguing that the arts generate
employment, enhance social cohesion, or reduce crime, which in
turn indirectly supports economic growth. Thus, despite a rationale
of searching for evidence for art's social or economic benefits. deep-

seated, unquestioned cultural norms and values pertaining to what counts as beneficial or has a positive transformative potential inform the way that impact is quantified. Conventional impact studies tend to be commissioned by organizations that support or fund the arts, which means that the findings of these studies tend to advocate various benefits and economically viable qualities of the arts, thus serving as advocacy reports rather than as research.

A further problematic aspect of the domain of impact studies is that it tends to predominantly value the arts along instrumental lines. The problem is not, as Belfiore convincingly argues, that a certain instrumentality is applied to the arts. Rather, the problem 'lies in the way in which the attribution of value to the outcome of aesthetic encounters has become part of the technocratic machinery of cultural policy-making' (Belfiore, 2015, p. 96). Mostly quantitative understandings of value tend to determine whether or not a certain artistic practice is worth investing in. Thus, even within the economic logic, a very narrow understanding of 'more is better', underwritten by governmental policies of austerity and privatization, remains largely unquestioned (Fotiadi, 2017). Economic understandings of impact thus assume far more policy-related influence and importance than other, less utilitarian and more interpretive, subjective approaches. The political philosopher Wendy Brown argues that neoliberalism is 'an order of rationality', i.e. not only a set of economic policies or an ideology, but also a political imaginary, an order of reason that seeps into all human domains in the most unexpected ways and in manifold forms of articulation (2015, pp. 10–11). Every human need and desire becomes valued in economized terms, which doesn't necessarily just mean monetary terms, but a logic of profit, benefit, growth and expansion. This also extends to those spheres that were historically governed by different values, such as the arts, interpersonal relationships, children's upbringing, education, health and well-being, ecology, or spirituality. Impact studies in the arts, particularly those that seek to prove and rationalize the benefits of the arts and demonstrate them as worthy of receiving structural or financial support, face the risk of succumbing to a neoliberal logic, even while they may claim to be championing the arts.

I would like to move away from such an evidence-based, economically rationalized understanding of impact towards a more ambivalent, open-ended notion, encompassing diverse dimensions and modes of interrelations between artworks and the societies they emerge from and respond to. The study of impact cannot be separated from the conditionalities and agendas of who is interested in theatre's impact and to what ends. The evaluation of impact is not an end in itself (Isar and Anheier, 2007, p. 4). What form a study takes largely depends on who commissions the research, to whom the results are presented, and how these results are used in policy making or structural decision making. Further, impact need not only be perceived as the effect of the big on the small, the powerful on the weak, or of institutions on individuals, but can also be meaningfully addressed from a multi-directional, systemic perspective, i.e. how non-institutionalizable acts and collective bodies in turn transform the structures into which they are placed, by which they may be restricted or empowered, but which never entirely constitute or define them. Impact need not be only positive and beneficial, and it is also the critical task of scholars to pay attention to negative aspects. This does not necessarily imply that it is a rejection of an artistic practice or its efforts altogether. There are many forceful arguments suggesting that participation need not have the same function in the arts as it does in other areas of public life, given that aesthetic criteria need not always tally with the criteria of democratic citizenship. To have the feeling of being excluded or invisible within the safe space of the theatre may be a powerfully disturbing aesthetic experience, enabling and triggering reflection precisely because it is set at a distance from exclusion and invisibility in society, however notional that distance might be. The socially critical participatory potential of an artwork may indeed lie in its not being 'useful' or 'applicable' in any empirically verifiable sense.

A number of scholars have made a case for such a critique of participatory art by suggesting that, instead of insisting on its being inclusive, cohesive and socially relevant, performance could counter-intuitively combat the ideology at work behind these commodified norms and not attempt to be a model consummation of macro-political causes. This critique has at least two variations. First, it is argued that meaningful impact through participation need not equal cohesiveness and consensus among participants, for dissent, disagreement, conflict and respect for alterity are as important to democratic political life as inclusivity, usefulness and cohesion, and the careful education that nurtures these is provided in the spaces and textures of the aesthetic. This strand of critique is most prominently developed by Claire Bishop, building on Chantal Mouffe's distinction between the *politics* and the *political* and a mobilization of Rancière's notion of dissensus (Bishop, 2012; Mouffe, 2013; Rancière, 2010). With a different emphasis, Irit Rogoff notes her suspicion towards so-called accessible artworks, or more specifically towards the demand for art to be accessible, which results in what she views as the instrumentalization of the question of *access* towards a client-oriented *accessibility* (Butt and Rogoff, 2013, pp. 71–73).

Secondly, it is argued that the appearance of categories such as (inter)activity, cohesion, personal encounter and conviviality within the framework of art projects may well be a signal of their absence or disappearance in civic life in general and must therefore be regarded with caution. In *Artist at Work: Proximity of Art and Capitalism* (2015) the dance scholar Bojana Kunst maintains that 'the production of sociality signals that art is actually closely intertwined with the processes of the disappearance of the sociality and political articulations of the public' (Kunst, 2015, p. 52). Qualities such as communication, sociability or creativity have now become financialized in their logic and integrated into neoliberal economic roles in such a way that their radical function as artistic concepts has been altered. Hito Steyerl notes in a similar vein that 'what used to be work has increasingly been turned into occupation' (Steyerl, 2011, p. 48), thus having no end, product or concrete instrumental relation, and this shift from work to occupation has also included the work of art becoming the occupation of art, so that instead of an end product, art consists of activity, which is deemed to be its own reward.

Curiously, just as 'uselessness' is invoked as a means of expanding what counts as impact, so also 'usefulness' as an aesthetic category can be invoked as a means of critiquing art's commodification. In her 'Introduction on Useful Art' (2011) the Cuban-American artist and curator Tania Bruguera proclaims that it is time 'to put Duchamp's urinal back in the restroom'. Bruguera's statement is neither a conservative dismissal of Marcel Duchamp's work, nor of the conceptual shift in modern art that this canonical work of 1917, titled *Fountain/ La Fontaine*, came to be representative of. She is not claiming that a urinal is not an art object in any given tradition of art criticism and must therefore be kept out of the sanctified exhibition spaces of art institutions. Rather, her statement is a reversal and expropriation of Duchamp's gesture, a call to take art and its institutions to places where it may be endowed with a lived purpose, where it does not remain a commodity or utilitarian item, but has the capacity to shift perspectives and sensibilities. Bruguera's statement may be interpreted as a call to rethink the task of the art world, not by turning the work of Duchamp into a formula and bringing more and more ready-made or day-to-day objects into formal art spaces, but rather by honouring the critical logic of its appearance. Duchamp's urinal, in its own moment, was a provocation to art institutions and their taken-for-granted modes of production and consumption of art. By installing an object of everyday life in an art gallery, he sought to draw attention to the interdependent relationship between what becomes an artwork, the contexts of its reception, and its institutional affiliations. Its status as art consists in its revelation of the *logic* of the artwork in a particular system of art (Meireles, 2007, p. 183). It is thus no coincidence that Bruguera referred precisely to Duchamp in order to make a point that seems, at first glance, to be at odds with Duchamp. Art objects such as *The Fountain* followed the Dadaist impulse of making the distinction between art and life useless, by bringing into focus the logic by which objects come to be regarded as art or not. Bruguera's call for a return of the urinal from the art gallery to the toilet seeks to both employ and undo this conceptual impulse provided by Duchamp, in order to pursue a project of what she terms 'useful art' (*arte útil*).

This is not a simple repetition of the debate between engaged art in opposition to art for art's sake. Even when taken literally, Bruguera's proposition poses intriguing questions. For what would it mean to return the use value to the urinal that is now elevated to the status of a canonical artwork, with its attendant art-historical debates and processes of commodification? What would it mean to allow it to become the thing it stood for, and simultaneously retain its exchange value in terms of its history as a provocative artwork? The gesture suggested by Bruguera calls for closer attention to the forms of participation that the artwork might generate when 'put to use', and thus claims the recognition of these operations as art. It invites a recognition of the paradigm shift that occurs when the aesthetic judgement of art is linked to its use or application, particularly to the participatory experiences it accesses.

Sometimes the radical potential of an artistic practice lies in its usefulness, and at other times in its refusal to be useful. If both usefulness and its inverse can be regarded as modes of critical practice in relation to participatory art, how then to make sense of a category that can mean so many, sometimes contradictory, things at different moments, and is nevertheless claimed as a distinctive aesthetic mode? Teatro Siluetas is acutely conscious of this dialectic. The play *Afuera* repeatedly references the systemic violence towards women in Central America. 'Are you lesbians in real life?' asks a school pupil during an after-performance discussion in rural Ciudad Quetzal, Guatemala, and when Teatro Siluetas members say 'Yes', the classroom bursts into a round of applause, a mix of embarrassment and admiration. The 'lesbian' comes to life by stepping out of the fictive construction of the performance, she is given the possibility of existing, not as a victim of abuse or as a potential threat but as an embodied subject, recognizable, reachable. Such moments reveal how restrictive it is to draw a neat line dividing the seemingly symbolic space of the theatre and the presumably real space of social and political coexistence, as if the former were a mere service provider or pet animal offering solace and entertainment to the latter, or as if the latter by definition could safely exclude the unruly realms of imagination and the impractical dimensions of the aesthetic. The participation of audiences in the life of a performance and the impact of performance on their lives are questions that need to be answered in ways other than the purely functional, or in terms of costs and benefits. The relevant issue is not a definition of participatory art and its formats, but rather an elaboration of the problems highlighted through participation in its multiple expressions and histories.

The history of the term 'participation' in the field of public policy and international development has no doubt influenced its trajectory in the arts, particularly in terms of the strong preference for participatory art forms in programmes funded through developmental schemes. Perhaps both the quest for the positive social impact of the arts as well as scepticism towards the imperative of 'usefulness' can be traced to the ascendancy of 'participation' in the context of international development.[4] The political economist and development theorist Pablo Alejandro Leal explains the rise of the term 'participation' as 'a new battle horse for official development' as coinciding with the so-called structural adjustment programmes imposed on most countries of the Global South by the World Bank and the International Monetary Fund beginning in the 1980s (2011, p. 71). Using the debt of poor countries as leverage, a sweeping array of privatization, austerity and trade liberalization policy measures were imposed on countries in Africa, Latin America and South and Southeast Asia, most of which were euphemistically labelled as people-friendly, bottom-up approaches, in which terms such as participation, empowerment and civil society were rediscovered as blueprints of governance (Cornwall and Eade, 2010). Leal reads the concept of 'participation' as having been particularly co-opted and sanitized, because it is drawn from a paradigm in which the principal objective is not institutional development or stability, but social justice and structural change (2011, pp. 71–72). From its historical association with radical pedagogy (Freire, 1968), social movements and direct action (Fals-Borda and Rahman, 1991), and citizenship rights (Chandhoke, 2003), the notion of 'participation' can be observed as mutating its way into the status-quo-ist vocabulary of 'maintaining relations of rule, neutralizing political opposition and ... taxing the poorest' (Cornwall and Brock, 2005, p. 1046).

The problem is, of course, not simply a matter of a concept being disembowelled into hollow jargon. As Wendy Brown has argued, the matter of real concern is the absorption of a concept into the neoliberal political imaginary, into an all-pervasive order of rationality (Brown, 2015, pp. 10–11). The concept of participation is thus mobilized in the maintenance of the interests of the powerful, an insidious shift from being a collective, autonomous demand to becoming a managerial imperative, which allows the state to devolve its responsibilities on to citizens, financializing citizenship into a form of entrepreneurialism and re-centralizing in the guise of decentralization (Brown, 2015,

Pearce, 2010, p. 15). On a smaller scale, the 'tyranny of participation' could imply that participatory processes are dealt with as a matter of technical administration, overriding legitimate concerns through a focus on methodological revisionism (Cooke and Kothari, 2001). The call for wider and deeper participation in public affairs, where even the most disadvantaged citizens have a say in matters that affect their lives, is reduced to questions of format or procedure: crowd-sourcing takes the place of collective action, user-generated content management systems mimic equitable access, do-it-yourself and self-service become attractive as consumer mandates rather than as political tools. Critics of neoliberalism repeatedly point out the dangers of focusing exclusively on participation as a developmental tool or a method in project work, at the cost of ignoring the broader ideological or political canvas or the underlying processes of active citizenship. The received wisdom of the overwhelming benefits of participation need to be weighed against the experiences in the field (Hickey and Mohan, 2004, p. 1). The methods of audience participation may be well intentioned and based on progressive democratic principles; however, if they are deployed in ways that undermine these principles, they become coercive or 'tyrannical' (Cooke and Kothari, 2001). Conversely, even under clearly repressive conditions, collective participation may prove to be effective in contesting pervasive norms. The mere performance of a play on lesbian relationships in the parish hall of a small town in Guatemala may be impactful in ways that neither the play nor its audiences may fathom or have been able to foresee. No regularities can be projected on to participatory practices, nor should the concept be underpinned by a linear or evolutionary idea of impact (Cleaver, 1999).

The debate between the utopian ideal and the watering down of participation seems to have moved on with what seems to me a significant conclusion, namely that the critical recognition of the dangers of co-optation should not imply that the concept be discarded altogether. The task of revaluing participation, whether in social development theory or in the arts, lies in the extent to which practices are firmly committed to societal and structural transformation rather than to the objectives of statecraft or mere formal innovation (Hickey and Mohan, 2004). Reading political and social discussions of participation covering four decades of transnational development policy turbulence, it becomes evident that there is sufficient commitment by scholars and activists to the ideals of the concept for them not be satisfied with a critique of the ways in which participation is contorted into a neoliberal rationality, however necessary and indispensable such a consistent critique might be. How therefore to critique participation and its attendant quest for impact in a constructive way, as something one cannot do without? How might this stance be understood in the realm of the arts, given that the notion of participation circulates in aesthetic, cultural, social-political and economic realms in very different ways?

The problem of aggregation

One of the critical challenges in studying participatory theatre's impact lies in determining its scale, scope and intensity by paying attention to the particularities of every specific instance. We could start by asking what exactly we refer to when we speak of participatory theatre: a single performance, the work of a theatre group, a tour or festival, a play script, the acting skills of one actress, or a certain formal characteristic? When we speak of impact, what are the time and geographical ranges we seek to or are able to address? Are we interested in individuals or communities, in the short or long term, in the local or regional or transnational, and why? Being explicit and specific about the grids of our frameworks is crucial, simply because different understandings of the arts, of communities and of the scope of impact will lead to different outcomes (Guetzkow, 2002). In the case of Teatro Siluetas' show *Afuera*, the framework of analysis might be restricted to a single performance, or its entire production history, i.e. all the performances in different locations, or additionally include the documentary film that can be viewed online. If one is interested in addressing the impact of the process of performance making on the actresses and their social environments, the framework might be extended to the entire process of conceptualizing, rehearsing and producing the performance. It can be further expanded to include the ways in which the performance circulated to other parts of the world, through donor agency reports, or by way of invitations to the theatre group members to LGBTQI events, and academic scholarship. This selection depends on what we can access in depth and what we are interested in finding out. If we ask the question of the impact of Latin American lesbian feminism on the practice of collective, collaborative dramaturgy, we obviously need to attend to the rehearsal and conceptual processes as well as to the specificities of lesbian feminism in Guatemala and El Salvador far more than to audience responses. If we are interested in the impact of the performance on attitudes towards sexuality among young adults, we must look for ways to access and communicate with young adults who have seen the performance, independently from or in addition to what may be available to us via documentation or reports by the theatre group.

The broader question here is that of aggregation, namely how to interconnect the micro with the macro levels. How can we claim with any certainty that there is a connection between the ticket sales for the show and a growing acceptance and liberal attitude towards homosexuality in society? Causality is a tricky principle when it comes to studying the arts. It is a fallacy to claim, for instance, that urban audiences in Guatemala were more receptive to the topic of lesbianism than rural audiences, *because* there was more laughter and applause in the former than in the latter. There is no direct causal link between applause for a show and the social openness towards a taboo topic that is the subject of the show. On the contrary, it is well known that what is widely accepted and appreciated by audiences within the imaginative space of performance may equally meet with hostility and violence on the streets (Butler, 1988). Audience laughter during a scene when two women kiss on stage may well be an expression of embarrassment, ridicule or even of a sense of disgust, just as the laughter of teenage school pupils at a performance in a high school may be an indicator of a healthy emotional receptiveness and curiosity towards sexuality and love, or indeed a mix of emotions. It requires heightened caution and sensitivity as a viewer and researcher to distinguish between appreciative and disapproving responses and draw conclusions based on them.

Taken together, the specificities of the performance and its interaction with its contexts or situational settings form a conceptually open arrangement rather than a fixed observational perspective of participation (Cohen and Uphoff, 2011, p. 43). As a methodological guideline, it suggests that the internal dynamics and modalities of participation cannot be entirely viewed at a remove from its external modes of circulation. The crucial implication from this for analysis is that, unlike many debates in the arts on autonomy vs. heteronomy, this model envisions an artwork's self-contained, aesthetic features (its 'autonomy') being thought in continuum with, rather than in opposition to, its interconnectedness to the world and the context it is situated in (its 'heteronomy'). It can be observed that the interest in understanding participatory modalities and conceptualizing them in relation to the problems of society is a shared problem that is pursued in different ways in the social sciences and in the arts. Finding ways to study and interconnect audience participation in performance with performance participation in its immediate and broader social, cultural, political or economic environment seems to be one of the most pressing tasks of scholarship on participatory art. This partly involves being attentive to the fluctuating boundaries between the aesthetic and the non-aesthetic rather than seeking a disciplinary cartography that can supposedly contain and settle them. It might be achieved through an investigation of how the political or social premises underlying the call for participation are reimagined through an aesthetic register, such as modes of representation or theatrical devices such as allegorization, de-familiarization or distancing. Conversely, it could pertain to how artistic strategies of shaping audience participation render visible the failures and possibilities of people's participation in the public sphere, as in works that problematize exploitative labour conditions or political repression by mimicking them, over-identifying with them or making them evident through a process of exaggeration (BAVO, 2007; Holmes, 2009).

Gareth White's *Applied Theatre: Aesthetics* (2015) proposes expanding the kinds of activities considered relevant to a participatory aesthetic, suggesting that we should look not only at performances as distinct works, but place them in a longer-term aesthetic continuum with workshops, rehearsals, after-talks, meetings with the artists, try-out sessions, installations and other para-theatrical events (2015, p. 61). The research group 'Assemblies and Participation' based in Hamburg, Germany, similarly seeks to connect dimensions and contexts of participation, by asking which new forms of assembly and participation can be imagined today, and how they might be honed within the realm of theatre and performance to be adequate to the needs and demands of democracy and social action (Burry et al., 2014). Formats such as lecture-performances, school classroom activities or assemblies in public spaces are explored in this study through participatory artistic means. The now defunct Indonesian journal of performing arts, *Lebur*, offers another instance of a multidisciplinary and unorthodox approach to cultural politics and questions of participation outside of formal academic platforms, thus including actions taking place in the streets, in market squares and on university campuses.[5] Such analyses attest to the myriad ways in which participatory performance and civic participation intersect.

Institutional impact

One of the possible ways to resolve the problem of aggregating the relation between the performance and society at large is to define and delimit the analysis to specific societal institutions, and examine the points of contact between the performance and these institutions. These could include artistic and cultural venues but also community centres, schools, universities, prisons or church-run institutions. Such institutions can be regarded, in the sense of Louis Althusser, as ideological state apparatuses, which reinforce the dominant ideology without using repressive force or violence (Althusser, 2014).[6] The performance *Afuera* premiered on 26 January 2012 in the Teatro de Bellas Artes of Guatemala City, a cultural institution under the aegis of the Guatemalan Ministry of Culture and Sports. Laia Ribera Cañénguez, a member of Teatro Siluetas, describes in an interview the difficulties in finding a venue that was willing to host this particular performance, because theatres did not want to risk their reputations by hosting a group that openly talked about lesbianism (2015, p. 246). The fact that Teatro de Bellas Artes hosted the event might be interpreted as a mark of the critical capacity of the institution. In showing its support to an independent lesbian feminist production in the face of widespread institutional caution and conservatism, it effectively took a public stance in support of reflecting on the social issues that the performance addressed. Who made the decision to include the performance in the programme? Were there prior connections to members of the theatre collective? Perhaps it lost some of its regular audience members in the process, perhaps it accessed a different public, or perhaps it led to new international connections All these aspects could form the focus of an investigation. Similarly we could inquire into the impact on those institutions that hesitated or categorically refused to host the performance. Was there an internal discussion prior to the decision, how were the hesitations regarding the play formulated, how did the institutions perceive their own social responsibility? Since the performance toured to various other countries and was shown in venues such as universities, schools and church centres, the institutional responses and afterlife of the performance offer possibilities for analysing its social impact on institutions with which it came into contact. Since these institutions made it possible for people who would presumably never buy a ticket to go and see the show in Guatemala City, to view the performance in a familiar environment, it is no exaggeration to claim that the outreach of the performance expanded greatly by virtue of being shown under the purview of these rural institutions.

The performance also triggered some discriminatory responses from institutions. In Costa Rica, the performers were asked to leave a café where they had gathered after a show, since the owners felt that the presence of lesbians would be a bad influence on children (Cañénguez, 2015, p. 247). In anticipation of protests or objections to the play, the theatre group took security measures at the performance venues, to prevent damage to property or personal injury. One of the performers was asked by her family to leave Guatemala, in order not to blemish the family's reputation. This indicates that performances (or public perceptions and projections of what a performance is about) can trigger very real social repercussions, which are enacted by institutions. These can come from strangers as well as from families and close networks. These impacts can consist of a motley of negative and positive responses, ranging from sentiments of moral outrage and offence on the one hand to accolades and praise from the press on the other.

In all this, the performance realistically constitutes but one of several factors that impact on institutional attitudes, policies or practices.

There is thus at best an indirect correlation between the level of participatory involvement of an institution and the extent of public impact it may have. The models of institutional participation can thus range from contributory or collaborative, to co-created and hosted projects, without one necessarily being better than others (Simon, 2010, p. 187).

Impact on individuals

Yet, while it might be possible to gather statistics on the demographics of the audiences, and make qualified observations about the ways in which a performance influences, critiques or interacts with institutions, this still leaves open the question as to how to qualitatively assess a performance's impact on individuals. Audience responses have served as the primary route for assessing the individual dimensions of impact (Bennett, 1990). While this study does not have the scope to address the methodological and theoretical complexities of audience and reception research, I would like to underline one point, at the risk of overstating the obvious, namely: every utterance about a performance and the impact it has on an audience member needs to be carefully contextualized. It cannot be taken at face value or viewed as a validation for an external, objective reality. Precisely because our access to these contexts is likely to be limited, great caution is called for in deriving generalizations. In the case of *Afuera*, the overwhelmingly positive and supportive responses of audience members towards the performance stand in contrast to a social and political climate that is extremely hostile to those who do not conform to the norms of heterosexuality. How to make sense of this disjunction? To find an answer to this question, it is worthwhile examining some of the individual responses more closely.

Interaction with audiences, specifically with young people and women from working-class and indigenous backgrounds, was an important motivating factor for Teatro Siluetas. The performances thus regularly featured after-talks with the public. They also offered the opportunity for audience members to write down their questions anonymously on a piece of paper, in case they did not feel comfortable asking something directly. One such note they received asked the unassuming question: 'Es bonito ser lesbiana?' (Is it nice to be lesbian?). Cañénguez cautions against reading this remark as an innocent response from a simple, good-hearted, rural woman (2015, p. 249). Rather, she suggests contextualizing such positive responses against the backdrop of a society recovering from a protracted civil war, in which self-pride and respect for a community's identity had become important means of recovering from violent conflict. The play's choice of deliberately not depicting lesbians as victims, and not speaking with tones of self-pity and resentment, allowed for diverse forms of audience empathy and identification. This also explains responses such as the following: 'I thought I was coming to see a lesbian play and I wanted to show my solidarity, but through the play I ended up thinking about my own relations, my construction of gender and I felt that it spoke to me very personally' (Cañénguez, 2015, p. 245). Instead of serving an identity politics, i.e. speaking primarily to those (few) who might self-identify with the protagonists of the performance, and thus treating lesbian subjectivity as a state of exception, *Afuera* looks for grounds of commonality with audiences. The specific loneliness that the figures in the play experience might thus be accessed as a universal, human emotion. One struggle for human dignity and recognition is not equivalent to, but also not separable from, another. When audience members say they are *touched* or *moved* by witnessing the vulnerability of another body or by the life story of another person, we are compelled to widen our understanding of impact to include not only social, political or economic *effects*, but equally psycho-physical *affects*: those forces other than or complementary to rationality, linearity, causality and cognition, which propel us in various directions in our lives and worlds (Gregg and Seigworth, 2010). These cannot be measured or valued in any empirical manner, but require an interpretive register that can encompass subjective, visceral, emotional, experiential and sensorial traces.

Gradations of participation

The problem of aggregation, i.e. the relationship between participatory art and its social impact, can be further described in terms of a spectrum of various levels of intensity of participation. Pablo Helguera proposes such a multi-layered typology based on formal criteria, distinguishing between so-called single-encounter events and those artworks that involve participation over a longer period of time (Helguera, 2011, pp. 14–15). *Afuera* combines both these levels, employing a longer term collaborative process between lesbian activists in creating a performance and touring to several places, as well as single-encounter events, eliciting audience participation in after-performance discussions. To this quantitative distinction Helguera also adds qualitative components. In the case of single-encounter events, he distinguishes between nominal and directed participation, i.e. where the public participates via contemplation and detached reflection, as 'regular' spectators, or where audiences are asked to follow certain pre-scripted instructions. In those practices involving a lengthier process of interaction, Helguera further distinguishes between a creative participation on the one hand, i.e. where audiences provide ideas or inputs within a structure pre-determined or devised by the artist or given in the method, and a collaborative participation on the other, i.e. where responsibility for the artwork's structure and content is shared between the artist and audiences, who become collaborators or co-creators (Helguera, 2011, pp. 15–16). A further threefold distinction proposed by Helguera is based on the conditions of participation, namely that between voluntary (i.e. active and willing), non-voluntary (i.e. mandated, prescribed) and involuntary (i.e. unknowing or coincidental) modes of participation, a categorization derived from a study on social work by John Poulin (2011, p. 15; 2000). By framing participation in terms of being voluntary, involuntary or non-voluntary, Helguera makes a useful technical distinction, for instance between a performance in which one is given certain tasks to perform without having the option not to perform them (non-voluntary), and an art installation that involves stepping on objects in a public space, without being aware of an intended interactivity with those objects (involuntary).

Jen Harvie reads these gradations of conditions with reference to the efforts of participants in terms of labour and leisure, terms belonging to a political economy of participatory art (2013). Harvie asks what kinds of labour are immanent to different forms of participation, under what conditions they serve as a form of outsourcing or crowd-sourcing, potentially dumbing down audiences, and when they might lead to a heightened awareness of the conditions of work in socially committed art (Harvie, 2013, p. 60). Regarding the performance by Teatro Siluetas, these questions can only be answered with reference to the specific circumstances of its staging and its reception. To some extent such gradations of participation, from low to high intensity, from short- to long-term, correspond to the categories proposed by Sherry Arnstein in her often-cited essay 'A Ladder of Citizen Participation' (1969). Arnstein was a member of a Washington-based research institute on community development and advisor to the city administration on issues such as citizen participation, following the student protests of 1968 across the world and the growing civil rights movement in the United States. Her typology of participation follows a hierarchical, juridical scheme, with the rungs of the ladder gradually moving from a less desirable manipulative concept of (non)-participation to the most desirable models of participation involving full citizen control.[7] To what extent is this applicable to artistic practices, and how would it reflect the relationship between participatory art and the societal settings in which they take place?

The play *Afuera* attempts to highlight the otherwise marginalized perspective of lesbians in Central America, thus locating the voices of a minority centre-stage and demanding of the majority that they be quiet, listen and pay attention. The idea that the participation of as many as possible is the ultimate aim of participatory art is called into question, instead proposing a scenario that privileges a minoritarian perspective. This remains the case even when the performance is staged for an audience consisting largely of children or young adults. It would thus be inappropriate to claim that a fully collaborative, citizen-controlled or child-centred art project is better or more desirable than one involving minor gestures of participation, to the extent that the former may be dull and one-dimensional, whereas the latter may offer valuable provocations or imaginative moments (Fletcher-Watson, 2015, pp. 29–30). The distinction between benign and undesirable forms of participation not only depends on the conceptual set-up of a performance practice, but is equally subject to the energetic unpredictability of a live moment. It may thus be necessary for theatre practitioners to move up and down the rungs of Arnstein's ladder of participation, as it were, shifting from a relatively authoritative position, which allows them to gain the trust of adolescent participants, to a collaborative position that leaves certain decisions and questions open to them (Fleishman, 2016).

Critics such as Bishop and Rogoff have pointed out that the aesthetic criteria of judgement regarding participatory art cannot be identical to the juridical, sociopolitical criteria of citizen participation in public life. Rather, this judgement demands the recognition and valuing of the act of participation in all its facets with a critical distance, from placatory involvement to co-ownership, from critical intervention to collaborative creation. Yet conversely, social justice movements and community-led organizational formations have often served as inspirational models and spaces of learning for artists (Finkelpearl, 2013, p. 12), and have in turn catalysed and stimulated the concatenation of artworks and projects into such movements (Cohen-Cruz, 2010; Raunig, 2007). Seen together, these two positions span from detachment to involvement, and from participation in the artistic encounter being either a means or an end in itself. The cultural sociologist Pascal Gielen maps these poles of the debate in terms of the gradation between what he terms as 1) the subversive and the digestive, i.e. ameliorative functions of art on a vertical axis, and 2) the auto-relational vs. the allo-relational practices on a horizontal axis (2011, p. 22). He argues that community art projects are located across various points of this grid, thus combining aesthetic or professional artistic standards and functions (i.e. the auto-relational, which emphasizes individual artistic goals and the subversive/critical function of art in the modernist sense), as well as criteria of sociability and embeddedness in the commons (i.e. the allo-relational, drawing upon art in its social context and the digestive or integrative functions of art). The difficulty of artistic interrogation lies not (only) in identifying the Weberian ideal-types from which certain practices depart, or in contrast to which they can be seen as hybrid practices, but rather in conceptualizing the possible, imaginative horizons they are seeking out. In that sense, the old problem of categories is worth revising in order to find new interstices and rifts, in which emergent practices locate their scope (Bharucha, 2007, p. 400). The formal typologies presented here may certainly be useful as introductory tools of schematization.

However, they ought to be employed as helpful points of departure and not as the main means of analysing and interpreting participatory art, as they remain schematic and tend to simplify complex, at times illegible and locally embedded, practices to a standardized, abridged grid.

In thinking through the challenges of what the impact of participatory theatre and performance might be, and how to critically approach it, I thus argue against a purely policy-oriented notion of impact that is underwritten by a rationale of utility and profitability. Instead I propose studying impact in its varied dimensions and inconvenient registers as well as in its unique contexts, while making as transparent as possible the objectives that inform us as researchers, and specifying the scope and scale of the areas in which one can realistically make claims of impact. Such an interpretive approach also requires methodological experimentation and a stretching of disciplinary horizons. To speak of the impact of a performance such as *Afuera* in Guatemala and El Salvador requires a heightened sensitivity towards and awareness of the sociopolitical context, and an openness to discuss issues and events that take place outside of the theatre in the strict sense. This involves a combination of performance analysis, supplemented by ethnographic research, audience research, social development as well as a close contextualization of the events that happen around and beyond the performance itself: from after-talks to press criticism to public interventions to everyday events. Arts scholarship offers us several typologies and ways of categorizing various formats of participation. The challenge of making use of this nomenclature in analysis lies in tracing and bringing to life the situatedness, the contradictions and the historicity of such participatory moments.

Participation continues to retain a discursive ambiguity; it oscillates between being a buzzword and a fuzzword (Cornwall and Brock, 2005), between offering the promise of emancipation and serving as a mechanism of maintaining the status quo (Burzynska, 2016), both in the realm of social development as well as in the arts. Critical readers might well wonder whether that ambiguity is only being further reinforced rather than resolved by thinking participation together with impact, thus insisting on a contextual appraisal. Indeed, it is true that the tension surrounding the concept is sustained throughout this study. The tension is not resolved by the fact that I am less interested in a formal definition of participatory art and more in an investigation of the problems it poses – not which version of participation is the right one, but how participation occurs in ways that do not close down its potentials. In the case of *Afuera*, which is, strictly speaking, not a participatory theatre work, since it does not involve any audience participation on stage, I am interested in the larger parameters of how a theatre collective engages participatory forms of devising and collaboration, as well as the ways in which the performance seeks out different audiences and attempts a conversation between the performers in the collective and members of the public. Participation may sometimes be an end in itself, worth aspiring to because a collaborative, non-hierarchical communication in artistic processes is deemed worthwhile, no matter the outcome. At other times participatory formats may serve as a tool, a means to achieve a desired end, namely the articulation and acceptance of lesbian subjectivities in a broader social climate of violence and discrimination. Yet participation is also, or ought to be, more than a means and not only an end in itself.

Notes

1 The presentation of the case study *Afuera* in this chapter is based on an interview I conducted with Laia América Ribera Cañénguez from Teatro Siluetas, as well as documentary material. See Cañénguez (2015).
2 Consider, for instance, the role of radio plays in inciting violence during the Rwandan genocide (Thompson, 2007). More recently, the use of blackface on stage has been heavily criticized in Germany and the Netherlands, pointing to the negative effects of caricaturing blackness, making its racist and discriminatory gestures invisible (Hoving and Essed, 2014).
3 Another way of explaining the emergence of *creación colectiva* practices is that they were a response to the absence of a national canon or of local contemporary playwrights who would supply texts for performance. My thanks go to the manuscript peer reviewer for pointing this out.
4 Participatory artistic practices appear in social science literature in three interconnected ways: first, from an anthropological or sociological perspective as cultural articulations and practices, studied in terms of the ways in which they forge a sense of identity or social cohesion or mark cultural difference (García Canclini, 2005; Turner, 1975); second, as a therapeutic

and pedagogical tool, thus in terms of the transformative potential of the arts at an individual or collective level (Da Costa, 2010; Osnes, 2014); and third, as a tool or methodology for inquiry, data gathering and for generating insights that would not have been accessible through conventional methods such as interviews, focus group discussions or participatory observation (Guhathakurtha, 2008; Kaptani and Yuval-Davis, 2008).

5 The archive of *Lebur Theater Quarterly* (2004–10), Teater Garasi / Garasi Performance Institute, can be found via lebur.teatergarasi.org. Thanks to Ugoran Prasad for bringing this body of work to my attention.

6 In an influential essay originally published in 1970, the philosopher Louis Althusser argued that the state and its subjects share not only a legal or territorial relationship, but also a psychological one, marked by ideology. A state controls its subjects not only through law-enforcement institutions and agents such as the police or the courts, but equally, and in a far more heterogeneous and decentralized manner, through cultural apparatuses such as schools, religious bodies, the social institution of the family, and the media. These so-called 'ideological state apparatuses' ensure that citizens comply with and subjugate themselves to state control by willingly and unquestioningly believing that their position within the state and its structures is a natural one. Althusser argued that through these ideological state apparatuses, subjects are hailed into being, they learn to recognize themselves and others and acquiesce to the place allocated to them, a process he termed 'interpellation' (2014).

7 Arnstein's ladder of citizen participation begins with manipulation and therapy on the lowest rungs, which she characterizes as non-participation, moving further up to informing, consultation and placation (degrees of tokenism) and ultimately to partnership, delegated power and citizen control (degrees of citizen power) (1969, p. 217).

3

Unsolicited gestures of participation

Gesture is always the gesture of being at a loss in language. (Agamben, 1999, p. 78)

The theatre of the oppressed for women's empowerment in India

In May 2013 I spent two days as a participant-observer of a community theatre workshop for rural women leaders in the small town of Karur in Tamil Nadu, south India. The workshop was part of a year-long train-the-trainer programme using the methodology of the 'theatre of the oppressed', which ended shortly before the national parliamentary elections in India in May–June 2014. I took part in one out of nine workshops, so my observations are not intended to offer a comprehensive study of this particular case or of the style of facilitation of one specific practitioner; rather, the workshop offered an opportunity to reflect on the minor gestures that challenge and trouble widespread conceptions of participation, both in the arts, as well as in the sociopolitical realm. Making use of an inductive analysis, I draw broader conclusions from this specific instance. What caught my attention in the workshop were the various instances of what I would like to call unsolicited participation, moments wherein participants responded to the theatre exercises and workshop framework in ways that went beyond the roles and options offered to them. What do these uninvited forms of participation tell us about the relationship between participatory methods in theatre and the communities they seek to serve? What place do they occupy in existing conceptualizations of participatory art? A close examination of one workshop setting, identifying instances and gestures of unsolicited participation,

80

reveals that these are at times defiant, at times cooperative, and at times evasive; it is no straightforward task to classify them as either subversive or subsidiary to established formats of participation. They may be perceived as reassuring to theatre practitioners regarding the efficacy of their participatory methods, or conversely as an indication of the methods not being adhered to, or, indeed, as participation without method or pattern. I will suggest that the concept of the 'gesture' is more accurate than the 'act', as the concerned moments are not legible in terms of intentional, full-fledged signifying acts, but as minor, small movements in the larger frame of theatrical action.

The workshop in question was initiated by S. Jothimani, a local Congress Party official and former general secretary of the Indian Youth Congress. Jothimani received a pilot grant from a Congress Party-led scheme called the Rajiv Gandhi National Women's Progress Scheme (*Rajiv Gandhi Rashtriya Mahila Vikas Pariyojana*), to kick off a grassroots participatory movement of women from her own district of Karur, which could then potentially serve as a model to be copied and implemented in other districts and states. She was given one year to demonstrate to the national party leadership that she could 'mobilize' a large number of rural women leaders, an extraordinarily absurd suggestion, as if a rural women's movement could be spreadsheeted into an administrative timetable. Nevertheless this was a challenge that Jothimani chose consciously to face, with and despite its contradictions. During a personal conversation on 28 April 2013, she mentioned that she stumbled upon the idea of using the theatre of the oppressed via a colleague, who had heard of this methodology during a visit to the USA.

The one-year framework was no doubt related to the election schedule, and in hindsight, following the massive losses of the Congress Party across India, including in Karur, one might speculate that the impossibly contradictory idea of a top-down 'grassroots' rural women's movement was a desperate bid to drum up last-minute political support for the Congress. The workshop was open to members or affiliates of any political party, though there was a preponderance of Congress Party members.[1] Given the abrupt end of the training shortly before the elections in 2014, the absence of any follow-up activity despite strong interest and willingness among the participants, and the programme's disowning by the Congress Party candidate, it is not unjustified to conclude that the workshop series served as a cover for campaigning and recruitment activities. Participants whom I interviewed in 2015 expressed their deep disappointment at the discontinuation of the training, though they were all too keenly aware that it was an attempt to tap into the significant rural female voter population prior to the elections.[2] Why they took part in the workshops, despite being cognizant of what was widely perceived as 'the empty promises of political parties, who appear right before and disappear right after the elections',[3] is a crucial and pertinent question that strikes at the crux of the problem of participation.

The choice of Karur for such an initiative was not coincidental. The town of Karur is the capital of the eponymous district, located in the southern state of Tamil Nadu in India. With a population of approximately 1 million and counting approximately 200 villages stretched across nearly 3,000 square km, this district has a significant agricultural economy, and is increasingly becoming an important hub of the export-focused textile industry, as well as the construction industry. The invited participants of the workshop were about 15 women (and a few men) from the broader network of the Congress Party and allied organizations in the district of Karur. Some were seasoned party workers. In India they are sometimes referred to as 'barefoot party members' who are involved in party activities at a village and district level. Others were schoolteachers or community centre volunteers. Most of the women were from agrarian communities in Karur district. They do not work on their own land but toil as seasonal labourers on land owned by others during the agricultural season. For the rest of the year they engage in different types of informal labour, from selling flowers or street food to working in the textile and construction industries. They were invited to the workshop by word of mouth and with the offer of food and the reimbursement of travel expenses, and some of the women nurtured the hope of securing further employment in the National Women's Scheme.[4] As is common in such settings, most of the participants did not know about the methodology of the theatre of the oppressed and had differing ideas of what the workshop would be about. It was more than evident that coming to the workshop for even three days required significant commitment in time, arranging child care and acquiring 'permission' from husbands or extended family members, and their motivation cannot simply be reduced to their receiving a minor monetary compensation. They are not subalterns in Gramsci's sense of having no access to social mobility, but belong to a liquid working class heralded by globalization in the 'threshold regions' of the Global South, with all its markings of precarity, caste and gender discrimination, as well as a flexibility in labour conditions that is post-Fordist without ever having been properly Fordist. The participants could not be easily lumped together as belonging to the same 'community', for the differences in caste, religious, economic and educational background, not to speak of political affiliations, were enormous, despite their sharing certain common features as rural or semi-rural women from the same region.

The workshop was conceptualized and conducted by Radha Ramaswamy, a community theatre facilitator and founder of the Bangalore-based NGO Centre for Community Dialogue and Change (CCDC). As an educationist who quit the formal education system after she came across the theatre of the oppressed in a workshop setting in the US in 2010, Ramaswamy has been using this methodology as a facilitator in various community and educational projects in India ever since. Like the participants in the series, she too was acutely aware of the problematic assumptions and premises of the women's mobilization programme in Karur, and yet, rather than declining on political or principled grounds, she opted consciously to work with the challenges of the given conditions, thus demonstrating a grounding in praxis and a commitment to developing a theory out of the concrete event and situation, rather than approaching it with a ready-made formula or template, or waiting for the ideal conditions to arrive.[5]

All the people involved in the Karur workshop series, whether the facilitator, the participants or the local Congress Party leader, clearly recognized the contradictions and problems inherent to the proposed aims of the theatre training and yet chose to work together and move on, notwithstanding the benevolent dangers of top-down calls for participation. Clearly a grassroots mass women's movement cannot be willed into existence, especially not by a political party with a history of poor governance, corruption and inefficiency, and a track record of offering little support to existing civil rights and social justice movements. And yet the theatre workshops offered the possibility of instrumentalizing to the best possible extent the terms and conditions of participatory governance, to steer belief in the power of the state towards the realm of play and experiment.

Towards a critique of the critique of participation

I went to the workshop with a hypothesis about participation in theatre. This hypothesis was not entirely proven wrong, but it was complicated by the observations I gathered during my brief presence in Karur. The hypothesis may be summarized as follows: when citizen participation comes as a requirement from the ruling powers, the people who are meant to be its beneficiaries either refuse to participate or do so by making a bad job of it.

This hypothesis is supported by critical literature from different disciplines, both in the humanities and social sciences. Sherry Arnstein's ladder of participation attempts to distinguish between the political implications of different modes of citizen participation, from a manipulative or placative participation to full citizen control (1969). Arnstein argues that purely tokenistic forms of citizen participation can at worst lead to non-participation or at best to a form of therapy or consultation. Similarly in the anthology entitled *Participation: The New Tyranny?* (2001), the development sociologists and geographers Uma Kothari and Bill Cooke offer a fierce critique of the field of development cooperation and its tyrannical imperative of participation. They argue that participatory development can serve to both conceal daily oppression and simultaneously ensure that participants remain subjects of development, obscuring larger structural injustices by emphasizing micro-level modes of participation (Cooke and Kothari, 2001, pp. 11–14).

In the arts and humanities, the critique of participation is routed through an examination of the relationship of artists and artworks to audiences, against the backdrop of the neoliberalization of the arts, with attendant restrictions on the political conditions of the arts, and questions of precarity and contingency. The critique of participation in the arts pursues four core arguments. Here I include various domains of the arts, wherein participation has become a debated topic, such as community-based or applied theatre and performance, immersive performance and the visual arts. The first line of critique refers to the contexts of participatory art, and claims that in a political climate that instrumentalizes culture and art for the aims of governance while simultaneously censoring dissident expression, audience participation in the arts can become a rhetorical tool of social engineering.[6] The second argument, following from and closely related to the first, maintains that such practices tend to prioritize their potential for social cohesion and relationality at a micro-level at the cost of the possibility of a critical, ambivalent or antagonistic stance, thereby both overstating their claim to be social practices as well as raising the question of their very status as art.[7] The third strand of critique of participatory art observes that methodological revisionism alone is insufficient to bring about a participatory citizenship or a radical aesthetic. Such practices may expand the genre of participatory art and add formal varieties, but they do not specifically offer new ways of conceptualizing participation through the arts.[8] The fourth strand argues that artistic practices involving audience participation raise questions around labour, exploitation and custodianship, all of which affect the social and material relations of power in the arts.[9]

My own previous experiences as a facilitator showed that in such participatory theatre, where the terms on which people should participate are decided in advance, people end up regurgitating what they think they are supposed to do, rather than articulating their own voices or opinions. People may well take part in the theatre practice, but the result is aesthetically uninteresting and therefore undermines the idea that participatory theatre instils social or epistemic transformation (Bala and Albacan, 2013). I was quite convinced that this was because they did not ask for it themselves, but rather it was dished out to them as recipients of some seemingly benevolent ideal. One may well have ample participation, but that does not necessarily translate into an interesting aesthetic process or outcome: 'In other words, participation is easy. The creation of a new energy is the challenge' (Ziemilski, 2016, p. 178).

All these points of criticism may seem to indicate an outright rejection of participatory community art forms, yet this was not the case. A certain caution towards the larger promises of participation did not offset the need for a renewed critical engagement with the concept and its performative practices. I initially assumed that the workshop participants would simply resist or refuse participation, if they did not have a stake in its objectives. However, I left the workshop in Karur realizing that the participants did not resist participation in the way we understand resistance to be oppositional, but instead took part in all kinds of unsolicited, unscripted and unexpected ways. True, the results of many of the exercises and games could be perceived as dull and uninspired; the participants seemed at times to be copying instructions mechanically, representations tended to be stereotypical, narratives tended to be stock and repetitive. Yet there was more to it; it could not be written off so easily as an instance of the rigidity of participatory community theatre interventions mirroring the rigidity of a heavily NGO-ized and bureaucratic public sphere (Kerr, 1991; Plastow, 2014). These were extremely charismatic and intelligent women and men, all of them – facilitator, organizer and target group. The parameters of their participation could not be properly recognized because they did not have a place in my existing grammar of participatory art, with notions such as 'empowerment', 'antagonism', 'transformation', 'the breaking of the fourth wall' or the 'do-it-yourself artwork', which suggested that participation in art was willed and guided by larger sociopolitical goals, seeking either cohesion or a transformation of the status quo through agency, opposition and resistance. However, several moments during the workshop made me reconsider this simplistic assumption. This seems pertinent not only to the specific developmental context of the theatre of the oppressed, but also in terms of a broader theorization of participation in the arts. In the following, I will elaborate on three such instances of unsolicited gestures of participation.

The Colombian hypnosis – variation high-/low-status exercise

One of the workshop exercises was a variation of the exercise known in Boal's *Games for Actors and Non-Actors* as the 'Colombian hypnosis' (Boal, 2002, p. 51). It explores status relations between so-called high vs. low positions. One person from the group volunteers to play the role of a high-status person, i.e. someone in a powerful position, or an 'oppressor' in theatre of the oppressed terminology. The task of this person is to ensure that their status is not impinged upon. The others in the group belong to the low-status category. Their task, in the course of the exercise, is to try to win over the high-status person, to make the oppressor capitulate, as it were. The rule of the exercise was that only the technique of hypnosis could be used as a means of communication, guiding a person's movement by holding a hand to their face, which is imagined as being hypnotically led by the hand, thus guiding the partner around the space in the desired direction without speech or the use of direct physical force.

One volunteer, who took on the role of the high-status person, came across as having difficulties with this exercise. Instead of using her high-status position to 'hypnotize' others, she seemed to be defending herself and viewed herself as under threat. My initial reaction was that she did not understand how to use the hypnosis technique, or did not grasp the difference between the low- and high-status positions. The group sitting around her in the circle joined the facilitator in shouting instructions out to her. Some tried to intervene to catch her attention. At one point, the high-status volunteer closed her eyes, yet still attempted to manoeuvre the low-status opponent away. Generally speaking, one cannot use the hypnosis technique with the eyes of the hypnotizer closed, so it seemed that she did not comprehend the rules. At another moment, two other participants in the group approached the high-status volunteer with two different tactics: one threw a scarf over her head, also a slight transgression of the rule of no physical touch; and the other tried to ridicule and make faces at the high-status volunteer, who remained seemingly adamant about holding her hand out to hypnotize the other, though she could not see whom she was manoeuvring, since her head was covered.

During the debriefing after the exercise, the high-status volunteer repeatedly stated that she was 'proud that she survived', or that 'she did not allow the attacks to lessen her determination', or that 'she stood it out on her own' and 'overcame all barriers'. Though she was supposed to be playing the high-status position, her actions and reactions indicated that she in fact felt that she was the oppressed, that the entire group was against her, and that it was she who had to fight them. Was this a case of her performing the task of participation badly, or was it an intelligent deconstructive twist of the exercise, an undermining of the binary between high and low or between oppressor and oppressed, a refusal of the victim or perpetrator role, even for the sake of an exercise? The manner in which the volunteer playing the high-status role improvised her role, gesturing towards what was not written in the role at all, indicated to me that she was seeking to set her own terms of participation.

Blindfolded walk with objects

This sensory and cooperation exercise is known by different names. It involves creating a path of obstacles made out of everyday objects, after which one person has to walk along the path blindfolded, without touching or stepping on any of the objects. The aim of the exercise is that everyone collectively helps the blindfolded person across by giving signals such as clapping, making sounds to indicate where they are and warning them about approaching barriers, all without using words. The instruction was that everyone had to be very quiet, so that the blindfolded person could clearly hear the guiding signals. Yet there was a lot of noise and chatter during this exercise at the beginning. Listening to the conversations while I stood at the side, I realized that some of the women were genuinely concerned about the safety of their objects, which they had placed on the floor in the centre of the room. I heard, for instance, someone commenting: 'I hope she doesn't step on and damage my water bottle, otherwise I will need to buy another one.' Another person hesitated to place their plastic sandal as an object in the space, removing it with a remark to another participant that it 'looked so cheap compared to other leather sandals', and replacing it with a handkerchief. Obviously, the placing of everyday objects would not have been an issue at all if done in a middle-class setting, yet in this context the everyday object was not an ordinary and thus dispensable one, but precious and acutely indicative of class and social differences.

When the group did become quiet, they appeared to circumvent the fun of the exercise by simply guiding the blindfolded person around the objects, rather than through them. This was clearly not a violation of the rules of the exercise, nor was it a demonstrative act of disregard, nor an explicit resistance to the terms of the exercise through a refusal to participate. What appeared at first glance to be a misunderstanding and simplified application of the exercise was perhaps a more complex attempt at participation by way of a reimagination of the exercise, with special care for the everyday objects used. Participation in the exercise was indeed solicited; however, the manner in which participants interpreted the rules of the exercise was unexpectedly non-compliant with the proposed terms of participation. The gesture of participation can thus be interpreted as one of simultaneous omission and commission, on the one hand not following the rules of walking through the maze of objects, though without any confrontation or oppositional stance, while on the other hand adjusting the aim of the exercise to protect the objects used as mere props. It would be futile to judge an omission in a theatrical context using juridical criteria, such as the breach of expectations, non-compliance or intentionality. Rather the omission itself becomes a form of commission through its processual, embodied effects Non-participation can thus cover a range of expressive forms of leaving out or non-doing (Gronau, 2008).

The uninvited guest

A third instance of unsolicited participation took place during the last part of the workshop, when four sub-groups were formed, and each sub-group was asked to devise a two-minute improvised scene, wherein they were meant to show some situation of oppression from their own lives, using image theatre and other theatre of the oppressed techniques taught in the earlier parts of the workshop. One of the sub-groups presented a short scene with an actor who had not previously been part of the workshop. This new participant was the watchman of the building where the workshop was held, which happened to be a local engineering college. He was not an official participant in the workshop, and nobody knew his name. Rather he was a curious onlooker, who occasionally passed by to watch the exercises. When it came to staging the group scenes, it turned out that this watchman was in the role of the main character in a scene. The plot of this rough improvisation was that a woman could not pay the fees for her son to study in the school, and the school administrative official, played by the watchman, was rude and insensitive to her, humiliating her in public because she did not have the money to pay for her son's education. From my conversations with others in the group, it was not clear how the watchman managed to join the final performance. Some thought that he had asked if he could also act, saying that he enjoyed acting very much. Others thought that it would be good to include him in the role since they felt it should be played by a man, and there were not many men available. His involvement was certainly not perceived as an intrusion by any of the other participants. The facilitator expressed her surprise at the participation of someone who had so far been an almost invisible onlooker, but did not make an issue of it. The uninvited participant turned out to be enthusiastic about his role as an administrator and gave a rather long speech, much longer than the two-minute time frame allocated to the group, and had to be stopped by the facilitator when he started changing the plot.

These glimpses from the workshop pose the question as to how to make sense of these kinds of unsolicited participation or misinterpellation, which are partly para-theatrical, partly social-behavioural phenomena and in any case closely interlinked to the aesthetics of the participatory theatre practice.

Between oversight and overestimation

There are two common responses offered by current scholarship and thinking in the field, both of which carry their own dangers: I refer to these responses as 'oversight' at one end of the spectrum, and 'overestimation' at the other end. By oversight I mean that this kind of participation is not taken seriously or is totally ignored. It is not difficult to read this workshop as an example of community theatre work that is chaotic and of a low artistic quality, because the participants are not professionals, they seem to misunderstand the exercise and its execution is artistically unpolished. The workshop is not a concentrated and focused space, as compared to a professional theatre environment. These occurrences tend to not be mentioned in the reports of developmental agencies or in theatre scholarship.

The other kind of response, overestimation, carries the danger of reading too much into these acts of participation. I believe that it is crucial not to over-confidently conclude that these acts are oppositional, counter-hegemonic, subversive, examples of resistance and so on. Overestimation is thus the flipside of oversight in some senses, to the extent that it also stems from an insistence on searching for the efficacy of community theatre. The examples of unsolicited participation could lay bare an antagonistic or oppositional dimension, but they could also serve to reassert the status quo. They could be just as much mollifying as disruptive. One could not therefore conclude that these were implicit acts of criticism of the Congress Party or of the idea of a state-run women's movement. Not every act of unruly participation is transgressive. It would be incorrect to claim that the participants belonged to one homogeneous group that was subject to state negligence or control in the same way, just because they seemed homogeneous from afar. It would be oversimplifying to read subversion or resistance into these acts of misinterpellated participation.[10] It would also be incorrect to see those on the formal, planning side of the workshop as a homogeneous group with the same interests. The local politician, the theatre facilitator and myself as theatre researcher each had very different investments and positions towards or within the scenario. Each approach to participation is marked by contingencies and ambivalences of varying degrees.

I came to the workshop with a hypothesis about participation in the arts, which argued that when citizen participation comes as a requirement, the people who are meant to be its beneficiaries either refuse to participate or sabotage it in other ways. At the end of the workshop I was beginning to realize the shortcomings of this hypothesis. During the short span of my participant observation in Karur, I noticed that the women and men in the workshop did not so much refuse to participate, but rather offered a rearrangement of the terms of participation, which could at times be very sophisticated. So where there is a formalized conception of participation, there seemed to emerge corresponding organic, non-formalized, non-conforming and unsolicited acts of participation.

Current conceptions and literature about participatory art tend to make a distinction between 'good' and 'bad' kinds of participation. There is an assumption that 'good' participation is bottom-up, horizontally organized, aesthetically autonomous and opening or paving the road to some kind of broader institutional, social or political transformation. The theatre of the oppressed is often considered or considers itself as belonging to this category. On the other hand, it is assumed that there is also a 'bad' kind of participation, which is top-down, inherently reflecting the model of neoliberal, entrepreneurial governance, whereby participation becomes a means of placation, minimizing friction or the devolution of public responsibility. Even where it may be innovative, it is ultimately more aligned to the creative industries or to regimes of governmentality, to sustaining the funding possibilities for NGOs, and not to critical practice (Bishop, 2012).

Observing the unsolicited acts of participation in the workshop, this division between a benevolent and a malevolent approach to participation seems unsatisfactory. Perhaps it is more accurate to say that there are two dimensions of participation, which can be found together: the formalized dimension, for example the description of the rules and games in Augusto Boal's handbook *Games for Actors and Non-Actors* or the concept that every trainer designs and uses in their facilitation of the workshops, as well as the non-formalized, unsolicited dimensions of participation. The workshop facilitator, Radha Ramaswamy, with whom I discussed this hypothesis, argues that the methodology of the theatre of the oppressed does in fact have a formal place for such uninvited interventions, and thus they cannot be viewed as outside of or opposed to the formalized concept, but are very much a part of and an outcome of it.[11] While this may be valid to some extent, I believe it is important to acknowledge the possibility of a kind of participation that one may never be able to anticipate, as qualitatively different from what is instructed or exacted from participants, as external to the methodological framework. To attribute the inventive inputs of the participants solely to the genius of the workshop method would not do justice to the fact that it is not just the workshop participants who benefit from the method, but conversely also the repertoire of theatre practice itself and the mindsets of the facilitators, researchers and organizers, which are enriched by their contributions. Without this possibility of suspending the assumption of the benevolence of the theatre practice and the good impact it will necessarily have, participation in the arts will remain conceived as something offered to those who do not have its possibilities, as filling a gap, and therefore as something that justifies constant supervision, facilitation and intervention.

Gesture as the other side of language

So how then to make sense of the coexistence and intertwining of both formalized, scripted modes of participation and those volatile, unexpected practices that emerge from the minute cracks of particular situations? Their oscillating relationship can be conceptualized in different ways. It can be compared, for instance, to the difference between *langue* and *parole* in the structuralism of Saussure, with *langue* being the formal, diachronically accumulated grammar and vocabulary of a language, and *parole* being the informal, synchronic diversifications and variations of a language in its constant usage (Saussure, 1986). However, in this distinction, *parole* is generated from the *langue* and *langue* regularly adapts itself to *parole*, whereas in the case of the two dimensions of participation, I believe there is more tension and power dynamics in their relationship; they are not simply two sides of the same coin that complement each other. The gestures of unsolicited participation in the workshop seek to remain illegible to the established discursive procedures of participatory theatre, they resist formalization without necessarily opposing it, and can thus often not even be recognized as resistant.

It could also be compared to de Certeau's distinction between strategy and tactics, in the sense that tactics, like unsolicited gestures of participation, are makeshift by nature, they belong to the quotidian, they are very specific to the local and disperse and proliferate within technocratic structures (de Certeau, 1984). Yet for de Certeau, tactics are like rhetorical tropes, which manipulate the rules of grammar but are nevertheless themselves grounded in very clear rules. Also the fact that in participatory art we are dealing with physical, embodied moments and not text or speech alone makes it difficult to speak of a strategic participation and a tactical participation along the lines of a linguistic distinction. Possibly the opposition between grammar and slang is more applicable, as the colloquial quality of slang captures a range of registers, from body language, sounds and intonations, to regional nuances and differences between social classes, as opposed to the rule-dominated logic of grammar. The gestures of participation in the workshop can be regarded as both internal and external to the rules of spoken language; they supplement language and yet are indispensable to speech.

Another comparison is that between 'politics' and 'the political' as elaborated by Chantal Mouffe. In Mouffe's conception, 'politics refers to the ensemble of practices, discourses and institutions that seeks to establish a certain order and to organize coexistence in conditions which are always potentially conflicting. The political refers to the dimension of antagonism which can take many forms and can emerge in diverse social relations' (Mouffe, 2013, pp. 2–3). I find this attractive because it acknowledges and gives place to conflicts and heterogeneous positions, yet its application to the arts is not straightforward, as aesthetic processes are not political in the same way as the political processes that Mouffe discusses.

Diana Taylor's notion of scenarios offers a further useful point of comparison in the discipline of theatre and performance studies. Scenarios are frameworks or broad outlines of practices, 'meaning-making paradigms that structure social environments, behaviours, and potential outcomes ... [featuring] milieux and corporeal behaviours such as gestures, attitudes, and tones not reducible to language' (Taylor, 2003, p. 28). Scenarios thus importantly include more elements than text, narrative or plot, and reflect the diverse layers and systems at work in order for practices to enter or exit the repertoires and archives of cultural imaginings. In relation to the workshop I describe above, it is productive to view the uninvited interventions of the participants as parts of a scenario, at least as a minor scenario, although it is more difficult to identify them as meaning-making paradigms in the sense suggested by Taylor. The observation that a scenario cannot be reduced to language and consists of an entire range of embodied articulations is pertinent here.

In all these conceptions, the non-formal articulations maintain a tense and ambivalent relation to language; not language as in a particular spoken or written utterance or statement, but the very way in which language takes (its) place. They seem to be enabled by language, even as they hint at its inadequacy. 'Gesture is always the gesture of being at a loss in language,' remarked Agamben, 'it is always a "gag" in the literal sense of the word, which indicates first of all something put in someone's mouth to keep him from speaking and, then, the actor's improvisation to make up for an impossibility of speaking' (1999, p. 78). This remarkable interpretive association between the two meanings of 'gag' is worth some reflection. In his essay on Max Kommerell's literary criticism, Agamben departs from an understanding of gesture as an element that is closely tied to language even as it does not exhaust itself in the linguistic. Gesture is thus 'the other side of language' (Agamben, 1999, p. 78), the hint within or at the edge of language at what is unspeakable. Agamben's witty remark around the 'gag' suggests that there is something put to silence behind the spontaneous, light-hearted improvisation of an actor on stage, namely 'the muteness inherent in humankind's very capacity for language, its speechless dwelling in language' (1999, p. 78). Or, read differently, it is the impossibility of language that produces gestures.

Could it thus be that, as far as the Karur workshop participants were concerned, the entire theatre of the oppressed programme and the political party set-up that brought it about belonged to the realm of top-down measures, of benevolent structural blocks, to the place that language takes? Gagged by these frames of participation, within which it is impossible for them to be truly heard or to articulate themselves, did they consciously or unwittingly resort to spontaneous improvisatory gags that unsettled or rearranged the rules of the game? Could it be that the more the demand for loud, visible acts of participation, the more it led to their scattered gestures of unsolicited participation?

In his study *Performance Affects: Applied Theatre and the End of Affect* (2009) James Thompson argues, among other things, for the importance of silence not only as a narrative element and essential component of storytelling, but also as a form of participation, which does not easily translate into the coda of *effect* but nonetheless has a strong *affective* force (2009, pp. 56–77). Documenting his own experiences as a theatre facilitator in a camp for internally displaced persons in Sri Lanka, Thompson traces a fine web of interrelations and links between the involvement of external agencies in a seemingly local theatre project and the public ramifications and discourses of the war. He questions the assumption that theatre must be expected to give voice to people's experiences, or that telling stories is a necessary precondition for 'healing' or 'relief', common tropes in the arena of humanitarian aid. Thompson argues not only that such assumptions are blatantly insensitive to culturally specific modes of coping with painful experiences, but also that the insistence on telling stories and sharing the experience of war and displacement, even in the 'safe' space of the theatre, can even cause harm. Thompson's reflections on the possibility that contesting versions of a real event might result in a breach of trust between participants in a workshop, and his observations on the need to respect the desire to find cohesion and reconciliation rather than insisting on depicting all sides of a conflict, demonstrate the difficulties of embracing an agonistic or oppositional approach to participation, particularly in an already conflict-laden environment. In *Humanitarian Performance* (2014) Thompson traces how narratives of suffering and saving form contentious political strategies in places of war, which often serve the agendas of humanitarian agencies rather than those who have suffered (Thompson, 2014, p. 25).[12] In the case of the theatre of the oppressed workshop that I attended, the affective force of participation lay not so much in the formal theatre exercises, but in the way in which the rules of the exercises were quietly altered. What I hope to suggest is that we need to think these two dimensions together in their plurality and ambivalence, the gestures of participation as the other side of the formal conditions of participation. The unexpected gestures of participation are attempts at reimagining and reformulating in aesthetic and theatrical terms the larger, sometimes deafening call for citizen participation. They are thus neither a rejection of nor a co-option into a pre-determined regime of participation, but an embodied engagement with it.

Notes

1 The fact that some of these Congress Party members later defected to a different party shows that party membership need not necessarily be a sign of ideological affiliation in the Indian electoral context.

2 In August 2015 I interviewed via telephone five of the most regular participants and core group members. In June 2014 I interviewed Radha Ramaswamy, who kindly gave me the video documentation of all nine workshops and also offered valuable feedback on initial drafts of this chapter. My communication with Jothimani Sennimalai was restricted to one personal conversation in 2013 followed by sporadic email correspondence.

3 Telephone conversation with Participant 1, 5 August 2015 (translation SB).

4 Telephone conversations with Participants 1 and 2, 4 and 5 August 2015 respectively (translation SB).

5 Conversation with R. Ramaswamy, 10 June 2014.

6 Elaborations of this argument in the field of community arts are to be found, for instance, in Kerr (1991), Ahmed (2002) and Plastow (2014). See also Miessen and Kolowratnik (2013) and Ray, Raunig and Wuggenig (2011) for an appraisal of the contexts of visual arts and architecture.

7 Well-known examinations of this aspect are Bishop (2012), drawing on theorizations by Rancière (2010) and Mouffe (2013); see also Rogoff (2005). For perspectives from community-based or applied arts, see Thompson (2000, 2008), Conroy (2015), and from the field of immersive performance, see White (2012).

8 The point is made most pertinently in relation to participation in development policy (Cooke and Kothari, 2001). In theatre and performance studies, see the special issue of *Performance Research* (Cull and Gritzner, 2011), and in relation to contemporary visual arts, see Rebentisch (2012, 2015).

9 Harvie analyses the economic conditions of participatory performance in the UK in depth (2013); Kunst focuses on the field of contemporary dance and on the implications therein of shifting notions of labour/ work (2015); the edited volume *Work, Work, Work* offers critiques of neoliberal economy in relation to visual arts and museum-based practices (Widenheim et al., 2011).

10 In *The Misinterpellated Subject* (2017), James Martel complicates the Althusserian notion of interpellation by investigating the ways in which those who are not meant to be the intended addressees of the call of the state nevertheless come forward and respond. These misinterpellated subjects, Martel argues, challenge the scene in which they arrive and thus carry a radical potential. In the case of the workshops where I observed exactly such moments of unexpected, uninvited responses, I would be more cautious in claiming the grounds for a new form of political subjectivity, even as I fully agree that misinterpellations are poignant gestures of participation.

11 Conversation with R. Ramaswamy, 10 June 2014.

12 In earlier writings, Thompson is closer to Claire Bishop's argument for sustaining a contradictory complexity, in his plea for retaining a sense of bewilderment in theatre's social practices rather than straining to resolve or simplify them (2008).

4

Vicarious gestures of participation

The more frequently we interrupt someone engaged in an action, the more gestures we obtain. (Benjamin, 1973a, p. 24)

Invitations to in-between places

The idea for the performance project *Where We Are Not* (2009) by the Amsterdam-based Lebanese artist Lina Issa emerged out of the artist's own legal situation at the time. Issa's application for an extension of her Dutch residence permit had been rejected, and she was awaiting the outcome of her appeal. She thus found herself in a situation where it was difficult to leave the Netherlands, for if she did so, she might have been refused re-entry. These circumstances created a peculiar situation where she was not yet fully legalized in her place of residence and simultaneously was unable to travel to her home country without potentially negatively affecting her chances of legalization. As an artistic response to this predicament, she collaborated with the performance artist, choreographer and dancer Aitana Cordero, who travelled to the Lebanon for ten days in 2008 as Issa's stand-in, messenger and recording device. Prior to this, Cordero had conducted an artistic research project in 2005 entitled *Do You Want to Use Me?*, in which she invited artists to use her body as material for their own solos.[1] Issa's invitation to be replaced by someone on a journey home thus fitted well with Cordero's invitation to make her body available to another artistic imagination.

Cordero stayed with Issa's parents and visited different people and places, in an attempt to trace what constituted the idea of 'homecoming' for Issa. She performed several tasks that Issa assigned to her, all relating to intimate and individual ways of inhabiting a place as one's home. These tasks were outlined in an elaborate diary that Issa gave to Cordero just before she boarded the flight to the Lebanon. They included instructions such as: 'Kiss my aunt as you cup her head with your hands and give her my greetings, say: "*Lina betsalem ậlay kteer*"', or 'Go with Nagham to the spot called "Balayet" where we used to play as kids, smell the soil there, take a look at the texture of the rocks, the people, the houses. [...] Find a moment to give the lemon, salt and knife to Nagham and ask her to peel it.' Cordero herself also kept a diary of her visit to the Lebanon in her mother tongue, Spanish, noting her own experiences as a stand-in, including notes on how the tasks assigned to her were carried out, but also the frustrations and misunderstandings that arose from the performative experiment, from being a receptor on behalf of someone else, from the poetic attempt to embody another person's desires and expectations, from the inability to transmit a sense of homecoming, or from inhabiting the transformations that a body experiences in migration.

The results and experiences of this experiment of taking someone else's place were shared by Cordero and Issa in the form of a staged performance/reading entitled *Where We Are Not*, which I attended in 2009 at de Brakke Grond, an experimental arts centre in Amsterdam. During this event, which was restricted to a maximum of six audience members at a time, visitors were first asked to wait in a room, which was bare but for a few chairs and a video screen showing the heads of two women next to each other, lying on a rooftop, with the sound and image of wind blowing in their hair and faces. The only instruction given to participants was to select four people from the group to go to the next room at the point when everyone instinctively felt that eight minutes were over. This time passed awkwardly, not unlike in a waiting room in a railway station or airport or immigration office, with time being allocated in a seemingly exact manner, but the perceived waiting period inevitably feeling extremely long and heavy. Those who stayed behind obviously waited even longer until they were called to the next room. The second room had a table with Issa's handwritten diary lying on it, which participants were invited to read through at leisure, together or individually. It served as the first direct source of information about the journey: a book with personal impressions about her family members and places of emotional attachment and personal history, as well as elaborate day-by-day instructions and general profiles of the country, the language and the food, a personalized *Lonely Planet* travel guide of sorts. It later transpired that one of the audience members was in fact a stand-in, who discreetly offered bits and pieces of contextual and background information to the others. One by one, visitors were then personally welcomed by Issa and Cordero to join them at a table in the third room. The visitor was asked to select one page from the diary of Cordero's visit to the Lebanon placed on the table. Cordero then read out in Spanish what was written on this page and subsequently translated her own text into English. In my case, the page I chose pertained to a particular day on which she was meant to visit a friend of Issa and take a walk with him. The diary notes commented on the difficulties and challenges encountered by Cordero in executing this task, as well as a number of personal impressions and thoughts. In the course of the conversation, which was the first time that Issa and Cordero had spoken to each other after the substitute journey about this incident, the tensions inherent to the concept of this performance artwork became apparent. For the artist Lina Issa, *Where We Are Not* 'is not about anywhere, but about those places we carry with us in our bodies' (Issa, 2009). Indeed, one might conclude that it is about the way that places only ever exist in the way we carry them in our bodies and memories.

In the follow-up project entitled *If I Could Take Your Place*, initiated in 2010 within the framework of an artist residency in Sweden, Issa reversed the idea of the 'stand-in'. Here she placed an advertisement in newspapers in Sweden and the Netherlands, offering to replace people in specific situations for a given period of time:

> Did you ever want to be in two places at the same time? Did you ever have a desire or need that 'someone else' – takes your place in a certain situation? – does or says something, that you never dared to say or do yourself? – visits something from your past or future, bringing a memory or a message? – goes in your place to work, or fulfils your daily rituals in your place? Can I take your place? For an hour, a day, or a week ... (Issa, 2010)

She received 33 responses and eventually 'replaced' nine people.[2] The occasions for the temporary substitutions varied in terms of the nature of the activity, but all the requests had a strongly affective dimension: one person asked Issa to take over her personal sadness and suffering for one weekend, so she could go away on a trip. Another person, himself a photographer, requested that she replace him for a day in his job of collecting garbage near a highway, and take pictures of the trash, since he wanted to see how someone else would view the same objects he dealt with on a daily basis. Other requests included meeting with a sorely missed friend, or having dinner with a former husband. These are occasions on which a person's physical presence is commonly regarded as indispensable, on which one cannot be substituted by anyone else. Possibly, the poetic audacity of the idea evoked in the advertisement could only beckon equally audacious counter-requests. In both projects, the artist creates an overlap between the artistic sphere and the sphere of social life through the figuration of the stand-in. In *Where We Are Not*, it is the life of the artist into which another artist figuratively and physically steps, whereas in *If I Could Take Your Place* it is the artist who steps into other people's lives and homes.

The theatricality of participation

Issa's 'replacement' projects might seem somewhat odd and unlikely choices for a discussion about participatory art. In the public presentation of *Where We Are Not*, the thrust of the performance installation was neither on activating spectators and transforming them into performers, nor was it devised as an immersive experience. Audience participation consists at the simplest level in being or becoming aware that one is invited to be a witness to or a part of a conversation and an intimately shared experience between Issa and Cordero. The conversation takes on a quality of heightened perceptibility, a theatricality that is inherent to any situation of encounter between the seer and the seen. I use the concept of theatricality here in the sense of Elizabeth Burns to refer to certain historically and culturally determined 'modes of perception' common to both theatre as well as social life, where the condition of being aware of being a spectator creates a theatrical frame (Balme, 2001; Burns, 1972, p. 13). Tracy Davis argues that the condition for theatricality as an artistic and social phenomenon is the audience's awareness and consciousness of being spectators. To take a walk and casually notice an animal grazing in a field does not create a theatrical situation, but to buy a ticket for a circus performance and watch the same animal on stage applauded by the circus audience creates theatricality by way of the heightened perceptibility of the situation through the self-awareness of being spectators (Davis, 2003, pp. 129–30). This theatricality is potentially applicable to any act or event, both within and outside the artistic realm, where there is a self-aware presence of spectatorship. By being aware of taking on the position of spectator, the act or scene viewed is marked as perceptible. Participation here is not about activating spectatorship, which would in a sense imply that spectatorship is in itself passive and thereby in need of alteration, a critique prominently raised by Jacques Rancière (2009). Rather, it is about a joint effort at making things worth paying attention to, in a way that foregrounds this effort as a central concern.

In the realm of the performance itself, different people jointly contribute to this work of spectatorship. Cordero does not employ a realistic approach to the task of feeling someone else's sense of home. Rather, she assumes her position as a spectator of someone who is not there, and attempts to embody this presence next to an absence. She recounts being taken by Issa's father on an early morning beach walk and feeling uncomfortable when he started singing a song, realizing that it was addressed not to her but to Issa (Issa and Cordero, 2008). At the same time she takes the idea of replacing Issa and following her instructions as literally as possible. She eats whatever she is offered by her hosts or asked by Issa to eat, even if it is much more than she would want to eat herself. She does not contact any of her own friends or family during the time she is there. In her diary she records her visceral and emotional responses to various situations and tasks she is asked to perform: a sense of awkwardness in conversations, loneliness, or a gut feeling of familiarity and shared circumstance. Issa's friends and family constitute another type of spectatorship, as they too are made aware of their own perceptions of the relationship to her, enhanced or irritated by Cordero's presence. Visitors to the performance/reading *Where We Are Not* perform another type of spectatorship, at times trying, through the diaries, to piece together what actually took place in the Lebanon, at other times asking questions that led to a conversation between everyone present.

Language plays a prominent role in heightening the sense of being a spectator. Not understanding what is being said or implied is a recurring experience for Cordero, a consistent reminder that she is not at home and is attempting to take someone's place. It points to the very way in which our notion of home has so much to do with the way in which we relate to language as our own or as foreign. The fact that English is a foreign language not only for herself but also for Issa's family creates a situation whereby language necessarily stands in the way of participating in someone else's sense of home, even as English makes basic communication possible. The use of English also offers a reassuring common ground – at least everyone is attempting to step out of their own language to make the other feel at home. It also suggests a comforting, though entirely illusory hope that a shared mother tongue might possibly imply a shared sense of home. Writing a diary in Spanish becomes a way of returning home, releasing herself from the awkwardness of English and the fragments of Arabic that she might have learnt to grasp. For Issa too, the invitation to Cordero was extended in English, which is not her first language. Yet her diary notes and instructions to Cordero contain repeated references to Arabic words and their pronunciation. These serve more than the purpose of easing communication, in the manner that a travel guide might include simple phrases in the language of the place being visited. Rather they point to the centrality of language, not in conveying meaning, but as an affective register of home. To learn a new language or to take the trouble to speak and falter in a second or third language are ways of de-familiarizing one's sense of home, of undoing a stable sense of how language is owned and made into one's home.

In terms of its broader political implications, theatrical spectatorship as a mode of witnessing is what makes it possible for Issa's state of semi-legality to become visible, and for empathetic connections to be formed. It makes it possible to imagine being in a similar position, and also to imagine others in far more precarious situations. Here, instead of positing spectatorship as a passive position assumed by the audience, theatricality suggests that the participation of art in the public sphere has the capacity to make people realize that a seemingly simple act of witnessing, when consciously undertaken, can potentially help to generate public reflection and action on issues that may otherwise remain hidden. Cordero notes that in conveying a message to Issa's parents, she could become an observer of their pain in missing their daughter, who had migrated to Europe, and also witness the pain of being a daughter who misses her parents. Her body is both a conduit and a catalyst for a gush of emotions, memories and interactions (Covington-Ward, 2016).

Issa's projects bear similarities to the work of the Palestinian-American conceptual artist Emily Jacir, specifically the project *Where We Come From* (2001–03), in which she asked 30 Palestinians living in different places, 'If I could do anything for you, anywhere in Palestine, what would it be?', and then carried out their wishes by proxy, documenting the process (Jacir, 2003).[3] The wishes ranged from sentimental and personal requests such as meeting long-lost relatives or drinking the water in an ancestral village, to simple, practical wishes, such as playing football with street children or paying a bill. Jacir's work highlighted the difficulties and restrictions in the mobility of Palestinians under occupation, difficulties that become apparent and visible precisely through the transposition of an unfulfilled wish on to a person with an American passport. As Edward Said eloquently remarks in a comment on Jacir's work, 'her compositions slip through the nets of bureaucracies and non-negotiable borders, time and space, in search not of grandiose dreams or clotted fantasies but rather of humdrum objects and simple gestures' (2003, p. 106). Similarly Issa's conceptually inspired replacements are deprived of utility and causality; they are not devised to serve the purpose of literal replacement, but rather they make it possible to pay attention more carefully to the predicament of one who is unable to go home, unable to pursue a desire for any number of reasons. Like Jacir's wish-fulfilments, Issa's acts of replacement too remain 'phantasmatic, vicarious, ghostly' (Demos, 2013, p. 103). Whereas Jacir uses the art gallery to show her work, Issa deploys the live, interactive component of performance in the public presentations, while also including video installations, radio shows and visual objects such as the diaries as a part of the presentation.

In *If I Could Take Your Place* the respondents are asked to participate by withdrawing from the scene in order to witness someone else enter and occupy their roles. Spectators are entirely absent; we only receive second-hand accounts through the narrations of Issa and a few of her collaborators, and given that it is work in progress, possible future formats of involving audiences might still evolve. Our access to these moments as spectators is indirect and heavily mediated through Issa's own narrative and framing. This implies that there is no primary audience for the artwork, and indeed the categories of performer, spectator or artwork are called into question, for is it not the artist who becomes the spectator of someone's life for a short period of time? It is impossible to find empirical evidence of how someone was replaced, or to measure its efficacy. In contrast to *Where We Are Not*, where the stand-in Cordero was explicitly asked not to take photographs, Issa prominently uses visual images as a means of giving form and visibility to her own process of being a stand-in in *If I Could Take Your Place*. An image of a living room sofa or a dining table set for two, pictures of garbage or of the key to a house – these objects stand in for the relations people have to them. During a public presentation in Sweden in 2010, some of the people who asked Issa to replace them spoke about what they did during this period, as well as about their motivation in responding to the advertisement (Issa, 2010). The collaborators themselves can be partly regarded as audiences; they alter their mode of perception of their own lives and attempt, albeit hypothetically and imaginatively, to step out of their own shoes by asking someone else to step into them for a moment. One of them shared her experience of saying goodbye for a weekend to Issa, handing over her mobile phone, computer passwords and keys and getting into a train.

The sociality of self-making

Issa's own account of taking someone's place has a confessional, personal, sentimental tone. She speaks of sitting on someone's couch and crying, feeling the sorrow they have asked her to feel, or feeling anxious about meeting someone to convey a personal message to them. Despite the overlaps between the artistic and the social realms in both projects, the discursive and physical gesture of standing in for someone else does not actually result in enacting or becoming that which it names, even temporarily. It is the artistic framing that makes it possible to imagine such a replacement. The gesture of offering to take someone's place is one of extending the scope of imagining how we are made. At the same time, to be moved by and towards the other, to attempt to share or expose oneself to others' wounds and sufferings, can profoundly alter one's own sense of being a stably determined, self-driven individual. Cordero views her participation in the project *Where We Are Not* in terms of a generosity to put aside her own wishes or inclinations, to be vulnerable and expose herself to whatever the situation brings, to be willing to submit to the instructions of another person and dispossess herself of her own visibility.[4] Judith Butler and Athena Athanasiou reflect on this performative aspect of dispossession when they distinguish between its two valences: dispossession in a negative sense as a state of being stripped of rights, land and entitlements, and dispossession in a positive, performative sense as the capacity to show solidarity with the less privileged, including those one does not know or never could know (Butler and Athanasiou 2013, p. 3). What is important in the distinction is the search for ways of positively connoting dispossession without necessarily relating it to possession, identitarianism or ownership.

The playful idea of standing in for others evokes such larger questions of what it means to participate in collective processes of imagining and transforming selfhood. In listening to the account of how Issa slept in someone else's bed or performed an intimate ritual of familiarity on someone else's behalf, or of how Cordero visited the village where Issa was born together with her father, one is invited to reflect on how ideas of selfhood are both socially imagined as well as emergent from the struggle against social norms and regimes (Butler and Athanasiou, 2013, p. 67). At the same time, the point of the artistic effort at vicarious participation is not to unveil some hidden core or arrive at an ultimate self-truth; as Butler argues, 'it is not to say that we do not require recognition; rather it is to say that recognition is always partial, and that our capacity to practice freedom critically depends on that very partiality' (2013, p. 68). In asking someone else to take her place, and offering to take others' places herself, Issa approaches participation in multi-directional way, where the self is dispossessed of its fixity as it seeks to enter other lives and realities in their very difference. A sense of distancing and detaching oneself from one's seemingly self-assured fantasies of the self becomes a necessary pre-condition for reaching out to and building a relation with another, a relation that is always precarious and partial. The solidarity in the gesture of vicarious participation lies not so much in recognizing and finding the so-called 'other' or in respecting and celebrating differences, but rather in being prepared and willing to deconstruct the fixity of one's ideas of oneself, a gesture that can be either potentially transformative or disorienting, depending on who is expected to perform this gesture and to what end.

The replacement projects place those involved in a peculiar relationship to time and space. In being required to dwell in a certain place with all the senses, to smell, touch and feel the things and people that remind Issa of her own subjective sense of home, Cordero is asked to approach this home without any self-assurance, in fact to imagine what it might mean to be uprooted from the specificity of site. She is asked to visit Issa's home, but to visit it as a home from which Issa is palpably absent, and thus to imagine what Issa feels in not being able to visit home herself, to observe that absence, to give it more priority than her own presence. In the act of travelling together with Issa's mother in a car, watching her drive and explain the lyrics of a favourite shared song, Cordero is invited to experience the moment in a way that brings past, present and future together all at once – someone else's past, her own present, and an unclaimed anticipated future.

Artistic gestures and social gestures

I have thus far referred to the aesthetic principle of participation in Issa's projects in terms of offering a gesture of participation, rather than enacting or fulfilling the call for participation. The idea of selfhood, something seemingly natural and organically connected to oneself, is interrupted and made strange, it is broken down into distinct moments and gestures, each artificial or incomplete on its own, but together creating a scenario that lends itself to reflection and critically intimate appraisal. This has strong resonances with the Brechtian concept of *Gestus*, which has served as a rich resource in theatrical experimentation, obviously extending beyond the scope of participatory theatre and performance alone.[5]

Brecht's concept of *Gestus* differs in two important ways from what is commonly implied in the English term 'gesture'. First, whereas 'gesture' is widely used with reference to the outward expression or bearing of an inner feeling or attitude, Brechtian *Gestus* refers not to 'the fulfilment or realisation of an intention or of an expectation but rather its disruption and suspension. It entails not so much expression as interruption And it is this that makes it eminently theatrical' (Weber, 2008, p. 98). *Gestus* calls situations into being, brings their smooth movement to a halt, as it were, making a situation perceptible in its details and its contradictions by interrupting any assumed direct link between inner feeling and outer expression. It is thus an essential means of achieving the effect of de-familiarization, which Brecht theorized in his *Short Organum for the Theatre* (1949) as necessary in order to cultivate a critical and politically constructive spectatorship. *Gestus* is the purposive arresting of movement, and thus of self-identification with movement, a technique that seeks to lay bare inconsistencies at various levels: 'the coherence of the character [*die Einheit der Figur*] is in fact shown by the way in which its individual qualities contradict one another' (Brecht, 1964, p. 196 no. 53).

While it is not uncommon to make use of a stand-in or replacement in certain sports or in the theatre, the interruption or de-familiarization in Issa's works is derived from the replacement taking place in the quotidian realm, outside of the conventional spaces of art, and most importantly, with no role-playing involved, while simultaneously being framed as an art project. Issa does not try to act like the person she is replacing, nor does Cordero claim to behave or feel like Issa. Instead the projects explore the Brechtian adage of bodily *Gestus* preceding feelings, ideas and thoughts. In his essays on amateur theatre, Brecht remarks, 'kneel down and you will begin to pray', or 'crying is caused by sadness, but sadness is also caused by crying', implying that it is possible to evoke certain psychological states and forms of self-identification by performing the gestures and actions that accompany them (cit. in Esslin, 1986, p. 30). However, whereas

Brechtian actor training revolves around exploring the relation of the actor or actress to the character and figure through the critically observant incorporation of the character's gestures and movements, Issa's participatory work deals with exploring how one person's feelings and relations to places and other people can be transmitted to another person by adopting the gestures and actions that accompany their feelings in a non-artistically framed situation, and observing this very process in the presence of spectators.

Second, *Gestus* specifically interconnects the embodied, somatic dimension with the social and historical dimension of a physical gesture.

> The realm of attitudes [*Haltungen*] adopted by the characters towards one another is what we call the realm of gest [*den gestischen Bereich*]. Physical attitude, tone of voice and facial expression are all determined by a social gest [*Gestus*] [...] The attitudes [*Haltungen*] which people adopt towards one another include even those attitudes [*Äußerungen*] which would appear to be quite private, such as the utterance of physical pain in an illness, or of religious faith. These expressions of a gest [*diese gestischen Äußerungen*] are usually highly complicated and contradictory, so that they cannot be rendered by any single word and the actor must take care that in giving his image [*Abbildung*] the necessary emphasis he does not lose anything, but emphasizes the entire complex. (Brecht, 1964)

The relation between *Haltung* and *Gestus* is significant here. In John Willett's translation of the *Short Organum for the Theatre*, the term 'attitude' is used both for *Haltung* as well as *Äußerung*. While 'attitude' reflects the way one faces or perceives something, it does not capture the physicality of *Haltung*, literally, 'bearing', nor the sense of 'articulation' or 'expression' in the term *Äußerung*. Brecht uses both the Latin form *Gestus* as well as the German term *Haltung*, which can both be translated in some contexts as 'gesture'. However, *Gestus* is both a manner of 'bearing' as well as of 'articulation'; it is the material from which seemingly individual utterances and expressions emerge. Brecht speaks of 'gestural material', which appears to be but never is fully private. This gestural realm shapes how individual figures bear themselves towards one another, in the old-fashioned sense of 'bearing' as both carrying and moving. In another often-cited example, Brecht comments that the gesture of 'warding off a fly is in itself not yet a social *Gestus*; warding off a dog can be one if it expresses the struggle of a poorly clad person against watchdogs' (1967, p. 609). *Gestus* thus combines physical, formal elements with social and political implications and configurations. Every singular theatrical event, Brecht continues, has a founding *Gestus*, the so-called *Grundgestus*: a moment, an arrested movement, that captures the gravity of an entire scene or social situation: 'Richard Gloster courts his victim's widow. The child's true mother is found by means of a chalk circle. God has a bet with the devil for Dr. Faust's soul' (Brecht, 1964). These physical gestures are never only individual expressions, they are always also the performative montage of a social habitude, of the inequalities and the violence inherent to them.

Walter Benjamin famously explained Brecht's concept of *Gestus* with reference to what he terms a family scene:

> Epic theatre, then, does not reproduce conditions but rather, reveals them. This uncovering of conditions is brought about through processes being interrupted. A very crude example: a family row. The mother is just about to pick up a pillow to hurl at the daughter, the father is opening a window to call a policeman. At this moment a stranger appears at the door. [...] In other words, the stranger is suddenly confronted with certain conditions. [...] The more far-reaching the devastations of our social order (the more these devastations undermine ourselves and our capacity to remain aware of them), the more marked must be the distance between the stranger and the events portrayed. (Benjamin, 1973b, p. 5)

For Benjamin, Brecht's epic theatre was radical in its use of the *Gestus* to both interrupt as well as dynamize and enrapture such moments. The interruption of action leaves the viewer or reader wondering as to what could happen next, and what happened earlier, what led to this moment, what is the larger condition it evokes. It is less the image and story evoked by the gesture than the moment of suspension and suggestiveness that intrigued Benjamin most. He understood the *Gestus* as rendering the possibility of understanding through 'rapture', a deep recognition of the history and larger purport of an event (Butler, 2014b).

In the course of researching Issa's replacement projects, I was repeatedly reminded of this scene from Benjamin's essay on Brecht. A stranger appears, a scene comes to a halt mid-way, a gesture is brought into being. The mother in Benjamin's *tableau vivant*, preparing to hurl a pillow at her daughter, is suddenly confronted by a stranger. In *Where We Are Not*, it is a stranger who bears herself as that daughter. If the stranger takes the place of the daughter, do we as spectators, listening to an account of that *Gestus*, then, hypothetically, become Benjamin's stranger? Does she become the stranger who perhaps brought a different scene to a halt? How do we participate in such a scene, witnessing someone hurl a pillow (in a later essay by Benjamin, the pillow is replaced by a bronze bust) at someone else? How do we adequately, appropriately bear ourselves (*Haltung*), articulate ourselves (*Äußerung*) faced with the prospect of possible violence? There is a specific kind of temporality to this gesture – a stranger appears, something comes to a halt – it compels us to think about what could have been, what will have occurred. What matters is not so much what actually took place, but what the interruption made it possible to imagine.

I do not wish to suggest that the performance projects *Where We Are Not* and *If I Could Take Your Place* are Brechtian; however, I propose that a Brechtian-influenced understanding of gesture as a physical movement that is simultaneously a social attitude is a useful category for understanding and thinking the participatory aspects of these works. To ask someone to take your place or to request to take their place is an imaginative question that is merely literalized by the gesture of replacement and casting. It is an invitation to think of the performer as well as the one being replaced, each in their historical, gendered specificity, and to ask what it means to adopt this specificity in an embodied way. To offer to replace someone is at best a gesture of participating in someone else's sense of home and self: it suggests the possibility but of course does not achieve or fulfil it. It is effective as a gesture precisely because it dwells in that twilight zone between speech, image and act; it belongs neither to the realm of authenticity nor to the realm of artificiality, it is both beyond linguistic expression as well as inseparable from it (Kolesch, 2010, p. 228). The work of being a stand-in is different from role-play and different from voyeurism. It is a gesture, a hint at sharing an experience, pointing towards what must remain external to the gesture. Participation in such a performance thus does not consist in immersing oneself in the subjectivity of another person or situation, but in being repeatedly reminded of the situatedness of one's own subjectivity. These gestures don't flow into each other to create one unifying experience, but rather consist of a series of interruptions of that experience. So there is the pretence of stepping into someone else's position, by receiving the key to their apartment and the password to their email account – mere gesture. There is the suggestion of transmitting an experience that cannot be narrated but must be embodied, and yet this experience is mediated to the audience as narration or as record. It is presented to the public using familiar formats of storytelling.

Issa's projects can be seen as gestural, physical and visceral in undertaking specific actions, yet evocative and suggestive in what these actions might mean. They envisage the participation of audiences and artists as constantly moving between the physical and the imaginative, the kinaesthetic and the symbolic, the instrumental and the signifying registers, in the way that the bodily gesture also constantly moves between these registers. The activities undertaken by Issa and Cordero in the gesture of replacing someone enable them in a peculiar way to access and revise routines, or, as Carrie Noland convincingly points out in her study of agency and embodiment, 'to sense the discrepancy between what gestures *mean* (the meaning bestowed by cultural convention on theme and therefore on the subjects performing them) and what gestures makes us *feel* (the sensations we experience while performing them)' (2009, p. 212). The gap between the cultural meaning of a gesture and the way gestures are sensed and experienced is widened when the experience is narrated or represented in a different format to an audience that was excluded or absent from the moment, always producing more and other than it intends in the process. This discrepancy or widened gap between physical movement and meaning implies that gestures performatively 'bring a body into being', just as bodies potentially bring new, different gestures into being (Noland, 2009, p. 212). The word 'potentially' needs to be emphasized here, for it would be fallacious to hastily conclude that the participatory gesture is a radical performative per se. Its fragility and contingency make it extraordinarily difficult to translate and put to use as a political concept. Both *If I Could Take Your Place* and *Where We Are Not* allegorize displacement and consider its political implications: the privilege of mobility in some cases juxtaposed with the quandaries of forced migration in others, or the freedom, however hypothetical, to step outside of one's own skin and predicament, as opposed to the freedom to hide or reveal what one deems as one's own.

Notes

1 Conversation with Aitana Cordero, 20 April 2017.
2 The Dutch newspaper advertisement specifically mentions that it is for an art project. 'Call for Participants: May I offer to take your place? For one hour, one day, one month. I am searching for other ways of experiencing myself, the other and the city' (courtesy Lina Issa).
3 Conversation with Lina Issa, 19 February 2015.
4 Conversation with Aitana Cordero, 20 April 2017.
5 I retain the German original *Gestus* with its capitalized nominal Latin form with reference to Brecht's theatrical-political concept, since the commonly cited translation by John Willett as 'gesture' or 'gest' is misleading for several reasons (Jameson, 1998, p. 99).

5

Delicate gestures of participation

Freedom, rather, possesses the strange capacity to hide itself in the gesture that expresses it. (Flusser, 2014, p. 164)

An audience that sleeps?

Going off to sleep during a performance is usually regarded as a sign of boredom, lack of attentiveness and lack of interest on the part of spectators. The sight (or sound!) of audience members falling asleep might be perceived as an indication of the performance's failure to engage, entertain or enthuse and thus a failure to fulfil what are widely considered to be the basic functions of the artist. The status and respect accorded to an attentive, alert and perceptive spectator is widespread in theatre and performance theory, even if the forms and expressions of this perceptiveness have been differently conceived in various historical moments and in diverse cultural paradigms. Since falling asleep, with its attendant gestures of yawning, dropping off, stretching out tired limbs or snoring, is a physiological phenomenon, it is rarely openly condemned or looked down upon when it happens within the frameworks or spaces of performance, for it is regarded as an uncontrollable and accidental 'natural' response, at best tolerated as an expression of a person's fatigue or exhaustion (Reiss, 2014). In most theatre and performance theory, a spectator who sleeps is an absent spectator, and certainly a non-participant spectator.

In the urban intervention *Nomad City Passage*, conceived by the visual artists Rebekka Reich and Oliver Gather, and performed in Düsseldorf, Linz and Cologne between 2005 and 2009, this premise is inverted. Participants were invited to spend a night camping at various everyday or representative urban locations, in public squares, in skyscrapers, in shopping malls and in school rooms. Upon arrival, they checked in by filling in a form, in which they were asked three questions about their relationship to the particular site.[1] They were then provided with a tent, an air mattress, towels and a torch. Audience participation consists of the deceptively simple act of around twenty people pitching tents on the site, spending the night there and leaving the next morning after sharing breakfast together. The artists as well as the proprietors or caretakers of the site also joined the campers. The latter were invited to introduce the site to visitors in terms of its history, its infrastructure, its function and to share their personal experiences of inhabiting or working in that particular space. There was no other artistic or entertainment programme on offer, and visitors were free to discover and explore the spaces and interact with each other in whatever way and to whatever extent that they chose.

Social interaction between participants and the site is integral to the project. The encounter and interaction take place in a specific kind of urban space, highly determined in its daily usage, but rendered with a different potential of sociality when approached through the act of spending a night on a camp site as part of an art project. The spaces can also be seen as participants, interacting with the human visitors.[2] In the video documentation of the project, Oliver Gather comments on this deliberate reduction of authorial design and foregrounding of the site, by arguing that the appropriation of the spaces by the participants can only take place when there is a minimized steering of the experience as event (Reich and Richter, 2011). Some participants experienced this minimal dramaturgy as an adventure, since it was not clear what might happen.[3] Others, such as the following participant who camped on a golf course in Düsseldorf with his 10-year-old son and friends, remarked on being initially disappointed with its strong resemblance to a 'regular' camping experience:

Lying in the tent at night I thought to myself: was I disappointed by the ordinariness of the site? Was it me who did not recognize what was special about the situation? ... I wondered whether the shopping mall might have been a more interesting choice. ... In hindsight though, I see it differently. That one night has very gradually changed my sense of perception of places. I have since passed by many places and wondered what it might be like to spend a night here. I now tend to speculate more about the possibilities of a site and question its given definition.[4]

The project was launched in Düsseldorf, Germany, in 2005, with a follow-up in 2009 in Linz, Austria, and Cologne, Germany. In Düsseldorf, it was the prestige-laden image of the city centre as a prosperous, post-industrial hub of museums, media houses, expensive shopping streets, tennis and golf clubs that informed the choice of camping sites. In Cologne, the camping sites were located on the top floors of six prominent skyscrapers in the city, with the city skyline being the space that informed the choice of sites.[5] In Linz, the project was conducted within the framework of the Austrian Festival of Regions, with the theme in 2009 being 'Normality' ('Normalzustand'). The camping sites were chosen from various locations on the city's periphery, with a focus on their 'normality' or ubiquity: an indoor rock climbing gym, a hardware supermarket, a hydroelectric power station, a shooting range, a school building and the lawns of a housing complex. Similar to most site-specific performance work, the sites in *Nomad City Passage* did not simply form backdrops or podiums for human interaction but were approached as active participants in their own way. Since they were not empty or directly public spaces, permission had to be sought from their regular occupants to temporarily inhabit the spaces in a manner that was alien to their day-to-day usage, and the ideas and responses of the proprietors played a role in the way the spaces were thrown open to the public. The artists attest to the difficulty of gaining permission and access to the spaces, with the preparatory work often involving long and tedious communications and bureaucratic procedures.[5]

Participatory urban interventions in a project-based art world

The fact that *Nomad City Passage* can be located across the domains of performance, scenography, urban design and installation art is evidenced by its funding sources, including the Municipal Urban Planning Department, a forum on contemporary architecture as well as various arts funding agencies and arts festivals. Participation is a central concept to *Nomad City Passage*, which explores lived experiences of urban spaces, asking how the sites of a city are experienced by its inhabitants, and how they relate to it in direct, palpable ways. It approaches city planning not as a given, static fact but through what the artists call 'the occupation of carefully chosen sites using the archaic principle of encampment' (Reich and Gather, 2005, p. 2). In this sense, it can be called an immersive participatory artwork, in the way that it seeks to prepare the conditions for enabling the participants' own version of the space and leaves open the question of how the invitation is taken up by them. Yet precisely because of its minimal framework, it is difficult to place *Nomad City Passage* in terms of genre. It is not a performance, an installation or a workshop, and in the artists' view it belongs more to the domain of the visual arts than to the performing arts. The term 'urban intervention' seems appropriate from a performance studies perspective, since the focus is on a scenographic encounter with urban architecture and public spaces. The spatial dimension is approached not in geometric or geographical but in social, interstitial terms.[7] This term conjures a history that has influenced both the trajectory of theatre and performance as well as that of the visual arts in a European and North American context in the twentieth century: from the *dérives* of the Situationists in France in the 1920s, to the Fluxus movement and happenings and land art in the USA in the 1960s and 1970s, to the urban experiments of the 'independents' in Brazil in the 1970s and 1980s.

The documentation of *Nomad City Passage* uses the word 'project', which is not insignificant given the political economy underpinnings of this term in contemporary art. A 'project' may take any format, and can also be located outside of traditional genre boundaries, and this is most likely the intended usage of the term. However, the idea of the project as the unit of artistic activity came to prominence via the increasing influence of management discourses in the 1990s, similar to terms like 'network', and has come to stand for what Luc Boltanski and Eve Chiapello have famously called 'the new spirit of capitalism'. In their eponymously titled book, Boltanski and Chiapello argue through their critical appraisal of management books of the 1990s that the 'project' has become representative of the typical format of economic activity in Western societies: an activity of limited duration and with a high level of intensity, which serves as an occasion and a reason for connections between people in a network and requires a process in which several persons or institutions collaborate on a short-term basis (Boltanski and Chiapello, 1999, pp. 104–105). They observe that as traditional jobs are on the decline, people become increasingly involved in a wide range of self-managed activities in the form of projects, all of which depend on and in turn generate encounters, leading to more activities. The project serves as a catalyst for people's involvement and active, enthusiastic participation, despite or precisely because it only lasts for a short period of time (Boltanski and Chiapello, 1999, p. 110). They diagnose the phenomenon of the project as a term pertinent not only to activities within managerial capitalism, but also to those activities that are explicitly critical of the project's precariousness and its dynamics within neoliberal capitalism, thus claiming that its transience and flexibility and ability to absorb criticism make it into one of the pillars of the 'projective city' (Boltanski and Chiapello, 1999, p. 111).

Boltanski and Chiapello's analysis of the cultural and political economy of the project and network further stresses its feature of 'being called on to participate' (1999, p. 126) and its requirement of participants to be constantly active and interactive, dissolving personal and professional life. The growing prominence of the project in critical artistic contexts is therefore analysed as inseparable from this broader paradigm shift of the work ethic. At the same time, the growing popularity of the 'project' concept in the 1990s did not emerge from a vacuum, but can be traced back to early Romanticism in European art history and to the philosophical critique of the artwork as being unable to adequately depict or represent infinite reality. By referring to *Nomad City Passage* as a project, the artists thus ally it conceptually to the notion of a work of art as always necessarily fragmentary, work in progress, never comprehensive or all-encompassing.

'The fall of sleep'

Nomad City Passage is no doubt motivated by a critical view towards the spatial and regulatory frameworks of this 'new spirit' of capitalism, even as it does not claim any easy possibility of stepping outside them, or being unaffected by them. It playfully deploys spaces of consumer leisure, productivity and symbolic power, visiting these sites not during their usual periods of restlessness and buzz of activity, but rather during the times when they are not used and are generally inaccessible. Visitors are called upon to participate not by busying themselves with any curated or designed activities on the site, but by going to sleep. Sleep itself thus becomes valued as a conscious, corporeal, intimate activity, as non-passivity on the one hand, and simultaneously as an act of defiance towards the demands of what Jonathan Crary calls the 24/7 world, on the other. For Crary, non-stop activity and sleeplessness, specifically the idea of reducing the need to sleep, characterize the contemporary economic order, which makes sleep into 'a human need and interval of time that cannot be colonized and harnessed to a massive engine of profitability' (2013, pp. 10–11). The invitation for the project announces in a matter-of-factly worded subtitle: 'everybody is heading home. we're staying. to sleep.'[8] Sleep is announced here in what could be read as a tone of defiance, not in the form of a loud slogan on a banner, but more reminiscent of a mobile phone text message, abbreviating punctuation rules for speed and convenience, typed into a gadget that never sleeps, or whose 'sleep mode' merely means that it can be readily activated at any given moment. The critical aesthetic qualities of *Nomad City Passage* are derived from the fact that sleep remains a profoundly ambivalent, evocative and delicate matter. Sleep is foregrounded as a mode of participation in the urban intervention, thus ironically questioning common-sense conventions and assumptions around audience participation in theatre and performance theory.

The various locations in which the tents were set up in three different cities assume a theatrical dimension when experienced through the minute details that become perceptible only when one is lying down, preparing and waiting for sleep to arrive, when conversations have come to an end, lights have been switched off and the body is ritually prepared to rest. The location's sounds and smells and nooks and corners begin to come to life. It is the camera that then remains awake and charged, recording some of these sounds and impressions: the curious sounds of the machinery of a water pumping station, the circumferential streaks of city lights from the top floor of a skyscraper. Participants whom I contacted in 2015, between six and ten years after their single night's camping experience, curiously and surprisingly remembered sensorial details such as the eerie creak of an empty school classroom at night, the mist drops on the golf course in the early morning, or the odours of the turf floor of a tennis club.[9] One participant, who camped on a golf course, remembered that most members of the group woke up rather late in the morning, and had to hurry to break down their tents because of a horse racing event that was about to start at the same venue.[10] Another participant, who camped at a hardware store in Linz in 2009, remarked in an interview:

> My strongest memories are from the morning: for one thing, having breakfast together with the other participants. [...] And then, going to the staff rooms to brush my teeth. On the way I encountered the first customer who walked into the hardware store. This situation was very intriguing and also funny. I woke up feeling 'at home' in this huge hardware store and it was thus awkward that people were suddenly walking around the place shopping on the spot where I had only recently pitched my tent.[11]

Even the phrase 'waiting for sleep to arrive' renders sleep an actor or actress in the wings of the stage whose entry is awaited by the spectators. Yet the arrival of sleep can never be planned or foretold with certainty. Jacqueline Rose notes in her reading of Freud's *Interpretation of Dreams*: 'Sleep ... cannot be willed. It only comes inadvertently. [...] we never know what will happen – or exactly where we are going – when we go to sleep' (Rose, 2003, p. 110). Simultaneously, when we say that we 'go to sleep', it is as if it is not sleep that comes to us, but we who must go to it. In *Nomad City Passage*, the collective performance of sleep oscillates between being an intense, active, dynamic experience on the one hand, and a non-performance, an absence of activity on the other. It raises the question of the relation between the omission and commission of acts and the concept of the performative. Whereas performativity is predominantly understood as a productive and generative concept, it might be asked what is the performativity of seemingly non-productive aspects of human action, such as silence, hesitation or sleep (Gronau and Lagaay, 2008, p. 11; Lagaay and Lorber, 2012). Going to sleep need not be seen as a negation or refusal of participation but indeed as a form of participation that enables the emergence of a different sociality and inhabitation of space, somewhere between doing and non-doing.

One participant remarked in email correspondence:

> In Germany, one doesn't just sleep in the middle of the city centre on a public terrain. Or if one does so, as a homeless person, a partygoer, or a protestor, it is always an act of transgression and always comes with a host of restrictions. I can remember exchanging glances with other participants as we pumped up our air mattresses in front of the Gehry buildings[12] – a feeling of trespassing over an invisible threshold and a feeling of reassurance in observing other participants doing the same.[13]

Although a sense of transgression and awkwardness was palpably felt, the event had a remarkably quiet and delicate dramaturgy. A highly pre-determined and charged site such as the Gehry commercial complex in Düsseldorf presents its own means of restricting even a temporary occupation and transformation of the space. At the same time, the transformation is not sudden but over the passage of time. This mixture is expressed in the word 'passage' in the title *Nomad City Passage*, conjuring the association of a transit or journey from one state to another, as well as a physical passage or route. Jean Luc Nancy's philosophical essay on sleep, entitled in French *Tombe de sommeil*, literally translates as the tomb or tombstone of sleep, as if a physical monument could stand for a passage of time, the unit with which sleep is measured. However, the word *tombe* also resonates with *tomber*, 'to fall', thus strikingly associating the act of 'falling asleep' with the passage from one state to another, with sleep as a liminal state between wakefulness and death (Nancy, 2009). The English translation of Nancy's essay is notably *The Fall of Sleep*, a phrase that imaginatively captures both the fall or decline of the value of sleep in a modernity marked by an economy of sleepless wakefulness, as well as the act of falling, dropping without control into the intoxicated stupor of consumerism, which is also associated with sleep. In German, *die Passage* is further used in compounded form in words such as *Einkaufspassage* (shopping mall) or *Filmpassage* (cinema centre), or with reference to a passage from a text, film, a musical piece and the like. The project evokes all these associations: in its choice of quotidian spaces with a predominantly commercial or entrepreneurial dimension; in the suggestion that these spaces, despite their overwhelming, monumental, symbolic power and architectural pre-determination, become vulnerable when used in unintended ways (*tombe* as monument/tombstone and *tomber* as falling); and in the association of the tent as equipment that accompanies a journey or transit, pitched along the way, a liminal space of shelter during the passage from night to morning or from one place to another.[14]

In the video documentation accompanying the project in Cologne, aptly titled 'Obere Etagen' [Top Floors], a term that colloquially refers to the top levels of a hierarchy as well as the top floors of a building, Reich remarks:

> [our] notion of immortality or perpetuity is also linked to our skyscrapers. Symbols of power they certainly are, and simultaneously so delicate. How delicate they are, we came to realize in the course of researching the project [...] how difficult it can be to make these places accessible, especially to strangers. (Reich and Richter, 2011)

The vulnerability and susceptibility of a commercial skyscraper becomes apparent when confronted by the delicacy of the act of 25 people setting up tents to sleep on its 41st storey for one single night. Its spectacularity is a reminder of Guy Debord's well-known lines from *The Society of the Spectacle*:

> As long as necessity is socially dreamed, dreaming will remain a social necessity. The spectacle is the bad dream of a modern society in chains and ultimately expresses itself in nothing more than its wish for sleep. The spectacle is the guardian of that sleep. (Debord, 1967, para. 21)

Debord's cry against consumer culture and commodification is dialectically contrasted in *Nomad City Passage* with the monumental buildings and sites of this consumerism literally, gently, unassumingly being called upon to guard the sleep and the dreams of their visitors, to be the stage on which society can recuperate itself from its maelstrom of endless activity, speed, vigilance, mobility and wakefulness, to reach higher levels in the very act of sleeping, as it were. The fragility of consumer spectacle is contrasted with the defenceless, exposed state that people are in when they are asleep. Reich points out in the video documentation that participants displayed a noticeable forthrightness and critical honesty when it came to choosing the spot on which their tent was to be set up, in their location preferences in the allotted site, in the way they sought to establish a familiarity and a sense of comfort in the space, as a way of protecting themselves for the experience of sleep (Reich and Richter, 2011). In Cologne, the familiarity and normality of sleep was sought in an unfamiliar environment, namely the top floor of a commercial skyscraper. In Linz, on the other hand, the sites themselves, which were quotidian, mostly public spaces, were de-familiarized through the acts of camping on them.

Crary introduces a social critique into this existential dimension, arguing that 'sleep cannot be eliminated, but it can be wrecked and despoiled [...] the injuring of sleep is inseparable from the ongoing dismantling of social protections in other spheres' (Crary, 2013, pp. 17–18). To fall asleep is thus to become imperilled in a way that makes evident how a certain 'precariousness' is a shared condition, common to all (Lorey, 2015). In response to Crary, one could say that sleep is not simply a state of passive vulnerability, nor can it conversely be hailed as a radical form of resistance to commercialization. In artistic practices such as *Nomad City Passage*, sleep retains a certain delicate ambivalence that renders it a counter-intuitively potent gesture of participation.

The poetic politics of camping

Nomad City Passage does not explicitly draw connections between the personal and the biopolitical dimensions of sleep in the way Crary does; it is not foremost a commentary about how sleep is beleaguered by post-industrial capitalism or about camping as a political act. In its minimal artistic design there is no tokenistic reference to or representation of homelessness, to the tourism and leisure industry and its economy of providing comfort and relaxation, to the deterioration of housing for the poor, or to the larger, now ever more current political topics of refuge and asylum, although it does not require a great stretch of the imagination for a participant to make these connections. When camping is evoked as an archaic principle of temporarily inhabiting a site and moving on, the mobility of some immediately conjures the immobility of others (Budgen, 2000, p. 155). The leisurely pleasure of camping summons the idea of the camp as a place of refuge from persecution or danger for others, or as a site of visible, collective occupation. The urban interventions in Linz, Düsseldorf and Cologne took place between 2005 and 2009, long before tents occupied the Maidan, Tahrir Square, Gezi Park, Zuccotti Park, Bahrain Central Square and the city centres in Barcelona, Lisbon and Athens. Yet they took place only shortly after the sleep-in blockades of anti-nuclear and anti-militarist activists in Germany, the UK and France in the late 1990s, the joyful celebrations of the *Reclaim the Streets* movement, the tent occupations of the alter-globalization activists in Seattle in 1999 or Genoa in 2001 (Notes from Nowhere, 2003) and the tent city of youth protesting the presence of the Syrian army that appeared in Martyrs' Square and Riad al-Solh Square in central Beirut in Lebanon in February 2005, following the assassination of the former prime minister Rafik Hariri (Bayoumi, 2005).

Nomad City Passage took place in an artistic context before camping in public spaces started to become a subject of interest to art museums and exhibition circuits as an act of artistic activism.[15] At the same time, it evokes a rich legacy of artworks at the crossroads of performance, scenography, architecture and the visual arts. In interviews, the artists reference the conceptual art, land art and body art traditions emergent in the US in the 1960s and 1970s, particularly the work of Allan Kaprow, John Cage, Robert Smithson, Georges Brecht and Chris Burden, remarking that these historical connections may not have been apparent to them at the time but became evident later.[16] However, unlike the avant-garde experiments of that time, which often sought to test the borders of participation and see how far they could allow themselves to go in stretching the limits of existing artistic conventions, *Nomad City Passage* seeks a subtle and non-spectacular exploration of urban space as lived and embodied.[17] Rather than being challenged and provoked, audiences are welcomed with hospitality and carefully informed about what the artists' intentions are. It is the absence of planned events and activities that enables the spaces to be viewed with a different eye, distanced from their usual utilitarian inhabitation.

The tent becomes the space for an intimate quotidian act of wearing one's nightclothes and going to sleep, withdrawing from the presence of others. Whether in outdoor or indoor environments, the tents were not only a means of protecting and marking one's place of sleep, but also served to ensure that participants would have the right to be left in peace and not be pulled into the limelight.[18] At the same time, the tent is one among several others, and the participants all huddle together, as it were, each in their own tent. In the choice of sites, in the choice of camping gear provided to participants and the documentation and framing of the events, *Nomad City Passage* carefully refrains from romanticizing sleep as a universal, ahistorical and uniformly pleasant phenomenon or from nostalgically conjuring a representation of what it once was and no longer is. Instead of overtly politicizing the event or introducing any narrative frames, the artists choose to configure it in terms of hospitality and interaction between site and visitors. Participants are personally introduced to the space and guided through it. The permission granted by the caretakers and proprietors and the invitation extended to outsiders are essential conditions of possibility for their participation. As Gareth White has argued with reference to the theatre, the invitation to participate is itself an authored process, 'making the audience participant more productive of signs and affects, more complex as a site of perception and action' (White, 2013, p. 195). This implies that the way an invitation is made, the manner in which it is extended, is co-constitutive of the aesthetics of participation, similar to the way in which the invitation is accepted, taken up and enacted by its recipients. Reich points to the multiple layers of participation, remarking in an interview:

> To us, the participants were conceived of not so much as participants but more as guests, to whom we, as hosts, extended an invitation. We had the role of mediating between the actual occupants of the spaces and the visitors, being responsible for the guests feeling safe and welcome. At the same time, we saw ourselves too as guests in the space.[19]

Such an affective dimension immediately renders audience participation in the artwork and the artwork's participation in urban spaces different in significant ways from sociological and political concepts of participation. Where social theory conceives of civic participation in terms of belonging, or of being a part of some larger entity or social unit, the aesthetics of *Nomad City Passage* emphasizes participation in a counter-intuitive way: it becomes possible to participate precisely because of *not* being a part of some shared community ideal. The invitation to spend a night in a hardware store together with 25 people is attractive simply because it makes possible the thrill of participation without belonging, commitment or affiliation. This does not mean that the paradoxes of social interaction are not recognized in social or political theory. As Reich points out, social theorists such as Richard Sennett in *The Fall of Public Man* (1977) recognized early on how the attempt to generate intimacy and closeness between white-collar workers in large, shared workspaces in fact led to a greater sense of perceived isolation and withdrawal from public affairs (Sennett, 1993).[20] The tents in *Nomad City Passage* paradoxically gesture both towards the intimate social contact denied to people in commercial public spaces on the one hand, as well as towards the necessary distance required between people in order for them to be sociable and invested in participating in civic life, on the other. Participants can be sociable and communicative because of the possibility of having the tent as a space of withdrawal, and they can perceive the spaces as public only when their utilitarian or commercial function is put aside, however temporarily.

On the archive of ephemeral experiences

Not having personally attended any of the events and only accessing the project several years after its completion, the available documentation on *Nomad City Passage* became an important source for my exploration of its participatory aesthetics, in addition to personal communication with the artists and several former participants, and one employee who works at one of the sites. The documentation takes the form of two videos and a paper collage. The first video, entitled 'Normalzustand' ('Normality', 2009), relates to the six camping events in Linz, and the second film, entitled 'Obere Etagen' ('Top Floors', 2011), documents the six overnight stays in Cologne's skyscrapers.[21] In all three locations, a photographer and/or a filmmaker was invited to attend the events and offer an audiovisual documentation and exploration of their own experience, rather than simply executing instructions from the artists. 'Normality' is a collage of images and ambient sounds from the six camping sites in Linz, with no narrative commentary or dialogue, played in fast-forward mode, thus compressing the passage of time and providing an atmospheric record of the sites in their transition from being quotidian spaces such as supermarkets or school buildings, to the arrival of the visitors, the gradual occupation of the spaces, the hours of quiet in the night and their departure in the morning. The curatorial concept of the documentation in 'Normality' emphasizes participation in spatial terms, i.e. how people approach and inhabit, take part in and contribute to the life of each space. Interestingly, space takes on more of an audio than a visual dimension, as the fast-forward mode allows for a cursory glance at the space, whereas the audio clips record minute details in real time. In contrast, the video documentation 'Top Floors' in Cologne emphasizes the social and communicative aspects of audience participation, featuring moments of encounter, astonishment, mundaneness and the very physical acts of setting up and breaking down the tents on the top floors of the skyscrapers, overlooking the cityscape from above. The voice-over narrative in the video features comments by the artists and the custodians of the sites.

What is the status of the documentation in relation to the event, in terms of the question of participation? For the analysis of works such as *Nomad City Passage*, the documentation is not a simple record of an event, but rather a transposition of various facets of the event into a different medium.[22] The paper collage, for instance, entitled 'Album' (2014), pieces together various moments of the process of developing the idea and comprises various physical records, such as newspaper articles and images, official permission letters and technical clearances, notes from the registration forms of participants, offering a panorama of participant motivations and relations to the site, in itself a valuable pool of audience research data. In response to questions about the relationship of visitors to the site, in this case a skyscraper in Cologne, visitors explain how they view it as a landmark or orientation around the city, or remember it since its construction following the demolition of a previously existing building, or how they find it the most ugly building in the city and wish it could be removed from the landscape.[23] Access to such documents, especially given the absence of an opportunity to participate directly in the event, provides a rich archive for analysing various aspects of people's participation in the artwork and the artwork's participation in public life.

The role of new (implying electronic) technologies in participatory works is a recurring topic in the scholarship on immersive performances, as their adaptation to the artistic context raises questions of liveness, simultaneity, presence and co-creation. Technological developments over the twentieth century have accorded a large-scale dimension to participation, giving importance to the question of the number of participants, the (technical) ease or access of participation, or the wide reach across regions and social groups, regardless of the objectives or quality of participation (Huybrechts, 2011, p. 24). The reliance on user-led technology in theatre and performance as a tool to enhance audience participation has become commonplace: from audience members being asked to wear headphones, or follow instructions on mobile devices, to using interactive screens, communicating with other spectators or people outside of the performance space during the performance, to radio ballets, simulations and games. The application of electronic technology in performance to seek the active, physical or virtual participation of audiences in co-creating the performance has been variously read as heralding 'an unsettling and,' or exhilarating process of becoming aware of the fusion of senses' (Machon, 2013, p. 143), or dismissed as 'ornamental, illusionistic devices perpetrating a treachery on the audience' (Schechner, 1973, p. 77).

Beyond these judgements of their moral value, with the resultant sifting of seemingly good or bad kinds of participation, the role of technologies in relation to the question of participation draws attention to its sites, modes and means (Magelsen, 2014). Where, how and through which forms or formats does participation 'occur' or fail to do so? How is the experience of participation in art grounded in and distributed across mind, body, space, objects, dialogical exchange or non-verbal social interaction? In what ways does technology influence this experience, where participation might mean 'playing a game' in some cases, and 'eavesdropping on a conversation' in other situations, where immersive participation can range from a sensory immersion (large screens, powerful sound environments, haptic experiences) to an imaginative immersion (identification, empathy, problem solving, cooperation and communication) (Susi, 2014, pp. 192–193)? On the one hand, it is evident that the incorporation of different media into the staging and scenographic elements of theatre has been a part of theatre history for centuries and need not be regarded as unique to the twentieth century. On the other hand, it is undeniable that they are now being increasingly studied and appreciated in terms of how they reconfigure formal aesthetic dimensions and conventions of the theatre. In performance theory, they have led to revised conceptions of what liveness and co-presence mean (Giannachi and Kaye, 2011), how the strict boundary between production and reception is broken down (Harvie, 2013), questions about the authenticity or the spectacularity of participatory technologies (Huybrechts, 2011) and about the ensuing questions of authorship, collective bodies and collaboration (Cull and Gritzner, 2011).

Yet in conjunction with the question of documentation and archive, the issue is one of finding what Josephine Machon terms 'a lasting ephemerality'; thus fleeting, momentary experiences that lead to lasting embodied memories (Machon, 2013), and a mode of transmission that can be accessed by those who were absent. The video and printed documentation of *Nomad City Passage* attempts to retain a sense of the ephemerality of the experience, with fleeting images and sounds, the light gradually shifting from evening to night to morning, ending with the spaces returning to exactly the same situation that existed before the camping took place. The documentation, however, also invites the question of what is politically and culturally at work in the deployment of these forms at a given moment in time, in what ways the generation of technologically aided, shared experiences and encounters in the sphere of art is related to larger modes of government or emergent forms of subjectivity in complex, contradictory ways (Kunst, 2015).

What I am trying to say is that the problem of archiving and documentation is more than a methodological or technical concern, and touches on the status of participation in the context of the visual arts alongside the category of 'contemporary art'. Participation and collaborative creation are often considered as among the main characteristics of contemporary art; thus a genealogy of participatory practices is often inseparable from the genealogy of what has come to be known as contemporary art. Boris Groys offers a two-pronged explanation for this: first, the absence of a so-called 'inner value' of contemporary art, i.e. its merit being dependent not on internal, formal or verifiable aesthetic criteria, but on how it is valued or appreciated by its public (Groys, 2008, p. 20). The physical involvement or engagement of museum or exhibition visitors could thus be either a direct affirmation of this absent 'inner value' of the artwork or, conversely, a critical response by the artists to it. A second explanation is to be found in the commercialization and commodification of the visual art market, which, according to Groys, leads to the devaluation of art and the separation of artists from the public, thereby compelling artists and audiences to search for 'the binding value of art ... in non-commercial – if not directly anti-commercial and simultaneously collaborative – practice' (Groys, 2008, p. 21). In both arguments, participation is presented as the positively connoted response to two interconnected problems: to the absence of autonomous artistic value and to the commercialization of modern art.

Juliane Rebentisch similarly identifies the category of participation as central to contemporary art, but draws a different, more convincing conclusion in her analysis. Rebentisch connects the rise of an experiential, participatory approach to a paradigm shift in aesthetic theory, whereby the idea of a distinct, autonomous artwork is called into question. The phenomenon of audiences participating in the making of an artwork goes hand in hand with the crisis in modern art, with its loss of faith in aesthetic universalism or in a truth-led aesthetic (*Wahrheitsästhetik*). Aesthetic experience can no longer be presented in pure or abstract, universalizable terms. It is thus relayed to the level of the particular, and in the process becomes inseparable from the dimension of intersubjectivity, i.e. the dimension of human interaction. The question of participation in contemporary art is thus one of aesthetic experience and thereby becomes tied to the question of participation in social life, thus to the problem of intersubjectivity in art. This intertwining of aesthetic experience and intersubjectivity leads to vastly divergent results in terms of how this participation takes shape and what its aims are (Rebentisch, 2013, pp. 59–60). Rebentisch argues that the increasingly active role assigned to viewers in contemporary art, specifically installation art, should not be mistaken for interactivity, but rather indicates 'the constitutive role of the viewer for the ontology of the work of art *in general*. [...] "the inclusion of the beholder" places installation art in direct relation to a central problem of modern philosophy: the problem of an ontology founded on the subject–object distinction' (Rebentisch, 2012, p. 15). Participation thus becomes the concept with which the philosophical problem of the subject–object distinction is rethought, namely the distinction between artwork and experience, or between artist and viewer.

This view is shared, though differently framed, by Janet Kraynak. In her influential essay on Bruce Nauman's installations entitled 'Dependent Participation' (2007), Kraynak argues that the shift towards audience participation in visual art was historically motivated by a combination of three reasons: first, it follows a Marxist model of realigning the relationship between subjects and objects and thus between viewers and artworks; second, it follows a post-structuralist model of critiquing authorship and thus leads to artworks that trouble the notion of authorship; and third, it follows a model of collective creation in opposition to a view of art that is of consumptive value to bourgeois elites (Kraynak, 2007, pp. 228–229).

All these analyses of the historical emergence of participatory practices present them as being responses to a set of problems. These are not simply formal or aesthetic problems but are complementary to broader social concerns. The problem of the gap between artists and their audiences emerges as complementary to the problem of social inequalities and hierarchies; the question of ascertaining universal aesthetic standards or values is inseparable from the question of cultural or historical universalism. Participation becomes the category for registering ruptures in the social-political and the artistic spheres, even as it is deployed as an antidote to the quandaries that these ruptures pose.

Participation in *Nomad City Passage* touches precisely on this question of the relationship between aesthetic experience and intersubjectivity. This relationship is not conceived as staking a claim to rights, citizenship, privileges and public goods or community, nor as holding the promise of taking part in something universal and ahistorical. Rather it remains a fleeting, short-lived inhabitation of a space, taking care to leave as few traces as possible and not seeking any material alterations in the space. The urban intervention is intensely low-key and involves an inconspicuous though intimate presence, rather than a participation through 'productive' activity. In Rebentisch's words, 'the possibility of participation itself becomes the material to reflect upon, by which the visitor is enmeshed in a certain sense, and which can touch him or her much more intensely than the reduction of aesthetic experience to practical participation might have it' (2015, p. 38). It is thus not so much a matter of the practical effectiveness of participation or its absence, but rather the question of the potential or possibility of participation that *Nomad City Passage* delicately gestures towards. One participates by reflecting on the terms of one's participation. The visceral aspect of participation is complemented by the reflection and observation of one's own participation. The seemingly immediate relation to the site remains in tension with one's awareness of the artistic transformation of the site (Rebentisch, 2013, p. 88). In *Nomad City Passage* this tension holds true for the participants, as well as for potential future audiences who can only access reflections of or reports and documents of the project. Not its clarity of message or pronounced allegiance to a cause, but its ambiguity and permeability between private and public, between individual and collective experience, characterize the participatory quality of the act of collectively pitching a tent in an urban space.

Notes

1 The questions were: 'How do you know about this site?', 'Why did you choose this site?', and 'Would you miss this site if it no longer existed? Why?' Email correspondence with Rebekka Reich, 17 August 2015 (translation SB).

2 This has some similarities with Bourriaud's concept of the 'relational aesthetic': 'an art taking as its theoretical horizon the realm of human interactions and its social context, rather than the assertion of an independent and private symbolic space' (Bourriaud, 2002, p. 14). However, one could modify this to the extent that the assertion of an independent symbolic space in *Nomad City Passage* is not separate from or in opposition to the realm of human interactions, but rather emergent from it. It also has congruencies with Claire Bishop's definition of participation in art, wherein 'people constitute the central artistic medium and material' (Bishop, 2012, p. 2). However, here too one could say that

people and places together constitute the central artistic medium and material.

3 Email correspondence with Participant 4, 14 August 2015 (translation SB).

4 Email correspondence with Participant 5, 9 August 2015 (translation SB).

5 The interior spaces of the top floors were the preferred sites, although in two cases, roof terraces were also used because of the prominent location of the skyscrapers in the city and the unsuitability of the interior spaces. Conversation with Rebekka Reich, 22 January 2016).

6 Email correspondence with Rebekka Reich, 15 June 2015 (translation SB).

7 Email correspondence with Oliver Gather, 17 August 2015 (translation SB).

8 'alles geht nach hause. wir bleiben. zum schlafen' (Reich and Gather, 2009).

9 I contacted 11 people from an estimated total of 250 participants and received seven responses by email and via telephone.

10 Email correspondence with Participant 1, 18 June 2015 (translation SB).

11 Email correspondence with Participant 2, 2 July 2015 (translation SB).

12 Landmark prestige buildings in the harbour centre of Düsseldorf designed by US architect Frank O. Gehry, consisting of three contrasting building complexes and appearing like a giant sculpture, with twisted towers, shiny mirror walls and asymmetrical floors.

13 Email correspondence with Participant 4, 14 August 2015 (translation SB).

14 Email correspondence with Rebekka Reich, 10 August 2015 (translation SB).

15 Several recent publications and catalogues of exhibitions, not only in Europe and the US, indicate the increasing interest in 'artistic activism' (Achar and Panikkar, 2012; Holmes, 2009; Steierischer_Herbst, 2014; Weibel, 2015).

16 Telephone conversation with Rebekka Reich, 10 August 2015 and O. Gather, 17 August 2015 (translation SB).

17 Telephone conversation with Oliver Gather, 17 August 2015 (translation SB).

18 Telephone conversation with Oliver Gather, 17 August 2015 (translation SB).

19 Telephone conversation with Rebekka Reich, 10 August 2015 (translation SB).

20 Email correspondence with Rebekka Reich, 22 January 2016.

21 'Normalzustand' (Normality), 2009, length: 6 min. 15 sec., Linz, format: 1-channel monitor (small), PAL video (25fps 1920x1080), colour, audio: stereo, by Rebekka Reich; 'Obere Etagen' (Top Floors), video, 2011, length: 19 min. 25 sec., Cologne, format: 1-channel monitor, PAL video

(25fps 1920x1080), colour, audio: stereo, by Marcus Vila Richter and Rebekka Reich.

22 Email correspondence with Rebekka Reich, 10 August 2015 (translation SB).

23 Email correspondence with Participant 6, 15 June 2015 (translation SE).

Conclusion: between image, act, body and language

I have argued throughout this study that participatory art practices need to be understood in conjunction with the anxieties and contradictions that accompany them. Whether or not this is a formally constitutive characteristic worthy of naming as a genre is, in my view, less important than finding ways to account for and be responsive to the questions it poses. This is the place that this study departed from, yet oddly, it also the place it finds itself arriving at. For if this study has inquired into some of the conditions for and articulations of participation in the arts, it has also turned out to be an investigation of the ways in which participation is already circumscribed by the questions we ask of it, such as the social impact of participatory art, or its specific aesthetic features. The frictions in this endeavour will have become apparent to the perceptive reader: on the one hand I attempt to identify commonalities and systematic coherences in a field named as participatory art, and on the other hand I seek to analyse it in terms of its deviations from, and incommensurability with, a systematic narrative, in the emphasis of unruly, subtle, non-formalizable modes of participation. I treat participatory art as an inherited category, looking at its diverse, specific operations, or disciplinary routes and historical legacies. At the same time, I try to alter the terms of received wisdom by extrapolating principles and observations from the confines of one disciplinary arena into another. I search for ways in which affiliation to a given type of participatory practice might be described, only to find that formal coherences are perforated by aspects that exceed those same terms of affiliation. The analysis of participatory art and the conceptualization of participation in and through art thereby become intertwined in complex ways.

Finding ways to study and interconnect participation in performance with performance's participation in its immediate and broader social, cultural, political or economic environment seems in my view one of the urgent tasks of scholarship. I have suggested that this partly involves pulsing the fluctuating but ever-existent boundaries between the aesthetic and the non-aesthetic, rather than seeking a disciplinary cartography that can supposedly contain and settle them. It also involves taking into account strategies of participation in the realms of artistic practice in the ways they render visible the failures and possibilities of people's participation in the public sphere. Terms such as the 'artwork', the 'production' or 'the artist' prove inadequate when considering that process, experience and encounter, rather than finished, authored works, are central to most participatory art forms. The gestures of participation are to be found in the most unexpected places and take on various hues and shapes. I argue throughout this study that the concept of participation in the arts should neither be restricted to a purely formalized reading, nor be elevated to a normative status, but rather should be open and alert to those issues and truth claims that come to light through the specific contexts of performance, contexts that need not be deemed antithetical to or incongruous with formalized models of participation in and of performance. This does not imply a dilution of the category of participatory art, implying that everything can be participatory in some way or other, but is rather a plea to take into consideration the precise modes of intersection between the dimensions of participation in art and the contexts of art's participation in social processes in the theorization of the category. Participatory forms in the arts must not be construed as abstract models with a self-governing aesthetic; they are not at one with themselves, but are burdened by the wider conjuncture of our times, 'forms of living in the world' in which a coerced or obligatory participation repeatedly exhausts our capacity to live up to the utopian demand for participation (Sangari, 2002).

The interpretation of participatory practices through the register of the gestural is my attempt to rethink participation while accommodating its contradictions and disquietudes. The notion of the gesture is not a transcendental key with which to unlock some final, proper significance and truth about how to resolve the paradoxes of participation once and for all, but rather one that I believe allows for renewing and revisiting the questions and stakes in it. Its provisionality and counter-intuitive suggestiveness are its limitation as well as what remain its hopes.

Thinking about gesture has fascinated many disciplines and traditions, from the natural sciences to sociology to philosophy, linguistics and the arts. Often the study of gesture pursues the search for its underlying rules and patterns, tying it to language, human physiognomy, to the relation between the body and the soul, or between individuals and societies, and to value systems. I have found these extensive possibilities of the concept to be methodologically helpful, offering a way to reflect on the paradoxes of participation in the arts. In mapping out the concept, gesture recurs as a foil to four interconnected realms: language, the body, the image and the act. Gestures have been referred to by the social theorist Marcel Mauss as 'techniques of the body': they are enabled by social or cultural norms and customs and are acquired and naturalized through a process of learning or imitation. They in turn feed back into and transform the social or the cultural, which allows us to claim that each society has its own gestures. Through this structuralist intertwining of the individual body and the social body, gestures come to be understood as 'physio-psycho-sociological assemblages' (Mauss, 1973, p. 85). Gestures are thus both the outward expression of the psychic as well as the physical internalization of the social. They can be both involuntary or given in the human body apparatus, as well as culturally imposed and acquired; they can be unskilled and skilled, routine or effortful (Noland, 2009, p. 6). Gestures can constitute a language or aesthetic system of their own, as in the Indian conception of *abhinaya*, gestures that link body, breath, narrative and repositories of meaning in a highly codified and yet open form. They can equally be theorized as supplementing and supporting language, or taking its place when language becomes impossible (Agamben, 1993).

Here too, when it is said that gestures are a system of non-verbal communication, the contextual, social element is critical. Whether or not they bear meaning, gestures are inevitably hinged to the social framework from which they emerge. The gestures of language are inseparable from imagery, they bring forth images, hint at grasping language through a different, non-discursive dimension (McNeill, 2005). At the same time gestures are themselves dynamized images, they introduce observable movement into an image, with a beginning and an end. A gesture is an image on the way to becoming an act, or conversely, it is the halting of an act in its transition to image, the condensation of an act, interruptions that generate *tableaus* or frozen images. A gesture may bear the potential of an act, but is not yet an act. Similarly, participatory art possibly gestures towards a broader civic participation, but is not yet or not necessarily its accomplishment. Theatre theory, specifically Brecht's work on the *Gestus*, has widely employed the concept to refer to its capacities to generate highly charged moments (Brecht, 1964).

In the way that the gesture speaks to both the body and to language, to the image and to the act, to the individual and to the collective, I find it offers a fruitful path to reflect on the operations of participatory art. In their being situated between the image and the act, I regard the gestural aspects of participatory art as being situated at the juncture between the visual and the performing arts. Shannon Jackson has referred to this cross-pollination of vocabularies and modes of perception – visual arts employing theatrical modes and theatre moving closer to scenographic or architectural modes – as typically characterizing participatory works (Jackson, 2011, p. 6). Participatory practices in the theatrical domain thus tend to generate moments of interrupted action, bringing the flow of acts to a temporary halt, giving rise to unexpected gestures. Participatory practices in the visual arts domain, on the other hand, appear to set still images into motion, putting their temporality to work, calling gestures into being.

In its mediation between the body and language, I find the notion of the gesture aptly captures the paradoxes of participatory art. Just as gesture is enabled by language and at the same time emerges in the place where language is muted or incapable, 'the other side of language', as it were (Agamben, 1999, p. 78), so participation in art is both enabled by authoritative discourses as well as 'gagged' by them. One side of the paradox of participation is that there are rules of participation given to us, set by art institutions, genres, specific practices or cultural conventions. They invite and enable participation. The other side of the paradox is that the freedom or desire to participate can never be restricted only to these pre-determined modes of participation. With reference to the political sphere, Judith Butler argues that to participate only according to the rules would imply that sooner or later one becomes subject to the rules (Butler, 2014a). So the question of participation is: who sets the terms? The gestures of participation may remain illegible to the established discursive procedures of participatory theatre; they resist formalization without necessarily opposing it, and may thus not even be recognized as resistant. A thin line separates the two sides of potential and limitation, of enabling participation (giving it a bodily possibility) and regulating it (fixing it in rules), demarcating the contours of its genres.

In terms of the notion of the gesture as an assemblage of the physical, psychic and social (Mauss, 1973), moving between the individual and the collective body, I find this resonant with an understanding of participatory art that encompasses both people's participation in artworks and processes as well as the participation (or non-participation) of art in public life. Rather than speaking of its measurable, quantifiable impact, I have argued for an 'inconvenient' understanding of the means and ends of participatory art, in order not to limit the appreciation of these practices to which version of participation is the right or most impactful one, but to appreciate how participation occurs in ways that do not close down its potentials. Expressions of critique towards institutions may involve embracing institutions or setting up counter-institutions, a critique that is not necessarily oppositional, or may not be conventionally considered as 'artistic', but nevertheless involves 'artful' acts of criticality, in that they reveal the mechanisms of institutional power that so forcefully shape theatrical practices and the scholarly discourses that accompany them. To that extent, a gestural appraisal of participatory art is a plea not to reduce the understanding of participation to a matter of verifiability. In some cases, a work may be participatory in the way that it allows us to reflect on the (im)possibility of participation, more than in the implementation of this possibility (Rebentisch, 2015, p. 38). It imaginatively gestures towards it without necessarily acting upon it.

I wish I could end with the confidence that participatory artistic practices will lead the way in revamping and injecting fresh life into a notion that is currently becoming a frenzied euphemism for voluntary subordination and a profit-oriented drive to self-enhancement. Can small hopes stand against big data, big capital, or even bigger planetary collapses? Gayatri Spivak writes: 'We must know what mistake to make with a specific text and must also know how to defend that mistake as the one that will allow us to live' (2012, p. 28). It is in this inconvenient sense that I regard the study of participatory art as an intended mistake – no guarantees or certainties, only gestures of spiritedness.

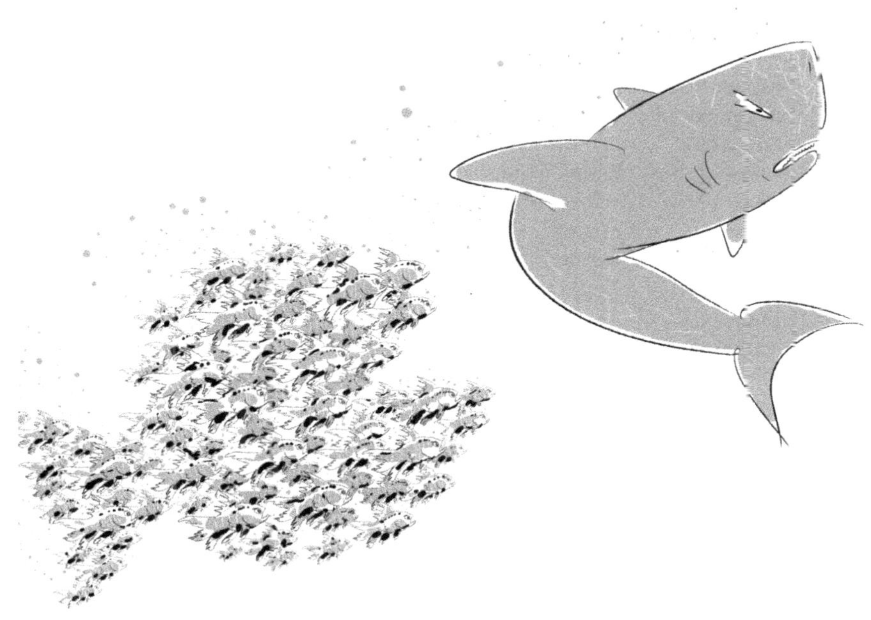

Bibliography

Achar, D., and Panikkar, S. (eds) (2012). *Articulating Resistance: Art and Activism*. New Delhi: Tulika Books.

Agamben, G. (1993 [1978]). Notes on gesture. In *Infancy and History: Essays on the Destruction of Experience*. Trans. Liz Heron. pp. 135–140. London: Verso.

Agamben, G. (1999). Kommerell, or on gesture. In *Potentialities: Collected Essays in Philosophy*. Ed. D. Heller-Roazen. pp. 77–85. Stanford, CA: Stanford University Press.

Ahmed, S. J. (2002). Wishing for a world without 'theatre for development': demystifying the case of Bangladesh. *Research in Drama Education: The Journal of Applied Theatre and Performance*, 7(2), 207–219.

Ahmed, S. J., and Hughes, J. (2015). Still wishing for a world without 'theatre for development'? A dialogue on theatre, poverty and inequality. *Research in Drama Education: The Journal of Applied Theatre and Performance*, 20(3), 395–406.

Alston, A. (2016). *Beyond Immersive Theatre: Aesthetics, Politics and Productive Participation*. London: Palgrave Macmillan.

Althusser, L. (2014 [1995]). *On the Reproduction of Capitalism: Ideology and Ideological State Apparatuses*. London: Verso.

Anderson, M. B. (1999). *Do No Harm: How Aid can Support Peace – or War*. Boulder, CO: Lynne Rienner Publishers.

Araeen, R. (2003). Dak'art 1992–2002. *Third Text*, 17(1), 93–106.

Arnstein, S. (1969). A ladder of citizen participation. *AIP Journal of the American Planning Association*, 35(4), 216–224.

Bala, S., and Albacan, A. I. (2013). Workshopping the revolution? On the phenomenon of joker training in the Theatre of the Oppressed. *Research in Drama Education: The Journal of Applied Theatre and Performance*, 18(4), 388–402.

Balfour, M. (2004). *Prison Theatre: Theory and Practice*. London: Intellect.

Balme, C. (2001). Metaphors of spectacle. Theatricality, perception and performative encounters in the Pacific. In Erika Fischer-Lichte et al. (eds), *Wahrnehmung und Medialität*. pp. 215–231. Tübingen/Basel: Francke.

Barok, D. (2009). On participatory art: an interview with Claire Bishop. https://multiplace.sk/pipermail/mtp-teoria/2009-July/000165.html. Accessed 9 February 2018.

BAVO (ed.) (2007). *Cultural Activism Today: The Art of Over-Identification* Rotterdam: episode publishers.

Baxter, V. (2013). Senzeni na (What have we done?) Educational theatre in southern Africa. In A. Jackson and C. Vine (eds), *Learning Through Theatre: The Changing Face of Theatre in Education.* 3rd edn, pp. 209–228. New York: Routledge.

Bayoumi, M. (2005). Diary: in Beirut's tent city. *London Review of Books,* 27(9), 34–35.

Belfiore, E. (2015). 'Impact', 'value' and 'bad economics': making sense of the problem of value in the arts and humanities. *Arts and Humanities in Higher Education,* 14(1), 95–110.

Belfiore, E., and Bennett, O. (2008). *The Social Impact of the Arts: An Intellectual History.* Basingstoke: Palgrave Macmillan.

Benjamin, W. (1966). *Versuche über Brecht.* Ed. R. Tiedemann. Frankfurt am Main: Suhrkamp.

Benjamin, W. (1973a). *Understanding Brecht.* Ed. and trans. S. Mitchell and A. Bostock. London: Verso.

Benjamin, W. (1973b [1966]). What is epic theatre? In *Understanding Brecht* Ed. and trans. S. Mitchell and A. Bostock. pp. 1–13. London: Verso.

Bennett, S. (1990). *Theatre Audiences: A Theory of Production and Reception.* London: Routledge.

Bharucha, R. (2007). The limits of the beyond. *Third Text,* 21(4), 397–416.

Bishop, C. (2012). *Artificial Hells: Participatory Art and the Politics of Spectatorship.* London: Verso.

Boal, A. (2000 [1974]). *Theater of the Oppressed.* London: Pluto Press.

Boal, A. (2002). *Games for Actors and Non-Actors.* London: Routledge.

Boltanski, L., and Chiapello, E. (1999). *The New Spirit of Capitalism.* London: Verso.

Bourdieu, P. (1984). *Distinction: A Social Critique of the Judgement of Taste.* London: Routledge and Kegan Paul.

Bourriaud, N. (2002). *Relational Aesthetics.* Ed. S. Pleasance, F. Woods and M. Copeland. Paris: Les Presses du réel.

Brandl-Risi, B. (2011). Getting together and falling apart: applauding audiences. *Performance Research,* 16(3), 12–18.

Brecht, B. (1964 [1949]). A short organum for the theatre. In *Brecht on Theatre: The Development of an Aesthetic.* Ed. J. Willett. pp. 179–205. London: Methuen Drama.

Brecht, B. (1967). *Gesammelte Werke. Große kommentierte Berliner und Frankfurter Ausgabe.* 32 vols. Frankfurt am Main: Suhrkamp.

Brine, D. (ed.). (2008). *The Live Art Almanac – Vol. 1*. London: Live Art Development Agency.

Brown, W. (2015). *Undoing the Demos: Neoliberalism's Stealth Revolution*. New York: Zone Books.

Bruguera, T. (2011). Introduction on useful art. http://www.taniabruguera. com/cms/528–0-Introduction+on+Useful+Art.htm. Accessed 24 March 2016.

Budgen, S. (2000). Book review, *The New Spirit of Capitalism* by Luc Boltanski and Eve Chiapello (1999). *New Left Review*, 1(1), 149–156.

Buenaventura, E. (1970). Theatre and culture. *TDR/The Drama Review*, 14(2), 151–156.

Burns, E. (1972). *Theatricality: A Study of Convention in the Theatre and in Social Life*. London: Longman.

Burri, R. V., Evert, K., Peters, S., Pilkington, E., and Ziemer, G. (eds) (2014). *Versammlung und Teilhabe: Urbane Öffentlichkeiten und performative Künste*. Bielefeld: Transcript.

Burzynska, A. (ed.) (2016). *Joined Forces: Audience Participation in Theatre. (Performing Urgency #3, House on Fire)*. Berlin: Alexander Verlag.

Butler, J. (1988). Performative acts and gender constitution: an essay in phenomenology and feminist theory. *Theatre Journal*, 40(4), 519–531.

Butler, J. (2014a). Performing the political. Oslo: the first supper symposium. http://www.thefirstsuppersymposium.org/index.php/en/symposium-2014/video-2014. Accessed 9 February 2018.

Butler, J. (2014b). When gesture becomes event. Paper given at the 'Performance Philosophy' international conference, Le Laboratoire des Arts et Philosophies de la Scène (LAPS), Paris. https://youtu.be/iuAM RxSH--s. Accessed 9 February 2018.

Butler, J., and Athanasiou, A. (2013). *Dispossession: The Performative in the Political*. Cambridge: Polity Press.

Butt, G., and Rogoff, I. (2013). *Visual Cultures as Seriousness*. Berlin/London: Goldsmiths, University of London and Sternberg.

Cañénguez, L. A. R. (2015). Outside and onstage: experiences of the lesbian feminist theater collective Teatro Siluetas from Guatemala and El Salvador. In A. Tellis and S. Bala (eds), *The Global Trajectories of Queerness: Re-thinking Same-Sex Politics in the Global South*. pp. 241–262. Leiden: Brill/Rodopi.

Chandhoke, N. (2003). *The Conceits of Civil Society*. New Delhi: Oxford University Press.

Chatterjee, P. (ed.) (1998). *Wages of Freedom: Fifty Years of the Indian Nation-State*. New Delhi: Oxford University Press.

Chinyowa, K. C. (2015). Participation as 'repressive myth': a case study of the Interactive Themba Theatre Organisation in South Africa. *Research in Drama Education: The Journal of Applied Theatre and Performance*, 20(1), 12–23.

Cleaver, F. (1999). Paradoxes of participation: questioning participatory approaches to development. *Journal of International Development*, 11(4), 597–612.

Cohen-Cruz, J. (2010). *Engaging Performance: Theatre as Call and Response*. London: Routledge.

Cohen, J., and Uphoff, N. (2011). Participation's place in rural development: seeking clarity through specificity [1980]. In A. Cornwall (ed.), *The Participation Reader*. pp. 35–56. London: Zed Books.

Cole, C. (2009). *Performing South Africa's Truth Commission: Stages of Transition*. Bloomington, IN: Indiana University Press.

Conroy, C. (2015). Editorial: aesthetics and participation. *Research in Drama Education: The Journal of Applied Theatre and Performance*, 20(1), 1–11.

Cooke, B., and Kothari, U. (2001). *Participation: The New Tyranny?* London: Zed Books.

Cornwall, A., and Brock, K. (2005). What do buzzwords do for development policy? A critical look at 'participation', 'empowerment' and 'poverty reduction.' *Third World Quarterly*, 26(7), 1043–1060.

Cornwall, A., and Eade, D. (eds) (2010). *Deconstructing Development Discourse: Buzzwords and Fuzzwords*. Warwickshire: Practical Action Publishing and Oxfam.

Cortés, E., and Barrea-Marlys, M. (eds) (2003). *Encyclopedia of Latin American Theater*. Westport, CT: Greenwood Press.

Covington-Ward, Y. (2016). *Gesture and Power: Religion, Nationalism and Everyday Performance in Congo*. Durham, NC: Duke University Press.

Crary, J. (2013). *24/7: Late Capitalism and the Ends of Sleep*. London: Verso.

Cull, L., and Gritzner, C. (2011). Special issue 'On Participation.' *Performance Research*, 16(4).

Da Costa, D. (2010). *Development Dramas: Reimagining Rural Political Action in Eastern India*. London/New Delhi: Routledge.

Davis, T. (2003). Theatricality and civil society. In T. Davis and T. Postlewait (eds), *Theatricality*. pp. 127–155. Cambridge: Cambridge University Press.

de Certeau, M. (1984). *The Practice of Everyday Life*. Trans. S. Rendall. Berkeley, CA: University of California Press.

de Saussure, F. (1986 [1916]). *Course in General Linguistics*. Trans. R. Harris. 3rd edn. Chicago: Open Court Publishing.

Debord, G. (1967). *The Society of the Spectacle (La so société du spectacle)*. Trans. K. Knabb. Bureau of Public Secrets. http://www.bopsecrets.org/SI/debord/index.htm. Accessed 9 February 2018.

Demos, T. J. (2013). *The Migrant Image: The Art and Politics of Documentary During Global Crisis*. Durham, NC: Duke University Press.

Derrida, J., and Ronell, A. (1980). The law of genre. *Critical Inquiry*, 7(1), 55–81.

Dinesh, N. (2015). Delusions of singularity: aesthetics, discomfort and bewilderment in Kashmir. *Research in Drama Education: The Journal of Applied Theatre and Performance*, 20(1), 62–73.

Dreysse, M., and Malzacher, F. (2008). *Experts of the Everyday: The Theatre of Rimini Protokoll*. Berlin: Alexander-Verlag.

Esslin, M. (1986). Brecht and the scientific spirit of playfulness. In G. Guinness and A. Hurley (eds), *Auctor Ludens: Essays on Play in Literature*. pp. 25–36. Philadelphia, PA: John Benjamins.

Fals-Borda, O., and Rahman, M. A. (eds) (1991). *Action and Knowledge: Breaking the Monopoly with Participatory Action Research*. New York: Apex Press.

Fernandez, D. G. (1996). *Palabas: Essays on Philippine Theater History*. Manila: Ateneo de Manila University Press.

Finkelpearl, T. (2013). *What We Made: Conversations on Art and Social Cooperation*. Durham, NC: Duke University Press.

Fleishman, M. (2016). Applied theatre and participation in the 'new' South Africa: a possible politics. In J. Hughes and H. Nicholson (eds), *Critical Perspectives on Applied Theatre*. Cambridge: Cambridge University Press.

Fletcher-Watson, B. (2015). Seen and not heard: participation as tyranny in Theatre for Early Years. *Research in Drama Education: The Journal of Applied Theatre and Performance*, 20(1), 24–38.

Flusser, V. (2014 [1991]). *Gestures*. Trans. N. A. Roth. Minneapolis, MN: University of Minnesota Press.

Fotiadi, E. (2009). *Participation and Collaboration in Contemporary Art: A Game without Borders between Art and 'Real' Life*. Amsterdam: University of Amsterdam DARE.

Fotiadi, E. (2017). Von autonomer zu allgemein anwendbarer Kunst. In M. Warstat, F. Evers, K. Flade, F. Lempa and L. Seuberling (eds), *Applied Theatre: Rahmen und Positionen*. pp. 251–273. Berlin: Theater der Zeit.

Freire, P. (1968). *Pedagogy of the Oppressed*. New York: Herder and Herder.

García Canclini, N. (2005). *Hybrid Cultures: Strategies for Entering and Leaving Modernity*. Minneapolis, MN: University of Minnesota Press.

Giannachi, G., and Kaye, N. (2011). *Performing Presence: Between the Live and the Simulated*. Manchester: Manchester University Press.

Gielen, P. (2011). Mapping community art. In P. De Bruyne and P. Gielen (eds), *Community Art: The Politics of Trespassing*. pp. 15–33. Amsterdam: Valiz.

Gramsci, A. (1996). *Selections from the Prison Notebooks*. Ed. Q. Hoare and G. N. Smith. New Delhi: Orient Longman.

Gregg, M., and Seigworth, G. J. (eds) (2010). *The Affect Theory Reader*. Durham, NC: Duke University Press.

Gronau, B., and Lagaay, A. (2008). *Performanzen des Nichttuns*. Ed. B. Gronau and A. Lagaay. Vienna: Passagen Verlag.

Groot-Nibbelink, L. (2015). *Nomadic Theatre: Staging Movement and Mobility in Contemporary Performance*. Utrecht: Utrecht University Open Access Repository. https://dspace.library.uu.nl/handle/1874/310682. Accessed 9 February 2018.

Groys, B. (2008). A genealogy of participatory art. In R. Frieling (ed.), *The Art of Participation: 1950 to Now*. pp. 18–31. San Francisco: SFMOMA.

Guetzkow, J. (2002). *How the Arts Impact Communities: An Introduction to the Literature on Arts Impact Studies* (Working Paper 20). Princeton, NJ. https://www.princeton.edu/~artspol/workpap/WP20%20-%20Guetzkow. pdf. Accessed 9 February 2018.

Guhathakurtha, M. (2008). Theatre in participatory action research: experiences from Bangladesh. In P. Reason and H. Bradbury (eds), *The SAGE Handbook of Action Research: Participatory Inquiry and Practice*. 2nd edn. pp. 510–522. London: Sage Publications.

Haraway, D. (2004). The promises of monsters: a regenerative politics for inappropriate/d others. In *The Haraway Reader*. pp. 63–124. London: Routledge.

Harpin, A., and Nicholson, H. (eds) (2017). *Performance and Participation: Practices, Audiences, Politics*. London: Palgrave Macmillan.

Harvie, J. (2013). *Fair Play: Art, Performance and Neoliberalism*. Basingstoke. Palgrave Macmillan.

Heemstra, M. van. (2009). Sudanese theatre on violence and responsibility: an interview with theatre director Walid Al-Alphy. *Kracht van Cultuur*. http://www.krachtvancultuur.nl/en/current/2009/october/people-cave. html. Accessed 9 February 2018.

Heinicke, J., Kalu, J. K. Möbius, J., Siouzouli, N., and Warstat, M. (eds) (2015). *Theater als Intervention: Politiken ästhetischer Praxis*. Berlin: Theater der Zeit.

Helguera, P. (2011). *Education for Socially Engaged Art: A Materials and Techniques Handbook*. New York: Jorge Pinto Books.

Hickey, S., and Mohan, G. (eds) (2004). *Participation: From Tyranny to Transformation. Exploring New Approaches to Participation in Development*. London: Zed Books.

Holmes, B. (2009). *Escape the Overcode: Activist Art in the Control Society*. Eindhoven: Van Abbemuseum and What, How and for Whom.

Holstein, J., and Gubrium, J. (2011). The constructionist analytics of interpretive practice. In N. K. Denzin and Y. S. Lincoln (eds), *The SAGE Handbook of Qualitative Research* 4th edn. pp. 341–358. London: Sage Publications.

Hoving, I., and Essed, P. (eds) (2014). *Dutch Racism*. Leiden: Brill/Rodopi.

Hughes, J., and Parry, S. (2015). Introduction: gesture, theatricality, and protest – composure at the precipice. *Contemporary Theatre Review*, 25(3), 300–312.

Huybrechts, L. (ed.) (2011). *Participation is Risky: Approaches to Joint Creative Processes*. Amsterdam: Valiz.

Isar, Y. R., and Anheier, H. (eds) (2007). *The Cultures and Globalizations Series. Vol. 1: Conflicts and Tensions*. London: Sage Publications.

Issa, L. (2009). Where we are now: documentation. https://vimeo.com/18746079. Accessed 9 February 2018.

Issa, L. (2010). What if, if I could take your place? Unpublished document.

Issa, L., and Cordero, A. (2008). Where we are not. Radio M2M programme, 24 April 2008. Amsterdam: Radio M2M.

Jacir, E. (2003). Where we come from. *Grand Street*, 72 (Autumn), 95–105.

Jackson, A. (2007). *Theatre, Education and the Making of Meanings: Art or Instrument?* Manchester: Manchester University Press.

Jackson, S. (2008). What is the 'social' in social practice? Comparing experiments in performance. In T. Davis (ed.), *Cambridge Companion to Performance Studies*. pp. 136–150. Cambridge: Cambridge University Press.

Jackson, S. (2011). *Social Works. Performing Art, Supporting Publics*. London: Routledge.

Jameson, F. (1998). *Brecht and Method*. London: Verso.

Kaptani, E., and Yuval-Davis, N. (2008). Participatory theatre as a research methodology: identity, performance and social action among refugees. *Sociological Research Online*, 13(5). http://www.socresonline.org.uk/13/5/2.html. Accessed 9 February 2018.

Katsiaficas, G. (2004). Aesthetic and political avant-gardes. *The Journal of Aesthetics and Protest*, 3. http://www.joaap.org/new3/Katsiaficas.html. Accessed 9 February 2018.

Keidan, L., Mitchell, C., and Mitchelson, A. (eds) (2010). *The Live Art Almanac – Vol. 2*. London: Live Art Development Agency.

Keidan, L., and Wright, A. (eds) (2013). *The Live Art Almanac – Vol. 3*. London: Live Art Development Agency and Oberon Books.

Kerr, D. (1991). Participatory popular theatre: the highest stage of cultural underdevelopment? *Research in African Literatures*, 22(2), 55–76.

Kester, G. (2011). *The One and the Many: Contemporary Collaborative Art in a Global Context*. Durham, NC: Duke University Press.

Kolesch, D. (2010). Die Geste der Berührung. In C. Wulf and E. Fischer-Lichte (eds), *Gesten: Inszenierung, Aufführung, Praxis*. pp. 225–241. Munich: Wilhelm Fink Verlag.

Kolowratnik, N. V., and Miessen, M. (eds) (2013). *Waking up from the Nightmare of Participation*. Utrecht: Expodium.

Kraynak, J. (2007). Dependent participation: Bruce Nauman's environments. In Tanya Leighton (ed.), *Art and the Moving Image: A Critical Reader*. pp. 228–245. London: Afterall.

Kunst, B. (2015). *Artist at Work: Proximity of Art and Capitalism*. Winchester: Zero Books.

Lagaay, A., and Lorber, M. (eds) (2012). *Destruction in the Performative*. Amsterdam: Rodopi.

Leal, P. A. (2011). Participation: the ascendancy of a buzzword in the neoliberal era. In A. Cornwall (ed.), *The Participation Reader*. pp 70–82. London: Zed Books.

Lehmann, H.-T. (2005). *Postdramatic Theatre*. Trans. K. Jürs-Munby. London: Routledge.

Lorey, I. (2012). *Die Regierung der Prekären*. Vienna: Turia and Kant.

Lorey, I. (2015). *State of Insecurity: Government of the Precarious [Die Regierung der Prekären]*. Trans. Aileen Derieg. London: Verso.

Machon, J. (2013). *Immersive Theatres: Intimacy and Immediacy in Contemporary Performance*. Basingstoke: Palgrave Macmillan.

Magelsen, S. (2014). *Simming: Participatory Performance and the Making of Meaning*. Ann Arbor, MI: University of Michigan Press.

Martel, J. (2017). *The Misinterpellated Subject*. Durham, NC: Duke University Press.

Matzke, A., Weiler, C., and Wortelkamp, I. (eds) (2012). *Das Buch von der angewandten Theaterwissenschaft*. Berlin: Alexander Verlag.

Mauss, M. (1973 [1935]). Techniques of the body. *Economy and Society*, 2(1), 70–88.

McNeill, D. (2005). *Gesture and Thought*. Chicago: University of Chicago Press.

Meireles, C. (2007). Insertions into ideological circuits, 1970–1975. In W. Bradley and C. Esche (eds), *Art and Social Change: A Critical Reader*. pp. 181–187. London: Tate Publishing and Afterall.

Miessen, M. (2011). *The Nightmare of Participation (Crossbench Praxis as a Mode of Criticality)*. Berlin: Sternberg.

Mouffe, C. (2013). *Agonistics: Thinking the World Politically*. London: Verso.

Myers, M. (2011). Now everybody sing: The voicing of dissensus in new choral performance. *Performance Research*, 16(3), 62–66.

Nancy, J.-L. (2009). *The Fall of Sleep [Tombe de sommeil]*. Trans. C. Mandell. New York: Fordham University Press.

Nicholson, H (2011). *Theatre, Education and Performance*. Basingstoke: Palgrave Macmillan.

Nicholson, H. (2013). On visiting forgotten tombs. In T. Noorani, C. Bencowe and J. Brigstocke (eds), *Problems of Participation: Reflections on Authority, Democracy, and the Struggle for Common Life*. pp. 83–90. Lewes: Authority Research Network Press.

Noland, C. (2009). *Agency and Embodiment: Performing Gestures/Producing Culture*. Cambridge, MA: Harvard University Press.

Noonan, E. (2012). *The Strange Career of Porgy and Bess: Race, Culture, and America's Most Famous Opera*. Chapel Hill, NC: University of North Carolina Press.

Notes from Nowhere (2003). *We Are Everywhere: The Irresistible Rise of Global Anticapitalism*. London: Verso.

Osnes, B. (2014). *Theatre for Women's Participation in Sustainable Development*. Oxford: Routledge.

Özengi, Ö. (2010). Disneyland as a degenerate utopia. http://www.pilvitakala. com/texts/Disneyland_as_a_Degenerate Utopia.pdf. Accessed 29 March 2016.

Pearce, J. (ed.) (2010). *Participation and Democracy in the Twenty-First Century City*. Basingstoke: Palgrave Macmillan.

Peterson, W. (2012). Discipline and pleasure: dancing inmates in Cebu's provisional detention and rehabilitation centre. *About Performance*, 11, 41–62.

Plastow, J. (2014). Domestication or transformation? The ideology of Theatre for Development in Africa. *Applied Theatre Research*, 2(2), 107–118.

Poulin, J. (ed.). (2000). *Strengths-Based Generalist Practice: A Collaborative Approach*. Belmont: Cengage Learning.

Rancière, J. (2002). The aesthetic revolution and its outcomes: emplotments of autonomy and heteronomy. *New Left Review*, 14, 133–151.

Rancière, J. (2009). *The Emancipated Spectator*. London: Verso.

Rancière, J. (2010). *Dissensus: On Politics and Aesthetics*. London: Continuum.

Raunig, G. (2007). *Art and Revolution: Transversal Activism in the Long Twentieth Century*. Los Angeles: MIT Press.

Raunig, G., Ray, G., and Wuggenig, U. (eds) (2011). *Critique of Creativity: Precarity, Subjectivity and Resistance in the 'Creative Industries'*. London: MayFlyBooks. http://mayflybooks.org

Ray, G., and Raunig, G. (eds) (2009). *Art and Contemporary Critical Practice: Reinventing Institutional Critique*. London: MayFlyBooks.

Rebentisch, J. (2012). *Aesthetics of Installation Art*. Trans. Daniel Hendrickson with Gerrit Jackson. Berlin: Sternberg.

Rebentisch, J. (2013). *Theorien der Gegenwartskunst zur Einführung*. Hamburg: Junius.

Rebentisch, J. (2015). Forms of participation in art. *Qui Parle: Critical Humanities and Social Sciences*, 23(2), 29–54.

Reeves, M. (2002). *Measuring the Social and Economic Impact of the Arts*. London: Arts Council of England.

Reich, R., and Gather, O. (2005). *Nomad City Passage*, Düsseldorf: documentation. www.nomadcitypassage.de. Accessed 9 February 2018.

Reich, R., and Gather, O. (2009). *Nomad City Passage*, Linz. Unpublished document.

Reich, R., and Richter, M. V. (2011). Obere Etagen [Top Floors]: video documentation. https://youtu.be/yxFWbEtZOyM. Accessed 9 February 2018.

Reiss, B. (2014). Sleep's hidden histories. *Los Angeles Review of Books*, 15 February.

Roces, M., and Edwards, L. (2010). *Women's Movements in Asia: Feminisms and Transnational Activism*. London: Routledge.

Rodriguez, J., Piercy. M., and Felipe, L. (1996). Mujer inconveniente. Trans. Roselyn Constantino. *Debate Feminista*, 7(13), 448–451.

Rogoff, I. (2005). Looking away: participations in visual culture. In G. Butt (ed.), *After Criticism. New Responses to Art and Performance*. pp. 117–134 London: Wiley Blackwell.

Rogoff, I. (2008). Turning. *E-Flux Journal*, November (0), 1–10.

Rose, J. (2003). On not being able to sleep: rereading *The Interpretation of Dreams*. In *On Not Being Able to Sleep: Psychoanalysis and the Modern World*. pp. 105–124. London: Chatto and Windus.

Röttger, K. (1992). *Kollektives Theater als Spiegel lateinamerikanischer Identität: La Candelaria und das neue kolumbianische Theater. Kollektives Theater als Spiegel lateinamerikanischer Identität*. Frankfurt am Main: Vervuert.

Said, E. (2003). Emily Jacir. *Grand Street*, 72 (Autumn), 106.

Sangari, K. (2002). *Politics of the Possible: Essays on Gender, History, Narratives, Colonial English*. London: Anthem Press.

Schechner, R. (1973). *Environmental Theatre*. New York: Applause.

Schechner, R. (2002). *Performance Studies: An Introduction*. 2nd edn New York: Routledge.

Scott, D. (2004). *Conscripts of Modernity: The Tragedy of Colonial Enlightenment*. Durham, NC: Duke University Press.

Sennett, R. (1993). *The Fall of Public Man*. London: Faber and Faber.

Simon, N. (2010). *The Participatory Museum*. Santa Cruz, CA: Museum 2.0.

Singer, Mi. (1959). *Traditional India: Structure and Change*. Philadelphia. PA: American Folklore Society.

Spivak, G. C. (2012). *An Aesthetic Education in the Era of Globalization*. Cambridge, MA: Harvard University Press.

Steierischer_Herbst (ed.) (2014). *Truth is Concrete. A Handbook for Artistic Strategies in Real Politics*. Berlin: Sternberg.

Steyerl, H. (2011). Art as occupation: claims for an autonomy of life In C. Widenheim, L. Rosendahl, Mi. Masucci, A. Enqvist and J. H. Engqvist (eds), *Work, Work, Work: A Reader on Art and Labour*. pp. 47–56. Berlin/Stockholm: Sternberg and Iaspis.

Susi, T. (2014). Embodied interaction, coordination and reasoning in computer gameplay. In L. Shapiro (ed.), *The Routledge Handbook of Embodied Cognition*. pp. 184–194. Abingdon: Routledge.

Taylor, D. (2003). *The Archive and the Repertoire: Performing Cultural Memory in the Americas*. Durham, NC: Duke University Press.

Taylor, D., and Townsend, S. (eds) (2008). *Stages of Conflict: A Critical Anthology of Latin American Theater and Performance*. Ann Arbor, MI: University of Michigan Press.

Thiong'o, N. wa (1998). *Penpoints, Gunpoints, and Dreams: Towards a Critical Theory of the Arts and the State in Africa*. Oxford: Clarendon Press.

Thompson, A. (ed.) (2007). *The Media and the Rwanda Genocide*. London: Pluto Press.

Thompson, J. (ed.). (1998). *Prison Theatre: Perspectives and Practices*. London: Jessica Kingsley Publishers.

Thompson, J. (2000). It don't mean a thing if it ain't got that swing: some questions on participatory theatre, evaluation and impact. *Research in Drama Education: The Journal of Applied Theatre and Performance*, 5(1), 101–104.

Thompson, J. (2008). *Applied Theatre: Bewilderment and Beyond*. Oxford: Lang.

Thompson, J. (2009). *Performance Affects: Applied Theatre and the End of Affect*. Basingstoke: Palgrave Macmillan.

Thompson, J. (2014). *Humanitarian Performance: From Disaster Tragedies to Spectacles of War*. Calcutta/London: Seagull Books.

Thompson, J., Hughes, J., and Balfour, M. (2009). *Performance in Place of War*. Calcutta/London: Seagull Books.

Thompson, N. (2012). *Living As Form: Socially Engaged Art from 1991–2011*. New York: MIT Press.

Turino, T. (2008). *Music as Social Life: The Politics of Participation*. Chicago: University of Chicago Press.

Turner, V. (1969). *The Ritual Process: Structure and Anti-Structure*. Chicago: Aldine Publishing.

Turner, V. (1975). *Dramas, Fields, and Metaphors: Symbolic Action in Human Society*. Ithaca, NY: Cornell University Press.

Underiner, T. (2004). *Contemporary Theatre in Mayan Mexico: Death-Defying Acts*. Austin, TX: University of Texas Press.

van Erven, E. (2001). *Community Theatre: Global Perspectives*. London: Routledge.

Weber, S. (2008). *Benjamin's Abilities*. Cambridge, MA: Harvard University Press.

Weibel, P. (ed.). (2015). *Global Activism: Art and Conflict in the 21st century*. Cambridge, MA: MIT Press.

Weiss, J. (1980). New theater in Colombia: interview with Patricia Ariza and Beatriz Camargo. *Theater*, 12(1), 22–25.

Weizman, E. (2011). Prologue: the paradox of collaboration. In M. Miessen (ed.), *The Nightmare of Participation (Crossbench Praxis as a Mode of Criticality)*. pp. 9–12. Berlin: Sternberg.

White, G. (2012). On immersive theatre. *Theatre Research International*, 37(3), 221–235.

White, G. (2013). *Audience Participation in the Theatre: Aesthetics of the Invitation*. Basingstoke: Palgrave Macmillan.

White, G. (ed.) (2015). *Applied Theatre: Aesthetics*. London: Bloomsbury Methuen Drama.

Widenheim, C., Rosendahl, L., Masucci, Mi., Enqvist, A., and Engqvist,

J. H. (eds) (2011). *Work, Work, Work: A Reader on Art and Labour*. Berlin/ Stockholm: Sternberg and iaspis.

Willett, J. (ed.) (1974). *Brecht on Theatre: The Development of an Aesthetic*. 3th edn. London: Methuen Drama.

Williams, R. (1983). *Keywords: A Vocabulary of Culture and Society*. 2nd edn. Oxford: Oxford University Press.

Wulf, C., and Fischer-Lichte, E. (eds) (2010). *Gesten: Inszenierung, Aufführung, Praxis*. Munich: Wilhelm Fink Verlag.

Ziemilski, W. (2016). Participation and some discontent. In A. Burzynska (ed.), *Joined Forces: Audience Participation in Theatre. (Performing Urgency #3, House on Fire)*. pp. 168–179. Berlin: Alexander Verlag.

Index

EU authorised representative for GPSR:
Easy Access System Europe, Mustamäe tee 50,
10621 Tallinn, Estonia
gpsr.requests@easproject.com

www.ingramcontent.com/pod-product-compliance
Ingram Content Group UK Ltd.
Pitfield, Milton Keynes, MK11 3LW, UK
UKHW020038170726
72141PUK00036B/285

The Way of Prophetic Leadership

The Way of Prophetic Leadership

Retrieving Word and Spirit in Vision Today

Jennifer Campbell

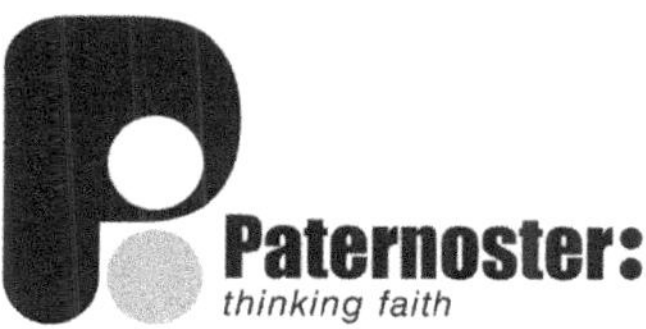

First published 2015 by Paternoster
Paternoster is an imprint of Authentic Media Limited
52 Presley Way, Crownhill, Milton Keynes, MK8 0ES.
authenticmedia.co.uk

British Library Cataloguing in Publication Data
A catalogue record for this book is available from the British Library
ISBN 978-1-84227-835-2
978-1-84227-084-9 (e-book)

Author's Note: The use of 'Word' in the text denotes the person of
Jesus Christ and 'word' refers to the Scriptures or the Bible. In all cases
in the Quaker material the word 'Light' is capitalized when it refers to
the person of Jesus Christ. Spelling, punctuation and grammar have
been retained in all citations, titles and details of publication in all works
consulted. Reference numbers for broadsides, pamphlets and microfilm
refer to the collections the Bodleian Libraries, the University of Oxford.

Cover Design by David McNeill (www.revocreative.co.uk)

Dedicated to all members of the worldwide St Thomas'
Order of Mission

Contents

 Contents

Abbreviations

BA	*An Apology for the True Christian Divinity*, Robert Barclay, 1869
CB	*Support of the Faithful*, Claude Brousson, 1699
CC	Calvin's Commentaries, 1965
CI	*Institutes of the Christian Religion*, John Calvin, 1961
CDa	*A Cry from the Desart in Prophetical Extracts*, 1707
CDb	*A Cry from the Desart* (2nd edn), 1707
CDc	*A Cry from the Desart*, 1707
GTD	*Gospel-Truth Demonstrated*, George Fox,1706
IP Works,	Isaac Penington, 1784
J1694 Journal,	George Fox, 1694
J1902 Journal,	George Fox, 1902
J1911 Journal,	George Fox, 1911
J1925 Short Journals,	George Fox, 1925
J1997 Journal,	George Fox, 1997
JPL Pastoral Letters,	Pierre Jurieu, 1689
JR Reflections,	Pierre Jurieu, 1689
WGF Works,	George Fox, 1831
WW Works,	John Wesley, 1985–89

Preface

Thus says the Lord: Stand at the crossroads, and look, and ask for
the ancient paths, where the good way lies; and walk in it and
find rest for your souls (Jer. 6:16).

Out of the whirlwind which is life in the hurly-burly of the
twenty-first century, comes the sanest word from the Christian
Scriptures: find rest for your souls. And how might we do this
as church leaders in the West managing decline, or stretched to
a limit managing busyness? We are instructed to pause at the
crossroads of our lives, or the lives of our churches, fellowships or
organizations, and take a breather: stop the frenzied casting about
for vision from this or that source and petition God to show us the
good ways. And when our spiritual eyes are opened we shall see
the road ahead. The trick then is to walk on it.

Visionary leadership or (Dare we mention it in these days of
aversion to anything too supernatural?), prophetic leadership is
a handmaid which is coupled closely to our quest for the ancient
paths. Lest we fear rash outcomes of such a heady spirituality,
we must ground Christian leadership in a union of Jesus Christ
the Word and the Holy Spirit the truth-giver. These concepts
are integral facets of a prophetic prism: the marriage of the two
hands of God, the synergy of Word and Spirit in prophecy for
the full release of dynamic, forward-thinking kingdom ministry.
However, we dare not fall back or stagger on the threshold of
the future. We must be bold and step into the new. If perchance
the Western church were to recover an ancient path set out in the
New Testament, viz. the structure of the fivefold ministry as an
open door to all, would the saints of God finally reach maturity

and be the witness we are meant to be? Moreover, if this pattern were to be infiltrated at every level by the gift of prophecy, might the vision of God be sharpened, clarified and shine brightly? This book seeks a futuristic vision by means of a backward glance into the past, a past littered with glittering examples of inspiring prophetic leadership in two unrelated moves of the Holy Spirit in seventeenth-century France and England.

I am indebted to church leaders who have pointed up the workable nature of the fivefold ministry: Mike Breen, erstwhile Superior of the St Thomas' Order of Mission (TOM), Peter and Anne Findley, leaders of Network Church, Sheffield, and countless nameless, faceless leaders in TOM, strenuously and courageously bringing the kingdom of God to earth across the globe. My thanks are due to those who aided and abetted the project in 2013: Professor Kathleen Coleman, who hosted me at Harvard University and edited the draft material; Dr Mike Parsons of Paternoster, who assisted in the final edits; Keith and Anne Crawford, Jamie and Liz Smith, for their hospitality during periods of research and writing; many friends in England, Europe, South Africa and America, whose friendship lent spiritual and prayerful impetus to my resolve. Finally, I owe my thanks to the north Wiltshire community among whom I live and with whom I share my life, for their sense of humour and staying power throughout my endeavours. Despite all practical and spiritual assistance, however, any matters of infelicitous style, inconsistencies or errors are mine alone.

Jennifer Campbell
Shaw Green, Ashton under Hill
8 April 2014

Foreword

Near the southern tip of Jennifer Campbell's native country of South Africa lies a little town called Franschhoek. The name, from the Dutch for 'French corner', enshrines the memory of its first settlers, 176 Huguenot refugees who arrived at the Cape of Good Hope in 1688, moving halfway across the world to escape religious persecution in France. The wine-farms that they established beneath the mountains along the Berg River, bearing names like 'Provence' or 'Dieu Donné', still testify to the nostalgia of those first owners for their homeland, coupled with their belief in the grace of God.

The Cape of Good Hope is only one of many parts of the world where the Huguenots sought refuge. Their French names are enshrined in prominent institutions and toponyms as far apart as La Trobe University in Australia (named for Charles La Trobe, Huguenot descendant and Lieutenant-Governor of Victoria) and Revere outside Boston, the site of the first public beach in the United States (called after Paul Revere, prominent in the American Revolution, whose father, Apollos Rivoire, passed on both elements of the anglicized version of his name to his son). Part of Jennifer Campbell's concern in this book is to chart the formation of the first Huguenot communities in France who rejected Catholicism and with the leaders who inspired them to follow a new path—a new path spiritually, leading them to new paths in the literal sense that would take them to some of the furthest corners of the known world.

At virtually the same time as the Huguenots were rejecting traditional Catholic teaching and practices in France, across the Channel in England, which had been officially Protestant since the Reformation a hundred years earlier, the Quaker movement emerged at the end of the English Civil War. Often regarded as a radical form of Puritanism, Quaker teaching is rooted in an unmediated personal experience of God, which is frequently manifested in the 'quaking' from which its adherents derived their popular name. The Quakers, too, briefly suffered persecution after the restoration of the monarchy under Charles II, and, like the Huguenots, some of them sought a new life and religious freedom abroad, especially in North America, where they played a significant role in shaping colonial history. The best-known of the early American Quakers is William Penn (1644–1718), who founded Pennsylvania. The formation of the Quaker movement constitutes the other main area of investigation in this book.

Huguenots and Quakers rejected the established Church—Catholicism in the case of the Huguenots, for the Quakers the Church of England. Hence they also turned away from the formal liturgy and ecclesiastical hierarchy that characterized it. But to bracket them together on that basis would be to elide distinct differences between them. The two movements evolved independently of one another and espoused different principles: the Huguenots were willing to bear arms in defence of their religious beliefs, while the Quakers espoused pacifism; the Huguenots tolerated slavery, whereas the Quakers were abolitionists; the Huguenots cultivated prophetic ecstasy, while the Quakers practised discernment through silence; Huguenot teaching was rooted in the Bible, whereas for the Quakers the Bible was subject to interpretation by the Spirit working independently within each member of the community.

To different degrees, the early Huguenots and Quakers were both guided by a union of Word and Spirit. In this book, Jennifer Campbell examines the two movements as crucibles of prophecy. She seeks first to uncover the mystical teachings and visionary leadership of their founders: for the Huguenots, ultimately John Calvin (1509–1564) but more immediately Pierre Jurieu (1637–1713), a French intellectual who spent part of his life in exile in Rotterdam; for the Quakers, first and foremost George Fox (1624–1691), who dedicated his life to preaching and the founding of the Quaker movement. She then traces prophetic utterance—including that of women and children—in the early communities formed by each of these movements. Juxtaposing Huguenots and Quakers in four separate chapters, she relates the role of the prophet to each of four other categories of ministry: apostle, teacher, pastor, and evangelist.

Huguenots and Quakers, driven from Europe for upholding their dissident religious principles, played a seminal role in the colonial enterprise of the seventeenth century, and in so doing they changed the world. Reaching back to the moment from which both movements took their inspiration, Jennifer Campbell offers a model for prophecy that poses a challenge to the conventional roles of clergy and laity in the Church of the twenty-first century. She does not sanctify those early Huguenots and Quakers or attempt to hide their errors, quarrels, and misjudgements. Rather, through extensive archival research, she is able to let their leaders, beset by crisis and armed with conviction, speak in their own words from their age to ours.

Kathleen M. Coleman
James Loeb Professor of the Classics
Harvard University
Easter Day, 2014

Introduction

These people who have been turning the world upside down have
come here also (Acts 17:6).

This book is inspired by the ever-present question in the Western
church: why is the manifest evidence of revival throughout Chris-
tendom marked by powerful signs and wonders, yet in Europe
– the cradle of Christianity – the gospel is proclaimed largely by
word, without 'a demonstration of the Spirit and of power' (1 Cor.
2:4)?

Equally teasing is the notion that the Western church is not
turning the world upside down, but that the world is being sent
to Europe to rekindle the seeds of revival. The European church,
in desperate need of its mission revived, is in dire straits without
visionary prophetic leadership, in order to understand the times
and to know what to do in them, by possessing the mind of Christ
(cf. 1 Chr. 12:32; 1 Cor. 2:16). If we are instructed to strive for the
spiritual gifts, and especially that we may prophesy (1 Cor. 14:1),
then surely the gift of prophecy must have particular moment for
vision and leadership? Is prophecy not the distinguishing element
between godly and worldly patterns of leadership? For if the Lord
God does nothing without revealing his secret to his servants the
prophets (see Amos 3:7), then it is essential that the prophets
make known the mind of God, in order that prophetic leadership
guides the church: 'Where there is no prophecy, the people cast off
restraint' (Prov. 29:18). And yet, today, prophecy is often seen as a
Cinderella gift, the very last to be considered, or omitted entirely
in the piles of Christian leadership manuals, invariably pickled in
a practical amalgam of who, what and how on the one hand, and

on the other so innovative and wide off the mark as to stray from biblical roots. Invariably there is a turn to secular literature, over-abundant with inherent genius in leadership models, but giving rise to interesting notions, which, like so many wandering barks, may take the church off course, heedlessly and recklessly. And those still in wide-eyed wonder at the joy of following Jesus are bored to tears with safe (but dull) instruction on leading others.

This book has its embryonic beginnings in a conscience trou-bled by the current lack of robust theological research in the field of prophetic leadership, and by the paucity of serious spiritual reflection on the topic within the contemporary church. Chris-tian prophecy often stops at the instant of receiving vision from God, and falls short in its attempt to understand, with *prophetic* insight, the ways and means or the strategies for the implementa-tion of such a vision. Presumably this problem stems from the fact that prophets are not necessarily leaders, or that leaders are not prophets. The church cries out for prophetic *leadership* more than gifts of prophecy, i.e. leaders who are prophets and prophets who are leaders, so that vision might be received and acted upon. Natu-rally such a journey is a risk. To open the door to the supernatural interventions of a boundary-breaking God is never predictable or certain and always an adventure.

Prophetic Leadership in a Vision of Word and Spirit

The general scope of this work is an engagement with God as a spiritual being, with Jesus Christ as fully human and totally divine, and with the Holy Spirit and all the *charismata* (gifts or graces). By embracing the totality of the biblical witness, including all the supernatural oddities and absurdities, there is more likelihood of an holistic appreciation of the full measure of the role of prophetic leadership today.

In all probability, this venture is likely to be a rocky ride and it is essential that prophetic leadership hold to a steady course. For this reason a recovery of the full meaning of a marriage of Word and Spirit is entirely necessary, in order to attain to an equilibrium in any agenda of prophetic leadership. By this is meant that if 'the testimony of Jesus is the spirit of prophecy' (Rev. 19:10), then all prophetic leadership should begin and end with the person of Jesus Christ, the Word of God, to whose life and witness Spirit-inspired prophecy testifies. At the same time, and running on a parallel track, is the work of the prophetic Holy Spirit, under whose impulse and influence the prophet speaks or writes: 'no prophecy ever came by human will, but men and women moved by the Holy Spirit spoke from God' (2 Pet. 1:21). The trick in visionary leadership, therefore, is to join and hold together the full measure and action of both Word and Spirit, so that the mission of the church is both generated and sustained by robust prophecy. It is incumbent upon leadership to uphold a union of Word and Spirit to avoid disastrous consequences spilling over from flakiness, as an investigation of the supernatural dimension leads, somewhat inevitably, to the difficult issue of mysticism and its relationship to prophecy. To hold true to a wise path, by means of an intelligent grasp of the complex nature of spiritual reality, is the task of prophetic leadership.[1]

James A. Wiseman, a Benedictine monk and professor in the School of Theology and Religious Studies at the Catholic University of America, pinpoints the essence of mysticism. It has less to do with absorption, so that the individual personality is lost, and more to do with a consciousness of the presence of God. From the Greek word *myein*, meaning 'to close', for example, to close the eyes or lips, connoting something hidden or secret, is derived the words *mysterion* ('mystery') and *mystikos* ('mystical'). In the Old Testament, a council of those who are party to God's secrets are 'Sons of God' or heavenly councillors, those to whom the thoughts of God are made known (Dan. 2:28, cf. Mark 4:11; 1 Cor. 2:7; 4:1). Elias Marion, one of the French Huguenot prophets, hears God say: 'Within a few days I will discover my mysteries unto thee.' The affective side of mystical writing has held it to be a special state of consciousness, which, surpassing ordinary experience through union with the transcendent, can be party to unusual or exotic states of vision and ecstasy.[2]

The cogent study of popular religion and transatlantic spiritual enthusiasm by Clarke Garrett, an American professor, traces the commonalities within German pietism, the early Methodists, the Great Awakening, the French Huguenot prophets and the Shakers. The term 'enthusiasm', originating in ancient Greece, is the notion of someone possessed by a god. Garrett argues that it does not represent an irrational departure from orthodoxy, but that most cultures believe in the supernatural spirit possession of earthlings. Widespread Pentecostalism, with its demonstration of glossolalia (tongue speaking) and Spirit baptism, is evidence of the very human desire for the indwelling immediacy of divinity experienced through the senses. Spirit manifestations must be tested, and for this reason the partnership of Word and Spirit: do such manifestations testify to Jesus Christ?[3]

Prophetic Leadership in the Huguenots and Quakers

In order to test the union of Word and Spirit in prophetic visionary leadership, we investigate two independent spiritual movements on either side of the English Channel during the seventeenth century. We are fired by the courage, daring audacity, sheer forthrightness and utter devotion to God of two groups of people blindsided in the extremities of persecutions and wars: the Protestant French Huguenots and the Nonconformist English Quakers. This work is governed by multivalent disciplines: on one level it is an historical synopsis, on another level it is a deeply theological analysis, and on still another it is a spiritual reflection. Although it cannot pretend to be an all-encompassing historical review of two highly significant church struggles, the book is nonetheless an attempt to draw out lessons from history as these pertain to the topic of visionary leadership.

The period under investigation comprises a generation, an interval of seventy years between 1640 and 1710, spanning the early Quaker founders and the first and second stages of Quakerism, and the intensified Huguenot uprisings in France to the aftermath of the war in the Cévennes. The work is a theological retrieval of visionary leadership: the way in which leaders saw and heard God in the pressurized political and religious cauldrons of their day, and the methods they used to set fire to their visions. It is also a spiritual reflection, as it seeks to grapple with the mysteries of faith under extreme persecution, the empowerment of ordinary people (particularly the potential of the ministry of women and children), familiarity with the supernatural visitations of angels and miracles, and the interpretation of Scripture in the social milieu and religious custom of the hurly-burly of daily life.

Two brief observations from leading contemporary scholars begin to acquaint us with the field. In his magnificent book, which covers a century and a half of Huguenot life and religion, an English historian, Geoffrey Treasure compares this church with the early Christians of the Roman catacombs. He applauds their conviction and courage, their will to be a people set apart, and suggests that the reader will find the record of these men and women of faith impressive, even inspiring: '[T]he mindset is constant. Huguenots were not afraid to be strangers in their own country. Faith was all.' In his thoughtful reflection on Quaker spirituality, Douglas V. Steere (1901–95), an eminent American Quaker ecumenist, notes the singularity of the freedom to worship God in any pattern, from the Quaker origins in the ferment of the revolutionary Commonwealth, to the present day. He raises the pertinent question of the significance of lay ministry, by underlining Quaker openness to hearing God, and challenging the view that the Apostolic Age is over and that the Holy Spirit speaks only through the Magisterium of the Church.[4]

Prophetic Leadership in the Fivefold Ministry

To guide the topic of Word and Spirit in visionary leadership we must set parameters in order to narrow the argument to a secure biblical framework. The fivefold pattern of ministry enunciated in the Letter to the Ephesians provides a way of testing the thesis of Word and Spirit in vision, and especially as this pertains to our study of the Huguenot and Quaker movements:

> The gifts he gave were that some would be apostles, some prophets, some evangelists, some pastors and teachers, to equip the saints for the work of ministry, for building up the body of Christ, until all of us come to the unity of the faith and of the knowledge of the Son of God, to maturity, to the measure of the full stature of Christ. (Eph. 4:11–13)

The underlying notion behind this Pauline order of ministry is a leadership arrangement designed to obtain the maximum potential from the members of the body of Christ. Key gifts of people are established to lead others and to promote ministry and a unity in faith – on a wide church canvas this is an ecumenical venture. There is an expectation of an integral synergy between the 'offices' in the fivefold pattern as they work together to achieve the objective of Christian maturity. The prophet stands alongside the apostle to envision and assist in pioneering new mission developments; the evangelist works tirelessly to bring into the fold those straying sheep; and the teacher and pastor educate converts into wholeness of life and witness. Although the prophet stands alone as a gift to the church, the importance of the relatedness of prophecy to the other four ministries cannot be too strongly emphasized. Without prophecy the vision is impoverished and the ministry the poorer. In view of the injunction to strive especially for the gift of prophecy, we must raise the bar, by raising the question of the integration of the gift of prophecy into the fivefold leadership sequence. Naturally this would exclude the prophet, who presumably already operates in prophecy, and reduce the pattern to four. How might prophecy be understood, therefore, as the most important primary gift, as well as an anchoring influence on the leader as apostle, teacher, pastor and evangelist? Each of the four ministries will be examined in 4 chapters in relation to Huguenot and Quaker leadership.

Chapter 1 discusses apostolic visionary leadership as an agent for change amid persecution and opposition, by seeing and hearing God, and by implementing vision through the written word, prophetic action and worship. Both Huguenot and Quaker movements are adept at transcending barriers, so that leadership is not confined to the acceptable norm, but embraces the differences of gender and age. Both groups of people are a tenacious witness to Jesus Christ and demonstrate the inspiration of the Holy Spirit by word and deed. They pass the test as apostolic movements in that they have persisted to the present day, due in no small measure to the firm foundation of the organization of their meetings and services.

Chapter 2 is an examination of the prophetic evangelist and the role of the Holy Spirit in a crucible of war and dissent. As both Huguenots and Quakers are fervent preachers, believing in their cause with wholehearted conviction, the movements grow numerically and geographically. Although much of the Huguenot prophesying is in a godly manner, some clearly is not. Fanaticism must be tested and the Quaker call to silence and discernment of the word is a good foil to untested Huguenot zeal. This is especially evident in the question of war: the Quaker Peace Testimony stands in direct opposition to the Huguenot call to arms.

Chapter 3 considers the prophetic pastor as one who testifies to the person of Jesus Christ. The Huguenot Church of the *désert*, based on an understanding of Christ as the only foundation, is steered by lay pastors who exhibit an extraordinary Christlikeness and carry their witness as visionary lights in the darkness. The early Quaker testimony to Christ within is no less a light in the prevailing gloom of dissention from established religion, and their pastors are no less real and relevant. However, later developments in Quaker theology turn on the thorny problem of Christ the Light. The issue is that if all are enlightened with a spark of divinity at creation, then the importance of a necessary atonement (salvation offered the human race through the reconciling work of Christ) must be raised. Is this a doctrine of universalism, that all shall be saved? Huguenot orthodoxy, as a pastorally prophetic witness to the saving action of Jesus Christ, trumps a Quaker doctrine wide open to deviation from Jesus Christ towards an Ultimate Reality.

Chapter 4 is a reflection on the union of Word and Spirit in the prophetic teacher of the Bible. The prophetic biblical exegesis in Huguenot and Quaker teachers and preachers represents a good example of the inseparability of the Spirit and Christ in the written word. The inspiration of the Holy Spirit is clearly at work in the texts examined, which bear witness to Christ. The difficult argument in early Quakerism, that the Spirit has supremacy over Scripture, is extremely pertinent as it applies to leadership. It is a reminder to leaders that the dead letter of the law cannot save, but also that the living testimony to Christ in the whole of Scripture puts the Bible in a unique relationship to the Spirit.

1.

Apostles of Prophetic Vision

I know and confess, moreover, that we occupy widely different positions; still, because I am not ignorant of the place in his theatre to which God has elevated me, there is no reason for my concealing that our friendship could not be interrupted without great injury to the Church (John Calvin 1509–64).[1]

As we begin the process of analyzing prophetic visionary leadership, by an examination of the foundational role of the apostle, it will be necessary to drill down carefully to the roots of the Huguenot and Quaker movements. Although the genesis of each is quite different and seemingly worlds apart, there are common factors that characterize them both as apostolically constituted and with which, therefore, we are concerned. Both religious groups are fiery elements in an explosion of spiritual moment as sparks fly on either side of the English Channel – the cauldron of political revolt, religious uprising and social upheaval is a catalyst for change. Both movements have leading roles: one without the other diminishes our script, which is played out in the theatre of God's activity in the second half of the seventeenth century.

Huguenot Apostles: Radical Vision in the Church of the *Désert*

Then thy soft flowers distill upon the Soul,
And all the Frenzy of the Mind control;
Reduce the Wretch, by Rage and Passions blind,
To Exercise the Opticks of his Mind;

Thy balmy Dews, the raging Storms restrain,
And Cool the Fermentations of his Brain;
Assisting Reason in her just Defence,
And Hand in Hand, Conduct him to his Sense;
Disperses all the Vapours that remain,
Brings him to act, and so restores the Man (Daniel Defoe 1661–1731).[2]

In order to make sense of the background to the French resistance to Catholicism in the seventeenth century, we examine two theologians whose writings were to guide, direct and inspire – for good or ill – fiery Huguenot zeal. The first is John Calvin, the French-born Protestant reformer who lived as an exile in Geneva, but to whom the Huguenot struggle can be traced, if only in part. The other part belongs to Pierre Jurieu (1637–1713), a French activist professor at the Reformed Academy of Sedan, who lived as an exile in Rotterdam, dominating the French Protestant crusade, if only from afar. Examined together they help our purpose: the discovery of the motivations and impulses behind the struggle for religious freedom. In the religious constellation of post-Reformation Europe, ablaze with new thinking and brightly lit by new modes of spirituality, these two stars are leading luminaries, their beams shining ever brighter, thanks to the invention of printing. In this early modern period, revolutionary ideas and apocalyptic prophecy – a prodigious portion of Protestant controversial literature – are more readily available to the masses. Apocalypticism, derived from the Greek word *apokalypsis* meaning 'unveiling', is a set of beliefs about the end of the world, especially a sudden cataclysmic end and the triumph of good over evil. The works and words of our two writers feed the besieged Huguenot soul: one positions a persecuted church on secure foundations and the other fires it with apocalyptic fervour. In a volatile world of persecution, the calmer writings of the first thinker serve to temper the excitable tenor of the second.

Our two theologians are separated by a century. Although the label was already in existence, Pierre Jurieu denies being Calvinist, claiming that French Protestants acknowledge no other head except Jesus Christ. As far as Jurieu is concerned, John Calvin is not the first reformer of France or Geneva. He is preceded by Ulrich Zwingli (1484–1531), Jacques Lefèvre d'Étaples (1455–1536), Guillaume

Briçonnet (1472–1534) and Peter Martyr Vermigli (1499–1562). He is an expounder of scriptural truths taught by earlier reformers, not an original thinker. Jurieu's hard line contrasts with seventeenth-century reformed theologians, notable scholars and clergy, institutes and commentaries, whose citations and praises of Calvin are frequent. For our purposes in this work, we acknowledge the debt owed the reformer by the French Huguenots in rooting their struggle in both Word and Spirit – the centrality of Jesus Christ and the inspiration of the Holy Spirit.[3]

In Jurieu's critique of Calvin lies the difference between a reformer constrained to bring about change in the church and a radical revolutionary committed to overturning an existing structure. Calvin's legacy is a Protestantism legitimated to defy state authority and operate independently, but grounded consistently in the minutiae of church organization and moral discipline and in the rigour of intellectual and un-mystical theology. A century later Jurieu's polemical rhetoric, underlined by the right to revolution and unlimited people power, was not suppressed within academy walls but burst out to help fuel an angry peasant revolt in Languedoc. Both theologians demonstrate the spirit of creative Protestant protest, i.e. prophetic criticism. By virtue of the living character of the revelation in Jesus Christ, the Protestant principle espouses a dynamic renewal and re-examination of church. The reformed church must always be a church which is reforming itself (*ecclesia reformata, ecclesia semper reformanda*). As we track the course of the French Huguenots we shall see the outworking of this principle in the short term, in a prophetic apostolic movement which is in constant adjustment to its variable environment. In the long term we perceive a lasting impact by visionary church leaders on society at large. And with an eternal perspective we reflect on the spiritual challenge of the union of Word and Spirit as a catalyst for groundbreaking internal church reform and outward apostolic enthusiasm.

The right to resist

The end of the sixteenth century sees the establishing of the reformed churches of Calvin, Zwingli and John Knox (c. 1513–72), the *Eglises réformées* or *ecclesiae reformatae*. Books and the printing press ignited Calvin's teachings like wildfire in Catholic France. By 1552 he had 10 per cent of the nation's allegiance. By 1555 the Reformed Church of Paris, significant for its number of pastors and martyrs, had been established. The year 1555 marks the return of French-speaking Genevan-educated pastors and missionaries who had fled from France to the safety of the Swiss *Eid* or Federation. The word 'Huguenot' may be derived from the Francophone attempt to pronounce *Eidgenossen*, 'comrades of the Eid'.[4]

By 1559 France boasted a fully-fledged federal Calvinist Church with decentralized and presbyterial structure, a national synod and a statement of Calvin's theology, the Gallican Confession. It cut across class lines, embracing aristocrats, nobility, students, clerics, artisans, merchants and professionals, but it lacked in rural appeal. In the main, Huguenots had no support from the peasantry, who appeared to lean largely toward the magical and incantatory religion of Catholicism. The very 'bookishness' of Calvinism and its reliance on abstract formulae, often legal, made it the home of the educated. These people lived sparsely scattered and in the minority, in a broad sweep from Normandy to Paris to Burgundy, south to the Rhône valley and across to the Atlantic; only in the Cévennes mountains and Languedoc plains are they in the majority.

The old French province of Languedoc stretched over the Cévennes into the valleys of the Upper Loire to the north and into the Upper Garonne to the west, to the Pyrenees to the south and the Rhône hills on the east. Its terrain comprises mountains, ravines, chestnut forests, vineyards and fertile fields. By 1573 Languedoc had separated into a Huguenot enclave with its own federal system of government. As we shall see, inflammatory rhetoric and peasant revolt in the 1670s in this region ignited fires of resistance in the Cévennes that is known as the Camisard War (1702–1704).

Quentin Skinner, a leading expert in modern intellectual history, cogently sets out the development of the Huguenot theory of revolution in his seminal work on the foundations of modern political thought. He makes it clear that Calvin's early doctrine of passive political obedience is anchored to the Pauline idea of non-resistance to an authority which is divinely ordered. This view gives no legitimacy to active resistance against a ruler who enforces idolatry or condemns true religion. However, within Calvin's political thought are embedded the seeds of potential revolution, which are watered by the Lutheran argument for forcible resistance by Calvinists in the 1550s.[5]

The Lutheran constitutional theory of resistance argued that, when a superior magistrate persecutes his subjects, then by the law of nature and by true religion and worship of God the inferior magistrate must resist, in accordance with God's mandate. To the question of resistance to an 'idolatrous sovereign', the Calvinist answer is to avoid a rash response and to do nothing contrary to God's laws. Calvin's later development of the Lutheran argument of forcible resistance is to employ the private-law theory against a king who, going beyond the bounds of office, opposes God by enforcing tyrannical edicts forbidding his worship. Such rulers are to be forcibly laid low. Calvin must abandon the central Reformation tenet that magistrates rule by divine providence and ordinance, and he accomplishes this complicated manoeuvre by a claim which for Protestants is revolutionary.[6]

'Popular' magistrates, i.e. those who act on behalf of the people, are 'appointed' to moderate power over kings, and perform an 'act of nefarious perfidy' if they fail to do so. This is a breach of conduct and a 'fraudulent betrayal of the liberty of the people'. Such a practice of elected officials introduces a concept based on legal humanism, adding a secular and constitutional element to the argument of lawful resistance, and broadening the basis of support for embattled Huguenots. Skinner points out that the Huguenots sought to 'sustain their revolutionary conclusions with arguments drawn from legal and historical as well as purely theological sources'. By the late sixteenth century, the right to resist lawfully an idolatrous or tyrannical government was integral to Calvinism. The broadened base of resistance included not only magistrates but also individuals and then the whole body corporate, authorized to engage lawfully in acts of political violence. These radical theories are developed by François Hotman (1524–90) in his work on the fundamental constitution of France, *Franogallia* (1573), Theodore Beza (1519–1605) in his work *The Right of Magistrates* (1574), and Philippe Du Plessis Mornay (1549–1623) in his work *The Defence of Liberty against Tyrants* (1579). Although these writers represent the heritage of Calvinist political thought and opposed the idea of populist insurrection, they continued to advance the notion of defensive and lawful political resistance on the grounds of conscience and constitutionalist ideology.[7]

From 1560 to 1600, the drama of European religion and its wars was played out in France and a Calvinist resistance movement led to open conflict in eight religious wars. The abjuration of Protestantism by Henry IV (1552–1610), reinforced by Pope Clement VIII, culminated in the extension of a limited religious toleration to the nation in the Edict of Nantes (1598), heralding the cessation of religious wars and peace for France. The troubles began again with the succession and re-catholicizing policy of the despotic Louis XIV (1638–1715), legislator of 300 decrees which eroded Huguenot religious and personal liberties (1660–85). His cruel persecution saw the first systematic use of violence, as billeted troops of soldiers, the dreaded *dragonnades*, intimidated and assaulted Huguenots in a campaign of coerced conversions to the king's religion (1681–85).

There is a terrifying and inhumane religiousness in the catalogue of atrocities: ministers who refused to recant were evicted from the country, newborn babies were baptized and reared into Catholicism, Protestant schools and academies were closed, 570 Reformed temples were placed under interdict or demolished. Finally, in 1685 the terrible Edict of Fontainebleau, otherwise known as the Revocation of the Edict of Nantes (or Revocation), ended the last period of legal existence of the Reformed Church in France. In a drive for religious uniformity Protestants were precluded from holding public office and pressurized to convert to the majority religion. The Revocation was ushered in with frightening brute force. The remaining 243 temples were destroyed and a 'wilderness church' (see Rev. 12:6), in armed resistance to the state, was birthed in Languedoc. Between 1685 and 1705 it is estimated that at least 200,000 had fled the country. This is likely to be an underestimation that does not take into account the numbers of those dying on an extremely difficult journey. Until the Edict of Versailles in 1787 and the Napoleonic Code in 1804, Huguenots were stateless persons, either living illegally in France or emigrating illegally. On both counts the penalty was imprisonment or the galleys.[8]

Heiko Oberman, an eminent historian and theologian of the Reformation, discusses the matrix of Calvin's reforming ideas, which may be applied with ease to the Huguenot resistance. Its indomitable character owes much to the cornerstones of Calvin's biblical theology: the glory of God, the secret operation of the Holy Spirit, the growth of the kingdom, the danger of idolatry and the strategy of Satan. Calvin's preface to the first French translation of the Bible (1535) by Pierre Robert Olivétan integrates all these themes into the one history of the covenanting God. In his comments on the liberation from Egypt, the reformer has God accompany the Children of Israel night and day on their flight, 'present among them as a fugitive himself'. In the history of persecution, God himself is the first refugee, trekking with the people of Israel through the desert. God is the compelling spokesperson for all European refugees, diaspora or transients-in-exile; as he is trekking, '*mannum porrexit*', 'he stretched out his hand'. Oberman summarizes the reformer's superb theological insight of God wandering with us: 'the abyss as the deadly flight *from* God and the growing insight in the life-giving refuge *with* God'. We shall see how Calvin's exodus theme is interwoven in the history of the French Refuge. We shall also see how his objectives in the establishing of the church on solid foundations are taken up and extended to accommodate a church in exile. A church community in flight, being on the move, is naturally apostolic. This does not, however, preclude order and structure. We shall discover that Calvin's principles of church government served to root the resistance in a movement that lasted.[9]

The dark night of French Protestantism is part of a wider and greater cosmic battle by German, Dutch, Swiss and English Protestants against Catholic forces perceived as diabolic. In France this period of persecution, embodied in the thirty-year reign of terror of Louis XIV, is also a season of awakening to the roots of the primitive church, a resurgence of the early Reformation. For the nuances of these echoes we turn to the rhetoric of Pierre Jurieu.

The duty to resist

Two notes played with loud repetition are quintessential sounds on the Huguenot score and distinguish the pitch of Pierre Jurieu: anti-popery and prophetic millennarianism. Millennarianism is derived from the Latin words, *mille* meaning 'thousand' and *annus* meaning 'year'. It is the belief that the kingdom of God will be established on earth for a thousand years, with Christ ruling as king before the final end and the judgement (Rev. 20). The underlying cadence in Jurieu is a return to true religion in France. His teaching method is tuned to steel Huguenot resolve in its anti-papist battle. His didactic is set within an apocalyptic composition of Antichrist, i.e. anti-papist diatribe. Jurieu accomplishes his purpose by joining his political anti-Catholic campaign to his Antichrist diatribe, i.e. anti-popery prophetic millennarianism. These violent utterances, which are found in all his works from 1681 to 1686 and coincide with the escalation of *dragonnades* terror, not only direct the course of anti-Catholicism but could be seen to sanction the use of arms by the Huguenot *fanatiques*.

Jurieu believes that the papal throne is the seat of Antichrist, but his reaction to mass conversions is not anti-monarchist. His appeal to the French king is for the destruction of the false church and the erection of the true church. He is self-appointed prophet to all European Protestants, warning them in a letter that this false church is an irreconcilable enemy of the Reformation and urging them to unite against its tyrannous invasion: 'Popery is a monster that devours without ceasing, and that never says, it is enough: can it be imagined that when it hath finished in France, and put that country into the same condition as Hungary, and Bohemia, that it will stop there?' In his pastoral letters to French Protestants published at least monthly, Jurieu promises that God will deliver his church and encourages the people to 'endeavour to discover the illusions by which we are assured that the seducers will attempt to deceive you', by which he means the methods used to enforce conversions. In the letters he attempts to expose the falsity of the teachers of papist books. He compares the subscriptions given the *dragonnades* in exchange for the safety of estates, or freedom from torture, with offering of incense to idols. The invasive nature of popery is a worry also to exiled French ministers in Germany. In a letter to their brethren in England they warn against accepting the spirit of popery in the misguided belief that 'it will be content to re-establish itself in England, without aiming to destroy the Protestant religion'. They mistrust this religion, declaring that it 'employs the sword and fire to extirpate that which it calls heresy'.[10]

In his book, *The Accomplishment of the Scripture Prophecies* (1687), Jurieu plainly states that the Antichrist, the Beast, is popery. By a series of intricate deductions in the light of the Book of Revelation, the year 1689 is designated to be the fall of popery. Naturally the work was a sensation, selling nearly ten thousand copies by the end of 1687. In it Jurieu predicts the deliverance of the true church from the grip of popery. Its demise, however, will not be without bloodshed: 'For that empire shall fall with noise, wars, troubles, effusion of blood'. Thus Revocation is met with divine destruction. Jurieu sanctions the right of revolution but not without reliance on some appropriate authority. He defends the right of the *populus* to have a certain amount of rightful authority. The people can do no wrong. The people have unlimited power if they choose not to delegate authority to the ruler. Divine providence justifies the means to the end and there are no laws or rights which are independent of God's laws.

For Jurieu even the secular can be the agent of divine intervention and God may be found in all natural events. Thus when William of Orange arrives on 15 November 1688 to protect the Protestant church and liberty, Jurieu declares on 15 March 1689 that the refugees should fight against France, not on the basis of the rights of oppressed French subjects, but as their duty to their new rulers. William is God's champion of Providence and Jurieu looks to him to enforce the true religion. It would not be fair to accuse Pierre Jurieu as advocating violence, but it is impossible to divorce his inflammatory anti-papist rhetoric from the volatile contemporary context, which he observed from his safe Dutch haven and which he influenced by means of his copious correspondence. His thoughts on war may be interpreted thus: victims of religious tyranny cannot turn the other cheek forever, illegal assemblies are applauded and some bearing of arms is justified. It is important to note that some Huguenots were unhappy about the violence of Jurieu's tone.[11]

Faith under fire

Having set out key visionary and foundational ideas of John Calvin and Pierre Jurieu and presented certain historic data as essential background components to the Huguenot struggle, we must dwell, however briefly, upon the convolutions of justice in a campaign which was designed to wipe out all vestiges of the religion and which incited both Catholic and Protestant rage.

Our source for the twenty-year-old persecutions pre-Revocation is a detailed short account by a Reformed minister, Jean Claude (1619–87), which was first published in France in 1686 and then translated into English; the copy was ordered to be burned by the French ambassador and the printers were imprisoned, fined and ruined. M. Claude lists six methods of persecution: suits and trials in courts of justice; deprivation of offices and employments; reinterpretations of the Edict of Nantes; new laws and regulations; tricking amusements; inciting and animating people with hatred against Protestants. Examples of religious trials in state courts include saving one's own skin by betraying another Huguenot: 'I plead out against an heretic, I have to do with a man of a religion odious to the state, and which the King is resolved to extirpate.' Or recantation: 'You have the remedy in your own hands; why do you not turn Catholic?' Or the innocent condemned by false witnesses. These are all attempts to make New Converts (*Nouveaux Convertis*). By 1686 the numbers of New Converts testified to the demise of Calvinism. Examples of cleverly contrived contravention of the Edict of Nantes include the rule that all natural children should be instructed in the Roman Catholic religion and the imprisonment of those at least 40 years of age who had not been 'catholicized' at birth. The curtailment of liberty of conscience is a violation of the Edict: children aged 7 should abjure Protestantism and embrace Catholicism under pretence, and could never return to the Protestant faith. Catholics could not change their religion.[12]

These contraventions were extremely problematic for Huguenots as they suppressed Calvin's strict catechisms (1537 'Instruction de Foy', 1541 Genevan Catechism): It is the duty of parents and the church to instruct their children through teaching, the sermon, and instruction on Sunday afternoons culminating in a confession of faith in the midst of the congregation. Given the extremities of these measures it is unsurprising that by 1685 the majority, particularly notables and clerics, had accepted nominal Catholicism, even in the traditional Huguenot strongholds in the south-east.[13]

Against a backdrop of renunciation of Calvinist beliefs we must enquire into the reasons for renewed Protestant vigour in faith after the Revocation of the Edict of Nantes. It would be excusable to surmise that the intensification of persecution would undermine the Huguenot cause, but the opposite is the case. The movement caught fire. The origins of the 'Eglise du "Désert"' (Church of the desert or *désert*) may be traced to the Dauphiné after the Revocation. On a Sunday shortly after the Revocation 100 persons attended the first clandestine assembly. From that moment illegal gatherings persisted even though secret worship meetings were broken up by the *dragonnades*. Calvinist practices had always continued in private but after the Revocation Calvin's instructions are even more closely followed. He writes from personal experience, calling the church to worship at all times and, especially during persecution, to remain faithful to the written Bible. His instruction in his commentary on the psalms is clear-cut and uncompromising: gather to pray, sing psalms and hear a preacher (in the early days of Calvinism one not ordained). Those subject to severe persecution he exhorts to brace their faith:

> I would have them to understand that the small measure of experience which I have had by the conflicts with which the Lord has exercised me, has in no ordinary degree assisted me, not only in applying to present use whatever instruction could be gathered from these divine compositions [i.e. psalms], but also in more easily comprehending the design of each of the writers.[14]

Thus it is that Mme Sybil de Brozet of Vigan declares that on account of many people being clapped in chains 'there were frequent meetings in woods and caves of the earth'. M. Elias Marion reflects on the joy of hidden meetings: 'These [inspirations] did expel sorrow from our hearts, in the midst of dangers from the enemy, as also when hunger and cold oppressed us in the caves and deserts; the most heavy cross we bore, was a light burden, because the intimate communion the gracious God vouchsafed us, afforded relief and comfort.' We note the regularity of the communion service, as Marion goes on to testify: 'we continued to give the holy supper of the Lord in the assemblies, two successive Lord's-days every quarter.' Two years after Revocation, an exiled Jurieu writes to encourage persecuted Protestants in their fight for faith: 'For more than four months time there have been assemblies almost every day in Cévennes, and in the adjacent parts, for the offering up prayers and supplications to God, sometimes in woods, and at other times in caves, and rocks, and dens of the earth.' The geographic areas referred to as 'adjacent parts' are Dauphiné, Vivarais, Velay, the plains of Languedoc and the mountain valleys of the Cévennes.[15]

If the reason for this spiritual ferment is the rippling effect of a radical vision on a persecuted people, then what precisely is its impetus? For this we must investigate the ways in which Huguenot resistance was steered in a prophetical manner so that a persecuted church on the run, dispersed not only within the mountainous region of south-east France, but exiled outward and around the world, could have a lasting effect on its times and on the countries in which it lodged. We see the incendiary flame of peasant revolt and the inspiration of the Holy Spirit. Holding in our minds the delicate balance in Jurieu between sanctioned unrestrained violence and a people's right to revolt against unjust tyranny, we attempt to understand the outworking of the role of prophecy, particularly in the Cévennes crucible, in an apostolic movement comprised of soldiers, uneducated peasant leaders and pastors, children and women. In the tradition of the ancient prophetic message, Jurieu attempts to overcome the tests and tragedies of life in a synergy of religious and political themes, with the result that the Apocalypse of Daniel, the persecution of the righteous and the final victory of the Lord are all joined together. From his Amsterdam hideout his apocalyptic publications in 1686 fire the cinders of unrest in Languedoc and fuel the rebellion in unhappy men and women.

As early as the 1670s peasant tax revolts in Languedoc seem to be instigated by an evangelistic and prophetic zeal – the last shall be first. The age of prophecy had dawned in a longing for social class inversion. Famine impoverishes Protestant peasants; local clergy and central authorities exact cruel tithes and unjust taxes. By 1680 the leaders of the revolt have moved from the papist Vivarais to the Huguenot Cévennes, where the outworking of revival is uniquely different from other regions. Here the fight is not simply political but deeply spiritual – a battle for the very soul of the Cévennes. Here psalms and not folk songs are sung over babies in the cradle and psalms instead of drinking songs accompany the festivities of artisans and peasants. Even the northern French language, *langue d'oil*, is subversive. It had infiltrated the south through the medium of the Bible and the Protestant texts, viz., the *Catechisms* of Calvin and the psalms of Theodore Beza. When a religious mystic speaks *en langues*, i.e. in a strange tongue inspired by the Holy Spirit (1 Cor. 14), it is in fluent French and not in *langue d'oc*, the language of the Cévennes, a dialect spoken in eight southern regions and associated with the working class.[16]

The crushing Revocation aims to annihilate the psalms, Bibles and preaching of the Protestants. Denuded of spiritual leadership, brutally repressed by unjust taxation and a severe economic climate it is little wonder that these people unwillingly accept the terms of the Revocation but live in constant guilt-ridden anxiety as to their betrayal of belief systems. Could one suspect even the sanest of their number to be subject to neurosis and hysteria which feed the seedbed of fanaticism to break out in prophetic agitation? Or is this an unfair assessment of the apparent anointing of the region by the Holy Spirit?

Faith on fire

Calvin's idea of God travelling with his people is pivotal in understanding the Huguenot Church of the *désert*, especially in its experience of the angelic realm. Calvin clearly believes in angels and their diverse functions, as his various comments on the matter demonstrate. God bends to our human frailty by 'the power and ministration of [legions of] angels' appointed to watch over, protect and defend us (Psalm 34:7). His interpretation of Peter's angel in Acts 12:15 debunks the belief that each person has two genii, one good and one bad as an 'unholy fabrication', but maintains that 'the whole heavenly host keeps watch for the safety of the Church, and therefore that, according to the need of the moment, sometimes one angel, sometimes many angels, are protecting us with their support' as 'beams of the divine splendour are our servants'. He asserts that angels are part of the 'consolation and the strengthening of our faith' and are 'dispensers and administrators of God's beneficence toward us'. God delegates the angels to protect those whom he has undertaken to guard.[17]

In a Calvinist way we see God hidden with his people in secret places late at night when singing is undetected by the *dragonnades*. In illicit assemblies bereft of pastors lay *prédicants* who have been hurriedly appointed imitate conventional Protestant worship by preaching sermons, singing psalms and urging repentance from papal idolatry. And in the desert are heard from the sky angelic voices and thousands of angels singing over them songs of deliverance, men walk barefoot and unharmed over burning coals, newborn infants speak up to refuse Catholic baptism and people weep tears of blood. Numbers of child and teenage prophets are in the vanguard. Violent and irresistible manifestations like shaking, choking and convulsions are familiar and often public, and will characterize future *inspirés*, i.e. inspired prophets. New and young prophets appear with the same physical symptoms. The *évanouissement* or swoon of the Dauphiné prophets becomes a prophetic sign of repentance in the uninspired. Visions proliferate and even the uninspired fall to the ground. More aggressive is the woman praying out loud in court for the conversion of her judge, someone smashing a crucifix and another rescuing a captured *inspiré* from three priests.[18]

Faith in the fire of the Holy Spirit

These strange phenomena are related in depositions which the Huguenot exiles themselves gave in London between November 1706 and March 1707. Records of interrogation are held in archival collections in France as well. The sworn testimonies defend the divine inspiration of the *inspirés*, denounced in January 1707 by a Huguenot Church council in the Savoy, London. Given under oath and, therefore, as far as we know, scrupulously accurate, they are an official record of prophecy, miracle and protest in the Cévennes. They provide an insider view, each having a common literary form: person, place, date, location of prophet, gender, age, content and physical manifestation. The collation of these testimonies is the work of François-Maximilien Misson, a celebrated author, a son of a refugee minister and an influential supporter of the French *émigrés* in London. His diligent research results in a well-documented piece which includes face-to-face interviews with French prophets. Their story circulated as *Le Théatre sacré des*

Cévennes ('The Sacred Theatre of the Cévennes'). It is one of the principal extant contemporary sources for the phenomenon of prophesying in this region. It is the live account of the plight of twenty-three *émigrés* and three *inspirés*. The English translation, *A Cry from the Desert*, is by John Lacy, a well-to-do Presbyterian gentleman educated in Latin and Greek. It gives a sympathetic portrayal of the work, emphasizing proof and verification. In his preface to the volume Lacy notes that in the region of Languedoc there is a 'powerful testimony of Jesus, animated by immediate inspiration, whereof the ensuing treatise contains an history'. He tells us that he is happy to go public with his findings, as he is certain of the authenticity of the French *inspirés* in England, having visited them all in person and having heard all objections to them. A quotation from Acts 4:20 on the title page of *A Cry from the Desert* sets the scene for what follows: 'We cannot but speak the things which we have seen and heard.' The depositions will be assessed more closely in Chapter 2 as we test Huguenot prophecy. What follows are 5 examples of vivid eyewitness accounts, which illustrate the genre of storytelling and give us a sense of the unfolding human drama in Languedoc.[19]

John Vernett of Bois-Chastel in the Vivarais, who was a teenager at the time, gives an objective testimony of inspired speech delivered in the *langue d'oil*, the sophisticated northern French language: 'The most agitation my mother had was of the breast, which made her have great gulpings of the throat. She spoke at the time of inspiration only French, which surprised me exceedingly, because she never before attempted to speak a word in that language, nor has since, to my knowledge; and I am certain she could not do it.' Isabel Charras of Les Roches attests that good French is always used and that 'during their discourse then they spoke in the manner as if the Divine Spirit had spoken in them; saying, I tell thee, I declare to thee, my child'. The term 'child' is probably apt, as, according to Charras, children of 5 and a half and 7 years of age have the gift of inspiration. Concerning a revelation of the Holy Spirit enabling visions of angels, John Castanette of St John de Gardonnencques sees and hears one of the inspired in St Jan call out, 'Behold there the dove that descends upon Cabritt', at which the said Cabritt falls into an ecstasy and proclaims, 'Do ye not see those angels rejoicing to see us here?' There are powerful stories of prophetic warning and physical protection. James du Bois of Montpellier gives evidence of open-eyed enraptured *inspirés* gazing into heaven to see 'armies of angels, sometimes those angels engaged against armies of men'. John of Cabanel signs his name to his attestation that a young *inspiré* warns a worship assembly to disperse, as they had been betrayed. No one heeds the warning, and within an hour the militia of Anduze fall upon the congregation, taking fifteen captives.[20]

The sacred theatre of the Cévennes

Arguably the depositions may have been given the title, *Le Thêatre sacré des Cévennes* ('The Sacred Theatre of the Cévennes') with the knowledge that drama features fairly prominently in Calvin: *spectaculum*, 'show' or 'spectacle', 23 times; *histrio/histrionicus*, 'actor' or 'acting', 6 times (*Institutes*); *theatrum*, 'theatre', 7 times (*Institutes*, innumerable times in the rest of the corpus). In Calvin 'theatre' is a metaphor for creation, with God in the central role and human beings as spectators: 'By saying God manifested it he means that man was formed to be a spectator of the created world, and that he was endowed with eyes for the purpose of his being led to God Himself, the Author of the world, by contemplating so magnificent an image' (commentary on Rom. 1:19). The created order is praised by Calvin as 'this most beautiful theatre', or '[t]his magnificent theatre of heaven and earth, crammed with innumerable miracles'. Angels, too, are spectators in the drama of the church: 'God willed to appoint the angels to care for our salvation. Consequently, they attend sacred assemblies, and the church is for them a theatre in which they marvel at the varied and manifold wisdom of God'.[21]

In the human drama of the rocks and caves of the wilderness theatre we see God centre stage: sung psalms, Bible readings and preaching are all for the praise of his glory! The actors, however, are also people: the assembled congregations, the inspired prophets, children and little ones performing the word of the Lord for his delight. A cynic might question the purity of this performance of prophetic utterance and agitated emotion. We would do well to judge it against Calvin's warnings. In his commentary on 2 Samuel 6 he has David leaping like a pagan but he is at pains to explain that joyful dance cures our wild, disorderly lusts in order that 'we may learn to rejoice in him'. He notes our *profane* rejoicing, but maintains that 'we are *cold* [my emphasis] when it comes to rejoicing in God!' However, we are not to be as hypocrites, who 'leaped and danced with great devotion showing signs of great ardour, and yet had nothing but falsehood in their hearts, mimicking true devotion like apes!' Far from quenching outward displays of emotion, Calvin encourages the use of all the senses in worship: 'For if we do not fully taste his goodness, it will escape us and soon vanish, leaving us unmoved. Hence we need to exercise ourselves in it and employ all our senses in it – our feet, our hands, our arms and all the rest – that they all might serve in the worship of God and so magnify him.' He urges yearning affections for God, 'hearts fired with a zealous and burning desire'. He instructs us to seek the ministry of the Holy Spirit, who indeed teaches and tempers our emotions, but also lifts us out of inertia and dullness, arousing in us 'assurance, desires, and signs [Rom. 8:26].'[22]

Given the extremities of the Huguenot plight it is highly likely that the theatre of the desert is a place for the cleansing of pent-up emotions in players and audience. In the synopsis of tragedy as drama and not narration by Aristotle (384–322 BC), people perform actions so that 'by evoking pity and terror it brings about the purgation (*catharsis*) of those emotions'. Similarly music purges 'those who are very susceptible of the passions of pity or terror, or whose passions in general are easily excited; they will perceive a kind of purgation or unburdening of the mind, accompanied with some degree of pleasure'. We may well find elements of very human catharsis in the drama of the desert church – trances, tears, visions, psalm singing and ecstatic speech. We may also find divine interventions when God performs through his people. If these are instances of the Holy Spirit working, then it is as well to heed Calvin's injunction for a serious consideration of Scripture – for a balanced and discerning perspective: 'Therefore, however fitting it may be for man seriously to turn his eyes to contemplate God's works, since he has been placed in this most glorious theatre to be a spectator of them, it is fitting that he prick up his ears to the Word, the better to profit'. This is particularly relevant when we consider the question of war and the Camisard rebellion.[23]

Women in the theatre of the Holy Spirit

Huguenot women are resilient under religious pressure; no doubt strengthened by the Holy Spirit with supernatural courage. A daughter watches her condemned mother with 'head shaved by the hangman, bare-footed and in her shift, holding in her hand a lighted torch', a brave symbol of her faith. Noblewomen who hold assemblies have their castles and woods destroyed and are sent to the notorious state prison, 'the manufacture of Bourdeaux'. Some manage to escape, but others are imprisoned for twenty years, 'glorifying God by their sufferings'. The wife of a colonel of the regiment of Picardy is nearly murdered at home by two assassins on assignment from a popish priest; she hides in a wood for two years until providentially found by her husband.[24]

The hideaway church in ravines and rocks of the earth is the arena for the extraordinary spectacle in seventeenth-century France of women teachers and preachers. Women anointed by the Spirit of God take centre stage. In his memoirs the Marquis de Guiscard describes 'the many thousands of women in the Cévennes, who, without ceasing, prophesy and sing psalms (though they are hanged up by hundreds)' without the knowledge of their families. One Sunday in 1697 in Dauphiné, a girl preacher astounds her listeners with a lamentation on the sins of the nation which have caused the 'deplorable condition of the churches of France'. She cites and applies many biblical texts with 'holy gracefulness and ardent zeal', and with such eloquence 'that it affected us strangely'. The writer leaves the Meeting, 'pierced to the very heart and soul, and full of the impressions of those wonderful things that faithful servant of God had pronounced'. He makes it quite plain that the gifts, learning and fluency of the young girl are attributed solely to the inspiration of the Holy Spirit. There are many such examples in the eyewitness accounts. Outside the crucible of the Cévennes women are not granted the same spiritual status. Lists of exiles in London, for example, show no women prophets, male secretaries failing to account for wives and followers. Inspired women begin to speak only in 1707 and by the end of that year they number fourteen. Secretaries are obliged to record their utterances.[25]

Women stand at their posts in the Cévennes. A courageous mother to her son, 'before he is removed into another world', announces with incredible resolve, 'I am fully resolved to do my duty, even to my last moment'. Statistics of the Huguenot evacuation post-Revocation show less than 10 per cent *émigrés*, of whom only a quarter are women. Evacuee women and young girls are found travelling exhausting distances; some disguise themselves as men or stain their faces; others feign insanity or pretend illness. Their lives are in constant danger from thieves or unscrupulous sea captains who rob and throw their live cargo overboard. As in the great escape of the Hebrew slaves from Egypt with feet shod and staff in hand (Exod. 12–14), here too, there is a feeling of silent and hasty flight.

The Camisard theatre of war

The question of prophecy and violence will be discussed more fully in Chapter 2. We merely note the primary facts of the case of the Camisard War: the outbreaks of prophesying in forbidden assemblies, the tipping point in a prophecy which ignites an attack by a frenzied band of peasants on the town of Pont-de-Montevert, and precipitates the war – a desperate struggle for liberty of conscience. The Camisard War was fanatical guerrilla warfare in which 40,000 lives were lost on both sides. The word 'Camisard' could derive either from an obsolete French word, *camisade*, meaning 'night attack', or be patois for the white shirt or tunic worn by the peasant class, *camisole*. The Camisars were the 3,000 guerrilla fighters who fought violently against royal troops ten times their number. The worst of the revolt was over by 1704 with sporadic fighting until 1710 and a timely peace in 1715.[26]

The loose ends of the saga of the Church of the *désert* are drawn together by Antoine Court (1696–1760), who is convinced that the interests of the Huguenots have not been served by the 'fanatical' or 'military' route. Obedience to Scripture and trust in divine providence is the only choice. With clear vision and organizational ability he sets up a Huguenot synod on 21 August 1715 at Montèze – the first for fifty-five years. Elders are elected, regulations drawn up and the *Confession of Faith* (1559) reaffirmed. A rigorous theological programme, based on the French Reformed Confession drawn up by Calvin is taught. Students preach outside in the rocks and ravines with an audience who are encouraged to comment and discuss. As an apostolic founder, Court visits thirty-one churches in Lower Languedoc and the Cévennes, covering over 300 miles, holding 'desert' assemblies, preaching and administering the sacraments. With a price on his head he preaches to vast crowds. By 1729 there are 200,000 confessing Protestants and 120 churches, each with an eldership supported by a provincial synod. Court discourages prophesying and silences the prophetesses.[27]

After the failure of the Camisard revolt 8,000 people sought refuge in Vaud in Lausanne or the Swiss cantons or Brandenburg-Prussia. Huguenot prophets fled from the Midi, i.e. Languedoc and the Cévennes, into areas already inspired by Pietism. Some 30,000 fled to Germany, to the small city-state of Geneva and the Swiss canton of Neuchâtel. In these regions, colonies of reformed Protestants received full religious liberty and established their own economic, political and cultural structures. In Switzerland and Germany the Huguenot population had none of the sufferings, nor the elations of the Camisard rebellion, which affected the general Protestant sensibility throughout Europe. Among dispersed Huguenots there was a craving for the spiritual purity and sense of God's presence experienced during the times of the Church of the *désert*.[28]

Quaker Apostles: Dissent and the Birth of Vision

> The seventeenth century is fruitful of sects, and some of them wild and monstrous, they were still more fruitful in the number of genuine, holy, and devoted Christians. It was not an age of fanaticism only, but of pure and undefiled religion (William Orme, 1787–1830).[29]

A comprehensive survey of the birth of Quakerism is not possible in a chapter: the sheer number of works available for consultation in a short work on prophetic leadership precludes such an analysis. We shall attempt merely to set a course, to put down historical markers as signposts to point the way to the question of vision in the light of Word and Spirit. Thus at the outset we shall lay a foundation and raise theological themes in an initial discussion, which will be more thoroughly examined in successive chapters.

The turbulence of the English Civil War (1642–51) is a catalyst for the energy of a new spiritual movement under the influence of an illumination granted George Fox (1624–91), aided by writers and publishers, which ignited an apostolic lay movement inspired by prophetic signs of difference, and startling the establishment into a persecuting mania. The more familiar notes of Quaker aversion to social convention, viz. rejection of the swearing of oaths, and, doffing of hats, and adoption of going naked as a sign, conducting silent meetings and espousing pacifism will be discussed as they arise, in relation to Word and Spirit in prophetic leadership.

Lest we lose our way and forget our primary purpose – overwhelmed by the volume of seventeenth-century works, the moderns, and contemporary scholarship – we will prepare a map for the journey. Our first task must be to set out a trajectory for discussion and mark out a path, by means of which we may trace the source for the ideas intrinsic to the evolution of Quakerism as a vibrant visionary movement. The advantage of the vast ocean of Quaker scholarship is its numerous lighthouses, pinpricks of brightness illuminating the landmarks – those significant viewpoints, ideas and philosophies. This overview will highlight select aspects of the debate, drawing on the classifications by Michael Graves, a specialist in rhetoric and communication, and Pink Dandelion, leader for the Centre for Postgraduate Quaker Studies at Woodbrooke Quaker Study Centre in Birmingham. Graves provides a helpful guide to plot a course through a brief literature survey. He identifies five currents within the sea of Quaker analysis: mystical, prophetical, Puritan, contemporary and feminist. Dandelion navigates two undercurrents in contemporary waters: metatemporal and sociological (i.e. without any contribution to a theological discussion).[30]

William C. Braithwaite, a British scholar specializing in the early history of the Society of Friends charts the nineteenth-century Quaker turn to the mystical or the metaphysical, viz. the union between God and humanity. He expounds on an ultimate Reality holding together the whole of life, making no distinction between the human and divine. He summarizes the interpretation of Quakerism as mystical theology in the influential works of Rufus M. Jones (1863–1948): the mystical self or the human spirit is not only joined to, but is connatural with the same Spirit which upholds the universe. This universal spiritual experience emanates in a light called Christ, a light that is moral or it cannot be called light. Braithwaite critiques the assumption that salvation is only a moral change; it must be a process of life and death, birth and rebirth. Jones organizes the reshaping of religion into something spontaneous that is dependent on direct spiritual intercourse, i.e. mysticism, 'a type of religion which puts the emphasis on immediate awareness of relation with God, on direct and intimate consciousness of the Divine Presence. It is religion in its most acute, intense, and living stage'. He defines 'spiritual religion' as different from 'unspiritual' church, and draws a line of continuity from the late second-century ecstatic prophetic Montanists to the Quakers. He argues that for spiritual reformers the inherent greatness of our essential nature is that which is of God in us. As we arrive at a concept of God by gazing and not by reason, Jones asserts that Quakerism, as a religion of inward life and power instead of dogma, is, therefore, the final break with Protestant theology. We note that an introduction by Jones, linking Quakerism to mysticism in Braithwaite's first edition on Quaker beginnings (1912) is omitted in the second edition (1970), on the grounds of new research which questions this link.[31]

For Rufus Jones the primacy of personal experience means that Quakers reconstruct the meaning of salvation with a new interpretation of God and also a transformed eschatology. The doctrine of eschatology, from the Greek word *eschatos*, meaning 'last', is teaching concerning the resurrection, the afterlife, death, judgement and the end of the world – the total consummation of God's purpose. Douglas Gwyn, a Quaker author, teacher and pastor, isolates a strand of prophetism in Jones's appreciation of the elements of apocalypticism and revelation in Quakerism. He surmises that Jones's reading of the Quaker message suggests that heaven and hell are inward dispositions, either requiring an adjustment to God's will or being out of step with it. Gwyn, however, represents the metatemporal contemporary current of realized eschatology, i.e. the kingdom of God as a present reality on earth, so that the 'taking away of the veil' can never be a mystical condition contained within the heart and removed from the human environment, but is integral to the world. If the form of this world is passing away (1 Cor. 7:31), then the whole of the created order is part and parcel of the scheme of God's redemptive work. Gwyn argues that George Fox, the principal spokesperson of early Quakerism, expresses his apocalyptic vision in 'experiential and socio-political terms'.[32]

Rosemary Moore, a seventeenth-century Quaker historian in the metatemporal stream, discusses Quaker relevance to the political scene in the establishment of the kingdom of God on earth. She posits that although the movement was not millennarian in the strictest sense of the word (as were the Baptists and Calvinists), it was extremely political and, therefore, millennarian. At times of millennarian fever people live with a strong sense of the proximity of the final age. The upheaval in a world turned upside down by the English Civil War is just such an epoch: a wide-eyed openness to a new parliament and a hopeful expectancy for just economic systems and fair distributions of wealth. Moore claims a political programme for George Fox, suggesting that he sees politics and religion as the two sides of a coin, and that all evil rulers will be cut down. Lewis Benson, an authority on the writings of George Fox, seeks to maintain his position as a proponent of Quaker prophetism by postulating that Fox is a revolutionary, and not a reformer: 'Everything that is distinctive in Quakerism is related to his teaching about Christ the Prophet'. This teaching is not, however, concerned only with individual salvation, but with corporate righteousness and the right way for the entire community. Benson regards George Fox as the sole exponent of the theme 'Christ as a prophet like Moses [see Deut. 18:18].'[33]

Contrary to the analyses of Quakerism as mystical, prophetic, apocalyptic or metatemporal, the mainstream understands the movement to be one Christian group among many who drew on earlier spiritual insights at the time of the English Civil War. The Quaker scholars Hugh Barbour and Geoffrey Nuttall defend the case for Puritan roots. In the 1560s the word 'puritan' came to be used of religious persons in England who sought to 'purify' the reformed Anglican Church of vestiges of popery. The Puritan protest is levelled at the episcopate, at vestments and ceremonials. Puritan piety leans heavily on Scripture, the experience of conversion, regular self-examination and a rigorous moral and ethical code of conduct. Some Puritans formed separatist breakaway groups, for example, Presbyterians, Baptists and Independents. Barbour regards the Quaker way as a mutation within Puritanism. Nuttall remarks that Puritans and Quakers are 'much of a muchness' in simplicity, sincerity and separateness, but notes their ultimate conflict over the initial working of the Spirit: with the Bible (Puritan) or without the Bible (Quaker). Puritan piety makes no attempt to seek communion with God's Spirit except within the bounds of the revelation through Christ in Scripture. Quaker sensitivity is towards God, whose creative power can work independently of the Bible. Whilst commending Nuttall for establishing the continuity between radical Puritans and the Quakers, Gwyn criticizes his work for failing to grasp the inner integrity of Quakerism.[34]

We will attempt to disentangle these intertwined, yet diverse strands of Quaker theology, as we traverse themes of Word and Spirit in prophetic leadership. In order to grasp the nuances of the historical background to our study, we must plough the field of seventeenth-century English Dissent and grapple with the problem of masterless men, as it is in this particular domain that we situate Quaker origins.

English Dissent

As we seek to understand the dynamic of popular revolt, we use as a grid the Arab Spring, kick-started by a Tunisian man in December 2010, who burned himself to death in protest at his treatment by police. Mob insurrection, fuelled by the military, spread like wildfire to resist and topple regimes in the Middle East and North Africa one after the other, like a pack of cards. Over the centuries the English radical proves to be no stranger to rebellion, and the first half of the seventeenth century is no exception: the infiltration of wars and rumours of wars from the Continent stoke the fury of anti-state sensibilities. English Puritans are hand in glove with continental Calvinists, within whose ranks the fiery French Huguenots feature dramatically. Ecclesiastic French reform is resisted by a committed Roman Catholic monarchy; ecclesiastic English reform faces an ambivalent half-Protestant half-Catholic monarchy. The despotic persecution endured by the French Huguenots far exceeds that meted out to the English Puritans, due no doubt to alliances with loyal monarchists advocating the reform of the state Church of England.

A hundred years of sombre Puritan leadership, hard at work in the persons of these self-appointed hounds of heaven, sanitizes the political air of the English parliament, pricking the conscience of commoner and gentry alike, ruining laxity and frivolity. The apocalyptic fervour which had helped fuel the Protestant Reformation in Europe had forced Christians into a choice between good and evil, for or against the papacy. The Catholic Church is Babylon and a weapon in the hand of Satan; the pope is Antichrist; but the true Protestant Church is the New Jerusalem. Likewise it is an apocalyptic hope in the English reformers, seeking to bring about a purified church from the ashes of a 'burned' church, which sparks the execution of Charles I in 1649 – 'a clearing of the way for King Jesus'. Christopher Hill, a distinguished modern historian makes the point that the spread of Quakerism would have been impossible in the 1650s without the antecedent millennarian excitement: Christ has come to reign in all men now that the King is dead.[35]

The overturning of the monarchy by the Army of the Long Parliament launches a fragile republic or Commonwealth that lasts only eleven years (1649–60). Under the Lord Protector Oliver Cromwell (1599–1658), the Puritans and breakaway sects enjoy a measure of religious toleration. The Restoration of the monarchy in 1660 sees the accession of Charles II and the cessation of these religious freedoms. These are, however, the masterless men in the footsteps of Daniel, publicly refusing to bow down and worship the golden statue of the established Church of England, which is perceived to be in the pocket of king or statesmen. Anti-monarchical ferment seethes in the underbelly of religion, pickled and potted with sectarian religious, economic and political aspirations. Sects abound: Levellers, Diggers, Fifth Monarchists, Seekers, Ranters, Baptists, Muggletonians and Quakers. Outside the established church is the English or Welsh worshipper: the Anabaptist, Brownist, Separatist or Free Churchman – labelled derisively a Dissenter or Nonconformist.

The refusal to render to Caesar the things that are God's is the essence of Dissension. The genesis of organized Nonconformity is to be found in the 1662 Act of Uniformity or Ejection and the expulsion of 1,800 clergymen for refusing, on the grounds of conscience, to submit to the church. Herein lies the origin of a pluralist society which passed the Toleration Act in 1689 – an enduring legacy of the Dissenters – and learned to live in peace. Although the Ejection threw all sects into a common furnace it failed to establish a united front. Quakers, never having been in the fold, could not be ejected from it. Notwithstanding the similarities between early Quakerism and Puritanism, the former was more radical in the application of its spiritual regime. Its outspoken voice of conscience was a severe challenge to a growing religious toleration. Such modifications in Dissenter practice were an attempt to offset the animosity of gentry who were offended by seemingly harsh religious sentiments.

Quaker Dissent

The name Quaker is itself indicative of the radical nature of the sect, as its origin may be traced to 1650, to a legal examination and a year's imprisonment for George Fox. Fox recalls that in his cross-questioning, Justice Bennet of Derby 'first called us Quakers because we bid them tremble at the word of God'. Fox was incarcerated on the grounds of violating the first statute of the Blasphemy Act (August 1650). One can only surmise that Fox's bold teaching on the experience of Christ within pushed back the boundaries of conservative religion, threatened churchmen everywhere and so rattled the secular authorities at the first sniff of civic disobedience that he was deemed safer within than without prison walls. However, Quakers *did* tremble when the power of the Lord came upon them so that the name was equated with tremblers. In his theological treatise, *An Apology for the True Christian Divinity*, the prominent Scottish Quaker, Robert Barclay (1648–90), describes the transition, in a meeting under the prevailing power of truth, from physical tremblings to praise:

> Sometimes the power of God will break forth into a whole meeting, and there will be such an inward travail . . . like the going of two contrary tides, every individual will be strongly exercised as in a day of battle, and thereby trembling and a motion of the body will be upon most, if not upon all, which, as the power of truth prevails, will from pangs and groans end with a sweet sound of thanksgiving and praise.[36]

Elizabeth Bathurst, who describes herself as 'one of the least of the flock of Christ', writes a letter in 1679 to Friends (a word synonymous with Quakers): her greeting, in the familiar terminology of 'quaking' and 'trembling', is not only a word of comfort, but also identifies their unique call to Christ. She addresses them as 'you Friends of the Bridegroom, that mourn for his withdrawing, and eat your bread with quaking, and drink your water with trembling, as those who find no comfort till you do enjoy him'. Edward Burrough's salutation at the head of his pamphlet to Friends, *A Trumpet of the Lord Sounded out of Sion* (1656) gives a flavour of the universal disdain in which Quakers are held, in contrast with the tender love in which they are held by the Lord: 'To all you who are in the light of eternal life . . . who are not known to the world (though by it scornfully called Quakers) even you doth the Lord also remember with everlasting kindness, and infinite love.'[37]

To summarize Quakerism by means of another derogatory phrase, used by a seventeenth-century critic, as 'the fag-end of reformation', does the movement an injustice. The stripping of all vestiges of organized religion, by the abolition of the ordained ministry and all seven sacraments, smacks less of the Reformation of the church and more of a revolution of the heart. Such a heart transplant is made possible by the removal of altars, pews and pulpits, enabling worship at any time. Silent waiting for the power to come, for God's message to be inwardly declared, is the essence of the new truth: Christ has come to teach his people himself and is already present whatever you are doing. George Fox and the early Quakers spearhead something new: a fresh revelation and outpouring of truth, a trumpet call to announce the present reality of the Day of the Lord after the Civil War.[38]

In the printed text the Quaker heralds are the First Publishers of Truth, for now is the time of the common man, both men and women, and for the release of gifts of leadership, preaching, prayer and writing. George Fox's *Journal*, which was written retrospectively by his stepson-in-law, Thomas Lower at the dictation of Fox himself, was never published in his lifetime and only disseminated in its present form in the twentieth century. With hindsight its events and personalities, while not deliberately distorted, are likely to have undergone modifications, either by Fox or by the editors in light of present experience, in order to show the power of the Lord over all. The corpus of George Fox comprises 5,000 items listed in *The Annual Catalogue of George Fox's Papers*, compiled between 1694 and 1697, edited and printed by Henry J. Cadbury in 1939. There are 2,100 broadside sheets, tracts, pamphlets and books, 1,750 letters, 2,900 unpublished works and 1,150 lost pieces.[39]

Apostolic foundation 1643–52

As we shall see, George Fox preaches a missionary gospel from his own experience, but his visionary propensity takes him beyond the conquering of sin, in an age of preaching about it, to lift his eyes in second sight and a divine vision to be passed on to all. We may discover the source of his illumination in three parts, tabulated as encountering Christ, combating the Devil and perceiving the harvest. These disclosures or 'openings' occur during 'the first workings of the Lord' and serve as a rudder to guide the early Quaker enterprise from its inception to the end of the seventeenth century. The pious 19-year-old Fox, grief-stricken at the lewd conduct of professors of religious faith in his home town of Drayton-in-the-Clay (now Fenny Drayton) in Leicestershire, cries out to God in prayer. The Lord speaks: 'Thou seest how young people go together into vanity and old people into the earth; and thou must forsake all, both young and old, and keep out of all, and be as a stranger unto all.'[40]

This instruction is obeyed to the letter: the youth leaves home in September 1643 to live for four years in a spiritual desert, traversing solitary countryside with the Bible clasped to his breast, beset by inner turmoil and temptation in his desire for God – a thirst not sated in his travels throughout England, by dialogue either with clergymen or with ordinary seekers of truth. He is at war within and without: his heart is in turmoil while his journey is frustrated by the spiritual ignorance he finds in priest and Dissenter alike, even those 'tender' towards him. The 'openings' of God show him that training at Oxford and Cambridge fails 'to make a man fit to be a minister of Christ', that God dwells not in buildings (steeplehouses) but in the heart, and in his people who together are his temple. He learns to forsake earthly succour and to savour his apartness 'much as a stranger, seeking heavenly wisdom and getting knowledge from the Lord'. These are moments of rapturous communion, transporting the young man, as he says, 'into such a heavenly joy that I thought I had been in Abraham's boscm' and anchoring him in the love of God.

Fox is steadfast in his growing convictions and undeterred by his family's anxiety for his mental safety, or by their priest's accusation that he pursues the folly of 'new lights'. At the age of 23 his perseverance is rewarded in a remarkable auditory experience, whose lasting effect is to govern his life's work. He hears a voice saying, 'There is one, even Christ Jesus, that can speak to thy condition . . .' Immediately he is convinced that Christ himself is the Opener: 'I knew him not but by revelation, as he who hath the key did open . . .' This divine message is the wellspring and fount of all future teaching in early Quakerism. Fox understands Christ's inner witness that bypasses every intermediary, viz. priest, teacher or Scripture, to be the very core of belief and the one thing necessary for faith (see Luke 10:42). Christ is come to teach his people.

Douglas Gwyn identifies Fox's contribution to Quakerism in view of covenant theology. He compares the Puritan 'covenant of grace' (available to the predestined) and its 'spirituality of anxiety' ('profession without possession') with Fox's teaching as 'a covenant of light' and with Quakerism as a covenant of 'experience rather than inference'. It is through surrender to the Light that one is led to participate in the covenant with God.[41]

In these early struggles Fox's chief combatant is the Devil masquerading as depression and deep darkness. However, once again the divine voice sounds to encourage him that the battle belongs to the Lord: 'Thou Serpent, thou dost seek to destroy the life but canst not, for the sword which keepeth the tree of life shall destroy thee' (Gen. 3:24). The young seeker is lifted by the love of God into a mystical epiphanous illumination, whose duration is undisclosed but whose intense spiritual pleasure causes him to admire the greatness of the love 'opened unto me by the eternal Light and power'. The powerful Light shows him that the tempter's mission is forever destroyed by Christ who sits 'atop' the Devil (cf. Eph 1:20–22), and that this 'secret belief' raises him, with Christ, above his trials (cf. Eph. 2:6). Next appears a 'pure fire', a 'refiner's fire' in him, by whose glowing effervescence he rightly discerns his own thoughts and sighs, distinguishing between the groans of the flesh not submitted to Christ, and the groans of the Spirit 'which did open me, and made intercession to God' (Rom 7:23,24; 8:26). By the power of this invisible Spirit he is able to detect all false hearing, seeing and smelling, which sit 'atop' the Spirit and draw one out of the Light by Devilish deceit. These fresh revelations inspire Fox's teachings and galvanize the great meetings outdoors: 'For in that day the Lord's power began to spring, and I had great openings in the Scriptures.' Some years later the founder writes poetically to Friends concerning the power of God to 'bind, to chain, to limit, to frustrate, that nothing shall rise nor shall come forth, but what is in the power' to 'open every spring, plant, and spark, in which will be your joy and refreshment'. He exhorts them to believe that, despite the freezing properties of wintry storms and temptations, 'the same light and power will go over the tempter's head'. The act of dispelling evil is, however, a conscious cognitive exercise, requiring an active lifting of the eyes to the Light of life. Fox cogently spells this out in a fragment of a letter, instructing Friends that whenever a mist of darkness threatens to cloud and veil belief, 'to the measure of the life of God in you all take heed, that with it your minds may be guided up to the living God, from whence *Light* and *life* doth come, and virtue, and strength, and nourishment . . . that the knowledge of the glory of God in the face of Christ Jesus, ye may all come to enjoy'.[42]

Gwyn interprets Fox's teaching as 'a spirituality of desolation', in which the falsely constructed self is deconstructed, through deep surrender to the power of the Light and to the new will and way of God. Early Friends experience 'a harrowing participation in the cross of Christ and an equally profound sense of emergence into a new creation'. For Fox, however, recreation does not terminate at the personal but is extended to embrace the whole of the created order (Col. 1:19,20). Through Christ, humankind is restored to the original condition of Eden to be in full unity with creation. Geoffrey Nuttall argues that George Fox is contemporaneous with seventeenth-century magic, quackery and Rosicrucianism (metaphysics and alchemy) at one end of the spectrum, and astronomy, chemistry, botany, medicine and metallurgy at the other. A common thread in these practices and disciplines at the time is the unity of the world in God, who alone reveals its secrets, and the penetration of the divine spirit into all created things.[43]

We have noted that the motivation for Fox's gospel, which drives him to preach and teach in barns, fields and steeplehouses, is the coherence of his conviction (his word is 'convincement') of the power of the love, life and Light of Christ over all human sin and failing. Gospel truth is indeed magnified by his audio-visual epiphanies, but the magnitude of a future harvest is revealed to his apostolic soul only in 1652 on Pendle Hill in Lancashire. In the light of the sun he sees people materialize before him like fine dust, as thick only as particles or specks on the earth. These masses are those who shall be brought home to the Lord so that there may be one shepherd and one sheepfold on earth. His eyes are riveted towards the north, transfixed by a visionary image of a great company of people. These are they who will accept him and hear his message – a prediction concerning the origins of Quakerism in the north-west of England. Retrospectively, an older Fox reflects on the work of the propagation of the gospel as the performance of many important, yet different tasks: 'Some speak to the conscience; some plough and break the clods; some weed out, and some sow; some wait, that fowls devour not the seed. But wait all for the gathering of the simple-hearted one: for "they that turn many to righteousness, shall shine for ever."' To those ministering out in the world in 'unbroken places', Fox counsels against taking the whole meeting of Friends 'to suffer with and by the world's spirit'. Here he breaks down the specific role of the apostle, advising that three to six persons, strong and mature in the truth, should go to the 'unbroken places and thresh the heathenish nature'.[44]

Braithwaite's statement that George Fox was the most powerful spiritual leader of his time is probably true. He points out the signs of an extraordinary apostolic vitality which are demonstrated in the fervency with which Fox prophesied, in his expectation that holy living is a requirement even in the army and navy, in his belief that divine wisdom is the only test for right conduct in mundane affairs, not only in speech or dress but also in business dealings. The spiritual exaltation felt by Quakers is on a par with the experience of the apostles at the first Pentecost (Acts 1,2): 'To the earnest-hearted Puritan a life of strict religion had meant exact obedience to a Divine law; to the Quaker it became the communion with a living Presence within his heart, so that the earthly life was felt to be a part of the larger eternal life.'[45]

Fox's agenda in practice is based on distinctives which, arguably, mark him as an original and not one of a kind, and if not the only founder of early Quakerism, at least the movement's main vision holder. Nuttall summarizes these basic tenets thus: Christ says this and the apostles say that, but what do you say? And what you do say can only be told by an experience of the Spirit of Christ within and not by the Scriptures. The manifestation of the Spirit gives spiritual meaning to the written word and for this process Quakers are required to live in the power which transports into paradise and triumphs over sinful susceptibilities. The expectation that the Lord's power enables everything to be turned to love exemplifies the hope in George Fox. The phrase 'the power of the Lord' in various combinations of words ('power of God', 'the Lord's power' or 'power of the Lord') is a catchphrase in the *Journal* and is used more frequently (388 times) than any other expression.[46]

In the preceding paragraphs on English Dissent we touched on the locus for the birth of Quakerism against a backdrop of English Puritanism, Protestantism and sectarianism, but neglected the tangible influence of Catholicism. Therefore, in a Catholic broadsheet of 26 October 1673 we note four statements of faith: the differences between Catholic and Quaker beliefs providing a springboard into the deep waters of the early Quaker creed. We take up the case for mystical theology as a dissenting ideology that is framed by Steven Ozment, an American historian of the early modern and modern periods, in order to clarify the dissenting standpoint of George Fox.[47]

Point one of the broadsheet enunciates the infallibility and divine inspiration of Holy Scripture, except for 'some things hard to be understood' in the Bible, in which case Catholics 'submit our private judgments to the judgment of the church, represented in a free general council'. We hear George Fox cry out: No man over me – the inner witness is enough! Ozment remarks that medieval mystical writings 'set forth what can fairly be called the latent revolutionary possibilities of the Christian religion'. He rightly asserts that mystical theology feeds on the 'exceptional, on God's freedom to communicate immediately with men, to speak more conclusively in the depths of the individual heart than through all the official writings and ceremonies of even the most holy institution'. We note the impulse of unified persecution, mysticism and authority, as it compels direct speech, in the Quaker claim to a legal right to speak. Despite it being a secular offence by an act of parliament, Fox preaches in Bootle after the sermon is over, ignoring the vehement protest of priest and volatile congregation:

> I told him [the priest] he had his hour glass by which he had preached, and having done, the time was free for me as well as for him . . . And he accused me that I had broken the law in speaking to him in his time in the morning, and I told him he had broken the law then, in speaking in my time.[48]

Point two of the broadsheet drives home the fact that images do not have any divinity or virtue in themselves as objects of worship, but 'as instruments, which we find by experience, do often assist our memories, and excite our affections'. The blatant defence of the use of visual aids in worship is anathema to the centrality of the invisible Light and Word in the teaching of George Fox – themes we shall pursue in successive chapters. Ozment reminds us that mystical theology, as a direct transaction between the soul and God, works without mediators. Its power to convince and persuade resides in a severe austerity. God speaks more authoritatively through an ass or a ragged prophet, more intimately through ascetic denial of body and spirit, than he does through the pulpit or sword. On the same afternoon in Bootle, Fox reins in the restive crowd, recalling it to Christ its teacher and only Light:

> So I called all people to the true teacher, out of the hirelings . . . for the Lord was come to teach his people himself by his spirit, and Christ saith, 'Learn of me; I am the way' which doth enlighten every man that cometh into the world, that all through him might believe; and so to learn of him who had enlightened them, who was the Light.[49]

Point three hammers out the notion of merit, that although works give no added value to our justification that is in Jesus Christ alone, meritorious works do provoke us to diligent observance of the commandments for the reward of obedience. On this topic we hear Fox expostulate: 'What, you still expect to *cultivate* [my emphasis] godliness!' Ozment nails down a solution offered to a doubting and imperfect world in the perfection and certitude of mystical theology. By means of the free gift of grace it is possible to become like Adam pre-Fall, knowing the very 'godness in God' which the first man knew at his creation. As we track Fox's teaching, we will see clearly this emphasis on the soul's receptivity to enlightenment, in contrast with the received tradition in Catholicism, viz. the exercise of mind and will in pleasing God.

Point four, the moral law i.e. obedience to magistrates and civil powers for conscience' sake, is a big bone of contention for Fox, who defies magistrates for the sake of conscience and in obedience to God. It is widely broadcast that Fox and his companions have so singular a response to judges and justices of the peace that these civic leaders 'were not able to answer us one word in twelve'. The Quaker vision speaks to disillusioned radicals after the Civil War. Ozment again, on the potentially anti-intellectual and anti-institutional aspects of mystical theology, reflects the substance of Quakerism as 'a refined challenge, always in theory if not in daily practice, to the regular, normative way of religious salvation'.[50]

Dandelion's ordering of four key ideas characterizing contemporary Quakerism (Evangelical, Conservative, Liberal) helpfully demonstrates the four points enunciated above from a twenty-first century point of view: corporate divine guidance without voting (the principle of no human authority); direct inward encounter with God and forms of worship which facilitate this (the anti-imagery principle); spiritual equality of all, the priesthood of all believers (all can minister, as all are created in the image of Christ); peace pacifism and aversion to war (the principle of obedience to God before magistrate).[51]

First apostolic period 1652–60

We may demarcate two periods in first-generation Quakerism which correspond to the manoeuvres of English politics. As we have traced the backdrop to early Quakerism in the tumult of civil war and abolition of monarchy, so we must grasp its birth

in the comparative freedom of a republic and the heady days of
Commonwealth. This first stage, 1652–60, connotes eight years of
vibrant apostolic vitality in groundbreaking principles and practices. A visionary apocalyptic hope, bred by the belief that they
are at the brink of the world's end, stiffens the Quaker spirit of
no compromise as the true church. The Light signifies the imminent Day of the Lord. The second phase, 1660–1700, correlates
to the Restoration and the Conventicle Act (1664) of Charles II,
which banned Nonconformist and unlawful religious meetings,
until the accession of William III and the Edict of Toleration (1689)
ended persecution. In a stabilized political climate a thrilling
pioneering movement adapts itself, settling into a Society of genuinely devoted and holy Christians. Its natal source is the Pendle
Hill vision in 1652 where Fox 'is moved of the Lord to sound out
his great and notable day . . . and from thence went forth, as the
Lord had shown him'. On that night he writes down his revelation 'concerning the day of the Lord and how Christ was come
to teach people himself by his power and spirit [sic]' in a paper
to priests and professors, which appears to have been circulated
far and wide – the wellspring for the fulfilment of Fox's vision of
'a great people in white raiment by a river's side coming to the
Lord'. These multitudes, convinced by the liberating truth of Fox's
preaching, are imparted a divine energy by the inspiring Spirit to
shape the world into their purposes, so that as world-changers
they establish Quakerism in all centres of the empire. People
'living of the first and great convincement' are from all strata of
society: trading and yeoman classes, merchants and gentry. For
the purposes of our ongoing discussions we shall employ the writings of early worthies of repute: Richard Farnsworth (c. 1630–66),
William Dewsbury (1621–88), Edward Burrough (1634–63) and
Isaac Penington (1616–79).[52]

These first Quakers are prophets, not theologians, for whom
the work of Christ in the heart in the *present* is the focus for religious thought and experience. In diverse ways they keep alive
the central message of George Fox, whose doctrinal teaching is
collected into a compendium of papers and works, *Gospel-Truth
Demonstrated* – a radical critique of state-sponsored church and
the new Puritan establishment, and a restatement of the revolutionary groups pre-Restoration. A paper from 1660 condemns all

invented practices detracting from true worship: popery, altars, crosses, images, representations, praying for the dead, bishops, cardinals, tithes, swearing oaths, organs, bell, book and candle, and many other doctrines 'contrary to the Scriptures, and the apostles' doctrine, where all things were to be done freely, and in love'. To be a Friend is to 'tremble at the word of God, by which all things were made and created', and to be always'[p]raying in the Holy Ghost, keeping ourselves in the love of God, singing in the Spirit'. God is that higher power transcending all things – both civic authority and transgressor – and to whom we must be subject, for conscience' sake. Thus to compel any person against their conscience is to sin against Christ.[53]

For the refined Puritan, Isaac Penington, who joined the despised Quakers and was imprisoned for five years without legal warrant, the place of study is his heart: a living inward experience of Christ can never be replaced by the dryness of doctrine. Thus he writes that apostles and ministers are 'to be governed by his Spirit, and spiritually, and not after a fleshly manner'. The reliance upon the Spirit for radical discipleship is the key: 'Can the least true change be wrought in the heart, without the operation of God's Holy Spirit and power there?' Penington sums up the inner disposition of the Quaker tuned to the pursuit of God: 'The thing that we wanted, and mourned after all our days, in our fervent strains and ways of profession, without the knowledge of this, is now met with.'[54]

Second apostolic period 1660–1700

By the death of George Fox in 1691 and the close of the seventeenth century, the Society of Friends had peaked in popularity and worldly prosperity. Judging by the continual and prolonged animosity it succeeded in arousing, we may assume that it had not become a white elephant in the religious stall. In contrast, the years 1702–55 are the days of tradition, haemorrhaging a cautious, inoffensive and prosperous body of people. During the second apostolic phase subtle emphases, favoured by scholars and gentlemen, steer a visionary apocalyptic campaign towards pragmatic organization and a steadying reasoned logic. William Penn (1644–1718), founder of the state of Pennsylvania, for whom freedom of conscience is a passion, upholds a practical and not a millennarian doctrine. He is a transition between the earlier prophetic enthusiasms and the later 'calmer, politer Quakerism', preparing the way for the Quietist impulse of the eighteenth century. Richard Baxter (1615–91), the archenemy of English religious sects and parties, sums up the situation: 'But of late one William Penn is become their leader, and would reform the sect, and set up a kind of ministry among them.'[55]

Robert Barclay, a Scot educated in Paris at a Calvinist theological college, underwent convincement and joined the Quakers in 1666, attracted by their love for one another and their manner of life. His faith is subjective and emotional: he becomes a fool for Christ's sake, parading the streets of Aberdeen in sackcloth and ashes, weeping in distress and calling for repentance. He also seeks objectivity in faith by attempting to harmonize the old and new thought in a systematic manual of Quaker principles, *An Apology for the True Christian Divinity*. An example of Barclay's process is the question of corporate judgement and the individual. The strengthening of church government by Fox results, somewhat inevitably, in individual subordination to those to whom the leading of the meeting has been allotted. To the Fox adage, 'To your own, to your own', i.e. to the light within, is added, 'Keep the unity'. The problem thus arises: should an individual assent to the judgement of the body, or wait to be convinced before accepting it? Fox's idea of silent waiting for the discernment of the Spirit is Quaker vision at its most extraordinary and singular. The tension between the limits of individual spiritual liberty and church government is not a new issue. While the big cat George Fox is in prison in 1666, the little mice play and sign a letter, which calls for the submission of individual guidance to the corporate sense of the church, i.e. to elders who are authoritative and sound in faith.[56]

Pioneering First Publishers of Truth

Within their short history of less than four hundred years the Quakers have produced a prodigious crop of writings, many of which are classics in their own right. Apart from the *Journal* of George Fox, this productivity includes, in the early period the letters of Isaac Penington and the journal of John Woolman (1720–72). Later writings comprise the influential *Quaker Strongholds* by the aristocrat Caroline Stephen (1834–1909), the *Testament of Devotion* by Thomas Kelly (1893–1941) and the works of Rufus M. Jones. Thus the development and interpretation of Quakerism appears to lean as much upon the record and discourse of prominent Friends as upon the inspiration of Scripture and the leadings of the Spirit.

The self-proclaimed First Publishers of Truth argue their case, set out their propositions and write furiously to themselves, to each other and to the world at large in journals, letters, broadsides and pamphlets. Nothing daunted, the critics respond to the growing force of the sect, and objections to the heretical Fox are widespread and published over-abundantly. George Fox's work, *The Great Mistery of the Great Whore* (1659), is a compilation of replies to over 100 anti-Quaker books and statements, one of these a book co-authored by the English Christian writer and preacher, John Bunyan (1628–88), *Some Gospel Truths Opened*. Fox protests that Bunyan has not comprehended his teaching and proceeds to affirm the real union between Christ and believer, 'flesh of his flesh and bone of his bone', as the touchstone of belief. Fox asserts that salvation proceeds from the Light who is, and was, Christ. Christ within the believer is the same as 'Christ without', the person who died in Jerusalem. He strongly challenges Bunyan's accusation that his preaching of Christ within is a new gospel. Those who eat his flesh have it within and this is not a new gospel. The crucified Christ within is the same crucified Christ without.[57]

Like a dog obsessed with a bone the critics will not let go of the argument. A summary of the grounds on which Quakers are condemned is published, with competing subtitle, *The Great Mystery of the Little Whore is farther Unfolded* (1712): for denying that Jesus of Nazareth is the same as Christ the Son of God; for undervaluing the death and sufferings of Jesus Christ and exalting their own; for denying the Scriptures to be the written word of God; and for rejecting the ordinances of baptism and the Lord's supper. Richard Baxter (1615–91), a Puritan church leader, adds a further anxiety to the general concern. Although he admits that the tremblings and vomitings of the earlier meetings have ceased, the fact that they 'pretended to be violently acted on by the Spirit' leads him to question the apparent activity of the Spirit in the later meetings: 'He that pretendeth to be moved by the Spirit speaketh; and sometimes they say nothing, but sit an hour or more in silence, and then depart.' Baxter's published list of offending parties lumps the Quakers together with other sectarian groups whose common crime is 'to set up the light of nature, in men, under the name of Christ, and to dishonour and cry down the church, the Scripture, the present ministry, and our worship and ordinances'.[58]

Pioneering women of conscience

Quaker women are remarkable for their active role as First Publishers of Truth, as their prodigious output, which goes beyond the religious sphere, bears witness. To name but a few: Dorothy White writes to parliament, London and the nation during the last years of the Commonwealth; Anne Downer Whitehead writes to king and parliament in 1670; Joan Whitrow to King William in 1689; Rebecca Travers writes tracts defending Quaker religious tenets against non-Quaker detractors; women write against false worship in the Church of England and against justices of the peace who imprison Quakers. In a written document, 7,000 women petition parliament against the tithe. Margaret Askew Fell Fox (1614–1702) of Swarthmoor, wife of a judge of assize and vice chancellor of the Duchy of Lancaster, is an especially impressive First Publisher of Truth. Of her 171 published documents there are thirty-one calls to repentance, fifty-four statements of religious doctrine, eighteen polemical tracts against ministers and officials, ten on women's meeting activities and sixteen complaints of persecution. Kunze argues that Fell's literary output, compared with other literate English women of the period, marks her out as one of the exceptional women of the seventeenth century and one of the chief controversialists of early Quakerism.[59]

The principle of spiritual equality, but social inequality is stamped into post-Reformation belief and practice. All are created in the image of God, both women and men sharing in the work of creation. The structure of society, however, is still patriarchal: women are dependent on men economically, legally and politically; in public spheres, vocationally or in business they do not have the same rights or rewards; they have no say in the state, education or the church. During the revolutionary period 1640–60 the sects hold the common view of a limitation of women in society and a restriction to childbearing and homemaking. There is some emancipation in Quakerism: women preach, teach and venture on mission. These women are highly motivated strugglers for justice and civil rights and they are prepared to endure punishment and penalties for their stance. Women constrained by Quaker authority turn to mission to Ireland, Holland, Italy (including specifically Venice), America (including specifically Maryland) and Jamaica. The apostolic endeavour in planting the Society of Friends in foreign parts is irrefutable. The establishment of the first women's meeting outside London by Margaret Fell is an example of the pioneering spirit in the Quaker women and leads us on to the Meetings of Sufferings.

Pioneering Meetings of Sufferings

George Fox evolved his strategy for organization in prison. An internal order and system rapidly evolved, which had the knock-on effect of checking extravagant individualism. A General Meeting for Friends was dependent on the itinerant ministry of travelling ministers and elders, as well as a settled body of elders. The structure comprised a Yearly Meeting in London, a Quarterly Meeting for every county or group of counties, a Monthly Meeting for small groups of congregations, and the Meeting for Sufferings. As a persecuted dissenting sect, the early Quakers are often subject to inhumane abuse. Consequently George Fox appoints meetings in open places, fields, moors or mountains, which are guided by 'the wisdom of God', so that Quaker truth may be protected from the world and 'all burdens may be kept off, and taken away'. These Meetings of Sufferings keep records of the persecutions. On the basis of the scattering of the persecuted apostles in the New Testament, Fox also instructs his flock to meet in homes and encourages travelling apostles to preach from house to house, like Paul. His words to the Friends are calming and pacifying: 'And let not our meetings be broken up, but let us have our meetings peaceable in the fear of the Lord God and edify one another to pray in the Holy Ghost, and to build one another in the holy faith.'[60]

In a climate of religious harassment, these sentiments are almost impossible to obey, as is evident from the Quakers' written records. An example of the nature of the provocation is the prohibition issued to William Dewsbury, 'a ringleader of the persons called Quakers', who is forbidden 'to go up and down from place to place teaching, until he receives approbation of some persons, who shall be thought fit to judge how agreeable his principles are to truth and peace'. The response of a Friend, Mr R. Crane, to the breaking up of meetings, arrests and imprisonments is to ask why the authorities are blind to the necessity of worship. Can they not see that Quakers 'cannot cease to meet together, to worship the living God in the Spirit of truth, as he hath manifested?' He argues that 'England's laws are made to preserve and protect the good Protestant people of the same, in all their just rights, and not to destroy them.'[61]

Friends everywhere in England catalogue their sufferings in detail; the county of Wiltshire is no exception to the unrelenting injustices perpetrated by the law in complicity with pliable priests. The offences include refusing to swear oaths and give tithes to the priest, harbouring inflammatory literature, speaking in church and meeting to worship. At a peaceable meeting in Stapleford (1685) 'the priest of the parish came to the meeting with officers, and violently forced them to go before two justices without any warrant who tendered them the oath, and for refusing to swear committed them to prison'. A Friend in Mardon (1687) suffered imprisonment for twenty years for his testimony against tithes but he outlived his adversary, the priest who had informed against him. The priest's successor, however, had extracted from the Friend, in lieu of a tithe, two sheep, one lamb, beans and bushels of wheat and barley.[62]

In Devizes (1662) a Friend is sitting with other Friends 'waiting upon God in his own house', when he is accosted by a constable and officers who 'came into his house, and with violence hauled him and some other friends away before two Justices'. A compromise is offered: if the Friend vows never again to hold a meeting in his own house he need not swear the oath. Naturally he refuses the bribe and is sent to prison for several months. Twenty years later in Devizes (1682), at the order of the mayor, officers descended upon a peaceable meeting and 'plucked all the Friends out that were there assembled'. The next morning the same officers were threatened by the mayor and ordered to inform on all those above the age of 16 who were present at the meeting. On pain of fines, therefore, and contrary to law, they swore against the meeting, 'some through envy, others for fear'. The informers were then granted a warrant and all Friends in the town who had been informed against were fined to the amount of £64, levied on their goods or chattels. In Urhant (1658) a Friend goes to the steeple-house and speaks a few words after the sermon and prayer by the priest. In a great rage, the priest sends for the officers and obtains a warrant from the justice, before whom the offending party must appear. A fine of £5 is levied and for refusing to pay the culprit is condemned to prison for three months. Mr Crane argues that the exaction of tributes and taxes ought to ensure a peaceable life, instead of which the Quakers 'behold nothing but cells, vaults, and nasty holes in prisons amongst felons, and murderers'.[63]

Restoring Apostolic Visionary Leadership

In this chapter we have been concerned primarily with the source of vision. We wished to establish a comprehensive view of the dominant impulses which compel a persecuted people to take an unflinching stand on their rock of faith, when the creed to which they have confessed their allegiance is under fire from the combined power of state and church. Both Huguenot and Quaker movements have as their combustive element the union of Word and Spirit which inspires and motivates steadfast faith. Christ is the Word as performance in the sung liturgies, visions and sermons in the Church of the *désert*. Christ the Word within is prophetic and apocalyptic in the mouth of the early Quaker. In both movements, leadership is inspired by vision: dreams, inspirations and illuminations are granted by the Spirit and impel the resistance to conformity, mediocrity and faithlessness to the Lord. Leaders are men, women and children and fulfil, therefore, the prophecy in the Book of Joel: 'Then afterwards I will pour out my spirit on all flesh; your sons and your daughters shall prophesy, your old men shall dream dreams, and your young men shall see visions' (2:28). Testimonies, whether written or oral, arise from heartfelt personal encounter with Jesus Christ and the Holy Spirit and are often in a context of persecution and struggle.

We may ask how these insights relate to the question of *apostolic* visionary leadership. As we have discovered, the church of the Huguenots in the latter part of the seventeenth century is a church in perpetual flight. It is a church on the run from the authorities, fleeing to the desert places so that it may worship God according to the tradition of its founding fathers. This desert exile is not confined to France; *émigrés* find the freedom to worship in a diaspora as far afield as America and South Africa, as well as the British Isles and Europe. In this sense the entire Huguenot enterprise is an apostolic movement driven by visionary leaders. The marks of a confessing church, which has stood in the crucible and not buckled, are imprinted on this apostolic people. The vision is carried to the nations and influences trade, commerce, industry, church and mission. The genius of George Fox succeeds in galvanizing and organizing with purpose Meetings of Friends in his own country and across oceans, so that the Society has survived to the present day. The impact made by the Quaker Peace Testimony and the stand taken on civil rights issues remains a living witness. Quakers in business and commerce have left a legacy of good ethical practices.

2.

Prophetic Evangelists on Fire

> For I decided to know nothing among you except Jesus Christ, and him crucified. And I came to you in weakness and in fear and in much trembling. My speech and my proclamation were not with plausible words of wisdom, but with a demonstration of the Spirit and of power . . . (1 Cor. 2:2–4).

In light of the extreme views of both Huguenots and Quakers, an examination of evangelism in the power of the Holy Spirit is probably unlike most analyses of the topic. A brief checklist of what we might expect to find in these two movements includes the following shared characteristics: preaching is impromptu and reliant on the Spirit; the content of the message is a biblically based call to turn to God in an arena of the end times; the word which is believed is lived out so that the life of each believer is a testimony to Jesus; inspired preaching has little to say about the historic life of Christ, but much to say about the inner experience of Christ. A point of dissimilarity concerns the question of violence. The view that a Christian may participate in war or insurrection is shared by both groups, until the Quaker Peace Testimony gains a foothold and becomes a primary foundation stone of the movement.

Huguenot Evangelists: Prophecy in the Theatre of War

> But all of you are kindlers of fire,
> lighters of firebrands.
> Walk in the flame of your fire,
> And among the brands that you have kindled! (Isa. 50:11).

In our discussion of the theology of Pierre Jurieu, we highlighted an apocalyptic note, an undying optimism which fuelled the hopeful intercession of a people enslaved by the dictates of an imposed Catholicism – a belief system to which they were vehemently opposed. In our treatment of the idea of legitimate resistance in Calvinism, we understood the overtone of such a theory played out in context – a rightful duty to rebel against unjust religious rulers in the thought of the Camisard freedom fighters. Intertwined with these two strands of apocalyptic fervour and justified rebellion is a strand which we must now attempt to disentangle, the vexed question of prophecy in the Huguenot resistance. We may state the dilemma thus: prophetic utterance is a canopy over a clandestine community and a shelter in the storm, a voice for the voiceless, an inspiration for the afflicted, a guide through tribulation, a light in the darkness and a signpost to deliverance, but it is also a justification for war. The power of prophecy to overturn an existing order and instigate permanent change, for good or evil, can be seen in the upheavals in south-eastern France. Our task is to investigate the problem and draw conclusions.

As we seek to chart the course of prophecy we cannot help be impressed, as the writer of *The History of the Edict of Nantes* (1695) appears to be, by the sheer numbers of the inspired, the child preachers. He writes: 'It is well known, that noise the shepherdess of Crêt, and a multitude of children of both sexes, who of a sudden became *preachers* [my italics] have made in Dauphiné and the Vivarais; how they, falling into a certain kind of ecstasy, said things represented to us altogether wonderful.' Prophets not only speak awe-inspiringly, but they do so as preachers of the gospel. Prophets can be evangelists who declare the message of Christ in a prophetical way. These numbers of faithful souls – men and women, girls and boys – prophesied faithfully, and accurately, suffering imprisonment or death for their witness.[1]

The reactions of critics at the time to the French prophesying will be discussed under the topic of discernment at the end of the chapter. Present-day scholarship, particularly that which concerns the Camisard War, tends to a contemporary understanding of apocalyptic texts, divine vengeance and the liberty of conscience. French historians agree on the question of apocalyptic influence. Philippe Joutard pinpoints an apocalyptic outlook which is more predominant in Languedoc than in the Cévennes. Emmanuel Le Roy Ladurie perceives an apocalyptic overtone characterized by convulsive and prophetic hysteria: economic crises as punishment for the Revocation, judgement in the swallowing up of the king's armies, light on the Catholics and the arising of a new people. An American historian, Hillel Schwartz argues for vehement opposition to the Camisard *inspirés* as a millennarian sect in England. A British Calvinist minister, Alan Clifford dismisses the spurious remedies for oppression as charismatic extremism. Moshe Sluhovsky, a teacher at the Hebrew University in Jerusalem, examines the Huguenots in the perceived connection of their possessing spirits, and in particular an exorcism which threatened the fragile peace between Catholic and Protestant. Clarke Garrett highlights the religious excitement spawned by the rivalry between the Catholic and Protestant religious systems, but refutes the idea that prophecy is the cause, as the entire region had been violent for decades and the government savagely repressive. He argues that in the aftermath of the many witchcraft cases throughout the seventeenth century it is not surprising that the Spirit-possessed in France were denounced, not as frauds, but as devil-possessed.[2]

To understand the high energy voltage in the topic of prophecy in France during the late 1600s, a brief sketch of the notions of devil possession, and the Convulsionary movement in the early modern period, is necessary. The idea of possession is understood to mean the entry of the Devil, or devils, to a greater or lesser degree, into a human body. The marks of a possessed person are clairvoyance, speaking languages previously unknown, and enormous physical strength exceeding the body's normal capacity. The attempt to make connections (or deny them) between epilepsy and supernaturally caused states of ecstasy has a long tradition. An apparent case of epilepsy, discovered by a famous French medical theorist, Jean Fernel, in 1548 to be an instance of possession, is used in many other cases from then on to demonstrate demonic possession. Conversely, others try to prove that epilepsy is not supernaturally caused. Fraudulent malpractice in anti- Huguenot propaganda is employed to con the masses. For example, a person speaking as a 'devil' pronounces as the truth the doctrines of the Immaculate Conception (Mary as sinless) or the Mass as the very flesh and bones of Christ (transubstantiation), and trounces as heretics Huguenots who will not believe these statements. For Calvinist Huguenots these papists perform a magical and idolatrous ceremony in the Mass.[3]

The Convulsionary movement has its origins in the first recorded instance of 'agitations' or 'convulsions' in 1731, following the death in Paris, in 1727, of a saintly deacon, François de Pâris. Aimée Pivert, already suffering from some kind of nervous disorder, is placed upon his tomb and experiences 'involuntary spasms or convulsions and amazing contortions of her limbs, almost, some claimed, as if she were possessed'. The agitations continue with the same intensity until she is cured, precipitating streams of worshippers who flock to the grave and witness numerous miraculous healings. These mass phenomena, engendering a sect of people in frenzied convulsions attributed to the inspiration of the Holy Spirit, through the intercession of M. Pâris, greatly alarm the authorities. More worrying is the fact that the Convulsionaries believe themselves to be the agents of a programme of social regeneration and spiritual revival. And more troublesome still is their attempt to comply with this divine mission, by directing into Paris, after January 1732, waves of millennial and revivalist religious fervour – anathema to the institutional church. Kreiser argues that this is an example of the close link between religion and politics in the structures of the *ancien régime*. The upheavals in the Cévennes are another clear example. Groups of anti-'illuminist' critics, disturbed by religious enthusiasm of any sort, oppose the violence of the 'pentecostal' ecstasies. Their denunciations turn on the perception that the *oeuvre des convulsions* are signs of *illuminisme*, of the visionary fanaticism which had characterized the Camisards in the Cévennes.[4]

Testing the spirits in Calvin's light

There are two concepts in Calvin which we may utilize as good judges of prophecy. The first test is the trait of hypocrisy, which is pretending to be what one is not, a notion in Calvin's lectures on the Book of Daniel between June 1559 and April 1560. He directs his remarks to the persecuted French church: '[T]o all God's faithful servants who long for Christ's kingdom to be well ordered in France . . .' He is acutely conscious that their religion is driven out with 'threats, terrors, steel and flame', but is critical of those who are beset with a 'strange blindness' and others who 'refuse to have their passions bridled; and since hypocrisy occupies the sense of all, they love the darkness and fear to be brought into the light'. His commentary on Daniel 4:27 explains that true righteousness is known by its external witness, and that hypocrites are those who believe that they serve God with many ceremonies, but do not live rightly with their neighbour. Love, and not pretence, therefore, is the touchstone for righteousness. Hand in hand with right behaviour is a habit of restraint. Calvin's commentary on the judgement upon the Ammonites in 2 Samuel 10, is revealing in light of his views on legitimate resistance: '[W]e see that this people, who could have lived peaceably, started a war by their recklessness and presumption . . . Hence, let us be careful to attempt nothing which is illegitimate. For we shall suddenly have to pay a painful price afterwards.' He pursues his point emphatically: '[L]et us keep from being reckless, and whenever we are tempted to undertake drastic action, let us immediately beat down the temptation.'[5]

The second test in Calvin is the discernment of spirits (1 John 4:1). In the *Institutes* he remonstrates with fanatics who, like the lawless sect of the Libertines, are carried away by frenzy. These fanatics are 'swollen with pride': disobedience, hypocrisy, idolatry and superstition. He implores them to recognize the Holy Spirit, who may be 'discerned by a most certain mark', and to remember that Satan masquerades as an angel of light (2 Cor. 11:14). He condemns any other spirit which 'foists another doctrine upon us', judging that it 'justly deserves to be suspected of vanity and lying [Gal. 1:6–9]'.[6]

Testing the spirits in Wesley's light

John Wesley (1703–91), the founder of the Methodist Movement and a revivalist of the eighteenth century, is a good guide to our period, being himself spiritually awakened in a new birth and conversant with the French prophets in England. Not only highly educated, he is also well rounded, appealing to Scripture, reason, the Church Fathers and experience in doctrinal matters.

He refutes the accusation of his critics that his spirituality 'rests only on ecstasies', denying that he has ever had any such ecstasy, and judging his 'spiritual estate' by two conjoint factors – the progress of his heart and his life. In relation to experience, his position rests on two premises: a differentiation between divine inspiration and 'enthusiasm', i.e. false or imaginary inspiration, and an acceptance that not all experiences are out of order simply because some experiences are untrustworthy. His standpoint on enthusiasts is that, believing they are inspired by God, they think they can 'attain the end without the means' – a short cut to true spirituality without the proper divine help. This 'false, imaginary inspiration is enthusiasm' as it 'contradicts the Law and the Testimony'. Wesley's *only* legitimate test for experience is that it must conform to the testimonies, both of Scripture, and of awakened Christians who have passed through the new birth, i.e. it must be related to the ultimate manifestation of the divine law, the receipt of the Holy Spirit in the individual soul. Of the testimony of Scripture he writes: 'It is easily discerned that these two little words – I mean faith and salvation – include the substance of all the Bible, the marrow, as it were, of the whole Scripture.' The testimony of an awakened conscience is described thus: 'But everyone must follow the dictates of his own conscience in simplicity and godly sincerity [2 Cor. 1:12]. He must be fully persuaded in his own mind [Rom. 14:5], and then act according to the best light he has . . . every man must judge for himself, as every man must give an account of himself to God [Rom. 14:12].' Wesley fixes on knowledge of communion with God as a gauge for the soul's happiness, insisting that it is 'in the testimony of his Spirit that all our works please him; and, lastly, in the testimony of our own spirit that "in simplicity and godly sincerity we have had our conversation in the world" [2 Cor. 1:12]'.[7]

Wesley applies his test on meeting a convert in June 1739 whose progress is hindered by French prophets: 'I endeavoured to point them out; and earnestly exhorted all that followed after holiness to avoid, as fire, all who do not speak according to the Law and Testimony.' His nervousness is apparent in a purposeful meeting that same year between a French prophet, a young woman, and Wesley, 'To try the spirits, whether they be of God.' He observes convulsive motions in every part of the woman's body, which might be 'either hysterical or artificial'; he hears words from Scripture, spoken in the person of God about the imminent coming of Christ, which could be spoken by anyone well versed in the Bible. He judges that the French prophets have no validity in themselves, and yet they may be from God: 'But I let the matter alone; knowing this, that "if it be not of God, it will come to nought [Acts 5:38–39]".' Garrett's conclusion is that for Wesley the distinction between authentic sacred theatre and its feigned or satanic counterfeit depended on the occasion. If God chose to show his power in these ways, then so be it.[8]

Ecstatic preachers

For the concept of trance or ecstasy we pass to the tradition enunciated by the Franciscan theologian, Bonaventure (1217–74). His sentence in *Soliloquia* 2.2, no. 12 goes to the heart of Christian mysticism: 'O soul, I would say that you exist more truly where you love than where you live.' By this he means that while we are at home in the body we are sojourning away from the Lord, but when the soul of Paul, for example, 'sojourns away from the body' i.e. in ecstasy, he is present with the Lord (2 Cor. 5:8). The phrase 'sojourns away from the body', is a translation of *peregrinari a corpore*, 'to sojourn abroad' (Latin Vulgate), and *ekdemeo*, 'to go abroad, to emigrate, to live abroad' (Greek text). The way of the mystic in Bonaventure provides a framework in which we may try to grasp the trances and ecstasies of the French *inspirés*. In the tribulations of their persecuted souls they may well have asked with him, 'How shall a man be able to live a life of heaven on this earth, in this *vale of tears*?' And as a means of overcoming their trials they may well have answered with him, 'If you see and love the things of heaven, how could you fail to live there, for in your daily life you resemble the heavenly spirits.'[9]

The rather fanciful notion of prophesying while asleep may be illumined, to some degree, by Calvin's thoughts on sleep. He argues that it is by the spirit (by this he understands the soul or intelligence) that we grasp and conceive the invisible God, and not by means of the body or bodily senses. In the state of sleep the body is at rest but the wakeful spirit is capable of intimations of divine forecasts: 'Therefore the spirit must be the seat of this intelligence. Indeed, sleep itself, which benumbs man, seeming even to deprive him of life, is no obscure witness of immortality, since it suggests not only thoughts of things that have never happened, but also presentiments of the future.' For Calvin, if the quest for the immortal is in every human being, then even our sleep patterns are touched. He substantiates his view by citing the Roman poet Ovid (43 BC–AD 17/18): '[W]hile all other living things being bent over look earthward, man has been given a face uplifted, bidden to gaze heavenward and to raise his countenance to the stars.'[10]

For our purpose in this study of prophesying, the point to be noted is that contact with the divine leaves some effect on the body, which may be called an altered state of consciousness, and it is at that precise moment of change in the *inspiré* that those watching, and those experiencing, both certify the ecstasy to be genuine. As opposed to those who object that 'the preparatory agitations of the bodies of the people of the Cévennes, may be imitated; from which they conclude that they are the effects of imposture', Elias Marion, one of the Camisard commanders, insists that they are 'the sure tokens of the presence of the Spirit of prophecy, in any sincere person'.[11]

Although the physical manifestations associated with the outbreak of prophecy in the Dauphiné do not assume different aspects from the prophesyings experienced in the Cévennes, there are two distinct periods of prophetic activity related to these two geographical areas. The first signs occur in the Dauphiné after the Revocation in 1685, between 1688 and 1689, spreading thereafter to Vivarais and Velay. It is not until 1700 that prophesying appears in the Cévennes, heralding a second season – and a Holy War. The first phase is a time of repentance and consolation; entire villages turn back to God in penitential prayer in response to prophetic words of comfort. In the second interval after 1700, prophecy is a catalyst for drastic action; a wide orbit of dispersed communities in the Cévennes is startled into taking up arms in response to the immediacy of prophetic utterance. It could be argued that a fifteen-year span gives birth to the children of a new generation of *inspirés* in the Cévennes, not all of whom speak and act in the purity of the first wave in the Dauphiné; to this we shall now turn.[12]

Our anonymous writer of the *History of the Edict of Nantes* is fascinated by the ecstasies of a little Huguenot prophet, the 15-year-old

Isabeau Vincent, 'the shepherdess of Crêt', who lives with her uncle in the Dauphiné, her father having recanted to Catholicism. Trance-like or asleep she preaches messages of repentance urging apostates back to the true Protestant creed. Unsurprisingly, she is physically apprehended by the authorities after four months and secured safely in a Catholic convent, but not before many young people have followed her example.[13]

After extensive examination, so as to be sure of his facts, Pierre Jurieu publishes his reflections on the miracle of the Dauphiné shepherdess. He dates Vincent's first ecstasy to 12 February 1688: duration several hours, diagnosis apoplexy or natural lethargy, no violent motions, health unimpaired. On the second night she falls into 'a kind of a profound sleep, out of which it was not possible to fetch her', despite pulling, thrusting, calling, pricking and pinching. She is in 'an entire and absolute privation of all sense; which is the true character of an ecstasy'. In this elevated state she utters 'many excellent and divine matters' in a clear and intelligible voice, her expressions 'very vigorous and touching', her motions 'graceful and well-ordered gestures'. She awakens, emerges from her ecstasy and returns to her natural, ignorant state of being: a poor, uneducated girl, whose 'instruction hath been wholly neglected'. Medical examination shows neither sickness nor bodily infirmity. After speaking for three to five hours she is not fatigued, and remembers nothing of her speeches. Jurieu does detect, however, a subtle change, an adaptation to her 'congregation' after five weeks of prolonged preaching. To that point she always speaks in her own 'vulgar' language (*langue d'oc*) for the benefit of her hearers – her provincial countrymen. On the arrival of curious visitors from the north she speaks in the correct dialect of a Parisian (*langue d'oil*) – a language she does not know, O miracle of miracles!

Jurieu notices that her discourse is unusually dissimilar to the preachers of the day: '[I]n a manner very singular, and always full of good sense; and it being out of the ordinary rules of method, it gives the greater character of divinity to what she saith.' The substance of her talks is the biblical text, from which source she refutes the papal controversies, quoting parts of the Mass in Latin. Jurieu takes note of her addresses to the converters to Catholicism, the 'merchants' and 'truckers for souls', who have changed their religion and sold their souls for money. Even her father is moved to confess his renunciation of Protestantism. Her relatives marvel at 'something in her that even sparkles', which seems to increase at her capture, transportation to Grenoble and examination in Crêt. She endures interrogation for fifteen days with shaven head, stripped of clothing (a search for charms), and exorcisms by priests. Her ecstasies persist in prison and she preaches from her room at the very top of the prison so that all the street can hear.

The ecstatic prophecies of Isabeau Vincent are delivered on the eve of the judgement day predicted by Pierre Jurieu, April 1689 – the promised divine intervention for Protestants. Her words nourish millennial hope in the people of Languedoc. Jurieu, however, along with other wise men in the country, will not discuss these prophecies, except to say that they promise the church 'a very sudden deliverance'. He does, however, offer a defence of ecstasy, logging it as one of those supernatural 'accidents', or miracles, which confound the laws of nature. The thought of his day posits a God who is in the *machine* of nature and in its laws. Jurieu rebuts this proposition, countering the argument of an unmoved God by asserting that God 'in the most part of his actions, hides himself (as it were) behind his creatures', but also '*acts* both in his creatures, and by his creatures' [my emphasis]. God is the 'soul of the whole machine, that it cannot advance one line without him'. Thus 'accidents' occur when God breaks his own laws and 'comes in freely, and by a special dispensation'. By this supposition we are to understand that God is the agent of these rather wonderfully whacky manifestations and outpourings of Isabeau Vincent, which arguably produce spiritual growth in the kingdom of heaven, as well as being numerically advantageous for the Huguenot cause.[14]

As we focus on the second prophetic wave we observe that in the Cévennes the outbreaks of prophesying are marked by the same phenomena as those in the earlier period, but are the very warp and woof of the Camisard War and at the heart of its guerrilla rationale and strategy. Ragged armies of peasant soldiers are led by inspired bands of prophets, in utter complicity with the local populations of the desert regions, who feed, shelter, guard and protect their interests from the ever-watchful dragoon troops.

Public ecstatic preachers

Jean Cavalier, chief commander of the Camisard army, testifies to the very public ecstasy of a pious soldier, Compan, who is called upon to administer communion on the Lord's Day to his troop gathered in a wood. As the oral tradition is a key to inspiring the faith of the Church of the *désert* we have another, livelier account of the story, handed down by Compan to his friend, Matthew Boissier, who in turn tells it to the London tribunal. Compan, encircled by the soldiers, is caught up in a terrifying visionary trance, in which he sees the flames of the bottomless pit. In his ecstasy he enacts the fierce battle to draw near to God, his body flung backward physically towards the fires 'more than forty feet', and tempted by an 'awful voice which debarred him the gate of heaven, by upbraiding his unworthiness'. Undeterred, he arises in the confidence of God's mercy and valiantly arrives at the door of heaven, signifying to the assembly that he sees 'armies of angels attending the throne of God, and myriads of glorified saints clothed in white, singing forth anthems of praise and adoration. He himself, in sympathy with them, sung [sic] sweetly' – the troop witnesses this with delight. The utterly enlivened Compan then preaches for two hours 'under the dictates of the same Spirit'.[15]

In his deposition, Compan himself describes the vision of the gate of heaven, certain words of which hint at the ongoing drama, which is the theatre of the Cévennes. In recalling his ecstasy he speaks of 'the sacred scene of this vision', and by so doing points to spiritual enactment in a public arena in which God, as the principal lead, declares the magnitude of his greatness. This sense of a wide open vista is captured, in a less passionate comment, by a critic reflecting on the inspired visionaries: 'They said, they saw the heavens open, the angels, paradise, and hell.' The same writer is impressed at the scale of these divine dramas: audiences number four or five hundred in the smallest assemblies, three or four thousand in the greatest. Before daybreak and from every hamlet they come hurrying to the assembly, women, men, children, even babies, 'pierced through the woods, leaped over the rocks, and flew to the place of appointment', as though to some giant amphitheatre. In the earthly auditorium the prophet has centre stage; having been 'under agitations of body for a while, he began to preach and to prophesy', proclaiming that it is 'the Holy Ghost that speaks to you though my mouth'. Elias Marion asserts categorically that a 'foreign and superior power makes me speak'. He supports the belief in the direct speech of the Holy Spirit, who himself forms words in the prophet's mouth, accompanied by agitations, or motions, and with a great constraint (see Mark 13:11).[16]

Mme M.R. of Montpellier has the account from a near kinsman, an eyewitness to the healing miracle of two young Camisard soldiers, in the full glare of the watching public. They are condemned to the wheel, all their limbs are broken, and then they are cast into a fire near the scaffold. Notwithstanding the flames they walk away healed. Soldiers with bayonets pull them back into the fire, where 'with praises and adorations, they breathed out their souls to God'. Even M. Basville, the Intendant (steward or quartermaster), moved perhaps by this public display of God's grace, reproves the soldiers for their merciless action. This dramatic sign of God's intervention may be recounted a hundred times over in the history of the Church of the *désert*, but one example of his protection in a landscape of repression stands out vividly.[17]

The trial by fire at Sérignan is an apocalyptic event, demonstrating the nearness of God to the persecuted. The fact of its verification in a deposition, by an important person like Jean Cavalier, adds to its significance. The location could be the tile kilns or woodlands in the vicinity of Cannes, a theatre for inspired prophets to preach, not only in words, but also in prophetic signs. In the face of the gathered assembly of 600 soldiers and several hundred others, one of the company falls into an ecstasy and pronounces there to be a traitor (presumably a Catholic spy) in their midst. They close ranks, encircling two men on their knees, convicted and terrified out of their wits, crying for mercy. While their fate is being decided, the same *inspiré* proclaims a trial by fire to show that God is present in judgement and protection. Wood is collected – dry pine branches, thorny shrubs and woody stems – and a fire prepared in a ritual space for a prophetic statement, a collective rite of purification, the cleansing of the Protestant soul from Catholic burning of their temples. Wearing only his *camisole blanche*, the white shirt made of incendiary linen or cotton fabric, the *inspiré* steps into the flames, five to six feet above his head, making pronouncements. He is still in a state of ecstasy when he walks away from the fire without a singe mark. This is prophetic preaching as a public spectacle.[18]

At this point in the discussion it would be easy to concur with the writer of the *History of the Edict of Nantes*: 'I am not very credulous of things of that nature, but rather inclined to mistrust the relations of what is uncommon and supernatural.' He admits that the spirit of his age (the seventeenth century) is quite different from the Jews of antiquity, who received everything from God who 'moves, as it were with his own finger, the agent-wheels of this world', and that we should permit ourselves 'to suspend the judgment awhile', until we have further information and 'sufficient light' on these matters. Illumination may be granted as we apply the schema of 'Allegoric Divinations', the handmaid to prophecy, expounded in a pamphlet of 1702. The writer sets out three types of prophetic phenomena: apparition, vision and dream. An example of the first two may be identified in the narrative on public prophetic preaching outlined above, and the third addressed in the topic of deluded prophecy.[19]

First, that God ruled Israel by apparitions, viz. angels and prophets – particularly those with second sight who live in 'deserts, and places and states forlorn'. Apparitions are public and include judgements and miracles. We see these characteristics in the preacher prophets ruling the desert assemblies, in the miracle of healing broken limbs, in the judgement on spies through the second sight of an *inspiré*, and in the throngs of angels in the skies. Secondly, vision is public and for the satisfaction of God's public will. Compan's visionary ecstasy overwhelms the troops with a sense of something beyond the natural, lifting their eyes to that which is supernatural and clearly of God. Thirdly, dreams are given privately and for private information, but concern things public. An example of this type is the biblical dream in the narrative of two different men named Joseph: a prisoner has a dream interpretation which saves Egypt from famine (Gen. 41); a husband dreams of Egypt, which saves the child Jesus for the salvation of all (Matt. 2). We shall consider the dream as we reflect on prophetic direction in a state of war.

Up to this point our discussion has revealed that although prophecy is unusual in its *essence* – inspiration, direction, challenge and confrontation – it has not led to *actions* that are contrary to the character of God. The situation alters as we address the topic of prophetic utterance and violent acts between 1701 and 1704 in Languedoc and the Cévennes

Deluded ecstatic preachers

There are several flashpoints for the Camisard insurrection. In 1701, *fanatiques* in prison number 350 and those condemned to slavery in the galleys number 40. Against this backdrop the first incitement to violence against Catholics in the same year is in the village of Vallérargues, where a week-long prayer meeting for the Holy Spirit troubles the authorities, leading local priests to carry out investigations, only to find groups of people listening to prophets. When the priests attempt to arrest the village notary on the charge of possession, the crowd becomes actively hostile and pelts the priests with stones. Led by the notary they attack the church, break the altar and crucifix and throw the vessels of the Mass into a sewer. They enter the prior's house and destroy statues and books. At this point the violence is against the physical forms of Catholic worship. The rituals of anti-iconoclasm are signs of destruction against all vestiges of Catholicism in the villages.[20]

The second critical breaking point is a dream by an *inspiré*, Abraham Mazel. In his deposition, he testifies that before he received 'positive and repeated commands from the Spirit, to take up arms', he dreamed of very fat black oxen browsing upon the plants in a garden. He is instructed to drive them out but chooses to ignore the directive until a second urgent command propels him into action. Next he receives an 'inspiration', which appears to be an interpretation of the dream: the garden is an emblem for the church and the oxen are symbols of the priests who lay the garden to waste. A few days later the Spirit gives him another public 'inspiration' (the second urgent command), which appears to be advance notice to prepare to take up arms in the cause of the Lord. He claims that others present in the public assembly confirm, in like manner, these protestations. He declares that being very loud in his ecstasies he gives offence to some, while others lift their eyes in admiration to heaven. In his deposition Mazel stresses that these repeated warnings are only general, by which he must mean that no exact detail for their application has been given. On 21 July 1702, as the company meets for worship near the mountains of Lausere, he is taken with violent agitations and is commanded to undertake a rescue operation, to take up arms to deliver fellow Huguenots held in prison in Pont-de-Montevert.[21]

Thus it arises that on 24 July 1702 the Archpriest and Inspector of Missions, Abbé du Chayla, who had oppressed the miscreants of Protestantism in that town for fifteen years, faces the fury of a crowd of sixty peasants wearing linen blouses and carrying ancient muskets, axes, scythes and knives. As they march in military step they chant a metrical version of Psalm 74, 'O God, why have you cast us off forever? Why does your anger smoke against the sheep of your pasture?' The priest's house is set on fire and he is killed; the peasant band kneels around the murdered man singing psalms. The next day, following divine orders, they kill the curé of Frugières and destroy the images and altars of the Catholic Church in the town. This incident sparks a full-scale rebellion, which spreads from Lower Languedoc to the Cévennes. Violent deeds are justified by religious explanations. For Huguenots schooled in apocalyptic imagery, the Catholic Church is Babylon, the mother of whoredom and the archenemy of true faith. Thus the only rationale for the brutal death of Abbé La Pize, prior of Saint-Martin-de-Bobaux, is that he remains in the Babylon church. In 1702 he is visited by a band of Camisards, who fell him with three musket shots in the stomach and kill him with swords.[22]

Bloodshed and apocalyptic warning and promise go hand in hand. A Camisard soldier, with face disfigured, is found dead. He is a *prédicant*, in whose pocket is discovered the text of a sermon which proclaims that in the year 1705 Louis XIV and all France will rally to Protestantism and beg forgiveness of Huguenots – but only after a bloodbath. However, after a decisive defeat in 1704 under Jean Cavalier, most of the Camisards had surrendered by 1705. The Holy Spirit seemed to have stopped speaking and many prophets went into exile. Sporadic outbursts of insurgency characterized the decade until 1710 and an eventual peace in 1715. The message and methods of the remnant prophetic community in England remained unchanged from 1715. Isaac Hollis, the French

Prophet whom John Wesley was to encounter a few years later, stated that 'they expect such a dispensation from God, that all the *gifts* of the primitive times should be restored, as working miracles, prophecy, healing the sick, raising the dead'. The convulsions and gasping that had stirred up Cévennes audiences were considered bizarre in Switzerland and prophetic *émigrés* were absorbed into the Huguenot exile communities, nothing more being heard of them.[23]

Accomplishment of prophecies

Pierre Du Moulin (1568–1658), a Protestant minister in Paris, summarizes the view of prophetic 'accomplishment', which is contemporaneous with his times. In the preface to the volume he reminds the reader that it is one thing to prophesy and quite another to speak of the fulfilling of prophecies. On the one hand revelation is inspired from above, but on the other hand fulfilment is experienced through memory and an insight into the times. His view is that the accomplishment of prophecies lies in history because the predictions given are confirmed by later events. Du Moulin's rule is that to predict successfully the accomplishment of two out of ten prophecies before the event is better than to predict ten after the event. We see this principle strikingly at work in many of the deposition texts. The difficult factor to reconcile with our twenty-first century mindset, sanitized by our political correctness, is that each of these predictions is intended for the protection, guidance and warning of Huguenots at war, a war which, arguably, they had started.[24]

The embarkation of the fleet is disrupted, but not stopped, by a tempest predicted by Jean Cavalier. He foretold that no one would be lost, and it was so. The same Jean Cavalier is seen and heard by a witness to be 'under the like inspiration. To my knowledge, those under inspiration, who were in arms with me, gave frequent directions for our conduct, in the affairs of war.' Warnings of spies and encroaching dangers in battle are frequent. A young man tells his mother or sisters, 'I say to thee, my child, speak no more at present', warning them of some dangerous person coming to the house, and it was always so. A witness tells of two sons and three daughters of a neighbour who go to worship. Three are massacred in the assembly, and the survivors testify that they were forewarned of their deaths while in a state of inspiration. In Anduze a poor girl of 14 or 15 is serving her mistress in her chamber when she is taken with convulsions. She speaks out clearly, but with hesitant trembling, in French, which is against the custom, given her rank and age. She tells her mistress: 'My child, my child, I acquaint thee, thy brethren at this moment are engaged with the enemy; but I fight for them; be not troubled; I assure thee the enemy shall be beaten.' Two or three hours later the news arrives that the Camisards had routed a detachment of the king's troops about six miles away. When the girl 'came to herself' she was unable when asked to repeat what she had just spoken.[25]

Fulfilment of prophecies

The sound of the trumpet blast from Zion to announce the day of the Lord's vindication is the clarion call of the Church of the *désert*. Bolstered by the biblical passage, Joel 2:28,29, armies of children are the vanguard of the genderless prophetic move of the Spirit of God:

> Then afterwards
> I will pour out my spirit on all flesh;
> your sons and your daughters shall prophesy,
> your old men shall dream dreams,
> and your young men shall see visions.
> Even on the male and female slaves,
> in those days, I will pour out my spirit.

The words and deeds of children are a witness to the evangelistic import of the prophesying. Each of the following examples is a cameo of some aspect of the gospel message. The gospel transcends all barriers of age and gender: James Brisson of Brignon swears that he 'saw and heard, at several times, a great number of inspired persons, of every age and sex', claiming a number nearer to 'four hundred'. The message of the gospel defies physical hurdles – gravity in this case – and is a revolutionary call to repentance among the Huguenot youth. The teenager, John Vernett, witnesses his friend, James Reboux, an *inspiré* with the agitations, sitting upon a rock with others and falling some seven or eight feet down to a road. He is unharmed, although his agitations continue violently in all parts of his body. Brandy cannot revive him and when he stops shaking he speaks powerfully, in a way which moves them and calls them to repentance.

The recurring theme of repentance, even in the mouths of babes and sucklings, takes the prophecy from Joel to an extreme. A witness alleges that at his entrance into the room, a baby of fourteen months, never having spoken, suddenly speaks up distinctly in French, in a small child's voice but loud enough for the twenty gathered in the room to hear. It is an exhortation to repent. Children of 5 and 7 have the gift of inspiration, fulfilling the prediction of Jesus that out of the mouths of 'infants and nursing babies' praise of God has been prepared (Matt. 21:16). It is also a fulfilment of the prophecy that 'a little child shall lead them' (Isa. 11:6). The Holy Spirit produces changed lives, as John Cabanel of Anduze attests: those who receive the gifts of inspiration immediately forsake lewdness and frivolity to lead sober, pious and exemplary lives. Some of the inspired are successful at reconciling neighbours previously estranged. A young *inspiré* not only moves the company to tears with his impassioned plea for repentance, but also exhorts them to pray without ceasing. Clearly the Church of the *désert* is the locus for an outpouring of the Spirit en masse to empower the small and insignificant to proclaim the gospel.[26]

Discernment of prophecies

John Quick (1636–1706), the English Nonconformist divine, has a sympathetic view of the Camisard violence, noting that 'it was but impossible but that some persons transported with a blind zeal or by the motions of their natural choler which they could not always master, should break out into intemperate actions or expressions, especially when as they saw their nearest relations murdered before their very faces without any legal trial, only for serving God'. His remark, that the violence of murders and massacres 'made very many sober persons contrary to their former resolutions to grow impatient', is insightful but diametrically opposite to the Huguenot preacher, Claude Brousson (1647–98). Brousson, notes Quick in his biography, disapproves of these excitable and

feverish unrestrained outbursts of frenzied passion, which he calls
'transports', i.e. states of being carried away, or transported on the
strength of an emotion so that one is beside oneself. He implores
his brethren, who act in the 'spirit of fire, zeal and indignation', to
remember that the 'weapons of our warfare are spiritual' (2 Cor.
10:4), that the gospel shall be preached with a spirit of sweetness
and love, and with the sword of the Spirit, the Bible. Brousson
himself had acted for the defence of Protestants in Nîmes as
a lawyer, until his distress at the Revocation compelled him to
identify more closely with the resistance, and ejected him into a
ministry preaching to the Church of the *désert*. He was betrayed,
arrested, imprisoned in the Citadel at Montpellier and executed
on 4 November 1698—broken on the wheel.[27]

The Catholic critique is quite unforgiving of the Camisard
enterprise. Jean-Baptiste Louvreleul (b. 1660) condemns the operation as 'a hunting of savages', not a 'just war', and is unable to
write his volume, *The history of the rise and downfall of the Camisars*
(1709) as a militaristic account, as though 'opposite armies meet
in the field'. He traces the source of 'this fanatic rage' to William
du Serre, a Calvinist knave of Dieu-le-fit in Dauphiné, whom he
accuses of managing the first school of fanaticism in France by
gathering a 'parcel of boys and girls', indoctrinating them with
anti-papist propaganda and millennial prediction and instructing
them in the ways of pretended ecstatic agitations and convulsions.
He purports that the exiled Pierre Jurieu infected their enthusiasm and controlled the content of the prophecies from Geneva.
Instead of these 'wild notions' he asserts that 'The dove is a mild
and peaceable bird; such is the church of Jesus Christ which being
animated with the Spirit of God is all sweetness and goodness'.
David-Augustin de Brueys (1640–1723), the Catholic author of
the tome, *The History of Fanaticism in our Times*, regales his readers
with the enthusiasm of this crazed 'sect', which 'spread itself, like
a flood, with such a torrent, that a conflagration blown with a
wind does not spread faster from house to house, than this fury
flew from parish to parish'. Words and phrases such as 'idiots' and
'people as savage almost as the half-brutes of America' sum up his
verdict of this prophesying madness. His version of a Dauphiné
sausage machine manufacturing little prophets between June
1688 and February 1689 concurs rather too readily with that of

Louvreleul: 'They struck themselves with the hand, they fell on their backs, they shut their eyes, they heaved with the breast, they remained a while in trances, and coming out of them with twitchings, they uttered all that came into their mouths' – spoken curses against priests, the pope, the church, blasphemies against the Mass, predictions of the fall of popery.[28]

Having studied the ecstasies at close quarters, the English writer of the depositions *A Cry from the Desert*, John Lacy, has no wish to be subject to the peculiarities of these manifestations. However, on the very day he delivers the manuscript to the printers and while in a state of utter passivity, he himself is singularly taken by the agitations. He believes them to be generated by a 'superior agent'. For a week he is preoccupied in 'mental prayer and acts of resignation', until his tongue is involuntarily moved by a 'superior power', and he speaks in revelations.[29]

A treatise on true and false prophecy by four Protestant Frenchmen in 1707 is biased in favour of the authors' own countrymen, and, in particular, Elias Marion. The writers pontificate at length on the subject. True prophecy, which has more of the divine than the human in it, enlightens the prophet 'as by the glimmering of lightning', and helps to see in a flash. False prophecy is beset as if with rage and distracted madness, like many a modern prophet who is 'sick of a violent distemper out of his senses'. None of these observations apply to M. Marion, 'for I know of a certainty', testifies John Daudé under oath, 'that it was truly the Spirit or angel of God that spoke . . . for the time he was possessed'. The consistory of the London Huguenot Church in the Savoy is overtly antagonistic to the movement, banishes *inspirés* from Holy Communion and accuses Elias Marion of publishing prophecies filled with blasphemy and sedition: 'a pseudo-prophet, an abominable, detestable and diabolic blasphemer, a disturber of the peace, heretic and imposter, publisher of false, scandalous and seditious libels'.[30]

Schwartz notes that contrariwise, Jeanne-Marie Bouvier de La Mothe, popularly known as Mme Guyon (1648–1717), the French Quietist, sees no need for new prophets in this last age and writes against the French Prophets, for 'their impetuosity, for speaking in God's person, and for mistaking external marks of inspiration for the simple, intimate peace of the Lord. The true "interior silence" never promoted bodily agitation, she explained, no matter how violent one's inner turmoil'. Mme Guyon herself is under intense scrutiny, judgement and imprisonment for her radical views on the passivity of the soul, works condemned at the time by the Catholic Church. We see the turbulence of the age and the church's struggle to accept new modes of spirituality. Sluhovsky comments on the early modern period and the perceived danger in the new practices, 'namely, the triangular relations among God, lay uneducated believers (including all women), and the Devil'.[31]

Quaker Evangelists: Prophetic Publishers of Truth

> It is a mighty thing to be in the work of the ministry of the Lord God and to go forth in that. It is not as a customary preaching; but it is to bring people to the end of all outward preaching (George Fox).[32]

In Chapter 1, I suggested that the transition from the first to the second apostolic phase in early Quakerism is the result of a gradual settling down into established conventions of belief and practice. If we focus only on the reasons for this loss of spiritual momentum, and seek the significance of an evolutionary, progressive and acceptable refinement of Quakerism, it will be to the detriment of recovering what is essentially a movement of preaching for the conversion of souls. Therefore our task in the present chapter is to contemplate those first fiery Friends, drawing out the distinctive element of prophetic evangelism, and allowing the successful propagation of the gospel message to speak for itself.

If we are appalled by the antics of these early Quakers, which appear somewhat unseemly to our sophisticated milieu, we ought to remind ourselves of the superstitious fabric, the stuff of the early modern period. The Quaker enterprise was successful precisely because it awakened these fascinations. The prophecies of Nostradamus (1503–66), black and white magic, spell and incantations are all part and parcel of an otherwise sceptical and materialistic attitude. It was said that the English were wont to carry 'an old prophecy about with them in their pockets, which they can produce at pleasure to promote their designs'. A frank admiration for the mysterious and the magical, and a wide-awake pursuit of soothsaying and prediction to sway political outcomes, sets the seventeenth-century Englishman in a world apart from the pragmatic politicking of our contemporary era. Serious politicians like Oliver Cromwell consult astrologists. The political philosopher, Thomas Hobbes (1588–1679), declares that prophecy was 'many times the principal cause of the event foretold [the Civil War]'. John Selden, a jurist and lawyer, extols supernatural intervention in the various challenges of life: 'Dreams and prophecies do thus much good; they make a man go on with boldness and courage, upon a danger or a mistress; if he obtains, he attributes much to them; if he miscarries, he thinks no more of them.' Despite Protestant hostility to magic, Hill reminds us that the Reformation, by its abolition of mediators and its stress on individual conscience, had opened the door to a direct address by God to the elect, and stimulated the spirit of prophecy. The prophet as interpreter of the stars, popular myths or the Bible is the new profession in the revolutionary decades.[33]

Radicalized preachers

It is this atmosphere, charged with new thought and alive with seditious ideas, that our study must penetrate, to trace the preaching of the early Quakers and in particular George Fox. Is there anything especially different about his message? There is little a Puritan could object to in the simple piety of his words, and contemporary language, in the sects of the day is not dissimilar: inner experience, the light within, the perfection of the soul. And yet great crowds of seekers gather in hundreds to hang on his every word, irate priests grind their teeth at him and, to magistrates and justices of the peace, Fox is a rabble-rousing fiend. An explanation to this quandary appears to be in the combined effect of the word preached and the word acted upon, so that early Friends are not only hearers, but they are doers of the word (cf. James 1:22–25), and the Quaker witness is *both* to the Word, Christ within, *and* to the Spirit, the power for the intended action.

The first half of the explanation for the popularity of the Fox phenomenon, which is gauged by the unusually significant response to the glad tidings, is in the receptivity of the listeners, in the attentiveness of the multitudes to the utter conviction, in the messenger, of the truth of the revelation received (cf. 1 Thess.

1:5). Fox is a speaker sincerely persuaded of the truth he bears. We recall that the *Journal* points to 'the power of the Lord' over all and upon all, as the mighty strength of 'convincement', and never to George Fox. For Fox, the power of God is directly opposed to the empty form of religion, expressed by Paul as 'holding to the outward form of godliness but denying its power' (2 Tim. 3:5). He teaches that to be without true form is to go from the Light, from the Spirit and power of God, into confusion and emptiness. He is not disputing the fact that men and women of God have the 'form of sound words, the form of godliness'; it is form without power or a powerless form only that he decries: 'for they deny the power; and do not only so, but quench the Spirit, and grieve and vex it, and hate the light'. A spiritual pressure on the heart, however, is not the same as the flowering of overt illegal actions, stemming, as the authorities believe, from a preacher's incendiary words and inciting a swift response: trial and imprisonment.[34]

A second part of the answer to the rage incurred by the Fox followers, therefore, is in the inner 'leadings' of Friends into acts of defiance and civil disobedience which destabilize the status quo. Each Friend, with that which is of God resident in him or her, is believed to be prophetic, and the very life and bearing of each Friend is a testimony to Christ. Dressing in sackcloth at the high cross, quaking during a Catholic Mass or interrupting a service – each is a kind of spiritual 'prophetic' protest. Confrontation with authority figures of priest and magistrate in steeplehouse or court, refusal to pay the tithe, or anti-state publications are protests of a radical political ilk. These actions are the outward expression of Christ within.

After the fashion of street preachers and print propagandists, early Quaker preaching is flamboyantly rhetorical. Its edgy raw revivalism reverts to primitive Christianity and vocal inspiration. For Quakers the *charismata,* or gifts of the Spirit, are rightfully theirs, and permission to do church differently is given by the charismatic church of the New Testament. All who preach from God's power are true prophets, legitimate speakers of his word with no special learning. Troves of priceless treasure are stored in human jars of clay, and earthly vessels carry the word of the Lord. George Fox implores Friends to 'Take heed of hurting the gift' and quotes Scripture: '"These shall be as my mouth" [Deut.

18:18], saith the Lord, for his work is great, and his gifts diverse. And therefore all mind your gift, mind your measure; mind your calling and your work.' Higginson, a Friend contemporaneous with Fox, describes the preaching of a sermon as 'whatever comes into the mouth' (*quicquid in buccam venerit*). This impromptu preaching style, without prior intentional preparation at all, flings wide open the possibility of interventions by the prophetic Spirit. As every word spoken is perceived and received as the direct communication of the very voice of God, then all communication, in some sense, is prophetic. For this reason there is the injunction for careful consideration, so as to be spare in one's speech: 'let your words be few'. Quaker preachers must be *moved* to speak, a practice not customary in pulpit preaching of the day, ruled as it was by the prepared sermon based on biblical text, lectionary or church calendar.[35]

Rather unsurprisingly, we have only ten sermons extant before 1687, all by George Fox. Most importantly, preaching is a 'matchmaker' preparing the way for the Lord: the word of Christ is introduced to the listener and is then left to do its work, independent of human intervention. It is the inward Light of Christ that converts, not the preacher, who must speak from the Word's voice within – Christ come to teach his people. Quaker preaching puts a moratorium on all Puritan expressions of the Love of God, by its judgement on guilt and the gravity of immediate revelation. The same Christ, who previously was preached with objectivity and detachment, is now located within: God in Christ, experienced as speaking innerly, is the spiritual core of Quakerism.[36]

Domesticated preachers

As early as 1658, the stress is less on individual preaching and more on the corporate witness, as the responsibility for witness-bearing falls upon all Quakers. Thirty years later, by means of a gradual process of 'routinization', individual speaking is apt to be brought under the corporate control of the rules of a Society and an appeal to right reason. The delay of the Second Coming ushers in the expectation that Quakers will embody the kingdom of God on earth, as a new society. The hallmarks of this body of people will be stability and prosperity. Without a strong eschatological vision, or a vigorous belief in the imminence of Christ's coming again, prophetic preaching is emptied of its vital power. If Christ is fully revealed now, in the present age, then there is no real urgency for the propagation of the gospel. This is the start of a process which leads, somewhat inevitably, to a doctrine of universalism, i.e. that all shall be saved, which shall be discussed in Chapter 3.[37]

Discerning the Holy Spirit

The impetus for early Quaker evangelism is to convince those stuck in the 'dead forms . . . at ease and rest, as though they were in the true heaven', that they who are strangers to the way of life may become partakers of it with Friends, who having tasted 'the love, goodness, and power of God, dwell in the sense and feeling of his love and power'. These words of Richard Farnworth, a companion of Fox, bring us to the matter of distilling the exact nature of this power. Is it enough to categorize it only as a 'sense and feeling', when denying the power seems synonymous with quenching the Spirit? Isaac Penington is adamant that the Spirit will teach the believer to cry and mourn 'at length to speak to the Father for the preservation and nourishment of his life'. He distinguishes the human sighs of the flesh, the false fire, from the cries of the Spirit – the live coal, the fire from the altar purging lips and speech. We recollect the counsel of Fox to Friends to differentiate between the groans of the Holy Spirit and those of the flesh. And yet, as Phyllis Mack, an American historian argues, the early Quakers seem to have been emotive feelers. In the stillness engendered by an expectant waiting upon the Lord's visitation, inhibitions dissolve into tears, groans, staring and shaking. Feelings of endearment and loving tenderness are expressed in terms of fluidity: bowels yearn for God; I feel God in me; I smell his sweetness. These emotions are powerful passions of the soul and undoubtedly often inspired by the Spirit of God. Do they represent the power of which Fox speaks? The question must also be put as to whether Quaker vehemence, in the defiance of social convention, is authentically of, in and through the 'prophetic Spirit'.[38]

One answer lies in the understanding of the emotions, which for Quakers should be authentic and not stilted public ritual, as in the etiquette of bowing or kissing. The inner affection should be genuine and not crowd-pleasing, as in the oppressive practice of whipping or imprisonment. If the phenomena of involuntary quaking, shaking, partial paralysis and weeping are, in themselves, social comment, then we may conclude that the deliberate attempt to let go of pride and bodily control is a demonstration by that most public of social critics, the Holy Spirit, in order to counteract displays of false emotion in ritual. If this answer is not entirely satisfactory, it is because human emotion is not entirely trustworthy and not all physical manifestations can be called a response to the Holy Spirit. We turn to the person of the Holy Spirit in early Quakerism to ascertain the attributes which might characterize a visitation by the Third Person of the Trinity.

The doctrine of the Holy Spirit, recorded by George Fox in 1661, is orthodox New Testament teaching. The Spirit is the life-giver who quickens the soul, the strengthener for the battle against the flesh and the Devil, the sanctifier of the ministry and the fellowship. Fox describes the role of the Spirit in salvation as being above that of the Bible: one may possess 'all the Scriptures of the saints' but 'except a man be born of water and the Spirit, he cannot enter the kingdom' (cf. John 3:5, 5:39–40). No visionary sight is accorded anyone by virtue of his own spirit: 'in the first birth following his own spirit he sees nothing'. It is the Spirit of God who discerns the heart, to see those who serve God in a new spirit, and with spiritual weapons to discern error. These ones 'speak to one another with new tongues, and [are] filled with the Spirit of understanding'. Fox clearly links the Spirit to the testimony of Jesus in prayer and prophecy: '[And the Spirit makes intercession to God for them, in that they have profiting in their prayers, and the Spirit is the testimony of Jesus the Spirit of prophecy, by which they see what they are to pray for, and give the man understanding of the supplication.' And, finally, the Spirit is the discerner of unclean spirits which 'like frogs can creep in every hole, rock, and mountain' and 'are proved proud, heady, and high-minded, amongst the spirits of error'. An older Fox maintains the view as fervently as the younger Fox, that without the Spirit it is not possible to know the Lord or the Bible: '[A]ll must come to that Spirit, if they would know God, or Christ, or the Scriptures aright, which they that gave them forth were led and taught by.'[39]

This is an age of extremes: some sects ban the Bible altogether, others disallow all further reading except the Bible, still others warn against the letter of the Bible and aim for a spiritual sense alone. Does the pursuit of new lights allow the freedom to interpret Scripture in whichever way pleases the reader, without recourse to any other book or learning from the universities? We shall investigate these questions in Chapter 4. Suffice at present to note Fox's belief that, as Friends waited and listened diligently to his word in the Light of Christ, they received 'the pouring down of the Spirit upon us, and the gift of God's holy eternal Spirit as in the days of old, and our hearts were made glad, and our tongues loosed, and our mouths opened, and we spake with new tongues'.[40]

Robert Barclay shows plainly the view, evolved and concretized in the second phase of Quakerism, that as the Light is in everyone, God can save without Scripture. The Second Proposition of the *Apology* states unequivocally that not only are 'divine inward revelations' the means by which God manifests himself 'by the testimony of the Spirit', but they are the *only* way in which God can make himself known. The Third Proposition elaborates on the assumption that a saving illuminative word is implanted in all, 'a seed of the kingdom, this saving supernatural and sufficient word' (cf. James 1:21), with the propensity to 'grow up and redeem the soul'. Insofar as the redeeming work of the soul is concerned, the Spirit has primacy over Scripture as 'the first and principal leader', who is 'more originally and principally, the rule' and whose testimony is 'more excellent, than all reason'.[41]

Discerning the spirits of the prophets

In his remark on the New Testament principle that the Spirit of the prophets is subject to the prophets (1 Cor. 14:32), Isaac Penington gives a lead in defining the benchmark for Quaker discernment: 'Everyone feeling a measure of the Spirit in himself, is thereby taught to own and be subject to greater measure of the same Spirit in another.' By this we may understand the power of owning the gift of prophecy, not only as an individual, but also as a body or community of people. In the preferment of the voice of the Spirit in another, we see the operation of an unspoken rule among the early Friends, viz. the authority of the will of Christ as it depends on the wellspring of fellowship, and the reliance, therefore, on springs of life rather than on the authority of a tradition or a system. Early Quakerism is empowered and energized by that which is prophetically of Christ, so that the prophet or, for that matter, the entire Society of Friends lives with a seer-like vision, seeing into the true value of everything and acting on the impulse of that insight. Each individual is thus offered the opportunity to lead prophetically and, if appropriate, to take others along in the venture.[42]

In contrast to ownership of the gift of prophecy by all, the later settled phase of Quakerism brings a charismatic movement under control and, by 'the power of disownment', subordinates individual guidance *at all times* to the corporate sense of the church. The Society compresses and confines into a structure of accountability to elders the legitimacy of those ministers who previously were answerable only to the Spirit of God. Barclay's Tenth Proposition, the instructions to ministers, constitutes a radical departure from the mission of the early Quaker evangelists. Limits are placed on those teaching in the spheres of the world: a programme must be advanced with graded teaching; there are to be no rash or 'aggravated reflections' or 'prophesyings'; instead of unrestrained and intense publications there are to be schedules which rehearse rhetorical questions. In short, all is to be led by moderated diplomacy: peaceable and inoffensive.[43]

The appeal to 'churchy' behaviour, which is understated and reasonable, is a far cry from the rugged individualism and compassion of the founder of the Quakers. We recollect George Fox's quest for truth, the questions he puts to the leaders of churches throughout the country, and frustration at their insipid answers. We remember his lonely travail in prayer, his reading of Scripture and his wrestling with the demons within. We realize that, if at any time he had bowed in despondency to the lethargic spirit of these leaders, the Quaker vision would have aborted, but for the intensity of the spiritual wave on which he appears to have been carried. We recollect his divine 'openings', the result of his obedient submission to the Spirit of God, one of which, logged in a *Journal* entry in 1647, gives us a sense of the power of the Holy Spirit with which Fox is anointed. Even at this pivotal moment we surmise that Fox has a choice: to listen to reasonable caution in the voices of others, or to respond to the heavenly vision (cf. Acts 26:19).

A dying friend has 'great prophecies and sights' concerning Fox. For fourteen days after the burial of this man there is an anointing upon Fox, such that many thought him to have died. The *Journal* declares the reason for the consternation: 'For I was very much altered in countenance and person as if my body had been new moulded and changed.' It is during this spiritual sleep that Fox is granted a gift of discernment, whereby he sees plainly in which spirit people speak, i.e. from Satan or from God (1 Cor. 12:10). This discerning gift begins at once, in the vision itself, in which Fox sees the beauty of the Lord, gazes at the inexpressible 'greatness and infiniteness of the love of God' and peers 'into that which was without end'. But he is also acutely aware of the 'ocean of darkness and death' through which his temptations have driven him, and the 'eternal glorious power of Christ', through which he has been delivered. A futurist vision of fields 'white unto harvest' (cf. John 4:35) is granted the young man. His evangelistic heart is moved to tears by 'the seed of God lying thick in the ground, as ever did wheat that was sown outwardly, and none to gather it'.[44]

The ability to distinguish between spirits hones the preaching of the gospel to give Fox, as evangelist, a razor-sharp edge. Seven years after this extraordinary and life-transforming epiphany, he transcribes *A Word from the Lord, to all the World*, a somewhat grandiose title for a work, written to all professors in the world, which seeks to address the condition of Everyman. Fox passes on the illumination given him concerning the discerning ability of the Light. The Light is the professors' Teacher and helps them not to stumble. Fox prays that the Light will open their understanding to self-knowledge, to 'let you see yourselves, which eye is the light, and this light will let you see God' (cf. Matt. 6:22,23). For Fox the Light is within all people and he points a finger at false prophets, who deny the enlightening power of the Light to be in everyone. This sticking point in Fox is not without its paradoxes, as we see in a comment made a quarter of a century later. The Quaker writer of a pamphlet links the Light and the power of discernment, by declaring that those who ignore the guideline that the spirits of the prophets are subject to the prophets do so because they are devoid of light. Does the Light reside in a human being *in toto* or does it evolve, dispensing truth as it grows, and was it there in the first instance? These are questions to which we shall return in Chapter 3.[45]

Discerning flatterers and Friends

The company of Friends in the first generation keeps to the rules of discernment and wages war on any spirit found to be contrary to the purity of the Quaker way. The message preached must be undiluted and uncontaminated by any impure spirit of the age. Against a millennarian backdrop – an excitable anticipation of the closure of the epoch and the imminent end of the Pope – the indomitable Margaret Fell, 'Mother of Israel', plays a key role in her task as chief exhorter and admonisher. As they await *the* Day of the Lord in these days of testing, false teachers are on the rampage and Fell demands faithfulness from Friends. The 'Daughter of Sion' must 'keep to the true testimony of God in their own hearts, and to the true touchstone, that God has placed in them; and not believe every spirit, but try the spirits, whether they be of God [1 John 4:1]'. Fell prophesies against the clergy, pronouncing that the twisted words of the serpent, you 'shall be as gods' (Gen. 3:5), have now come to pass in its seed, which has inveigled itself 'into the highest dress; he is now got into the profession and words of truth itself'. For Margaret Fell and all the First Publishers of Truth, the doctrinal touchstone is to profess Christ the Light, his Spirit and his truth within. The spirit of Antichrist is in the form of the trappings of religion and is pretence. It knows only Christ without and does not have him within, in the experience of the heart.[46]

In a similar vein and in straightforward words of rebuke, Edward Burrough berates priests, prophets and teachers for their 'filthiness in preaching for hire, and for gifts, and for rewards, and in making a prey upon the people'. The Quaker tirade against falsity and flattery in religion has designs not only upon the state church or organized religion, but also upon teachers and sects who 'have the form of godliness but want the power'. The temper of Edward Burrough, in his epistles to Richard Cromwell Lord Protector (1658–59), is uncompromising, yet conciliatory. He advises the Protector not to persecute the sects as they will perish or fight against each other. He is completely confident that 'the good, old way, and truth, and the pure religion only will remain', by which he means the purity of the Quaker way. He warns the politician against the burden of 'wild raw flatterers' in sheep's clothing, who will use him for their own ends. His advice is to 'shake off such spirits from thee'.[47]

Prophecy in war and peace

In the first decade of their existence, Quakers are by no means pacifist and show a willingness to be associated with the use of violence. Many Quaker leaders in the early movement are ex-soldiers, having been enlisted in Cromwell's army. After their 'convincement', Friends organize petitions, sign up for military service and support the activities of the army, not finding this incompatible with their principles. When the political climate is more to their liking in 1659, some re-enlist in the army or submit suitable candidates for office in the militias.[48]

Edward Burrough is one of many like-minded political radicals in the 1650s. He assumes that Friends will serve parliament in the Civil War and not desist from political activity. In a letter to Oliver Cromwell, delivered into his hands at Hampton Court a month before his leader's death in 1658, Burrough speaks prophetically to the Protector about the double duty of the word of God. First, it will 'beat down the nature into which temptations enter . . . and it will bring thee to know a birth immortal born in thee'. This is the saving side to the word felt in the heart – a spiritual battle waged against the enmity of the flesh (cf. Rom. 7). Second the word will 'bring thee to war against and to overcome all thy enemies, which will defile thee or betray thee'. This is the saving side to the word felt in the world – a physical battle fought against individual people or nations, in this instance Spain. Burrough instructs Cromwell, who holds the honour of being 'the Lord's ploughman', to plough up the land of Spain and tread down their idol gods. It appears that to combat the idolatry in the Catholic Church is a service to God and merits the taking up of arms.[49]

The founder believes implicitly that the hand of the Lord is over all the nations to thwart evil. In a letter to a Friend, George Fox encourages his reader to feel that hand stretched out, 'for a mighty work hath the Lord to do in other nations', and predicts that 'their quakings and shakings is but entering'. Therefore the Quaker campaign to enlist Oliver Cromwell in the Lord's army is a sincere attempt to convince him of the prophetic power of the Lord God, whose hand is stretched out over *him*. The salutation in a letter from George Fox to Cromwell (the original copy delivered in November 1657) is quaintly endearing. He addresses him in the words, 'Oh! Oliver', and then proceeds to counsel him as a spiritual friend, dispensing prophetic insight into the political arena. Having stated his case that, if Cromwell had been faithful to God, then Holland, Germany, France and Turkey would have bowed to him, and Spain would have 'withered as in winter', Fox presses home his point. Cromwell must endeavour to be kept in the power of God and live in it, so that he will 'live over all, and stop and cross and tread under the intents of wicked men'. Clearly Fox is not advising Cromwell to be a passive leader, but monitors his spiritual health in order to steer him into successes in war. In a second letter, Fox is more explicit as he pleads for a united front in a religious war against the Pope. He wishes Cromwell to 'invite all them that profess against the Pope in all nations to join with thee against him, and . . . not lose thy dominion nor authority . . . and let thy soldiers go forth with a free willing heart, that thou may rock nations as a cradle'.[50]

By 1660, Quaker reaction to a changed political scene heralds a new direction in their philosophy of war. The failure of the army of 'God's Commonwealth', the Restoration of the monarchy and subsequent persecution of Quakers, together with the hostility of the outside world, are factors which combine to initiate a sea change: the principle that force is wrong. Correspondents with the king show the beginnings of the transition. In her letter to Charles II (1660), Anne Gilman demands to know what the Quakers have done, that at his command soldiers should come 'into our peaceable meetings in a warlike manner, as if some great enemies were to be conquered'. She defies the king to control their worship: '[W]e cannot bow to the imagination of men concerning the worship of our God.' In the persecution maelstrom of 1660, with 1,400 Quakers imprisoned in London and in county jails, George Fox writes to Charles II and his council. He is still the prophetic spokesperson of the Lord, reminding the king of his duty to give the sword to 'violent men without mercy, and compassion, and distinction', and to 'order the rude people'. But he defends the Quaker cause, stating that 'our principle is, and hath been, not to revenge ourselves'.[51]

The Declaration of 1660, signed by George Fox and eleven others, and given to the king on 21 November 1660 (January 1661 in the new calendar), is the first official declaration of pacifism in all circumstances and the beginning of an absolute refusal to accept civil or military office. It opens with the statement that 'Our principle is, and our practices have always been, to seek peace and ensue it, and to follow after righteousness and the knowledge of God.' As this principle pertains to war, the *Declaration* states: 'All bloody principles and practices, we, as to our own particulars, do utterly deny, with all outward wars and strife and fightings with outward weapons, for any end or under any pretence whatsoever. And this is our testimony to the world.' In a century committed to warfare, the *Declaration* is a witness of prophetic and far-reaching importance, whose rippling effects are felt in our own age.[52]

This remarkable testimony to peace has the consequence of the translation of warlike metaphors into the terminology of spiritual battle – demonstrated by the flurry of literature at the time. One example illustrates this predilection. Elizabeth Bathurst writes that as Quakers follow 'our leader, Christ Jesus, our captain and commander, so shall we become as a well-disciplined army, marching on in order, everyone keeping our ranks, and making war in righteousness with the prince and powers of darkness'. For Penington the battle is internalized: 'The fighting in the gospel is turned inward against the lusts, and not outward against the creatures.'[53]

Prophecy in speech and silence

Fox appears ambivalent in his instruction to submit to the higher power, as it is not clear whether that means God or the authorities. To resist earthly powers is to resist God. Ordinances of kings and governors are to be obeyed, unless they are contrary to the command of God. This has direct bearing on Quaker speech and silence, especially with respect to the swearing of oaths. The Quaker ownership of the religious freedoms – partly recognized as the choice to speak or not to speak – is a line drawn in the sand to distinguish a movement from a sect. Because Christ establishes the simplicity of a Christian's words, 'Let your word be "Yes, Yes" or "No, No"' (Matt. 5:34–37; cf. Jas. 5:12), the Quaker stand against complicated oath swearing is legitimated, although the penalty for civil disobedience stands firm. For refusing to swear the Oath of Allegiance, both George Fox and Margaret Fell are penalized with praemunire, i.e. the forfeiting of estates and imprisonment at the king's pleasure. To take the Oath of Allegiance (March 1659) is to 'declare in my conscience before God and the world, that our Sovereign Lord King Charles is lawful and rightful King of this realm', and to promise not 'to depose him or rulers in his lands, or raise an army'. The Quaker disengagement with the affairs of the world, on the grounds of allegiance to a higher power, marks out a boundary which smacks more of sectarian withdrawal than of prophecy. On the other hand, the intensity of direct speech in a meeting, where any Friend has permission to pronounce as the very voice of the Lord, is the dynamic of prophetic speech. As we have seen, the control of that liberty in the second period leads to speech and action which are far less threatening to the authorities than in the earlier period.[54]

It is a debatable point whether plain speech, as the defiance of social convention, is truly prophetic. As in the swearing of oaths, plain speaking is literalism taken to an extreme. For a Quaker, the act of bowing or curtseying, doffing the hat or using titles gives worldly honour and defers to worldly pride. They are empty gestures. The literal meaning of 'farewell' is to 'be well'. For a Quaker to greet a person with 'farewell' is to wish well also upon any evil intent. To call a person 'your humble servant', when one is not, is a lie. Renaming the days of the week, i.e. first day to seventh day, is a refusal to accept the idolatry of pagan gods, after which the days of the week are named. This blatant dissension from social norms and customs is a very public practice, taking place in the public eye and in the public domain. As we have seen, Friends are jailed for resistance to swearing oaths of allegiance; they are also imprisoned for defying the established conventions of politeness in salutations and greetings. These are part of the routine of daily life; 'plain speech' offends and is a thorn in the flesh.[55]

We turn to the prophetic action of silence, as a means of discerning issues of right and wrong, with reference to the work by George Keith in 1687, which purports to reflect on the first signs of this practice, continued to that day, and indeed to the present day in Meetings worldwide. It is the Lord who first taught the Quakers about silent meetings, directing them to gather, teach and pray 'in the light, wisdom, power and quickening Spirit of God'. Keith explains that the word is to be brought without mixture, by which he means it must have nothing of the speaker in it. The word is first to be rooted, tried and tested in the speaker: in order to have 'free passage in the mouth', it must first have 'command and dominion over the heart'. The mouth, 'as the instrument of word and Spirit of God', if under the control of the speaker, will 'reel and flagger in its expression, and be apt to speak the words of the wisdom and spirit of man than of God'. Under such a burden, early Quakers wait for the Lord to open their mouths. In some instances, as they wait in silence, one person is the vessel of 'an occasion of great refreshment' to the whole meeting. Keith exhorts the Friends not to stay away from Meetings, as strength and help is channelled through mutual support, one to another (Job 3:13; Zech. 2:13). The postscript is a copy of a letter written from Germany by Stephen Crisp to George Keith, pointing out the value of waiting in silence. Friends who savour the life within will come to feel 'daily quicknings thereby, and will have power over the nature that is dead in Adam to all good works, and especially to waiting upon God with a steadfast and stayed mind'.[56]

Prophecy in sign and sight

The core text for the concept of the sign in early Quakerism is Isaiah 8:18. Early Friends are called to be 'signs and portents' to their generation. In assessing the strange sensation of going naked as a sign, we come to the bizarre aspect of the first Friends. In his remarks on 'Nakedness a sign or figure', Richard Farnworth uses a passage from Isaiah 20:1–5 to support the notion. The prophet is commanded to strip the sackcloth and sandals from his body and to go about for three years as a sign to Egypt and Cush (the upper Nile region). We are not told if the loins are clad or whether Isaiah is stark naked. In such a way stripped and barefoot, will the king of Assyria lead away the Egyptian captives and Cushite exiles. Farnworth expounds on the prophetic implications of such an act in his own day: '[T]o put off their gawdy attire, and to go in sackcloth, and to be a figure to the people . . . that would be a wonder to this generation.' He then draws an analogy, somewhat far-fetched, between the action of Isaiah and the crucifixion and death of Jesus Christ, who went naked and barefoot for three days. He goes on to assimilate this fanciful idea to the 'prophetic' strippers, who show people that they are 'all uncovered, and their shame and nakedness appear before the Lord, and before all, it would make them startle'. William Simpsons, a specialist at going naked as a sign, has no qualms about doing this in London, Cambridge, Colchester and Walton. The motive for being a sign for the Church of England is to bring shame upon it, by showing its spiritual poverty. The naked body shows the current or future spiritual condition of a city or parliament, or even the state of the Quaker. As a body is naked, so is a congregation without the Spirit of the Lord. We may, on the one hand, question the validity of these actions as true prophetic evangelism, and, on the other, remark the impact of dramatic spectacle upon folk who are still fascinated with the magical and supernatural.[57]

The Quaker way of evangelism is to allow the revelatory illumination of the state of the soul to be shown by the Light shining in the heart. This Light executes God's business and lifts the burden from the preacher. Penington advises evangelists on the mission field 'not to prescribe to them [potential converts] in a lordly way, either in what they should believe or practise; but in the light and in the power of the Spirit, to make their way into every one's conscience in the sight of God, ministering to every one in the Spirit according to their capacity and growth'. Margaret Fell gives an evangelistic call to those in the bondage of darkness, begging them, as they love their own souls, to turn to the light of Jesus, so that 'they may come to be learned and taught by him'. She tells all people everywhere to hearken to the law and to the testimony written in the heart, so that they may come to know the revelation of Jesus. To see in the Light is providential and irreplaceable by any other kind of visionary sight.[58]

At times George Fox 'sees' in dreams, which he catalogues and distinguishes into three types, lest they 'mash or confound all together'. There is the dream caused by an overworked busyness; the dream which is the whisperings of Satan; and the dream which is the speakings of God. Fox's vision of the harvest fields, which we have examined quite closely, demonstrates that the way he 'sees' the purposes of God is by revelation. God shows him his heart and his designs, and it is this knowledge, thoughtfully processed and acted upon, that advances the mission.[59]

Reclaiming Prophetic Preaching

As we situate the gift of prophecy within a volatile French climate of inexorable oppression, tyrannical persecution and a rising tide of discontented mob fever, we are bound to acknowledge the dangerous effect of a 'prophetic' word swept up in a strong current of popular opinion, emotion en masse, or the sway of a prophet. Similarly, in the drama of English politics, we see extreme actions, which are founded on inner convictions played out in the lives of Friends. At this point, the advice of Calvin, to beat down the temptation to reckless action, is essential.

The French depositions that we have examined demonstrate no evidence of prophecy ever discerned by others, either by the gathered company or by the company of *inspirés* or by the Bible. The Quakers appear to vacillate between testing a word or an action by mutual consensus, and allowing an individual conscience free reign. For Fox, the way of discernment is by means of the Light, rather than by Scripture. The advice of Calvin to test the true and false spirit is a necessity, not an option. As we have seen in our survey of the prophesying during the Camisard War, there are consequences for the church in untested prophesying. Lest prophecy becomes a caricature of the God-given gift, meticulous attention ought always be given to the 'weighing' of prophetic utterance. The advice of John Wesley, to discern all prophets and prophecies according to the Law and the Testimony and to distinguish between divine and imaginary inspiration, is essential. However, as we have also seen in our overview of the prophesying after the Revocation and before the Camisard War, we abandon at our peril the treasure of true and pure prophecy. Its power to teach, convert, and bring faith to life is unquestioned. We have observed the power of prophetic evangelism in drawing many people to Christ in the mission of the early Quakers. If, for fear of deception, we abandon prophecy altogether, we throw the baby out with the bath water by choosing to neglect a gift which has the potential to reap a great harvest for the mission of God.

3.

Prophetic Pastors of the Heart

As the Holy Spirit in Scripture imposes on all bishops the necessity of teaching, so in the ancient Church it would have been thought monstrous to nominate a bishop who would not by teaching demonstrate that he was a pastor also. Nor were they admitted to the office on any other condition (John Calvin).[1]

In this chapter we are dealing with the content of the pastoral ministry of the church, raising the question of a conventional and orthodox Jesus Christ: should the Christian proclamation give way to a mysterious and mystical Christ with whom all streams, and finally, all religions can identify? In this respect we use the Huguenot testimony – the depiction of Christ with whom most in the evangelical stream can identify – as a foil to the Quaker view of Christ the Light within, which begins slantwise and continues its journey towards a universal inner Light.

Huguenot Pastors: Testimony to Christ in the Crucible

'But I see four men unbound, walking in the middle of the fire, and they are not hurt; and the fourth has the appearance of a god' (Daniel 3:25).

Having examined in some depth the inspirations of the French *inspirés* and notwithstanding the difficulties associated with the perceived 'madness' of such ecstasies, we must concede that the evidence for the primary role played by the person of the Holy Spirit is overwhelming: accurate prediction, words of knowledge and wisdom, other tongues, gifts of healing, prophetic signs and wonders. We also recognize that evil spirits have been at work and that the prophesying at times is impure or mixed; the human intentions and motives of the *inspirés* are not always divorced from the word they bring. We return, therefore, to our union of Word and Spirit, to the concept of both Christ and the Holy Spirit as an integral partnership in prophetic visionary leadership. It is essential that we establish a clear idea of the rootedness of the pastor in Christ in order that Spirit-inspired prophetic leadership remains grounded in Christ and reflects a Christlike character. It is a distinct possibility that if the Church of the *désert* had listened to the moderate advice of Claude Brousson, the fevered excitement of the radicals would have abated and war could well have been averted, or at least conducted as a military campaign and not as grim and gruesome guerrilla warfare. The words of an anonymous French sonnet, in honour of Brousson, gently remind us of the worthiness of the imitation of a virtuous man and are an echo of Paul's injunction, 'Be imitators of me, as I am of Christ.' To imitate Brousson is to copy his testimony to Jesus Christ, which is the Spirit of prophecy:

> He died for the truth,
> And his passing is worthy of envy
> And worthy to be recited.
> Pastors, with whom he was a companion,
> Show honour for the character
> Whom heaven has bestowed on you!
> To honour his memory eternally,
> To aspire to the same glory,
> And to be worthy of it, imitate his virtues.[2]

Christ the foundation in the Calvinist Church

Calvin's teaching on the foundation of the church universal is crystal clear. All pastoral work rises or falls upon this unshakeable Calvinist rock. He employs Paul's instructions to the squabbling, misguided congregation of Corinth as an exact principle to be applied to all Reformed churches. For our purpose it is a plumb line by which we may test the practices of the Church of the *désert*.

An irrefutable logic guides the simplicity of Calvin's commentary on 1 Corinthians 3:11. Christ is the one and only foundation on which the church of Corinth is founded: 'For no one can lay any foundation other than the one that has been laid; that foundation is Jesus Christ.' And yet still the Corinthians, who had been properly founded on Christ by Paul's teaching, have itching ears for the novelty of the new. The fact that these people refuse to adapt themselves to the teaching of true ministers shows that they are following other kinds of dogma, and by so doing are not building up the church but demolishing it: 'For what is more destructive than confusing believers well grounded in pure doctrine, with a new kind of teaching, so that they are not sure where they stand and turn this way and that?' He drives home the point, asserting that teaching dissenting from the true foundation is 'hay, wood, stubble' (1 Cor. 3:12), remarking pithily that it is 'fabricated in men's minds, and then thrust upon us as oracles of God'.[3]

In the *Institutes* Calvin insists that our primary doctrine is 'that we might learn Christ'. The church that is properly built on Christ manifests the 'testimony of Jesus', but only if 'He alone is set up for righteousness, redemption, sanctification, wisdom, satisfaction, cleansing, in short for life and glory'. Christ is not only the head of the church and the one to whom all spiritual headship belongs, but also its *only* mediator and guide (Eph. 4:1–15). Angels are *not* mediators but are themselves in need of a head, i.e. Christ, 'through whose bond they might cleave firmly and undividedly to their God'. With a backward glance at the Old Testament, Calvin ties his notion of headship to the New Testament. The angel who accompanied the Israelites through the wilderness is indeed Christ: '[E]ven then he was already the Guide of the Church, of which He was the Head.'[4]

Calvin then proceeds to bind Christ and the Spirit. It is plainly his belief that the Holy Spirit completes the ministry of Christ in the body corporate and in the individual believer. It is by the Spirit that we are drawn to Christ. The manual *Instruction in Faith* elucidates this drawing power: 'By the power of the Spirit, Christ makes, upholds, maintains, and vivifies all things; by it he justifies, sanctifies and purifies, calls and attracts us to himself in order that we may obtain deliverance.' By the indwelling Spirit we are enlightened 'and fully know how great are the riches of the divine goodness which we possess in Christ'. By the Spirit our hearts are inflamed 'with the fire of ardent love' and 'without the Spirit there is in us nothing but darkness of understanding and perversity of heart'.[5]

As we dig deeper into the Reformed religion, it is easy to spot the essence of this union between Christ and the Spirit. The idea of 'reformation', i.e. 'to form again' (French, *réformer*), and 'protestant', i.e. to protest (Latin, *protestari*), is not in the sense of protesting against, for example, Catholicism, but witnessing or declaring publicly to something, in this case the Christian faith. Calvin's *Instruction in Faith* is written to inspire the simple folk of Geneva with the positive tenets of faith and not as a Catholic diatribe. The Spirit in early Protestantism is an inspiration to revive and rebirth the person and work of Christ, as foretold in Israel's prophecy. Pastors are the carriers of the message. They are ministers of the word and not narrators of their own dreams and inventions. They are ordained to 'teach the pure doctrine, administer the sacraments, and by their good example instruct and form all to holiness and purity of life'. For Calvin, the pastor is the pivot for the unity of the church. Pastors are the pillars of the building without whose ministry the church topples. Those who despise this order and discipline withdraw as heretics from the society of the church, damaging not only the body of Christ, but God himself. Thus the role or office of pastor is not only to point the way to Christ, but also to *be* Christ to the people as a symbol of unity. We bring these insights to bear upon the gift of the prophetic pastor to the Church of the *désert*.[6]

Christ the foundation in the wilderness church

Just as in the early days of the reformation of the French church, the Church of the *désert* is in the process of the reformation and retrieval of Calvinist rootedness in Christ. We have seen that the leadership of this movement is often in the hands of ecstatic prophets, and that it was necessary for the wider church community to test the message. Sir Richard Bulkeley, second baronet, a moderate Anglican and member of the Royal Society in Ireland, takes upon himself a thorough investigation and discloses his findings in a letter to a friend. We learn that the doctrine taught is exactly in line with Calvinist orthodoxy. God, through Jesus Christ, will restore to humankind what has been lost through corruption and degeneracy. Through Jesus Christ the whole of creation will be revealed in its primitive beauty and we shall regain the perfection of Adam and his immediate communion with God. Bulkeley compares this with the teaching of Scripture, viz. that we shall regain in Christ what we lost in Adam in a kingdom governed by the Spirit of God. These actions upon our imperfect state are gradual: perfection and the restoration of our 'primitive purity' shall only come to completion when the Lord comes again.[7]

Elias Marion, the radical Camisar exiled to London, prophesies the advent of the Lord, the arrival of God in his temple. This could mean that the Parousia (the Second Coming) is close at hand, as we have seen in the apocalyptic writings of Pierre Jurie, or that a divine visitation to the church is imminent. The prophecies are unclear. What is certain is that his epiphany will herald a new foundation built upon Jesus Christ, the Prince of Peace. The prophecy is alive with apocalyptic imagery. The gospel narrative of the Messiah's triumphal entry into Jerusalem feeds the drama of a city on tiptoe, in longing expectation for the arrival of its king. Jerusalem (London?) is the church at the centre of the new age and the home of the Lord, a spiritual building not made with hands (cf. Hebrews 9:11) and founded on a victorious ruler who comes to establish his sovereignty over the nations of the world:

> I will build my house with new foundations. Take courage, Jerusalem, rejoice: behold thy king, who is about to enter, in glory and triumph into thy house. Behold him, who brings peace to Zion. Behold him, who comes to assemble the nations of the earth together, and to subject them to his laws. Behold, behold, my child, the glory of the earth, the Prince of Peace.

The universal dimension in the oracle is a contrast with the domestic domain in the following divine message given by Marion and addressed personally to the people of God. Whereas the previous prophecy concerning Christ as the new foundation is spoken as an ephemeral abstraction to the church at large, this revelation is a plea to its heart. We hear the voice of God claiming lodgings in a home cleansed and surrendered to his will. These attitudes of heart are the sturdy foundations required to establish an edifice hosting the Lord. In the words of the appeal, 'Answer me, answer me', we hear the strains of reciprocal relationship: God demands a response from his people. Here we begin to touch on the personal and pastoral aspects of church: 'Answer me, answer me, if thou hast an house to give me. Must I not prepare thy heart, if thou wouldst have me to lodge with thee? Can I lodge in a frail house, in an habitation that totters, and that is not subject to my will?'[8]

Bulkeley is quite clear in his own mind that only God can know the secrets of the heart and that no created being has that privilege. Nevertheless, he has to confess that his 'most secret thoughts have in various instances, and upon different occasions, been revealed to me by some of the inspired persons'. Clearly the clergy of his day do not have this 'extraordinary communication with God', which was enjoyed by the primitive church, and now by these inspired prophets. If ministers of Christ were in contact with God they would not abandon their congregations, either physically, by fleeing from persecution, or figuratively, by not tending to their needs. This is the nuance in the prophetic message spoken by the Lord through Marion. It is an example of the close tie between God and the prophet, who takes on a pastoral function to speak as a divine mouthpiece to the church, ministers having failed in their duty: 'Know that I will manifest thee in a few days, to my people. I will bring thee forth myself, into the assemblies (of people;) and will make thee cry out against those faint-hearted (and) fearful wretches, who have forsaken their flock.' The sense of immediacy in these prophetic promises and predictions builds up the church on the foundation of Christ, unites believers in a bond of courageous endurance in persecution, and stimulates a vision of hope in precarious times.[9]

The testimony of Jesus in pastors

Michael Buckley describes the impulses in seventeenth-century French spirituality, which for our purposes may be woven together in a threefold cord: the rise of mysticism, humanism and creation, and the leap of faith out of the pit of unbelief. In summary, these influences may be ordered thus: mysticism as oneness with God and absorption into his will; spirituality as a statement about being human; the journey from scepticism to piety and apostolic mission. We find these aspirations running through the narrative of the Church of the *désert*, especially as we consider its pastoral oversight. Bearing in mind the high view in Calvinism of the minister of the gospel, and with limited sources of meditations, prayers and biographic detail, we shall seek to trace the 'testimony of Jesus' in the pastors of the desert. We hope to find in them a narrow way which bypasses two deviant and opposite paths: a Christ-less cross and a cross-less Christ. The former may be described as an impersonal, sterile Christianity with a legalistic, forensic work of atonement, a saving cross devoid of the person of Jesus. The latter path emphasizes the person of Jesus, his attributes and grace, but underplays the saving work of the cross.[10]

As we have seen in our examination of French theological trends in Chapter 1, the words of Pierre Jurieu, the highly educated pastor and professor, played an important role in stirring the turbulent waters of the Huguenot resistance. His writing proves not to be limited to political apocalyptic, but to cover all aspects of Christian life and behaviour. In his discourse, *A Plain Method of Christian Devotion*, Jurieu offers us a vignette on the tradition of mysticism as a passage, journey, or means to attain union with the divine. Love is the source and spring of all devotedness to God. The soul's union with God is described by means of a marital image – the embrace of lover and beloved. In the contemplation of the beauty and goodness of God, the affections are aroused and the soul is overcome with 'violent desire and longing after union with him, and cries out with the spouse, *Let him kiss me with the kisses of his mouth, for his love is pleasanter than wine*' (cf. Song of Songs 1:2). The effect of these pursuits renders the soul in such a state of 'sprightliness and lively joy' that it runs to its exercises of prayer and meditation to hasten its piety. Just as a flying eagle intent on assuaging hunger travels with speed, so the true devout flies with rapidity, surmounting all obstacles in its course. The absorption with celestial contemplation translates the soul out of itself and out of the orbit of the material world. Unseeing and unhearing, it attains ecstasy, the ravishment of the soul.[11]

Jurieu is quick to admit that the course of true love is not a permanent state of bliss and that the soul is subject to the changes

and chances of life. The soul suffers the infirmity and failing, dullness and sadness of the condition of humanity. Herein lies the integration of humanity and divinity in the soul, which is a shadow of
the two natures in Christ, completely divine and yet fully human.
In Jurieu we see that the heart of the relationship is love towards
the person of the Lord and thus the pitfall of a Christ-less cross is
avoided. We find, too, at the centre of this discourse, the cross of
Christ in the desire for the spiritual disciplines. Thus the pitfall
of a cross-less Christ is avoided. The mystical mood in Jurieu is
matched by the preaching of Claude Brousson, a short example of
which will be analyzed in Chapter 4.[12]

Using the seventeenth-century Protestant Bible, Brousson
preached fifteen times in the Cévennes, the landscape of rocky
ravines and caves exacting from him remarkable spiritual consolation for a threatened, secret cell. A brief illustration shows this
pastoral artistry in a mystical vein. The sermon, entitled 'Mystic
Dove', is an allegoric exposition on the Song of Songs 2:14: the dove
(conventional symbol for the Spirit) in the cleft of the rock is a metaphor for the Woman of the Apocalypse (Rev.12), who is identified as
the bride of Jesus Christ (see Rev. 22), alias the church in hiding in the
desert (Ps. 119:114). The meaning is plain, although the hermeneutical method is complicated. God has such love for this dove, for the
church infused by the Holy Spirit, hidden and at home like a dove
in the cleft of a rock, that he longs to see and hear her: 'O my Dove
that art in the clefts of the rock, hidden in the steep places, let me see
thy countenance, let me hear thy voice: For sweet is thy voice, and
thy countenance is gracious.' The last phrase, 'le regard mystique de
notre foi', that is, 'the mystical gaze of our faith', is understood to
mean the loving look the church community gives to her Lord.

Brousson knew well the loving intimacy with Jesus Christ. His
biographer writes: 'He was even sick with the love of God, the
glories thereof overflowing his feeble nature. Christ's left hand
was under his head and his right hand did embrace him [Song
of Songs 2:6].' These passages, in the intensity of warm affection
between the Lord and his flock, demonstrate the effect of the
person of Jesus upon Brousson – not a Christ-less cross. At the
heart of Brousson's sacrificial ministry, and explicitly in his death,
is a cross shape – his broken body cruciform on the wheel. He has
not crafted for himself a cross-less Christ.

John Quick's biography, *The Life of Monsr. Brousson* is a hagiographic portrayal of a missionary pastor who is 'like unto a pelican in the wilderness and an owl in the desert'. Ordained as one of the *prédicants* (lay preachers) in a kind of guerrilla network, Brousson joins the resistance, relentlessly repressed but filling the void left by the flight of the Huguenot pastors. He is a refugee sleeping under trees, on a dunghill, on faggots, and underground in holes in the earth. He is a person in exile, enduring hunger, fatigue and fainting, and a Huguenot in hiding from betrayers and enemies. He is zealous – sold out for the cause of Christ – preaching up to twenty-five times in eight days in three-hour meetings and at least three to four meetings mostly at midnight, for two years. He labours in prayer for three hours up to three times a day. His prayers are fruitful and reap abundant harvests as he pleads for repentant hearts. On one occasion 5,000 people kneel on the bare ground and with streaming faces renounce the papist ways in worship. He writes many sermons, letters and prayers to the besieged church from his desk, 'the table in the wilderness'.

Quick recounts his story very movingly and, having met Brousson on one occasion in 1694, gives a vivid reflection of his life. The work was published in 1700, two years after Brousson's imprisonment and execution. A telling remark by his executioner is an insight into the measure of the man: 'I have put to death two hundred convicts, but none have ever made me tremble like M. Brousson.' His sheer courage and audacious commitment to the church struggle marks Brousson not only as a saintly pastor, but, more importantly for our purposes in this study, as a prophetic pastor. His identification with Christ as he lays down his life for the church is a prophetic sign, a 'testimony to Jesus'. In the life and action of Brousson we see, too, the threefold cord of French spirituality: union with Christ in his outrageous love for God, knowledge of the human creation in his trials and tests, and a piety shown forth in apostolic fervour to advance the growth of the church in the Cévennes.

The testimony of Jesus in people

We remind ourselves again of the assertion by John Lacy, in his preface to *A Cry from the Desert*, of the faithfulness of the wilderness church to the sacrament of the Lord's Supper and to the reading of Scripture as the supreme rule of faith for everything. Lacy's enquiry into the piety of the *inspirés* in England leads him to conclude that in every way their conduct is above reproach. In addition to their private prayer, fasting and reading of Scripture, they are diligent in their attendance at public worship and communion. From Bernard, the Protestant gardener, we understand that his utter steadfastness in clinging to the Bible is a conviction handed down through the generations (see 2 Tim. 1:5): '[S]o worship I the God of my fathers; believing all things which are written in the Law and the Prophets.' We learn that his daily habit of musing upon the words of the Bible is his guide for life. His vast knowledge of the Bible is evidenced in his quoting of innumerable texts to convince his mistress of her need of salvation. From his meditations he is able to discern the truth or falsehood of the error, superstition and idolatry in practices, especially those of the Catholic religion.[13]

From numerous accounts of atrocities perpetrated we select a few short statements in order to grasp the enormous pressure on Huguenots to recant, even in the years preceding the Revocation. In a fictitious dialogue between two papists, Jurieu contrives to show that the Huguenots are 'good Frenchmen, brave, sincere, faithful in their commerce, true friends' and cries out in the mouth of a persecuted gentleman: 'Must so many efforts be used to force from us that French heart that God and birth has given us . . . and to inspire the people with a spirit of fury against us.' D'Auborn, a French Protestant minister, writes to a colleague in London, ever hopeful that the forbearance of prisoners of conscience will soften the hearts of their persecutors:

> I having (with many others) languished a long time in prison, for the sake of a good conscience, afflicted with much sickness, by reason of my close confinement, which blessed by the name of God enabling me I have born with patience; though many have died unpitied of their cruel persecutors, yet the cry of innocent blood may in time make them cry, How hard it is to kick against the pricks.

In similar vein and on the good authority of a maritime officer, Jurieu endorses the perseverance of the Huguenot saints: 'Here are six hundred galley-slaves of the religion called Protestant, who by their patience move compassion from the most hard-hearted and unpitiful of their officers.' The saintly Advocate of Stemenebaud, Monsieur Lewis of Marolles, whom all Paris beheld preaching in his chains in the spirit of the old martyrs, came to Marseilles 'laden with a chain of fifty pound weight about his neck, and a violent fever'.[14]

The testimony of Jesus in division

Clearly the ministry of the pastors of the Church of the *désert* is toward a fraction of the Protestant church in France, specifically those in rebellion against the state and the state church. How do we understand the unity of the church for which Christ died in light of schism and division? How does a faction display a testimony to Jesus? Did the Huguenot Church manifest a witness to Christ in its separation from the norm? We will tackle these questions with reference to Calvin's *Institutes* and to letters and papers from French and English Dissenters.

Calvin notes that the fundamental starting point for unity is our mystical union with Christ (*unio mystica*), whereby we put on Christ and are grafted into him, making us one with him, a union occurring essentially through preaching and the Lord's Supper. Thus the benchmark for unity is word and sacrament, and any church in which both these marks exist may be safely embraced, to the extent 'that we must not reject it so long as it retains them, even if it otherwise swarms with many faults'. Calvin advocates condonation of 'delusion in those matters which can go unknown without harm to the sum of religion and without loss of salvation'. He recognizes that the invisible church, comprising true believing members of Christ, is comingled with the visible church, that is, hypocrites who bear only the name and outward appearance of Christ. He argues for tolerance of these in that 'a rigorous discipline does not always flourish as it ought'. Pierre Jurieu is among those who advanced the idea of these fundamental articles, which formed the basis of liberal projects of union in the seventeenth century.[15]

Charles Owen, an English Protestant Dissenter (c. 1720), conforms to Calvin's ideal as he sets out the principle of separation and schism and its application to the Church of England

and the Catholic Church. This principle applies equally well to the Huguenot Church in its quarrel with French Catholicism. Protestants allow that as the Catholic Church holds to all the essentials of Christianity it is the bearer of salvation. However, as it puts its members under obligation to prefer the authority of the church rather than the oracles of God, i.e. the Bible, its practices and the imposition of its own inventions leads to a separation. Owen is emphatic that it is separation and not schism. The only rule that a Protestant is obliged to obey is 'the best light he can get from Scripture', and not blind obedience to an institution or magistrate. By following the dictates of Scripture the Huguenot Church is binding itself to the 'testimony of Jesus'. In separating itself from idolatrous practices it is being obedient to the Lord of the Bible and loosening itself from the mastery of religious practice. We see these beliefs concretized in the writings of the Revocation period.[16]

The gentleman of Dauphine confides in his Genevan friend his observations concerning the matter of the Lord's Supper. On Easter evening he hears the girl preacher, Isabeau Vincent exhort the assembly to abstain from veneration of the Catholic Mass, and to communicate the Lord's Supper to one another. She denounces the Mass, likening it to a pair of silver plates, gay and glittering on the outside but void on the inside. By adoring 'that which is but bread, and by serving the creature in the place of the creator', we offend God. A night-time vigil in the home of her parents is the occasion for a sleeping Isabeau's refutation of the Catholic doctrine of the Real Presence of Christ in the elements of bread and wine. One watcher listens attentively. He hears her say: 'Take, eat this body that hath been crucified for you; and do not believe that Jesus Christ is there in body and soul; for his is in heaven. It is by faith that we are to penetrate into this mystery.' She is dismissive of the practice of indulgences, 'They sell a mass for five pence, and eight for forty pence', and persistent in her challenge: 'Do not go to the mass, for it is a great sin, and a mortal sin; for you abuse the talents that God hath given you.' The little prophet judges the superficial cheap grace of the indulgence – money for a mass offered for the forgiveness of sin – on another occasion reported by Pierre Jurieu. She restates the doctrine of the atonement, that the sacrifice of Christ is the vehicle for forgiveness, not any other monetary sacrifice: 'In one word, there can be no sacrifice, where there is no remission of sin.'[17]

A false Christ in the diaspora

Jean-Baptiste Louvreleul, the author of the work *The History of the French Prophets*, is an opponent of the inspired prophets of the Cévennes in exile in England. He writes in order to refute their vindication in the depositions compiled as *A Cry from the Desert*. The test Louvreleul employs is upon the practice of the prophets: if it is in contradiction to gospel doctrine, morality and humanity, they are hypocrites, and if it is inspired, it is by the spirit of the Devil. He finds that they are indeed hypocritical in that they claim (in the preface to the depositions) to be above the laws and statutes of the realm which 'condemns an intent in any prophecy to make insurrection and rebellion'. However, in the same breath they also 'declare against the detestable notions of setting up Christ's kingdom by arms; they vent no prophecies injurious to Her Majesty, or any of the honourable personages of this realm'. If they are against the use of arms, he asks in exasperation, 'Why did they preach and prophesy so many thousands into destruction? Why do they glory in their barbarous exploits there?' He judges them to be hypocrites, leading many into deception and brutality: 'Were not they the men that deluded the multitude by their hypocrisy and invited them to commit so many savage cruelties?' He gives the example of two fanatics, tried and executed as criminals by the High Court at Nîmes in March 1704. Lewis Jonquet, aged 28, is 'a noted rebel, brigadier to Cavalier's troops and convicted of the most barbarous cruelties'. Great Mary, aged 30, under the false name of prophetess of Lussan, caused the deaths of an 'abundance of innocent persons by her deceitful revelations; and by making of gatherings had procured considerable supplies of money and provisions, for the support of Cavalier's men, among whom she kept continually'. Louvreleul's test is applied to the conduct of insurgents who claim to be lovers of peace and yet instigate war.[18]

The advice of an English gentleman to a bishop concerning the French enthusiasts is that they require a magistrate's control, for 'it is necessary that the people should have a public leading in religion'. He is more light-hearted in his disparaging dismissal of enthusiasm: 'Revealed religion . . . [is] . . . little better than frenzy and infection. 'Tis all panic, from the beginning to the end.' The acid test of hypocrisy is put to use in the diaspora, particularly in

London, a bowl of plenty for Huguenots in the great scattering after the Revocation. Many flee to the city and are on trial for the genuineness of their beliefs, none more so than 'pretended converts', up for sale in a 'market for conversions'. These insincere impostors embrace the Protestant religion when the good folk of the church reach out with financial aid for the plight of the refugees. John Armand Dubourdieu, a Protestant minister in the Savoy has a yardstick for these so-called proselytes: alms are to be given first to the 'old Protestant', our friend and relation, whose faith cannot be questioned, before the novice or one whose sincerity cannot be assured.[19]

The judgement of Calvin upon human reason is that it is mastered by many forms of deception and does not choose according to the excellence of the immortal nature: 'Rather like an animal he follows the inclination of his nature, without reason, without deliberation.' The faculties of the eyes of the mind must be opened. This is a process and not the work of a day. How do we do what is right? Calvin's rejoinder is 'that he discern good by right reason; that knowing it he choose it; that having chosen it he follow it'. But how do we choose the good when the reason is impaired? His answer is that we do not even aspire to do good 'except by the impulsion of the Holy Spirit'. We arrive back at the point of departure in this chapter, the necessity of the union of Christ and the Spirit for discerning pastoral leadership.[20]

The true Christ in the diaspora

For a Calvinist to return to foundations is to accede once more to there being salvation in Christ alone, to repent of sin and to cleave to Christ. One of the ways in which this theology is transmitted to the Church of the *désert* is through the medium of prophecy. These messages not only arm the besieged for battle but more importantly lead them to lean on Christ himself and not on human leaders. In each of the following inspired messages delivered by Elias Marion we pinpoint scriptural inferences from which we deduce christological content, i.e. data associated with the person and work of Jesus Christ.

First, we examine an example of a prophecy defining the work of Jesus Christ as healer. Psalm 51 is the penitential context for this prophecy, in which a visitation by the divine healer to the church will repair the damages wrought by sin: 'You desire truth in the inward being; therefore teach me wisdom in my secret heart' (v. 6). To the body corporate in France – disjointed and at loggerheads within itself – this is a hopeful word. The prophecy confirms the text Ephesians 2:20,21, which describes the church 'built upon the foundation of the apostles and prophets, with Christ Jesus himself as the cornerstone. In him the whole structure is joined together and grows into a holy temple in the Lord':

> I will visit the most hidden parts of thy heart: I will join what thou, by sin, has disjointed. I will make whole again what thou, by thy lusts, hast broken.

Secondly, we turn to prophecies which tell of the wonders of the love and blessings of God for his children. The christological sense we may extract from these sentences is in not one but many Bible verses – a bouquet of fragrances. Here is Christ with priestly benediction in his hands (Matt. 19:13,15; Mark 6:5; 8:23,25), Christ the giver of the Holy Spirit at Pentecost (Luke 11:13), Christ in advent glory and majesty at his Second Coming (Matt. 24:30):

> I will lay my hands upon my people. They shall receive my grace and my blessings in abundance. Behold, my child, a new Pentecost. Behold, behold, behold, my child, I am coming down visibly upon the earth!

We hear the heartbeat of a lover: Christ reaches for his children to hold them in an intimate embrace. This prophecy is an echo of the words of the Saviour longing for Jerusalem to return to his wing as a hen gathers her chicks (Matt. 23:37):

> Have I not embraced thee? I come now to take thee in my arms. I come now to set thee upon my lap.

Thirdly, prophecies show the Son of Man with refugee status and nowhere to lay his head (Matt. 8:20), his identikit that of the typical French exile. Here is the identification of Christ with his persecuted people, offering the hope of brightness renewed as his face shines upon them:

My child, I would rest my head upon earth; (but) I have no place of abode. I have no habitation upon the earth: I am driven away from all places: I am wandering, I tell thee, like the things of nought. My child, my face is going to shine upon the earth.

Christ will not leave them orphans but shall come to their rescue in their wilderness retreats. From thence they will be driven out and scattered like sheep. The good shepherd shall seek them out (John 10:1–15):

Stand your ground firmly in your places of retreat. I shall come to seek you out, and to drive you from thence.

Fourthly, an example of a prophecy couched in apocalyptic language but with a turn of phrase so immediate as to actualize it in the present day: Marion's prediction of 'new churches' may well be, as Schwartz suggests, the creation in London of a new desert church, a response to the active hostility to the Huguenot ministry in the city:

My child, the world will be much deceived, when I shall come, in a few days, upon the earth, to make a new world. I will have a new people: I will lodge them in new churches: they have corrupted those, which are built upon the earth.[21]

Christlikeness in the diaspora

The promise of Christ to tabernacle with his people in the dispersed church must surely produce in them the virtues associated with his indwelling. John Lacy tabulates the true characteristics of a prophetic messenger: humility and lowliness of mind. He discloses that in all those interviewed and observed he finds nothing but the temper of union, love, tenderness, confession, forgiveness, likemindedness, brotherly affection, sweetness, sympathy, goodness, charity and peace. Such saintliness is the fruit of the Spirit, not of the evil one.[22]

In the testimonies we find tears of repentance, sadness, joy, pleasure and pain. There is much evidence of deep repentance for sin and forsaking idolatry. A young man, Alexis, exhorts the assembly to forsake their sins 'so pressingly, that they all burst into tears', and will not leave them in peace until they are all 'firmly resolved for amendment'. Tears at times are of blood, a sign of extreme identification with Christ. For example, a maid of the upper Cévennes had her inspiration and said in it that 'great tribulation would come upon that country, insomuch that it would become a new world . . . and by thunder and lightning destroyed, she crying out loud to God for mercy, and at that moment shed tears of blood'. It is testified that Elias Marion set them to prayer, and after a moving discourse they were called upon to draw near, at which point the entire assembly 'burst into tears' of contrition, and upon receiving the message that their broken hearts were restored by the Lord they wept 'tears of joy'. Marion himself lies prostrate before God in an attitude of intercession for mercy and then is 'seized with ecstasy', during which he tells us that his soul is under these aforesaid apprehensions and he 'poured forth tears of blood, in great plenty; the blood was florid, as if spun directly from the veins, my cloths were stained with it, and the earth likewise; these tears came out upon the anguish of my mind, and this was discernible to a great number present, at noon-day, near a place called Vernedes'. How may we discern such activity if not by wise and discerning pastoral leaders who themselves bear the imprint of Christ in their labours.[23]

Evidence for the spiritual frame of mind characterizing Huguenot leadership is in a document, the Toulouse statement (May 1683), which perfectly describes the loyalty of ordinary churchmen to the cause of Christ. Sixteen laymen pledge 'to be converted sincerely to God', in love, piety and humility, by seeking the help of the Holy Spirit in reading and constant meditation on the Scriptures. They disavow demonstrations on temple ruins, consenting to gather instead in quiet meetings in homes, fields, gardens and woods. Such an assembly, although unlawfully constituted, is still a church gathered for worship, for song, for divine instruction, for the sacraments and the solemnization of marriage. In the absence of ordained ministers, elders and deacons shall preach and pray. The key to the belief system of these laymen is the premise that they shall obey God rather than the king. By so doing they shall keep a clear conscience before the Lord – a piety exceptional in its allegiance to God. They are true

Protestants in that they 'protest [declare, witness] in the face of heaven and earth that, with the grace of God, in the interests of whom they are exposing themselves to so many disgraces, they will continue to glorify him in spite of the most terrible calamities'. These sixteen laymen are also the new leaders of a new reformation, a movement faithful to its foundations and yet reforming itself to meet new challenges.[24]

Quaker Pastors: Testimony to Christ Within

> Therefore keep to the witness of God in yourselves, and that is the Word of the Lord to you; and then you will have the just weight, and measure and balance, and true understanding, to answer the just principle of God in everyone (George Fox).[25]

In our analysis of the Huguenot resistance we have seen, too, that an adherence to Calvin's doctrine of Christ the foundation is a stabilizing force for good, in light of enthusiastic Spirit-filled prophesying. We must now apply the same principle of balance between Word and Spirit to the pastoral enterprise in Quakerism. Clearly the Quaker evangelist is a man or woman on fire with the Spirit of God, burning with a word received in the Light of Christ. What is less clear, in both messenger and message, is the person of Jesus Christ: how does Quakerism exhibit, or bear witness to, the character of the historic Jesus? As we turn to an examination of the prophetic pastor, it is this dilemma, a rather knotty problem that requires disentanglement. As we deal with the notion of the testimony of Christ within, the inevitability of the charge of universalism – that all shall be saved – confronts us. Is George Fox advocating a general salvation for all, by means of 'the just principle of God in everyone'? How might his view that the Light enlightens everyone be interpreted in a pastoral manner?[26]

The essential George Fox: Christ within

The Light metaphor in George Fox is drawn from John's Gospel (1:4–9, 3:19–21, 8:12, 9:5, 12:35,36,46). Fox is untroubled by the being and origins of the Light as a matter for philosophic speculation or mystical experience. It is the activity of the Light which is his primary concern. This inner Light, or Christ within, or the Spirit of Christ shows up the marks of evil and is the lynchpin of the unity between the Creator and the creature. The essence of Foxian spirituality is that the testimony of Jesus consists not chiefly in a creed to believe, but in a life to live. His preoccupation with the lordship of Christ ensures that the crucified Christ is integral to his thinking regarding the Light within.

In a pastoral letter entitled 'To Friends concerning the cross of Christ', Fox states that the rule of Christ begins and ends at the cross. To dwell in the cross in the world opens the way to the love of God: 'The cross . . . overturns the world in the heart. Which cross must be taken up by all who follow Jesus Christ out of the world.' Submission to the reign of Jesus is, for Fox as pastor, a complete action, never a half measure. In a telling metaphor he deals a death blow to the human ego, by establishing the right of Christ to rule from the centre of the soul: 'We must not have Christ Jesus, the Lord of life, put any more in the stable amongst the horses and asses, but he must now have the best chamber, the heart, and the rude, debauched spirit must be turned out.' By an intricate interlocking of Word and Spirit Fox then hammers home the way in which the heart is harnessed to Jesus: 'Therefore let him reign, whose right it is, who was conceived by the Holy Ghost, by which Holy Ghost you call him Lord, in which Holy Ghost you pray, and by which Holy Ghost you have comfort and fellowship with the Son and with the Father.' Fox is less concerned with the outward event of the cross than with the inner state of the recipient of the atoning work of Christ. The way of the cross is the path to perfection, which the Quaker has already entered, by means of the restoration offered by Christ.[27]

The word 'Light', therefore, is employed by Fox to describe the active presence of Christ, although there is general consensus as to its interchangeability with other terms prolific in his writings, viz. inward Christ, seed, root, the principle, the Light of Christ and the Spirit. For example, the Pauline idea of Christ as the seed is connected with the Light in a pastoral sense (see Gal. 3:16,19,29). Friends are encouraged to 'Mind the Light, and dwell in it, and it will keep you atop of all the world; and the seed of God mind, and know it, and in it be content.' Christ is the 'Royal Seed'. This term means that the inheritance of God is promised to Christ who is the seed of Abraham, and to those belonging to Christ the promises are given. Fox encourages the Friends to '[d]well in the seed which is heir of the promise of life eternal, and dwell in the profession of that', and to make faith a regular practice: '[I]n all your doings (and words) be faithful to the Lord, and to men; let this be your daily exercise.' The work of Christ is understood as a response of the heart, by obedient listening to the Light within.[28]

To be a child of the Light is to receive the power of the Light that speaks within. In his doctrinal exposition, 'The Pearl Found in England', Fox utilizes the metaphor of the fine pearl to expound on the prophetic word brought by Jesus Christ (Matt. 13:44–46). We find a fistful of biblical allusions in the image: 'And the pearl that hath been hid in the earth is found [Matt. 13:46], and the morning star is risen, and the day is dawned, and the true light shines [2 Pet. 1:19], and wisdom . . . cries in the streets to the simple ones [Prov. 1:20], and for all to fear God.'

The kernel of the view of Light put forth by Fox, in a descriptive piece entitled 'The Spirit of Man the Candle of the Lord', is that its source is not natural but divine: 'And so Christ [who] is the Light, who enlightens every man that comes into the world with his divine Light . . .which is not a natural light, or a created light, but a spiritual, heavenly, and a divine Light.' This high view of the Light of Christ is linked to the comparison between the spirit of a human being and a candle of the Lord (see Prov. 20:27, Ps. 18:28), so that the Light is that 'which enlightens every man's spirit that comes into the world, his candle'. David, the writer of the psalms, had his candle lit and saw the state of the Jews, and looked 'beyond all their figures and shadows, to Christ Jesus, and called him Lord: So that made him a prophet, and a seer, that he saw afar off'. Divine inspiration is granted 'all the prophets of God, whom God hath lighteth their candles, their spirits, by his Spirit and Light', so that these enlightened Old Testament writers 'saw Christ Jesus, who was to come to end their Law, with all their types, figures and shadows'. In the New Testament Christ is the Light and speaks to his disciples, whose spirits, their candles, he had enlightened: 'Ye are the light of the world.'[29]

The analogy of the candlestick is commonplace in religious writings of the day to describe the person as a whole, both body and soul. In a petition by a zealous group of young apprentices to the Lord Mayor and Council of London in 1659, the candlestick connotes the light of the Lord in the body corporate. The warning is that 'should the Lord remove his candlestick out of his place (as we have cause to fear he will, unless we do repent) . . . a dark and dismal night of black and gloomy ignorance, error and profaneness will envelop our valley of vision'. George Fox employs the image to marry the candle, the candlestick and the work of Christ in the human being. He explains that when the Spirit lights the candle (i.e. the spirit) in the candlestick (i.e. the body, soul, mind and conscience), then one 'may see Christ that died for them, and is risen for them'.[30]

The tricky part of Fox's train of thought is that the Light is in everyone prior to conversion: 'For unbelievers in the Light are grafted into old Adam, in transgressions. And the believers in the Light (which is the life in Christ) are grafted into Christ the Word, by which all things were made and created.' How may we make sense of the conundrum in George Fox that the unconverted soul has the Light, and yet that all are still to receive the Light? For Fox the spirit of the human being is created from birth with something of the divine essence implicit within it: 'And is not this [breath of life] that cometh out from God, which is in God's hand, part of God, of God, and from God, and goes to God again [Gen. 2:7]?' At this point we understand Fox to mean that germane to the breath of life is the soul's potential for eternity, as it is 'taken up into God': 'And does it not speak of a human soul, an earthly soul, and is earthly, immortal? Cannot it die nor be killed? And is not that which came out from God, which God hath in his hand, taken up into God again?' Fox stresses, however, that this work of God in the soul 'which Christ the power of God is the bishop of' can only be achieved by Christ, who is 'of God's being'. The power of Christ brings a restored perfection: 'For being made whole, they are made perfect, for sin wounds; for the ministry of God was to bring people to the perfect man, "to present them perfect [cf. Eph. 4:13; 5:27]".' By this Fox implies the redemptive action of God, who in Christ reconciles the world to himself (see 2 Cor. 5:18,19). But we are still left with the problem of the stages of enlightenment: 'Christ, the great heavenly prophet, hath enlightened every man that cometh into the Light [John 1:9], and so have the Light of life, and not come into condemnation.' At this point in the argument we shall assume that this statement means that Christ enlightens at the moment of conviction, not that all are endowed with enlightenment at their creation.[31]

The essential George Fox critiqued

Fox's perplexing stance on Christ within drew much criticism from writers of the day. Francis Bugg's publication in 1712 states four objections to the Foxian 'heresy' concerning Christ. First, faith in Jesus Christ as he is in heaven above, which is a critique of the emphasis on a heavenly being. Secondly, the denial that Jesus of Nazareth is also Christ the Son of God, which is a judgement on a perceived inability to hold together both human and divine natures in Christ. Thirdly, an undervaluing of the death and suffering of Jesus Christ, which is an attack on the Quaker focus on their own sufferings. Fourthly, the rejection of the ordinances of baptism with water and the Lord's Supper with bread and wine, which is a criticism of the Quaker neglect of traditional church ordinances. Rosemary Moore pinpoints the problem for the contemporaries of Fox: 'The Quakers' intense experience of Christ, or as the light of Christ, which led them to blur the distinction between Christ and themselves, was difficult to reconcile with a belief in Jesus as man.'[32]

Clearly the idea of a real union with Christ is still the touchstone of Quaker belief. Fox makes this plain in a compendium of replies to over a hundred anti-Quaker books and statements. One of the agendas of the 100-page defence, entitled *The Great Mistery of the Great Whore* (1659), is the attempt to show the close relation between Christ and the believer as 'flesh of his flesh and bone of his bone'. In his introduction to the work, Ellis Hein defends Fox by stating that the founder is not arguing on the basis of theology or theory, but as one to whom God has been revealed and who can, therefore, speak to all states of the human condition. Fox's reply to the critique of John Bunyan and John Burton, 'Some Gospel Truths Opened', is set out in meticulous question and answer style. He tackles their accusation that Quakers deny that Christ has come in the flesh, by contending for the witness of Christ within, which does not deny his incarnation. To the allegation that dependency upon the righteousness of Christ within is the spirit of the Devil, the rejoinder is that the one who died at Jerusalem is the same as the one within. Bunyan and Burton assert that not only is the teaching of Christ within a delusion, but it is also a new gospel. Fox is emphatic: the crucified Christ within is the same crucified Christ without. He goes so far as to say that 'if there be any other Christ but he that was crucified within, he is the false Christ', and conversely, 'he that hath not this Christ that was risen and crucified within, is a reprobate'. On the latter point Fox is categorically clear: '[N]one know the Son of God but by revelation, and with the Light', so that to be out of the Light of revelation is 'odious'.[33]

Wilcox raises the pertinent questions in relation to the doctrine of atonement in early Quakerism, which takes its cue from its founding father. A preoccupation with Christ within diminishes the objectivity of the reconciling work of Christ. Atonement is not an external event as much as it is an inner work of the heart – the concentration on personal perfection. The cross translates the believer into an already achieved perfected state, which not only conflates the processes of justification and sanctification, but also undermines the preaching of the cross for salvation.[34]

Christ as Light and seed to early Friends

Although not an entirely original term, being ascribed to some continental Baptists and a few of the Seekers, the phrase 'Children of Light', by which the earliest Quakers were known, captures the very essence of George Fox's teaching. The pastoral emphases in early Quakerism, i.e. that of the 1650s and 1660s, demonstrate the Light to be a searching spotlight on the ego, with power to save from self-will or self-deception. The outworking of these revelations permeates the First Publishers of Truth, affecting the Quaker walk of faith. By drawing on the imagery of Light and seed, Margaret Fell is able to develop pastoral lessons for her readership. She discusses Jesus as the one who calls his chosen seed out of captivity: 'By this Light, which is the life of the law, doth he call the seed out of bondage still.' She writes of a saving Light to the Gentiles, and urges those desiring to live in virtue and grace to 'wait in the Light, which shines in your conscience, for this fountain of life is the Light of men'. For those who obediently wait in his Light, Christ is 'a fountain of gardens, and a wellspring of living waters, and streams from Lebanon'. Fell instructs the Friends to turn inwards, to the law written on their hearts, whereby they shall find peace and comfort for their souls. Hearing the word of the Lord is a priority and comes directly via 'the preacher of righteousness', who is given as 'a witness to the people, a leader, and a commander . . . whose name is called the Word of God'. Spiritual food for the journey of faith comes by way of the cross, as gathered Friends wait in silence, imbibing 'the invisible virtue and life which comes from the living God', and experiencing 'the hidden manna'.[35]

For early Friends, the Light must shine into the conscience to awaken right action. The pastoral Penington declares that the only means of enlightening and saving a man from his utter death and darkness is 'the light of the Spirit of Christ, shining in his dark heart and conscience'. An early document, 'The Epistle to the Reader' (1653) by Edward Burrough, assigns the practice of discernment to the Light. As Friends rely on the Light within they will own a capacity to distinguish between good and evil, right and wrong, God and the Devil, truth and error. The Light is 'a sufficient teacher to lead us to Christ . . . to receive Christ, and to witness him to dwell in us'. The counsel of William Dewsbury, in an early epistle (1655), for dealing with anyone found in deception, is not to speak behind that person's back, but to 'declare and witness forth the mind of the living God against the deceit, and it [the witness] will cut it [deception] down'. In this way the brother or sister, 'the pure holy seed', is set at liberty from captivity.[36]

Christ as shepherd to early Friends

The pictorial representation of Christ the shepherd in the Quaker literature gives equilibrium to the intangibility of the imagery of Light and seed. Pastors are to follow in the footsteps of the good shepherd and imitate his ways (see John 10:1–18). Anne Gilman explains the task of pastoral ministration within the Society, in an extended metaphor of the suffering shepherd, 'who in all our afflictions is afflicted', and reaches out to the afflicted by means of 'the angel of his presence' who 'is known to support in the time of our need'. On the problem of straying sheep she advises that 'if any lamb among you be suffered to go astray, the shepherd's crook is to be known to catch them to the fold'. She establishes an order in pastoral care, by placing the Friends firmly in the care of God, rather than one another: '[H]ere is no need of sheltering one under another, for the Lord is the shelter of those that put their trust in him.' But Christ is also the Lamb to be followed (see Rev. 14:4), and the one with whom Friends are to identify: 'turn not your backs in the day of the Lord's controversy, but follow the Lamb; this is the day of tribulation. We have to follow him in our age.'[37]

The vocation of a Quaker minister is set out cogently by Penington, who isolates its primary task as the keeper of the conscience of the flock. Friends are not to idolize or imitate pastors who administer truth that emanates from themselves rather than Christ, or who go 'further than the Spirit leads, guides and persuades them', and are, therefore, 'running into religious practices, without the Spirit'. His instruction to pastors is to focus on a pure conscience, which is the 'the main thing in religion'. The work of the pastor is 'to know the guide, to follow the guide, to receive from him the Light whereby I am to walk; and not to take things for truths because others see them to be truths'. Burrough does not mince words in his message to monarchs and rulers: ministers are sent by God, not the state, which has no right to meddle in spiritual affairs outside of its jurisdiction. At times the work of pastors will be contrary to the state: '[T]he Lord will have a ministry in this nation purely of his own . . . and such a ministry you shall not be able to hinder.'[38]

Christ as the fellowship of early Friends

It is plain to see that the single desire of the hearts of the Friends is experience and not knowledge. The answer of Penington to the question of how Friends want the Lord to appear to them epitomizes this longing for union with Christ: 'We wanted the power from on high, we wanted life, we wanted the presence and fellowship of our beloved; we wanted the knowledge of the heavenly feed and kingdom, and an entrance into it.' To abide in the Spirit of Christ, by distinguishing this sweet fellowship from an earthly and worldly spirit, is the strenuous Quaker requirement. The lover of the Light will have a tenderized conscience and will be willing to go to the mountain of the Lord to receive his precepts and to walk in his ways, which are the commands of Christ (see Mic. 4:2). For the early Quakers the truth about themselves does not arise from the guidance or opinions of others, as much as it does by a turning to the Christ within. The pattern of silent meetings is, therefore, the conduit for the act of clearing the channels of communication to enable Christ to speak. The notion of hearing the Lord amid the commotion of life is fine-tuned in early Quakerism.[39]

In practice, an individual brings a pertinent 'concern' before a small committee of clearness, a group of people whose task it is to bring clarity by discerning the proposition set before it. There is silent and expectant waiting in the Light as the group probes for an outcome. Communal deliberation may result in one of three options: go, or yield for a time to personal refiring, or no. In the case of an affirmative 'yes', approval of the 'concern' must be sought from the relevant Meeting, by means of harmonious and unanimous acceptance of the 'concern'. Modifications may be made. For example, in the absence of a parent the financial needs of a family may be met. Holy obedience to the directive of the Spirit must then be demonstrated, even if this means crossing oceans. The 'concern' of William Penn required him to leave his wife in delicate health – it is recorded that she desired he should go – and to travel 'under concern'. His famous 'Holy Experiment' in Pennsylvania is the consequence of his submission to the judgement of the fellowship. The respect paid to the innovator of the idea, and the due regard given to all, to the 'commonest he', is characteristic of Quaker equality.[40]

The evolution of Christ in the Society of Friends

As we have seen, the early Quaker vision of the Light is linked to an inward experience of Christ who has come to dwell in the heart. There is, however, continuity between inner and outer witness: Christ is both 'come and coming', in radical inward transformation, but also in social change – a new dispensation as a present reality, on earth. Gradually but inexorably, there is an eschatological shift during the later period, i.e. the 1670s and 1680s. Restoration is located in the heart, not in nations. As we have discovered,

Friends of the early awakening are fired by a visitation of Christ the Light and are compelled to be signs of difference in society. The later phase evolves into a religion of 'mystical light', viewed impersonally and disassociated from the person of Jesus Christ, who is a 'divine principle, universal and pre-existent'. The inward turn is also an affirmation of the divine principle already present in all people: 'What the Quakers sought within themselves was that of God in every person.' Robert Barclay, the influential scholar and vocal representative of this progression, expresses its sentiment thus: '[W]e have desired people earnestly to feel after God near and in themselves, telling them that their notions of God, as he is beyond the clouds, will little avail them, if they do not feel him near.'[41]

In order to expound on the divine principle, Barclay picks up the seed analogy in Proposition 5 in the *Apology*. His explanation of the seed – the grace and word of God by which all are enlightened – is confusingly complex. On the one hand the seed is *not* 'the proper essence and nature of God precisely taken, which is not divisible into parts and measures'; on the other hand the seed *is* 'a spiritual, heavenly, and invisible principle, in which God, as Father, Son, and Spirit dwells'. Barclay argues that there is a 'measure' of the divine life 'in all men as a seed', which of its own accord 'draws, invites, and inclines to God'. Barclay will have it both ways: that which is of God in all inclines to God, and that which is of God in all is not the substance of God. What precisely, then, is the divine principle? It is the seed, which is a vehicle of God in which God and Christ dwell. The seed is not a joining principle, i.e. a way of union with Christ. Neither is the seed identified as the conscience or reason or human nature, being separate from all that is human. However, Barclay will have it that the seed is present *as* Christ and *in* all, even in those who resist God. By means of an allegorical exegesis of Amos 2:13, he argues that if something of Christ is already present as a pure seed residing in everyone, then Christ is in all, even in his crucified state. As a cart is pressed under sheaves, so is Christ crucified in the ungodly: 'In this respect then, as he is in the seed which is in all men, we have said Christ is in all men, and have preached and directed all men to Christ in them, who lies crucified in them by their sins and iniquities.' At this point Barclay might be accused of a drift towards the inevitability of all being saved, i.e. a doctrine of universal salvation. However, his refusal to embrace the notion of perfectionism, which is prevalent in the early Friends, demonstrates not only his belief in ongoing sanctification, but in conversion itself '[F]or if all the saints, the least as well as the greatest, be perfectly justified in that very hour wherein they are converted, as our adversaries will have it, then they have remission of sins long before they die.'[42]

Having reflected on later evolving definitions of Christ, it is essential that we address a related issue, viz. can we trace the roots of the trend towards a blurring of the human and divine in the human being to the founder himself? Are there inklings in George Fox of a Gnostic or Docetic Christ? Taking the outcome of these questions into consideration, we must then judge the usefulness of early Quaker theory to the practice of prophetic pastoral leadership today.

The evolution of a Gnostic Christ in the Society of Friends

Contrary to previous studies, which place George Fox in an apocalyptic framework (the Quaker scholars Douglas Gwyn and Rosemary Moore, for example, uncover a fierce apocalypticism), an American writer, Glen D. Reynolds attempts to adopt him as a Christian Gnostic. Reynolds defines Gnosis as 'an individual's discovery through revelation and baptism that they are divine, with a part of their body (soul, seed, light) being consubstantial to the redeemer figure of Christ'. Christian Gnostic belief holds to the union between the divine element in an individual and Christ, stresses inner revelation, devalues Scripture and discards communion or baptism as outward rituals. In order to support his thesis that Fox is essentially a closet Gnostic, Reynolds leans heavily on the writings of John Owen (1616–83), a Puritan and vice chancellor of Oxford University. Owen dismisses Quakerism on the grounds that it diminishes the historic Christ and stresses the revelatory Light being Christ, with a subsequent deification and freedom from sin and temptation in the believer. Reynolds summarizes his findings in a list of characteristics shared by both Gnostic and Quaker creeds: the acceptance of spiritual and divine perfection, an anti-historical stance, reliance on revelation, and a reduction of the authority of Scripture. Reynolds argues that for Quakerism, as for Gnosticism, conduct is secondary to union, so that Foxian spiritual transformation supersedes ethical and moral issues.[43]

We have seen that the writings of George Fox reveal an ardent seeker whose union with Christ is real and dynamic. Is the achievement of such a spiritual state to be called Gnostic? In the works of Fox it is difficult to disentangle the physical from the spiritual, as his use of language for the divine indwelling is in the terminology of divine sonship, and the difference is somewhat blurred. There is the oft-quoted statement, in a letter to Oliver Cromwell in 1654, that he is the son of God: 'God is my witness, by whom I am moved to give this forth for the truth's sake, from him whom the world calls George Fox, who is the son of God.' One must agree with an editorial comment that more has been read into this statement than was intended by Fox. The young man was not a trained theologian, and in all probability based his thought on Romans 8:14: 'For those who are led by the Spirit of God are sons [huioi (Greek) = sons] of God' (transliteration). Similarly, the use of the phrase 'sons of God' for all God's children is insufficient proof of Gnosticism in the writings of Fox. Does Fox propose that the soul receives part of the divine essence at the birth of the individual, with a potential capacity for knowledge of God? It may appear so in the following agonizingly convoluted theology:

> Is not that of God that came out of him? And is not the earthly and human of the ground? And is not that mortal? And is that which is immortal human? And does thou say it is human, and is not that earthly? And where doth the Scripture of the prophets, Christ or the apostles, tell people of a human soul?

The close affinity between Christ and the divine, eternal nature of the soul is elaborated upon in graphic imagery, as Fox upbraids spiritually undiscerning priests for their lack of understanding of the enlightening Light:

> ... [Y]ou are stumbling at such as are become the sons of God, adopted sons and heirs, and of the flesh and bone of Christ, and of his mind and spirit ... [you] who come to the light in their own particulars and receive it, and with it comprehend darkness ... [you] do not know the soul from eternity to eternity.[44]

In these writings, which, we may say, are concerned with a soul that is potentially divine, there is a confusing opacity, on a par with the discussions on the divine essence already present in the seed in Adam. It may be safer to assert that the very haziness of the descriptions of the divine/human seed, Light and soul, are so obscure as to preclude a direct link with Gnosticism. In support of Fox, Graves maintains that in the early period the 'inward light' is 'not the *intrinsic* [my emphasis] part of the human psyche that shone *outward*, but the *inward* enlightening of God to every person'. The paucity of a robust theology in Fox and the first Friends, however, opens the door to fresh interpretations of Christ in the second period of Quakerism.[45]

The evolution of a Docetic Christ in the Society of Friend

The idea that Jesus Christ only appeared or seemed to be human is the central tenet of Docetism, which believes that the human form of Christ was an illusion. In this respect the remarks of Braithwaite on the inadequacy of George Fox's christology are helpful, as we attempt to trace the argument about Christ into the present day. He argues that Quaker theological 'woolliness' is aided and abetted by a philosophical Dualism in the thinking of the age. Locating the natural and the divine into two separate categories assists the failure in Quakerism to reach a unified conception of the person of Christ. Jesus Christ is merely a vessel through which the divine life works; the historic Christ is not given a full place in the purposes of God. Braithwaite declares that the Foxian expression of the Quaker experience promotes spiritual passivity, as it omits to teach an active faith which reaches out for God. The lack of a proper conception of human personality and obedience to an indefinable principle of life leads to the consequential collapse of faith, and a 'disastrous vagueness' in Quakerism.[46]

The theology of Penington exemplifies a dualistic Jesus Christ. It is governed by a verse in the Letter to the Hebrews, which lends welcome support to a theory explaining the co-existence of the divine and human in Christ. Penington does not slight the manhood of Christ, but lays the emphasis upon the *life* which took upon itself the manhood. He distinguishes between 'that which is called the Christ, and the bodily garment which he took. The one was flesh, the other spirit . . . the body of flesh was but the veil, Heb. 10:20. The eternal life was the substance veiled'. The one was the body prepared, in which the life appeared, and the other was 'the life, or Light itself, for whom the body was prepared'. In a discussion on the Light which shines in the conscience of the heathen, Penington convincingly displays the natural and the divine as a separation into two compartments. Christ is the real thing, the wisdom of God and the 'substance' itself, which the Lord brings forth under a 'veil' and which is the equivalent of 'the body prepared': the physical body of the human Jesus.[47]

Does an allegation of a Docetic Christ matter for pastoral practice? On the one hand, we have the sensitive Penington, whose instructions to Friends are laden with pastoral insight and practice arising from an encounter with the Lord. Reflecting on the experience of early Friends, he writes of the 'gospel-religion', which began in the inward demonstration and evidence of the Spirit of God: 'Can the Gospel-ministry, or gospel-work in any heart, be carried on without it?' On the other hand, there is the gradual fading of an earlier fiery vision into a way of Quakerism which is less distinctive although, it can be argued, hardly less compelling. Braithwaite sums up the problem of a divine/human paradox in the turn in later Quakerism to the idea of mystical union. In the notion that the mystical self is joined to another, the issue that cannot be avoided is that the spirit in us is the same Spirit which upholds the universe. He asserts that integral to contemporary spiritual trends is the lack of distinction between the human and the divine, and the belief in an ultimate Reality which holds together the whole of life. This 'Other' may well be named the 'inner light', a new term for contemporary liberal Quakerism. It goes without saying that evangelicals will find this brand of mysticism extremely problematic on the grounds that if the cross and the light are available to all, then this bypasses the real effectiveness of the life and death of Christ. One must also query a pastoral ministry which, in its attempt to be relevant to all, takes these vital orthodox Christian beliefs fairly lightly, and yet names itself Christian.[48]

An example of such liberalizing tendencies is found in Ambler's Experiment, a present-day project attempting to marry Quakerism rooted in Christian tradition to a universal philosophy. Rex Ambler, an English theologian, claims that the key to the *Works* of George Fox is a meditative process, which is the basis of an entire pattern of life. In a letter to Friends, Fox advocates a three-step process to overcome temptation. The first step is to see oneself in the Light of Christ, as it shines in the conscience to reveal sin and evil. The second step is to stand still in the Light, opening oneself to the truth. And thirdly, by standing still in a submission to the Light, one hushes the temptation. Ambler uses this method of meditation to suggest that the intellect, morality, integrity and feeling are not to be submitted to God as the ultimate Reality; on the contrary, they make up the path, as the acts of obedience following such states of meditation will show a submission to the Light within. Whilst meditation of this nature is not only fashionable today, but can be an effective means to calm the self into responsible action, it is important to note that it is entirely divorced from Scripture and the person of Jesus Christ. As we shall see in Chapter 4, this is far from the practice of waiting in the Light that is discussed in the writings of George Fox and the early Friends: the silent Meeting is interrupted by a flow of words from Scripture, and Christ the Light is never far from the participants' lips.[49]

Revisiting Prophetic Pastors

In our concluding discussion on the French Huguenot pastors, we noticed especially that the testimony to Christ, as the Spirit of prophecy, is in constant reformation and pressed into new shapes under the strain of persecution. In light of the distressing scenarios played out in the wars of religion and, more specifically, upon the Huguenot populace –the weight of taxation, the pressure to recant, the door to escape, the doorways to prison, torture or execution – we are reminded that Calvin's primary doctrine is 'that we might learn Christ'. As we considered the Huguenot resistance, active in the diaspora in the Cévennes and among displaced émigrés further afield, we realize that they understood that all things happened for the good as they looked to Christ, the 'the pioneer and perfecter' of their faith (Heb. 12:2). Is there a substitute for such loyalty and perseverance, under persecution, to the testimony of Jesus?

The early Quaker witness, in relation to the person of Jesus Christ, is fraught with conflict of a different sort, in its diversion from traditional religion: the issue of an inward experience in the Light versus the historic incarnate Lord. Despite their disparate ways, do we find sympathetic soundings between the Huguenot and Quaker faith in Christ? Garrett would have us accept that the Quaker doctrine of the inner Light preserved the same Pentecostal tradition that the French prophets embodied. A superficial view might agree with this summary: both movements are passionate about the power of the Lord and uphold with ferocious tenacity their inner witness to the truth. The nuances in Quakerism, however, must preclude such an easy assumption. The inability to sustain a coherent and robust christology in the early days leads to a confusing picture of Jesus Christ, which evolves over time into an ultimate Reality with which all faiths can concur. In the cold light of day when all is said and done, the issue boils down to this: pastoral prophetic leadership, according to conventional Calvinist principles, is more reliable than a Foxian experiential prophetic testimony.[50]

4.

Prophetic Teachers of Scripture

At another time I saw the great love of God, and was filled with admiration at the infiniteness of it . . . and how by Jesus, the opener of the door by his heavenly key, the entrance was given (George Fox).[1]

In a final chapter we are concerned with the problem of tired teaching systems devoid of divine encounter and dependent only on intellectual prowess to instruct the believers. How might we revive the prophetically inspired Bible teacher? A Calvinist way provides a bulwark against heresy and false teaching in its fixed and unshakeable hermeneutical method. The Huguenot Church remains consistently open, however, to a fresh breath of the Holy Spirit upon the words of Scripture, which invigorates its prophetic witness. A Quaker way has as its touchstone not the Bible, but the testimony of Christ within. This controversial point, of working from a personal experience of God to its confirmation in Scripture, is open to severe criticism but is not without an irrefutable dynamic and inner logic of its own.

Huguenot Teachers: Prophetic Spectacles of Scripture

Sometimes I am deceived by a fair dream:
I believe I truly see myself
In thine entourage, most honoured Queen,
As I used to be, in thy curtained chamber,
In which thou hadst me sing in divers tones,
Those songs of thine which are the sacred psalms.
Clément Marot (*c.* 1496–1544), *Epistre a la royne de Navarre*
trans. M.A. Screech.[2]

Our brief survey of the Cévennes crucible has underlined the critical role played by spontaneous prophetic speech to inspire the Church of the *désert*, and at times to direct both the flight of the Huguenot émigrés and the fight of the Camisars. We are left with questions about the reliability of a prophetic witness dependent only on direct inspiration to hear, with utter clarity, the voice of God. Are the discourses of sleeping prophets and ecstatic visionaries the only way in which the Church of the *désert* was guided? Was disciplined Calvinist 'bookishness' abandoned? How was the Huguenot resistance oriented to the Bible? In order to grasp the part played by Scripture during the times of violent uprising and revolt in the Huguenot resistance, we must seek to understand the supremacy of the Bible for the Calvinist. Calvin's theology on the inseparability of Word and Spirit in Scripture, its impact on preaching and discernment of false teachers, is particularly important for our assessment of the Huguenot movement as it struggles to keep its own unique identity. The question of the unity of Word and Spirit is important for our task of understanding how prophecy works in the Church of the désert. For this we employ the method of the literal-prophetic hermeneutic and establish its outworking in scriptural exposition by Huguenot teachers. We shall examine the Psalter as the inspired teacher of the desert in war and in the diaspora.

The supremacy of Scripture in Calvin

Calvin's axiom is the non-negotiable authority of Scripture for all the theology that is and can be known. All else is speculation. His teaching is less about dogma and more about the whole of life. He attempts to bring together morality and religion. This is crystal clear in his treatise addressed to the city of Geneva, 'Confession of Faith which all the citizens and inhabitants of Geneva and the subjects of the country must promise to keep and hold' (1536). His high view of the Bible is set out thus:

> First we affirm that we desire to follow Scripture alone as rule of faith and religion, without mixing with it any other thing which might be devised by the opinion of men apart from the Word of God, and without wishing to accept for our spiritual government any other

doctrine than what is conveyed to us by the same Word without addition or diminution, according to the command of our Lord.

Calvin's treatise stresses that spiritual doctrine is a door into the kingdom of God and this entry point is the sacred text of Scripture. He wishes the church to grasp fully the primacy of Scripture, and to realize that he is not the author of these intimations and that those who read them must know that they are 'truly from the Word of God'. He instructs his readers: '[T]ake them not at all as from us, but as from him from whom they proceed, that you similarly consider of what importance and consequence they are for the maintenance of the honour of God in this State and the conservation of the Church in its integrity.'[3]

Calvin's most decisive utterance on the role of the Bible is in his analogy of the 'spectacles of Scripture'. He cites the usefulness of spectacles for old or bleary-eyed men with weak vision who are unable to read the most beautiful words, and compares it with Scripture, which 'gathering up the otherwise confused knowledge of God in our minds, having dispersed our dullness, clearly shows us the true God'. By this Calvin means God 'opens his own most hallowed lips' to instruct the church. Calvin reads the Bible as a Renaissance man, exercising the second of the two methods of allegorical interpretation, whereby significance is gleaned not through fable and examples, but through types and ideas in the story. The actual text is a mirror for the living God, just as the invisible God is set before us in the story of Moses 'as a mirror in which his living likeness glows'. Calvin is at pains to show that all other means for the search for God will lead only to perplexity. By using the analogy of spectacles he drives home his point concerning the absolute necessity of Scripture for knowledge of God: 'For just as eyes, when dimmed with age or weakened by some other defect, unless aided by spectacles, discern nothing distinctly; so, such is our feebleness, unless Scripture guides us in seeking God, we are immediately confused.' The poet Clément Marot expresses the same idea, that the text itself is a mirror to describe the Word which is Christ: 'And so my brethren, we must mirror ourselves in the word of God, which is the word of Jesus Christ, which is the law of perfect freedom of the children of God, the Gospel law: and always have it before us, ever mirroring ourselves in it . . . Let his Word be ever our mirror.'[4]

For Calvinists, all sources for knowledge of God are untrustworthy. For them, secular literature is not of equal value to sacred writing and they are suspicious of fiction. The purpose in writing is to praise God and there is no relation between sacred and profane texts. The revealed word of God is pre-eminent and the purpose of all writing is to magnify God's word. Calvin's successor, Theodore Beza, is rigorous in his denial of any writing not inspired by the Bible. This judgement on literature explains the abundance of biblical text quoted in the depositions, the stories of the French refugees which we examined. In order to be validated as a true witness, each eyewitness account has to demonstrate knowledge of Scripture. Likewise the plain and unembellished narrative (1690) of two émigrés, a mother and daughter from Champagne, is not explicitly religious or spiritual. The writing of the mother, Marie de La Rochefoucauld, is not biographical, and although her flight from site to site in France and England has the potential for allegory, she does not make use of the geographical terrain as a vehicle for her experience. It is a factual confession (*reconnaissance*) composed for an audience, the Huguenot community in England, about their circumstance and faith. Her daughter, Suzanne de Robillard, dutifully includes a Bible text: 'During the voyage and after arriving, I taught them and myself with the twenty-seventh Psalm ['The LORD is my light and my salvation'], which, it seems to me, suited me very well.'[5]

Word and Spirit in Scripture in Calvin

Just as the primacy of Scripture is foundational for faith, so the unity of Christ and the Spirit in Scripture is fundamental for the teaching of faith. 'Word and Spirit belong inseparably together' is the heading for the third part of Calvin's exposition, 'Fanatics, Abandoning Scripture and Flying Over to Revelation, Cast Down All the Principles of Godliness'. The principle may be stated thus: Christ is the interpreter and fulcrum of Scripture, which remains lifeless in us unless the Spirit brands the dead letter on our hearts with the life-giving properties of Christ (Phil. 2:16; 2 Cor. 3:6). As this action of the Spirit relates to the preaching of the word of Christ, Calvin explains that the Spirit completes the work of Christ, confirming it by his word. Preaching is the 'ministration of the Spirit' (2 Cor. 3:8). Calvin's commentary on Galatians underscores this point. Paul's oratory is not by word but by the 'power of the Spirit', present to reveal Christ crucified in a tangible way. A representation of Christ by means of the power of the Spirit will 'penetrate into consciences, so that men may see Christ crucified and that his blood may flow'.[6]

Claude Brousson, the apostolic pastor to the Church of the *désert*, provides a good example of the combined power of Christ and the Spirit in the word of preaching. Brousson's text is the Song of Songs 5:2, the voice of Christ the Beloved. The narrator of this event, a Frenchman, describes his conversion to his children:

> Kneeling on the ground, but our souls rising up to heaven, we heard, first, the ten commandments, then the prayer for confession of sins; and, in the same attitude, we sang with hushed voices the first part of the fifth psalm, after which came the exposition of the divine words . . . and, lastly, our participation in the holy supper.

Brousson said that 'the Holy Sprit has had mercy on us and has reconquered our souls'. Herein lies the key: the inner working of the Spirit within the preached word of Christ has converting power to bring about a change in the soul. John Quick writes that Brousson has the grace of God given him 'to preach his word in its native simplicity and purity, in the evidence and demonstration of the Spirit'. This preaching style is dissimilar in every respect from the fanatical teachers addressed by Calvin in his treatise.[7]

Calvin gives short shrift to 'giddy men' carried away by frenzy, who exalt the teaching office of the Spirit and abandon the teaching of Scripture. He interprets Isaiah 59:2 as a foreshadowing of the Christian way, arguing that the prophet does not 'bind the ancient folk to outward doctrine as if they were learning their ABCs; rather, he teaches that under the reign of Christ the new church will have this true and complete happiness; to be ruled no less by the voice of God than by the Spirit'. By this he means that the Christian community will be governed by the voice of Christ and the voice of the Spirit in Scripture. Calvin has a reliable method for testing 'new and unheard-of revelations', or anything which 'foists another doctrine upon us', or any person who carelessly forsakes Scripture to 'seize upon whatever they may have conceived while snoring'. He argues that the Spirit promised by Jesus does not teach from himself but instils in our minds what Jesus has handed on through his word (John 16:13). We notice again the cooperation of Spirit and Christ in the taught word. To those who suggest that the Spirit is not subject to Scripture, Calvin retorts that as the author of Scripture, the Spirit cannot vary or differ from himself by submission to human judgement. Calvin's stance is the inseparability of Spirit and Scripture. Although Paul was caught up into the third heaven, he was nonetheless an expert in the doctrine of the Law and the Prophets. Calvin notes his injunction to believers in 1 Thessalonians 5:19,20 not to quench the Spirit. At the same time Paul is balanced, as he 'does not loftily catch them up to lofty speculations without the Word, but immediately adds that prophecies are not to be despised'.[8]

Calvin addresses factions and sects within Christianity, viz. the Anabaptists and Libertines – particularly those which exalt the Spirit over the letter or delve into speculative thinking and doctrines of sinlessness – by labouring to disentangle their obscurities and drag them forcibly into the light. He urges the church not to forsake the plain language of Scripture, whereby the Lord accommodates himself: '[A]s a wet nurse coos to her baby, so He uses toward us an unrefined (*grossiere*) way of speaking in order to be understood.' Calvin's tough, uncompromising rebuttal of new-fangled teaching is echoed by the anonymous writer of a pamphlet entitled 'A Discourse of Schism' (1702): '[L]et us never give present assent to any new opinion that pretends Scripture.' This writer denounces private teachers who impose their fabricated doctrines upon the ignorant. The principle of public discernment should be applied, i.e. the duty of the church community, by means of the received revelation in Scripture, to assess teachers who traffic in new thought. Brousson urges his flock not to hold communion with 'ministers of Satan', by which he means Catholic priests, who have violated edicts and tormented the faithful with a thousand evils. We shall examine a sermon by Brousson in order to ascertain how he holds together the union of Christ and the Spirit in Scripture, and for this purpose we must now attend to the question of a literal-prophetic sense of Scripture.[9]

Literal-prophetic hermeneutic

The French humanist biblical scholar, Jacques Lefèvre d'Etaples (c. 1455–1536), sets out the principles of biblical interpretation: the literal-historical method, the Old Testament as historical narrative; and the literal-prophetic method, the coming of Jesus Christ as prophecy. Having investigated the traditional way of reading the texts for the literal sense, he discusses the idea that this 'is not the true literal sense' ('non verus litteralis sit sensus'), i.e. belonging to the letter. He researches the way in which Paul, the prophets and the evangelists had 'first committed the divine seed to the trenches, or ploughing, of our souls and opened a door of the letter of holy Scripture'. He then sees 'another sense' ['alium sensum'] which is plainly the intention of the prophet and of the Holy Spirit speaking in him. This he calls the letter, i.e the literal 'sense', which coincides with the Spirit and which is the view of the prophets or seers, those with open eyes. He goes on to state that for those who are not open-eyed, but nonetheless think they see, another literal sense assumes its place. This sense is a destroyer and opponent of the Spirit. This way of interpretation is to assign to David, the writer of the psalms, the role of narrator and not of prophet. But David himself spoke prophetically: 'The Spirit of the Lord spoke though me and his word is upon my tongue.' D'Etaples concludes that there is a two-fold sense: one is a faulty sense; those with unopened eyes are blinded and interpret divine things according to the flesh and human understanding; the other is the proper or particular way of interpretation ['proprium'], which belongs to those seeing and receiving illumination. The first is the deception, or fiction, of human reason; the second is the pouring in, or injecting, by the divine Spirit. D'Etaples explains how monks complain that, upon leaving sessions of teaching according to the literal sense, they feel depressed as though iced water had been thrown on a burning fire. He encourages the sense of Scripture that gives light and colour to the text.[10]

Huguenot rhetoric is alive with the literal-prophetic sense of Scripture. Preachers seem at a loss to apply anything other than a prophetic contemporary sense to the historic biblical narrative. One of the complaints in a catalogue of persecutions (1707) reads:

> If any minister spoke but of Egypt, of Pharaoh, of the Israelites, of the godly or the wicked (as it was difficult not to speak of these matters, when they explained the Scriptures), those spies never failed to report, that by Egypt and by the wicked, they meant the Catholic, by Pharaoh the King, by the Israelites, the pretended Reformed.

Deiadamia, a French Catholic, rich in the goods of this world but poor in the kingdom of God, is instructed about the wisdom and goodness of God by her gardener, who has a 'peculiar faculty of spiritualizing his employment, and making his business serve, like Jacob's ladder, to carry him from earth to heaven'. The literal-prophetic hermeneutic may be noted in a prophetic word given by a young woman on meeting an itinerant preacher on his journey to the churches in the Haut Vivarais: 'The sword thou hast seen at thy servant's side is my Word which will be in his mouth as a two-edged sword. This abundant dew thou hast seen fall upon his head is the same Word, which will live abundantly in him.' We recognize the imagery of the double-edged sword as a combination of texts from the books of Revelation (1:16; 2:12; cf. 2:16; 19:15) and Hebrews (4:12): We see that this 'sword', which is equivalent to the word of the prophet, is different from the 'sword' we came across in Chapter 2: 'I have not come to bring peace, but a sword' (Matt. 10:34).[11]

The literal-prophetic sense is also at work in prophetic utterance (or performance). It is reported in the assemblies that 'When the prophet had been under agitations of body for a while, he began to preach and to prophesy.' Elias Marion, one of the three French *inspirés* in London, issues several prophetic warnings for the city. Each is nuanced with a faint whisper of a familiar scriptural text. The prophecy, 'Yet a few days, and I will set this city on fire, and will inflame it with my word', is an echo of the reviving Pentecost flames over Jerusalem (Acts 1,2). When the Lord addresses the prophet in these words, 'My child, I tell thee, my truth is wandering; she can find no place of retreat upon earth. I must come, and cause room to be made for her – they have driven her away; they have cast her out everywhere', the listener (or reader) recalls the Lord Jesus himself saying, 'the Son of Man has nowhere to lay his head' (Luke 9:58), and that he is the truth (John 14:6). The metaphor of digging for truth in the following prophecy is a reminder of the parable of the pearl of great price, the pursuit of the ultimate gain: 'My child, my laws are now hid, but I come to discover the very depths of them. My children shall understand them, and know my will: they shall dig into them, and shall find the truth.' In these examples of prophecy we see the centrality of Jesus Christ as the Spirit draws out fresh meaning from biblical inferences.[12]

Literal-prophetic homiletic

Claude Brousson preached the same sermon, 'The Support of the Faithful in Times of Persecution' in several places in the wilderness on three separate occasions between July 1692 and September 1693. His text is Isaiah 41:14: 'Do not fear, you worm Jacob, you insect Israel!' He seeks to teach his listeners how to understand the 'sense' of these words, 'that though the literal sense of the prophecies of the Old Testament had respect to the church of Israel after the flesh; yet their mystical sense relates to the Christian church, which is Israel after the Spirit; and moreover, that those ancient prophecies have their chief and full accomplishment nowhere but in the Christian church'. He implores the assistance of the Holy Spirit in his exposition. We detect in the message the synergy of Christ and the Spirit in the moulding of the character of the Church of the *désert* by the Spirit to show forth the testimony of Jesus.[13]

Brousson limits himself to the mystical sense of the words as they relate to Christians. He is not very encouraging. The consolation of God is upon the refugee church, a 'worm', yet Christians are the heirs, like Jacob, of the heavenly food. Compared with God, who fills heaven and earth, they are but 'worms of the earth', or 'dust and ashes', who ought to remember their misery and nothingness. The sermon gets worse, not better, in a comparison between the 'worm' and its enemy. As Jacob strove with God and is wounded, so the Church of the *désert* is lamed and humbled in order to understand that, as Brousson put it, 'when we are benighted in affliction, as we are at this time, and when we fear the rage and fury of our enemies; that then it is our duty to humble ourselves before God in an extraordinary manner', with prayers and tears, until the church has 'disarmed (as it were) his almighty arm, and obtained his blessing and assistance'. He exhorts his congregations to meditate on the word of God 'with continual application of mind, and constantly pray to God for the assistance of his Holy Spirit; for 'tis by his Word and Spirit he fortifies our faith, and 'tis by faith we are enabled to repel all the fiery darts of the Devil'.

Literal-prophetic militant psalmody

We next consider the import of psalmody, and for this topic we must delve into the early days of Calvinism. Calvin's aim is to build a sound worshipping community. Brousson's sermon illustrates not only the literal-prophetic method of a Huguenot teacher, but also his aversion to the fight and his championing of the flight of émigrés. As we have seen, evacuees from the homeland or exiled worshippers to the wilderness face extreme penalties, sometimes death. The embattled church of the Refuge must take courage in the fight of faith and the constant companion and armour of its members is the Psalter. Brousson himself often faced martyrdom and reputedly recites a psalm when fearful for his life:

> Why art thou cast down O my soul? Why art thou disquieted within me? Hope still in God, who is the light of thy countenance and thy God. My life is in his hands. If he will have me die, 'tis not all the world can hinder it. And if I must die, 'tis better dying in the way of duty than in the neglect of it.

The steadfastness of Brousson is an echo of the depth of joy experienced by Calvin when he recites the psalms, 'girding and preparing himself for prayer', and especially in his many trials. He deems all secular music unsuitable for worship, but enlists it for the singing of psalms. For Calvin praise is merely prayer sung with warmth and passion, not simply popular hymns, but psalms to express the complexity of the journey of the soul. Liturgical psalm singing, therefore, is one of the marks of the fundamentally remoulded *Eglise Réformée*. Tracing the Calvinist way of psalm singing in order to grasp the intensity of Huguenot attachment to the psalms, our route takes us back to the evangelical French poet-in-exile, Clément Marot. Despite the condemnation of the psalms by the Sorbonne, his elegant prose translation endorsed its popular appeal. Calvin commissioned a musical setting for liturgical use and the two editions (1539, 1551), containing psalms by Marot and Thédore Beza, invigorated Protestant worship. The Psalter became a key text and active agent of Calvinist militancy, aided no doubt by the prohibition of scandalous public psalm singing in the vernacular in 1558 by Henri II. Psalms are sung to disrupt Catholic services, and are sung by prisoners on their way to prison and execution and as marching songs to rally civilians in war.[14]

Psalm singing is the warp and woof of Calvinist worship, and for the Languedoc Church of the desert the psalms are life-giving – a sustaining, dynamic force. The Psalter is an oasis to uplift the spirits of beleaguered Huguenots living in a spiritual drought. It is an arsenal and a battery of truth to defeat their persecutors. The psalms teach these Christians that persecution is a trial sent from God and surmountable by joy and praise. For these reasons the ban on psalm singing is not only an affront to worshippers, but a declaration of war and a guarantee of greater loyalty to Reformed piety. Jean Claude's list of new laws in the dark days of persecution tabulates the embargo on the singing of psalms in private houses, even in temples when the sacraments or processions passed by. Nothing daunted, a pamphlet written to French churches under the cross dictates the singing of a psalm at the beginning of an outdoor service, more psalms sung a cappella after the reading of biblical texts, a sung psalm to close. For morning and evening worship at home, one or two psalms are sung. An impartial observer states that in a desert assembly a prophet recites 'with his utmost strength' the prayer that Protestants pray before the sermon, followed by one of the psalms of Marot or Beza. Notwithstanding his healthy lungs and strong voice, Quick remarks that the high and lofty notes in French psalm singing take their toll on Claude Brousson, who leads his congregations so that they may sing the psalms musically. Thus the hidden church makes every attempt to keep the faith by fidelity to its liturgical tradition.[15]

Devotion to church practice is one thing, but a prophetic rendering of psalms to sanction the use of violence is quite another. At the outset of the attack on Pont-de-Montvert, the catalyst for the Camisard War, the assembled peasants gather to wait in prayer upon the directive of the Holy Spirit, and when told to go home and fetch their weapons they march on the prison, chanting Psalm 51, the penitential psalm. One can only surmise that their motive is to cleanse their own hearts before committing the acts of violence they believed to have been ordered by God. In these cases the question of the trustworthiness of such radical commands ordered by Spirit-possessed men must be set alongside the insights of Calvin delivered to churches in *extremis*.[16]

Calvin's letters to the persecuted Protestant church in Paris between 1557 and 1559 (some smuggled into prisons) show us the strengthening effect of psalms in war. For protection 'there is no safety except under the shadow of God's wings' (Ps. 57); for peace of mind and patience in persecution, God permits the shedding of blood of his servants, yet 'he fails not to treasure up their precious tears as it were in a phial, according to the expression of David in Psalm 56'; for the example of Jesus Christ, mocked and scoffed, there is a word for those tormented to stand fast on the word despite the mockers, and to keep to the law in the face of the snares of the wicked, because 'my heart standeth in awe of thy word' (Ps. 119). A higher prophetic insight shines through these lines of Scripture injected with the Holy Spirit, to give meaning to a church under extraordinary pressure. Our sufferings and triumphs, as individuals and as a church, are prophetically related to the sufferings and triumphs of Christ. For Calvin all the emotions of life – grief, fear, perplexity – are captured by the Spirit at work in the prophets, who 'laying open all their inmost thoughts and affections, call, or rather draw, each of us to the examination of himself in particular'. In the preface to his commentary (1557), he calls the psalms 'An Anatomy of All the Parts of the Soul'. It is this comprehensive view of the psalms, engaging intellect as well as heart, which garrisoned Huguenot defiance and is at the centre of spiritual renewal in France.[17]

Subversive song in the underground church

In his pastoral letter of 1 October 1688, Pierre Jurieu reflects on the singing of psalms as one of the remarkable activities of Isabeau Vincent, the girl prophet of Dauphiné. He remarks that 'she sings them very sweetly and agreeably too; and for the most part quite thorough'. He insists that Isabeau sings without knowing the psalms and without missing a note, which seems a little unlikely, given the high priority of the sung Psalter in Calvinism. Jurieu attests her knowledge of the *Pater Noster* (Lord's Prayer) and *Credo* (Creed) – two other pieces in learned liturgical practice. A gentleman of Dauphiné writes to a friend in Geneva, recalling the little prophetess singing ecstatically, 'with her eyes closed, putting out her hands one after another; after which she sings *Leve le cœur* ('Lift up your Heart') or some other psalm to the end'. There is no doubt that these songs of exhortation are sung to encourage the persecuted folk present and they are followed by Isabeau's exposition on several passages from Scripture, made in a good strong voice. We note that at all times she speaks in good French, except in her denunciations of the abuses of the Catholic Church, when she falls back into her own dialect to camouflage her subversive activity. An eyewitness testifies to the shepherdess singing Psalm 42 in her sleep, a ministry under cover, as it were, for she sings of 'hiding the word of God' and tells those who do not understand to leave the room. Another witness, in conversation with a friend, describes Isabeau's discourse on 'hiding the word'. She informs her congregation that when we are hidden in the word of God it becomes our 'fortress' and the wicked are 'disabled'. Therefore we are to 'search his word, and hide it in our hearts; and God by his grace will make his glory shine upon us'. She sings two or three verses of the commands of God in rhyme, contrasting these with the ways of the wicked (meaning no doubt the persecutors of the Huguenots), whose 'efforts and malice was [*sic*] like the stones flung against trees, and like feathers cast against the wind'. A cynical de Brueys rather disparagingly dismisses the testimony of the imprisoned Isabeau Vincent, using the simile of a bird singing. She

> did not do like some birds, who – sing no more when put into a cage, she talked rather more than ever. And then it was that she said to her judges, (what Mr. Jurieu has so much built upon in one of his Letters): 'Ye may put me to death, but God will raise up others to speak greater things than I have done.'[18]

Inspired psalms in the underground church

Calvin's perspective on psalm singing as divinely ordained is heightened considerably as we examine texts in which the skies over certain geographical regions in the Refuge resemble a celestial concert hall. Earth is invaded by heaven in a symphony of angelic psalms. We see the divine order of wilderness worship reflected, as in a mirror, in the music of the spheres. In the theatre of the Cévennes, this uplifting spectacle is a sign of God's gracious blessing and favour. Just as the heavenly host is a portentous marvel, celebrating the miraculous nativity of the Messiah Jesus Christ (Luke 2:13,14), so the angelic choir in Languedoc trumpets a victory. For the persecuted church in France this is 'a miraculous token of the will of God in those singings that have been heard in the air at the beginning of this persecution'. M. Vivens, a pastor in the Cévennes and a preacher in the desert church for two years, claims to have heard thirty or forty (angels?) at one time. M. Valles-cure, a gentleman of the Cévennes, hears five or six verses of Psalm 5 sung celestially. This particular psalm in twelve verses, a plea for the help of God over oppressive enemies, ends with the stanza, 'For you bless the righteous, O LORD; you cover them with favour as with a shield' – an entirely appropriate angelic refrain in the circumstances. The writer of a critical examination of the question of miracles states categorically that in these otherworldly harmonies they have identified 30 psalms of the Huguenot Church.[19]

Letters to Jurieu from his countrymen tell of trumpets in the sky and angels singing psalms. An imprisoned minister writes: 'There are a multitude of people that say they have heard in France the sound of a trumpet, and the singing of psalms, all coming out of the air.' He witnesses to hearing these phenomena in an 'infinite number of places', the first time on 1 April 1686, in Viane, Upper Languedoc. At other times he heard the sound of a trumpet, 'together with a harmony [angelic?] bearing much resemblance to the singing of our psalms'. He recollects hearing this harmony, together with a clerk and his uncle, all three so transported that they lift up their hands to heaven, 'ravished and charmed'. He hears either the trumpet or the harmony at Rovergue, Geuadan, Auvergue, the Forests, the Lyonnois, and a part of Savoy. He perceives that the trumpet sounds in the plains and the harmony in the vales, both day and night, although more distinctly at night. He simply will not accept that heavenly music is merely the singing of certain people in caves or woods in Viane and Berlière. Others have heard it as far away as the Cévennes. In fact, five men of Mazamet are in prison for having said they heard 'the sound of a trumpet, and the singing of psalms coming out of the air'. It appears that the heavenly songs increase in beauteous intensity, in tune with troubles in the vale of tears on earth. According to M. Descalmels: 'The trumpet sounds always as if an army were going to charge, and that [sic] the harmony is like a composition of many voices, and of an infinite number of musical instruments, and that [sic] sometimes more and sometimes less ravishing, according to the situation of the vales.' In all cases the heavenly music comforts and consoles a community ravaged by savage persecution.[20]

The Bible in the underground church

As we have seen, Calvin's starting point for doctrine as a doorway into the kingdom of God is Scripture. The converting power of the Holy Spirit in the Bible may be seen at work in the clandestine spiritual conversations between the Catholic Deiadamia and Bernard, her uneducated Protestant gardener. On separate occasions she stumbles upon him in the garden in spiritual pursuits: secretly reading aloud from his own Bible, unashamedly weeping at his devotions and praying for mercy. He tries to conceal the Bible. She demands the book that it may be consigned to fire and promises to protect his 'being conversant with a book so strictly by the church prohibited to the laity'. She is fearful of misuse and heresy – a powerful argument. The gardener retaliates in an impassioned speech, declaring that he would rather die than betray the Lord by sending the Bible, the way to salvation, to the flames. Deiadamia is convinced and relents of her plan, pondering instead on his words about sincerity in Paul's speech to Felix (Acts 24:10–21) 'in her night-thoughts' and 'labourings in her mind, through the gracious operation of the Holy Spirit'. Finally procuring a Bible in the vernacular, a French Bible, Deiadamia reads it at every opportunity. Exchanging her rosary beads, crucifix and legends of saints for frequent prayers, she finds 'abundance of joy and comfort enlightening her soul, so that she could not forbear breaking out into raptures of praises and thanksgiving, for the wonderful change, (by so strange and unexpected means) wrought in her soul'.[21]

It is important to establish the foundation on which the Church of the *désert* is built, that is, the bulwark of the operations of both Christ and the Spirit in Scripture. John Lacy, the English gentleman whose rigorous scrutiny of the Cévennes uprising is recorded in his preface to *A Cry from the Désert*, states categorically that Scripture is the 'touchstone' by which everything must be tried. Having cross-examined witnesses, he finds that the Scriptures are read as the supreme rule of the Huguenot faith. The Trinity is asserted. Jesus Christ is the cornerstone and the sacrament of his Supper is celebrated in the gatherings. In ecstasies under the operation of the Spirit the two great commandments are urgently enforced and other prayers practised, including those for Princes. Psalm singing is a constant. Lacy's interrogation concludes that 'This mission brings no new doctrine with it, nor advances anything different from the Scriptures.' Lacy is a Protestant of his time who believes in the democratization of the Bible. The grace of God, in anyone studying the Bible independent of scholars and clergymen, reaps its reward. He commends, therefore, the direct inspiration from the Spirit which he discovers in the Huguenot interpretation of Scripture: 'If mankind from the least to the greatest, shall ever come to be taught immediately by the Spirit of God, they will not need other instructors.'[22]

The sceptical de Brueys is quite out of his depth, baffled by the biblical knowledge evident in the youth of the rebel church: 'Persons of good sense, even Catholics themselves, knew not what to think of it; to hear little boys and young girls, of the dregs of mankind, who could not so much as read, quote many texts of the Holy Scripture.' Divine inspiration belongs to the illiterate and uneducated, and this radical view, which is the stance of the Huguenots, is summed up by a young Welshman of the same period, Arise Evans, who looks upon Scripture 'as a mystery to be opened at this time *belonging also to us* [my emphasis].'[23]

Quaker Teachers: Prophetic Openings of Scripture

> But the Spirit of light owns Scriptures, and the Scripture doth judge spiritual light, and they are one against the other, but are in unity (George Fox).[24]

The unusual approach which the early Quakers take to the Bible lays the movement open to charges of an unorthodox biblical hermeneutic. Notwithstanding the emphasis in the early stages of the Society of Friends, upon experience in the Light for the development of faith, the Bible is of supreme importance for the Quaker. Inevitably there were fanatics who wished to cast off its restraint, asserting that their experience is greater than the written word, but they are in the minority. The premise is that, because the Bible can *only* be understood correctly by the Spirit, it remains authoritative because the Spirit is changeless. We shall let the Quaker literature of the day speak for itself, allowing controversial issues to be addressed as they arise.

The place of Scripture in the teachings of George Fox

Our approach to George Fox and his attitude to the Bible will engage with three primary assertions in early Quakerism: first, the compelling appearing of Christ in the 'openings' of the heart; secondly, the distinction between the Spirit or spiritual word of Christ, and the Law or the word as a dead letter; thirdly, the proclamation of the word of Christ from immediate revelation, and not from the outward forms. The first supposition has its impetus in the high regard for the inward revelation above the written Scripture, and is a reaction to biblical authority as this is expressed in academic exegesis. For Fox, as for the later Quakers, God is the key to biblical hermeneutics, and the Spirit is the supreme interpreter of Scripture. Fox arrives at this fundamental tenet by means of the series of 'openings' that he experiences at the very beginning of his spiritual quest. Prior to these fresh revelations we recall his fruitless conversations with priests who are 'miserable comforters', and it grieves him to open his mind to one who is 'an empty, hollow cask'. These men, Fox says, 'could not reach my condition'. The divine openings are an X-ray upon his inner state of mind: they answer one another and are answered by the Scriptures. In an enlightening moment he is struck by the stupendous truth that only Christ Jesus can speak to his condition: '[T]here was an anointing within man to teach him . . . the Lord would teach his people himself.' In the same way that Christ opens the seals in the Book of Revelation (5:5), he opens the creature and the creation. Christ is the key which opens and shuts in visions, in openings. Christ is the true teacher. This cornerstone of belief, fixed firmly in place, remains unaltered in Fox's later doctrinal writings (1677): 'And the word of the Lord is to you, that God is come, and coming to teach his people himself, by his Son Jesus Christ.' Fox spreads abroad the message of the workings of Christ in the heart, 'we do earnestly desire and wait, that by the Word of God's power and its *effectual operation* in the hearts of men', the kingdoms of the world will be subjected to the kingdom of God. The teacher must lead people to the Spirit, who will instruct the heart in the truth of Christ, through Scripture:

> And I was to direct people to the Spirit, that gave forth the Scriptures, by which they might be led into all truth, and so up to Christ and God, as they had been, who gave them forth. And I was to turn them to the grace of God, and to the truth in the heart, which came by Jesus.[25]

The second concept tenaciously adhered to by Fox is that Christ is the power or Spirit that speaks through the words of Scripture, which is the 'letter' or 'form'. We may understand the distinction between Spirit and letter by means of public disputes between Fox and opponents to his teaching. In a dispute with an antagonist, Fox asks the assembly of people to take out their Bibles, saying, 'for I would make the Scriptures bend him'. He argues that, far from being a natural created light, the Word, i.e. Christ, is with God from the beginning and created all things. On another occasion he defends his views against any who assert that the Scriptures are above the Spirit and the angels: '[T]he Word was God and the Spirit gave forth Scriptures, and . . . he must know in himself both the Word and Spirit which reconciles to the Scriptures, to God, and to one another.' At another time Fox challenges an adversary, claiming that 'if all are in possession of the divine Light then it comes before the acquisition of the written Scriptures and itself teaches all the saints. All must have the Spirit of God too, or else how were they capable of grieving him.' In a treatise he pins down the progression: first is the Spirit within – the law or word in the heart – leading into all truth; and second is the Scripture, given forth by the Spirit. In obtuse rhetoric he asks: 'Were not all the Scriptures from the Spirit within? And were they not there before they came out? And must not all upon the earth have the Spirit within that gave it forth, before they can understand the Scripture without?'[26]

The third core notion in the thought of George Fox is the revelation of the Word of God through an immediate encounter, not through the written form. Scripture confirms the experience: 'Yet I had no slight esteem of the Holy Scriptures; but they were very precious to me: for I was in that Spirit by which they were given forth; and what the Lord opened to me, I afterwards found was agreeable to them.' The emphasis on immediate revelation renders erudite sermons useless and governs Fox's critique of the trained university men. Without a right sense of Scripture 'you run into all absurdities, that give your meaning to Scriptures, and by private interpretations have brought the world on heaps above the Scriptures. And who are in the faith, are in the healing of the sick, and removing mountains, and you who are out of the faith have brought whole nations into sickness, mountains, and rough places.' Presumably the quaint phrase, 'brought the world on heaps', is a description of the world foundering on heaped-up edifices of teaching elevated above the Bible. The revelation of Christ the teacher is the true message, which was lost through apostasy and is now regained and revealed to his servants the prophets, not least of whom is George Fox. Margaret Fell writes that '[h]e was the instrument in the hand of the Lord in this present age..[27]

The place of Scripture in the early Friends

William Penn reflects on the remarkable ability of George Fox to open the Scriptures: 'He would go to the marrow of things. and show the mind, harmony, and fulfilling of them with much plainness and to great comfort and edification.' This favourable observation is illustrated in the challenging question put to Margaret

Fell by Fox at their first meeting at her home in Swarthmoor: 'Art thou a child of light, and hast walked in the light, and what thou speakest, is it inwardly from God?' On hearing him open the Scriptures, Margaret Fell is 'opened' and 'cut to the heart' (cf. Acts 2:37), weeping bitterly and crying out: 'We are all thieves, we are all thieves; we have taken the Scriptures in words, and know nothing of them in ourselves.' This heartfelt cry cuts to the chase, drawing the distinction between the inner dynamic of the Spirit, and the outward 'form' or 'letter' of the Law. The priority of the revelation by the Light, as an experience in the heart, is emphasized by Fell in her writings to Friends: 'Therefore turn into the measure of the Light which ye have received from the fountain of Light, and see what ye have there in possession.' In the Light a person will also see what is *not* possessed: 'A house without a foundation is seen once you have turned to the Light.' In this statement Fell overturns the conventional interpretation of the story of the house built on the rock (Matt 7:24,25) – that the Bible is foundational for saving belief – by laying the emphasis on the saving power of the Light. She chastises those who 'may get all the words of the whole Scripture in your brains and comprehension', but deny the Light, and warns that the Bible 'shall be as a book sealed unto you, the depth and the mysteries of them ye shall never know'.[28]

In his preface to a treatise, Isaac Penington gets to the nub of the early Quaker view of experience and Scripture. He declares their creed to be a 'gospel-religion', but that it begins in the inward demonstration and evidence of the Spirit of God. For this reason, 'the Gospel-ministry, or gospel-work in any heart', cannot be continued without the power of the Spirit. Richard Farnworth isolates the conventional Quaker view on Law and Spirit: '[T]he letter is not the life [John 5:39,40] and power of God to salvation, but Christ and the Gospel is, where the letter or Scriptures declares and testifies of.' James Parnell lays an accusation of idolatry of the letter on priests and people. He remonstrates with them, declaring that by doting on the 'Scripture without' they 'take the authority from Christ' and give it to 'the dead letter'. Robert Barclay states the principle of priority more precisely than earlier writers: because Scripture gives a faithful testimony to the first foundation, they are a 'secondary rule, subordinate to the Spirit, from which they have all their excellency and certainty'.[29]

The writings of early Quakers are overrun with biblical inference, images, references in the margins, and direct quotation. Favourite Old Testament texts concern the Day of the Lord (Jer. 23; 31), and false priests (Ezek. 34). The central beliefs about the Light, the Word and the Spirit are taken from the Gospel of John, 1, 2 and 3 John, and the Book of Revelation. Rarely are the Synoptic Gospels utilized, but the letters of Paul and the Letter to the Hebrews concerning Jesus the High Priest are employed in their writings. Practices are defended with a battery of texts interpreted literally: quaking (Hab. 3:16; Dan 10:7; Acts 9:4); the men in the fiery furnace keeping their hats on (Dan. 3:21), oaths (Jas. 5:12); and the most controversial Quaker text, asserting that the holy men of the Old Testament were fully possessed of the Light (John 1:9).[30]

Early Friends use agrarian and pastoral imagery drawn from Scripture as they pass on their message to outsiders and strangers. Ploughing and weeding the rough and stony ground of the heart is seen to be the mission to the world: '[T]hy heart is highway ground; and as thorny ground without thee, so thy heart is as thorny ground.' Markets, fairs, streets, even churches, are battlegrounds for the conscience and abound with opportunities for openings from the Lord. As a strong oak living in its own strength, or a widow without a husband, so is the world without the Lord. Seed imagery is employed to denote the sowing of the word of God (Matt. 13:3–8: Mark 4:3–9; Luke 8:5–8): some is sown in stony, thorny ground and the same seed is sown in good ground. The scattering of seed in the soul of every human being is a work of divinity: 'So that, though all are not saved by it, yet there is a seed of salvation planted and sown in the hearts of all by God, which would grow up and redeem the soul, if it were not choked and hindered.' Friends are not to shrink back in fearful dread from the wild fields of the world. Instead, as 'children of the day' they are instructed to 'put on the armour of light, and have your feet shod now when we walk through thorny places' to engage in this spiritual war (cf. Eph. 6:10–20).[31]

Writers use biblical imagery to beautify their sentiments about Christ the Light. Christ is 'a fountain of gardens, and a wellspring of living waters, and streams from Lebanon . . . fountain of life . . . and there is no life to be found but in the fountain'. The text

Amos 2:13 is employed in a graphic metaphor to connote the weight of human sin set upon Jesus Christ: 'God is pressed down as a cart under sheaves, and Christ crucified in the ungodly.' A fistful of scriptural images is a powerful affirmation of the word of Christ: 'And the pearl that hath been hid in the earth is found [Matt. 13:45–46], and the morning star is risen [2 Pet. 1:19; Rev. 2:28; 22:16] and the day is dawned, and the true light shines [John 1:9; 1 John 2:8] and wisdom . . . cries in the streets to the simple ones [Prov. 1:20, Mic. 6:9], and for all to fear God.'[32]

Prophetic silence and Scripture

We have touched on the importance of the pattern established by George Fox of silent waiting upon God in order to hear his word. The less than laconic style, in the First Publishers of Truth does not agree with the accepted format of the few words spoken in a Meeting. One can only assume that, having heard the Lord so clearly on one point, Friends are quick to elaborate in many points. For the Quaker, silent fellowship in the Spirit of God, in which there are no spoken words, is the life of the gospel. Fox lays the foundational truth that, those who 'inwardly rove from the Spirit of God; so are gone from the silence, and stillness', that they possess 'the words of Christ and the apostles, but inwardly are ravened from the still life'.[33]

An early text (1658) by William Dewsbury concentrates upon the refreshing presence of Christ in its instructions to the 'dear lambs' called to take their rest in Christ and to lie down in the sheepfold. To enjoy the fragrance of Christ, the rule of thumb is to 'take heed of many words, at all times let them be few'. In order to teach this rule, Dewsbury writes an epistle to Friends to be read out in the Meetings, in which he exegetes the parable of the ten wise and ten foolish virgins (Matt. 25:1–13). The wise trim their lamps to await the return of the Lord; the foolish allow their lamps to run dry, and, by their absence in purchasing oil, miss the hour of the master's return. Dewsbury states that this passage will bring about a revelation to the heart, and a 'separation': presumably between those who do and those who do not practise the discipline of silence. We shall examine his exegesis, probing its value as a prophetic exercise in silence.[34]

Dewsbury begins by outlining the disadvantage of external clamour, which seeks 'to draw you every way, seeking to get your minds from the pure, to draw into the visible things, your affections there to captivate . . . in the fleshly wisdom'. He draws the analogy between these sorts of people, captured by earthly wisdom, and the foolish virgins. They are those who feed on the 'husks, the form and image of what you have enjoyed, or what you see in the vision'. He is scathing of this type of spirituality: it produces 'words without knowledge', like the foolish virgins, who turn away from pure wisdom to their own light, and are empty of the power of God. He compares these words, quickly spoken or belonging to others, with the beautification of the outside of the virgins' lamps. It is futile activity, like trees bearing leaves without fruit. He commands these people to 'silence flesh'. The wise, on the other hand, are those who wait for the movement of the Spirit, by topping up their oil – joy and gladness in the power of his love. The Spirit of truth bridles their tongues and keeps them from uttering idle words, as they wait in silence upon him. At the move of the Spirit upon the mind, there is a declaration 'from the living power the soul possesses and enjoys in Christ'. By the power of Christ the wise virgin 'keeps her lamp trimmed always, breathing and thirsting for him to manifest his power to take away sin'.[35]

This short exegetical exercise demonstrates the ability of the early Friends to draw out of Scripture, as from a living well, fresh water to saturate their weary souls. Dewsbury projects prophetic insight into a New Testament parable, picking out elements which correspond to the different feelings and responses to the practise of silence in Meetings, i.e. impatience and sluggishness, or alert attentiveness in quietness. As the letter is read, we can imagine that the sharp sword of a prophetic word will provoke self-awareness, dividing the Meeting into two: the 'separation' between the foolish and the wise, as predicted by the writer. The motivation for silence is the belief that the Lord wishes to speak his truth afresh, through the word of Christ gleaned by reflective rumination upon Scripture.

Penington describes meditation as waiting silently for God to give 'the key of knowledge', and not climbing up and over the door with human understanding, or 'dead knowledge'. The knowledge is received 'by the Spirit's opening the words which speak of them, or by inward immediate prophecies which form the word of life in the heart'. Penington advises a lengthy waiting period, so as 'to feel the thing itself which the words speak of', so that the words are preserved as a living spring and as leaven in the life of the recipient.[36]

Prophetic exegesis of Scripture

To grasp the early Quaker hermeneutical method, we must tackle the question of typology, particularly as it impacts on the interpretation of the Word as apocalyptic. We also wish to ascertain the prophetic significance of typological allusion. For Fox, the Bible in its entirety is interpreted in like manner: the text always points to the inward spiritual realities. Thus typology is the correlation between the outward and the inward: types in the biblical landscape are a reflection of the interior state of the soul, or the wider world. Friends see themselves in the types or figures in Scripture: the external figure is a type of the inward and spiritual reality. The truths of the Exodus experience are seen as a mirror to reflect the spiritual journey of Christians, 'that even as of old Moses by his rod divided the waves of the Red Sea, that the Israelites might pass; so God hath thus by his Spirit made a way for us in the midst of this raging wickedness'. Moses instituted outward ceremonies and observances in worship, which are types and shadows of the substance, 'until the *spiritual worship* should be set up', that is, inaugurated by Christ.[37]

How may we understand apocalyptic spirituality, or 'apocalyptic typology'? The former writings establish the Law, i.e. the Old Testament is a foreshadowing of the later covenant under Jesus Christ, i.e. the New Testament. Thus the creation in the Old Testament prefigures the resurrection in the New Testament. The old has gone and the new has come. For the early church, therefore, on the tiptoe of expectation, there is an apocalyptic sense of an imminent demolition of the present age, and a new beginning for the church. How are we to relate these typological ideas to the early Quakers? And how may apocalyptic inference be viewed as prophetic?

As we have seen, Scripture must be 'opened' by the Spirit before it can be comprehended in the heart. Apocalyptic references in the writings of Friends serve to precipitate spiritual crises and open hearts. The motives of the heart, as revealed in the actions of Cain, or Moses, or any other biblical figure, are inwardly applied. A revelation of Christ judges and condemns a sinful and apostate soul, and is a challenge to repent. If, for example, all evil is destroyed and there is nothing of Cain left in the Christian, then the goal of perfection has already been attained. If the inward disposition witnesses to the outward historic reality, then Jesus Christ, born of a virgin, is born in you. Christ, formally known only as a figure, type or shadow in the Old Testament, then as the historic incarnated figure of Jesus of Nazareth in the New Testament, is now known as the incarnate Christ of the Quaker heart. The types are mere shadows rooted in biblical history and prophetic signposts pointing to the coming of Christ – especially as executed by the brand new Quaker movement. Christ's advent abolishes the old, and, for Quakers, the priesthood is an especial target of this abolition: '[T]hen all the priests are put an end to, which were true types and figures of him.' Because the everlasting Priest has come, all figures of temple and priesthood are ended: 'There was a temple which God commanded; when Christ was come and risen, all outward temples were denied; and we witness one Priest . . . ten thousand witness one Priest, which is entered into the holiest, and all the priests and his hirelings are denied (Heb.9,10).' All tithes are ended: '[T]hough Abraham paid tithes to Melchizedek, who was a figure; when Jesus Christ the everlasting Priest was come, he put an end to all figures.' Prophecy is fulfilled, and the Quaker Children of Light herald the dawning of a new gospel day: away with steeplehouses, priests and tithes, or preaching from a preconceived body of knowledge![38]

Prophetic inspiration in Scripture

Three published works, dating from the second period of Quakerism and the mid-eighteenth century, are texts to guide us through the topic of prophecy inspired by Scripture. The first is a commentary on a portion of the New Testament; the second and third works are both narrative and descriptive, as they unpack the general idea of inspired biblical preaching. A prisoner, Charles Marshall, writes to inhabitants and neighbours in the West

Country in a letter entitled 'A Tender Visitation in the Love of God unto All People everywhere'. At first glance this short, energetic communiqué, composed in a genre not dissimilar to the pastoral epistles of the New Testament, may be seen to be just that, an exhortatory missive. It is, however, written in 1683, in the midst of persecution, but also in the settling-down period, when Quakerism is in danger of losing its cutting edge and adjusting to the norm to avoid trouble.

In light of contemporary circumstances, Marshall's despatch may be seen as a prophetic exhortation, appealing as it does to his readership (especially those teetering on the brink of disaster) to make a choice between two ways, the broad and the narrow (Matt. 7:13,14). Having utterly vilified the broad way, Marshall praises the entry to the 'pleasant way', where travellers shall drink of the 'brook of comfort and consolation'. The pilgrim must shoulder the cross of Jesus and lift up the 'spiritual standard' in the soul, to combat the temptation of beating a retreat to the broad way. This disposition is somewhat quaintly expressed: '[T]he holy Light and saving grace of God gives the sight, and makes a discovery of sin in its first arising.' As the doubting, yet-to-believe reader well knows, the sacrificial path of the crucified Christ, undertaken as a radical Quaker, is not without cost. These fearfully testing times are fanned out before the seeker, like a winnowing fork in the harvest:

> And so have our whole conversation changed, and become other men, not walking in the way most of our country-town or village walks in; we fear we should become a by-word and scorn of our neighbours and acquaintances; nay, we doubt our kindred and near relations would forsake us, and we should become as strangers unto them, and lose their respect, and it may be lose our employ and trade . . . and should we go to markets and fairs . . . and refuse to drink to excess . . . and not be vainly merry, as in times past we were, should be a derision and a by-word, and scorned by such who have been our companions in those things in times past.

All these misgivings are airily dismissed, as Marshall contemplates the peace and satisfaction of the soul – the reward for choosing the narrow path. One has the sense in these lines of an apostolic continuity, of a close affinity between an early Quaker and a New Testament apostle, who endured hardship and affliction for the sake of Christ, and for whom that gospel is never a second-hand experience, but a passionate choice between life and death.[39]

The Edict of Toleration (1689) is a milestone along the way to the cessation of religious persecution and relative peace between the state and the sects. The price of concord, however, is the loss of vitality, and for many Friends it is 'business as usual' – commercial enterprises boom and prosperity beckons and captivates. By 1696, when our tale takes us to the life of Samuel Bownas of Westmoreland (b. 1676), narrated in a composition entitled *An Account of the Life, Travels, and Christian Experiences in the Work of the Ministry of Samuel Bownas* (1756), we encounter a term: 'traditional Quaker'. This disparaging remark, by a woman preacher in the great Strickland monthly Meeting, points the finger (and she did wag her finger) at the 20-year-old Bownas, who hitherto had devoted his life to pleasure, and came and went from each Meeting as he pleased, unchanged. He is smitten and converted. Three weeks pass: he desires to testify 'of my own experience of the operation of the Spirit in my mind'. At the Meeting a great weight falls upon him and he is given words to speak, but out of shyness at his recently reversed condition and new reformation, he abstains. The following Meeting finds him feeling the 'weight' of the same 'concern', until he gets to his feet at the end of the Meeting and breaks out, 'with a loud voice', into inspired speech. His words are based on a collage of New Testament verses: 'Fear not them which kill the body, but are not able to kill the soul; but rather fear him which is able to destroy both body and soul in hell. I say, fear you him who will terribly shake the earth, that all which is moveable may be shaken and removed out of the way, that which is immoveable may stand' (Matt. 10:28; Heb. 12:26,27). This is the start of a ministry of inspired preaching.

As a preacher, Bownas becomes skilful in the matter of 'dividing of the word'. He examines the text, considering where the strength of the argument lies, but realizes that he often falls short in finding the most apt Bible verse(s) to support his point. He has to guard against formality, and the ease of employing an 'opening' already received, thus losing 'that divine spring which I had always depended upon'. He is shown that the Spirit can renew the old matter, which, 'opened in new life, was always new'. Bownas preaches and a Baptist is convinced that he has been wrong in his accusation that Quakers are heathen and do not use the Bible. In his sermon Bownas gives 'ample testimony of the value we put upon the Scriptures, earnestly pressing the careful reading of them, and advising to consider what they read, and to seek the Lord, by prayer, for assistance and power, that they might practice what they read'.[40]

A treatise by Bownas, *A Description of the Qualifications Necessary to A Gospel Minister* (1767), although a century later than the writings of Fox, retains the method of the early Quakers and is a good model for inspirational preaching from that period. In his comments on the reception of the inspired gifts of apostle, prophet, evangelist, pastor and teacher (Eph. 4:11), Bownas is emphatic that two disciplines are a prerequisite: sanctification by the Spirit of judgement and burning, and a strict examination of works and actions. He discounts all study and frequent reading, by which means preachers 'frame a set and studied speech in a regular way, methodically dividing, and sub-dividing their matter'. This ministry comes from the head and will do nothing for the hearers, 'having nothing of inspiration or power of the Spirit in it'. False inspiration is 'heady and stubborn'; those who speak are the judges of everyone who will not receive them as true ministers, 'by foretelling the ruin and downfall of all their opposers, working themselves up to a strange degree of imagination'. True inspiration is 'an inbreathing of the divine word into our minds, giving a true understanding of divine things', so that the hearers make wise choices. Bownas advocates restraint: not until both authority and power are received is there to be speech, so that the minister fits into the timing of the Lord for the delivery of the message.[41]

Women leaders inspired

George Fox offers biblically inspired wisdom to Friends, that they should 'live in the immortal seed and power of the Lord God', and then follows the injunction with the proviso that such living must be 'in the Spirit' (e.g. Rom. 15:13,30; 1 Cor. 3:16, 12:13; 2 Cor. 6:6; 13:13; Gal. 5:25), so that 'ye will have unity and peace, and the spiritual weapons, to cut down the spiritual enemies of your peace' (e.g. 2 Cor. 10:4; Eph. 6:12). We see the principle of biblical, Spirit-inspired unity in the Quaker women. Deathbed testimonies are an indication of the oneness and friendship which Quaker women feel towards one another; they are also true to the biblical record, which commands testimony as a way of overcoming evil, thereby maintaining the unified ideal of community (see Rom. 12:21; 2 Cor. 13:11; Rev. 12:11) and the 'bond of peace' (Eph. 4:3). The reason given by a Friend for the writing of such a text as the *Epistle of Love*, in honour of Anne Whitehead, is that so worthy a person ought to be remembered, 'nor her faithfulness be buried in the grave of oblivion . . . and the desire of my soul is, that we that are left behind, may walk in the same path, and that her past public testimony that she bore among you, may not be forgotten by you'. The inspiration of former saints will live on in the fellowship of the Holy Spirit. Elizabeth Bathurst, an outspoken Friend, summarizes this closeness, preferring mutual fellowship in the Spirit to that of her natural relations, former friends and acquaintances: '[Y]et you being that new kindred, spoken of by Christ, Matt.12.50, thus are you nearer to me by the union of his inward grace, than any unconverted thereunto can be.'[42]

The togetherness of women to one another, and to the body of Friends, is heartening, and reminiscent of the teams in the Acts of the Apostles. Quaker women travel frequently on mission in pairs, or stand together in solidarity with one another at the posts of protest in the town squares. This esprit de corps manifests itself in their common public image. At the height of fashionable wigs, high-heeled shoes and extravagant cosmetics, they preach with loosened hair in unadorned clothing, or don sackcloth at the high cross in a market square. They are an affront and a sign of contradiction in an affluent society. It is possible that the desire of Friends for perfection in prayer, work, friendship, and even sleep, resulted in dreams, auditory commands and visions in everyday life, in meetings and in prophetic actions. Women's inspiration is exhibited in bodily quaking during a Catholic Mass, in interruptions of services, in the confrontation with priests in church or magistrates in court, and in the publication of pamphlets, broadsheets, tracts and epistles, some of which they are inspired to give to Oliver Cromwell, or the Houses of Parliament, or to the cities of Oxford or London.[43]

The pamphlet *A Living Testimony*, signed by six women, expresses the heart of a woman's inspired witness. It is to shine the light within, 'the candle of the Lord', by placing it on a lampstand, so that all 'know our several works and services the Lord requireth of us in his Church' (Matt. 5:15; Mark 4:21; Luke 8:16; 11:33). Women are allotted a large, not equal, part in worship and church government. They are excluded from ministers' meetings, the management of finances, all executive decisions and the business side of the Yearly gatherings. Yet the establishment of separate business meetings for women – innovative in mainstream Nonconformist and Separatist groups – leads to their working with the poor. Despite a male-dominated hierarchical structure, certain individuals have sufficient impact in leadership in local Meetings, as well as forbearance in persecution, to ensure the continued existence of the revival.[44]

Women speaking justified

The enlightened approach of George Fox to the thorny question of whether or not women may lead, speak, teach or prophesy is set out plainly in his provocative treatise, *Women learning in silence or the Mystery of the Woman's subjugation to her husband*. The heading of the work is a quotation: 'Do not quench the Spirit. Do not despise the words of prophets' (1 Thess. 5:19,20), and is followed by a compilation of lengthy biblical citations (1 Chr. 16:22; Num. 11:26–28; 1 Tim. 2; Gal. 5:18; 2 Pet. 3; Eph. 5; Phil. 4) and a list of New Testament women (Phoebe, Priscilla, Aquila – who Fox presumably took to be a woman – Mary Magdalene). This reliance on the authority of Scripture permeates Fox's discourse on prophetic women. The 'daughters' who prophesy are to be received as 'the women-labourers in the gospel'. He asserts that those who will not have Christ reign in the female, as well as in the male, are against Scripture and Christ does not reign in *them* (2 Cor. 13:5–8). By using Scripture to conjoin prophesying and the testimony of Jesus (Rev. 19:10), Fox overcomes gender issues: '[I]f male and female have received the testimony of Jesus, they have received the spirit of prophecy.' In no uncertain terms he reprimands the opponents of women who speak: 'So be ashamed for ever, and let all your mouths be stopped for ever, that despise the spirit of prophecy in the daughters, and do cast them into prison, and do hinder the women-labourers in the gospel.' Fox's rejection of male supremacy comes from his utter conviction of the limitless freedom of the Spirit: 'And may not the Spirit of Christ speak in the female as well as in the male?' His view of gender equality is founded also upon his understanding of the undivided properties of the Light within: 'For the Light is the same in the male, and in the female, which cometh from Christ . . . one in all, and not divided.'[45]

Fox's view on gender equality is ahead of its time and goes a step further than the accepted stance of his day. In church circles at that time it was somewhat subversive, even revolutionary. It was held that women are made in the image of God, and are spiritually equivalent to men, but their total equality cannot be condoned, as woman was taken *from* man in the Genesis account and is, therefore, subordinate to man. This argument was used to foist upon the church the notion that women are spiritually equal to men, but not in the public sphere. Fox's views appear in the context of a telling account in the *Journal*. Heaven appears to be on the side of women, as Nathaniel Coleman of Slaughterford discovers to his consternation. In a passionate rage the gentleman leaves the house of a women's Meeting, but an angel with drawn sword confronts him, ready to cut him off. Filled with terror he returns indoors 'like a dead man', and declares his repentance before Fox. His repentance, however, is short-lived and he circulates a paper condemning the liberties accorded the Quaker women, beginning with the question, 'Was it not the command of God that a man must rule over his wife?' and continuing with the Pauline prohibitions on women speaking (1 Cor. 11:3–10; 14:34–35; 1 Tim. 2:11,12). Fox responds to Coleman and records his reasoning on the matter in the *Journal*. The Gospel-order establishes the sufficiency of Christ and the Spirit, so that all may exercise the priestly ministry of Christ, without distinction between male and female. Men are not at liberty to rule over other men's wives, widows or younger women; women are free to exercise their ministry in the affairs of the church, as they are in civil and temporal matters. If this order is adhered to, then the poor will be looked after, the young taught, the reprobate disciplined, and proposed marriages monitored more closely, and all members of the fellowship will be helpful to one another.[46]

Fox elaborates on these principles in his instructions for the administration of Meetings, in a paper entitled *To all the men and women's meetings everywhere.* He uses the letter to Titus to outline practical guidelines. He also addresses the question of involvement outside the church. Women are made in the same image of God, and join with men as 'meet-helps' (Fox's word for help-meets) to subdue the earth (Gen. 1:28), but also to subdue 'unrighteousness and all ungodliness, and that which they know doth dishonour God'. Through Christ women and men regain the dominion over Eden that they lost through sin, and they are re-established to rule: 'Christ makes them as kings and priests to reign upon the earth' (Rev. 5:10). This standpoint very definitely opens the door to the public arena, to interventions through the medium of printing, protest and prophetic displays. Radical activists of the 1650s, imbued and fused with the Light of Christ, went on to many exploits. There is a marked shift in the later period, from active testimony to insular modes of worship. With hindsight we may well ask whether Quaker women were tamed into what was seen to be normatively feminine.[47]

Women teachers and publishers

Quaker women writers are unrivalled in seventeenth-century print culture. Of the 3,853 Quaker texts published between 1650 and 1699, women are the authors of 220 (57 per cent). The early period (1650–60) spawned 334 prophetic texts, compared with forty-five texts between 1680 and 1690. Publishers who were Friends manipulated the market and strengthened the emergence of female printers. The driving force behind the printed word is the making known of the Word: print conveys the will of God, carries and shapes the motions of community, provides a moral code, defines what it is to be a Quaker, and conveys God's voice through believers and his prophetic word.[48]

A short tract by Margaret Fell, with a subheading 'Womens Speaking Justified, Proved and Allowed of by the Scriptures' (1666), employs many passages from the Old and New Testaments to defend the rights of women teachers and prophets. Fell is quick to concretize her beliefs in decisive action, using Scripture to justify her position. She writes four letters to Cromwell and letters to the military and council after his death. She also writes letters to Charles II, one of which is penned on 6/6/1666 (no doubt deeply significant) from her prison at Lancaster Castle, where she is held captive for three long winters, and was kept a year and seven months before being allowed home to see her children. Fell has no hesitation in chronicling, for the king's benefit, the deaths of hundreds of 'innocent, harmless, peaceable people', the result of the heinous atrocities meted out to her people for obedience to Jesus Christ. She requests a meeting with bishops and ministers of the land, 'that thereby they and we, might be tried by the Scriptures, which of us was in the error'. Of course these men refused such a trial, Fell surmises, because they 'feared that their cause would not hold stitch with the rule of the Scriptures'. She is resolute: they are 'out of the life and power of the Scriptures'.[49]

In the second period of Quakerism, we begin to see an intellectually advanced theological discourse which emphasizes the divine Light within instead of a religion of the book. This has consequences, not only for the view that an experimental knowledge of God's nature is possible without the Bible, but also for the way in which women are seen as the image of God. On 20 August 1678, after her dramatic 'Visitation in the Living Power of the Lord', Elizabeth Bathurst enters a Presbyterian meeting house. Her disruption of the service is to make a new appeal: God's mercy is held out to all humanity, not only the elect, and salvation is in response to the stirrings of the Spirit. In 1694 Margaret Marsin publishes a tract against the theory of predestination: she aims to reveal the truth of God's nature, as revealed in Scripture, in order to hasten the Second Coming. The main innovation of these two voices on the margins is an anti-Calvinist critique of patriarchy which is set out in tracts defending women's preaching and leadership. At the moment of Christ's sacrifice the inner Light is made available for all. As grace is free, inward and universal, so the office of bearing the truth about Christ is universal: to be received by women, as well as men. The election of men for dominant religious roles is as arbitrary as ordaining the smallest number for salvation.[50]

Redeeming the Prophetic Teacher

We have attempted to excavate the Calvinist biblical foundation on which the Huguenot enterprise was built, overlaid as the structure is with epiphanies and visitations of angels. This analysis has demonstrated that the unyielding attachment of the Church of the *désert* to the Bible was its mainstay in times of trouble. The security of this anchor outlasted the unreliable mix of true and false prophecy, sifted the good from the bad in a complex era of persecution, and ensured a good and permanent Huguenot heritage. In the same way, we have seen that prophetically inspired teachers, who remained faithful to the Huguenot legacy of utter rootedness in the Bible, kept the Church of the *désert* on track by a realistic assessment of the times. A brief survey of the Quaker literature has shown a somewhat different view of the Bible. A critique might base the case, somewhat cautiously, on several problem areas: if only the Spirit of God within and at work in the heart can interpret Scripture, then such interpretations can be subjective and unreliable; if the only guide is the Spirit, operating emotionally and tangibly through the words of Scripture, then individuals are always legitimated – rightly or wrongly; not even Scripture can overrule the absolute supremacy of the Holy Spirit; Quakerism is a religion of the heart, and Quakers hold the radical view that anyone, not only an elite minority, can interpret the Bible and understand it better than mere scholars. From these observations we may conclude that the task of the contemporary Bible teacher is to stress the Spirit within the text and not the letter of the law, the person of Christ and not the power of reason as the opener of Scripture, in order to draw out prophetical meaning for the present age. We might expect a prophetic teacher, therefore, to employ the tools of allegory so that the text is related to the maelstrom of everyday life in sign and symbol – a feature not uncommon to the listener flooded in mainstream television and Hollywood with sci-fi, *Doctor Who*, *The Chronicles of Narnia*, *The Hobbit*, to name but a few. If Jesus Christ is to emerge from the familiar biblical stories in a compelling fashion for the listener or reader, then the Holy Spirit should be invoked consciously and clearly in preparation, delivery and response: *Veni Creator Spiritus*; Come Holy Spirit and quicken the text, the mind and the heart.[51]

Conclusion

At the outset of this study on prophetic leadership, I posed what I perceive is a reason for the apparent lack of spiritual revival in the European church, viz. a dearth of visionary leadership which is proportionate to the church's neglect of the gift of prophecy. I put it to the reader that Christian vision is dependent upon the full dimension of the operations of both Word and Spirit working in tandem. I proposed that it is incumbent upon church leadership to embrace the totality of the biblical witness, especially the *charismata* – even if this requires an acceptance of Christian mysticism. In order to test the thesis that prophetic leadership is underpinned by a marriage of Word and Spirit, I flagged up two seventeenth-century revivals, the French Huguenot Church of the *désert* and the English Quakers. By way of setting parameters for an argument on leadership, I framed the discourse within the boundary of the New Testament church foundation of the five-fold ministry. I submitted the role of apostle, evangelist, pastor and teacher in each movement to a fairly rigorous scrutiny under the category of prophetic leadership.

From this examination of Word and Spirit in prophetic leadership I offer three conclusions. The first remark pertains to apostolic leadership. We learn that the waves of persecution levied against a movement or its exile from its place of origin, far from deterring faith, advance the gospel cause and grow the kingdom of God. The reason for this commitment is an overarching belief in the reality of a God who intervenes in the community under siege. The spiritual surges in both Huguenot and Quaker revivals are not high-flown words empty of meaning, but are impulses pregnant with the life force of the Holy Spirit in Word and deed. The exaltation of the name of Jesus Christ is not only in the word as it is preached, but also in the signs, which are a demonstration of the message: angel song, sackcloth, strange tongues, directive dreams, predictive words of knowledge, the Peace Testimony, inspired speech or silence, and a fellowship of love. In both these moves of God we observe the powerful effect of an active witness to Christ intertwined with the manifest presence of the Spirit.

How does this serve our quest for visionary leadership? Clearly both Huguenot and Quaker leaders have as the fulcrum of their mission the conviction that the church meeting or service must go on, despite every setback and disappointment. For the Protestant Huguenot and the Nonconformist Quaker, an ecclesial structure, in whatever form (a desert assembly or a Meeting of Sufferings), is inviolable. The gathered group is an immediate strength in times of pressure. The liturgical orderliness of the psalms of the Refuge is a garrison against recantation to Catholicism. The very 'bookishness' of Calvinism, in its adherence to the written word of Scripture, is a fortress in times of trouble. Likewise, the arrangement of the Friends' Meetings is a mighty bulwark to withstand the total onslaught of an irate establishment. The rhythm of the inspired sermon and silent tarrying in the Light is, in its own way, a liturgical order of service. The essence of what it is to be a refugee church or a Society of Friends is easily transportable. The gathering or assembly is a movable feast. As long as the raw material is discernible, i.e. ecstatic prophesying, psalmody, biblical exposition or silence, then worship continues in fields, homes, barns, mountain ravines or caves. The cohesion of a body of people, dependent on the leadings of the Holy Spirit and exercising the priestly ministry of Jesus Christ in times of turmoil, is an extraordinary feat of fearless courage. It is also a fine example of permanent apostolic endeavour, as the perpetuation of the two movements to the present day demonstrates.

The second deduction concerning the way of prophetic leadership impinges on the question of an evangelistic vision for an ingathering of a harvest of souls into Christ's kingdom. How might we correlate the gleanings from the writings of the Huguenot and Quaker prophets to the question of world evangelism? It is quite plain from our reading of the material that not all prophesying can be accredited to the prophetic Spirit. Indeed, some misguided prophets bring the word of the Lord into disrepute, as in the case of the *inspiré* Abraham Mazel. That which at first glance appears to be a prophetic word from the Spirit burns as a fire in the speaker. Once it is delivered it is in the hands of a crowd of nervous and highly charged individuals who, in the mood of the moment, leap into frenzied action at a nod from their commander. This example of extraordinary misdirected zeal (and subsequent warlike actions stemming from prophecies) threw the entire Huguenot prophetic enterprise into disgraced disarray. The attempts by Antoine Court to placate the critics trammelled the gift of prophecy and restricted it to the teacher or preacher. Prophets were shut down and prophecy banned from the meetings. The enlightened years of prophesying were a dim memory: ecstatic preaching, trance vision, words from the Lord on the lips of sleeping children, dreams and inspirations by day and by night. The great years of God's voice, trumpeted loud and clear in the skies above and in the mouths of the very young, to a persecuted church on the run, are over. Apart from the London *inspirés*, exiled charismatic leaders were not willing to run the gauntlet and risk the wrath of their colleagues. The gift of prophecy was harnessed, the baby was thrown out with the bath water, and the Church of the Refuge subsumed under mainstream Protestantism. Its unique charism, i.e. the gift of prophecy, was sacrificed to the interests of decent churchmanship. We must conclude that the harvest ingathering is impeded by this default position, as the Church of the *desért* showed a massive intake of lost souls and exponential growth, as a direct result of prophesyings.

The inspirations of Friends are similarly bridled in the later second period. The attempt by the leaders of the Quakers to curb the extremes of unusual behaviour, by means of a ruling that all prophets are subject to leadership, succeeds in domesticating and narrowing down an original charismatic vision. The sheer audacity of Spirit-directed inspiration and action drove the movement in its early stages and gathered in a large harvest, unprecedented among the Nonconformist groups in England. Quakers of the later era trod more warily, as upon eggshells, and inspirations are calmer and more thoughtful.

One must conclude that had the leadership of the Society strove to maintain a cutting edge, in an open door to prophetic inspiration from the Holy Spirit, its numbers would be far greater today.

The third comment engages with the leader as prophetic pastor and teacher. In both the Huguenot and Quaker revivals there is evidence of a powerful manifestation of the Holy Spirit in the assemblies and meetings. The voice of the Spirit is heard and actions follow accordingly. Strong pastoral leadership is, however, exercised to exert what can only be called 'equilibrium', a balance between Word and Spirit. By means of expository literal-prophetic homily, the besieged pastors of the Church of the *desért* seek to draw out allegorical lessons from the biblical texts in order to encourage Christlikeness. One can only surmise that these efforts induce in those undergoing torture or imprisonment a praiseworthy imitation of Christ. Huguenot lay pastors lead by example and display a remarkable restrained dignity reminiscent of Christ under pressure. Quaker leadership is equally grounded on Christ the Light, although a predisposition to a Gnostic or Docetic Christ subverts the historic Person. This is more than compensated for in an overflowing abundance of biblical passages in the written text: letters, sermons, warnings and admonitions are saturated with the voice of Christ the Light speaking through the words of Scripture. Despite the Quaker riddle, that the Bible is subject to the Spirit and simply confirms what the Spirit has already spoken, it cannot be denied that the early Quakers were people of the Book.

What is more revolutionary for the times than these theological niceties is the high regard, in both movements, for the position and ministry of women as prophetic pastors, preachers and teachers – in spoken and written word. It is as though the full weight of Word and Spirit – albeit radical for that age and conservative for postmodernism – is brought to bear upon this elevation. The testimony of Jesus Christ is in his honouring of women and the prophetic Spirit dispenses his gifts wherever he pleases. Women take their place alongside men in the struggle for Christian liberties. Women stand for the rights of the marginalized and oppressed, and for the gospel truth. Young girls teach their elders and young women publish their thoughts and feelings about the faith. Women pastor their families and friends in brave words of encouragement. Women travel abroad on mission to unexplored territories. Yet it is in the gathered meetings that the role of women is most noticeable in biblical teaching and prophesying – and in the Huguenot religion this is in the face of both genders. God is no respecter of persons and the whirlwind of prophetic activity frees women and exposes them conspicuously in the ministry of Word and Spirit.

How may we interpret these three concluding points in light of the present? First, to establish the full release of a visionary apostolic church we remind ourselves that the body of Christ has the mind of Christ (1 Cor. 2:16). A church or Christian fellowship, which is not only *au fait* with the *charismata*, but also actively operating in the gift of prophecy in the fivefold ministry spread across its leadership, has everything at its disposal to see the vision to establish a foundation on which a flourishing church may be built.

Secondly, to pinpoint the reluctance of church leadership to associate itself with the gift of prophecy is to charge these authorities with an over-conscientious control of prophetic leaders. The parable of the weeds sown among wheat (Matt. 13:24–30) instructs the church to leave the ingathering of the harvest to the Lord. The inevitability of words from God scattered among words from self or the Devil should not engender a fever of anxiety about the wrongheadedness of certain prophets at certain times in the church's history. Such parancia dumbs down the gift of prophecy and relegates it to a forbidden back burner. The Pauline injunctions are not to despise or forbid prophecy, but to seek this gift above all the others (1 Cor. 14:1, 1 Thess. 5:20).

Thirdly, the appropriate checks in prophetic leadership are inlaid within the fivefold ministry, which if applied will give the delicate balance necessary. Untested prophetic vision is anathema. On the one hand it is especially irksome if not contained within the guide rails of Scripture and is dependent solely on a subjective feeling or the Light within. On the other hand, a dream, vision or utterance may well have been sincere; it is the interpretation and application which can be troublesome and may lead to a retardation of the propagation of the gospel message. The function of a pastor and teacher, therefore, is to settle prophecy within community in the light of Scripture and the love of God so that the kingdom may be extended into the world.

Bibliography

Huguenot

Primary Sources

A Discourse of Schism, etc. 1702, Pamphlet 245.

A Hymn to Peace. Occasion'd by the Two Houses Joining in One Address to the Queen. By the Author of the True-born English-man [Daniel Defoe] (London: 1709), Pamphlet 282 (1).

A Letter from the Honest Protestant Dissenters To a Rt. Revd Occasional Friend (London: 1702), Pamphlet 245.

A Letter of several French Ministers Fled into Germany upon the account of the PERSECUTION in France, to such of their Brethren in England as Approved the King's Declaration touching Liberty of Conscience. Translated from the Original in French (1688), Pamphlet C 188 (33).

Aristotle. *Poetics* (trans. Kenneth McLeish; London: Nick Hern Books, 1999).

A Short Account of the Complaints, and Cruel Persecutions of the Protestants in the Kingdom of France (London: 1707).

Brousson, Claude. *The Support of the Faithful in Times of Persecution, or, A Sermon Preach'd in the Wilderness to the Poor Protestants in France. By M. Brousson, an Eminent Minister, who was broke upon the Wheel at Montpelier, Nov. 6. N.S. 1698* (London: 1699).

Bonaventure. *St. Bonaventure: Opscula, Second Series*, The Works of Bonaventure, Cardinal Seraphic Doctor and Saint, III (trans. José de Vinck; Paterson, St. Anthony Guild Press, 1966).

Calvin, John. *Institutes of the Christian Religion*, I.I to III.XIX, The Library of Christian Classics, Vol. XX (ed. John T. McNeill; trans. Ford Lewis Battles; London: SCM Press Ltd, 1961).

—. *Institutes of the Christian Religion*, II.III.XX to IV.XX, The Library of Christian Classics, Vol. XXI (ed. John T. McNeill; trans. Ford Lewis Battles (London: SCM Press Ltd, 1961).

—. *John Calvin: Works and Correspondence*, Electronic Edition (ed. Ford Lewis Battles, Henry Beveridge, Jules Bonnet, David Constable; Charlottesville, VA.: Intelex Corporation, 1995). Accessed 10 June 2013, Bodleian Libraries, University of Oxford.

—. *The Acts of the Apostles 1–13* (trans. John W. Fraser & W.J.G. McDonald, CC; Edinburgh: Oliver and Boyd, 1965).

—. *The First Epistle of Paul The Apostle to the Corinthians* (trans. John W. Fraser, CC; Edinburgh: Oliver and Boyd, 1960).

—. *Calvin: Theological Treatises* (with Introduction and Notes). The Library of Christian Classics, Vol. 22 (trans. J.K.S. Reid; London: SCM Press Ltd, 1954).

—. *Commentary on the Psalms* (abridged by David Searle; Edinburgh: Banner of Truth Trust, 2009)

—. *Commentary on the Book of Psalms* (trans. James Anderson, Vols 1–5 (Edinburgh: The Calvin Translation Society, 1845–9).

—. *The Epistles of Paul The Apostle to the Romans and to the Thessalonians* (ed. David W. Torrance & Thomas F. Torrance, CC; trans. Ross Mackenzie (Edinburgh: Oliver and Boyd, 1961).

—. *The Epistles of Paul The Apostle to the Galatians, Ephesians, Philippians and Colossians* (ed. David W. and Thomas F. Torrance, CC; trans. T.H.L. Parker; Edinburgh: Oliver & Boyd, 1965).

—. *Daniel I (Chapters 1–6)*, John Calvin's Lectures on the Book of The Prophecies of Daniel. Taken down by the effort and industry of Jean Budé and Charles Joinviller, Geneva 1561 (trans. T.H.L. Parker, Calvin's Old Testament Commentaries, Vol. 20; Grand Rapids: Wm. B. Eerdmans Publishing Company, 1993).

—. *Sermons on 2 Samuel Chapters 1–13* (trans. Douglas Kelly; Edinburgh: Banner of Truth Trust, 1992).

—. *Instruction in Faith* (1537) (trans. Paul T. Fuhrmann; London: Lutterworth Press, 1949).

—. *Treatises against the Anabaptists and against the Libertines: Tranlation, Introduction and Notes* (trans. Benjamin Wirt Farley; Grand Rapids: Baker Book House, 1982).

—. *Tracts and Letters*, Vol. 6: Letters, Part 3 1554–1558 (ed. Jules Bonnet; trans. Marcus Robert Gilchrist; Edinburgh: Banner of Truth Trust, 2009).

—.*Tracts and Letters*, Vol. 7: Letters, Part 4 1559–1564 (ed. Jules Bonnet; trans. Marcus Robert Gilchrist; Edinburgh: Banner of Truth Trust, 2009).

Daudé, John, with N. Facio, Charlies Portalés, Richard Holford, *A Preservative against the False Prophecies of the Time, or, A Treatise concerning True and False Prophets; with their Characters*, Pamphlet 273 (1), April 1707.

Dubourdieu, Jean Armand. *An Appeal to the English Nation: or, The Body of the French Protestants and the honest Proselytes, Vindicated from the Calumnies cast on them by one Malard, and his Associates, in a Libel, entitled, The French Plot found out against the English Church, etc. The Second Edition. With a considerable Addition, occasion'd by a French Pamphlet lately publish'd, entitled, The Abuse of the Confessions of Faith; and a remarkable Passage relating to the Bangorian Controversy* (London: 1918), printed by J. Roberts in Warwick Lane (Woodbridge, CN: The Eighteenth Century, Reel 5468 Nos. 1–23. Research Publications, 1992).

Du Moulin, Pierre. *The Accomplishment of the Prophecies; or the Third Booke in defence of the Catholicke faith, contained in the booke of the high and mighty King James. I. by the grace of God King of Great Brittaine and Ireland. Against the Allegations of R. Bellarmine: and F.N. Coëffetreau and other Doctors of the Romish Church* (trans. I. Heath; Oxford, 1613).

Fowler, Dr, Bp of Gloucester. *Reflections Upon a Letter concerning Enthusiasm, to my Lord *****. In another Letter to a Lord* (London: 1709), Pamphlet 282 (1).

Hobbes, Thomas, *The English works of Thomas Hobbes of Malmesbury/now first collected and edited by Sir William Molesworth,* Vol. 1 (London: 1839–1845), 11 vols.; *The Making of Modern Law* (Gale, 2013), Gale, Cengage Learning: http://galenet.galegroup.com/servlet/MOML?af=RN&ae=F100586935&srchtp=a &ste=14" (accessed 19 February 2013, Bodleian Libraries, University of Oxford)

Jurieu, Pierre. *The Pastoral Letters of the Incomparable Jurieu, Directed to the Protestants in France Groaning under the Babylonish Tyranny, translated: Wherein the Sophistical Arguments and Unexpressible Cruelties made use of by the Papists for the making Converts, are laid open and expos'd to just Abhorrence. Unto which is added, a brief account of the Hungarian persecution* (London, 1689).

—. *The Policy of the Clergy of France, to Destroy the Protestants of that Kingdom. Wherein is set down the Ways and Means that have been made use of for these twenty Years last past, to root out the Protestant Religion. In a Dialogue between two Papists* (London: 1681).

—. *The Sighs of France in Slavery, breathing after Liberty. By Way of Memorial. Done out of French* (London: 1689).

—. *A Plain Method of Christian Devotion: Laid down in Discourse, Meditations, and Prayers, Fitted to the Various Occasions of a Religious Life. Translated and Revised from the French of Monsieur Jurieu, By William Fleetwood, D.D. Late Lord Bishop of Ely* (London: 25th edn, 1724).

—. *The Reflections of the Reverend and Learned Monsieur Jurieu, Upon the Strange and Miraculous Exstasies of Isabel Vincent, the Shepherdess of Saou (Saov) in Dauphine; who Ever since February last hath Sung Psalms, Prayed, Preached, and Prophesied about the Present Times, an Her Trances as also Upon the Wonderful and Portentuous Trumpetings and Singing of Psalms, that were heard by Thousands in the Air (and many Parts of France) in the Year 1686: Taken out of the Pastoral Letters of the 1st and 15th of October last. To which is added, A Letter of a Gentleman in Dauphine, to a Friend of His in Geneva; Containing the Discourses and Prophesies of the Shepherdess. All faithfully translated out of the French copies, for Publick Information* (London, 1689).

—. *Seasonable Advice to all Protestants in Europe Of what Persuasion soever, for Uniting and Defending themselves against Popish Tyranny. Done out of French* (London: 1689).

—. *The Accomplishment of the Scripture Prophecies, or the Approaching Deliverance of the Church. Trans. from the French* (London: 1687).

Lefévre d'Etaples, Jacques. *Quincuplex Psalterium*, Fac-similé de l'édition de 1513, Travaux D'Humanisme et Renaissance, No. CLXX (Geneva: Librairie Droz, 1979).

—. *The Prefatory Epistles of Jacques Lefévre d'Etaples and Related Texts* (ed. Eugene F. Rice; New York; London: Columbia University Press, 1972).

Louvreleul, Jean-Baptiste (b. c. 1660) *Fanaticism Reviv'd, Book 1, The history of the rise and downfal of the Camisars: giving an account of their false pretences to prophecy and inspiration, their brutish carnality, their many bloody and inhuman Murders and Massacres of Persons of all Ages, Sexes and Conditions, and their horrid devastations of towns* and villages by fire. Collected from Original Letters, and the Testimony of Ey-Witnesses* (London: 1709), pp. 2–5, 15. Eighteenth Century Collections Online. Gale (accessed 27 July 2013, Harvard University Library).

—. *The History of the French Prophets. Their pretended Revelations, False prophecies and Hypocritical Behaviour, on that Account: with the many Bloody Murders, Barbarous Declarations by Burning, Horrid Sacriledges, and other Villanies committed by them, under Colour of Religion, in the Sevennes, and Parts Adjacent deliver'd Monthly as they happened from the Beginning of that Rebellion, till the Total Suppression thereof* (London: 1709).

Mission, Maximillien. *A Cry from the Desart: or Testimonials of the Miraculous Things lately come to pass in the Cévennes, Verified upon Oath, and by other Proofs. Translated from the Originals.* The Second Edition. With a Preface by John Lacy (London, 1707).

—.*A Cry from the Desart: or Testimonials of the Miraculous Things lately come to pass in the Cévennes, Verified upon Oath, and by other Proofs.* Translated from the Originals (London: 1707).

Misson, Maximillien. *Prophetical Extracts. Containing a very scarce Prophetic Piece, Intitled, A Cry from the Desart, or, Testimonials of the Miraculous Things Lately come to pass in the Cévennes, or southern parts of France. Verified upon Oath, and by other Proofs. Printed from the Original* (London: 1707).

Owen, Charles. *Plain-dealing: or, separation without schism, and schism without separation. Exemplify'd in the case of Protestant-Dissenters and church-men* (5th edition; London: 1720?) The Eighteenth Century Reel 3998, Nos. 1–33 (Woodbridge, CN: Research Publications, 1990).

Prophetical Warnings of Elias Marion, heretofore One of the Commanders of the Protestants, That had taken Arms in the Cévennes: or Discourse Uttered by him in London, under the Operation of the Spirit and Faithfully taken in Writing, whilst they were spoken (London: 1707).

Selden, John, *The table-talk of John Selden: with a biographical preface and notes (London: 3rd edn, 1860); The Making of Modern Law (Gale, 2013), Gale, Cengage Learning:* http://galenet.galegroup.com/ servlet/MOML?af=RN&ae=F100566559&srchtp=a&ste=14. (accessed 19 February 2013, Bodleian Libraries, University of Oxford)

The French Convert: Being a True Relation of the Happy Conversion of a Noble French Lady, from The Errors and Superstitions of Popery, to the Reformed Religion, by Means of a Protestant Gardener her Servant. To which is added, A Brief Account of the present Severe Persecutions of the French Protestants (London: 9th edn, 1736).

The General idea of Allegorick Language: Or the State of the Divine and Absolute Kingdom and Empire of Almighty God, Demonstrated, as most Real and Apparent in a Summary State and Ratio. By the author of the New Jerusalem (London: 1702), Pamphlet 245.

The Prophetical Warnings of John Lacy, Esq; Pronounced under the Operation of the Spirit; and Faithfully taken in Writing, when they were spoken (London: 1707).

Warnings Pronounced by Elias Marion, 1706. Pamphlet 273 (1).

Wesley, John. *The Journal of the Rev. John Wesley, A.M.*, Vol. II (ed. Nehemiah Curnock; London: Charles H. Kelly, 1909–1916).

—. *The Works of John Wesley: Sermons II, 34–70*, Vol. II (ed. Albert C. Outler; Nashville: Abingdon Press, 1985).

—. *The Works of John Wesley: Sermons IV, 115–151, Vol. IV* (ed. Albert C. Outler; Nashville: Abingdon Press, 1987).

—. *The Works of John Wesley: The Methodist Societies History, Nature, and Design*, Vol. IX (ed. Rupert E. Davies; Nashville: Abingdon Press, 1989).

Secondary sources

Backus, Irena & Philip Benedict, eds, *Calvin and His Influence, 1509–2009* (Oxford; New York: Oxford University Press, 2011).

Bell, Mark R. *Apocalypse How? Baptist Movements during the English Revolution* (Macon: Mercer University Press, 2000).

Coats, Catharine Randall. *Subverting the System: D'Aubigné and Calvinism*, Sixteenth Century Essays and Studies, Vol. XIV (Kirksville: Sixteenth Century Journal Publishers Inc., 1990).

Cosmos, Georgia, *Huguenot Prophecy and Clandestine Worship in the Eighteenth Century: 'The Sacred Theatre of the Cévennes'* (Aldershot: Ashgate, 2005).

Chappell, Carolyn L. '"The Pains I Took to Save My / His Family": Escape Accounts by a Huguenot Mother and Daughter after the Revocation of the Edict of Nantes', *French Historical Studies*, Vol. 22, No 1 (Winter 1999), Duke University Press, pp. 43–61.

Clifford, Alan, C. *Calvin Celebrated: The Genevan Reformer and His Huguenot Sons*. A Contribution to the John Calvin Quincentenary 1509–2009 (Norwich: Charenton Reformed Publishing, 2009).

Diefendorf, Barbara, B. *Beneath the Cross: Catholics and Huguenots in Sixteenth-Century Paris* (New York; Oxford: Oxford University Press, 1991).

Dupré, Louis & Saliers, Don E. in collaboration with John Meyendorff, *Christian Spirituality: Post-Reformation and Modern, World Spirituality* (London: SCM Press Ltd, 1990).

Garrett, Clarke. *Origins of the Shakers: From the Old World to the New World* (Baltimore; London: John Hopkins University Press, 1988).

Grubb, Arthur Page. *Jean Cavalier: Baker's Boy and British General* (London: George Allen & Unwin Ltd, 1931).

Gwynn, Robin. *Huguenot Heritage: The history and contribution of the Huguenots in Britain* (Brighton: Sussex Academic Press. 2nd rev. edn, 2001).

Higonnet, Patrice L.–R. *Pont-de-Montevert: Social Structure and Politics in a French Village, 1700–1914* (Cambridge, MA: Harvard University Press, 1971).

Howells, R.J. *Pierre Jurieu: Antinomian Radical* (Durham: University of Durham, 1983).

Kreiser, B. Robert. *Miracles, Convulsions, and Ecclesiastical Politics in Early Eighteenth-Century Paris* (Princeton: Princeton University Press, 1978).

Le Roy Ladurie, Emmanuel. *The Peasants of Languedoc* (ed. George Huppert; trans. John Day; Illini Books; Urbana, Chicago: University of Illinois Press, 1976).

Lane, Belden C. *Ravished by Beauty: The Surprising Legacy of Reformed Spirituality* (New York: Oxford University Press, 2011).

Neuser, Wilhelm H., ed. *Calvinus Sacrae Scripturae Professor: Calvin as Confessor of Holy Scripture*, International Congress on Calvin Research 20–23 August 1990, Grand Rapids (Grand Rapids: Wm. B. Eerdmans, 1994).

Prestwich, Menna, ed. *International Calvinism 1541–1715* (Oxford: Clarendon Press, 1985).

Ridholls, Joe. *The Spirit of the Desert: The Life of Antoine Court* (London: Epworth Press, 1968).

Saillens, Reuben. *The Soul of France* (London: Morgan and Scott Ltd., 1916).

Schikora, Henning. *The anointing of the Holy Spirit on France: Reflections on the prophetic movement in the Cévennes in the Seventeenth and Eighteenth centuries* (Mas David, Vézénobres, n.d.).

Schwartz, Hillel. *The French Prophets: The History of a Millenarian Group in Eighteenth-Century England* (Berkeley: University of California Press, 1980).

Schwartz, Hillel. *Knaves, Fools, Madmen, and that Subtile Effluvium: A Study of the Opposition to the French Prophets in England, 1706–1710* (Gainesville: University Presses of Florida, 1978).

Screech, M.A. *Clément Marot A Renaissance Poet discovers the Gospel: Lutheranism, Fabrism and Calvinism in the Royal Courts of France and of Navarre and in the Ducal Court of Ferrara,* Studies in Medieval and Reformation Thought, Vol. LIV (Leiden, New York, Köln: E.J. Brill, 1994).

Skinner, Quentin. *The Foundations of Modern Political Thought,* Vol. 2: *The Age of Reformation* (Cambridge: Cambridge University Press, 1978).

Sluhovsky, Moshe, *Believe Not Every Spirit: Possession, Mysticism, & Discernment in Early Modern Catholicism* (Chicago & London: The University of Chicago Press, 2007).

Treasure, Geoffrey, *The Huguenots* (New Haven & London: Yale University Press, 2013).

Utt, Walter C., and Strayer, Brian E., *The Bellicose Dove: Claude Brousson and Protestant Resistance to Louis XIV, 1647–1698* (Brighton: Sussex Academic Press, 2003).

Walker, D.P. *Unclean Spirits: Possession and exorcism in France and England in the late sixteenth and early seventeenth centuries* (London: Scolar Press, 1981).

Quaker

Primary sources

A Collection of the Sufferings of the People called Quaker in Wiltshire from the year 1653 (1699/17). Wiltshire and Swindon Archives.

A General Epistle to all who have believed in the Light of the Lord Iesus and are called of God to follow the Lamb through the Great Tribulation. F.H. n.p. (1684)

A Letter sent to the King from M.F. Here is also thereunto Annexed a Paper written unto the Magistrates in 1664. which was then Printed, and should have been dispersed, but was prevented by wicked hands. n.p. n.d.

A Living Testimony From the Power and Spirit of our Lord Jesus Christ in our Faithful Womens Meeting and Christian Society (London: 1685).

An Account of the Life, Travels, and Christian Experiences in the Work of the Ministry of Samuel Bownas (London: 1756).

A Message to the Present Rulers of England. Whether Committee of Safety, (so called) Councell of Officers, or Others whatsoever (London: 1659).

An Explanation of the Roman Catholikes Belief, concerning these four Points: Their Church; Worship; Justification; and civill Government. Broadsides 2 Nos. 77–170 (Wood 276A/2 Special Collections), CIII. Given to the recipient 26 October 1673, n.d. n.p.

Bathurst, Elizabeth. *An Epistle to such of the Friends of Christ As have lately been Convinced of the Truth as it is in Jesus* (1679) n.p.

Barclay, Robert. *An Apology for the True Christian Divinity, as the same is held forth and preached by the people, in scorn, called Quakers*. Original edition in Latin – first English edition, 1678 (Manchester: William Irwin, 13th edn, 1869).

—*An Apology for the True Christian Divinity, as the same is held forth, and preached by the people, Called, in Scorn, Quakers; Being a full explanation and vindication of their Principles and Doctrines, by many arguments, deduced from Scripture and right Reason, and the testimonys of famous Authors, both antient and modern, with a full answer to the strongest objections usually made against them, Presented to the King* (1678), n.p.

Bownas, Samuel, *A Description of the Qualifications Necessary to A Gospel Minster, containing Advice to Ministers and Elders, how to conduct themselves in their Conversations, and various Services, according to their Gifts in the Church of Christ* (London: 1767).

Bugg, Francis. *A Finishing Stroke; or, Some Gleanings, Collected out of the Quaker Books. By Way of Prologue. Never before Publish'd. The Great Mystery of the Little Whore is farther Unfolded* (London: R. Wilkin, King's-Head, 1712).

Burrough, Edward. *A Trumpet of the Lord Sounded out of Sion which sounds forth the Controversy of the Lord of Hosts* (London, 1656).

Cole, James. *The Last Testimony of That faithful Servant of the Lord and Minister of Jesus Christ, Richard Farnworth. Whereunto is Prefixed A brief Testimony concerning his Life Death, and Travels, etc. To which is added A few words of Exhortation unto those that believe in the Light of the Lamb* (London: 1667).

The Cry of Newgate, with the other Prisons, in and about London: In which dismal Holes, and Cels, are immured about three hundred persons, of the Innocent People of God, called Quakers, for no other Cause, but for their unspotted Testimonies in God, held in clear Consciences. To you Magistrates, Priests, and People of this City of London, and elsewhere, whom these may concern, are these Words uttered (London, 1662).

Dewsbury, William. *The Discovery of the great enmity of the Serpent against the seed of the Woman, which witnesseth against him where he rules, both in Rulers, Priests and People: Whose hearts are now made manifest in his great day of the Lords power; wherein he is sending his Sons and Daughters in the power of his spirit to run to and fro to declare his word* (London, 1655).

—. *The Faithful Testimony of the Ancient Servant of the Lord, and Minister of the everlasting Gospel William Dewsbury: in His Books, Epistles and Writings, Collected and Printed for future Service* (London, 1689).

Farnworth, Richard. *The Holy Scriptures From Scandals are cleared. Richard Farnworth* (London, 1655).

—. *The Pure Language of the Spirit of Truth: Set forth for the confounding false Languages, acted out of Pride, ambition and deceit. Or, Thee and Thou, In its place, is the proper Language to any single person whatsoever* (London, 1656).

Fell, Margaret. *A Call unto the Seed of Israel, That They may come out of Egypts Darkness, and House of Bondage, unto the Land of Rest* (London [1668?]).

—. *To the General Council of Officers. The Representation of divers Citizens of London, and others Well-affected to the Peace and Tranquility of the Common wealth. London, 1659. Broadsides 2 Nos. 77–170* (Wood 276A/2 Special Collections), CVIII.

—. *Womens Speaking* (London: Pythia Press, 1989). Original 1666.

—. *A Brief Collection of Remarkable Passages and Occurrences Relating to the Birth, Education, Life, Conversation, Travels, Services, and*

Deep Sufferings of that Ancient, Eminent, and Faithful Servant of the Lord, Margaret Fell: But by her Second Marriage Margaret Fox (London, 1710).

—. *A Testimonie of the Touch-stone, for all Professions, and all Forms, and Gathered churches (as they call them) of what sort soever to try their ground and foundation by and A Tryal by the Scriptures, who the False Prophets are, which are in the world, which John said should be in the last times by Margret Fell. Also, Some of the Ranters Principles Answered* (London: 1656).

'*For the King and his Council*'. From Friends of Truth and Innocency, G.F. and J.S. (London, 16 November 1660).

Fox, George. *A Journal or Historic Account of the Life, Travels. Sufferings, Christian Experiences and Labour of Love in the Work of the Ministry, of that Ancient, Eminent and Faithful Servant of Jesus Christ, George Fox; who departed this Life in great Peace with the Lord, the 13th of the 11th month, 1690,* I (London: Thomas Northcott, 1694).

—. *The Journal of George Fox*, 2 vols, ed. from the MSS by Norman Penney (Cambridge: University Press, 1911).

—. *The Journal of George Fox; Being an Historical Account of his Life, Travels, Sufferings, and Christian Experiences,* 2 vols (London: Headley Brothers, 1902).

—. *The Journal of George Fox* (ed. John L. Nickalls; Philadelphia: Religious Society of Friends, rev. edn, 1997).

—. *The Works of George Fox*, Vols 1–8 (State College, Pennsylvania, PA: New Foundation Publications, George Fox Fund, 1990). Reprinted from 1831 edn. Published by M.T.C. Gould, Philadelphia, with new introduction and edited by T.H.S. Wallace.

—. '*The Power of the Lord is Over All*': *The Pastoral Letters of George Fox* (ed. T. Canby Jones; Richmond: Friends United Press, 1989).

—. *A Collection of Many Select and Christian Epistles, Letters and Testimonies. Written on Sundry Occasions, by that Ancient, Eminent, Faithful Friend and Minister of Christ Jesus, George Fox,* Vol. 2 (London: T. Sowle, White Hart-Court, 1698).

—. *A Word from the Lord, to all the World, all Professors in the World; Spoken in Parables* (London: Giles Calvert, 1654), Vol. 4/21 Library of the Society of Friends.

—. *The Short Journals and Itinerary Journals of George Fox* (ed. by Norman Penney; Cambridge: Cambridge University Press, 1925).

Gospel-Truth Demonstrated, in a Collection of Doctrinal Books, Given forth by that Faithful Minister of Jesus Christ, George Fox: Containing Principles, Essential to Christianity and Salvation, held among the People called Quakers (London: 1706).

Good Counsel and Advice, Rejected; By Disobedient men. And the days of Oliver Cromwells Visitation passed over; And also of Richard Cromwel his Son, late Protectors of these Nations (London: 1659).

Gilman, Anne. *An Epistle to Friends; Being a Tender Salution To the Faithful in God every where. Also, a Letter to Charles, King of England, etc. (London: 1662).*

Keith, George. *Benefit, Advantage, and Glory of Silent Meetings, Both As it was found at the beginning, or first breaking forth of this clear manifestation of Truth, and continues to be found by all the Faithful and Upright in Heart at this Day* (London, 1687).

Marshall, Charles. *A Tender Visitation in the Love of God unto All People everywhere, Particularly unto the Inhabitants of Wiltshire, Gloucestershire and Bristol. And to my Neighbours in and above Tetherton, Calloways, and the adjacent Towns and Villages* (London: Andrew So[a]wle, 1684). Wiltshire and Swindon Archives.

Orme, William. *The Life and Times of Richard Baxter: with a Critical Examination of his Writings*, Vol. 1 (London: James Duncan, 1830).

Parnell, Jmes. *The Stone which the Builders have rejected, the same is now become the Head of the Corner: or, Christ Exalted into his Throne: And the Scripture owned in its place*, n.n. n.p.

Penington, Isaac. *Knowing the Mystery of Life Within: Selected Writings of Isaac Pennington in their Historical and Theological Context*, selected and introduced by R. Melvin Keiser & Rosemary Moore, MS transcriptions by Diana Morrison-Smith (London: Quaker Books, 2005).

—. *The Works of the Long-Mournful and Sorely-Distressed Isaac Penington, whom The Lord, in his tender Mercy, at length visited and relieved by the Ministry of that despised People called Quakers.* Vols 1–4 (London: 3rd edn, 1784).

Sound Advice to Roman Catholics: Especially, The Residue of Poor, Seduced, and Deluded Papists in England, who obstinately shut both Eyes and Ears, against the clearest Light of the Gospel of Christ, and surest Evidences of Scripture and Reason. To which is added, A Word to the People called Quakers. By I.O. (London: 1689).

The Daughter of Sion Awakened, And putting on Strength: She is Arising, and shaking herself out of the Dust, and putting on her Beautiful Garments. M.F. n.p. 1677.

The Oath of Allegiance, Enacted 13.Jacobi, Cap.4. Which Oath was solemnly taken by every Member of both Houses of Parliament, Rump and all (March, 1659). Broadsides 2 Nos. 77–170 (Wood 276A/2 Special Collections), CXLIII.

The Oaths of Allegiance and Supremacy (London: 1672). Broadsides 2 Nos. 77–170 (Wood 276A/2 Special Collections), CXLIV.

To the right Honourable, our right vvorthy and grave Senatours, the Lord Mayor, Aldermen, and Commonalty of the City of London in Common Council assembled, The most humble Petition and Adress of divers young men, on the behalf of themselves and the Apprentices in and about this honourable City. Monday 5 December 1659 (London, 1659). Broadsides 2 Nos. 77–170 (Wood 276A/2 Special Collections), CVII.

Townsend, Theophila. *An Epistle of Love to Friends in the Womens meetings in London, etc. To be read among them in the Fear of God,* n.d. n.p.

Wiltshire Friends. Sufferings from 1653 to 1756. 1699/18. Wiltshire and Swindon Archives.

Secondary sources

Ambler, Rex. *Light to live by: An exploration in Quaker spirituality* (London: Quaker Books, 2002).

Apetrei, Sarah. 'The Universal Principle of Grace: Feminism and Anti-Calvinism in Two Seventeenth-Century Women Writers' (Gender and History, Vol. 21 No. 1, April 2009), pp. 130–145.

Bauman, Richard. *Let your Words be Few: Symbolism of Speaking and Silence among Seventeenth-Century Quakers,* Cambridge Studies in Oral and Literate Culture 8 (Cambridge: Cambridge University Press, 1983).

Barbour, Hugh. *The Quakers in Puritan England* (New Haven & London: Yale University Press, 1964).

Benson, Lewis. *What did George Fox teach about Christ?* New Foundation Publications, No. 1, Spring, 1976 (Gloucester: George Fox Fund).

—. *The Quaker Vision,* New Foundation Publications, No. 4, Winter 1979 (Gloucester: George Fox Fund).

—. *The Truth is Christ*, New Foundation Publications, No. 5, Summer 1981 (Gloucester: George Fox Fund).

Braithwaite, William C. *The Beginnings of Quakerism* (rev. Henry J. Cadbury; Cambridge: Cambridge University Press, 2nd edn, 1970).

—. *The Second period of Quakerism* (rev. Henry J. Cadbury; Cambridge: Cambridge University Press, 2nd edn, 1961).

Dandelion, Pink. *The Quakers: A Very Short Introduction* (New York: Oxford University Press, 2008).

—. ed. *The Creation of Quaker Theory: Insider Perspectives* (Aldershot: Ashgate: 2004).

Durham, Geoffrey. *Being a Quaker: A Guide for Newcomers* (London: Quaker Quest, 2011).

Gill, Catie. *Women in the Seventeenth-Century Quaker Community: A Literary Study of Political Identities, 1650–1700*, Women and Gender in the Early Modern World (Aldershot: Ashgate, 2005).

Graves, Michael P. *Preaching the Inward Light: Early Quaker Rhetoric*, Studies in Rhetoric and Religion 9 (Waco: Baylor University Press, 2009).

Gwyn, Douglas. *Apocalypse of the Word: The Life and Message of George Fox* (Richmond: Friends United Press, 1984).

Hill, Christopher. *The World Turned Upside Down: Radical Ideas During the English Revolution* (Harmondsworth: Penguin, 1984).

Jones, Rufus. *Quakerism: A Spiritual Movement* (Philadelphia Yearly Meeting of Friends, 1963).

Kunze, Bonnelyn Young. *Margaret Fell and the Rise of Quakerism* (Basingstoke: Macmillan, 1994).

Mack, Phyllis. *Visionary Women: Ecstatic Prophecy in Seventeenth-Century England* (London, Berkeley & Los Angeles: University of California Press, 1992), 1st paperback printing 1994.

Mills, J. Travis. *John Bright and the Quakers*, I (London: Methuen & Co. Ltd, 1935).

Moore, Rosemary. *The Light in their Consciences: Early Quakers in Britain 1646–1666* (Pennsylvania: The Pennsylvania State University Press, 2000).

Nuttall, Geoffrey F. *Early Quaker Studies and the Divine Presence* (Weston Rhyn: Quinta Press, 2003).

—. *The Puritan Spirit: Essays and Addresses* (London: Epworth Press, 1967).

—. *The Holy Spirit in Puritan Faith and Experience* (Oxford: Basil Blackwell, 1947).

Ozment, Steven, E. *Mysticism and Dissent: Religious Ideology and Social Protest in the Sixteenth Century* (New Haven; London: Yale University Press, 1973).

Priestland, Gerald, *Reasonable Uncertainty: A Quaker approach to doctrine*, Swarthmore Lecture 1982 (London: Quakerbooks, reprinted 2007).

Scully, Jackie Leach & Pink Dandelion, eds, *Good and Evil: Quaker Perspectives* (Aldershot: Ashgate, 2007).

Steere, Douglas V., ed. *Quaker Spirituality: Selected Writings,* The Classics of Western Spirituality (London: SPCK, 1984).

Taylor, Kay. S. 'Society, Schism and Sufferings: The first 70 years of Quakerism in Wiltshire', June 2006, unpublished PhD Thesis, University of the Weset of England, Bristol [© K.S. Taylor].

Trevett, Christine. *Quaker Women Prophets in England and Wales 1650–1700*, Studies in Women and Religion, Vol. 41 (Lampeter: The Edwin Mellen Press, 2000).

—.*Women and Quakerism in the Seventeenth Century* (York: The Ebor Press, 1995).

Weddle, Meredith Baldwin. *Walking in the Way of Peace: Quaker Pacifism in the Seventeenth Century* (New York: Oxford University Press, 2001).

Watts, Michael. *The Dissenters: From the Reformation to the French Revolution*, I (Oxford: Clarendon Press, 1978).

Wilcox, Catherine M. *Theology and Women's Ministry in Seventeenth-Century English Quakerism: Handmaids of the Lord*, Studies in Women and Religion, Vol. 35 (New York: The Edwin Mellen Press, 1995).

Wildwood, Alex. *A faith to call our own: Quaker tradition in the light of contemporary movements of the Spirit*, Swarthmore Lecture 1999 (London: Quaker Books, 2010).

Wiseman, James A. *Spirituality and Mysticism: A Global View* (New York: Orbis Books, 2006).

Endnotes

Introduction

[1] See Jennifer Campbell, *Light on Prophecy: Retrieving Word and Spirit* in *Today's Church* (Milton Keynes: Paternoster, 2012), pp. 63–6, 92–4.

[2] James A. Wiseman, *Spirituality and Mysticism: A Global View* (New York: Orbis Books, 2006), pp. 7–11; Elias Marion, *Prophetical Warnings of Elias Marion, heretofore One of the Commanders of the Protestants, That had taken Arms in the Cévennes: or Discourse Uttered by him in London, under the Operation of the Spirit and Faithfully taken in Writing, whilst they were spoken* (London: 1707), hereafter *Prophetical Warnings*, p. 10.

[3] Clarke Garrett, *Origins of the Shakers: From the Old World to the New World* (Baltimore; London: John Hopkins University Press, 1988), hereafter *Origins of the Shakers*, p. 2.

[4] Geoffrey Treasure, *The Huguenots* (New Haven & London: Yale University Press, 2013), p. 387; Douglas V. Steere, ed. *Quaker Spirituality: Selected Writings, The Classics of Western Spirituality* (London: SPCK, 1984), hereafter *Quaker Spirituality*, pp. 6–7.

1. Apostles of Prophetic Vision

[1] John Calvin, 'To Melanchthon' (105), *Letters of John Calvin II in John Calvin: Works and Correspondence*, Electronic Edition (ed. Ford Lewis Battles, Henry Beveridge, Jules Bonnet, David Constable; Charlottesville, VA.: Intelex Corporation, 1995), p. 377 (accessed 10 June 2013, Bodleian Libraries, University of Oxford).

2 *A Hymn to Peace. Occasion'd by the Two Houses Joining in One Address to the Queen*, By the Author of the True-born English-man [Daniel Defoe] (London: 1709), Pamphlet 282 (1), pp. 4–5.

3 Richard A. Muller, 'Reception and Response: Referencing and Understanding Calvin in Seventeenth-Century Calvinism', in *Calvin and His Influence, 1509–2009* (ed. Irena Backus and Philip Benedict; Oxford; New York: Oxford University Press, 2011), pp. 182–201; John Calvin, *Tracts and Letters*, Vol. 6: *Letters, Part 3 1554–1558* (ed. Jules Bonnet; trans. Marcus Robert Gilchrist; Edinburgh: Banner of Truth Trust, 2009), p. 319, n.1. For an examination of the place of Pierre Jurieu in historical studies, ecclesiology, political authority and the sociology of dissent, and for the range of his writings see R.J. Howells, *Pierre Jurieu: Antinomian Radical* (Durham: University of Durham, 1983), hereafter *Pierre Jurieu*, pp. 7–9,11–73.

4 Meic Pearse, *The Age of Reason: From the Wars of Religion to the French Revolution, 1570–1789*, The Monarch History of the Church, Vol. 5 (Oxford: Monarch Books, 2007), pp. 44–52 and Garrett, *Origins of the Shakers*, p. 16.

5 Quentin Skinner, Part 3, 'Calvinism and the Theory of Revolution', in *The Foundations of Modern Political Thought, Vol. 2: The Age of Reformation* (Cambridge: Cambridge University Press, 1978), hereafter *Foundations*, pp. 189–348. This work is the source for the material for the Calvinist argument on the right to resist in the following paragraphs. Skinner's translations of Calvin on pp. 232–3 are from John Calvin, *Institutes of the Christian Religion*, in Opera Omnia, ed. Baum et al, 1559, p. 1116.

6 *Foundations*, pp. 231–34,304–14.

7 *Foundations*, pp. 191–4,208,217–9. For *The Lutheran constitutional theory of resistance, The Confession and Apology of the Pastors and other Ministers of the Church at Magdeburg, 13 April 1550*, see p. 208.

8 Hillel Schwartz, *The French Prophets: The History of a Millenarian Group in Eighteenth-Century England* (Berkeley: University of California Press, 1980), hereafter *French Prophets*, pp. 12–14; Georgia Cosmos, *Huguenot Prophecy and Clandestine Worship in the Eighteenth Century: 'The Sacred Theatre of the Cévennes'* (Aldershot: Ashgate, 2005), hereafter *Huguenot Prophecy*, pp. 1,25, n. 14; Philippe Joutard, 'The Revocation of the Edict of Nantes: End or Renewal of French Protestantism?' in *International Calvinism 1541–1715* (ed. Menna Prestwich; Oxford: Clarendon Press, 1985), pp. 339–68 (p. 346), cf. Garrett, *Origins of the Shakers*, pp. 35–6.

9 Heiko A. Oberman, 'Initia Calvini: The Matrix of Calvin's Reformation', in Wilhelm H. Neuser, ed. *Calvinus Sacrae Scripturae Professor: Calvin as Confessor of Holy Scripture*, International Congress on Calvin Research 20–23 August 1990, Grand Rapids (Grand Rapids: Wm. B. Eerdmans, 1994), hereafter *Calvinus*, pp. 113–54 (pp. 152–4).

10 Jurieu, *Réflexions sur la cruelle persecution que souffre l'Eglise réformée de France* (1685), see Howells, *Pierre Jurieu*, pp. 30,37,43,45–6; Pierre Jurieu, *Seasonable Advice to all Protestants in Europe Of what Persuasion soever, for Uniting and Defending themselves against Popish Tyranny.* Done out of French. (London: 1689), pp. 7–10; Pierre Jurieu, *The Pastoral Letters of the Incomparable Jurieu, Directed to the Protestants in France Groaning under the Babylonish Tyranny, translated: Wherein the Sophistical Arguments and Unexpressible Cruelties made use of by the Papists for the making Converts, are laid open and expos'd to just Abhorrence. Unto which is added, a brief account of the Hungarian persecution* (London: 1689), hereafter *JPL*, pp. 3–6; *A Letter of several French Ministers Fled into Germany upon the account of the PERSECUTION in France, to such of their Brethren in England as Approved the King's Declaration touching Liberty of Conscience. Translated from the Original in French.* 1688 [Pamphlet C 188 (33)], pp. 6–7.

11 *Pierre Jurieu, The Accomplishment of the Scripture Prophecies, or the Approaching Deliverance of the Church.* Trans. from the French (London: 1687), p. 59; cf. Howells, Pierre Jurieu, pp. 38–59.

12 *A Short Account of the Complaints, and Cruel Persecutions of the Protestants in the Kingdom of France* (London: 1707), hereafter *Short Account*, pp. 46–7,51–3,64–7; Garrett, *Origins of the Shakers*, pp. 16,17; cf. Schwartz, *French Prophets*, pp. 12–14.

13 Nobuo Watanabe, 'Calvin's Second Catechism: Its Predecessors and Its Environment', in Neuser, *Calvinus*, pp. 224–5,227.

14 From John Calvin, *Introduction, Commentary on the Book of Psalms* (trans. James Anderson; Edinburgh, 1845; republished Grand Rapids: Eerdmans, 1949), p. xxxix, in John Calvin, *Commentary on the Psalms* (abridged by David C. Searle; Edinburgh: Banner of Truth Trust, 2009), p. xix.

15 Cosmos, *Huguenot Prophets*, p. 39, *A Cry from the Desart: or Testimonials of the Miraculous Things lately come to pass in the Cévennes, Verified upon Oath, and by other Proofs. Translated from the Originals* (London: 1707), hereafter *CDc*, pp. 78,89,93; *JPL*, p. 12.

16 Cf. Emmanuel Le Roy Ladurie, *The Peasants of Languedoc* (ed. George Huppert; trans. John Day; Urbana; Chicago; London: University of Illinois Press, 1976), hereafter *Languedoc*, pp. 266–72.

17 John Calvin, *Commentary on the Book of Psalms*, Vol. 1–5 (trans. James Anderson; Edinburgh: The Calvin Translation Society, 1845–9), Vol. 1, 1945, pp. 562–3, cf. Vol. 2, p. 340, Vol. 3, pp. 23,485–7, John Calvin, *The Acts of the Apostles 1–13* (trans. John W. Fraser and W.J.G. McDonald, CC; Edinburgh: Oliver & Boyd, 1965), p. 343, cf. John Calvin, *Institutes of the Christian Religion*, I.1 – III.19, The Library of Christian Classics, Vol. XXX (ed. John T. McNeill; trans. Ford Lewis Battles; London: SCM Press Ltd, 1961), I, 14,7,), hereafter *CI*, pp. 166–7.

18 Schwartz, *French Prophets*, pp. 14–20.

19 Cosmos, *Huguenot Prophecy*, pp. 2–25, Schwartz, *French Prophets*, pp. 79–80. See also Robin Gwynn, *Huguenot Heritage: The history and contribution of the Huguenots in Britain* (Brighton: Sussex Academic Press, 2nd rev. edn, 2001); *A Cry from the Desart: or Testimonials of the Miraculous Things lately come to pass in the Cévennes, Verified upon Oath, and by other Proofs. Translated from the Originals*. The Second Edition. With a Preface by John Lacy, London, 1707 (Author Maximillien Misson), hereafter *CDb*, pp. vi–vii, *Prophetical Extracts. Containing a very scarce Prophetic Piece, Intitled, A Cry from the Desart, or, Testimonials of the Miraculous Things lately come to pass in the Cévennes, or Southern Parts of France. Verified upon oath, and by other proofs* (1707: London), hereafter *CDa*.

20 *CDa*, pp. 18,20–1,23–4,26,36,24.

21 Belden C. Lane, *Ravished by Beauty: The Surprising Legacy of Reformed Spirituality* (New York: Oxford University Press, 2011), pp. 57–85, 285, n.16, see pp. 60–1 for theatre in Geneva, John Calvin, *The Epistles of Paul The Apostle to the Romans and to the Thessalonians*, CC (ed. David W. Torrance and Thomas F. Torrance; trans. Ross Mackenzie; Edinburgh: Oliver & Boyd, 1961), p. 31, *CI* I, 14,20, p. 179, *CI* II, 6,1, p. 341, cf. *CI* I, I, 5, p. 52, *CI* I, I, 1, p. 35, *CI* II, III, 20,23, p. 881.

22 John Calvin, *Sermons on 2 Samuel Chapters 1–13* (trans. Douglas Kelly: Edinburgh: Banner of Truth Trust, 1992), pp. 267–9, *CI* III, 20, 3, p. 852, III, 20, 5, p. 855.

23 Aristotle, *Poetics* (trans. Kenneth McLeish; London: Nick Hern Books, 1999), p. 9, the note cites Aristotle, *Politics* 1, 8, Ch. 7, *CI* I, 6, 2, p. 72.

24 *Short Account*, pp. 10–14; *The French Convert: Being a True Relation of the Happy Conversion of a Noble French Lady, from The Errors and Superstitions*

of Popery, to the Reformed Religion, by Means of a Protestant Gardener her Servant. To which is added, A Brief Account of the present Severe Persecutions of the French Protestants (London: 9th edn, 1736), hereafter *French Convert*.

25 *CDa*, p. 23, *An Extract of Some Minutes of Mr Matthew Boissier (Aged about 48). Written and signed by his own hand, and left with one of his Acquaintances at London*, in *CDa*, pp. 13–17; Schwartz, *French Prophets*, p. 83, JPL, pp. 371–2.

26 Schwartz, *French Prophets*, p. 22; Alan C. Clifford, *Calvin Celebrated: The Genevan Reformer and His Huguenot Sons. A Contribution to the John Calvin Quincentenary 1509–2009* (Norwich: Charenton Reformed Publishing, 2009), hereafter *Calvin Celebrated*, p. 130. For social class on the eve of the Camisard wars, see Patrice L.–R. Higonnet, *Pont-de-Montevert: Social Structure and Politics in a French Village, 1700–1914* (Cambridge, MA: Harvard University Press, 1971), hereafter *Pont-de-Montevert*, pp. 16–29; for a description of the social factors influencing the attack see pp. 30–44.

27 Clifford, *Calvin Celebrated*, pp. 132–7.

28 Garrett, *Origin of the Shakers*, pp. 36–9.

29 William Orme, *The Life and Times of Richard Baxter: with a Critical Examination of his Writings*, Vol. 1 (London: James Duncan, 1830), hereafter *Richard Baxter*, p. 123.

30 Michael P. Graves, *Preaching the Inward Light: Early Quaker Rhetoric*, Studies in Rhetoric and Religion 9 (Waco: Baylor University Press, 2009), hereafter *Preaching*, p. 10; Jackie Leach Scully and Pink Dandelion, eds, *Good and Evil: Quaker Perspectives* (Aldershot: Ashgate, 2007), hereafter *Good and Evil*, p. 12. For Quaker gender historiography and contemporary feminist trends see Kay S. Taylor, 'Society, Schism and Sufferings: The first 70 years of Quakerism in Wiltshire', June 2006, unpublished PhD Thesis, University of the West of England, Bristol [© K.S. Taylor], pp. 19–22. For contemporary openness to new lights see Alex Wildwood, *A faith to call our own: Quaker tradition in the light of contemporary movements of the Spirit*, Swarthmore Lecture 1999 (London: Quaker Books, 2010). For a comparison with Hugh Barbour's early Quaker testimonies in *The Quakers in Puritan England* (New Haven & London: Yale University Press, 1964), hereafter *The Quakers*, pp. 160–80, see Geoffrey Durham, *Being a Quaker: A Guide for Newcomers* (London: Quaker Quest, 2011), p. 89. For a contemporary view on Quaker doctrine, see Gerald Priestland, *Reasonable*

Uncertainty: A Quaker approach to doctrine, Swarthmore Lecture 1982 (London: Quakerbooks, reprinted 2007), p. 16.

31 William C. Braithwaite, *The Second Period of Quakerism* (ed. Henry J. Cadbury; Cambridge: Cambridge University Press, 2nd edn rev., 1961), hereafter *Second Period*, pp. 394,396; Douglas Gwyn, *Apocalypse of the Word: The Life and Message of George Fox* (Richmond: Friends United Press, 1984), hereafter *Apocalypse of the Word*, pp. xiii–xxiii; Rufus Jones, *Quakerism: A Spiritual Movement* (Philadelphia Yearly Meeting of Friends, 1963), hereafter *Quakerism*, pp. 55–60,81,98,112–115.

32 Jones, *Quakerism*, pp. 112–15. For the historical development of Christian eschatology from the early church to the Reformation see Mark R. Bell, *Apocalypse How? Baptist Movements during the English Revolution* (Macon: Mercer University Press, 2000), hereafter *Apocalypse*, pp. 13–22. Douglas Gwyn, 'Apocalypse Now and Then: Reading Early Friends in the Belly of the Beast', hereafter 'Apocalypse Now and Then', in *The Creation of Quaker Theory: Insider Perspectives* (ed. Pink Dandelion; Aldershot: Ashgate: 2004), hereafter *Quaker Theory*, pp. 127–48 (pp. 127–29).

33 Rosemary Moore, *The Light in their Consciences: Early Quakers in Britain 1646–1666* (Pennsylvania: The Pennsylvania State University Press, 2000), hereafter *Light in their Consciences*, pp. 60–74; Lewis Benson, *What Did George Fox teach About Christ?*, New Foundation Publications, No. 1, Spring, 1976 (Gloucester: George Fox Fund), hereafter *George Fox*, pp. 3–14; Lewis Benson, *The Truth is Christ*, New Foundation Publications, No. 5, Summer 1981 (Gloucester: George Fox Fund), hereafter *Truth is Christ*, pp. 9–31. For Quakerism as a third kind of Christianity different from the church of Rome and from Protestants, yet a denomination within Protestantism, see Lewis Benson, *The Quaker Vision*, New Foundation Publications, No. 4, Winter 1979 (Gloucester: George Fox Fund), hereafter *Quaker Vision*, p. 25.

34 Dandelion, *Good and Evil*, p. 12; Barbour, *The Quakers*; Geoffrey F. Nuttall, *The Puritan Spirit: Essays and Addresses* (London: Epworth Press, 1967), hereafter *Puritan Spirit*, pp. 170–6. For sectarian groups see Geoffrey F. Nuttall, *Early Quaker Studies and the Divine Presence* (Weston Rhyn: Quinta Press, 2003), hereafter *Early Quaker Studies*, pp. 5–12; for Puritan mysticism see Geoffrey F. Nuttall, *The Holy Spirit in Puritan Faith and Experience* (Oxford: Basil Blackwell, 1947), hereafter *The Holy Spirit*, pp. 146–7; Geoffrey F. Nuttall, *Studies in English Dissent*

(Weston Rhyn: Quinta Press, 2002), pp. 83–96; Gwyn, *Apocalypse of the Word*, pp. xiii-xxiii; for further reading on the topic of English Dissent and the term, 'masterless men' see Christopher Hill, *The World Turned Upside Down: Radical Ideas During the English Revolution* (Harmondsworth: Penguin, 1984), hereafter *World*; Michael Watts, *The Dissenters: From the Reformation to the French Revolution*, I (Oxford: Clarendon Press, 1978); Bell, *Apocalypse*.

35 Hill, *World*, pp. 96–7.

36 George Fox, *The Journal of George Fox* (ed: John L. Nickalls; Philadelphia: Religious Society of Friends, rev. edn, 1997), hereafter *J1997*, p. 58; William C. Braithwaite, *The Beginnings of Quakerism* (ed: Henry J. Cadbury; Cambridge: Cambridge University Press, 2nd edn rev., 1970), hereafter *Beginnings*, pp. 54–7; Robert Barclay, *An Apology for the True Christian Divinity, as the same is held forth and preached by the people, in scorn, called Quakers* (Manchester: William Irwin, 13th edn, 1869), hereafter *BA*, pp. 224–5. Original edition in Latin – first English edition, 1678.

37 Elizabeth Bathurst, *An Epistle to such of the Friends of Christ As have lately been Convinced of the Truth as it is in Jesus* (1679), n.p., p. 97; Edward Burrough, *A Trumpet of the Lord Sounded out of Sion which sounds forth the Controversy of the Lord of Hosts* (London: 1656), hereafter *Trumpet*, p. 33; See Catherine M. Wilcox, *Theology and Women's Ministry in Seventeenth-Century English Quakerism: Handmaids of the Lord*, Studies in Women and Religion, Vol. 35 (New York: The Edwin Mellen Press, 1995), hereafter *Women's Ministry*, Endnotes 3, p. 12 for references to quaking in comparison with Wesley revivals.

38 Pink Dandelion, *The Quakers: A Very Short Introduction* (New York: Oxford University Press, 2008), hereafter *Introduction*, p. 7.

39 George Fox, *A Journal or Historic Account of the Life, Travels, Sufferings, Christian Experiences and Labour of Love in the Work of the Ministry, of that Ancient, Eminent and Faithful Servant of Jesus Christ, George Fox; who departed this Life in great Peace with the Lord, the 13th of the 11th month, 1690*, I (London: Thomas Northcott, 1694), hereafter *J1694*; George Fox, *The Works of George Fox*, Vol. 1, *The Journal*, introduction by Douglas Gwyn and specific introduction by John H. Curtis (State College, Pennsylvania, PA: New Foundation Publications, George Fox Fund, 1990). Reprinted from 1831 edn. Published by M.T.C. Gould, Philadelphia, hereafter *WGF* [permission to quote granted by T. Wallace, Foundation Publications]; George Fox, *The Journal of*

George Fox; Being an Historical Account of his Life, Travels, Sufferings, and Christian Experiences, 2 vols (London: Headley Brothers, 1902), hereafter *J1902: George Fox, The Journal of George Fox*, 2 vols (ed. from the MSS by Norman Penney; Cambridge: University Press, 1911), hereafter *J1911*; George Fox *J1997*; George Fox, *'The Power of the Lord is Over All': The Pastoral Letters of George Fox* (ed. T. Canby Jones; Richmond: Friends United Press, 1989), hereafter *Pastoral Letters*, pp. iii,187; Hill, *World*, p. 231.

40 Nuttall, *Puritan Spirit*, p. 186. References that follow are to Fox, *J1987*, pp. 3–21. For the phrase, 'Christ is come to teach his people' see *J1987*, pp. 104,107,109,143,149–50.

41 Gwyn, 'Apocalypse Now and Then', in *Quaker Theory*, pp. 134–5.

42 Fox, *J1987*, pp. 13–19, pp. 282–4; George Fox, *A Collection of Many Select and Christian Epistles, Letters and Testimonies. Written on Sundry Occasions, by that Ancient, Eminent, Faithful Friend and Minister of Christ Jesus, George Fox*, Vol. 2 (London: T. Sowle, 1698), p. 59.

43 Gwyn, 'Apocalypse Now and Then', in *Quaker Theory*, p. 135; Nuttall, *Puritan Spirit*, pp. 194–203, see pp. 198–200 for the understanding of light and the creation as unsullied and unfallen in the Hermetic writers, e.g. Henry Vaughan.

44 *J1987*, pp. 103–4, William Penn, 'Extracts from William Penn's Preface to the Original Edition of George Fox's Journal, 1694', hereafter 'Preface', in *J1987*, pp. xxxix–xlviii (pp.xl–xli), cf. J. Travis Mills, *John Bright and the Quakers* I (London: Methuen & Co. Ltd, 1935), p.4, n. 2; Fox, *WGF*, Vol. 7; *The Epistles*, Vol. 1, pp. 18,22–3.

45 Braithwaite, *Beginnings*, pp. 513–23.

46 Nuttall, *Puritan Spirit*, pp. 177–93, Canby Jones, *Pastoral Letters* vi, p. 187.

47 For the following discussion, see An Explanation of the Roman Catholikes Belief, concerning these four Points: Their Church; Worship; Justification; and civill Government. Broadsides 2 Nos. 77–170 (Wood 276A/2 Special Collections), CIII. Given to the recipient 26 Oct 1673, n.d. n.p. See Steven E. Ozment, *Mysticism and Dissent: Religious Ideology and Social Protest in the Sixteenth Century* (New Haven; London: Yale University Press, 1973), pp. 1–2.

48 Fox, *J1997*, pp. 149–50, cf. Hill, *World*, p. 106.

49 Fox, *J1997*, pp. 149–50.

50 Fox, *J1997*, p. 250.

51 *Introduction*, p. 2.

52 See Braithwaite, *Second Period, Beginnings*; Wilcox, *Women's Ministry*, pp. 3–15,17–55; Penn, 'Preface', in *J1987*, pp. xl–xli,104; Barclay, *BA*, pp. 324–350.

53 George Fox, *Gospel-Truth Demonstrated, in a Collection of Doctrinal Books, Given forth by that Faithful Minister of Jesus Christ, George Fox: Containing Principles, Essential to Christianity and Salvation, held among the People called Quakers* (London: 1706), hereafter *GTD*, pp. 227–42; Gwyn, *Apocalypse Now and Then*, pp. 132–3.

54 Isaac Penington, 'An Examination of the Grounds or Causes Which are said to Induce the Court of Boston, in New-England, to make that Order or Law of Banishment, upon Pain of Death, against the Quakers', in *The Works of the Long-Mournful and Sorely-Distressed Isaac Penington, whom The Lord, in his tender Mercy, at length visited and relieved by the Ministry of that despised People called Quakers*. Vols. 1–4 (London: 3rd edn, 1784), hereafter *IP*, 1, pp. 345–450 (pp. 439–40); Penington, *The Seed of God, and of his Kingdom, Treated and Testified of According to the Scriptures of Truth, and according to True Experience felt in the Heart from the God of Truth*, in *IP*, 4, p. 419.

55 Wilcox, *Women's Ministry*, pp. 3–15; Dandelion, *Introduction*, p. 15; Barclay, *BA*, pp. 324–350, *Richard Baxter*, p. 114.

56 See Braithwaite, *Second Period*, pp. 334–40 for the early life and religious changes in Robert Barclay; Barclay, *BA*, pp. 246–7; Braithwaite, *Beginnings*, p. 248.

57 Fox, *The Great Mistery of the Great Whore* (1659) in *WGF*, pp. 337–46.

58 Francis Bugg, *A Finishing Stroke; or, Some Gleanings, Collected out of the Quaker Books. By Way of Prologue. Never before Publish'd. The Great Mystery of the Little Whore is farther Unfolded* (London: 1712), p.2; Orme, *Richard Baxter*, pp. 112–113.

59 Bonnelyn Young Kunze, *Margaret Fell and the Rise of Quakerism* (Basingstoke: Macmillan, 1994), hereafter *Margaret Fell*, pp. 4–5,7,131–42.

60 J. Travis Mills, *John Bright and the Quakers*, I (London: Methuen & Co. Ltd, 1935) pp. 14,15; Fox, *The Epistles*, Vol. 1, in *WGF*, Vol. 7, pp. 22–23,'For the King and his Council'. From Friends of Truth and Innocency, G.F. and J.S. London, 16 November 1660, p. 5.

61 William Dewsbury, *The Discovery of the great enmity of the Serpent against the seed of the Woman, which witnesseth against him where he rules, both in Rulers, Priests and People: Whose hearts are now made manifest in his great day of the Lords power; wherein he is sending his Sons and Daughters in the power of his spirit to run to and fro to declare his word.'*

(London: 1655), hereafter *Discovery of great enmity*, p. 5; *The Cry of Newgate, with the other Prisons, in and about London:* 'In which dismal Holes, and Cels, are immured about three hundred persons, of the Innocent People of God, called Quakers, for no other Cause, but for their unspotted Testimonies in God, held in clear Consciences. To you Magistrates, Priests, and People of this City of London, and elsewhere, whom these may concern, are these Words uttered, By R. Crane.' (London: 1662), hereafter *Cry of Newgate*, pp. 6,8.

62 'Wiltshire Friends. Sufferings from 1653 to 1756', Wiltshire and Swindon Archives (1699/18).

63 'A Collection of the Sufferings of the People called Quaker in Wiltshire from the year 1653', Wiltshire and Swindon Archives (1699/17), *Cry of Newgate*, p. 5.

2. Prophetic Evangelists on Fire

1 *The History of the Edict of Nantes*, 1695, in Vol. 3, part 3, pp. 1016 etc. Trans. from French, in *CDa*, hereafter *Edict of Nantes*, pp. 5–8.

2 See Cosmos, *Huguenot Prophecy*, pp.4–8 for a survey of the literature; Le Roy Ladurie, *Languedoc*; Hillel Schwartz, *Knaves, Fools, Madmen, and that Subtile Effluvium: A Study of the Opposition to the French Prophets in England, 1706–1710* (Gainesville: University Presses of Florida, 1978), hereafter *Knaves*; Hillel Schwartz, *The French Prophets: The History of a Millenarian Group in Eighteenth-Century England* (Berkeley: University of California Press, 1980), hereafter *French Prophets*; Clifford, *Calvin Celebrated*; Moshe Sluhovsky, *Believe Not Every Spirit: Possession, Mysticism, & Discernment in Early Modern Catholicism* (Chicago & London: The University of Chicago Press, 2007), hereafter *Believe Not Every Spirit*, pp. 20–21,197; Garrett, *Origins of the Shakers*, p. 40.

3 D.P. Walker, *Unclean Spirits: Possession and exorcism in France and England in the late sixteenth and early seventeenth centuries* (London: Scolar Press, 1981), pp. 5–12,76–77; for further reading on the reaction to the French prophets in England and analyses of devil possession, illness and the supernatural, see Schwartz, *Knaves*; for an overview of the question of devil possession in the Catholic Church, see Sluhovsky, *Believe Not Every Spirit*.

4 B. Robert Kreiser, *Miracles, Convulsions, and Ecclesiastical Politics in Early Eighteenth-Century Paris* (Princeton: Princeton University Press,

1978), pp. ix–xi, p. 286, cf. pp. 359–60,173–4,271–4; for further reading on convulsionaries, pp. 243–75.

5 John Calvin, *Daniel I (Chapters 1–6)*, John Calvin's Lectures on the Book of The Prophecies of Daniel. Taken down by the effort and industry of Jean Budé and Charles Joinviller, Geneva 1561, Calvin's Old Testament Commentaries, Vol. 20 (trans. T.H.L. Parker; Grand Rapids: Wm. B. Eerdmans Publishing Company, 1993), pp. 1,4,145; John Calvin, *Sermons on 2 Samuel Chapters 1–13* (trans. Douglas Kelly; Edinburgh: Banner of Truth Trust, 1992), p. 456.

6 The Libertines were a sect numbering between four and ten thousand and led by Quinton of Hainaut in 1534, together with Bertrand of Moulins and Claude Perceval, followers of the originator, Coppin. They opposed Calvin's strict order and discipline in Geneva, and Calvin opposed them. Some were exposed for immorality, heresy and pantheistic mysticism. See John Calvin, *Treatises against the Anabaptists and against the Libertines: Translation, Introduction and Notes* (trans. Benjamin Wirt Farley; Grand Rapids: Baker Book House, 1982), hereafter *Anabaptists*, pp. 163–73, CI I, IX, 1–3, pp. 93–6.

7 John Wesley, *The Works of John Wesley: The Methodist Societies History, Nature, and Design*, Vol. 9 (ed. Rupert E. Davies; Nashville: Abingdon Press, 1989), hereafter *WW*, pp. 115, 130; John Wesley, *WW: Sermons II, 34–70*, Vol. 2 (ed. Albert C. Outler; Nashville: Abingdon Press, 1985), Sermon 43 (2), p. 156, Sermon 39 (9), p. 85; John Wesley, *WW: Sermons IV, 115–151*, Vol. 4 (ed. Albert C. Outler; Nashville: Abingdon Press, 1987), Sermon 120 (17), p. 67.

8 John Wesley, *The Journal of the Rev. John Wesley, A.M.*, Vol. II (ed. Nehemiah Curnock; London: Charles H. Kelly, 1909–1916), pp. 226, 136–7, Garrett, *Origins of the Shakers*, p. 79.

9 Bonaventure, *St. Bonaventure: Opscula, Second Series*, The Works of Bonaventure, Cardinal Seraphic Doctor and Saint, III (trans. José de Vinck; Paterson, St Anthony Guild Press, 1966), *Soliloquy* 2.2, 12, p. 87; M.A. Screech, *Ecstasy and the Praise of Folly* (London: Duckworth, 1980), pp. 152–4.

10 Calvin, *CI*, I, 1, 15, pp. 185–6, cites Ovid, *Metamorphoses* I, 84 ff.

11 *Prophetical Warnings*, pp. xx, cf. Cosmos, *Huguenot Prophecy*, p. 58.

12   Cosmos, *Huguenot Prophecy*, pp. 57–8, *The History of Fanaticism in our Times*, etc. By Mr De Brueys, of Montpellier (1692), a shortened version in *CDa*, hereafter *Fanaticism*, pp. 8–12, cf. Henning *Schikora, The Anointing of the Holy Spirit on France: Reflections on the prophetic movement*

in the Cévennes in the 17th and 18th centuries (Mas David, Vézénobres, n.d.).

13 *Edict of Nantes*, p. 5. For the descriptions in the following paragraphs to the ecstasies of Vincent, see Pierre Jurieu, *Reflections Upon the Miracle hapned in the Person of A Shepherdess of Dauphine. Made by the Reverend and Learned Mons. Jurieu, in his Pastoral Letter Of the 1st of October, Anno 1688, in The Reflections of the Reverend and Learned Monsieur Jurieu, Upon the Strange and Miraculous Exstasies of Isabel Vincent, the Shepherdess of Saou (Saov) in Dauphine; who Ever since February last hath Sung Psalms, Prayed, Preached, and Prophesied about the Present Times, an Her Trances as also Upon the Wonderful and Portentuous Trumpetings and Singing of Psalms, that were heard by Thousands in the Air (and many Parts of France) in the Year 1686: Taken out of the Pastoral Letters of the 1st and 15th of October last. To which is added, A Letter of a Gentleman in Dauphine, to a Friend of His in Geneva; Containing the Discourses and Prophesies of the Shepherdess. All faithfully translated out of the French copies, for Publick Information* (London: 1689), hereafter *JR*, pp. 1–21,53.

14 *JR*, pp. 16–20.

15 *CDa*, pp. 57, 60–1.

16 *CDb*, p. 56, de Brueys *Fanaticism*, pp. 10,11, *Prophetical Warnings*, p. vii.

17 *CDa*, p. 125.

18 Cosmos, *Huguenot Prophecy*, pp. 109–26.

19 *Edict of Nantes*, p. 5. For references to the schema of allegoric divination, see *The General idea of Allegorick Language: Or the State of the Divine and Absolute Kingdom and Empire of Almighty God, Demonstrated, as most Real and Apparent in a Summary State and Ratio. By the author of the New Jerusalem* (London: 1702), Pamphlet 245, pp. 18–21.

20 Garrett, *Origins of the Shakers*, pp. 29–30.

21 *CDb*, pp. 93–4.

22 Arthur Page Grubb, *Jean Cavalier: Baker's Boy and British General* (London: George Allen & Unwin Ltd, 1931), pp. 30–4.

23 Le Roy Ladurie, *Languedoc*, p. 276, Garrett, *Origin of the Shakers*, pp. 140–1. For the French Prophets in London see Cosmos, *Huguenot Prophecy*, pp. 127–57, especially for printed libels in broadsides and dialogues, songs and pamphlets sold publicly in the market places, coffee-houses and streets of London. For a detailed historic overview 1706–7, see Schwartz, *French Prophets*, pp. 72–112.

24 Pierre Du Moulin, *The Accomplishment of the Prophecies; or the Third Booke in defence of the Catholicke faith, contained in the booke of the high*

and mighty King James. I. by the grace of God King of Great Brittaine and Ireland. Against the Allegations of R. Bellarmine; and F.N. Coëffetreau and other Doctors of the Romish Church (trans. I. Heath; Oxford, 1613), Preface, A2,A3,A4.

25 *CDa*, pp. 13–17,27,18,24,21,123–4.

26 *CDa*, pp. 18, 26–7,19,20,28,29.

27 Clifford, *Calvin Celebrated*, pp. 132–7; J. Quick, 'The Life of Monsr. Brousson', *Icones Sacrae Gallicanae* (1700), MS on deposit at Dr Williams's Library, London, DWL 6,38–39 (50), hereafter *Life*, in Clifford, *Calvin Celebrated*, pp. 114–128 (pp. 120–22); Cosmos, *Huguenot Prophecy*, pp. 41–2, n. 12.

28 Jean-Baptiste Louvreleul, Preface, *Fanaticism Reviv'd*, Book 1, in *The history of the rise and downfal of the Camisars: giving an account of their false pretences to prophecy and inspiration, their brutish carnality, their many bloody and inhuman Murders and Massacres of Persons of all Ages, Sexes and Conditions, and their horrid devastations of towns and villages by fire. Collected from Original Letters, and the Testimony of Ey-Witnesses* (London: 1709), pp. 2–5, 15. Eighteenth Century Collections Online. Gale. (accessed 27 July 2013, Harvard University Library); de Brueys, *Fanaticism*, p. 10.

29 *CDa*, pp. iv–vi.

30 A Preservative against the False Prophecies of the Time, or, A Treatise concerning True and False Prophets; with their Characters, Pamphlet 273 (1), April 1707, John Daudé, with N. Facio, Charlies Portalés, Richard Holford, pp. 1–36.

31 Schwartz, *French Prophets*, pp. 84,156–7; Sluhovsky, *Believe Not Every Spirit*, pp. 129–36.

32 Fox, *J1997*, p. 341.

33 T. Fuller, *Church History of Great Britain* (1655), II, p. 396, cited in Hill, *World*, p. 90; Hobbes, Thomas, *The English works of Thomas Hobbes of Malmesbury / now first collected and edited by Sir William Molesworth*, Vol. 1 (London: 1839–1845), 11 vols.; *The Making of Modern Law* (Gale, 2013), Gale, Cengage Learning:
http://galenet.galegroup.com/servlet/MOML?af=RN&ae=F100586935&srchtp=a&ste=14" (accessed 19 February 2013, Bodleian Libraries, University of Oxford).
John Selden, *The table-talk of John Selden: with a biographical preface and notes* (London: 3rd edn, 1860); *The Making of Modern Law* (Gale, 2013), Gale, Cengage Learning:

http://galenet.galegroup.com/servlet/MOML?af= RN&ae=F100566559&srchtp=a&ste=14; (accessed 19 February 2013, Bodleian Libraries, University of Oxford); Hill, *World*, pp. 87–91.

34 Fox, *WGF*, 8; *The Epistles*, Vol. 2, pp. 16–17.

35 See Graves, *Preaching*, pp. 1–2,12–13; Richard Bauman, *Let your Words be Few: Symbolism of Speaking and Silence among Seventeenth-Century Quakers*, Cambridge Studies in Oral and Literate Culture 8 (Cambridge: Cambridge University Press, 1983), hereafter *Words*, pp. 29,35, for the intricacies of preaching imagery, pp. 63–83; Fox, *WGF*, pp. 7,18.

36 Barbour, *The Quakers*, p. 230; William Dewsbury, *The Faithful Testimony of the Ancient Servant of the Lord, and Minister of the everlasting Gospel William Dewsbury: in His Books, Epistles and Writings, Collected and Printed for future Service* (London: 1689), hereafter *Faithful Testimony*, pp. 175–6.

37 Braithwaite, *Beginnings*, p. 529; Bauman, *Words*, p. 138; Wilcox, *Women's Ministry*, pp. 84–5.

38 Richard Farnworth, *The Last Testimony of That faithful Servant of the Lord and Minister of Jesus Christ, Richard Farnworth. Whereunto is Prefixed A brief Testimony concerning his Life Death, and Travels, etc. To which is added A few words of Exhortation unto those that believe in the Light of the Lamb* (London: 1667), pp.3,10; Penington, *Some Queries concerning Christ and his Appearances*, Vol. 3, in *IP*, I, 55; *The Axe Laid to the Root of the Old Corrupt Tree; and the Spirit of Deceit struck at in its Nature*, in *IP*, I, 297; Phyllis Mack, *Visionary Women: Ecstatic Prophecy in Seventeenth-Century England* (London, Berkeley & Los Angeles: University of California Press, 1992), hereafter *Visionary Women*, 1st paperback printing 1994, pp. 165–211.

39 George Fox, *Truth's Triumphs in the Eternal Power, Over the Dark Inventions of Fallen Man. The Quakers Just Allegiance is to hurt none of God's Creatures upon the Earth, and their Supremacy is the Power of God. Also some Particulars of what they own, and what they deny*, in *GTD*, pp. 227–42 (pp. 237–40); *J1997*. p.33.

40 *The Epistle to the Reader*, in *WGF*, Vol. 3, pp. 5–32 (pp. 12–13)

41 Robert Barclay, *An Apology for the True Christian Divinity, as the same is held forth, and preached by the people, Called, in Scorn, Quakers; Being a full explanation and vindication of their Principles and Doctrines, by many arguments, deduced from Scripture and right Reason, and the testimonys of famous Authors, both antient and modern, with a full answer to the strongest objections usually made against them, Presented to the King* (1678), n.p., hereafter *Apology*, pp. x, 114–5, 41–2.

42 Penington, *An Examination of the Grounds or Causes Which are said to Induce the Court of Boston, in New-England, to make that Order or Law of Banishment, upon Pain of Death, against the Quakers*, in *IP*, I, pp. 345–450 (p. 440), cf. Braithwaite, *Beginnings*, pp. 524–9.

43 Bauman, *Words*, pp. 144–7; *BA*, pp. 168–214.

44 *J1997*, pp. 20–21.

45 George Fox, *A Word from the Lord, to all the World, all Professors in the World; Spoken in Parables* (London: Giles Calvert, 1654), Vol. 4/21 Library of the Society of Friends), hereafter *A Word from the Lord*, pp. 1–8 (pp. 5–7); I.O., *Sound Advice to Roman Catholics: Especially, The Residue of Poor, Seduced, and Deluded Papists in England, who obstinately shut both Eyes and Ears, against the clearest Light of the Gospel of Christ, and surest Evidences of Scripture and Reason. To which is added, A Word to the People called Quakers* (London: 1689), p. 21.

46 M.F., *The Daughter of Sion Awakened, And putting on Strength: She is Arising, and shaking herself out of the Dust, and putting on her Beautiful Garments*, (1677), n.p., see *Postscript*, pp. 11,13.

47 Burrough, *To all the Priests, and Prophets, and Teachers of the People*, in *Trumpet*, pp. 10–12 (p. 10), Burrough, *Letters to Richard Cromwell*, in *Good Counsel and Advice, Rejected; By Disobedient men. And the days of Oliver Cromwells Visitation passed over; And also of Richard Cromwel his Son, late Protectors of these Nations* (London, 1659), hereafter *Good Counsel*, pp. 61–2,47.

48 Dewsbury, *Faithful Testimony*, p. 16; Hill, *World*, pp. 241–3; Meredith Baldwin Weddle, *Walking in the Way of Peace: Quaker Pacifism in the Seventeenth Century* (New York: Oxford University Press, 2001), hereafter *Way of Peace*, pp. 246–7, see Appendix 4, pp. 245–53,305, n. 1 for new directions in the *Quaker Peace Testimony*.

49 Burrough, *Trumpet*, pp. 9–10; Burrough, *Good Counsel*, pp. 31,35–6.

50 Fox, in *Good Counsel*, pp. 36,37.

51 Weddle, *Way of Peace*, pp. 245–6; Anne Gilman, *An Epistle to Friends; Being a Tender Salutation To the Faithful in God every where. Also, a Letter to Charles, King of England, etc.* (London: 1662), hereafter *Epistle to Friends*, p. 6; 'For the King and his Council'. From *Friends of Truth and Innocency*, G.F. and J.S. London, 16 November 1660, pp. 1–4.

52 Hill, *World*, p. 241; *J1997*, pp. 398–403 (p. 399).

53 Elizabeth Bathurst, *An Epistle to such of the Friends of Christ As have lately been Convinced of the Truth as it is in Jesus* (1679), n.p.; Isaac Penington, 'Somewhat Spoken to a Weighty Question Concerning the Magistrate's

Protection of the Innocent' (1661), in *Quaker faith and practice: the book of Christian discipline of the Yearly Meeting of the Religious Society of Friends (Quakers) in Great Britain (1995)* in *Knowing the Mystery of Life Within: Selected Writings of Isaac Pennington in their Historical and Theological Context* (selected and introduced by R. Melvin Keiser and Rosemary Moore; MS transcriptions by Diana Morrison-Smith; London Quaker Books, 2005), 24.21, p. 174.

54 Fox, 'A visitation to all you that have long had the scriptures', *WGF*, 4, pp. 76–89 (p. 87); *The Oath of Allegiance, Enacted 13. Jacobi, Cap. 4. Which Oath was solemnly taken by every Member of both Houses of Parliament, Rump and all* (March, 1659); Broadsides 2 Nos. 77–170 (Wood 276A/2 Special Collections), CXLIII, cf. G. Fox, *A Small Treatise concerning Swearing in the Old Time of the Law, with its use: And an End put to it in the Gospel by Jesus Christ: Who forbiddeth all Swearing, and sets up Yea and Nay instead thereof*, in *GTD*, pp. 469–82. For a detailed description of the Quaker testimony against swearing of oaths, see Bauman, *Words*, pp. 95–119.

55 See Bauman, *Words*, pp. 43–62, for the understanding of plain language and the rhetoric of impoliteness.

56 George Keith, *Benefit, Advantage, and Glory of Silent Meetings, Both As it was found at the beginning, or first breaking forth of this clear manifestation of Truth, and continues to be found by all the Faithful and Upright in Heart at this Day* (London: 1687), pp. 10–17,24.

57 Richard Farnworth, *The Pure Language of the Spirit of Truth: Set forth for the confounding false Languages, acted out of Pride, ambition and deceit. Or, Thee and Thou, In its place, is the proper Language to any single person whatsoever* (London: 1656), pp. 6–7; Bauman, *Words*, pp. 88–9,93.

58 *IP*, I, p. 349; Margaret Fell, *A Call unto the Seed of Israel, That They may come out of Egypts Darkness, and House of Bondage, unto the Land of Rest* (London: [1668?]), hereafter *A Call unto the Seed*, pp. 11–12.

59 *J1997*, p. 9.

3. Prophetic Pastors of the Heart

1 John Calvin, *Calvin: Theological Treatises* (with Introduction and Notes), The Library of Christian Classics, Vol. 22 (trans. J.K.S. Reid; London: SCM Press Ltd, 1954), hereafter *Theological Treatises*, p. 207.

2 An anonymous sonnet cited and translated by M.A. Screech, in *Clément Marot: A Renaissance Poet discovers the Gospel: Lutheranism, Fabrism and*

Calvinism in the Royal Courts of France and of Navarre and in the Ducal Court of Ferrara, Studies in Medieval and Reformation Thought, Vol. 54 (Leiden, New York, Köln: E.J. Brill, 1994), hereafter *Clément Marot*, p. 146.

3 John Calvin, *The First Epistle of Paul The Apostle to the Corinthians*, CC (trans. John W. Fraser; Edinburgh: Oliver and Boyd, 1960), pp. 73–5, 209–10.

4 *CI*, I,14,7, p. 166; *CI*, II,12,1, p. 464.

5 John Calvin, *Instruction in Faith* (1537) (trans. Paul T. Fuhrmann; London: Lutterworth Press, 1949), hereafter *Instruction in Faith*, pp. 51–2,72–3, n. 146, p. 88.

6 Calvin (trans. Fuhrmann; *Instruction in Faith*), pp. 8,10,72–3.

7 Schwartz, *French Prophets*, pp. 79–80. Richard Bulkeley, *Introduction, containing an impartial account of the prophets of the Cévennes. In a Letter to a Friend* (London: 1795), in *CDa*, pp. 1–30 (pp. 25–26).

8 *Warnings Pronounced by Elias Marion*, 1706, Pamphlet 273 (1), hereafter *Warnings*, p. 105, *Prophetical Warnings*, p. 72.

9 *Prophetical Warnings*, p. 72. See Bulkeley, pp. 25–26.

10 Michael J. Buckley, 'Seventeenth-Century French Spirituality: Three Figures', in *Christian Spirituality: Post-Reformation and Modern* (ed. Louis Dupré and Don E. Saliers, in collaboration with John Meyendorff; London: SCM Press, 1990), pp. 28–68 (pp. 29–30).

11 Pierre Jurieu, *A Plain Method of Christian Devotion: Laid down in Discourse, Meditations, and Prayers, Fitted to the Various Occasions of a Religious Life* (trans. and revised from the French by William Fleetwood, D.D., Late Lord Bishop of Ely; London: 25th edn, 1724), pp. 3–11.

12 For the extracts on Brousson in the following paragraphs see Quick, *Life*, pp. 114–28; Le Roy Ladurie, *Languedoc*, pp. 275.

13 Lacy, in *CDb*, pp. xiv, xii, *French Convert*, pp. 17,19,23–26.

14 Pierre Jurieu, *The Policy of the Clergy of France, to Destroy the Protestants of that Kingdom. Wherein is set down the Ways and Means that have been made use of for these twenty Years last past, to root out the Protestant Religion. In a Dialogue between two Papists* (London: 1681), pp. 3–4, 98–101, *The Copy of a Letter sent from A French Protestant Minister in France, to his Friend in London, with the following Relation. A. D'Auborn*, bound in the same volume with *French Convert*.

15 Calvin, *CI*, II, 4, 1, 12, pp. 1025,1026; *IV*, 1, 8, pp. 1021–2,1027, n. 21.

16 Charles Owen, *Plain-dealing: or, separation without schism, and schism without separation. Exemplify'd in the case of Protestant-Dissenters and*

church-men (5th edition; London: 1720?), The Eighteenth Century Reel 3998, Nos. 1–33 (Woodbridge, CN: Research Publications, 1990), pp. 7,9. The MS is to be found in the Bodleian Library, Oxford.

[17] 'A Letter From a Gentleman of Dauphine' in *JR*, pp. 50–5 (pp. 52–3), 'A sincere and true Relation', in *Continuation*, in *JR*, pp. 58,63; Jurieu, 'Pastoral Letter', in *JR*, pp. 1–21 (p. 5).

[18] Jean-Baptiste Louvreleul, *The History of the French Prophets. Their pretended Revelations, False prophecies and Hypocritical Behaviour, on that Account; with the many Bloody Murders, Barbarous Declarations by Burning, Horrid Sacriledges, and other Villanies committed by them, under Colour of Religion. in the Sevennes, and Parts Adjacent deliver'd Monthly as they happened from the Beginning of that Rebellion, till the Total Suppression thereof* (London: 1709), pp. A3,113.

[19] Reflections Upon a Letter concerning Enthusiasm, to my Lord *****. In another Letter to a Lord (insert in handwriting: By Dr Fowler Bp of Gloucester) (London: 1709), Pamphlet 282 (1), pp. 8–9, Jean Armand Dubourdieu, *An Appeal to the English Nation; or, The Body of the French Protestants and the honest Proselytes, Vindicated from the Calumnies cast on them by one Malard, and his Associates, in a Libel, entitled, The French Plot found out against the English Church, etc. The Second Edition. With a considerable Addition, occasion'd by a French Pamphlet lately publish'd, entitled, The Abuse of the Confessions of Faith; and a remarkable Passage relating to the Bangorian Controversy* (London: 1918), printed by J. Roberts in Warwick Lane (Woodbridge, CN: The Eighteenth Century, Reel 5468 Nos. 1–23. Research Publications, 1992), pp. 48–9. The MS is to be found in the Bodleian Library, Oxford.

[20] *CI* II, 2, 25, pp. 286–7.

[21] *Prophetical Warnings*, pp. 72–3; *Warnings*, p. 122; *Prophetical Warnings*, p. 128; Schwartz, *French Prophets*, p. 81; *Prophetical Warnings*, p. 105.

[22] *CDb*, pp. xiii,vi,xiv.

[23] *CDa*, pp. 28–29; *CDc*, p. 34; *CDc*, p. 87.

[24] Reuben Saillens, *The Soul of France* (London: Morgan and Scott Ltd., 1916), hereafter *Soul*, pp. 76–9.

[25] George Fox, *A Collection of Many Select and Christian Epistles, Letters and Testimonies. Written on Sundry Occasions, by that Ancient, Eminent, Faithful Friend and Minister of Christ Jesus, George Fox*, Vol. 2 (London: T. Sowle, 1698), hereafter *Collection*, p. 84.

[26] *Collection*, p. 84.

27 See Wilcox, *Women's Ministry*, pp. 17–55; *J1990*, p. 312; Fox, Letter 51,'To Friends Concerning the Cross of Christ, The Power of God', in *Pastoral Letters*.

28 *Collection*, pp. 67,91, cf. pp. 66–8,91,111,126.

29 Wilcox, *Women's Ministry*, p. 29; *The Doctrinals in WGF*, IV, pp. 164–76 (p. 166); Fox, *The Spirit of Man the Candle of the Lord: The Candle of the Wicked often put out. How the Lord enlightens the Spirit of Man, which is the Candle of the Lord; and who are the Candlesticks, and how Christ walks in the midst of his Candlesticks; and how the Candle of the Wicked is often put out* (1677), in *GTD*, pp. 626–42 (pp. 630, 629, 636).

30 *To the right Honourable, our right vvorthy and grave Senatours, the Lord Mayor, Aldermen, and Commonalty of the City of London in Common Council assembled, The most humble Petition and Adress of divers young men, on the behalf of themselves and the Apprentices in and about this honourable City. Monday 5 December 1659* [sic] (London: 1659), Broadsides 2 Nos 77–170 (Wood 276A/2 Special Collections), CVII; *GTD*, p. 630.

31 Fox, *Collection*, p. 144; Fox, *WGF*, III, pp. 339,181; Fox, *Collection*, p. 144; Fox, *WGF*, III, p. 374; Fox, *WGF* I, p. 77.

32 Francis Bugg, A *Finishing Stroke; or, Some Gleanings, Collected out of the Quaker Books. By Way of Prologue. Never before Publish'd. The Great Mystery of the Little Whore is farther Unfolded* (London: R. Wilkin, 1712), p. 2; *Light in their Consciences*, p. 105.

33 Fox, *The Great Mistery of the Great Whore* in *WGF*, III, pp. iii–iv, 337,338,339.

34 For an extended argument see Wilcox, *Theology and Women's Ministry*, pp. 17–55.

35 Braithwaite, *Beginnings*, p. 44; Fell, *A Call unto the Seed*, pp. 3,4,7,21–22,35.

36 'The Scattered Sheep Sought After', in *IP*, I, 106–25 (p. 117); Edward Burrough, 'The Epistle to the Reader', in Fox, *WGF*, III, 5–32 (p. 12); Dewsbury, *Faithful Testimony*, p. 23.

37 *Epistle to Friends*, p. 3; *A General Epistle to all who have believed in the Light of the Lord Iesus and are called of God to follow the Lamb through the Great Tribulation. F.H. n.p.* (1684), p. 3.

38 *IP, An Examination of the Grounds or Causes Which are said to Induce the Court of Boston, in New-England, to make that Order or Law of Banishment, upon Pain of Death, against the Quakers*, I, pp. 345–450 (p. 441); Edward Burrough, *Trumpet*, p. 15.

[39] A *Brief Account Concerning The People called Quakers, in Reference both to Principle and Doctrine*, in *IP*, III, p. 419.

[40] Cf. Steere, *Quaker Spirituality*, pp. 3–53.

[41] Wilcox, *Women's Ministry*, pp. 99,110, for scholarship in the changing vision, especially for the doctrine of depravity and the gulf between Calvinism and Quakerism; for the lack of theologizing on the imminent end of all things in William Penn, see pp. 104–6; Bauman, *Words*, p. 121; *BA*, p. 362; cf. Braithwaite, *Second Period*, pp. 388–92.

[42] *BA*, pp. 80–1,84,161.

[43] Glen D. Reynolds, 'George Fox and Christian Gnosis', in *Quaker Theory*, pp. 99–115 (pp. 101,102).

[44] George Fox, *The Journal of George Fox*, 2 vols (ed. Norman Penney; Cambridge: Cambridge University Press, 1911), hereafter *J1911*, I, pp. 161–2 (p. 161, n. pp. 425–6); *J1925*, p. 17; *WGF*, III, pp. 181,371.

[45] Graves, *Preaching*, p. 17.

[46] Braithwaite, *Second Period*, pp. 383–5,391,394.

[47] *IP*, I, 345–450, pp. 118–121.

[48] Penington, *IP*, IV, p. 419; Braithwaite, *Second Period*, pp. 394,396; Graves, *Preaching*, p. 17.

[49] Alex Wildwood, *A faith to call our own: Quaker tradition in the light of contemporary movements of the Spirit*, Swarthmore Lecture 1999 (London: Quaker Books, 2010), p. 81; See Rex Ambler, *Light to Live By: An Exploration in Quaker Spirituality* (London: Quaker Books, 2002); *WGF*, IV, pp. 20–21,43.

[50] *CI*, I, p. 74, Garrett, *Origins of the Shakers*, p. 46.

4. Prophetic Teachers of Scripture

[1] *WGF*, I, p. 76.

[2] Cited and translated by M.A. Screech, *Clément Marot: A Renaissance Poet discovers the Gospel: Lutheranism, Fabrism and Calvinism in the Royal Courts of France and of Navarre and in the Ducal Court of Ferrara. Studies in Medieval and Reformation Thought*, Vol. 54 (Leiden, New York, Köln: E.J. Brill, 1994), hereafter *Clément Marot*, p. 146.

[3] *Theological Treatises*, pp. 26,129,130,55.

[4] Calvin, *CI*, I, 6, 1, p.70 and n. 1,14,1, pp. 160–1; Jacques Lefèvre d'Etaples et ses disciples, *Epistres et evangiles pour les cinquante et deux sepmaines de l'an*, in M.A. Screech, *Clément Marot*, p. 178.

[5] Catharine Randall Coats, *Subverting the System: D'Aubigné and Calvinism, Sixteenth Century Essays and Studies*, Vol. XVI (Kirksville: Sixteenth Century Journal Publishers Inc., 1990), pp. 1–3; Carolyn L. Chappell, '"The Pains I Took to Save My/His Family": Escape Accounts by a Huguenot Mother and Daughter after the Revocation of the Edict of Nantes', *French Historical Studies*, Vol. 22, No 1 (Winter 1999), Duke University Press, pp. 1–61 (p. 59).

[6] *CI*, I, 9, 1–3, pp. 94–5; John Calvin, *The Epistles of Paul The Apostle to the Galatians, Ephesians, Philippians and Colossians* (ed. David W. and Thomas F. Torrance, CC; trans. T.H.L. Parker; Edinburgh: Oliver & Boyd, 1965), 3,1, p. 47.

[7] Saillens, *Soul*, p. 87; Clifford, p. 124.

[8] *CI*, I, 9, 1–3, pp. 93–6.

[9] Calvin, *Anabaptists*, pp. 187,169–73,214–5; *A Discourse of Schism, etc.* (1702), *Pamphlet 245*, p. 18; *Claude Brousson, The Support of the Faithful in Times of Persecution, or, A Sermon Preach'd in the Wilderness to the Poor Protestants in France. By M. Brousson, an Eminent Minister, who was broke upon the Wheel at Montpelier, Nov. 6. N.S. 1698* (London: 1699), hereafter *CB*, pp. 23–24.

[10] From Epistle 66, To Cardinal Guillaume Briçonnet, in *Quincuplex Psalterium. Gallicum. Romanum. Hebraicum. Vetus. Conciliarum*, Paris, Henri Estienne, 31 July 1509, in Jacques Lefévre d'Etaples, *Quincuplex Psalterium*, Fac-similé de l'édition de 1513, Travaux D'Humanisme et Renaissance, No. CLXX (Geneva: Librairie Droz, 1979); cf. Jacques Lefévre d'Etaples, *The Prefatory Epistles of Jacques Lefévre d'Etaples and Related Texts* (ed. Eugene F. Rice; New York; London: Columbia University Press, 1972).

[11] *Short Account*, p. 54; *French Convert*, pp. 13–14; Joe Ridholls, *The Spirit of the Desert: The Life of Antoine Court* (London: Epworth Press, 1968), p. 34.

[12] *Fanaticism*, pp. 8–12 (p. 10); *Prophetical Warnings*, pp. 72,122; *Warnings*, p. 105.

[13] *CB*, pp. 3–20. All references in the next paragraph are to this work.

[14] John Quick in Clifford, *Calvin Celebrated*, p. 123; John Calvin, *Commentary on the Book of Psalms*, Vols. 1–5, Vol. 1, 1845 (trans. James Anderson; Edinburgh: The Calvin Translation Society, 1845–9), hereafter *Psalms*, p. xxxvii; *CI*, III, 20, 33, pp. 896–7; Screech, *Clément Marot*, pp. 3–150; Barbara B. Diefendorf, *Beneath the Cross: Catholics and Huguenots in Sixteenth-Century Paris* (New York; Oxford: Oxford University Press, 1991), pp. 137,12.

15 *A Short Account*, p. 71; Utt, and Strayer, *Bellicose Dove*, p. 114; De Brueys, *Fanaticism*, p. 11; Clifford, *Calvin Celebrated*, p. 117.

16 Garrett, *Origin of the Shakers*, pp. 31–33.

17 Letter 457, To the Church of Paris, 15 March 1557, pp. 319–22 (p. 320), Letter 475, To the Church of Paris, 16 September 1557, pp. 359–63 (p. 360), in John Calvin, *Tracts and Letters*, Vol. 6: Letters, Part 3 1554–1558 (ed. Jules Bonnet; trans. Marcus Robert Gilchrist; Edinburgh: Banner of Truth Trust, 2009); Letter 523, To the Prisoners of Paris, 18 February 1559, pp. 18–20 (p. 20), in John Calvin, *Tracts and Letters*, Vol. 7: Letters, Part 4 1559–1564 (ed. Jules Bonnet; trans. Marcus Robert Gilchrist; Edinburgh: Banner of Truth Trust, 2009); Calvin, *Psalms*, p. xxxvii (trans. Anderson); cf. James A. De Jong, '"An Anatomy of All Parts of the Soul": Insights into Calvin's Spirituality from his Psalms Commentary', in Neuser, *Calvinus*, pp. 1–14.

18 Pierre Jurieu, 'Pastoral Letter Of the 1st of October, 1688', in *JR*, pp. 1–21 (p. 3); 'A Letter of a Gentleman of Dauphine', in *JR*, pp. 50–5 (pp. 51,54); 'A sincere and true Relation', in *A Continuation of the Reflections Upon the Miracle of Dauphine with An Examination of the Question, Whether the Time of Miracles be absolutely ceased?*' in *JR*, pp. 57–64 (p. 57), hereafter *A Continuation*; 'Another Relation of the same Subject, In Form of a Conversation', in *A Continuation*, pp. 65–8 (pp. 61–2); *Fanaticism*, p. 12.

19 *A Continuation*, p. 34.

20 *A Continuation*, pp. 33–4, 'A letter by M. de Besse, an imprisoned minister, from Lausanne, 25 May 1686', in *A Continuation*, pp. 36–7; 'A letter from M. Descalmels', in *A Continuation*, p. 38.

21 *French Convert*, pp. 15–39.

22 *Fanaticism*, p. 11; Lacy, Preface, *CDb*, pp. vii, xiv.

23 *CDa*, p.xii; Arise Evans, *An echo to the book called A voice from heaven* (1653); http://eebo.chadwyck.com/search/full_rec?SOURCE=pgimages. cfg&ACTION=ByID&ID=V154414 (accessed 23 April 2013, Bodleian Libraries, University of Oxford).

24 *WGF*, IV, p. 107.

25 Wilcox, *Women's Ministry*, pp. 57–93; *WGF*, I, pp. 90,72–3,76; Fox, *To All the Kings, Princes, and Governours in the whole World: And all that profess themselves Christians, and others, to read and consider. This was upon me from the Lord to write unto you, hereafter To All the Kings*, in *GTD*, pp. 603–25 (p. 603); *J1997*, p. 400; *J1694*, p. 22.

26 *J1997*, pp. 296, 332, 471–2; *WGF*, III, pp. 107–111.

27 George Fox, *A Journal or Historic Account of the Life, Travels, Sufferings, Christian Experiences and Labour of Love in the Work of the Ministry, of that Ancient, Eminent and Faithful Servant of Jesus Christ, George Fox; who departed this Life in great Peace with the Lord, the 13th of the 11th month, 1690,* I (London: Thomas Northcott, 1694); *J1694,* p. 20; *WGF,* III, p. 108; Margaret Fox, 'The Testimony of Margaret Fox concerning her Late Husband George Fox together with a brief Account of some of his Travels, Sufferings and Hardships endured for the Truth's sake', in Fox, *J1694,* hereafter *Testimony of Margaret Fox,* pp. i–ix (p. i).

28 William Penn, Preface, in *J1997,* p. xliv; *Testimony of Margaret Fox,* in *J1694,* pp. i–ix (p. iii); Margaret Fell, *A Testimonie of the Touch-stone, for all Professions, and all Forms, and Gathered churches (as they call them) of what sort soever to try their ground and foundation by and A Tryal by the Scriptures, who the False Prophets are, which are in the world, which John said should be in the last times by Margret Fell.* Also, *Some of the Ranters Principles Answered* (London: 1656), pp. 3–4,13.

29 Penington, *The Seed of God, and of his Kingdom, Treated and Testified of According to the Scriptures of Truth, and according to True Experience felt in the Heart from the God of Truth,* in *IP,* IV, p. 419; Richard Farnworth, *The Holy Scriptures From Scandals are cleared* (London: 1655), pp. 20–21; James Parnel, *The Stone which the Builders have rejected, the same is now become the Head of the Corner: or, Christ Exalted into his Throne: And the Scripture owned in its place,* n.d. n.p, pp. 3–5; *BA,* p. 41.

30 Moore, *Light in their Consciences,* pp. 51–9.

31 *A Word from the Lord,* in *WGF,* IV, pp. 34, 36; *BA,* pp. 114–5; *A General Epistle to all who have believed in the Light of the Lord Iesus and are called of God to follow the Lamb through the Great Tribulation,* F.H. n.p. 1684, p. 3.

32 Margaret Fell, *A Call unto the Seed,* p. 3; *The Doctrinals,* in *WGF,* IV, pp. 164–76 (p. 166).

33 *Concerning Silent Meetings,* in *WGF,* IV, p. 134.

34 *Faithful Testimony,* pp. 175–6, p. 16.

35 *Faithful Testimony,* pp. 16–20.

36 *The Axe Laid to the Root of the Old Corrupt Tree; and the Spirit of Deceit struck at in it Nature,* in *IP,* I, 291–4.

37 *BA,* pp. 11,281.

38 Gwyn, *Apocalypse,* p. 106; Wilcox, *Women's Ministry,* p. 79; Dewsbury, in *Discovery of great enmity,* pp. 17–18; Fox, *Word from the Lord,* p. 4.

39 Charles Marshall, *A Tender Visitation in the Love of God unto All People everywhere, Particularly unto the Inhabitants of Wiltshire, Gloucestershire*

and Bristol. And to my Neighbours in and above Tetherton, Calloways, and the adjacent Towns and Villages* (London: 1684), Wiltshire and Swindon Archives, pp. 3–10.

[40] Samuel Bownas, *An Account of the Life, Travels, and Christian Experiences in the Work of the Ministry of Samuel Bownas* (London: 1755), hereafter *An Account of the Life*, pp. 5,8–9.

[41] Samuel Bownas, *An Account of the Life*, pp. 16–17,25; Samuel Bownas, *A Description of the Qualifications Necessary to A Gospel Minister, containing Advice to Ministers and Elders, how to conduct themselves in their Conversations, and various Services, according to their Gifts in the Church of Christ* (London: 1767) pp. 8,21,22,25–27. See Graves, *Preaching*, pp. 131–53 for impromptu preaching and Quakerism.

[42] Fox, *J1694*, pp. 66–7; Theophila Townsend, *An Epistle of Love to Friends in the Womens meetings in London, etc. To be read among them in the fear of God*, n.d. n.p., p.2; Elizabeth Bathurst, *An Epistle to such of the Friends of Christ As have lately been Convinced of the Truth as it is in Jesus* (1679), n.p., p.97.

[43] Mack, *Visionary Women*, p. 165–6.

[44] *A Living Testimony From the Power and Spirit of our Lord Jesus Christ in our Faithful Womens Meeting and Christian Society* (London: 1685), p. 2; Christine Trevett, *Quaker Women Prophets in England and Wales 1650–1700*, Studies in Women and Religion, Vol. 41 (Lampeter: The Edwin Mellen Press, 2000), hereafter *Quaker Women Prophets*, pp. 251–7.

[45] Fox, *Women learning in silence or the Mystery of the Woman's subjugation to her husband*, in *WGF*, IV, pp. 104–10 (p. 109).

[46] *J1997*, pp. 666–8.

[47] *WGF*, pp. 169–75 (pp. 169,175); Catie Gill, *Women in the Seventeenth-Century Quaker Community: A Literary Study of Political Identities, 1650–1700*, Women and Gender in the Early Modern World (Aldershot: Ashgate, 2005), hereafter *Women in the Seventeenth-Century Quaker community*, pp. 145,185–7.

[48] Cf. Gill, *Women in the Seventeenth-Century Quaker Community*, pp. 1,4, 118,119,120,123,124,126,127.

[49] Margaret Fell, *Womens Speaking* (London: Pythia Press, 1989). Original 1666, Margaret Fell, *A Letter sent to the King from M.F. Here is also thereunto Annexed a Paper written unto the Magistrates in 1664. which was then Printed, and should have been dispersed, but was prevented by wicked hands*, n.p. n.d, pp. 2–4.

[50] Sarah Apetrei, 'The Universal Principle of Grace: Feminism and Anti-Calvinism in Two Seventeenth-Century Women Writers,'

Gender and History, Vol. 21, No. 1 (April 2009), pp. 130–146 (pp. 130–2,137,143).

[51] Cf. Garrett, *Origins of the Shakers*, p. 47; Hill, *World*, p. 95.

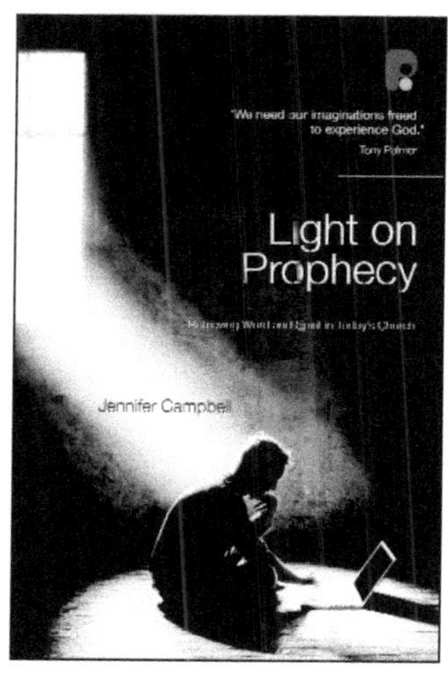

Light on Prophecy

Retrieving Word and Prophecy in Today's Church

Jennifer Campbell

The author correlates the vision and thinking of two powerful prophetic leaders: Hildegard of Bingen, a twelfth-century enclosed nun/mystic, and Dietrich Bonhoeffer, the twentieth-century German pastor/theologian executed by the Nazis. With a view to recovering a balanced and rounded theology of prophecy for the church today, she discusses the closely related workings of both the Word of God (viewed as Christ and the Scriptures) and the Holy Spirit in the works and lives of these famous Christians.

'Rarely do we encounter maturity, depth and wisdom when the subject at hand is the prophetic gift. Jenny Campbell's book is the exception. With rare insight she offers us a workable and thorough theology of Prophecy' – **Mike Breen, 3DM Global Leader.**

Jennifer Campbell is a lecturer in Christian Doctrine at Westminster Theological Centre, Cheltenham, UK. She is also the leader of Eaglesinflight.

978-1-84227-768-3

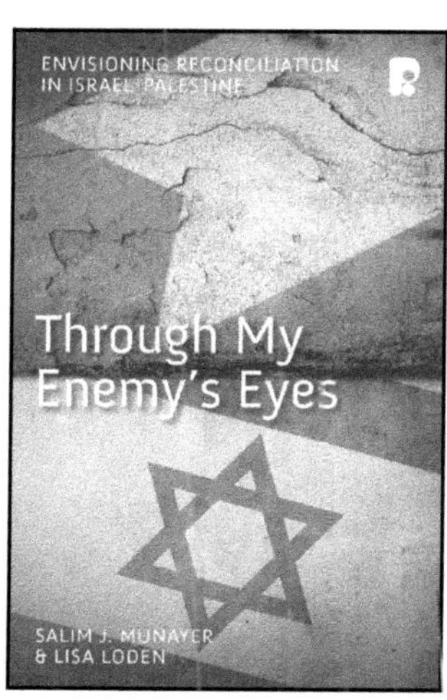

Through My Enemy's Eyes

Envisioning Reconciliation in Israel–Palestine

Salim Munayer and Lisa Loden

This unique book addresses reconciliation in the context of the Israeli Messianic Jewish and Palestinian Christian divide. This remarkable work, written in collaboration by a local Palestinian Christian and an Israeli Messianic Jew addresses head-on divisive theological issues (and their political implications); land, covenant, prophecy, eschatology. The struggle for reconciliation is painful and often extremely difficult for all of us. This work seeks to show a way forward.

'This is a unique conversation in which each partner gives full expression to all that they are and think and feel about themelves and the conflict in their land. Above all we come to share the hope and courage that shines through the pain and struggle.' *Christopher Wright, Langham Paternership.*

'Given the divides between their communities, this book is a remarkable achievement, a cry of hope from the land where Jesus walked.' *Chris Rice Duke Divinity School, US.*

Salim Munayer is on the faculty of Bethlehem Bible College. Bethlehem, Palestine and director of Musalaha Ministry of Reconciliation, Jerusalem, Israel. Lisa Loden is on the faculty of Nazareth Evangelical Theological Seminary, Nazareth, Israel, and Director of Advancing Professional Excellence, Israel.

978-1-84227-748-5 (e-book 978-1-84227-859-8)

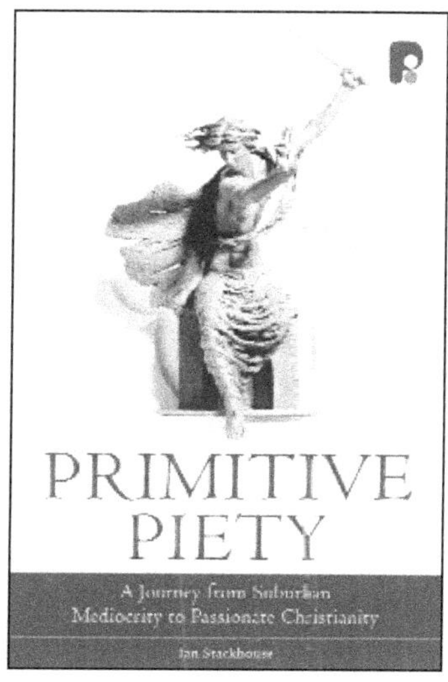

Primitive Piety

A Journey from Suburban Mediocrity to Passionate Christianity

Ian Stackhouse

In *Primitive Piety* Ian Stackhouse takes us on a journey away from the safety and pleasantries of suburban piety and into a faith that is able to embrace the messiness as well as the paradoxes of the Christian faith.

In a culture in which there is every danger that we all look the same and speak the same, Stackhouse argues for a more gritty kind of faith – one that celebrates the oddity of the gospel, the eccentricity of the saints, and the utter uniqueness of each and every church.

Ian Stackhouse is the Pastoral Leader of Millmead, Guildford Baptist Church.

978-1-84227-786-7

Alejandro Amenábar

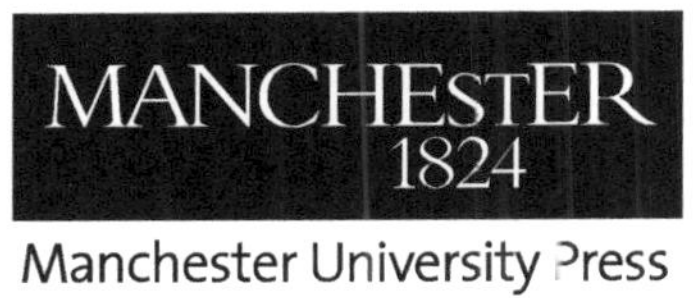

MANCHESTER
1824

Manchester University Press

Spanish and Latin American Filmmakers

Series editors:
Núria Triana Toribio, University of Manchester
Andy Willis, University of Salford

Spanish and Latin American Filmmakers offers a focus on new filmmakers; reclaims previously neglected filmmakers; and considers established figures from new and different perspectives. Each volume places its subject in a variety of critical and production contexts.

The series sees filmmakers as more than just auteurs, thus offering an insight into the work and contexts of producers, writers, actors, production companies and studios. The studies in this series take into account the recent changes in Spanish and Latin American film studies, such as the new emphasis on popular cinema, and the influence of cultural studies in the analysis of films and of the film cultures produced within the Spanish-speaking industries.

Already published

The cinema of Álex de la Iglesia Peter Buse, Núria Triana Toribio and Andy Willis

Daniel Calparsoro Ann Davies

Julio Medem Rob Stone

Emilio Fernandez: pictures in the margins Dolores Tierney

Alejandro Amenábar

Barry Jordan

Manchester University Press

Published by Manchester University Press
Altrincham Street, Manchester M1 7JA, UK
www.manchesteruniversitypress.co.uk

British Library Cataloguing-in-Publication Data is available

ISBN 978 0 7190 7589 6 *hardback*
ISBN 978 1 5261 3941 2 *paperback*

First published by Manchester University Press in hardback 2012

This edition first published 2019

The publisher has no responsibility for the persistence or accuracy of URLs for any external or third-party internet websites referred to in this book, and does not guarantee that any content on such websites is, or will remain, accurate or appropriate.

Contents

List of figures

Acknowledgements

My warmest thanks must go to Alejandro Amenábar himself, who generously gave me several hours of his time in interview, in the summer of 2005, in Madrid, not long after he had returned from promoting *Mar adentro* in the USA and Japan. His observations, recollections, anecdotes and good humour greatly enriched my knowledge and understanding of his films and their production. I am also grateful to him for dealing so well with subsequent queries and for sending me further details of his shorts by letter. I should also like to express my debt to Sra Magdalena Vázquez Béjar, Amenábar's lawyer, who was instrumental in arranging the above-mentioned interview and who, over the last few years, has been diligent in relaying further questions and queries to him. Also, a special thank you is due to Dra Margarita Lobo, of Madrid's Filmoteca Nacional. Without Dra Lobo's help as intermediary, it is doubtful whether I would have made the initial contact with Sra Vázquez and subsequently with her client, Alejandro Amenábar.

Regarding Amenábar's short films, I also wish to express my deepest thanks to Raquel Gómez Rosado, an early colleague and friend of Amenábar and drama student, who played Silvia in *Himenóptero*. Apart from a large package of visual materials, she provided me with opinions, anecdotes and clarifications concerning Amenábar's shorts and new information about the role of her father in his early career. I remain eternally grateful to her for these insights.

Among other colleagues in Spain, I am indebted to a number of people who, either directly or indirectly, have helped me track down elusive primary and secondary sources, including Antonio Sempere and Marimar Azcona as well as Vicente Sánchez Biosca, Juan Antonio Palau, Raquel Zapater and Arturo Lozano, at the Filmoteca de Valencia. I am also very grateful to Guillem Vidal Folch, Susana Herreras and of course Fernando Bovaira at Sogecine for helping with stills and permissions. A key acknowledgement must go to Executive Producers Alvaro Agustín and Jaime Ortiz de Artiñano of Telecinco Cinema, who gave me nearly two hours of their time in interview in April 2009 on the production background to *Ágora* and Spanish cinema more generally. A further thank you is owed to Santiago Juan-Navarro who kindly gave me access to a jointly written monograph on Amenábar, published in French, of which I was unaware.

This book would not have reached the publishers without the support of a number of institutions and individuals. It was completed thanks to a generous Research Leave Award from the Arts and Humanities Research Council during 2005–6. It also benefited from an AHRC grant for a shorter period of study leave in 2004. Moreover, the project would not have prospered had it not been for the support of the Faculty of Humanities at De Montfort University. I would like to thank my ex-Dean, the current Acting Dean and my former Head of Department, namely Professor Philip Martin, Professor Tim O'Sullivan and Dr Ian Hunter (who kindly helped me track down materials on Amenábar's favourite horror director, Peter Medak). I also owe a major debt of gratitude to a number of Hispanist colleagues who, in one way and another, have helped me bring this project to fruition: Professor Mark Allinson, Dr Santiago Fouz-Hernández, Professor Paul Julian Smith, Professor Chris Perriam and Dr Núria Triana-Toribio. Finally, thanks are also in order for the series editors and my publishers at Manchester University Press for their help and encouragement.

Barry Jordan

Note on other sources:

Reference in the text made to the interview with Amenábar in 2005 and correspondence with him since then is indicated as follows: 'Interview', 'Letter to the author' and 'Email to the author'. In the chapter on *Ágora*, the 'Interview' in question refers to my conversation with Alvaro Agustín and Jaime Ortiz de Artinaño in 2010. Translations and glosses are my own.

1

Young Orson, King Midas and the emerging auteur

Alejandro Amenábar has made only five main features over a 15–year period (1995–2009). His most recent production was *Ágora*, an ambitious and challenging reimagining of the historical epic, which was released in Spain in early October 2009. Yet his relative paucity of output has not prevented him from becoming Spain's most successful, celebrated and versatile filmmaker ever. In 1995 he abandoned his Film Studies degree at Madrid's Complutense University in order to shoot *Tesis* (Thesis), his first feature. This was an arty, Hitchcock-inspired version of the 'teen slasher' formula, which represented his own final-year dissertation on celluloid. Though the film was written with Penélope Cruz in mind, it was in fact the iconic child star of the Francoist art film, Ana Torrent (who had played Ana in Víctor Erice's *The Spirit of the Beehive*, 1973), who finally embodied the sexually ambiguous female lead. *Tesis* was also a manifesto film. Through the device of the 'snuff' movie, it warned its viewers to beware of Spain's explcitative 'telebasura' (trash television) and their own morbid fascination with screen violence. It also drew attention to the long standing disconnection between the national cinema and mainstream Spanish audiences, by underlining the appeal as well as the threat of American film imports. Paradoxically, though critical of American market hegemony, *Tesis* was widely admired by its publics (particularly the under-25s), precisely because its well-designed thriller format and strong production values did not look or feel Spanish at all, but American! In mid-1995 Amenábar was also the youngest ever feature director in Spain, at 23 years old, and the first to be let loose with a million-dollar budget (120 million pesetas approximately). Such precocity was unheard of and very soon journalists and film critics began referring to him as 'Orsoncito' (Little Orson) or 'el

Orson Welles español' (the Spanish Orson Welles), linking him to one of the most canonical and revered as well as controversial names in film history.[1]

Before its commercial release in Spain, *Tesis* was shown at festivals in Berlin and Annecy (France), where it attracted strong public interest and positive notices. Amenábar was valorised by critics for his competence in direction, scoring and screenplay, even though, at that time, he did not regard himself as a proficient scriptwriter.[2] In his review the *ABC* film critic E. Rodríguez Marchante was concerned by plotting excesses in the second half, but overall was very impressed by the youngster's grasp of suspense and thriller conventions, while also comparing him favourably with his great idol, Steven Spielberg.[3] Núria Bou and Xavier Pérez in the Catalan daily *Avui* went even further, claiming that Amenábar had already begun to show signs of 'una personalitat autoral' (an authorial personality) and a distinctive interest in certain thematic and moral concerns, which was motivated by 'la seva visió' (his own vision or worldview).[4]

Despite being based on the evidence of only one film and a good deal of wishful thinking, such auteurist spin was again evident in the extraordinary critical reception which greeted *Abre los ojos* (Open Your Eyes), Amenábar's second film, released in Spain in December 1997. Like *Tesis* this production was another generic hybrid, drawing upon resources not usually associated with Spanish filmmaking, i.e. Lynch-style surrealism and fragmented subjectivities, Philip K. Dickian musings on multiple realities, Hitchcockian suspense and male narcissism and the flawed but redeemable nature of our 'humanity'. But, unlike *Tesis* and its more accessible linear narrative, *Abre los ojos* was vastly more complex, ambitious and deep; also, its highly elliptical, flashback structure was a major challenge to audience intelligibility. In a poor year for national cinema, the critic Lluís Bonet proclaimed Amenábar's second outing as the achievement of 'un verdadero autor' (a real auteur) with an extraordinary capacity for 'la fabulación visual' (visual storytelling).[5] Even the usually parsimonious critic of *El País*, Ángel Fernández Santos, praised a brilliant and agile Amenábar as 'el dueño de un estilo propio y de una poderosa mirada sin equivalente' ('master of a personal style and a powerful gaze without equal').[6] By the beginning of 1998, and on the strength of only two feature films, many professional film critics and large sections of the Spanish media were heralding a new, star director and seriously promoting a 25-year-old Amenábar as an emerging auteur. Such emphatic hype, based on only two films, could have been a heavy burden to bear for such an inexperienced young filmmaker. Yet, rather than play safe by making another relatively small-scale, easily manageable, European horror-thriller co-pro, Amenábar surprised everyone by risking his growing reputation and career in a major transatlantic project with the moguls of 'independent' Hollywood.

Thanks to the Sundance Film Festival of early 1998 (where the film was showcased) and the intervention of the producer Paula Wagner, *Abre los ojos* came to the attention of her business partner Tom Cruise. In the 1990s Cruise was arguably the biggest, most successful and powerful, independent, actor-producer in Hollywood. Overwhelmed by Amenábar's film and dazzled by 'dream girl' Penélope Cruz, Cruise quickly acquired the remake rights with development money supplied by Paramount. The project became *Vanilla Sky* (2001), directed by Cameron Crowe, who had already worked with Cruise on the hugely successful hit *Jerry McGuire* (1996). Not only was *Vanilla Sky* a personal, star vehicle for Cruise and a challenging new twist on his 'hot shot kid humbled and redeemed' screen persona; it was also a virtual, sequence-for-sequence remake of the progenitor film narrative, but with a far less ambiguous ending. Genuinely impressed by his creative talent and sensing other opportunities on the horizon, Cruise also offered to co-produce another Amenábar project. This was a script devised for a low-budget art film, originally written in Spanish, called 'La casa' (The House) and set in Chile, which would finally become *The Others* (2001). Seen by Cruise as a potential Oscar opportunity, it would star his then wife, Nicole Kidman, supported by a strong Anglo-Irish cast.

Produced, financed, shot and initially edited in Spain, *The Others* was not only the most expensive Spanish feature of its day ($17 million), it was also the biggest-grossing, most successful film ever made in Spain (attracting 6.4 million spectators, taking €27 million in local admissions and grossing approximately $210 million worldwide, including $96.5 million in the USA – source: mcu.es). No other Spanish director, not even the mighty Almodóvar, had ever achieved a critical and commercial success of this type and on this global scale. It was also Amenábar's first foray into English-language filmmaking. This was a major challenge, particularly at the scripting, rehearsal and shooting stages, given the director's still uncertain command of English. The film also benefited from a large-scale distribution campaign in the USA and English-speaking countries, orchestrated by Miramax/Dimension Films, anxious for Oscar success. It was promoted globally as a classy, old-fashioned, ghost story cum horror-melodrama and inspired stylistically by the black and white, suspense thrillers of the early 1940s, including Hitchcock's *Rebecca* (1940). It was also heavily indebted to Jack Clayton's *The Innocents* (1961), his acclaimed adaptation of Henry James's novella *The Turn of the Screw*. Apart from being a stunning commercial hit, *The Others* was a major critical success, with Golden Globes and BAFTA nominations for Nicole Kidman. It also won eight Goyas (Spain's equivalent of the Oscars, awarded by the Spanish Film Academy) and, controversially, was the first ever English-spoken production to receive the Spanish Academy's Best Film Award. Also, for a beginner, Amenábar picked up the rudiments of deal-making in Hollywood very quickly, so much so that, rather than cross the Atlantic to work, he insisted on shooting the picture in Spain. Remarkably, his American producers agreed. We are bound to admire his determination, *sang-froid* and single mindedness. Such co-pro arrangements with independent Hollywood were totally unprecedented in Spanish film history and for a 29-year-old Spanish director, with only his third film, quite unique.

After completing a trilogy of genre hybrids located broadly in the 'horror-thriller' domain, Amenábar could have simply remained in his comfort zone, headed for Hollywood and made another thriller or two. But, despite the global success of his third picture, he was anxious to reclaim some of the control he had ceded to Cruise and Miramax during his stressful and frustrating encounter with independent Hollywood. Moreover, he was also afraid of being pigeonholed as just another imitator of Hitchcock and seen a mere 'maker of thrillers'. This perhaps explains why his fourth feature represented such a dramatic, indeed totally unexpected, change of direction in subject matter, style and generic focus. Returning to national stories and local referents, he embarked upon a project which he had first researched in 1998, but for which he was unable to find a suitable mode of dramatisation. This was *Mar adentro* (The Sea Inside, 2004), a strongly local and very polemical bio-pic. It was based on the memoirs, poems and other writings of Ramón Sampedro, a real-life, bedridden Galician paraplegic, whose legal and media campaigns for the 'right to die' had deeply divided Spain and brought Amenábar no end of grief from the Catholic Church and anti-euthanasia pressure groups. Generically and formally, *Mar adentro* constituted a decisive break with Hitchcock and the suspense thriller mould of his first three pictures. At the same time, it demonstrated once again that Amenábar was a serial risk-taker, self-confident enough to dramatise an incendiary legal case which was still sub judice. In so doing, he was also testing the treacherous waters of the 'issue' film, seeking to put a positive, indeed heroic, construction on Sampedro's bitter legal struggle for 'una muerte digna' (a dignified death).

Despite such dangers, the film was a major commercial success in Spain (with over four million admissions and nearly €20 million in box-office – source: mcu.es). But, because of its subject matter, no matter how hard the distributors tried (except perhaps for Japan), they could not find a viable commercial audience internationally for a 'right to die' film (this was particularly acute in the USA, where it grossed a negligible $2 million – source: imdb.com). By way of compensation, *Mar adentro* was an enormous critical success (winning well over thirty awards worldwide) and established Amenábar's reputation as a newly emerging, international auteur filmmaker, but one able to work successfully in more than one generic register. His elevation seemed complete with the award of the Oscar for Best Foreign Film of 2004, for *Mar adentro*. This brought him serious peer recognition from within the international film industry (especially from his idol, Steven Spielberg), while greatly enhancing his national standing and celebrity at home, as well as his global marketability. At the same time, back home, his Oscar was accompanied by astonishing levels of success at the Goya awards in Spain, in 2005, where *Mar adentro* won an unprecedented 14 of the 15 categories for which it was nominated. Having already seen Amenábar's film outperform his *La mala educación* (Bad Education, 2004) at the national box office, and with nothing to show from four Goya nominations, Spain's leading international auteur filmmaker Pedro Almodóvar and his producer-brother Agustín both resigned from Spain's Film Academy in deep dudgeon. They blamed the voting system for their lack of success, (notably the lack of information regarding the number of participants in each round of votes) as well as the Academy's alleged lack of generosity towards Almodóvar over many years. Amenábar was now the new face of Spanish filmmaking and appeared to have stolen the clothes of the national cinema's prickly 'pope'.

From its inception in mid-2005, the identity of Amenábar's fifth feature was kept under wraps for well over two years, until the funding was in place and the leading player, Rachel Weisz, had been signed. In Spain, between 2005 and 2007, rumours of possible film projects were rife, public interest and media anticipation were enormous, while local distributors and exhibitors complained that, without an Amenábar film to attract audiences, the home box-office would collapse. When the announcement came, and echoing the example of *Mar adentro*, Amenábar and his producers took the whole national industry by surprise when they revealed the nature of the new project: a sword-and-sandals historical epic, set in classical antiquity (fourth century AD) and dealing with aspects of the life and notorious death of a forgotten, female astronomer and philosopher, Hypatia of Alexandria. The film presented evident continuities with *Mar adentro*: It returned to the fictionalised 'bio-pic' template, focusing once again on aspects of the life and death of a pagan martyr. It also recycled and extended Amenábar's sustained critique of Catholicism (seen in *Abre los ojos* and *The Others* as well as *Mar adentro*), but this time going much further in condemning not only religious intolerance but all forms of fundamentalist belief systems which exploit terrorist violence in order to impose their views. The film also repeated Amenábar's usual practice of alternating in his films between a female and a male lead character. And as for the type of project, his choice of genre seemed extraordinary, even daring to the point of recklessness. No Spanish filmmaker in modern times had ever directed a 'peplum', even in the glory days of producer Samuel Bronston in the 1950s and the 60s and taking into account Spain's acknowledged reputation at that time as an excellent location for making historical epics. Hence, the enormous risk for producers in backing such a project, even one placed in the capable hands of a young Oscar-winner like Amenábar. Moreover the film's colossal budget was by far the biggest and riskiest ever devoted to a local picture and, in the end, wholly funded by national companies. However, the commercial fate of the picture would hang on its achieving successful international distribution and a guaranteed release in the massive American domestic market. All in all Amenábar's fifth film was his biggest and boldest gamble to date. It would test to the limit his creative, technical, promotional and marketing skills, for an unpromising, period art film, widely seen by buyers, critics and audiences as a 'hard sell' and strongly anti-Christian.

Following his Oscar success Amenábar has been increasingly regarded as a filmmaker who has already achieved auteur status. For example, on the back cover of the second edition of his book on the director, Antonio Sempere (2004) remarks confidently: 'Calidad y éxito se aunan en todos los trabajos de este autor, nacido en 1972' (Quality and success are combined in all the films of this auteur, born in 1972). On the international front Amenábar was even hailed as the new sensation of 2005 and even a rising film mogul. In the first issue of *Newsweek* (January 2005) he appeared nonchalant and moody on the magazine's front cover, with the caption: 'Alejandro Amenábar. Spanish Eye. The wunderkind filmmaker looks beyond Hollywood.' And, according to the inside feature, he was described as the 'Spanish director who made Kidman a star' and who 'is driven not by Hollywood' but 'by his own vision', thus reinforcing the classic auteurist stereotype.[7] By early 2006, on the twentieth anniversary of the Goya awards, Amenábar was also dubbed 'el señor Goya' (Mr Goya) by *El País Semanal* (reflecting his eight personal awards overall); he was thus feted as 'el chico de oro del cine español. Nuestro Rey Midas' (the golden boy of the Spanish cinema. Our King Midas).[8] Despite dismal international box-office returns for three out of five features (*Abre los ojos*, *Mar adentro* and *Ágora*), Amenábar has not made a bad film yet. He also heads a small group of commercially successful directors (Pedro Almodóvar, Agustín Díaz Yanes, Javier Fesser, Santiago Segura, Juan Antonio Bayona, Álex de la Iglesia, Fernando Trueba, Julio Medem etc.) on whom the Spanish film industry has come to rely for its economic well-being and critical reputation.[9] Yet, to what extent does the media construction of Amenábar as a brilliant, successful, international, auteur director hold water? What is the reality behind the hype and what sort of authorship do we mean?

Retracing authorship

The idea of the talented director as the crucial creative presence behind the film emerged with particular force in postwar Europe, initially through Alexandre Astruc's authorial analogy between writing and filmmaking via the 'caméra-stylo' (Cook 2007: 390). Astruc's proposition helped lay the foundation for later debates on authorship in French film criticism, notably in the influential journal, *Cahiers du Cinéma*, co-founded by Bazin in 1951. Such debates were made famous by Truffaut's vitriolic attack on France's dominant, commercial 'cinéma de qualité' and its studio hierarchies, which foregrounded the role and powerful status of the screenwriter (in 'Une certaine tendance du cinéma français', published in April 1954). Here, Truffaut berated a 'cinéma de papá' for its stuffiness and datedness, its emphasis on psychological realism, its overdependence on the literary adaptation and its privileging of the 'scénariste' (screenwriter) over the director as the source of filmic value. What was required, argued Truffaut, was a decisive shift towards the specifically cinematic, i.e. towards *mise-en-scène* and film style and a much clearer distinction between the *'metteur-en-scène'* (the competent director or technician, translator of script into image) and the figure of the *'auteur'*, whose creative talent and artistry deserved far greater recognition. All this was summed up in Bazin's article 'La politique des auteurs' (published in *Cahiers* in April 1957). But here, though he acknowledged the 'personal factor' in filmmaking, Bazin was reluctant to endorse the sort of extravagant, often ad hominem, auteurist criticism (then called 'author policy' or 'polemic') being developed by young cinephiles such as Truffaut, Chabrol, Rohmer, Godard and Rivette etc. Echoing the tenets of Sartrian existentialism, these young film critics celebrated concepts of artistic integrity and 'authenticity', where the individual filmmaker 'authors' his or her life and worldview on film through particular technical and stylistic choices. Such a view assumed a certain separateness or specialness for *Cahiers'* 'men of the cinema', a certain elitism, fostered by a rich diet of previously unavailable Hollywood films and the postwar traditions of the ciné club movement in France as well as the film festival circuit. These activities emphasised strong, creative (male) personalities whose film works transcended their contexts of production and reception (Stam 2000: 20). By contrast Bazin tended to argue that film gained its expressive power not through authorial stylisation or the recycling of narrative and technical aspects but through representational fidelity, i.e. realism. Moreover, as Bordwell argues, Bazin and his colleagues all acknowledged and indeed celebrated the fact that 'Hollywood displayed high-level achievements and that the real avant-garde was the advanced studio filmmaking of the sound era' (1997: 50). As a result and very controversially for the times, the 'young turks' of *Cahiers* sought to blur the boundaries between art cinema and commercial cinema by conferring auteur status on a number of major Hollywood studio directors, such as Ford, Welles, Hitchcock, Hawkes, Ray, Sirk, Lang etc. Even in the industrialised heart of darkness that was supposedly Hollywood, the pioneering Nouvelle Vague critics recognised the talent and distinction of certain commercial genre directors, whose powerful personalities, personal visions and creativity were able to rise above the constraints and standardising processes of factory filmmaking.

When translated into the context of Anglo-American film criticism in the 1960s, via Andrew Sarris, 'la politique des auteurs' mutated into 'auteur theory', shifting priorities from polemic to taxonomy. That is, it functioned as a (subjective) means of categorising and ranking American directors into rough league tables (variously designated as 'pantheon', 'second line', 'fallen angels' etc.), while demonstrating the general superiority of American filmmaking. This was done according to three rather vague and questionable criteria for authorship: (1) technical competence, i.e. the director's ability to master the techniques of filmmaking in an expressive fashion; (2) distinctive personal style, i.e. a set of visual and narrative choices which are recognisable and repeated across a series of films, such as Welles's use of deep focus and mobile camera; and (3) interior meaning, i.e. a consistent worldview, unique to the director. Accordingly, Sarris acclaimed those few 'brave spirits who had managed to overcome the gravitational pull of the mass of movies'.[10] Yet, as Maltby also argues, Sarris tended to marginalise and ignore what Bazin had famously referred to as the 'genius of the system' (i.e. the quality and the strong traditions of Hollywood genre cinema) and the many achievements of directors such as Raoul Walsh or Michael Curtiz, who were among the leading contract directors in the 1930s and 1940s, and at the top of their game in terms of their craft skills, as evidenced by *The Roaring Twenties* (1939) and *Casablanca* (1942) (Maltby 1995: 31).

Also, lest we forget, Bazin did not entirely accept the purist premise of 'la politique des auteurs', in the often bombastic form proposed by Truffaut and company. Bazin was wary of the idea of the auteur as a source of meaning, given his commitment to the freedom of the spectator and his view of the ideal filmmaker as an almost neutral, passive recorder, not a creative manipulator, of (admittedly staged) real world events (Cook 2007: 390–1). Indeed, Bazin believed that the *mise-en-scène* should be cleared of signs of individual style altogether, thereby letting the spectator engage with meaning freely, without being manipulated. Also Bazin was troubled by the practice of constructing filmic 'greatness' on the basis of regularities and supposed coherence 'found' by the auteur critic across a body of film work. This smacked of subjectivism and teleology, and seemed to leave out of account the social and historical contexts and constraints which invariably bear upon the process of filmmaking. He also stressed that the auteur inhabited a specific filmmaking ecology (or what Maltby calls, in relation to Hollywood, the 'multiple logics' of filmmaking, 1995: 30), shaped by economics, industrial practices, national trends, cultural precedents, social movements and the specialisation of production cycles according to genre etc. In short the auteur was always treated by Bazin as a 'function within a system of forces' (Stam 2000: 21). Bazin's preference therefore, was for an impure cinema, for hybrids, rather than for a fetishised, personal creativity or imagined purity, lying behind the images on screen. And, while a keen student of Welles, he also took a particular interest in the Hollywood western and the ways in which the strong authorial personality negotiates and interacts with genre. Bazin's coolness towards authorial hero worship and his acute understanding of the logics of commercial filmmaking arguably offer a useful perspective and corrective when analysing Amenábar as an aspiring popular, auteur filmmaker.

In the mid- to late 1960s, in response to major upheavals in cultural politics arising from May 1968, *Cahiers* criticism abandoned the auteur in favour of ideology, the filmic 'ideological apparatus' and the textual 'unsaid'. The dominant capitalist ideology was everywhere, it seems, and needed to be exposed. How was it that symbolic systems, such as cinema, sustained social and psychic relations of domination, subordination and oppression in capitalist societies? Could this be the key to explaining the defeat of the French left in 1968? Ideology was invariably embedded in all types of filmmaking, *Cahiers* argued, save perhaps for that special category 'e', examples of which might be salvaged from oblivion through oblique 'symptomatic readings' against the grain (Cook 2007: 450). Structuralism, semiotics and psychoanalysis, with support from Althusserian Marxism, all sought to displace the human subject as the source of textual creativity with a dreary, anti-humanist and pseudo-scientific view of 'language'. It was now language itself which spoke through us, unconsciously and unbidden and which authored those linguistic artefacts we once called 'texts' and 'utterances'. Auteur criticism now adopted the more rigorous and scientific methods of structuralism and post-structuralism. Astruc's nostalgic 'caméra-stylo' and the filmmaker as writer became rapidly redundant in the 'age of the reader' and an open-ended paradigm of 'écriture', according to Derrida. Sarris's 'pantheon' auteurs were thus relegated to the level of mere 'regularities' in textual organisation, their skills and creativity having been dissolved into the flow of the multiple signals and codes of the film text. And, until the arrival of cultural studies in the 1980s, film studies was quickly and successfully occupied for nearly two decades by faddish, repetitive and ultimately tiresome incantations from Marxism, psychoanalysis, linguistics and 'ideological critique'. Yet, miraculously, though marginalised and frequently written off, the notion of the film director as auteur refused to die. Indeed, the concept is still with us and is still crucial in the promotion and marketing of films, in much press and journal criticism and even in the confection of directorial lists and league tables. Also, the expansion of 'middlebrow' film entertainment, i.e. popular art cinema for wider audiences, has extended the life cycle of the film director as creative artist. Moreover, the boundaries between art and commerce, art cinema and commercial cinema have blurred significantly, as mainstream cinema has taken up many of the formal strategies which were once the preserve of the art film.

A shared, distributed, collective authorship?

In an inherently collective and collaborative form of activity such as filmmaking, where so many different elements and processes coexist, giving primacy to the work of the director in critical terms may seem counterintuitive and analytically suspect. Yet, in practice, before a mainstream fiction film can be made, a co-ordinating figure of some description is usually involved in virtually all of the key creative decisions arising from the development phase to post-production. Apart from finance, these decisions usually include script approval, casting, locations, production, costume design, details of performance and editing. Also, the film has to be pre-visualised or storyboarded and narrative ideas have to be mapped out, before handing them over to the various production and art design teams (Katz 1991: 4–6). This co-ordinating labour has been seen traditionally as the domain of the director, the overseer of the creative input and the person who knows (or is supposed to know), through his/her skills, habits and prior experience, what the film will look like and how best to achieve the highest possible level of integration of all the various contributions. This usually puts the director in the position of unifying the project and guiding the team(s) on what is required. But, unless we have reliable, empirical information confirming the co-ordinating and unifying roles of the director, it is difficult to assign credit to these administrative and creative functions. Also, how far should other teams and specialists be credited for their contribution to the fully integrated, final film product? The problem with 'auteur theory' is that it simply pays lip service to the notion of collaboration or teamwork before heading straight towards an evaluation of directorial input. Clearly, not all films are made by auteurs, nor are all auteurs directors; not every film has a single director, or a single guiding consciousness. Also, the critical implications of assigning filmic coherence, the integration of all specialist contributions as well as meaning to the sole figure of the auteur-director are highly problematic. They simply fail to reflect the complex realities of mounting and producing a film. More pertinently, to what extent is Amenábar the author of work usually attributed to him, such as scripting, shooting and scoring?

Let us consider a practical example from his period as a student filmmaker. One of the reasons why the producer-director José Luis Cuerda called the 19-year-old Amenábar a 'renaissance genius' and facilitated his break into feature filmmaking was his apparent 'jack-of-all-trades' authorship. That is, his unusual breadth of expertise and practical skills in virtually all filmmaking departments (even acting), as seen in the credits for the short *Himenóptero* (Himenopterus, 1992), his 'passport' into feature production. The film was reminiscent of Powell's *Peeping Tom* (1960) and Hitchcock's *Psycho* (1960). It also featured a version of Powell's Mark Lewis, called Bosco, played by Amenábar himself. Cuerda was also impressed by the very assured shooting style and the smooth flow of the film narrative. While making *Himenóptero*, Amenábar did the lion's share of the work on scripting, rehearsing, direction and editing as well as adding the sound and music. However, it was his university friend and flatmate Mateo Gil who actually shot most of the film, given that Amenábar was involved in an acting role. Moreover, as a performer, a strangely silent and autistic Amenábar (with just one line of dialogue) worked opposite three female speaking roles (played by Raquel Gómez, Nieves Herranz and Juana Macías) who carry the film. In other words, *Himenóptero* was very much a team effort and, had it not been for Gil's very assured use of the video camera and the strong female performances, Cuerda might not have been so impressed by the direction or camerawork. Of course this in no way seeks to diminish Amenábar's enormous contribution to the film or to gainsay his impressive range of skills. In fact it was Amenábar himself who took overall responsibility for the piece, especially in its crucial post-production phase. And it was his painstaking hard work and integration of all the creative elements which fashioned a highly competent, successful, prize-winning short. Moreover, compared to that of his competitors, the short's sound quality was deemed outstanding, this being the decisive factor which ensured for Amenábar his second short film award. So, at the level of student filmmaking, on the basis of the above information, we arguably do find a degree of personal integration and coherence which emerge from a small-scale collaborative effort, in which Amenábar played key roles in virtually all departments.

As regards his full-length features, much of the media and web coverage they have attracted gives the impression that every image, dialogue line and nuance therein proceeds from Amenábar's authorial consciousness. This is obviously wide of the mark, though he has nearly always co-scripted his films, tends to take personal control of editing and (until *Ágora*) soundtrack and sound mixing and insists on approving the final cut. Moreover, he is also generous in acknowledging the contributions of those he has worked with and never presents himself as a genius or transcendent 'intelligent designer'. Indeed, on *Tesis*, for example, feeling understandably jittery and not wishing to 'cagar' (mess up) his first big opportunity as a feature director, Amenábar suggested to producer Cuerda a 'joint direction' arrangement with Mateo Gil (Interview). This proposition was rejected (Heredero 1997: 105). As a compromise, although Gil did not co-script the film, he became Amenábar's personal assistant minder on set and a second pair of eyes, available to offer advice and alternative suggestions for set ups, as well as lighting and camera positions etc. On *Abre los ojos*, apart from co-scripting the film with Amenábar, Gil again worked as his personal assistant in much the same manner. He also collaborated on the early treatments of *Tesis* and he co-scripted and was on set during the shooting of *Mar adentro*. All in all, apart from *The Others*, a case can probably be made for regarding Amenábar's authorship thus far as strongly shared with Gil, since it is impossible to disentangle clearly what belongs to Amenábar and what to Gil.[11]

At the same time, on Amenábar's first three features, José Luis Cuerda and Fernando Bovaira intervened very extensively on the scripting and preparation of *Abre los ojos* and *The Others* respectively. In fact Cuerda was crucial in reshaping the whole narrative outline and philosophical/ethical basis of *Abre los ojos*, while Bovaira supervised the script development of *The Others*. In a rather different mode of auteurist intervention, Nicole Kidman was also very influential in reshaping the role of Grace in *The Others*. The sort of changes she persuaded Amenábar to make radically changed the concept of

Grace as a hysterical, conflicted, disagreeable, Catholic mother with a very dark side. Also we are unlikely ever to discover the true nature and extent of Tom Cruise's micro-management of the production (including his constant notes and queries to Amenábar and then Bovaira, after viewing the dailies) and the difficult editing phases of *The Others*. With regard to film crew, it is worth mentioning that in the editing room Amenábar tends to rely on a co-editor (such as Nacho Ruiz Capillas). In relation to *mise-en-scène*, after outlining his concept and requirements, he normally leaves production design, lighting and cinematography almost exclusively in the hands of the relevant specialists, such as Benjamín Fernández, Guy Dyas and Javier Aguirresarrobe, who provide him with options and designs. In relation to soundtrack and music, until *Ágora*, he was normally fully credited as the main composer. Yet, given his lack of formal training, he has usually relied on a series of professional musicians (such as Mariano Marín, Lucio Godoy and Juan Carlos Cuello) to correct, orchestrate, transcribe and prepare for recording the musical templates he creates at home on his keyboard and computer. He also indicated that in his fifth film he wanted to hand over responsibility for the scoring to a professional, just to see what happens (Interview). He did so by hiring the Oscar-winner Dario Marianelli to prepare the score for *Ágora*.[12]

Amenábar is a highly talented director, whose skills and experience are clearly honed and strongly enhanced by the expert support of many others. At the same time the various teams of specialists (from production and art design to editing, camerawork and costume design to sound mixing) all seek to identify with the project, share and shape the director's requirements and work together to realise the concept. As Bruce Kawin argues, such a collaborative enterprise is not simply the result but also evidence of a group effort; the integration and coherence of the finished film can also be largely credited to the shared objectives of its makers (1992: 300). But in the end Amenábar ultimately bears the overall responsibility for the finished product, while justifiably taking the credit for its successes as well as the brickbats for its weaknesses and failings.

Amenábar and genre

In an essay which traces the passage from the 'margins to the mainstream' of horror filmmaking in Spain in the 1990s, Andrew Willis underlines the importance of Amenábar's *The Others* (2001) in the process. He regards it as a film which in its time raised significantly the otherwise low critical and cultural esteem of Spanish genre filmmaking, particularly that of horror. He also sees *The Others* not simply as a catalyst but as the culmination of the rapid growth in 1990s Spanish horror, which helped increase levels of Hispanic co-productions and strengthen the global appeal and commercial viability of the genre at home and abroad (2004: 237). In other words, *The Others* was a key film whose success in terms of global audiences, box office and critical recognition lifted Spanish horror squarely into the international mainstream. In order to theorise recent trends in Spanish horror, Willis draws upon two concepts used by Jim Collins to study aspects of 1990s Hollywood genre production, those of 'eclectic irony' and 'new sincerity' (1993: 242–63). In Collins's schema, the first of these terms emphasises the collapse of generic boundaries, playful excess and 'ironic hybridisation', (e.g. the *Back to the Future* franchise), while the second eschews playfulness, irony, parody, overt cinephilia and self-conscious spoofery in favour of seriousness, narrative coherence, generic unity, 'good taste' and a broadly realist aesthetic (e.g. Kevin Costner's *Dances with Wolves* (1990). Alongside *The Others*, Willis places Guillermo del Toro's *El espinazo del Diablo* (The Devil's Backbone, 2001), seeing both films as examples of Collins's notion of 'new sincerity' filmmaking. Both films, he argues, consolidated public acceptance of Hispanic horror as an appealing, transnational, mainstream product; both also enjoyed major commercial and critical success worldwide; both satisfied dominant critical expectations by working within culturally 'respectable' gothic traditions and both have become assimilated into the ranks of 'serious' cinema, opening up spaces for other such works to do likewise (2004: 248–9). In other words, Hispanic horror has achieved significant mainstream distribution by going upmarket and appealing to more middlebrow audiences, while also catering to Spain's large youth market domestically. Willis describes this outcome as 'The victory of the serious' (2004: 247), i.e. a horror formula based on realism, narrative coherence, generic unity and art cinema style as opposed to the explicit violence, gore, parodic comedy and general semiotic excess which characterises Collins's notion of 'eclectic irony'. This is a useful point of entry for a brief consideration of Amenábar's attitudes towards genre and the ways in which his generic choices and film style have developed and interacted with his authorship.

Let us begin by recalling that a major turning point in the early 1990s in the revitalisation of the genre film in Spain was Álex de la Iglesia's début feature, the big-budget *Acción Mutante* (Mutant Action, 1992), produced by Almodóvar's company El Deseo (see Buse, Triana-Toribio and Willis 2004). Though not a massive box-office hit (368,289 spectators, €990,00 – source: mcu.es), the film marked a ground breaking broadside, in aesthetic and thematic terms, against the PSOE-sponsored art movie of the 1980s with its aggressive, 'in your face', lowbrow, counter-cinematic style. Against the depth and verisimilitude attributed to realism, de la Iglesia counterposed a visceral superficiality and anti-illusionism, with his two-dimensional, grotesque, comic-book characters and cheesy narrative. And against the relative stability of realist generic boundaries he offered fantasy, black humour, impurity and hybridity, through which he seemed to ridicule the cultural and social status of Almodóvar's effete 'niños bonitos e hijos de papá' (pretty, spoiled rich kids) and 'maricones diseño' (designer poofs). The film also led to a very successful follow-up, i.e. *El día de la bestia* (The Day of the Beast, 1995), which had a significant influence upon the grungy aesthetics of a new crop of abrasive, quasi-Rabelasian, parodic comedies. These included Juanma Bajo Ulloa's *Airbag* (1997) and Ray Loriga's *La pistola de mi hermano* (My Brother's Gun, 1997) as well as Álex as de la Iglesia's *Perdita Durango* (1997), *Muertos de risa* (Died Laughing, 1999), *La comunidad* (The Association, 2000) and *800 balas* (800 Bullets, 2002). Many of these films also took a much harder line against the didactic and politically correct agenda of the socialist art film, articulating a far more conservative political, sexual and moral outlook. By far the most successful film cycle in this vein was and continues to be Santiago Segura's *Torrente: el brazo tonto de la ley* (The Dumb Arm of the Law, 1998), *Torrente 2: Misión en Marbella* (Mission in Marbella, 2001) and *Torrente 3: El protector* (The Bodyguard, 2005). Made without any government subsidy, the first *Torrente* (1998) was Spain's biggest box-office hit of the 1990s, attracting three million spectators and nearly €11 million (source: mcu.es). It thus grossed double its nearest rival, Fernando Trueba's period musical satire *La niña de tus ojos* (The Girl of Your Dreams), starring Penélope Cruz (1998) (Heredero 1999: 314). *Torrente 1*'s appeal was based on its hybridity, i.e. its attractive combination of classic, mainstream American genre conventions (e.g. the 'fascist cop' movie, with echoes of *Dirty Harry*) and the local 'esperpento' or black comedy, comprising an ironic and exaggerated vision of certain social values and customs, laced with vicious black humour, surrealism, explicit violence, grotesque stereotypes and the recycling of forgotten Spanish film, television and musical stars and celebrities (Tony le Blanc, El Gran Wyoming, El Fary etc.). *Torrente* thus offered an array of recognisable if overblown signs of local and national 'Spanish' identities, which represent urban, lower- class, 'backdoor' Spain, in all its baseness, monstrosity and visceral prejudice. It also aggressively reaffirmed its deviation from and negation of the norms of 1980s subsidised art cinema (championed by Pilar Miró, Director General of Cinema, in Spain's Ministry of Culture (1983–85). *Torrente* presented itself as an 'anti-establishment' film on the basis of its unashamed commercialism and celebration of 'trash' cinema. Largely because of its playful sense of narrative and semiotic excess, the Torrente cycle can be seen as a commercially successful riposte to the hegemony of Hollywood in Spain's domestic market. It also provides a potential model of national cinema, one of transnational, ironised, generic hybridity, with rootings in Spanish media, cultural and even sporting traditions.[13] However, if it is able to compete nationally with dominant American action cinema whilst retaining clear signs of its local identity, its cultural rootedness and many of its localisms tend to impede intelligibility, universality and thus exportability and foreign sales.

Doing it straight

The ultra-violent, parodic, cartoon-like comedy style found in Álex de la Iglesia's first two feature films, as well as in Bajo Ulloa's *Airbag* (1997) and in the *Torrente* cycle, established a major stylistic register for Spanish popular genre cinema in the 1990s. Here, let us recall that, as a student and maker of shorts (and to some extent echoing Álex de la Iglesia), Amenábar was vaguely and temporarily attracted by the combination of Berlangian sardonic humour and the postmodern, parodic grotesque. Evidence of this can be found in his first short *La cabeza* (The Head, 1991), which I discuss in more detail in the following chapter. It is also visible in *Tesis*, especially in the early script treatments, which initially focused on a single male character, the 'porno-gore freak' Chema, and his engagement with the mechanisms and tricks of exploitation cinema. Amenábar has stated: 'Hay en mí una parte cutre que me hace reír mucho; pienso que si optara por la comedia, tiraría por ese lado' (Rodríguez Marchante 2002: 63) (There is a very vulgar side to me which makes me laugh a lot; if I ever chose to do comedy, I think I would explore this side of it). In his first short, *La cabeza*, Amenábar was unsure of how to resolve and close down the narrative. So he opted for a comic, cartoon-like finale, character-ised by violent decapitation, lots of fake blood, female hysteria and black humour. This appears to be the only moment in his entire filmography which relies on explicit screen gore (in *Tesis* Bosco's dismemberment of his female victims is largely suggested through sound rather than overtly displayed). Otherwise, even in his student days, though perhaps tempted, he was never seriously committed to developing a film aesthetic dominated by stylised, excess violence, by the parodic grotesque or by techniques of ironic distantiation. And, because of bigger budgets, in this area of filmmaking Amenábar believes that Hollywood achieves far better results on a technical level than any Spanish production (Rodríguez Marchante 2002: 163). Also, as someone who is physically squeamish towards violence, who avoids confrontation and also suffers physically when filming (Rodrí-guez Marchante 2002: 149–50), he derives no personal pleasure from screen violence as such, be it realistic or parodic. Besides, parodic horror may be fun and may provide scenarios for the masturbatory fantasies of adolescent boys, but it is not scary (Interview).

As a film spectator Amenábar argues that he has never been seriously scared by a screen ghost, vampire or werewolf. In his own films the supernatural is used as a metaphor for dealing with more worldly issues, including troubled family relationships or the exploitation and abuse of young children. Even the ghosts in *The Others* appear human and alive until the final revelation (Rodríguez Marchante 2002: 158). Amenábar believes it is far too easy for filmmakers nowadays to create screen scares using fake blood and CGI, which rather than scare tend to provoke nausea and disgust. Sadly, he argues, there is no lasting impression, the after-effect tends to be rather superficial, the spectator quickly becomes attuned to the visible excess and the affective impact quickly dissipates. Amenábar prefers to be scared by psychological horror and mystery, by the denial of information and the suppres-sion of clues, by the unknown and the unseen, and by being forced to share the point of view of the victim (Rodríguez Marchante 2002: 29–31 and 59). In this sense he diverges considerably from Hitch-cock, who preferred to build suspense on the basis of spectator power and omniscience over the characters. Amenábar prefers to delay the release of information and tease the viewer for as long as possible, maintaining confusion and uncertainty, until the catharsis of a surprise ending. Moreover, as a horror fan, he goes to the cinema to be genuinely scared, but not to throw up or be bombarded by special effects, which tend to destroy spectator immersion in the onscreen action: 'Lo que me gusta en realidad es el cine que da miedo, no el que da asco. No soy aficionado al gore. Me gusta tener la sensación de terror pero tiene que ser un terror limpio' (Heredero, 1997: 86) (What I really prefer is scary rather than gory cinema. I'm not a fan of gore, I like the sensation of horror but it has to be clean horror). For Amenábar what the horror director should be aiming to create are not only surface intensities but also a form of viewing engagement which helps unlock the dark spaces of the subconscious: 'Para mí, dejar un espacio a la imaginación es la esencia de las ansiedades, obsesiones e incluso paranoias latentes en nuestra conciencia colectiva. Despertarlas hará volver el espectador a los rincones de la infancia ... a aquel escalofrío' (Payán 2001: 48) (For me, leaving a space for the imagination is the essence of those anxieties, obsessions and even paranoias which are latent in our collective consciousness. By awakening these, we can take the spectator back to the dark corners of childhood .. to that shiver).

In 1997, talking about film horror and his admiration for Peter Medak's *The Changeling* (1980), Amenábar said: 'Creo que hay que devolverle al cine de terror el tono serio' (Heredero 1997: 103) (I think we need to go back to a horror cinema with a more serious feel). Amenábar admires a film like Medak's which relies on atmosphere not blood, conveys a strong sense of traditional suspense and horror, especially through its performances, the interactions of the gazes, the reactions to offscreen sounds and a sophisticated use of music and soundscapes. And even though the film exploits a supernatural element, 'lo hace de forma muy seria' (Heredero 1997: 103) (it does so in a very serious way). In other words, spectator pleasure is based on alignment and empathy with characters whose traumas and tragedies (seen and unseen) matter to us, who play out our anxieties in credible, realistic, ways and where film style is subordinate to storytelling. Amenábar thus prefers this straight, 'serious', rather classical, conservative delivery. This is so, in part, because it seems to fulfil its intended emotional effect on him, by engaging him affectively and intellectually, on a personal level. It also appeals because it reflects the styles of a number of his key filmic reference points, including Medak, Hitchcock, the Kubrick of *2001 A Space Odyssey, A Clockwork*

Orange, The Shining and the Spielberg of *Jaws* (1975) and *E.T. The Extra-Terrestrial* (1982). In other words, Amenábar sees spectator engagement and pleasure being better served by a suspension rather than a foregrounding of disbelief in the film diegesis.

To summarise, Amenábar was and is a cinephile and a horror buff; he is also a fan of the popular genre film, but of a type which aligns itself with art cinema (i.e. a form of cinema which is usually seen as unfettered by or beyond genre). Alongside Mateo Gil he also derives great pleasure and benefit in messing with and subverting the conventions, codes and forms of mainstream genre cinema. He is thus a filmmaker who tends to respect and to establish hierarchies of genre cinema, clearly demarcating his own tastes, and finding greater legitimacy, perhaps, in the thriller than in the horror genre, with a preference for the family melodrama and bio-pic over, say, the romantic comedy. Amenábar thus appears to want to distance himself somewhat from genres of low cultural status. He seeks legitimacy and distinction by disavowing the bad reputation of violent horror, 'horror gore' and its associated fan groups, in favour of a hybrid form of horror (dominated by the codes of the thriller) which privileges stylistic unity and coherence, symmetry, atmosphere, repeated motifs and realism. We might say that his kind of clean, 'serious' horror represents the more predictable, safe, more conservative end of the spectrum, i.e. horror suitable primarily for middlebrow tastes and middle-class audiences.

The contemporary auteur

Warren Buckland has argued persuasively that mastery of the film-making process (which he refers to as 'internal' authorship) is no longer a sufficient criterion for film authorship (2006: 14) nowadays. Today's auteur directors, he argues, also require control over external factors, including production, finance and deal-making; they thus need business acumen, managerial skills and the ability to create a brand image, in order to achieve market advantage over their competitors. Thus, in terms of defining contemporary authorship, a major scholarly shift over the last twenty years (see especially Corrigan 1991: 103–4) suggests that signs of authorship can be seen as traces not only in film texts themselves but outside of them too, in the domains where authorship and commerce intermingle. Here authorship emerges in the realm of what Catherine Grant (echoing Corrigan) calls 'a cultural and commercial intersubjectivity' (2000: 103), that is a zone or zones where the auteur can promote his/her status as organising agency and the motivating presence behind filmic textuality. As such, authorship emerges in the activities of film reception and consumption, in the traces left in journalistic, publicity and Web materials, promotional interviews, magazine photo shoots, festivals, award ceremonies and personal appearances, wherever the auteur figure functions as power broker, media star and celebrity marketeer. In short, signs of authorship arise in those areas which Genette calls 'paratexts', i.e. all those secondary texts and activities which surround and frame the main film text and shape its consumption and reception (1998: 52).

In this domain Almodóvar is arguably the paradigm case in Spanish filmmaking. Almodóvar's name will open a film since it offers a distinct brand image and track record, supported by his well-known production company (El Deseo, founded in 1985), jointly run with his brother Agustín. His name is enough to secure financial backing as well as a wide support network of financial institutions. It can also generate production and distribution partners and a host of 'associations' linked to an 'Almodóvar-branded' film product. Also Almodóvar's cleverly promoted and carefully designed photo shoots and marketing appearances at premieres, festivals, award ceremonies, stores and bookshops emphasise the centrality of his place, not only as the director but also as the multi-talented stand-in actor who can play all the parts of his own films. The ubiquity of Almodóvar's star image, always far bigger than that of any of his actors, has helped project him as the consummate promotor, performer and publicist of his own films, at home and abroad. By contrast Amenábar has been regarded very differently and though influential enough nowadays to attract financial, production and distribution partners for his films (notably via Fernando Bovaira and his company Mod Producciones), he has lacked any comparable media recognition, public image or star profile. In this connection, his almost total absence from the marketing and publicity campaign for *The Others* was symptomatic of his surprising lack of visbility and public recognition, outside of Spain and Latin America. Though far more adept than before as a 'mediático' (media-friendly celebrity), and having 'come out' in 2004, he remains shy and tight-lipped about his personal life and very discreet about his working relationships on and off set.[14]

He also finds it very difficult to shake off the image of an eternally youthful, polite, 'boy next door', a low-profile representation which still emerges in much of the media coverage, including Web interviews and blogs. In his amusing piece published just before the Oscar awards in February 2005, Ryan Gilbey recalls interviewing a 'schoolboy' called Amenábar in a London hotel, as if the young director had been 'dressed by his mother for prize giving day' (2005). Gilbey added jokingly that Amenábar was far too young-looking to be making the sort of gloomy, challenging, serious films he seems to specialise in.[15]

This book

In their monographic study of François Truffaut, Diana Holmes and Robert Ingram use their Introduction to comment on one of Truffaut's key shorts, *Les Mistons* (The Mischief Makers, 1957).[16] They argue that this short film provides the seed or kernel of the distinctive thematic and stylistic elements which reappear in the rest of Truffaut's considerable output (three shorts and 22 features). They even make the claim that the film is a crucial precursor and model for the Nouvelle Vague and indeed for French national cinema as a whole: 'The twenty-three fleeting minutes of *Les Mistons* are, then, pointers not only to themes and filmic practices which will nourish and sustain the later work, they are also a key to the Nouvelle Vague, to its approach to cinema and its desire to create a cinema that is French' (1998: 8). At the same time the authors also claim that *Les Mistons* 'is rich and diverse, open, like later films, to readings other than those intended by its author' (1998: 8), yet the approach they adopt towards Truffaut's filmmaking is still a strongly organicist one – that is, one of biological growth whose patterns and direction already appear to be laid down, already encoded into the filmic DNA of the model, foundational short. Claims for organic growth, clearly delineated patterns of meaning and recurring thematic issues may make sense following a full-scale review of a lifetime's filmmaking, such as Truffaut's. However, with Amenábar, it would obviously be inappropriate to make any definitive claims of this type, given his limited output and the fact that he is still in the early stages of a potentially long and glittering career. So, in order to avoid the potential pitfalls of metaphors of biological growth and authorial hero-worship, I have taken a rather decentred as opposed to an organic approach and a relatively empiricist rather than a thematic model for my main chapter analyses.

Chapter 2 contains a brief biographical profile of Amenábar, but the main focus is a detailed analysis of his shorts, and the ways in which a set of templates and devices (stylistic, narrative and thematic) begin to emerge from them as well as a series of working practices. Unsurprisingly perhaps, the shorts (of both Amenábar and Gil) appear to prefigure and underpin significant aspects of the features, especially in the first two thrillers. Chapters 3 to 7 provide the main body of the book and offer detailed accounts of Amenábar's five feature films to date. Though the approaches adopted and the menu of topics vary in each chapter, I seek to combine important aspects of contextual information (historical, social, industrial) with detailed production and reception notes. I also pay close attention to aspects of film form and style (e.g. the interplay in *Tesis* between classical Hollywood narration and 'art film narration', also the problems of viewer comprehension created by the non-linear diegesis of *Abre los ojos* and how Amenábar and Gil resolve these difficulties). However, my main focus is to explore the ways in which Amenábar appears to conduct experiments in generic hybridity in order to create a personal, auteur cinema which satisfies his cinephilia as well as his desire for ambiguity and profundity while at the same time demonstrating his commitment to the tastes and pleasures of film audiences. In my selections and mode of coverage of such material I have been guided in large part by questions already raised in scholarly writings on Amenábar, but also by other issues and evidence which have emerged during the research for this book.[17]

Notes

1 Welles made his film-directing debut and most acclaimed feature *Citizen Kane* (1941) at the age of 25. See also A. del Barrio and L. Pérez, 'De estudiante a director de cine', *El Mundo, Suplemento* (27 September 1995), 3–4.

2 A. Corral, 'Amenábar. La tesis del debutante', *Antena Semanal* (21 April 1996), 37.

3 E. Rodríguez Marchante, '*Tesis*: hay películas que matan', *ABC* (13 April 1996), 86; see also Carlos F. Heredero, 'La "*Tesis*" de Alejandro Amenábar', *Diario 16* (17 February 1996), 32.

4 N. Bou and X. Pérez, ' La fórmula de l'èxit', *Avui-Barcelona* (21 April 1996), 8.

5 L. Bonet Mojica, 'Nada ni nadie es lo que parece', *La Vanguardia-Barcelona* (24 December 1997), 40.

6 A. Fernández Santos. 'Celuloide en las venas', *El País-Madrid* (21 December 1997), 39.

7 Sean Smith, 'Finding the story inside', *Newsweek* (27 December 2004–3 January 2005), 68–70.

8 Rafael Ruiz and Gregorio Belinchón, '20 personajes para 20 años de Goyas', *El País Semanal*, no. 1531 (29 January 2006), 47.

9 With regard to Medem, it is worth pointing out that *Caótica Ana* (2007) was something of a watershed in his career. Apart from being a critical and commercial flop (attracting a mere 247,593 spectators, compared to 377,094 for *La pelota vasca* (The Basque Ball, 2003) and 1.3 million for *Lucía y el sexo* (Lucia and Sex, 2001, source: mcu.es), it triggered a serious reappraisal of his approach to filmmaking. In particular it seems to have created a new awareness of and concern for his lost national audiences, their tastes and preferences, and a determination to re-capture them. See his remarks in interview with Rocío García in 'Julio Medem empieza de cero', *El País* (27 June 2008), 38. Alas, Medem's supposedly commercial, 'comeback' film, his sexy lesbian romance *Habitación en Roma* (Room in Rome, 2010), imploded in Spain, attracting a mere 86,000 spectators and a disappointing €500,000 gross (source: mcu.es).

10 Andrew Sarris, *The American Cinema: Directions and Directors, 1929–1968* (New York: Dutton, 1968), 31.

11 Also, among his main collaborations, Amenábar has written music as well as working in other capacities for Guillermo Fernández's short *Al lado del Atlas* (Next to the Atlas, 1994), Mateo Gil's three shorts, *Antes del beso* (Before the Kiss, 1993), *Soñé que te mataba* (I Dreamed I Killed You, 1994) and *Allanamiento de morada* (Breaking and Entering, 1998) as well as scoring Gil's first feature *Nadie conoce a nadie* (Nobody knows Anybody, 1999). He has also scored José Luis Cuerda's very successful *La lengua de las mariposas* (Butterfly's Tongue, 1999).

12 Marianelli won an Oscar for *Atonement* (Joe Wright, 2007); he was also Oscar-nominated for *The Brothers Grimm* (Terry Gilliam, 2005).

13 For example the cast for *Torrente 4* includes a rare gamut of cameos including, among others, the late dictator Franco's eldest granddaughter (Carmen Martínez Bordíu), Esteso and Pajares (television comedy duo), Andreu Buenafuente (television comic and presenter), David Bisbal (successful solo singer) and Cesc Fábregas (professional footballer).

14 This same impression of shyness and reserve is evident when one visits Amenábar's official home page, hosted by ClubCultura. Despite its spooky soundtrack and vaguely interactive elements, the page quickly translates into rather conventional textual postings, such as the interview material on *Mar adentro*: see www.clubcultura.com/clubcine/clubcineastas/amenabar/mar03.htm. See also Núria Triana-Toribio, 'Auteurism and Commerce in contemporary Spanish cinema: *directores mediáticos*', *Screen*, 49:3 (Autumn 2008), 259–76. Triana-Toribio provides a useful insight into how media-savvy Spanish directors, such as Isabel Coixet and Álex de la Iglesia, exploit (in different ways) their official websites to enhance their commercial appeal as well as their auteurist credentials.

15 Ryan Gilbey, 'That's so Amenábar', *Independent on Sunday* (22 February 2005), 13.
16 D. Holmes and R. Ingram, *François Truffaut*, French Film Directors (Manchester: Manchester University Press, 1998).
17 To date, in relation to Amenábar scholarship, for example, we find one short study in Spanish, covering only his first two films (Sempere 2000, expanded in a revised edition in 2004 to include *The Others* and *Mar adentro*); a 170–page, book-length interview in Spanish, with an introduction and a final essay by ABC's film critic (Oti Rodríguez Marchante 2002); a volume of interviews, in the *¿Cómo hacer cine?* series, involving the main cast, management and crew of *Tesis* (Vera 2002). There are also several shorter interviews (Heredero 1997 and Payán 2001), several overview pieces (Jordan and Morgan-Tamosunas 1998, Stone 2002, Triana-Toribio 2003), and a growing number of scholarly articles and reviews (e.g. Allinson, Amago, Buckley, Hills, Jackson, Jordan, La Caze, Lev, Maule, Ortega, Perriam, Russell, Smith, White, Zatlin etc.). More recently I have also been pleased to receive notice and copies of a work written in French, a short, monographic study of Amenábar's first three films, by María Asunción Gómez and Santiago Juan-Navarro (2002) and a much more extensive volume of 11 essays, plus a very long interview with the director, edited by Professor Nancy Berthier, 2007. See the main bibliography as well as my review article of the Berthier volume in *Studies in Hispanic Cinemas*, 4:3 (2007), 199–212.

2

From film freak to jack-of-all-trades

Formative years

Alejandro Fernando Amenábar Cantos was born in Santiago de Chile on 31 March 1972, during the government of the Marxist president Salvador Allende. With a Spanish mother (Josefina Cantos) and a Chilean father (Hugo Ricardo Amenábar Wormald), he was the second of two brothers (Ricardo, the older sibling, was born on 4 December 1969). Within a year Allende's socialist experiment was near to collapse, undermined by widespread industrial unrest and mounting opposition from corporate business interests (supported by the CIA). Alarmed by the situation, which echoed the unstable political climate just before Spain's Civil War (1936–39) and Josefina's personal experience of wartime upheavals, Amenábar's parents decided to return to Spain at the end of August 1973. In so doing they managed to avoid by a couple of weeks Pinochet's military coup of 11 September, which overthrew the elected government and in which Allende himself perished.[1]

Amenábar arrived in Spain at the tail end of another dictatorship; his childhood and adolescence developed within a context of relative political stability. Over the next decade (which saw the death of Franco in November 1975, a new democratic constitution in 1978 and a new socialist government in October 1982, following a failed military coup in February 1981), the refugee family gradually resettled in and around Madrid. Amenábar spent nearly ten years at a private Catholic boys' school (the Padres Escolapios de Getafe, south of the capital), six as a day-student then four as a boarder (Berthier 2007: 209). Getting home at weekends and holidays invariably meant negotiating the treacherous Madrid ring road. This created all sorts of opportunities for experiencing hitching scares and crazy drivers, as well as crashes

and near misses (in the family car, driven by his mother), a fertile
motif in Amenábar's filmmaking (Rodríguez Marchante 2002: 31).
With the closure of the school in 1985/86, and much to his relief,
aged 14, he was transferred to the state-run Instituto Alameda de
Osuna, near Barajas and much nearer home. At religious school he
had been an obedient, academically outstanding, model pupil. At his
new school, as well as winning prizes for his short stories (Sempere
2004: 97), he continued to thrive in all of his BUP subjects (i.e. 'A'
levels, now called Enseñanza Secundaria Obligatoria or Compulsory
Secondary Education'. In fact, Amenábar never failed a course and
passed his school-leaving exams and university entrance (*Curso de
Orientación Universitaria*) with flying colours (Sempere 2004: 95–6).

More recently, in relation to his character and outlook as a youngster, Amenábar defined himself as: 'terco, cobardica y cinefilo'
(stubborn, timid and a film buff).[2] Behind this self-description we
discover a very unusual, excessively protective, upbringing, based
on 'un tipo de vida, muy chilena, muy de casa' (a very Chilean, very
home-based type of life), where his mother kept him indoors, with
only his brother Ricardo and the family dogs for company. He adds,
'A lo mejor, soy producto de una patología, pero a raíz de todo esto
yo desarrollé muchíssimo la imaginación' (I'm probably the product
of a pathology, but because of this I developed a very fertile imagination).[3] This is perhaps not surprising since, among other things, in
the Amenábar household of the mid-1970s and early 1980s, television viewing was virtually banned by his mother in favour of more
wholesome, creative pursuits such as reading, drawing and music
(Rodríguez Marchante 2002: 32). Such unusual house rules (echoed
in *The Others*) were unknown among Spanish families of the time. As
a result, as young nine- to ten-year-olds, the Amenábar brothers were
strictly rationed and allowed to watch only the occasional imported
cartoon series, but little else (Sempere 2000: 17). In response to such
heavy-handed screen censorship in the home, a young and imaginative Amenábar absorbed himself in superhero comics (Superman,
Batman, Spiderman etc.) which, in turn, inspired his creative writing,
his drawing skills and an early sense of narrative (Interview). He
also developed a voracious appetite for 'scary books' (adventure and
mystery stories, such as Enid Blyton's *Famous Five* series and Agatha
Christie's whodunnits) and a love of film music. And, having been
inspired as a child by John Williams's memorable score for *Superman*
(1978, Richard Donner), he developed an acute sensitivity to sound

which fed into his later fascination with film scoring.[4]

At around the same time his brother Ricardo (anxious to learn English) made contact with the Smiths, their neighbours in Paracuellos del Jarama (Herbert Smith was an American who worked at the Torrejón airbase and his wife Isabel was Spanish). With television effectively banned at home and with no cinema nearby, Amenábar now began viewing feature films on video, on a more regular basis.[5] It was in the living room of the Smiths' household that he was able to experience a range of forbidden screen delights and see for the first time a whole series of 1970s and 1980s Hollywood movies (Interview). Many of these have become horror and action adventure classics, including strong 'adult' titles such as *The Exorcist* (William Friedkin, 1973, *The Omen* (Richard Donner, 1976), *Alien* (Ridley Scott, 1979), *The Howling* (Joe Dante, 1980) and *The Changeling* (Peter Medak, 1980), as well as Spielberg's *Jaws* (1975), *Close Encounters of the Third Kind* (1977), *Raiders of the Lost Ark* (1981) and *E.T. The Extra-Terrestrial* (1982). However, despite being a regular viewer on Saturday mornings of *La bola de cristal* (The Crystal Ball, 1984–88), a Spanish television series and cultural magazine for children (which often featured 'Alaska' (Olvido Gara) and her band Dinarama as well as items on cinema and basic video technique), as yet there were few if any signs of the filmmaking prodigy to come.[6]

In terms of a career, Amenábar's early ambition, encouraged by his parents, was to study law or architecture not cinema (Interview). In anticipation his mother bought him the basic tools of the trade, including a set-square and a drawing/design board (Rodríguez Marchante 2002: 33). However, by the age of 16, when he himself realised that architecture demanded a serious command of mathematics (a subject in which he did not wholly excel), his evident talents for music, writing, drawing and storytelling all pointed in a rather different direction: the cinema. He had been told at school that Madrid's Complutense University ran a course in audiovisual and film studies and, in general, the university had a reasonable reputation at that time (Interview). Thus, some five years before the reopening of the National Film School (controlled by Madrid City Council, under the rubric of ECAM, or Escuela de Cine del Ayuntamiento de Madrid), Amenábar was accepted onto a course in Imagen y Sonido (Image and Sound), at the Facultad de Ciencias de la Información (Department of Information Sciences), at Madrid's Complutense University, which he joined in October 1990.

Nightmare at the Faculty

As Amenábar has frequently made clear, his experience as a film studies undergraduate in Spain in the early 1990s was not a happy one, rather it was 'bastante desastrosa' (pretty calamitous) (Rodríguez Marchante 2002: 33; see also Sempere 2004: 98–104). As the product of a traditional, bookish and very strict Chilean-Spanish family the young Amenábar was expected to reproduce in his higher education the outstanding results he had achieved at school. Also, as an incoming undergraduate, he was driven, ambitious and desperate to learn but with only the vaguest notions of filmmaking and anxious to shift into a much higher gear, intellectually and practically (Interview). He wanted to be challenged by his teachers and stimulated to explore in depth those practical areas of filmmaking which fascinated him, i.e. scripting, photography, *mise-en-scène*, editing and sound. Unfortunately, for Amenábar, his department failed comprehensively to satisfy even the most basic of these aspirations. And as a result, in a very short time, he went from being a brilliant to a very mediocre student. As he recalls amusingly in 'Aulas y jaulas' (*El País Semanal*, 18 May 1997), rather than a forum for intellectual discovery and excitement, his university experience was risible and embarrassing. His course was excessively theoretical and wide-ranging, improvised, lacking in coherence, badly delivered, largely irrelevant to his filmmaking interests, with little practical training and lacking technical support. Rapidly disillusioned and alienated mid-way through his first year, he soon abandoned his studies, as did his best friend, flatmate and regular collaborator Mateo Gil. Both stopped attending class, initially taking refuge in the cafeteria, using it as a noisy debating chamber on the merits of Spielberg, Hitchcock, Kubrick etc. But very soon, with money earned from odd jobs, they struck out on their own, determined to learn filmmaking by experimenting with shorts.[7] Motivated by a healthy scepticism towards the institution, these young dissidents soon found support and a certain countercultural identity among numerous undergraduate classmates, and as a gang of 'film freaks' they all shared, helped and learnt from each other. This rebellious fifth column also took great delight in mocking not only the evident limitations of their teachers but also those of their own national cinema. This is cleverly captured in *Tesis* in Chema's vicious in-jokes and put-downs at the expense of Spanish filmmaking.

As is well known, Amenábar learnt virtually nothing at university and failed to pass his degree course (including, it is said, 'Dirección' or Direction).[8] Since then, however, he has defended the Faculty in its role as an important meeting place for like-minded, creative people, with a passion for their craft (Interview). He mentions student actors, performers and filmmakers such as Sandra Gil, Raquel Gómez, Nieves Herranz and Juana Macías (all of whom worked with him), plus Sergio Rozas (who inspired the character of Chema in *Tesis*), Carlos Montero (through whom Amenábar first met Eduardo Noriega) and of course Mateo Gil, his best buddy and co-scriptwriter (Sempere 2000: 20). And, as he has pointed out more recently, 'Con la Complutense no tengo demasiada relación pero tampoco estoy enfrentado. Además, siempre les estaré agradecido por habernos concedido el permiso para rodar allí *Tesis*' (Letter to the author) (I'm not in close contact with the Complutense but nor am I on bad terms either. Besides, I'll always be grateful to them for giving us permission to shoot *Thesis* there). Moreover, despite their collective student 'nightmare', most of his contemporaries are now gainfully employed in Spain's audio-visual industries.

The Shorts

Amenábar's shorts constitute his own practical training ground in storytelling and film technique, a DIY solution to a dysfunctional and chaotic university department. They allowed him to road-test a series of narrative ideas, character types, staging options, shooting set ups, basic camera placement and technique (shot/reverse shot, the tracking shot etc.), editing options, sound effects and extra-diegetic music, as well as developing his cinephilia and even his own acting abilities (under his early stage pseudonym: Edmundo Morzwit). This invaluable experience gave rise to an important portfolio of ideas and options which would soon find their way into his main horror features. The 4 shorts in question are: *La cabeza* (The Head, 1991), as yet unreleased, *Himenóptero* (Himenopterus, 1992) and *Luna* (Moon, 1994/95), the latter made in two different formats: an original 30-minute, black-and-white version on Hi8 video – on which I base my comments – and a shorter 12–minute, colour version, made on 35mm film (thanks to the Luis García Berlanga script award of 1995, intriguingly co-sponsored by his old university department and as yet unreleased). Amenábar made all of his shorts together with his regular collaborator, Mateo Gil.[9] Given the latter's familiarity with photography, it was Gil who mostly handled the camerawork during this period (plus a cameo appearance in *Luna*), while Amenábar took care of direction, editing, sound, music and various acting roles.

The shorts also form the crucial phase in Amenábar's apprenticeship as an autodidact, 'jack-of-all-trades', student filmmaker, and underpin his early, rather neurotic, authorship. The films are strongly personal, autobiographical pieces, echoing Amenábar's and Gil's combined experiences of student filmmaking, odd jobs, family problems, hitch hiking, car accidents, scary pick-ups, equipment rip-offs, romantic rivalries, strained friendships, sexual harassment, confinement in the home and Amenábar's rather macabre fascination with death and the afterlife. They are also inspired by some of his favourite Anglo-American/Hollywood sources, such as Hitchcock's *Psycho* (1960) and Powell's *Peeping Tom* (1960), Kubrick's *2001. A Space Odyssey* (1969) and *The Shining* (1980), Spielberg's *Duel* (1971) and *Jaws* (1975), and Robert Harmon's *The Hitcher* (1986), among others. On the whole the shorts recycle but also significantly re-engineer the classic, 'shock inversion' template of the Hitchcockian thriller. Here the wholesome everyday world of the 'wrong person, in the wrong place, at the wrong time' is turned upside-down and his/her life is catapulted into a spiralling nightmare.

For most 18–19-year-olds, so completely disillusioned with their first year at University, the logical step would have been to change degree course or institution or find something else to do. Unwilling to sacrifice his directorial ambitions and concede defeat but also very anxious not to upset his parents, Amenábar continued as a registered, if largely absent, film student. On the up side, through a chance contact made by his brother Ricardo while hitching, Amenábar was introduced to Colin Arthur, head of a small special effects film company called Dream Factory, based in Madrid. And for a month during the summer of 1991 he worked there, sweeping up, helping to make models (such as a crocodile head for Álvaro Sáenz de Heredia's absurdist comedy *El robobo de la jojoya* (The Jewel Robbery, 1991) and seeing at first hand the inside of a small film workshop. He also borrowed some props from his boss, which he used to finish off his first short.

La cabeza (The Head, 1991)

Amenábar describes *La cabeza* as a 'ghost story ... shot on VHS' (Letter to the author). Elsewhere he adds, 'Lo planteé como un juego sin saber realmente lo que quería hacer más que colocar la cámara y que espero que no lo vea nadie' (I saw it as a game without really knowing what I wanted to do beyond positioning the camera and I hope no one else sees it) (cited in Gascó and Vitale 2005: 32). Filmed largely by Mateo Gil in and around Amenábar's family bungalow, made in black-and-white, and 15 minutes long, the short concerns a young woman (Ana, played by Sandra Gil, no relation to Mateo) who, on returning home, finds a message from her husband (Roberto, played by Amenábar) saying he will be late. By nightfall, and with no sign of Roberto, Ana thinks she notices an intruder. But, while she is vaguely aware that the latter might be her husband, a phone call informs her that he has just died in a car accident. On turning round, Ana beholds Roberto transformed into a charred, disfigured, bleeding zombie. Startled, she reacts violently by tearing off his grotesque head, which bounces around the room and out of the window, to a Warner Brothers-style cartoon soundtrack.

La cabeza probably began as an experiment with the new Sanyo video camera bought by Amenábar for his first term at university, which he was desperate to use (Rodríguez Marchante 2002: 35). But without a script, the shoot (spread over many weekends and holidays) turned into an improvised and very untidy practice exercise in camera placement and the creation of suspense. Any hopes of competing for glittering prizes were soon dashed by a poorly developed story line without an ending. Unsure of how to finish it, Amenábar borrowed some ghoulish model heads from Dream Factory, which Colin Arthur had made for Juan Piquer's cheesy *La mansión de Cthulu* (Cthulu's Mansion, 1991) (Rodríguez Marchante 2002: 36–7).[10] He then added the parodic, comic, gory finale (the first and only one in his entire filmography).

The short was made without any substantive knowledge of the main practical filmmaking disciplines, such as scripting/storyboarding, camera technique, *mise-en-scène* etc. Moreover, the Sanyo camera was a poor purchase with significant limitations, made by a technically illiterate Amenábar. Yet, despite its improvised and messy narrative, the film introduced a number of basic elements, many of which would be recycled in later shorts and features, including a fascination for horror and the ghost story; the lone, innocent figure in peril (here fear, hysteria and victimhood are gendered feminine, with Ana arguably reincarnated as Ángela in *Tesis* and Grace in *The Others*); the absent, returning male (physically disfigured, recalling César in *Abre los ojos*, but also perhaps prefiguring the mentally deranged Charles in *The*

Others and the atrophied Ramón Sampedro in *Mar adentro*); the trauma of seeing the love object 'doubled' as monstrous 'other'; the motifs of the female vigil and the haunting, the telephone warning, the car crash, the use of black humour, mistaken identities and the female as survivor (Ana neutralises the monster and overcomes the threat, as do Ángela and Grace). Technically, Gil also experimented with the tracking shot, but lacking a dolly he used an old tricycle (Rodríguez Marchante 2002: 39). Unfortunately, disagreements between Amenábar and Gil over the quality and coherence of their hybrid narrative (including its muffled sound) sparked a furious quarrel and a prolonged separation, leaving the short in limbo. Undaunted, and after his department refused him the use of an editing machine over the summer, Amenábar re-edited the film by buying his own unit (Interview). He also cleaned up the dialogue by revoicing Ana's part with help from drama student and friend Nieves Herranz. He also added a loud ticking clock to the creepy soundtrack, which he finally composed himself on his own Yamaha organ (Rodríguez Marchante 2002: 36). Even at this early stage his concern for sound quality (dialogue, effects and extra-diegetic music) is very noticeable. In 1991 the film was entered for a competition sponsored by Spain's Independent Association of Amateur Filmmakers (Asociación Independiente de Cineastas Amateurs). Quite unexpectedly, being praised for its surreal, comic ending and its promising sound quality, the unplanned short from hell took first prize. Reflecting on his experience, Amenábar comments 'La cabeza era un corto espantoso, de suspense, y ante su ineficacia Mateo Gil y yo optamos por hacer un final super gore, con la protagonista arrancándole la cabeza a otro personaje y la cabeza dando tumbos por toda la casa. La gente se meaba de risa y nos dieron un premio' (La cabeza was an awful suspense short, so useless that Mateo Gil and I decided on adding an excessively gory ending, with the main protagonist tearing off the other character's head, which bounced all over the house. The audience pissed themselves with laughter and they gave us a prize).[1]

Himenóptero (Himenopterus, 1992)

With his self-confidence boosted by competition success (and a substantial cash prize of 300,000 pesetas), Amenábar made peace with Gil. Also, among other bits of kit (including a professional tripod) he bought himself a brand new, state-of-the-art video camera (a Sony

V5000, with an excellent digital zoom and stereo sound) and quickly embarked on his second short, the exotically entitled *Himenóptero*. Initially conceived as another black comedy, it soon developed into a rather more serious and self-reflexive commentary on suspense filmmaking and the manipulation of the spectator, as well as a more controlled and coherent response to the rather chaotic *La cabeza*. Vaguely taking the form of a fake documentary or 'making of' featurette, the film opens by way of a black screen and a superimposed title, which names a setting (I.B. Villa de Madrid, an anonymous school, in reality Amenábar's own alma mater), the month (May) and the precise time, 7.45 pm. The use of black screen (possibly inspired by Spielberg's early features) will quickly become one of Amenábar's trademark opening and closing devices. With a cast of four characters (three female students and the weird, autistic, male camera operator called Bosco, played by Amenábar), this substantial, 31–minute piece follows over several days a group of media students, who hide out in a school after hours to shoot a horror-thriller short, devised by the sadistic, tyrannical female director Silvia (and Amenábar's screen proxy). Unfortunately, though she knows her character must demonstrate a credible fear of provocation and death, the lead actress María (played by Nieves Herranz) refuses to take the shoot seriously and her lack of commitment threatens to sabotage the entire project. Obsessed by achieving a 'corto decente' (decent short) and determined to punish María, cruel Silvia arranges her real death on film, firstly courtesy of Mónica (her co-actress, played by Juana Macías) whose attempt fails and then via a pact of blood with Bosco.

Recalling on a smaller scale the vast geometric patterns of the Overlook Hotel in Kubrick's *The Shining*, the horror setting is a modern, brightly lit, secondary school interior. Though it comprises a series of rather anonymous classrooms, landings, passageways and corridors, Amenábar manages to conjure up (through editing and an electronic soundtrack) a moody labyrinth of doors and hidden spaces, all suggestive of threats and lurking danger. With a further spatial nod to *The Shining*, the credit sequence rolls over a lower-ground-floor setting, i.e. the toilet/shower area, as the caretaker departs and the students emerge from hiding to set up their equipment. Here, expressing her relief at having the school to themselves, Silvia utters the line 'El instituto es nuestro' (The institute is ours), a line which Grace and the children will recycle and echo, a decade later, at the end of *The Others* with: 'La casa es nuestra'.

The opening shot of *Himenóptero* is an extreme, POV (point-of-view) close-up at ground level of a wasp in its death throes (hence the film title), already dissected and then filmed by Bosco, the psychotic cameraman (akin to Powell's youthful Mark Lewis). The film will end symmetrically, spatially and visually, with another insect close-up. Bosco's obsessive desire is to immortalise on videotape the precise moment of death; after chopping up the wasp, he practises again, varying the form of execution. He also films a beetle trapped in a toilet bowl, whose drowning is cross-cut with María taking a shower after being bullied by Silvia and covered in stage blood (Amenábar's homage to Hitchcock and *Psycho*). Here we see one of Amenábar's favourite visual figures, the juxtaposition of reality and fiction, real and fake death, humans and/as insects, as well as his evident cinephilia. On the final day of shooting, with little decent footage, and fearing discovery, Mónica fails to stimulate María sufficiently for her big death scene. Silvia then calls on Bosco to terrorise María for real, using a 'plano secuencia', i.e. one long, unedited, agonising take. Yet, just as he is about to plunge the stage knife into her abdomen (as happens in *Tesis*, during Ángela's dream), Silvia calls him off. She claims that his (genuine) murder attempt was just a joke, a mere fiction (contradicting her earlier assertion that screen fiction 'no es un cachondeo' (i.e. is no laughing matter). The film ends with the three young women in a consoling huddle on the lower stairs (curiously reminiscent of the final pietà in *The Others*) and with a crestfallen Bosco who, denied a human sacrifice, is forced to return to his wriggling insects.

With its much better narrative organisation, inventive camerawork, smoother continuity editing, credible performances, clear depth of field, well-judged music track and clean sound effects, this second short did extremely well at national competitions and film festivals (such as Carabanchel and Elche).[12] Among other plaudits, the film also won first prize and a Best Director award from AICA for 1992. Given its length and very acceptable integration of the main film techniques, it also confirmed that Amenábar was now getting the hang of achieving greater narrative coherence, given the film's circular structure and its symmetrical beginning and ending. On camera Mateo Gil was also improving his use of the tracking shot and high and low angle shots (including the zenith shot) and deploying the digital zoom (a key narrative feature in *Tesis*), for extreme close-ups. Through his editing Amenábar was also learning the value of cross-cutting and the matching of shots, to reinforce diegetic cohesion. He was also keen to display his cinephilia with his 'homage' to Víctor Erice (where Silvia plays dead for María, as Isabel does for Ana in *El espíritu de la colmena* (The Spirit of the Beehive, 1973)) as well as experimenting with sound sourcing. Also Bosco's robotic, intrusive gaze, via the camera eye, recalls not only Powell but also Kubrick. This is evident in the scene where the girls meet in a classroom to talk excitedly among themselves but exclude Bosco; he looks on from the corridor through the window, camera running, with his camera eye recalling the POV of Kubrick's rogue computer HAL, denied aural access to the chatter next door but able to lipread it.

With *Himenóptero*, at a more thematic level, the ontological boundaries between fiction and the real, reality and fantasy, playing dead and real death are effectively blurred. At the same time the spectator also enjoys a pleasurable, double scare. Firstly, we gaze on María, as a voyeur of her own victimhood and, finally, at her genuine fear of being stabbed to death. Secondly, we function as doubles for both Silvia and Bosco, as accomplices in their combined murderous voyeurism and sadistic scopophilia. Positioned behind and in front of the camera, as both voyeur and victim, the spectator enjoys the thrills and spills, confusions and vertigo of an ontological *mise-en-abyme*, which will become a further trademark of Amenábar's horror narratives and his more open, twisty, surprise endings. Also *Himenóptero* undoubtedly stands as the embryo and precursor of *Tesis* (with the educational setting, chases and long corridors, and with Bosco repeated as the villain) as well as a cautionary tale on media manipulation, screen violence and the world of the 'snuff' film. Here, though not mentioned by name, snuff is arguably prefigured by Bosco's taste for female murder on camera, evidenced by the uncut 'long take'.

Luna (Moon, 1994/1995)

The third short, *Luna*, ably illustrates the combined flair of Amenábar and Gil for fusing biographical detail, reworking genre conventions and subtly echoing important social issues of the period. At 30 minutes, and recalling elements of *Duel* (Steven Spielberg, 1971), *The Hitcher* (Robert Harmon, 1986), *Fatal Attraction* (Adrian Lyne, 1987), *Thelma and Louise* (Ridley Scott, 1991) and *Basic Instinct* (Paul Verhoeven, 1992), *Luna* is a psychological thriller, shot in black-and-white, with dialogue recorded partly in direct sound (car interiors) and the rest overdubbed. While maintaining strong verisimilitude by way of the improvised dialogues, the film begins on an upbeat note, only to descend into a nightmare, structured around inversions and reversals of gender and power relations. The threat of violence comes not from the male hitcher but from the pick-up driver, an attractive, manipulative *femme fatale* whose name is withheld. In the original story outline she murders her husband, puts his corpse in the car boot and seeks a hitcher to help bury the body. This action line was dropped in favour of the female serial killer, who preys on different male hitchers and who demands a submissive 'por favor' from her passengers before being allowed to ride.

The short is apparently based on a real incident experienced by Amenábar himself and begins and ends late at night on a dark, lonely, country road. The unnamed female driver (played by Nieves Herranz, who also co-scripted the piece and plays Ángela's sister Sena in *Tesis*) gives a lift to Alberto, whose car has broken down. He is a young encyclopaedia salesman, played by the Amenábar regular, Eduardo Noriega.[13] Following a stop for coffee at a service station and after much verbal fencing and emotional blackmail, Alberto refuses to go home with the insistent driver. Angrily taking a detour to the nearby woods, after a quarrel, she vents her rage at rejection by shooting him in the back as he tries to flee her car. Against the moonlit sky, there is a further struggle in the dark in which a wounded and enraged Alberto severely beats his opponent (echoing César's beating of Núria in *Abre los ojos*). A seemingly triumphal, bloodied kiss, shot in extreme close-up at ground level, between driver and passenger, is followed by the sound of two more gunshots, heard offscreen. The short closes with the same female driver, back on the road (though unseen), picking up her next victim and demanding her signature 'por favor', a supplicatory tag soon to reappear in *Tesis*. In a brief cameo by Mateo Gil, her new victim is uncannily dressed like Alberto.

As Amenábar has indicated (Letter to the author), *Luna* was in large part a stylistic exercise, comprising three longish dialogue scenes, sandwiched between a prologue and epilogue. His aim was to create tension and suspense, not through action but through a verbal duel of 'cat and mouse', ending in devastating violence. However (unlike *Himenóptero*) he dispenses with the intrusive, voyeuristic, subjective camerawork and shoots the dialogue scenes objectively using shot/reverse shot techniques. He also exploits the narrative possibilities of offscreen action and sound (devices consistently exploited in the features), for example, leaving the spectator guessing as to the victim of the final two gunshots.

Drawing heavily upon the sadomasochistic dynamics of the hitcher movie, erotic thriller and film noir, the short introduces a predatory, alienated, *femme fatale* who effectively entraps a weak and indecisive young stranger, as the viewer's screen proxy. As noted above, the piece also stands as the prototype for the violent, sexualised relationship between César and Núria in *Abre los ojos*, as well as the template for the car crash sequence. The female driver is also strongly reminiscent of Alex in *Fatal Attraction*, with whom she shares her loneliness, sexual obsessions, aggression, rage at rejection and a strong sadomasochistic streak, culminating in murder. Yet the reasons for her actions are not clear. She appears not to be an exploited, career woman fighting back against male oppression. And, given virtually no background, she recalls the anonymous, unseen truck driver in Spielberg's television movie *Duel* and the sphinx-like, seemingly motiveless figure of John Ryder in *The Hitcher*. Presenting her as a sadistic serial killer, the short indicates a profound concern with the threat of assertive female sexuality. Moreover, in a period (the early- to mid-1990s) when casual sex could be lethal, the short also seems to suggest that not all men are on the lookout for a fling. (Indeed, trapped in a potentially fatal love triangle, Alberto makes a point of ringing his girlfriend Teresa twice, from the bar, in order to confirm his whereabouts and the reasons for his delay and to provide reassurance of his fidelity.) Amenábar thus seems to have made a kind of anti-sex sex thriller; and, though AIDS is not mentioned by name, the subliminal message is that casual sex spells trouble and even death.

As in the second short, there is also a final twist. Just before the end sequence on the main road, the camera closes in on the unnamed driver's key ring (she has thrown away her car keys as a bizarre gesture of devotion to her victim). A metal plate bears the pseudonym or nom de guerre LUNA in capitals (recalling the close-up on Kane's boyhood sled and the name ROSEBUD, symbol of lost innocence and the trigger to the retrospective narrative). LUNA is the film title, but also a MacGuffin which is ironically echoed earlier in Alberto's dialogue, when he believes he is safely on his way home. It also refers to the female serial killer who works at night but above all to failed romance, alienation, rage and her refusal to accept rejection. And yet the sign fails to solve the puzzle. As with the previous short, the ending, identity and motivations of the young woman are left open, ambiguous, unresolved and a dangling tease for the audience. Also, the threat posed by LUNA, whoever she is, is still active and ongoing, very real and far from being contained. This lack of closure relates to genre (the thriller as cautionary tale about the deceptive nature of appearances) and to audience expectations (the twisty tale reminds the viewer that the serial killer is not male but female, suggesting that biological sex is no guide to gender, sexual or social identity). This play with inversion and identity also vaguely prefigures the type of surprise ending we find in *The Others*, where those who appear to be ghosts are in fact real and those who appear to be living are in fact dead.[14]

Coming Out

In September 2004, coinciding with the release of *Mar adentro*, Amenábar 'came out' publicly in interview and photo shoots in Spain's gay press. He had already done so indirectly, a year earlier, in interview, though no one seems to have noticed. He was replying to a question about the role of the gay review *Shangay Express* on its two hundredth issue in December 2003. Amenábar declared that the review 'ha contribuido a la normalización de los gays y nos ha ayudado a todos a salir del armario poco a poco' (has contributed towards the normalisation of gays and helped everyone come out of the closet, little by little).[15] In Spain, in the world of national celebrities and their gender preferences, this public acknowledgement by Amenábar of his own sexuality would not normally have given rise to major media interest, speculation or press comment. Gay identity in Spain is far less of an issue than it used to be, even for those working in the 'creative industries'. Though his preferences had been well known in filmmaking circles for some time, he had nonetheless jealously guarded his privacy for many years and had always been unhappy about what he regarded as prurient press intrusion into his personal life. His quiet, sober public image did not align itself with any gay stereotype or suggest any linkage with Spaniards who have come out more recently, such as the dancer and choreographer Nacho Duato or the television presenter Jesús Vázquez. Moreover, in his films there are no clearly indentifiable gay themes or characters.[16] With so little to go on, understandably perhaps, his revelation caught the Spanish media and wider society by surprise and for a while the news gave rise to considerable interest. Yet, in *Shangay Express*, he also stated: 'me asusta que la gente pueda meterse en mi vida privada pero, por otro lado, no me importa reconocer que soy gay' (I'm scared that people can intrude into my private life but, on the other hand, I don't mind admitting that I'm gay', reprinted *El Mundo* 2004; see also Sempere 2004: 46). In interview, offering a little background to his personal journey, Amenábar pointed out that he first came out at university, while a student. At that time he told a few good friends and then his family, though not his parents, it seems, until much later. He added that coming to terms with his gayness was not a serious problem, rather quite normal and he did so without difficulty, though he was aware of the wider world in which respect for personal sexual orientation was much less easy to achieve.

In an interview published in the gay magazine *Zero*, in response to a question suggesting that in his thrillers and even in *Mar adentro*, all his characters try to hide their true identities, Amenábar accepted that such a reading was possible but disagreed with it. Indeed, he stated that 'Mi condición sexual y mi cine no tienen demasiada relación. Nunca la he plasmado en una película' (My sexual identity and my cinema are not really closely related. I've never tried to embody this in a film).[17] Rather, in terms of personal tastes, Amenábar emphasises the purposes of his cinema as entertainment and escape, not as coded stories of repressed gay identity. And if he were to tell a gay story, he adds, 'la plantearía primero en términos heterosexuales ... la intentaría ver desde otra perspectiva, por miedo a ser demasiado auto complaciente' (Generelo 2004: 76) (Firstly, I'd pose it in heterosexual terms, try to see it from another perspective, for fear of being too self-indulgent). Clearly Amenábar regards his sexual identity not as a major personal or social issue, despite the fact that his films seem open to queer readings (as the editor of *Zero* makes clear). He has always been very scrupulous about protecting his private life ('me gusta que mi vida privada sea lo mas discreta posible' (I like my private life to be as discreet as possible) and has no wish for it to become a campaigning or polemical rallying point, though he is happy to add his personal solidarity to fellow gays who are yet to come out (2004: 77). 'todo lo que contribuye a normalizar la situación de los gays, me parece perfecto' (everything that helps normalise gay identity is fine by me). And while he prefers to control his public image, he is also anxious to be consistent: 'parte de esa imagen es ser coherente con lo que hago y digo' (2004: 81) (part of that image is to be consistent with what I say and do'). Hence Amenábar's quiet, cool and unfussy 'coming out'.

Notes

1 If he were ever to make a political film, says Amenábar, it would probably deal with the Pinochet coup and its consequences (Rodríguez Marchante 2002: 90).

2 Miguel Polo, 'Entrevista a Alejandro Amenábar', *Interviú*, Madrid (17 February 1997), 43–4.

3 Elena Pita, 'Entrevista a Alejandro Amenábar', *La Revista de El Mundo*, Madrid (16 February 1997), 15–16.

4 Curiously, the musical origins of Amenábar's interest in cinema emerged without him ever having taken any formal instruction in piano or music theory. It was arguably his practical experience, including much trial and error on guitar and electronic keyboards (including a Bontempi, Casiotone and several Yamaha units), which would underpin his musical and scoring abilities (Interview).

5 The Smith household became something of a refuge and oasis for the Amenábar youngsters, a source of escapism and distraction, especially since the Smith family had a video player and access to Hollywood films on tape (borrowed from the airbase), all of which in the early 1980s was still quite a novelty in Spain.

6 Between the ages of 9 and 13, Amenábar's adolescent cinephilia was based almost exclusively on video viewing. It was only from the age of 14, again thanks to his brother (who accompanied him), that he began frequenting the cinema in Madrid, especially the Cine Covadonga. The latter specialised in American and European double-bills of horror features, such as big screen versions of *The Exorcist*, *The Evil Dead* (Sam Raimi, 1980) and possibly films by Dario Argento such as *Phenomena* (1985), though Amenábar's memory is particularly hazy regarding his familiarity with Italian horror (Interview). For Amenábar, even at this stage, the attraction of such fare was arguably 'cinema as refuge' from the enclosure of home but also as a portal to danger, fantasy and forbidden pleasures, aesthetic and emotional. It was also a place where privileged, but repressed, young men could begin to make sense of the outside world, to encounter staged representations of sex, love and death and to see what might be expected of gendered behaviour, though relayed largely through American rather than Spanish or European narratives.

7 Mateo Gil already knew the basics of photography, an area in which Amenábar initially lacked any practical knowledge or skill and was anxious to learn. Also Gil's unusual, indeed esoteric, interest in Soviet montage cinema via Dovzhenko (rather than Vertov, Eisenstein or Pudovkin) represented the sort of intellectual challenge which Amenábar craved and which was lacking on their degree course. The same could be said, of course, of Amenábar's more 'popular' tastes in contemporary Hollywood commercial cinema, another important area also absent from their programme (Interview). Paradoxically, for his first feature,

the rather more 'arty' and intellectual of the pair, Mateo Gil, decided to accept an 'encargo' (based on a novel by Juan Bonilla, with the same title) which he transformed into a commercial genre film, the 'video gaming' thriller, *Nadie conoce a nadie* (Nobody Knows Anybody, 1999), for which Amenábar composed the score.

8 Following the release of *Tesis* in April 1996, public controversy arose over Amenábar's alleged 'fail' in Film Direction, because of the surname of one of his film characters, Jorge Castro. This coincided with the real name of the lecturer (Antonio Castro) who had allegedly failed him unfairly in Direction. Amenábar thus named his fictional Professor of Media Psychology Jorge Castro, as a deliberate 'dig' at his old Faculty nemesis. In a long, commented interview, published in *Interviú* in March 1997, the real Antonio Castro disputed Amenábar's version of events. Castro also claimed that he had not taught Amenábar Direction in the period 1993–95, but had taught a course on 'Narrativa' (Film narrative) and here he conceded that he might well have failed the youngster. Castro also claimed that Amenábar might have mixed up the two courses, replacing Narrative with Direction. But, he asked, was this an innocent slip or a deliberate, motivated error on Amenábar's part? Castro alleged the latter, in view of a wider political struggle developing at the time concerning the controversial funding and reopening of the National Film School, in which he claims Amenábar spoke in favour of it and against his old University department.

9 Following Amenábar's lead, during this period, Mateo Gil directed his first two shorts: *Antes del beso* (Before the Kiss, 1993) and *Soñé que te mataba* (I Dreamed I Killed You, 1994). He also appeared in main acting roles in his own films, with Amenábar taking up duties on the camera and post-production, including editing, sound and music.

10 Carlos Aguilar argues that the film was not Piquer's best work, indeed he describes it as a 'subproducto' (trashy spin-off), based on a Lovecraft story, starring Frank Finlay, which bombed commercially. He puts much of the blame on Arthur's weak models and poor special effects. See Aguilar 2005: 16.

11 Paula Ponga, 'El más listo de la clase: Alejandro Amenábar', *Fotogramas*, 1859 (December 1997), 118. It is worth adding that, at a very early stage, a version of the extra-diegetic, background music for *La cabeza* was composed by one of Amenábar's classmates, Alfredo Alonso. Unfortunately, when it was completed, the main theme was excessively sweet, melodic and romantic and therefore inappropriate for a horror short, which required a degree of tension and suspense before the comic ending. This suggests to me that Amenábar did not see himself, at least initially, as the obvious composer of his own music scores. Yet, in the absence of appropriate material, he had no inhibitions in trying his own hand. So, with his Yamaha organ, a cheap reverb unit and a very basic

multi-track recorder, he composed the music himself (Interview).

12 In light of the praise for his soundtrack on *La cabeza*, Amenábar did not hesitate to take on the much more challenging task of scoring the 31 minutes of *Himenóptero*. He did so on a newly-purchased Yamaha keyboard sequencer, with five in-built recording tracks, though he only later found out how they worked (Interview). Such additional technical knowledge allowed him to produce the music for Guillermo Fernández's short *Al lado del Atlas* (Next to the Atlas, 1994).

13 This was a job that Mateo Gil had actually done as a student and which he revisits in his 1998, multi-prize-winning short *Allanamiento de morada* (Breaking and Entering), which also boasts a subtitle: 'Basado en 1.749.358 casos reales (sólo en nuestro país)', (based on 1,749,358 real cases (just in our country)).

14 *Luna* won prizes for Best Film and Best Actress at the AICA competition of 1995. It also won the Berlanga script award of the same year, as noted elsewhere. The prize, in this case, involved the shooting on film of the winning script, funded by a well-known Madrid production company (Central de Producciones Audiovisuales). This translated into a much shorter version of *Luna* (12 minutes), but this time in colour and on 35mm film. With regard to the score, Amenábar was initially persuaded by a friend to use a small student orchestra from Madrid's Music Conservatory. But when the day came to record what he had transcribed from his own keyboard notations, he felt the tuning and cohesion of the amateur orchestra were far from perfect. In fact they sounded out of tune. In the end he mixed some of the recorded orchestral score with material he himself had already produced on the keyboard. Also, he decided that, unless he could rely on the services of a professional orchestra, he would continue to score his films himself and produce his own and other commissioned soundtracks. Also the 35mm film version of *Luna* (in which Amenábar is replaced in an acting role by Joserra Cardiñanos as the barman) has not been released.

15 These declarations were reprinted in *El Mundo* (15 September 2004).

16 However, there are occasional hints, such as the poster for *My Own Private Idaho* (Gus Van Sant, 1999, with its focus on marginal sexualities, especially male prostitution), hanging over Ángela's bed in *Tesis*. There is also the dialogue line in *The Others* 'Salid del armario, salid del armario' (Come out of the wardrobe, come out of the wardrobe), which was delivered by an adult voice addressed to the children but was later dropped. In this connection, Amenábar observes: 'conscientemente no he querido ir sembrando cosas o que se entrevea algo' (on a conscious level, I haven't really wanted to plant clues or drop any hints, Generelo 2004, 76).

17 See Jesús Generelo, 'De Amenábar a Alejandro. La verdad desde dentro', *Zero*, 67 (September 2004), 74–81.

3

The violent image: *Tesis*

It seems clear that, sooner or later, Amenábar's evident commitment to developing film narrative (already seen in his two 30–minute shorts) would find an outlet in a feature film. By a mixture of chance and design, his big break came early in his career thanks to the intervention of José Luis Cuerda, the left-wing auteur and the person credited with discovering Spain's filmmaking prodigy of the 1990s.[1] In 1993 Amenábar received a message from Cuerda, who wished to congratulate him on the success of *Himenóptero*. The director also wanted to know if he had any more ideas for film projects, whether shorts or features. However, Cuerda would never have heard of Amenábar at that time had it not been for another key figure in the chain of the youngster's discovery who, hitherto, has been overlooked. I refer to the academic and painter Juan José Gómez Molina, Professor of Drawing and Fine Art at Madrid's Complutense University and an old friend and staff colleague of Cuerda's from their days at Salamanca University in the mid-1980s.[2] It was Gómez who sent Cuerda a copy of *Himenóptero*, in which his daughter (Raquel) played the sadistic female director and whose label credited Amenábar as sole author of the piece. The concerned father wanted his friend's opinion about Raquel's performance and whether she had any prospects as a film actress. Cuerda was impressed by the young woman's acting abilities, but absolutely astonished by the quality of the film, mistakenly believing it to be the work of one uniquely talented individual. According to Cuerda, 'el corto estaba también interpretado y además fotografiado, musicado, escrito y dirigido por una sola persona ... todos estos trabajos hechos con impecable solvencia y con muchísimo talento' (Sempere 2000: 25) (as well as the acting, the short was also photographed, scored, written and directed by one person ... all these tasks carried out with impressive skill and a great deal of talent).

When Gómez revealed that the director was in fact a 19-year-old film student, Cuerda was taken aback: '¡Joder! Es un genio del renacimiento ... Si él cree que le puedo echar una mano en algo, que venga a mis rodajes aunque sea a mirar' (Vera 2002: 48) (Good grief! The lad's a Renaissance genius ... If he ever needs any help, tell him to drop by while I'm filming, even if it's only to take a look). In fact, Amenábar and his filmmaking side-kick Mateo Gil visited Cuerda on several occasions shortly after, while he was filming on the sets of *Tocando fondo* (Rock Bottom, 1993) and *Así en el cielo como en la tierra* (As on Earth as It Is in Heaven, 1994). Amenábar also gave him a copy of *Luna* (which Cuerda subsequently used as collateral when seeking finance for *Tesis*). From these early visits, and from the discussions which emerged, so impressed was Cuerda by Amenábar's 'jack-of-all-trades' authorship, his cinephilia and his sheer passion for filmmaking that he asked the youngster to send him a script for a feature with a view to 'moverlo' (Rodríguez Marchante 2002: 25) i.e. getting it produced. This was *Tesis*.

Over the summer of 1994, while supposedly studying for exam retakes (including Direction) and with Bernard Herrmann's score for *Psycho* playing in the background, Amenábar wrote up the definitive version of a script idea begun over two years earlier, entitled 'La tesis' (The Thesis).[3] The reworked and updated screenplay brought together in one story the topic of snuff movies and screen violence as mass entertainment, the manipulative power of the visual media and the university environment (which had let him down so badly) as a setting for criminal activity. Re-titled simply *Tesis* (The Thesis), and on advice from Cuerda, the script was then sent out to several production companies in Madrid. These included Camelot Pelis – for whom Amenábar had done soundtrack work on *Al lado del Atlas* (Next to the Atlas, Guillermo Fernández, short, 1994) – and Central de Producciones Audiovisuales (CPA), headed by Rafael Díaz Salgado, which had produced Cuerda's previous two films. It also made the 35mm colour film version of Amenábar's *Luna* in 1995, as part of the Luis García Berlanga Script Prize. Unfortunately, neither company showed any serious interest in *Tesis* and the project appeared to stall. Feeling disillusioned and ready to give up, Amenábar finally decided to ring Cuerda and asked him to look at the script.

After three days Cuerda replied positively, saying that he himself would try to raise finance for the film. Though he had directed ten features over the course of a twenty-year career in film and television, he reminded Amenábar that he had no money of his own, had never financed any of his own projects and was not a film producer. Indeed, just like his young protégé, facing his first full-length feature, Cuerda was also a total novice. Even so, he saw in *Tesis* 'una película pequeña, factible, para un productor novato como yo' (Ubeda-Portugués 2001: 216) (a small, manageable film for a first-time producer like me). On a more positive note, Cuerda was very well connected to official agencies, television companies, distributors and a whole range of film professionals. He was thus in a strong position to negotiate television pre-sales, government subsidies and distributor advances and advise on casting as well as a film crew.[4] Moreover, the production of *Tesis* gave Cuerda the opportunity to resurrect an old idea from the 1980s, i.e. the creation of a new, co-operative-style, production company, called Las Producciones del Escorpión (Scorpion Productions), ostensibly to make films by newcomers, beginning with Amenábar's first full-length feature. So, apart from being Spain's youngest ever feature director, Amenábar enjoyed the added distinction of having a new production company created with him in mind. Also, after *Tesis*, Cuerda offered the youngster a contract for two more films to be produced by Scorpion Productions. For a complete novice, at least in Spain, a three-film deal of the type offered by Cuerda was extremely unusual in the rest of the national industry.

Amenábar's idea of using 'snuff' as a pretext to critique Spain's trash television and increasing levels of screen violence (and, along the way, to portray some of his teachers as deviants, criminals and murderers) seems to have crystallised definitively through his reading of the last chapter of Román Gubern's study of extreme cinema and visual perversions (Rodríguez Marchante 2002: 49). Gubern's *La imagen pornográfica y otras perversiones ópticas* (1989) offers an analysis of taboo visual imagery across a range of subtypes, including erotic, pornographic, religious, proletarian, Nazi and snuff sources. The final chapter deals with 'la imagen cruel' (the cruel image), and the public's fascination with images of death, ranging from suicides on camera and execution clips to examples of 'snuff'. However, Gubern does not limit his view of such exploitation imagery solely to these instances of physical cruelty and murder. Rather, he widens his definition of perverse imagery to take into account the 'emotional pornography' of exploitative reality shows, in which he includes the Mexican *telenovela* (or soap opera).[5] It is this sort of lowbrow, trash television, rather than snuff films per se, which seems to have annoyed and deeply upset Amenábar (in terms of its exploitation values and flagrant voyeurism). Thanks to Gubern, Amenábar found the basis of a viable critique of trash television through 'snuff' (which was virtually unknown in Spain at the time) and which, as shown in *Tesis*, becomes part of the discursive flow of mainstream, scheduled, news and current affairs output because of its alleged 'public interest'.

In this chapter my main focus lies in the multiple interconnections between *Tesis* and genre. I deal with Amenábar's approach to Hitchcock and the suspense thriller. I seek to locate *Tesis* within the urban legend and traditions of 'snuff' filmmaking. I explore the film's main intertextual sources, including *The Silence of the Lambs* (1995, Jonathan Demme) and *Historias del Kronen* (1995, Montxo Armendáriz). I also consider the ways in which Amenábar deals with the gendered gaze and screen violence, and how he works through the contradictions between our voyeuristic fascination for violence and our ethical revulsion and disgust at what we see and hear. Additionally, I explore the kinds of film narration employed in *Tesis*, the ways in which Amenábar establishes his modes of audience address and the extent to which the film follows the basic rules of Hollywood storytelling. I also consider briefly the notorious Alcasser case, whose shameful treatment on Spanish television (by both public and private channels) formed a key ingredient in a rather chaotic and unregulated media context which Amenábar sought to denounce in the film. Before exploring these areas in more detail, I also provide a plot synopsis and seek to outline the film's contexts of production and reception.

Production and Reception

The overall shooting budget for *Tesis* was approximately 120 million pesetas or €720,000, rising to 170 million pesetas or just over €1 million, if we include additional expenditure, such as print copies for festivals, travel costs, press books and the purchase of extra film stock (see Vera 2002: 43). The project benefited from a 45 million peseta subsidy from ICAA (Instituto de Cinematografía y de las Artes AudioVisuales or National Film Institute), with the rest of the money provided mostly through distributor advances (Sogepaq, which handled international distribution and contributed 50 million pesetas and UIP Spain (United International Pictures), which organised the national release, 12 million pesetas.[6] A remaining portion of approximately 15–20 million pesetas came primarily from the partners of Cuerda's new production company, who invested in the venture by waiving their fees and by supplying equipment mostly gratis. These 'socios' included the executive producer (Emiliano Otegui), second unit head (Julio Madurga), the sound engineers (Goldstein and Steinberg) and Cuerda himself. They would be paid according to the size of their investment, once the film went into profit; by contrast, Cuerda's newly established co-operative, Scorpion Productions, received no income. Other investors, who took only half salary, included the cinematographer (the famous Hans Burmann), the art director (Wolfgang Burmann) and the editor (María Elena Sáenz de Rozas) as well as Amenábar himself (who took very little money), all of whom became associate producers (Vera 2002: 43). The actors (mostly unknown and untried) were paid minimal rates, apart from Spain's iconic child star Ana Torrent, who played Ángela, and the veteran local actor Xavier Elorriaga, who played Castro.[7] In many ways the film was a truly collective undertaking, with director, actors and many of the crew all risking their own money in a modestly budgeted project (See Vera 2002: 42–3; on Eduardo Noriega and Fele Martínez, see also Perriam, 2003: 174–85).

An extremely tight summer shooting schedule began on 21 August and lasted until 27 September 1995. The production took full advantage of real locations, including the faculty buildings of Ciencias de la Información (Information Sciences) and Farmacia (Pharmacy, connected by their filthy, narrow, underground tunnels) at Madrid's Complutense University. Amenábar managed to obtain permission to use these locations over the summer of 1995 without being charged. As noted earlier, he was genuinely grateful to the University authorities. Given the limited budget, actors and crew worked exhausting shifts of ten to twelve hours per day (from 8 am to 8 pm), five days a week, plus five hours on Saturdays (Vera 2002: 25). Also, feeling pressurised by Cuerda and the hugely experienced film crew he had assembled, a very nervous Amenábar stuck rigidly to what had been pre-prepared on storyboards by Sergio Rozas, a student friend and budding art designer.[8] However, because of financial constraints, not all scripted scenes were shot; in fact, some 48 scenes in all were eliminated (Rodríguez Marchante 2002: 61). Even so, Amenábar shot between 20 and 25 set ups per day (a huge number) while putting enormous additional strain on his actors by denying them retakes, apart from his star Ana Torrent, who struggled to decipher what motivated Ángela. In the process, Amenábar consumed enormous amounts of raw film (an extra cost not allowed for in the budget) which created an initial rough cut of near epic proportions. Mateo Gil suggests a first edit of almost 160 minutes, which was finally whittled down to 125 minutes, including credits; unfortunately, according to Gil 'el guión quedó masacrado' (Vera 2002: 33) (the script ended up in tatters).

On completion, alongside Isabel Coixet's English-spoken *Cosas que nunca te dije* (Things I Never Told You, 1995), *Tesis* was selected by Spain's National Film Institute (ICAA) to represent the country at the Berlin Film Festival, held in February 1996, in the 'Panorama' section for new directors. The film attracted much enthusiastic feedback and generally positive reviews (see, for example, see Carlos F. Herederc (1996: 32) and Paloma Leyra (1996: 72). However, in terms of the film's commercial release, it would have made better sense to have scheduled the Spanish premiere just after this very helpful international festival exposure. Unfortunately, this did not happen since the Executive Producer Emiliano Otegui, on behalf of Las Producciones del Escorpión, was unhappy with the film's distributor for Spain (UIP) over its choice of theatres, fearing the film would die within a week or two in inappropriate locales (Vera 2002: 45). Hence the decision to wait until early April 1996, when more appropriate and attractive venues became vacant (Rodríguez Marchante 2002 61). Meanwhile, a young, and by now 24-year-old, first-time filmmaker, encouraged by a successful but enormously costly visit to Germany (part-subsidised by ICAA and where he also used the internet for the first time), toured radio and television stations in Spain trying desperately to sustain a modicum of interest and public awareness for *Tesis*.

Released on 12 April 1996, on 40 prints and shown mainly in Madrid and Barcelona (Vera 2002: 45; Palacio and Cortell 1997: 965), *Tesis* did not achieve anything like satisfactory distribution, particularly in Spain's provinces. In Valencia, for example, the film was withdrawn after one week (*El Periódico*, 29 January 1997: 57). It ended the year in Madrid in only one art house locale, the Salas Renoir, playing to student audiences in the 'sesión golfa' (late-night showing). So, contrary to a great deal of hype and mythology, *Tesis* was hardly a runaway commercial success. In fact box office results during 1996 were disappointing, 'solamente satisfactorios' (only satisfactory, Palacio and Cortell 1997: 965), despite pre-sales of 100 million pesetas (Payán 2001: 45). However, all this would change by the end of the following year in the wake of the film's remarkable and wholly unexpected success at Spain's 1996 Goya Awards (staged 25 January 1997). Nominated in eight categories, *Tesis* won in seven (including Best Film, Best Young Director, Best Original Script, Best New Actor, Best Editing, Best Production Supervision and Best Sound Track). This was extremely rare for a film which had had a very poor commercial career initially and which had dipped below the radar well before the Goya nominations were announced on 27 December 1996. However, with seven Goya awards, such emphatic official plaudits and the ensuing free media publicity allowed the producers to practically relaunch the film nationally and internationally, hitting a far wider and more diverse market, well beyond its already proven appeal to Spain's under-25, teen and student audiences. This relaunch also led to the film's quite unprecedented success in the home video market and a much more self-confident and effective re-release campaign in most Spanish cities, which capitalised on Goya-driven publicity. By the end of 1997 *Tesis* had made over 200 million pesetas. And by 2000, apart from the sale of the remake rights to Jim Sheridan (of Hell's Kitchen, which have never been taken up), the film had been distributed in over forty countries worldwide (doing particularly well in Germany and Japan). In Spain, overall, it attracted 854,735 spectators and accumulated €2.65 million at the box office (source: mcu. es). But, as Amenábar points out, over its screen career the film has always done far better abroad than at home (Rodríguez Marchante 2002: 45).

Alcasser

On the 27 January 1993 the remains of three teenage girls, buried in a shallow grave, were found near the Tous reservoir, in the Valencia region. The bodies, in an advanced state of decomposition, belonged to Miriam García, Antonia (Toñi) Gómez and Desirée Hernández, who had disappeared on 13 November 1992 on their way to a discotheque. It seems that the girls had hitched a ride to the disco and were taken there by several men whom they probably knew but then they simply vanished. Their parents, from Alcasser (Alcacer in Castilian), a small town near Valencia, mounted a three-month search for their daughters, which developed into a nationwide media campaign to find them. The discovery of their mutilated bodies and their appalling state had a truly traumatic impact on the national consciousness of the whole of

Spain. However, with many television crews converging on Alcasser, desperate to secure interviews and live images of grieving parents, a national tragedy was exacerbated by the deeply prurient and irresponsible media coverage. The autopsy evidence showed that the girls had been put into an old shed, tied up and brutally beaten, with each subjected to multiple rapes and torture before being murdered with a single shot to the head from a 9mm pistol. The two main suspects were Antonio Anglés (with a serious criminal record for violent assault and Miquel Ricart (a petty robber), though local journalists suggested that these two young men were merely 'fall guys' for other more important criminals involved. The police investigation was chaotic and incompetent, papers and forensic evidence went missing and suspects' confessions were continually being altered. Inexplicably, Anglés was allowed to escape and has never been found. Ricart remains the only suspect to have been convicted, with a sentence of 170 years in jail. In 2005 the parents of the three girls finally received a compensation award from the Spanish state of €600,000 each in respect of legal failures and their suffering during the incredibly protracted thirteen years of the case (*El Mundo*, 4 July 2005: 45).[9]

The Alcasser murders became notorious in Spain in the early and mid-1990s, not only as embarrassing proof of comprehensive judicial bungling in an extreme multiple murder case but also for the sensationalist media coverage. As noted earlier, Spain's three new national commercial, television channels (Antena 3, Canal Plus and Tele 5, launched in 1990), as well as new local channels, were engaged in a fierce ratings war. The trial itself was covered by Canal 9 Valencia on a daily basis, with the most lurid aspects of the coverage being continually reheated and recycled by the main national news channels. And in the evenings, various television chat shows featured items on Alcasser, illustrated by explicit photographs of the girls' bodies, preceded by the usual 'health warnings'. We find something rather similar in the programme *Justicia y ley* (Justice and Law), which appears at the end of *Tesis*. In interview, Amenábar has denied that *Tesis* was influenced in any direct way by the Alcasser case. However, he has said that the film responded more generally to issues of media exploitation of the victims and their gruesome deaths and the 'emotional pornography' of prurient interviews held with their distraught parents on national television (interview). The latter included those conducted by Pepe Navarro with Fernando García (father of Miriam) or *Esta noche cruzamos el Mississippi* (Tonight We Cross the Mississippi, a very successful late-night magazine/chat show, on Tele 5, which ran from 1995 to 1997).[10] What is also intriguing is the fact that, following the release of *Tesis* in April 1996, many people in Spain began to 'reread' the Alcasser murders in relation to the multiple 'snuff' killings represented in *Tesis*. The film fed an appetite for explanations, however unfounded and conspiratorial, since it seemed to suggest the possibility that the rapes and murders of the young girls might have been deliberately planned in order to be recorded as a snuff film. So far, however, the idea that Alcasser was Spain's first authentic snuff murder and filmed account, 'ordered' by shadowy, powerful figures, appears to exist solely in the public imagination.

Synopsis

Ángela is on her way to University one morning. As it pulls into the station, the local train in which she is travelling hits a man and cuts him in half. The man has apparently committed suicide by jumping onto the line. Over the intercom the conductor indicates that the train has stopped short of the platform; the guard then advises passengers to move through two carriages to disembark but not to look at the body. Walking along the platform with other travellers, Ángela feels a sudden urge to gaze at the gruesome remains of the severed body but is physically prevented from doing so by a station employee.

Ángela is a final-year film studies student (Imagen y Sonido) at university in Madrid, in the early stages of planning her thesis on audiovisual violence. After showing him an outline of her project (which he regards as very measured and objective), she asks her elderly supervisor, the asthmatic Professor Figueroa, to search the Faculty archives on her behalf for films containing extreme violence. She also enlists the help of a classmate, the grungy weirdo Chema, who invites her to see his collection of soft- and hard-core porn as well as extreme, horror-gore movies. At his flat (a veritable shrine to film gore), Chema shows Ángela 'Fresh Blood', a compilation, 'mondo' tape containing images of executions, autopsies etc. At precisely the same moment, Figueroa stumbles upon an underground video storeroom (unlocked), picks up a tape at random (number 001) and leaves to watch it in a basement projection room. The following morning, Ángela finds him dead, perhaps of a heart seizure provoked by an asthma attack; fascinated by Figueroa's corpse, she touches his face (an action she repeats later with a screen image of a face). Rather than alert anyone, she removes the tape that has probably caused Figueroa's death and takes it home to watch. However, her fearful anticipation of what it might contain visually is so overwhelming that she is able only to listen to the soundtrack, on which she hears a woman's blood-curdling screams during a terrible beating.

Following the announcement in class of Figueroa's death, Chema works out that Ángela has the offending tape; they decide to watch it together. It is a snuff movie, a video recording of a real murder, in which a young woman is tortured and butchered by a masked assailant, dressed in black. Analysing the texture of the image, Chema recognises technical details about the type of camera used in the recording (especially the use of the digital zoom, a key feature of a Sony XT500) and notices (through almost imperceptible jump cuts) that the tape has been cleverly edited to hide the name of the perpetrator, someone known to the victim. In fact Chema thinks he knows the identity of the victim, a media student called Vanessa who disappeared two years earlier. Some time later Ángela sees a young man in the Faculty cafeteria called Bosco, who is also using an XT500 to film his girlfriend, Yolanda. Ángela tries to follow him but he chases her and corners her. He reveals that he knew Vanessa and went out with her. Ángela also discovers that the Faculty bought a batch of video cameras like Bosco's. She tries to tell Chema, but cannot find him.

With Figueroa dead, Ángela is assigned a new thesis supervisor called Jorge Castro, Professor of Media Psychology, who arranges a meeting with her to talk about her work. During an increasingly tense conversation, Castro confronts her with a CCTV recording of her theft of the snuff tape and demands its return. Warned by Chema to flee, Ángela runs out of Castro's office, fearing she might be the next snuff victim. The rest of the narrative comprises a series of false leads and red herrings, designed to create confusion over the identity of the serial killer. At the same time, Ángela is reluctant to involve the police or her parents and for unexplained reasons increasingly puts herself in harm's way and is trapped by Castro. At a major turning point she is rescued by Chema, who manages to kill Castro. Later, she rescues her sister Sena at a disco by (deliberately) falling into Bosco's clutches. In the dramatic denouement, as the snuff victim for a second time, she turns the tables on Bosco and shoots him, saving Chema in the process.

The epilogue of the film takes place in a hospital ward where Chema is recovering from his wounds. Ángela pays him a visit, brings him a gift of a book and, when she leaves, says she has abandoned her thesis. All the patients are glued to the television, where a reality show, *Justicia y ley* (Justice and Law) presents a report on the six victims of the serial killer, 'calling them las chicas snuff' (the snuff girls) and – invoking the defence of the public interest – promises to show clips from a snuff film. At this point, rather than follow the report and just as the news presenter warns the audience to prepare for the snuff material, Chema abandons his bed, runs after Ángela and leaves the hospital with her, thereby resuming their friendship or so it seems.

Film narration

Mateo Gil has argued that earlier generations of Spanish film directors, especially those now in their forties and fifties, are remarkably clever and well-read, 'Pero son narradores defectuosos. No controlan cuestiones de ritmo, de suspense y la planificación suele ser torpe' (Vera 2002: 36) (But they are poor narrators. They cannot control matters of rhythm and suspense and their organisation is usually clumsy). By contrast, 'la nueva generación narra mucho mejor' (the new generation narrates far better), i.e. young directors like himself and Amenábar are technically far more competent, are prepared to take chances and realise that 'el cine también es espectáculo' (Vera 2002: 36–7) (cinema also implies spectacle). In relation to its structure and modes of narration, *Tesis* tends to be viewed as broadly consistent with Hollywood story-telling principles. Amenábar himself acknowledges the influence of Hollywood style in the film's formal organisation and the fact that its main 'horror-thriller' intertexts are mostly American (Rodríguez Marchante 2002: 49–50). Talking of *Tesis*, he admits: 'Se puede decir que en *Tesis* he copiado de los americanos' (Vera 2002: 21) (You could say that in *Tesis* I've copied from the Americans). But to what extent does *Tesis* follow the principles of Hollywood film narration?

Bearing in mind the debates in film studies in the 1980s and 1990s concerning perceived shifts in narrational priorities from classical to post-classical Hollywood, Kristen Thompson argues that 'the ideal American film still centres around a well-structured, carefully-motivated series of events that the spectator can comprehend relatively easily' (1999: 8). Hollywood style thus continues to value such narrational principles as causality (cause and effect logic), clarity, unity, forward narrative progress, goal-oriented characters (through which action and agency are projected), verismilitude and a strong degree of closure. In short it is narrative form which has primacy over cinematic representation, story over style. Of course this is not to say that all Hollywood movies are perfectly closed, coherent narratives dominated by tight narrative causality, where all the holes are plugged and loose ends tied up. This is merely an ideal. In any Hollywood film we may well find inconsistencies, gaps, poor causality, unwarranted delays, right down to mistakes in continuity.[11]

In *Tesis*, with its symmetrical prologue and epilogue and the duplication of diegetic voiceovers (the guard's initial warning not to look at the body on the tracks, the final 'health warning' before transmission of the snuff clips in the reality show), the impression of circularity and closure appears strong. This is reinforced by the double causal structure and the satisfactory resolution of the two action lines: the hunt for and disposal of the serial killer and the apparent teen romance. Indeed, the solving of the first action line triggers the resolution of the other (Chema and Ángela finally get together, it seems, and she learns her moral lesson about the dangers of her masochistic voyeurism). The epilogue scene also allows Amenábar to move the film outside of the teen narrative and flag up his editorial concerns about the power of the look, youth alienation, screen violence and the ethical responsibilities of both television programmers and their audiences.

However, despite what Amenábar has called his 'guión de hierro' or iron script (Heredero 1997: 106), *Tesis* does not quite run like clockwork. As Mateo Gil has tried to explain, when compared to the classic template of the three-act script (with two main turning points before the finale), *Tesis* emerges as a 'mejunje extraño' (strange concoction) in which the turning points are not clearly set up (Vera 2002: 33). This is especially the case, so Gil argues, in the final quarter of the film, after the 'false climax' in which Chema accidentally shoots Castro. This is a moment when it is by no means clear whether the film has come to an end. In fact it continues for another 30 minutes, adding a series of confusing and laboured subplot elements. Rather than condense the action, the narration struggles to maintain tension and spectator interest when the identity of the serial killer is increasingly obvious. And, by unduly stringing out the ending, Amenábar arguably reveals a certain lack of experience and flexibility in being unable to cut quickly to a resolution. As Gil observes, 'estás esperando que acabe y se sigue alargando' (Vera 2002: 33) (you're waiting for it to end and it just keeps going). Such problems of retardation and narrative excess thus tend to weaken the impact of the final revelation in Bosco's garage. Also, in relation to verisimilitude and motivation, the three main fight scenes in the film (Chema versus Castro in the tunnels, Chema versus Bosco in the house/garage and the final shooting) are poorly choreographed and at least in the first two instances lack realism. Also, as Gil mentions, where did Ángela pick up the knife with which she cuts her bonds and where did she learn how to fire a gun? (Vera 2002: 33). In mainstream Hollywood filmmaking these imperfections of plotting and character motivation would have been fixed in order to ensure clear causality and plausibility.

In other respects *Tesis* also seems to diverge somewhat from the codes of Hollywood narration and contains features more properly associated with art film narration. For example, some of Amenábar's cause-effect linkages are rather vague and tenuous: Bosco's girlfriend Yolanda seems to disappear from view, as does Ángela's sister Sena, without explanation; also, the official investigations into Figueroa's death, as well as the murders of Castro and Bosco, are all loose ends which are left dangling. Another aspect which diverges significantly from Hollywood style is that of the enigmatic characters and their lack of background. In Hollywood narrative, characters provide the main sources of motivation, based on their traits and goals; these need to be carefully laid down and consistently developed. If characters then behave strangely, i.e. out of character, this needs explaining. By comparison, Amenábar's characters appear seriously underdeveloped and lacking in motivation. As noted earlier, this is probably due in large part to the extensive cuts made to the film in the editing process. This applies, for example, to Ángela whose introversion, masochism, fascination with death and 'fatal attraction' to Bosco emerge without clear background support or symptomatic behaviour. With Chema we know very little about him; about all we do know is that his parents do not live in Madrid and that his flat belonged to his recently deceased grandmother. As for Bosco (who uses his parents' bungalow), he is a virtual blank page, an enigma, with no background traits at all to explain his charisma, charm, misogyny, anger, God complex and sadistic, sexualised violence on women. Such ambiguous and diffuse characterisations suggest that Bordwell may be right in saying that the art film is a cinema of psychological effects in search of causes (1979/2002: 96).[12]

Audience address

In *Tesis*, despite its strong commitment to realism, Amenábar is continually managing and manipulating our involvement with and relation to the film text. One of his favourite moves, repeated in all five main features thus far, is his habit of opening the film using a black screen to attract our attention (in *Ágora* he uses a star field). Having done so, he then introduces a voice from within the film's diegetic world which appears to address the spectator and the screen character(s) simultaneously. We hesitate for a moment to check that we are the correct addressees of the message. This kind of opening seeks a double effect: On the one hand, it tries to confuse and destabilise the spectator's positioning in relation to the diegetic world portrayed on screen, blurring the line separating the two. On the other, it functions as a stimulus to our aural as well as our scopic drives. We are thus engaged by being (in) directly hailed from the screen. Such obvious manipulation makes us aware of our viewing activity and also draws attention to Amenábar's narratorial ability and power to both promise and deny visual and aural information and hence control our viewing pleasures. In short, as Jacques Terassa argues, Amenábar foregrounds the very ontological status of cinema itself while at the same time immersing the spectator in diegetic worlds of extreme situations.[13] Another widely exploited device is that of offscreen space and the ways in which Amenábar attempts to suggest the presence of things in the six main offscreen areas (i.e. that space which lies beyond the four edges of the frame, the space behind the set and the space behind the camera).[14] In *Tesis* Amenábar frequently alludes to these spaces by using the technical vocabulary of filmmaking such as 'shot/reverse shot' combinations and reaction shots, which are to be inserted into the taped interview with Bosco. At the same time he relies heavily on the use of ellipsis and places the most explicit violence offscreen, to be suggested indirectly, mainly via sound, the reaction shot, facial close-ups or bodily gestures.

Not surprisingly, *Tesis* has been championed by some critics and academics as a piece of work whose aesthetic agenda goes well beyond the level of affect and the delivery of visual hits, as one which is to be valued as a self-conscious construct aimed at cine-literate audiences (see Allinson, Lev and Buckley, though for a less positive view see Palacios 1998: 123). In addressing groups of film viewers in such a self-conscious way, *Tesis* also encourages a degree of alignment with the director, not so much in the sense of a flesh and blood Amenábar but more akin to the figure of an offscreen teller – that is, an 'implied artistic narrator' of the text, whose presence is felt in those technical and narrative choices which produce and cue our visual denial and our recognition of signs of mediation. The specific pleasure generated here is that of the appeal made to the viewer's or spectator's own skill, perspicacity and reading proficiency, resulting in a satisfying confirmation of the viewer's understanding of how the film makes meanings. This sort of 'intellectual' pleasure is of a rather different order to that involved in being immersed in the spectacle and visual intensity of a *Nightmare on Elm Street* slasher movie, for example. Noticing the functioning and purpose of technique (i.e. reading the snuff tape as Chema does) requires a certain degree of critical detachment, which then develops into a form of pleasure for the more self-aware or educated viewer. In the end we can posit at least two different – though not mutually exclusive – forms of viewer engagement and pleasure. One is based on spectacle and linked to fairly random visual intensities. The other is based on more self-conscious strategies of narration, repeated and marked with signs of authorial control and educated reader proficiency. In this sense *Tesis* is arguably far closer to the type of classic, pre-slasher horror found in *Psycho* (1960) and *Peeping Tom* (1962) than to *Halloween* (1979) and the *Nightmare on Elm Street* film cycle. At the same time Amenábar's film style and his more classical intertextual preferences arguably illustrate Bourdieu's proposition that 'tastes are perhaps first and foremost distastes, disgust provoked by horror or visceral intolerance ("sick making") of the tastes of others' (1984: 56). In other words, as he has declared on many occasions, Amenábar is not a fan of graphic 'horror gore' and probably regards those who see the horror genre as defined primarily by its 'visceral' address and the body count as unfortunate and perhaps even deluded.

Voyeurism and the gaze

In a straightforward, non-pathological sense, voyeurism has to do with the act of looking at the behaviour of others, who are unaware of our presence and our furtive gaze. All of us engage in this activity, though film viewing seems deliberately designed to intensify the act, since it positions us as spectators in a context where we are safely protected from the returning gaze of those figures we contemplate on screen. In a stronger, more extreme, sense, voyeurism is a type of sexual perversion, where the looker's preferred form of sexual stimulation arises from looking at the sexual parts and/or sexual behaviour of others. Voyeurism derives from our infantile 'scopcfilia' (i.e. sexual stimulation by looking or being looked at) and is the paired opposite of exhibitionism. In *Tesis* Amenábar sets up a vague approximation of this pairing though, intriguingly, it does not principally involve Ángela, who is not coded in her dress, look or behaviour, for the traditional exhibitionist, female role. The pairing has to do with Chema and Bosco, i.e. the contrast between the deeply voyeuristic, self-loathing, introverted film geek and the arrogant, self-confident seducer, who takes pleasure in looking and being looked at and engages in much self-display and showing off (see Rycroft 1968: 175 and 47).[15]

As noted earlier, films such as *Rear Window*, *Vertigo*, *Psycho* and *Peeping Tom* foreground and explore the complex relations and implications of voyeurism and the various viewing positions involved. The influence of *Peeping Tom* also seems to underpin certain features of the predecessor to *Tesis*, i.e. *Himenóptero* (1992). Like Powell's classic feature, Amenábar's second short is concerned self-reflexively with watching and being watched and the connections between being terrified by screen violence but being too fascinated to turn away. Like Amenábar's short, Powell's feature film explores the aggressive, predatory, murderous gaze of his young male filmmaker. But Powell goes much further and provides a rationale for the deep-seated compulsions which drive Mark Lewis to torture and kill his female subjects using the phallic leg of his tripod as a blade and murder weapon.[16] In *Peeping Tom* the spectator is positioned both in front of and behind the camera, i.e. aligned with both the assailant and the victim, and via the distorting mirror attached to the tripod leg, able to see the female victim witnessing her own monstrous victimisation, fear and death. This chilling 'double foregrounding' of the gaze (see Hayward 2006: 161–2), where the spectator experiences a double helping of abject fear and brutalism at the same time, creates a *mise-en-abyme* effect which Amenábar seeks to emulate in *Tesis*. He does so by transforming his characters into spectators as well as protagonists and victims of their own voyeuristic spectacle, exemplified in Ángela's repeated positioning as passive, voyeuristic fantasist as well as active snuff starlet. Via the gaze he also forces the spectator into occupying the roles of the characters, i.e. into experiencing Ángela's victimhood as well as the serial killer's fantasy of omnipotence. These classic positionings are repeated and recycled throughout the film, and are consistent with *Tesis*'s status as a 'rites of passage' story and cautionary tale, one in which role switching and the nature of the sadistic male gaze are revealed not only as murderous but deeply pleasurable and attractive.

One cannot deal with spectatorial pleasure, ways of looking and the gender-based organisation of the gaze without acknowledging the importance and impact of Laura Mulvey's pioneering article of 1975, 'Visual Pleasure and Narrative Cinema' (written in 1973).[17] Very much a product of its time, Mulvey's strongly politicised proposition was that all mainstream, commercial cinema (exemplified by classical Hollywood) was complicit in female oppression through its objectification of women, by way of the cinematic gaze, which (reflecting patriarchal ideology) was gendered male. Mainstream cinema thus reinforced patriarchy through its particular coding of the erotic; it organised and indeed 'naturalised' the male gaze by its co-ordination of the three looks: that of the camera, character and the spectator, whose gaze imitates the other two looks. Mulvey claimed that the male spectator (by identifying with the male hero on screen, his ego ideal), sought pleasure in looking and a controlling power through his eroticised, objectifying gaze at the woman. Subordinate and victimised, the female figure on screen was valued solely for her 'to-be-looked-at-ness'; but (according to Freud) she was also a potential source of disturbance for the male viewer, threatening him with castration anxiety. Such a threat could be diverted and contained either by a phallic, fetishistic look (which disavows female difference through its refocusing on a body part or fetish) or by the voyeuristic male gaze (often leading to the sadistic punishment of the female body on screen). Also, according to Linda Williams, if a woman character achieved a degree of agency, power or dominance in the film narrative, she was likely to come to a bad end and pay for her curiosity (i.e. sexual desire) with her life (1984: 85).[18] Moreover, the female spectator was denied a gaze of her own and on the whole had no active women characters to identify with. This being so, short of abandoning mainstream cinema, her only recourse was transvestism, i.e. she was obliged to occupy the dominant viewing position and adopt the all-powerful, male gaze.

Over the years Mulvey's speculative, pessimistic and puritanical schema of woman's oppression (unsupported by any empirical evidence of actual spectator behaviour) has been inspirational for feminist film criticism. But it has also been criticised for its monolithic, static, ahistorical view of gender and the cinema institution and its lack of opportunities for viewing positions for women, resistant or otherwise. Later feminist writers (such as Mary Anne Doane and Carol Clover) have successfully managed to prise open Mulvey's closed 'relay' of looks, especially Clover in her study of youthful male spectatorship.[19] Analysing the American slasher film of the 1970s and 1980s, Clover focused on the masculinised figure of the 'final girl', with whom male audiences are able to identify masochistically as narrative agent. Here, the popular slasher subgenre is reread as a more flexible form of cross-gender experience for young male audiences, as opposed to the phallic rigidity of Mulvey's dominating male gaze, arising deterministically from the cinematic apparatus.

As a whole film, *Tesis* is full of voyeurs, lonely people who inhabit their own audiovisual bubbles (some, like Amenábar himself, via headset technology and the Walkman) and gaze at each other but are unable to connect. Their atomisation and obsessive gazing are presented as signs of a sick, dysfunctional society, composed of isolated, unhappy individuals. And whether they admit to it or not, the disconnected, repressed, middle-class characters of *Tesis* are powerfully drawn to violent screen imagery. They derive intense stimulation and erotic pleasure from contemplating scenes of brutality and butchery which seem to speak to their repressed fantasies and fears, concerned principally with sexuality and sexual identity. Chema, for example, is the archetypal, introverted, horror geek, the hardened, experienced, but alienated consumer of extreme gore and grue. In one of the film's deleted scenes, while Ángela sleeps, he gazes upon her and fantasises about raping and ripping her to pieces, as he parodies his favourite screen monsters (see DVD Extras). So smitten is he by Ángela (but also so aware is he of his own lack of looks) that he is quite happy to pay for sex. Yet, beyond his voyeuristic, pornographic gaze, Chema is capable also of other forms of looking. Indeed he seems perfectly able to keep sexual desire in check while looking objectively at the snuff tape. Despite his poor eyesight, marked by his thick-rimmed glasses, Chema can thus mobilise something like an investigative gaze in pursuit of control over the image, rather than over women. Yet, in reality, they amount to the same thing, since Chema is little more than a shy, lonely voyeur and peeping tom, unable to engage with women and forced to film secretly his object of desire (Ángela) for his own private, masturbatory consumption. *Tesis* charts his journey towards some form of reconnection or resocialisation, with his own generation, through Ángela.

Bosco is also strongly attracted to Ángela, though not for true romance, despite his pretence. Rather he regards her as a challenge and an object for seduction, control and sadistic humiliation. Bosco even foregrounds the power of his gaze in his signature chat-up line: '¿De qué color son mis ojos?' (what colour are my eyes?). He fixes Ángela with his hypnotic, boyish, blue eyes, seeking to scan, investigate and possess her, indeed to construct her as his personal object of submission and violent gratification. His voyeurism is pathological (perhaps even insane), giving rise to extreme forms of violent, sadistic behaviour. What is at stake here? Is he a victim of child abuse or abandonment, perhaps? Are his serial killings repeated attempts at mastering a sense of loss, fear or pain through the torture and murder of his female colleagues? His brutality against women suggests a need to affirm his ownership and control of the male gaze while externalizing deep-seated anxieties and problems of male sexual identity.

On the surface Ángela is presented as an innocent and almost child-like figure in matters of sex, cinephilia and death ('yo no he visto la muerte' (I haven't seen a dead person), she says regretfully, voicing her lack of worldly experience but also, quite possibly, a repressed obsession with necrophilia). Her middle-class values also require her to feel disgust and repulsion at the sort of extreme violent imagery routinely consumed by Chema. She also resists the traditional mainstream codings of the exhibitionist film female: she is fastidious, does not wear make-up or revealing clothing (no plunging necklines or flimsy nightgowns), she is in no way provocative or flighty. Indeed, compared to Yolanda, she is barely sexual (until the disco sequence). She is the total opposite of Bosco's confident, masculine display, exuding prudishness and repression. Perhaps this is why her male suitors work so hard to fit her into their fantasy scenarios, and are driven by their desires to transform her into spectacle. Yet, as Denzin says of the contemporary female voyeur, 'Her gaze is still defined by the masculine eye, even as recent texts expose the limits of the male look and give women the power to gaze upon themselves and the male figure' (1995: 139).[20] Moroever, Ángela is secretive and devious, hardly upstanding or trustworthy (she lies and steals on a number of occasions), and above all, she hides her real motivations regarding her interest in screen violence. She also acts as the audience identification figure within the film diegesis, appalled but spellbound by images of extreme violence, echoing the prurient viewing habits of Spanish television audiences towards the tragic victims of the Alcasser murders.

The film charts the evolution of her reactive, childish voyeurism and the impossibility of her romantic fantasies. Initially, she consumes film violence by audio only, not through the gaze at all, but by reconstructing the scene of murder imaginatively on her own mind screen.[2] At Chema's flat (echoing Amenábar's own viewing education) she uses her fingers as a protective screen, peeking through them like a child; and, initially overcome by disgust, she is obliged to vomit Yet, fascinated by the torture and pain, she immediately returns to the small screen for more brutal horror. Over time Ángela develops a taste for extreme violence on video through her own (male?) gaze, overcoming her squeamishness and middle-class values and allowing her darkest fantasies to emerge. Her erotic dream (in which she seems aware of being filmed and where Bosco's bloody knife represents her fantasy of submission and sexual penetration) is further evidence of her deeply ambivalent attitude to sexual violence, underpinned by her disturbingly masochistic voyeurism. This sequence is recycled when Chema also films Ángela through her lounge window (as she fantasises intimacy using Bosco's beautiful image, freeze framed on the television screen). While this strategy of repetition is used by Amenábar to create doubt in the viewer over the identity of the serial killer, it also suggests a *mise-en-abyme* of voyeurism and the sexualised gaze, as the viewer looks at Chema, looking at Ángela, who is looking at, touching and kissing Bosco's screen image.

Tesis thus speculates not only on the social impact of a powerful, sadistic male gaze but also on a persistent female gaze which claims to be objective, analytical and non-violent but which thrills to female torture and murder. Behind the façade of Ángela's middle-class gentility we find deep-rooted, masochistic desires for self-endangerment and sexualised violence, indeed fantasies of rape and brutal, filmed annihilation. Through the snuff video Amenábar presents screen violence as real, authentic, credible, not as fictional or merely simulated. And through her contact with snuff videos and their powerful 'reality effect', Ángela's voyeurism is hugely stimulated, turned on by the illicit act of looking at and listening to the sounds and shocks of real murder. As a spectator of real, not fictional horror, Ángela unites and empathises with the victim, which seems to be the very *raison d'être* of her viewing activity. Through her Amenábar comments more generally on filmmaking and its consumption, not only on the sadistic impulses of horror-thriller filmmakers and cinematographers like himself and but also on the masochistic fascinations of his diegetic and non-diegetic spectators, including ourselves.

Hitchcock and the thriller

Hitchcock continues to be widely regarded as the consummate self-publicist and cinematic Svengali, able to bring to the surface our deepest, illicit, most compulsive desires and make peeping toms and serial killers out of all of us. His reputation as the 'master of suspense' made him into a global brand. His craftsmanship as a filmmaker also emphasised his meticulous preparation and prodigious ability to pre-visualise his films and storyboard them (akin to Amenábar's talent for pre-visualising and even pre-scoring his own films in his head). However, in practice, once his 'vision' collided with the daily realities of working on set, Hitchcock could be a monster, regularly bullying and abusing actors and crew. His need for control was legendary but was frequently compromised by his own inability to make compromises. He was a showman who was also a very private person, who liked titillating and tormenting his audiences in equal measure, but revealed little about himself or his private life. Perhaps his filthy, black humour (indebted to a deeper sadism) was a distraction to keep prying eyes at bay. In his films Hitchcock is concerned in part with the vicissitudes of identity, usually 'mistaken' identity, through which his male characters, accused of criminality (predominantly murder) and thrown into a maelstrom of fakery and illusion, struggle to prove their innocence. This provides opportunities for much character doubling and simulation, disguise and masquerade, fantasy and deceit, where characters projected their deepest fears and desires on to 'others'. Hitchcock thus trades freely on dualisms and juxtapositions such as reality/fantasy, sanity/insanity, the normal/abnormal and what lies beneath the outward 'ordinariness' of the lodger, the lover, the close friend or even one's spouse. In a Hitchcock film, while everything is motivated and has a reason for being on screen, nothing is what it seems. Also, via POV shots, the master liked putting the spectator into the position of the character (Jeff in *Rear Window*, Norman in *Psycho*) in order to experience first-hand Jeff's anxiety of helplessness (knowing a murder has been committed) or the prurient thrill of Norman's compulsive male voyeurism. In short, he sought to recreate the delightful buzz of inhabiting the skin of both the hero and the villain, and of switching sides, revelling for a while in what he called the 'impurity of our desires'.[22]

The importance of Hitchcock to Amenábar's filmmaking is undeniable (even *Mar adentro* resonates with echoes of *Rear Window*). Of course this relationship or dialogue deserves far more attention than can be given here. Also, the impact of Hitchcock on Spanish or Hispanic filmmaking more widely is a subject which is much underrated and arguably requires a great deal more research and analysis.[23]

Hitchcock's influence resurfaced in the 1990s in Spain, as young directors rejected the model of 1980s official heritage films concerned with the Civil War and turned towards American genre films, especially the thriller, as a vehicle for winning back young audiences and generating box office. Though Amenábar began making horror shorts aged 19, he seems to have encountered Hitchcock somewhat later. He was already reasonably *au fait* with the cinema of Spielberg, Cameron, Scorsese, Coppola, Kubrick and De Palma before he began any serious viewing (via video and television mainly) of the Hitchcock classics.

With *Tesis*, for example, Amenábar may not have necessarily wanted to shoot an American-style thriller, but he did want to put on film una historia que me tuviera agarrado a la butaca' (Heredero 1997: 97) (a story which kept me on the edge of my seat). Hence his preference for the thriller mode, 'se trata de un género casi matemático donde … puedes mantener la atención del espectador' (it's an almost mathematical genre where you can hold the spectator's attention), even though, he adds, certain American stereotypes and devices cannot and should not be adapted mechanically to the Spanish context (Heredero 1997: 97–8). Also, well-made thrillers, not overly tied to local culture or locality, could be exported, gaining their directors greater visibility, critical recognition and a foothold in foreign markets. And who better to guide the budding thriller filmmaker than the master himself?

However, Amenábar has developed something of a love–hate relationship with Hitchcock, though his attitude is largely one of admiration and indebtedness, especially in relation to his mastery of suspense: 'En Hitchcock, lo que más valoro es el suspense' (Payán 2001: 42) (What I value most in Hitchcock is suspense). In this regard, as Charles Derry reminds us, the suspense thriller seeks to plunge risk-averse (thrill-hating) figures into extreme situations where familiar objects, spaces and behaviours are made unfamiliar, threatening and destabilising.[24] Derry also suggests that suspense need not depend on resolving the case or explaining the enigma but on the viewer's expectations and fears of what might happen, based on the tightly controlled delivery of narrative information. Suspense is generated, he argues, via the interplay between narration and expectation, where what becomes suspended is time: 'time seems to extend itself ... each second provides a kind of torture for the spectator ... anxious to have his or her anticipation foiled or fulfilled' (1988: 32). In other areas Amenábar draws upon and seasons his films with Hitchcockian dark humour and the use of jokes (e.g. as voiced by Chema in *Tesis*, Nicholas in *The Others* and Ramón in *Mar adentro*, for example). There are also strong affinities in Amenábar's preparation and attention to detail, his creation of a 'team' of young actors and rehiring of personnel. And where Hitchcock's misogynist motto for audience engagement was 'torture the women', Amenábar appears more evenhanded in delighting in torturing both sexes, hysterics such as Núria and Grace, but also of the male variety, such as César and Ramón. Amenábar coincides to some extent with Hitchcock in his Catholic upbringing and his dialogue with guilt, death and the afterlife. He also emulates the master in his liking for the cameo appearance.[25]

Of course, unlike Hitchcock, who remade one of his own films (*The Man Who Knew Too Much* 1934/1956), Amenábar has consistently refused offers to remake two of his own: *Tesis* and *Abre los ojos*. Moreover, in interview in the 1990s, he saw his mentor on suspense as rather overrated: 'Los directores que más me interesan son Orson Welles y Alfred Hitchcock, pero creo que a éste se le ha sobre estimado' (Heredero 1997: 83) (The directors who most interest me are Orson Welles and Alfred Hitchcock, though I believe Hitchcock is overrated). In his films Amenábar parts company from Hitchcock in relation to his view of storytelling and the mechanics of suspense. Hitchcock claimed that letting off a bomb would give the audience, at best, a ten-second shock. But if the audience know that a bomb has been planted, the building of suspense can keep them in a state of heightened expectation for five minutes or more. Audience knowledge can thus be manipulated and exploited to provoke anxiety. Hitchcock also rejects the device of the 'whodunnit', preferring to expose the identity of the villain early on, in order to create tension around the pursuit. He thus prefers omniscient narration, with the villain left to improvise while the spectator looks on, already 'in the know'. By contrast Amenábar tends to favour even more traditional storytelling techniques (inspired by Agatha Christie), based on delay and denial of knowledge and the use of the surprise ending, elements of which Hitchcock strongly disapproved.

One of Amenábar's major contributions to Spanish filmmaking arguably lies in his overcoming of the great fear of the thriller in Spain. The thriller form, he says, is a tricky type of cinema which relies on the intricacy of plot mechanics and a balance between narrative excess (subplots, false trails, red herrings etc.) and strong verisimilitude in order to sustain viewer engagement (Payán 2001: 40). He also emphasises the manipulation of our perceptions via the exploitation and interplay of onscreen and offscreen space as well as the denial, misdirection and repression of narrative information The ambition of course, as Derry also indicates above, is to 'torture' the spectator by aligning him/her with the characters' vulnerabilities. while taking pleasure in their suffering. Amenábar's spectators are thus positioned to adopt the POV and inhabit the skins of very dark enigmatic and often very unsympathetic characters (Silvia and Bosco in *Himenóptero*, Bosco, Chema and even Ángela in *Tesis*, César in *Abre los ojos* and Grace in *The Others*). Hence the strong sadomaso-chistic drive of the thriller form, which nevertheless seeks to ensure the viewer's excitement at being trapped in darkness for two hours and willingly put through the wringer. In this field very few Spanish directors before him (Bajo Ulloa, Díaz Yanes, Uribe, Urbizu perhaps) have found success (Payán 2001: 40).[26]

Amenábar's thrillers also function as analogues of children's stories, allegories, fables and fairy tales, in which excess curiosity is met by a fall into danger, entrapment and severe punishment. Con-fused, angry, alienated, often paranoid, Amenábar's mainly young teen and 'twenty-something' protagonists in his shorts and features (Ana, María, Alberto, Ángela, César, Grace etc.) are made to suffer and given little respite, as they face overwhelming shocks and calami-ties in their vacuous lives. They tend to see themselves in crisis as innocent victims of a sick, image-obsessed society, or of mysterious 'others' who would wish to occupy their living space. By their own selfishness, narcissism, bad luck or sadomasochistic drives, they are invariably plunged into a repeating nightmare, stripped of their lifestyles, comfort zones, values and consoling fictions (such as looks and religion) and forced to confront their darkest selves. Largely authors of their own misfortune, their suffering is nonetheless thera-peutic and usually leads to some form of deeper understanding and self-awareness, or so it seems. Yet, as with Hitchcock, nothing is quite what it seems in an Amenábar film.

Intertextualities

As noted earlier, in its reworking of the suspense thriller format and its exploration of voyeurism and the gaze, *Tesis* bears the imprint of Hitchcock's *Rear Window* (1954) and *Psycho* (1960) and also Powell's *Peeping Tom* (1960). The film also acknowledges classical Hollywood in the form of *The Night of the Hunter* (Laughton, 1956), echoed in Chema's dialogues during second tunnel sequence. And, as Amenábar himself has indicated, in terms of its tones and atmospheres, *mise-en-scène*, low-level lighting set ups and extra-diegetic music, *Tesis* draws upon *Alien* (Ridley Scott, 1979), *Seven* (David Fincher, 1995) and *The Changeling* (Peter Medak, 1980) (see Payán 2001: 42 and Heredero 1997: 100). In short the intertextual field around *Tesis* largely comprises a mix of classical and contemporary Anglo-American cinema, reflecting the viewing experiences and tastes of Amenábar and Gil.

In relation to its Spanish and European sources, by 1994–95 Amenábar had seen very little European cinema, let alone European horror cinema (such as the Italian 'giallo') and, perhaps surprisingly, was even unacquainted with local Spanish 'auteurs maudits' such as Villaronga and Zulueta (Rodríguez Marchante 2002: 97). It was only after *Tesis* and *Abre los ojos*, for example, that Amenábar began to acknowledge the works of European horror *meisters* such as Michael Haneke (e.g. *Benny's Video*, 1992, and *Funny Games*, 1997) (Rodríguez Marchante 2002: 86–7 and 167; Berthier 2007: 180). As regards Spanish sources, apart from the early Berlanga, Amenábar has always been particularly effusive concerning the importance of *El espíritu de la colmena* (The Spirit of the Beehive, 1973), which he regards as an 'obra maestra' (masterpiece) (Heredero, 1997: 95). The impact of Erice's ode to the power of children's imagination and sibling rivalry can be seen throughout *The Others*. More specifically, *Tesis* contains strong echoes of this acclaimed art film in some of its atmospheres, lighting setups, dialogues in the tunnel scenes and in a 'playing dead' scene between Ángela and Bosco (reminiscent of Ana and Isabel), near the end of the film, which was shot but had to be cut (Rodríguez Marchante 2002: 94).

A more obvious though little explored Spanish source is arguably Montxo Armendáriz's 'youth movie' *Historias del Kronen* (henceforth

Kronen). The film was released in April 1995, shortly before Amenábar started shooting *Tesis*. *Kronen* was also the film in which Eduardo Noriega began his feature film career, appearing in a small role in a couple of scenes, before starring as Bosco in *Tesis*. Based loosely on the prize-winning novel of the same name by José Angel Mañas (though toning down the novel's distinctive racism, consumerism and macho nihilism), Armendáriz's realist, downbeat film version of *Kronen* did very well commercially though its critical reception was mixed.[2] The film also focused precisely upon the same social grouping which inter-ested Amenábar in *Tesis*, i.e. the contemporary, transgressive, urban youth of Spain's so-called 'X generation'. These were largely well-off, middle-class students, so-called 'pijos' (spoilt brats), looking for kicks and extreme excitement. In *Kronen*, during the summer holidays and using the heart of Madrid as their nocturnal playground, a group of friends and their girlfriends embark on a sustained, frenetic binge of sex, drugs, alcohol, heavy metal music and macho acts of bravado (e.g. climbing empty buildings, hanging from pedestrian motorway bridges, driving against the traffic). In pursuing excess, danger and violence, and putting their lives at risk, they seek somehow to assuage their emptiness, their lack of distinction and purpose, their anomie and aimlessness and their uncertain masculinities. This is strongly reminiscent of the sort of thematic territory covered by Amenábar in *Tesis*: youth alienation, nihilism, homoeroticism, sibling rivalry, a taste for sensationalist screen violence and a scorn for death as a badge of 'macho cool' (hiding gender insecurities). Also the prominence given in the film to the acclaimed American slasher *Henry, Portrait of a Serial Killer* (McNaughton, 1986/90, the group's favourite film) and refer-ences to 'snuff movies' (both verbally and at a birthday party, where Carlos tortures with alcohol teetotal, weakling Pedro, whose agony is captured on a camcorder, before his death) directly link *Kronen* with the narrative and thematics of *Tesis*. It is also worth noting that, in the casting of *Tesis*, the young rising star of *Kronen*, Juan Diego Botto, was screen tested for the role of Chema and was strongly favoured by producer Cuerda; however, in the end, Amenábar got his way and kept 'Fele' Martínez in the part, with Noriega already slated for the role of Bosco (Interview).

In his prologue to the published version of the script for *Tesis* (Guión *Tesis*, 1997: 11), Amenábar states rather coyly, without any elaboration 'Mi principal referente era *El silencio de los corderos*' (My main refer-ence point was *The Silence of the Lambs*). His reluctance to expand on this matter is telling. Even a brief comparison of the two works (which is all I can include here) demonstrates just how significant a source Demme's horror thriller was in relation to *Tesis*.[28] The brief notes which follow on narrative structure, character traits and patterning and the theme of maturation seek to illustrate how Amenábar subtly draws upon *The Silence of the Lambs* (henceforth *Silence*), exploring certain options and not others, while seeking to scramble, reassign, complicate and disguise some of his more likely borrowings.

Firstly, in terms of its narrative structure, let us recall that *Silence* exploits the classical 'deadline' format, the archetypal 'race against the clock' narrative. In *Tesis*, by contrast, Amenábar largely eliminates the tight, deadline structure, replacing this with a much looser, 'whodunnit' narrative design, cued not by Ángela but by Chema's recognition of Vanessa as the snuff victim. He happens to know the victim personally as well as the likely culprit and moreover has an erotic interest in Ángela. Also Amenábar works largely within what he knows. He replaces the FBI manhunt or police-procedural-driven narrative of *Silence* with a far more improvised, DIY search for the serial snuff killer, undertaken by two students. Yet, like Demme, he locates a substantial part of the action inside an educational institution, swapping the modern, well-lit, though aseptic FBI training base at Quantico for the gloomier, claustrophobic, gothic-like Faculty of Communications. Where the films converge, however, is in their mutual fascination for the novice female investigator (the trainee forensic profiler compared to the media or film researcher). Both are clever, both are young 'women in peril' and both are located in a male-dominated environment which suits the evocation of vulnerability and potential danger. However, they are of very different class backgrounds: Clarice is small-town, rural and lower-class; Ángela is city, suburban and middle-class. However, some of their goals are similar since both yearn to escape their backgrounds, though in opposite directions: Clarice seeks to leave behind her quasi-'white trash' social positioning (her orphan status and her bad memories) through upward mobility and a job as an FBI agent. By contrast Ángela is keen to abandon a stifling, bourgeois family context (especially her sneaky, snooping sister) by moving downmarket, and seeking a new identity among cinephiles and a more congenial, geeky, male-dominated, horror fan culture.

Secondly, regarding character construction and patterning, in *Silence* Clarice is obviously the main protagonist and 'Buffalo Bill' (i.e. Jame Gumb alias Jack Gordon) her principal antagonist (though with similarities in terms of class background). But where do we place Lecter, the evil genius? Is Lecter another antagonist or a parallel protagonist with his own goals or a mixture of both figures?

In *Tesis* Amenábar exploits a similar character pattern, reminiscent of the classic, 'erotic triangle'. Here I strongly suspect that Amenábar has borrowed various traits from the two main opponents in *Silence* and reassigned them to Bosco and Chema, in order to construct rival serial killer specimens (one real, the other a decoy). However, neither character is given a back-story or sufficient motivational basis to explain his behaviour. It is just possible that something of the smug and smarmy Dr Chilton migrates into Jorge Castro, the cool, suave, Professor of Media Psychology. However, Chilton's description of Lecter as a monster and a psychopath is repeated several times but via Chema, who describes Bosco, very early on, as 'ese psicópata' (that psychopath). If *Silence* is a film with a main female protagonist (a victim-heroine) and parallel male antagonists, whose backgrounds and motivations we understand to some extent, in *Tesis* (and in *Abre los ojos*) a similar pattern holds, though, in both cases, Amenábar's main trio remain obscure, puzzling and thinly drawn.

Thirdly, *Silence* traces Clarice's maturation process through her quest narrative. Helped by Lecter, she makes a successful journey towards tracking down and eliminating the serial killer as well as rescuing Catherine. She also graduates from FBI school and in the process guarantees herself a job in Crawford's department. From trainee cop to fully fledged agent, Clarice successfully negotiates her own passage to adulthood and professional recognition; hers is a path of growth, development and achievement, unlike that of Gumb, whose attempts at sexual transformation fail. Her victory over adversity is also a sign of her ability to deal with her own childhood traumas (loss of father, orphan at ten, upbringing in state institutions, her failure to save the spring lambs from a certain death). Demme provides the spectator with enough background information on Clarice to give her 'rites of passage' story adequate credibility and a satisfactory closure.

As for *Tesis*, on the surface, like Clarice, Ángela is also involved in a process of maturation and change, from naive, vulnerable object of male scrutiny and desire to a far more autonomous and less fearful young woman. She displays positive identification and empathy with other female victims of male violence and fulfils the role of the victim-heroine, showing traits of positive female agency and resolve. She also kills Bosco, saves Chema and helps expose the snuff ring, thus protecting other women from further attack. Yet, while she mirrors Clarice Starling in her rites of passage trajectory, her goals as a student are not fulfilled. She drops her thesis and (presumably) does not graduate (just like Amenábar). Also her quest is not aimed at the fulfilment of any career ambitions. Unlike *Silence*, which sidelines the romance aspect of the narrative, in *Tesis* teen angst and infatuation are brought centre stage. Ángela's investigation into Vanessa's murder is also simultaneously an attempt to fulfil her own desire by entering the eroticised world of the serial killer, to fulfil her 'death wish' as Bosco's snuff victim.

Like Ángela, Bosco also seeks some form of transformation and new identity, in his case through the carefully tortured and butchered bodies of young women. We have no screen 'pathology' to explain Bosco's actions, but it seems that a physically mature young man remains emotionally infantilised, taking out his childhood traumas on vulnerable young women, as if still in the suffocating grip of an over-protective parent (recalling Norman's mother in *Psycho* or Mark's father in *Peeping Tom*). As for Ángela, her desires appear driven by a deeply entrenched masochism and voyeurism, arising from some childhood disturbance. But we are never told why Ángela is an obsessive risk-taker, who wants to experience screen violence and death for real. In the epilogue to *Tesis* (which parallels the coda of the graduation ceremony in *Silence*), the romance aspect appears to be reignited when Ángela visits Chema in hospital. Echoing Lecter's darkly humorous jibe to Clarice: 'People will say we're in love', the purpose of the scene is to renew their friendship and reconnect them as a potential couple. Amenábar's ending to *Tesis* is also oddly prophetic, since it prefigures an ending in Thomas Harris's novel *Hannibal* (1999), where Clarice and Lecter join forces and strike out together as the outlaw couple in South America. Bizarrely, in Ridley Scott's flawed adaptation of *Hannibal* (1999), with Julianne Moore replacing Jodie Foster, Harris's provocative ending is junked and replaced by an absurd, gory, schlock horror finale, the very sort of closure which Amenábar would decry as weak, clichéd and unimaginative. Such a positioning perhaps explains why Amenábar so admires Demme's film. In part this has to do with Demme's visual restraint and his subtle treatment of violence; it also indicates how Amenábar seeks to provide the thrills of the horror movie to his middle-class audiences in *Tesis* without them feeling upset or self-conscious at watching what is, at bottom, an upmarket thriller-cum-slasher flic. In short Amenábar seeks distinction and kudos through his seriousness and his tight control of voyeuristic spectacle.

Tesis and snuff

The disturbing, though far-fetched, premise of *Tesis* is that the University Communications department secretly harbours a snuff movie production and distribution ring, organised by senior male staff and supplied with product by selected students. At the very core of Spain's publicly funded higher education system, we find the mantra of Professor Castro's free market philosophy for the national media put into practice.

But what do we mean by snuff and how does *Tesis* approach its putative audio-visual quarry? As Kerekes and Slater have shown (1995: 7–8), the origins of the term have been variously linked to the alleged filming of Sharon Tate's murder by the Charles Manson gang, to 'mondo' shock documentaries on video (such as the *Faces of death* Series) and to an exploitation film of the early 1970s (directed by Michael and Roberta Findlay) entitled *Slaughter* (1971).[29] This film was originally shot in Argentina, dubbed into English and released only very briefly in the USA. World distribution rights were then purchased by Allan Shackleton's Monarch Releasing Company. The film was re-released in 1976, with an added though fake and inept 'snuff' ending of mutilation and death (allegedly shot by Horacio Fredriksson and Simon Nuchtern) and with the title changed to *Snuff* (1976), thus inaugurating the urban legend. If *Snuff* gave currency to the term, with the promise of an actual filmed murder of a female actress, in reality *Snuff* was little more than an elaborate hoax. All of which raises a question mark as to whether snuff actually exists.

In the mid-1990s Amenábar himself was convinced that such material was extant and available, arguing that examples could be found in the USA, Canada, Finland, Switzerland and Sweden and that snuff could be defined as 'un tipo de cine que generalmente consiste en torturar a alguien, ejecutarlo, descuartizarlo y grabarlo con la cámara ... Casi no se conoce en España, aunque se comenta que aquí se han hecho *snuff movies* con animales ... El snuff representa el límite de la violencia audiovisual, es la máxima degeneración del cine sangriento' (Sempere 2000: 77) (a type of cinema which usually consists of torturing, executing and cutting up someone, while recording it on a camera ... It's almost unknown in Spain, although they say people have made snuff movies using animals ... Snuff represents the outer limit of audiovisual violence, the most repellent kind of gory cinema). In the 'Making of' feature on the DVD of *Tesis*, Amenábar reaffirms this point (see Extras).

In the absence of any extant examples of real snuff, a number of commercial and more extreme, 'shot on video', features have imaginatively laid down the parameters and conventions of a popular snuff aesthetic. These range very widely from Michael Powell's pioneering pre-snuff *Peeping Tom* (1960), arguably a strong intertext for *Tesis*, and include also *Emanuelle in America* (Joe D'Amato, 1977), *Last House on Dead End Street* (Roger Watkins, 1977), *Hardcore* (Paul Schrader, 1978), *Cannibal Holocaust* (Ruggiero Deodato, 1980), *Effects* (Dustin Nelson, 1980), *Videodrome* (David Cronenberg, 1982), *Special Effects* (Larry Cohen, 1984), *Henry, Portrait of a Serial Killer* (John McNaughton, 1986/1990), *Video Violence* (Gary P. Cohen, 1987), *Man Bites Dog* (*C'est arrivé près de chez vous*, Rémy Belvaux, 1992), *Mute Witness* (Anthony Waller, 1994), *The Brave*, (Johnny Depp, 1997), *8mm* (Joel Schumacher, 1999), *The Blair Witch Project* (Daniel Myrick and Eduardo Sánchez, 1999), the sequel *Book of Shadows: Blair Witch 2* (2000), *My Little Eye* (Marc Evans, 2002), *Snuff Movie* (Bernard Rose, 2005), *The Poughkeepsie Tapes* (John Eric Dowdle, 2007) and *Untraceable* (Gregory Hoblit, 2008). Snuff filming conventions would appear to include: a hidden, enclosed, dingy space (usually one room), a single, still camera, black-and-white, grainy film, but sometimes colour; the absence of sound, male camera operator as hooded torturer, the long take, minimal or no editing, specialist or taboo material, greater ease of dissemination thanks to video or camcorder technology, a clandestine and extremely expensive commodity, made to order. At the extremity of the exploitation film, snuff has emerged in many versions in mainstream commercial output (for example, in Joel Schumacher's *8mm*), primarily via the route of horror cinema and the serial killer/slasher subgenre.

In *Tesis*, in an early sequence, Chema shows Ángela (at her request) examples of screen violence (in fact a simulation of the 'mondo' documentary compilation *Faces of Death*, which is retitled *Fresh Blood*), dealing with scenes of death in combat, mangled accident victims, autopsies etc. Here Amenábar seeks to acknowledge and present to the audience something approaching a snuff tradition, something equivalent to pornography, which he calls 'snuff blando' (Sempere

2000: 77). Gradually, throughout *Tesis*, he connects this soft version to his own artistic recreation of illegal 'snuff duro' (hard snuff), involving recorded imagery and sound of the (simulated) slow humiliation, torture, murder and butchering of the Faculty media student Vanessa, one of Bosco's old flames.

In *Tesis*, snuff is represented as a perversely attractive form of taboo, ultra- violent imagery, which appeals to both male and female voyeurism, and somehow reflects an archaic human desire to confront death and look it directly in the face. Part of this appeal has to do with greater availability of video technology and the 'reality effect' of the snuff video image itself. In the early 1990s, during a period in Spain when digital technologies (e.g. mobile phones) were only just beginning to be developed and marketed and still without the internet Amenábar's Sony V5000 Hi8 video camera produced a digital image which convincingly captured the 'real'. His film interweaves film and video sequences into the narrative, alternately positioning the spectator before the diegetic world of the mainstream story and the digital world of the taboo snuff staging. By doing so Amenábar acknowledges his own video education, cinephilia and shorts. He also foregrounds the fact that his mainstream horror thriller has its origins in more marginal, extreme, exploitation film forms. And at the same time, through Ángela's POV, he dangles in front of the spectator the promise of a snuff image (with added soundtrack) as a portal to the marginalised 'real', or other world, of a recorded snuff murder.

Leaving aside Figueroa's case (of a media authority figure literally suffocated by overwhelming screen violence and an ironic confirmation of Chema's vicious joke about a 'deadly' national cinema), Amenábar also offers at least two contrasting modes of snuff consumption, that of masochistic Ángela, as a total novice and 'everywoman' figure, and that of Chema, as sadistic, experienced, cultish, fan boy. Firstly, viewing secretly at home, Ángela removes the snuff image from the screen and consumes the stolen tape via the audio track only (a defence mechanism against anticipation and over-stimulation but also a means of empathising with Vanessa while psychically replacing her as victim and thrilling to her pain). Secondly, at Chema's flat, she views fragmentarily by way of nervous glimpses shielded by her fingers, accompanied by a joke-strewn verbal summary (i.e. Chema's sadistic commentary, arguably more appropriate to a mainstream horror film and echoing Gumb's mockery of Catherine's imprisonment in *Silence*). The sequence also includes amusing match on action shots of ingestion (Chema snacking) and expulsion (Ángela vomiting), which emphasise the powerful 'bodily' impact of the snuff image on the female novice. Though distraught, Ángela keeps on watching, increasingly sensitive to the sound design of the tape (screams, chain saw, execution shot etc.). Thirdly, stimulated by watching the interview shots with Bosco, Ángela seeks to merge physically with Bosco's image onscreen, thus complementing her psychic audio connection to Vanessa with an attempted physical link to Bosco. Overall, if on a first viewing snuff is literally unwatchable because too powerful, with a little practice Ángela learns to look and consume, as shots of her reactive gaze are intercut with snippets of onscreen snuff material.

Though it presents snuff material throughout most of its running time, from the POV of our female screen proxy, as a set of brief but fragmentary, medium shots, tight close-ups and mainly partial views, *Tesis* also approaches the toxic subgenre from the position of the snuff 'practitioner', in his 'studio'. Here Amenábar imagines in some detail the pro-filmic snuff scenario, in which the masked assailant (in his well-lit garage) seeks to start proceedings with the sadistic humiliation of the victim via a verbal account of the staging of her murder. (This is a device which Amenábar repeats at the end of *Ágora*, thus linking the early Christian Parabolani militants with today's Taliban and Islamic jihadist propaganda videos.) In Bosco's case (now a seasoned craftsman), he takes great pains with his set up, checking audio and video levels, then proceeds to explain how he 'might' create his violent spectacle (demonstrating how uncertainty and improvisation increase his power of intimidation and 'life and death' over Ángela). Here Amenábar imagines a fairly thoughtful, even 'arty' aesthetic, with Bosco anticipating elaborate acts of stagy mutilation, for example using a severed hand as a tiara or an ear placed in the mouth: 'Esas mariconadas dan mucho juego' (Those touches are very stimulating). But, continuing the lecture, after Ángela passes out through loss of blood, Bosco will bring her round again and expose her guts whilst keeping her alive a little longer. Finally, with the victim exhausted and close to death, Bosco will administer the head shot, as if slaughtering cattle or sheep. (Ritual slaughter, originally based on animal sacrifice, is of course at the heart of jihadist decapitation spectacle.) Moreover, apart from violently dehumanising the female victim, as he speaks slowly and confidently, Bosco revels in his sadistic, Godlike power: '¿A que acojona?' (Are you not shitting yourself?). In some ways, these features echo Lecter's awesomely violent and highly stylised murder of Lt Boyle in *Silence*, in which the evisceration of the policeman is mentioned as a staging option in *Tesis*. Finally Bosco will butcher Ángela's body with a chain saw and dump it in a ditch, a possible reference to the more popular, downmarket, 'white trash' serial killer tradition of *The Texaschain Saw Massacre* (1976), mentioned earlier. All in all, Bosco presents himself as a monstrous, evil, though dedicated snuff artist, devoted to maximising entertainment value for his specialist clients through his sadism and his use of theatricalised murder as inventive spectacle.

Amenábar's 'thesis' on screen violence, partly introduced here, suggests that our natural voyeurism and rubbernecking at traffic accidents and urban suicides etc., if sufficiently stimulated, can draw us ever closer to stronger and more violent imagery (to soft snuff such as 'mondo' material), leading inexorably to a waning of affect and thus towards a taste for hard-core snuff. As our identification figure, Ángela takes this journey, beginning with her prurient voyeurism, passing through her interview with vampire Bosco, her dream sequence, her embrace of Bosco's screen image and above all her training (via Chema) in looking at and consuming the snuff tape. Moreover, if such extreme material reinforces the link between female exploitation and aberrant male voyeurism, sadism and rape, enacted in the snuff scenario, it also suggests that female voyeurs like Ángela are just as capable of becoming successful consumers of female abjection as the male variety.[30]

Endings

Tesis contains two endings, one which wraps up the investigation plot by uncovering the serial killer and another which contains Amenábar's editorial coda on the noxious effects of trash television. The penultimate scene shows Ángela freeing herself by cutting her bonds, wrestling the gun from Bosco and killing him with one shot (repeating earlier snuff execution clips and the fight scene between Chema and Castro in the tunnels). Here we return to the standardised generic ending of the mainstream slasher and action thriller, where the final girl eliminates the villain. Through Bosco's sadistic commentary, the scene also allows Amenábar to lay down metafilmically a set of conventions for snuff filmmaking within the framework of a mainstream horror thriller. The spectator is given access not only to the snuff victim's distress and suffering but also to the director's 'authorial vision' for his snuff film and is even allowed to occupy his authoritative position behind the camera. Amenábar thus creates a satisfactory narrative ending as well as a thematically dense and self-reflexive closure. The generic and industrial boundaries between mainstream film and marginal snuff video also become blurred. This suggests that mainstream horror and its related film pleasures rely for their power and effectivity not only on explicit graphic violence and effects but also on their hidden, marginal, 'offscreen' others, such as snuff, which Amenábar so skilfully imagines for us.

In the final scene Ángela visits a bashed-up Chema in hospital and via the gift of a book (*The Princess and the Dwarf* based on Oscar Wilde's fairy story *The Birthday of the Infanta*) asks him out for a coffee. They leave the hospital together, just as the television presenter announces the screening of the snuff clips, with the camera panning over the hypnotised gazes of the hospital patients. The scene re-establishes the 'romance' thread between Ángela and Chema; and this time, Ángela takes the initiative and Chema follows, thus reversing gender priorities and the power of the gaze, given Chema's embarrassment to return her look. The book motif (linked to a celebrated gay writer and literary icon) echoes and repeats the story recounted by Chema in the tunnels; it also foregrounds Amenábar's own literary tastes, and the reclaiming of reading books as opposed to consuming images as a subtle critique of the dangers of trash television. However, in keeping with the conventions of the suspense thriller, Amenábar elides the actual police investigation into the Bosco Herranz case, which we see only in the exploitation format of 'reality television' at the end of the film.

The promised snuff clips in the television programme (which resonate uncannily with the real media exploitation of grisly photographs in the Alcasser case) represent the mainstream appropriation of filmed murder as spectacle, under the guise of legitimate broadcast material, in defence of the public interest. No longer secret, hidden or censored, the broadcast of snuff imagery represents the terminus of a process, embodied in Castro's famous prescription for the national cinema, i.e. of giving the public what it wants. The epilogue also suggests that the migration of snuff into mainstream television output is merely the logical and inevitable outcome of a radical process of dumbing down, ratings wars, collapse of standards and the ubiquity of increasingly sensationalist and sexualised trash television output. Meanwhile, with a change to the ending of the fairy tale enunciated by Chema, in *Tesis* the beautiful princess (Ángela) teams up with the ugly dwarf (Chema). By exiting the hospital together and by choosing to turn away from the snuff material, Ángela and Chema provide an apparently positive though unusual mainstream film closure. They appear to acknowledge their common tastes and identities (i.e. Chema's horror fan subculture); they also seem to come to terms with their own voyeurisms and wish to move beyond their prior fetishes and fixations, self-loathing and death worship. They choose to be buddies, to walk away from their morbid curiosity about violence and death, abjuring its attractions and perhaps offering an empowered example to their fans in the audience of a conscious rejection of violence. However, the closure remains ambiguous, since it may well be that in Chema Ángela has found a soulmate who satisfies her desire to escape her social class and her masculine tastes in horror as well as her ambiguous sexual orientation.

Notes

1 See, for example, Heredero 1997: 113, Sempere 2004: 104–7 and Rodríguez Marchante 2002: 46–7. Regarding Cuerda's career, after studying law and being tempted by the priesthood, he trained as a documentalist in the 1970s with the state broadcaster TVE (Televisión Española); he also adapted Ernesto Sábato's *El túnel* (The Tunnel) for television in 1977. In 1982 he began a rather erratic filmmaking career, with a social comedy short *Pares y Nones* (Odds and Evens), then a futuristic television film *Total* (1985), followed by two years teaching filmmaking at Salamanca University. He returned to commercial directing in 1987 with *El bosque animado* (The Haunted Wood), winner of five Goyas, a surrealist fantasy, located in Galicia and the first of a series of rural comedies. His breakthrough film, which did very well internationally, was the period adaptation *La lengua de las mariposas* (Butterfly's Tongue, 1998), for which Mateo Gil led the second unit and Amenábar wrote the score. Since then Cuerda has made *Primer amor* (First Love, 2000) and a three–minute segment for the anti-PP, *Hay Motivo* project (del Amo/Aranda, 2004), as well as a further two period adaptations: *La educación de las hadas* (The Education of Fairies, 2006) and *Los girasoles ciegos* (The Blind Sunflowers, 2008), scripted by Cuerda and the legendary Rafael Azcona (who died in March 2008, aged 81, before release). The latter film was unsuccessful as Spain's Oscar entry for 2008/9 and, though nominated in 15 categories for the Goya awards, it won in only one, that of Best Adapted Script.

2 Gómez died in August 2007, aged 64, as a result of a tragic traffic accident. His role in supporting and providing studio facilities for the young

Amenábar as a novice filmmaker during his student days seems to have been crucial and deserves further investigation. Also, as well as attending the funeral, at the end of the year in Madrid's Círculo de Bellas Artes, Amenábar and Cuerda personally helped to launch Gómez's final book publication, *La representación de la representación: danza, teatro, cine, música*, published by Cátedra, an edited volume of essays on the relationship between drawing and other art forms.

3 In earlier versions *La tesis* (like the shorts) was primarily a self-reflexive, 'exercice de style' concerning the workings of suspense and the plot mechanics of the thriller. The wafer- thin narrative was set in a university media department where one student only, Chema, sought to experiment with film narration and style by making extremely gory shorts. Only later would Amenábar and Gil flesh out the story and add the other characters. It is worth repeating that Gil did not co-write the script of *Tesis* with Amenábar; rather, his intervention came earlier, mainly in helping to work out the over-elaborate plotting of the piece.

4 As it turned out, Cuerda found it relatively straightforward to raise the finance for *Tesis*, thanks largely to the input of Sogepaq/Sogecable and support from the Ministry of Culture. Because of new film legislation introduced in 1994, the government was offering substantial loans for new directors who were prepared to commit to making two or three features over a two-to-three year period, in order to achieve continuity in work (see Ubeda-Portugués 2001: 222–3).

5 Gubern's 1989 book was reprinted in 2005, by Anagrama Publishers. Also of interest here is a related volume by Gubern, *Patologías de la imagen* (Barcelona: Anagrama, 2004). See also Amenábar's interview with Carlos F. Heredero, in which he explains that his use of 'snuff' in *Tesis* is largely as a MacGuffin, that is a dramatic device used to sustain a thriller narrative as well as a pretext to deal self-reflexively with the morbid appeal of the violent image (Heredero 1997: 105).

6 It is worth noting that the biggest investor in *Tesis*, Sogepaq, was the film distribution arm of Sogecable, the pay-TV division of the parent company PRISA, owner of *El País* and many other media interests in Spain and abroad. Sogecable's film production arm Sogetel (which changed its name to Sogecine in 1997) had begun a policy in 1991 of signing up young, promising directors such as Julio Medem, Fernando León de Aranoa, Álex de la Iglesia, Icíar Bollaín, Gracia Querejeta etc. in order to promote a new, young, more commercially oriented, popular auteur cinema (Stone 2007: 36–7). On the strength of *Tesis* Amenábar quickly became a new 'fichaje' (signing) to the Sogecine stable of young auteurs. Unfortunately, in September 2007, owing to a debt crisis arising from complex legal wrangles over football re-transmission rights with Media Pro (a Catalan media content provider), plus the departure of Fernando Bovaira and Simón de Santiago and the collapse of PRISA's share price, Sogecine

halted its film production activity. However, it did manage to complete Cuerda's *Los girasoles ciegos* but failed to save Mateo Gil's rendering of *Pedro Páramo*, which was about to start shooting.

7 Initially Amenábar wished to cast Penélope Cruz as Ángela. She was approached and for a while appeared actively interested in the role. However, during the summer of 1995 she was committed to a leading role (Patricia) in another film (*Brujas*/Witches, Álvaro Fernández Armero, 1996) and could not comply with Amenábar's August/September shooting schedule, which could not be changed. She was also concerned by a sex scene in the script (i.e Ángela's dream/fantasy of intercourse with Bosco, which was very explicit in an early draft), especially following her controversial screen debut in Bigas Luna's *Jamón, jamón* (1992). It was Cuerda, it seems, who suggested Ana Torrent as a replacement. Given the difference in ages between Torrent (then 28 and living in New York) and Noriega and Martínez (22 and 20 respectively), Amenábar was not sure the combination would work. Yet, after reading the script and consulting her agent, Torrent flew to Spain, met Amenábar, was impressed by his self-confidence and accepted the role, even though she never quite understood what made Ángela tick (Vera 2002: 104–6).

8 Rozas was also Amenábar's template for the character of Chema, played by the novice actor Rafael Martínez, a first-year student of Dramatic Art, who had done a mere five months of Performance Studies. According to Mateo Gil, who attended most of the rehearsals (which for 'Fele' lasted an agonising six weeks), Amenábar sought to impose on him an almost robotic version of Chema, with manic attention to detail, rehearsing 'has-a el movimiento de un dedo' (even the movement of a finger – Vera 2002: 34). Despite his baptism of fire, following 'la técnica del espejo' (the mirror method, i.e. simply copying Amenábar's performance to the 'nth' degree), Martínez recalls that 'Alejandro era un chaval de 23 años y prácticamente se jugaba el futuro' (Vera 2002: 123) (Alejandro was a 23-year-old kid and was basically putting his future on the line). Amenábar's cruel, authoritarian style as a young, inexperienced director also recalls the neurotic behaviour of his fictional avatar Silvia, in *Himenóptero* (see Vera 2002: 34).

9 The abject failure of Spanish justice in the Alcasser case was merely one symptom of many which prefigured the wholesale politicisation and subversion of Spain's legal system following the Madrid train bombings of 11 March 2004. Here, the PSOE manipulation of the judicial investigation (which included suborning the judges, removing virtually all the forensic evidence, including 90 tons of train wreckage, and concealing the type of explosive used, to this day) was orchestrated by the Ministry of the Interior. Though fronted by Minister José Antonio Alonso, it was almost certainly Alfredo Pérez Rubalcaba (co-ordinator of Zapatero's election campain in 2004 and the GAL armed police units in the 1980s) who supervised the cover-up. For further information on the Alcasser

murders see: http://webs.demasiado.com/elpalleter/cartas.htm and www.kruela.ciberanika.com/alcasser/htm

10 Seen by Amenábar as a peddler of vulgar, dumbed-down, exploitation television, Navarro was nonetheless invited to 'simulate' an item from his own show for *Abre los ojos*, in which he interviews Dr Serge Duvernois on the subject of cryonisation. This is exactly the sort of 'freaky' item the Navarro show would normally have dealt with. Amenábar's use of the simulated interview, with Navarro himself in the chair, gives the sequence great credibility as well as strong intertextual resonance. The fact that Sofía says that she has seen the same piece thirty times also illustrates the deeply worrying nature of popular television viewing tastes in the mid- to late 1990s in Spain.

11 As Maltby reminds us, the logic of narrative coherence and continuity in films always competes with commercial imperatives. A film neither exists primarily as a coherent narrative nor is it necessarily dominated by narrative. Indeed, as Maltby notes, the main obligation on a movie is to make a profit by way of spectator pleasures, which engage and entertain audiences. In any case most commercial films tend to contain a good deal of excess, i.e. digressive material that escapes a unifying narrative structure. This is material which is mainly concerned with 'exploitation values', such as stardom, spectacle, technical wizardry, digressions which identify the movie as a commercial entity, and which offer the viewer a range of pleasures, not necessarily connected with narrative progression at all. See Richard Maltby, *Hollywood Cinema. An Introduction*, 2nd edn (Oxford: Blackwell, 2003), 14–19.

12 See David Bordwell, 'The art cinema as a mode of film practice', *Film Criticism*, 4:1 (Fall 1979), reprinted in *The European Cinema Reader*, Catherine Fowler (ed.) (London and New York: Routledge, 2002), 94–102.

13 Jacques Terassa, 'Les écrans noirs d'Alejandro Amenábar: des voix en quête d'images', *Le cinéma d'Alejandro Amenábar*, in Nancy Berthier (ed.) (Toulouse: Presses Universitaires du Mirail, 2007), 27–42.

14 See Nancy Berthier, 'Voir ou ne pas voir: la fonction du hors champ dans *Tesis*', *Le cinéma d'Alejandro Amenábar*, in Nancy Berthier (ed.) (Toulouse: Presses Universitaires du Mirail, 2007), 43–56.

15 Also according to Rycroft, post-Freudian notions of exhibitionism tend to view the condition as a 'manic defence against depression, frigidity or fear of loss of identity' (1968: 47).

16 Mark's sadism arises from his abuse by a father who has used him as a guinea pig in his experiments; he thus copes with his childhood trauma by projecting his repressions and rage through a repeated compulsion to murder. Powell's unusual take on this situation is to play Mark's sadistic father himself in a cameo. This finds a vague parental echo in *Himenóptero*, where the equally sadistic director Silvia is female and arguably a stand-in for Amenábar and quite possibly for his mother too. *Peeping Tom* is also

homaged at the beginning of *Himenóptero*, via the soundtrack, as the cameraman Bosco extends his tripod leg with an aggressive 'crack', recalling the 'camera as weapon' motif and the knife concealed in the tripod leg in Powell's film.

17 See, Laura Mulvey (1989), *Visual and Other Pleasures* (Houndmills, Basingstoke: Macmillan, 1989), 14–28.

18 Linda Williams, 'When the woman looks', in *Re-Visions. Essays in Feminist Film Criticism*, M.A. Doane, P. Mellencamp and L. Williams (eds) (Frederick, MD: The American Film Institute/University Publications of America, 1984) 83–99.

19 Carol J. Clover, *Men, Women and Chainsaws: Gender in the Modern Horror Film* (London: BFI, and Princeton NJ: Princeton University Press, 1992); see also Mary Ann Doane, 'Film and the masquerade: theorising the female spectator', *Screen*, 23:3–4, (September/October 1982), 74–87.

20 Noman Denzin, *The Cinematic Society. The Voyeur's Gaze* (London: Sage, 1995).

21 See Dominique Russell, 'Sounds like horror: Alejandro Amenábar's thesis on audio-visual violence', *Canadian Journal of Film Studies*, 15:2 (Fall 2006), 81–95.

22 See Robin Wood, *Hitchcock's Films Revisited*, Revised Edition (New York: Columbia University Press, 1998/2002), 151. See also Thomas M. Leitch. 'How to steal from Hitchcock', in David Boyd and R. Barton Palmer (eds), *After Hitchcock. Influence, Imitation and Intertextuality* (Austin: University of Texas Press, 2006), 251–70.

23 It is worth noting that Professor Dona Kercher delivered a paper on Amenábar's relationship with Hitchcock in November 2003, at the IRS, University of London, at the conference *Hispanic Cinemas: The Local and the Global*, 'Hispanic Hitchcock: the Direct Takes of Amenábar and De la Iglesia'.

24 Charles Derry, *The Suspense Thriller. Films in the Shadow of Alfred Hitchcock* (Jefferson NC: McFarland Press, 1988), 31. See also Steve Neale's section on the suspense thriller in Pam Cook (ed.), *The Cinema Book*, 3rd edn (London: BFI, 2007), 286–7.

25 For example, for *Tesis* he planned to include a short cameo sequence which involved him and Mateo Gil shooting film (with his parents also in shot) in the Faculty foyer. However, this was eventually excised. In *Abre los ojos* he appears as part of a trio of young men (plus Mateo Gil and Carlos Montero) who joke at César's expense as they exit the toilet. The same trio reappear as tuberculosis victims in *The Others* in one of the photographs in the 'Book of the Dead'. Also, it is worth recalling that Amenábar and Mateo Gil made a sort of brotherly pact very early in their relationship to appear in each other's films. Thus, Amenábar also appears in Gil's shorts and in his *Nadie conoce a nadie* (1998), as part of a group in the bar where Simón is playing chess. Moreover, in Javier Ruiz Caldera's pioneering

comic spoof feature *Spanish Movie* (2009), alongside Álex de la Iglesia, Juan Antonio Bayona, Jaume Balagueró, Paco Plaza and Andreu Buenafuente, among others, Amenábar amusingly re-creates one of César's 'phantom of the Opera' moments in the bathroom from *Abre los ojos*.

26　See Ann Davies, 'Can the contemporary crime thriller be Spanish?', *Studies in European Cinema*, 2:3 (2005), 173–83.

27　See Paul Julian Smith, 'Towards the Spanish youth movie: *Historias del Kronen*', in *Spanish Visual Culture. Cinema, Television, Internet*, Manchester: Manchester University Press, 2006), 75–90, especially 78–81.

28　See Yvonne Tasker, *The Silence of the Lambs* (London: BFI Publishing, 2002, 24–6. See also Mark Whitehead, *Slasher Movies*, 2nd edn (Herts: Cox and Wyman, 2003), chs 6 and 7.

29　See David Kerekes and David Slater, *Killing for Culture: An Illustrated History of the Death Film from Mondo to Snuff* (London: Creation Books, 1995). I am also grateful to one of my final-year students, Rostam Wiehl, for bringing to my attention the real case of the 'Dnepropetrovsk Maniacs (3 guys, 1 hammer)', from the Ukraine, as an authentic example of a teen, serial 'snuff' spree. Between mid-June and mid-July 2007, three 19-year-old classmates from wealthy, respectable families, brutally tortured and murdered 21 old people from their own town with a hammer and a screw-driver. Graduating from killing cats to pensioners, their modus operandi included recording the murders on a mobile and attending the funerals of their victims. Motivation? A macabre hobby which consisted of collecting 'memories' for their 'old age'!

30　There is insufficient space to develop the point here, but another aspect of Amenábar's thesis on violence is arguably a complement, if not a challenge, to the Mulveyan paradigm of the gaze outlined earlier. Mulvey argued that the visual pleasure of classical Hollywood cinema was male-defined and dominated by his gaze alone. She ignored, however, the sort of pleasures women viewers might take when looking at film, by arguing that female screen characters and women spectators are victims of patriarchy and both are punished on- and offscreen. Also, in terms of Mulvey's model, if women viewers like watching films where women characters suffer, then they could only be empathising and identifying with a male, sadistic positioning. In relation to 1970s feminism and gender politics, such an alignment with the suffering woman was politically awkward, while thrilling to her pain was definitely taboo. Since the 1970s, as noted above, writers such as Clover have shown how the alleged power of the sadistic male gaze has been much exaggerated, while the masochistic female gaze has been virtually ignored. Clover's analysis of the masochistic pleasures of horror spectatorship largely limits itself to young male viewers, while leaving the female reactive gaze relatively unexplored. The case of Ángela in *Tesis* and her powerful masochistic gaze might well provide a fruitful theme for further work.

4

Life, death and the Disneyland question: *Abre los ojos*

In *Tesis* a shy, sexually repressed, female media student, preparing a dissertation on screen violence, has a hidden appetite for danger and extreme movies. While investigating the disappearance and murder of a colleague, she expresses this repressed desire by falling in love with a gorgeous young 'pijo' (spoilt rich kid), an *homme fatal*, who is the prime suspect as the serial killer. She also enlists as her helper and side-kick the other potential suspect for the murder, a former close friend of the handsome playboy. Seemingly trapped in a deadly love triangle, Ángela saves her sister and male helper, slays the monster, abandons her thesis and then walks off with the decoy serial killer. Put like this, the plot outline of Amenábar's first feature echoes the conventions of a standard, Hollywood, 'teen horror' feature. Similar concerns seem to underpin the narrative outline of his second film. Here, at his twenty-fifth birthday party, a handsome young man flirts with his best buddy's date, spends the night with her and falls in love. His ex-girlfriend becomes insanely jealous and wreaks terrible vengeance. While the buddy recovers his girlfriend, the handsome young man loses not only his looks and the 'girl of his dreams' but also his mind. Once again a rather unpromising, cheesy romance underpins the often baffling, convoluted thriller narrative of *Abre los ojos*. In their co-written script it is clear that Amenábar and Mateo Gil recycle many of the narrative and character elements of the earlier feature. For example, the character patterning found in *Tesis* is simply repeated in *Abre los ojos*, with Eduardo Noriega and Fele Martínez reappearing as best buddies César and Pelayo. This time, however, the focus of attention is on the already familiar narcissistic playboy, who (like Ángela in *Tesis*) plays the role of an investigator, but this time of the murder of his own 'dream girl'. And while Sofía returns to Pelayo, César's egotism and betrayal of male friendship are seemingly punished via a prolonged and devastating nightmare of mental anguish and suffering.

Abre los ojos is without question an ambitious project, even audacious, in its striking timescale and generic remixing. It cleverly combines elements of teen romance, thriller, film noir, horror and sci-fi, cautionary tale, morality play and family melodrama. Also, if *Tesis* has its origins in the short *Himenóptero* (1992) and is strongly inspired by *Psycho, Peeping Tom* and *The Silence of the Lambs*, *Abre los ojos* is based on *Luna* (1994), and on Gil's two early shorts *Antes del beso* (Before the Kiss, 1993) and *Soñé que te mataba* (I Dreamed I Killed You, 1994). The film's 'life and death as a dream' and 'reality versus perception' problematic also sets up a vast array of possible intertextual links and echoes, from areas such as philosophy (e.g. Descartes, Hume, Nietzsche) literature (Cervantes, Calderón, Borges, Dick) and cinema. As well as acknowledging the surrealist traditions of Buñuel and Dalí, *Abre los ojos* clearly stands as a partial remake of Hitchcock's *Vertigo*, arguably its main intertext. It also pays homage to the German Expressionist masterpiece *The Cabinet of Dr Caligari* (Robert Wiene, 1920), as well as classic versions of *The Beauty and the Beast* (*La belle et la bête*, Jean Cocteau, 1946), *The Hunchback of Notre Dame* (William Dieterle, 1939), *The Phantom of the Opera* (Rupert Julian, 1925, with Lon Chaney) and *Dr Jekyll and Mr Hyde* (Victor Fleming, 1941). It also reveals its indebtedness to the more modern, erotic thriller, such as *Fatal Attraction* (Adrian Lyne, 1987) and *Basic Instinct* (Paul Verhoeven, 1992). It even pre-empts the last film made by one of Amenábar's most revered directors, Stanley Kubrick, and his mystifying, ambiguous *Eyes Wide Shut* (1999). The latter film starred husband-and-wife team Tom Cruise and Nicole Kidman and is concerned with the destructive effects of male jealousy (marital), dreams, fantasy and unsettling realities. And, echoing the pre-millennial moment of its making, *Abre los ojos* recalls any number of 'memory loss', 'mask' and 'virtual reality' films, from *The Lawnmower Man* (Brett Leonard, 1992) to *Memento* (Chris Nolan, 2000), *The Sandman* (J.R. Bookwalter, 1996) and *The Game* (David Fincher, 1997), and especially *Total Recall* (Paul Verhoeven, 1990), to name but a few. However, compared to *Tesis*, *Abre los ojos* constitutes a massive leap forward in ambition, formal complexity and risk. Amenábar and Gil weave a vast, intricate narrative and stylistic matrix, transforming a seemingly, dumb, adolescent story line into a dark parable of dreams, nightmares, death and resurrection.

Given its more problematic origins and the various complications which arose during pre-production, my approach in this chapter is guided by what Amenábar has said in retrospect about the film: 'Es una película muy compleja ... me quedaré con la duda de saber qué es lo que pudo ser si la hubiera planteado de otra manera' (Rodríguez Marchante 2002:106) (It's a very complicated film ... I'll always wonder what it could have been like had I approached it in a different way). My aim here will be to focus initially on certain background aspects such as scripting, title, casting and problems of narrative comprehension. These are followed by my attempt to clarify certain ambiguities in the film's narrative structure. I then offer a three-part analysis of what I consider to be the film's main and contrasting intertexts, which offer much food for thought in terms of its meanings and implications. These include Hitchcock's *Vertigo* (1958), perhaps the most obvious and widely acknowledged frame film, but also *The Matrix* (Wachowski brothers, 1999), a film released two years later than *Abre los ojos* but which is increasingly regarded as a key reference point. And, given the very powerful impact of contemporary American genre cinema on Amenábar and Gil as scriptwriters, I propose to locate *Abre los ojos* within the context of so-called 'yuppie horror'. Finally, I provide a brief commentary on and comparison between *Abre los ojos* and its American remake, *Vanilla Sky* (2001).

The idea

Amenábar claims that it was while recovering from a bad dose of flu and persistent nightmares in early 1996 that he first came up with the idea for what was initially entitled *El contrato* (The Contract), which only later would become *Abre los ojos* (*Open your eyes*). Just as he had researched snuff movies by reading Román Gubern's chapter on extreme cinema and used the topic as a premise for *Tesis*, he stumbled on the idea for his second film by playing some 'mind games' and 'what if' scenarios with actor colleague and friend Eduardo Noriega. They speculated on the question of immortality and how long it might be before science and technology were able to prolong life indefinitely, using cryogenic techniques (Sempere 2000: 87). Such 'transcendental questions' (a term used by César in the film dialogue when replying to Núria, just before the car crash), were posed against the background of Amenábar's first close encounter with the internet in 1996 (on a visit to Germany), where he found information on the cryonics company which would become the model for L.E.[1]

Arguably, Amenábar's original idea for *El contrato* was in no way groundbreaking or cleverly fleshed out. It involved a beggar who is forced by circumstance to sell his body for scientific experimentation in exchange for money (an echo, perhaps, of Amenábar's genuine concern for Madrid's 'street people', the lower orders and the poor). He then wakes up in some indeterminate future and discovers that he has been reanimated via cryonics, and that during his time in deep freeze he has been living in a dream (Rodríguez Marchante 2002: 65). As noted above, the notion of 'life/death as a dream' is a classic trope of most literary, philosophical and filmic traditions, to be found in many different cultures across the world. And, at least since Kubrick's *2001 A Space Odyssey* (1968) as well as *Alien, Blade Runner* and *Total Recall*, among a host of others, Amenábar's basic idea was already a well-worn staple of mainstream modern Hollywood science fiction and fantasy. However, in the context of Spanish filmmaking in the mid-1990s, the idea was unusual. Indeed, if the topic of the snuff movie was almost unknown in Spain, then a plot outline for a Spanish psychological thriller cum sci-fi film involving hibernation, virtual reality and Philip K. Dickian paranoia and alternative worlds was almost unimaginable.

The more distant origins of the film are largely personal and lie in part in Amenábar's memories of certain childhood and adolescent traumas, aspects of which he had already incorporated into his shorts: 'De algún modo, todo esto lo utilizo en mis historias' (Rodríguez Marchante 2002: 31) (In one way or another, I use all this personal stuff in my stories). These included the effects of a car crash involving a truck on the way to school, with his mother at the wheel. Afterwards his older brother Ricardo suffered prolonged nightmares and bouts of sleepwalking and screaming. This deeply disturbed behaviour scared the whole family, especially the young Alejandro (Rodríguez Marchante, 2002: 33).[2] Also, as noted earlier, another unnerving vehicular incident occurred when Amenábar was hitching back home from school by himself. He was picked up by a female driver, who became aggressive and intimidating (Rodríguez Marchante 2002: 46). This unpleasant incident clearly left a lasting impression on the youngster and reappears as the basis of the causal chain (as well as various dialogue motifs) for his third short film, *Luna* (1994). As noted in Chapter 2, in *Luna* the usual male-dominated, hitcher movie format is reversed, with the female driver murdering her innocent passenger. Similar action lines, character templates and relationships appear in Mateo Gil's early shorts, *Antes del beso* and *Soné que te mataba* the latter piece structured according to an elaborate series of flashbacks. Since Amenábar and Gil made their shorts together, these tended to reflect common narrative patterns, stylistic selections, motifs and thematic concerns which appealed to both filmmakers and were reworked by them. Moreover, the early shorts offered ample resources for regular raiding and recycling in both Amenábar's and Gil's main film features. This presents us once again with the problem of attribution, alluded to earlier, especially in relation to *Abre los ojos*, since it is difficult to separate what story input belongs to Amenábar and what to Gil. The problem also extends to the film script, since the producer José Luis Cuerda played a key role in supervising the progress of the script and its many revisions before submission to Bovaira.

Script development

It is worth reminding ourselves that *Abre los ojos* came into being because of the contract Amenábar had agreed with Cuerda, i.e. to make his first three feature films for Las Producciones del Escorpión. After *Tesis*, however, and as producer, Cuerda was anxious not to repeat the mistakes they had made on the first film. Some involved scripting, rehearsing and editing, but most of them arose from the constraints of a limited budget. Hence his decision to approach a much bigger, more financially solvent, national film company as co-producer on the project. This was Sogecine,the film production arm of Sogetel and part of the PRISA media group. Cuerda had a good relationship with the company and he knew he could rely on a highly competent and forward-looking young film producer called Fernando Bovaira, who had taken charge of the film division in 1996. In order to seal the contract, Cuerda needed to present Sogecine with a water-tight film treatment, a solid script and a cast list. According to Sempere, the treatment went through six different versions and the script at least three, until they were accepted (2000: 87). And, as Amenábar reminds us, scripting *Abre los ojos* was a much more gruelling assignment than *Tesis* since Cuerda insisted on supervising and editing the drafts until they reached a satisfactory standard (Rodríguez Marchante 2002: 65).

With regard to Amenábar's original outline, Cuerda as well as Gil concluded that the original scenario was too naive and clichéd, with too many holes and inconsistencies . At some point the beggar was dropped in favour of another Spanish 'pijo' (spoilt rich kid). Also, thanks to Cuerda, the revised plot line was much simplified and reoriented towards the psychological interiority and mental confusion of the main male lead, who mistakes one woman for another and, in his delirium, ends up murdering her. Of course the resemblance of this skeleton to the main plot line of Hitchcock's *Vertigo* (1958) was hardly coincidental. Indeed, after *Psycho* (1960), *Vertigo* was one of Hitchcock's most influential and canonised films, one about which Amenábar was arguably most enthusiastic. However, Cuerda was rather concerned that the script was too reminiscent of the Hitchcock classic, with perhaps too much emphasis being placed on César's personal loss, melancholy, delusions and downward spiral. The narrative was thus thinned out, which resulted in the deletion of a middle section, which greatly extended César's confusion between Núria and Sofía. Also Sofía was changed from a model to a drama student who works as a mime (a suggestion made, incidentally, by Mateo Gil) (Interview). And, for the sake of greater narrative clarity, Cuerda suggested shifting the motivation for César's trauma away from a technophobic critique of the the protagonist's 'dream life'. The cause of César's trauma was thus reoriented towards the disfigured seducer's own psychological make-up and the fact that he himself purchases a dream which goes wrong. In this way, through irruptions from his own subconscious desires, César himself would become a causal factor in the subversion of his own dream, by way of guilt feelings, self-loathing or masochistic self-punishment (an echo perhaps of Ángela in *Tesis*). Thus, despite his wealth, he would undermine his virtual happiness, through his own volition, because of deeper personality flaws and psychological defences, which allow personal guilt, responsibility and depression to be marginalised or denied.

Such an approach also coincided strongly with Cuerda's own liberal, left-wing, ethical stance towards human nature, 'ya que somos nosotros los que nos creamos nuestro propio infierno' (Rodríguez Marchante 2002: 66) (because we alone invent our own hell). [3] This now famous lapidary phrase (like others from the film such as 'Do you want to know the truth? It's unlikely you could bear it!') was eventually worked into the dialogue through the mouth of the L.E. Director, Serge Duvernois. The incorporation of this 'deus ex machina' figure came in the third version of the script, after further interventions from Cuerda. He suggested that, rather than have an ending which focused on the failure of the technology in the future, César's night-mare should stem from his own contradictions and from an inner, self-destructive desire to mess up his own dream. What is abundantly clear here is the strong degree of Cuerda's own personal involvement in rewriting the script and reorienting, while clarifying, character development, even though he is nowhere credited. As Amenábar has declared: 'Todas las intervenciones de José Luis Cuerda fueron fruto de decisiones de las que no me arrepiento, porque le dejé opinar y cortar mucho' (Rodríguez Marchante 2002: 66) (All of José Luis Cuerda's interventions came from decisions I have never regretted, because I let him give his opinion and cut a great deal).[4] Cuerda's crucial role in reconceptualising and supervising the scripting process of *Abre los ojos* thus reminds us that, even though Amenábar is routinely credited and often lionised by critics as sole author of his scripts, other major contributions (such as those of Gil and Cuerda) are patently crucial to the quality and viability of the writing. They also indicate that Amenábar's authorship is invariably team-driven, shared, distributed and collective in this area.

Cuerda also calculated that Amenábar's second film would benefit from the commercial and critical success achieved by *Tesis*, which had done very well after its relaunch, following its unforeseen Goya successes in January 1997. In two to three months *Tesis* had stimu-lated very positive 'boca oreja' (word of mouth) in Spain, which quickly transformed the film into a much more mainstream hit. It also attracted very positive press coverage. Amenábar's second feature could thus rely on a strong platform of public support and eager anticipation. What was wholly unexpected, however, was the unprec-edented degree of media interest in Spain's 'little Orson' and his second film. Television and press journalists pursued in enormous detail each phase of the shooting schedule, the post-production period and so on until the press screenings in mid-December 1997. According to Amenábar, such emphatic media attention and public curiosity were very welcome as free publicity and hype for the film but imposed considerable pressures and strains.[5] Needless to say, in his second outing, Amenábar could afford to be much more adventurous, and explore story lines and issues which would have been far too risky to undertake in a first film. All in all, had it not been for the success of *Tesis*, the producer Cuerda and his main partner Sogecine would have been very reluctant to proceed with a second film which, by compar-ison with the first, was no simple, reheated *Tesis* 2. Rather, it was a far more complex and challenging, multilayered narrative, though based on a trivial romantic premise, in which the unsympathetic, cocksure rich kid genuinely falls in love with the 'girl of his dreams'. It was also a leap into the unknown and a serious financial risk, compared to the budget constraints which affected *Tesis*. And if it did not work in the domestic market, it would very likely puncture the Amenábar bubble and derail his career (*Academia* 1999: 8).

Title

The change of film title from *El contrato* to *Abre los ojos* was also Cuerda's idea. He was struck by the powerful visual impact of the opening sequence of the film and by the insistent, repetitive, voice message, which fades in from black, recorded by Núria on César's clock radio. For Cuerda, the message was highly suggestive, enigmatic and very expressive: 'incluso era una llamada al espectador para que se fijase bien en las cosas que estaba viendo allí' (*Academia* 1999: 12) (it was also a cue to the spectator to focus carefully on what she/he was seeing there). In other words, by asking the audience to wake up, the film urges a more focused, critically alert form of looking, a more careful reflection on the 'seen' and, at the same time, an awareness of the trap of visibility and the visual, i.e. a heightened cautiousness when faced with the bedazzling effect of spectacle and glossy imagery. By comparison, the title 'El contrato' was seen as rather too flat, banal and explicit, too strongly tied narratively to the last 30 minutes of the film, where César recalls his life-changing, 'consumer' moment: his purchase of L.E.'s most advanced cryonics/VR package. Cuerda was concerned that Amenábar's original title would tilt the film too far towards a simplified, trivial parable of 'caveat emptor' or buyer beware. For Cuerda the science fiction section was not the crux of the film, merely the 'envoltorio' (container or wrapping) for a far more searching exploration of issues to do with the outlook and moral values embodied in contemporary, hedonistic, Spanish youth culture, particularly physical beauty and the importance of one's 'looks'. Also crucial was the treacherous nature of appearances as well as matters of love, friendship, alienation, betrayal and how to cope with a catastrophic loss of identity.

In many ways the change of title offered a far more suggestive, metaphorical hook to audiences, providing a number of entry points into the film. And, taking into account Amenábar's admiration for Kubrick, the new title was also emblematic of a feature he too considers essential in filmmaking: ambiguity.[6] As the device which opens and closes the film, the repetition of the line 'abre los ojos', in different contexts and with female voices, creates pleasing effects of symmetry and closure. It also cues the audience to compare beginnings and endings in order to gauge the nature of the contexts in play and the impact of the leading character's 'journey' towards some form of enlightenment or new awareness throughout the narrative. For example, at the opening of the film, the words are recorded by Núria, after a night of explosive sex. They are intended to remind César that he has not been having sex with a machine but has been with a real woman who has an identity and personality of her own and who demands his attention. At the end of the film the words (preceded by 'Tranquilo, tranquilo' – relax, relax – the very same words which are used to open *Mar adentro*) are spoken, we assume, by a nurse in a cryonics lab, where César is being encouraged to wake up after exiting his Virtual Reality dream, having been re-animated in 2147. What kind of new identity and reality is César being asked to contemplate? We are neither told nor shown anything, which leaves the next phase in César's new life tantalisingly open and the film ending cryptic and enigmatic.

The line, an obvious editorial tag, is also deeply intertextual and complicit with Amenábar's first film. Where *Tesis* opened and closed with health warnings recommending us 'not to look', to avert our gaze (from the mangled body in the railway station, from the corpses of the victims on television), *Abre los ojos* opens and closes with the demand that we look, watch closely, keep our eyes peeled in order not to be misled. This refers not only to looking in the realm of real-world experience but also to looking in the cinema. The line makes the simple metacinematic point that we should not confuse the film theatre with the world outside or mix up our own projections and fantasies with the reality of the 'other'. Hence the function of the line as a warning, which underpins the film not only as a cautionary tale but also as one concerned with ontological questions, i.e. the nature of reality and fantasy, as well as epistemological concerns, such as our attitudes towards trust, belief, scepticism and doubt.

Casting

As noted earlier, the new wave of young, first-time filmmakers who entered the Spanish film industry in the early and mid-1990s was accompanied by a rush of new acting talent. The commercial success of films such as *Días contados* (Countdown, Imanol Uribe 1994), *El día de la bestia* (The Day of the Beast, Álex de la Iglesia, 1995) and *Historias del Kronen* (Stories of the Kronen, Montxo Armendáriz, 1995) revealed an appetite among young Spanish audiences for edgy, contemporary roles, played by new, relatively unknown actors, such as Ruth Gabriel, Candela Peña, Santiago Segura and Juan Diego Botto, all Goya nominees in 1994 and 1995 for Best New Actor. In casting *Tesis*, Amenábar had also opted largely for unknown young actors (Eduardo Noriega, Fele Martínez, Nieves Herranz, Rosa Campillo). This is despite the choice of the legendary child star Ana Torrent as Ángela (this was Cuerda's preferred option and not Amenábar's, given that Penélope Cruz was unavailable). Among the seven Goyas won by *Tesis*, the prize for Mejor Actor Revelación (Best New Actor) went to Fele Martínez, an award which gave a complete unknown a flying start to his acting career. It also seemed to confirm Amenábar's ability to spot acting talent, which he has developed in subsequent features, especially *Mar adentro* and the film careers of Belén Rueda, Lola Dueñas, Mabel Rivera, Tamar Novas and Celso Bugallo.

For everyone connected with *Tesis*, the Goya 'bounce' was a welcome surprise and it radically changed the commercial fortunes of the film. It also had the effect of unifying the crew into a team, many of whom were anxious to be considered for work on Amenábar's next film. However, even with this boost to his self-confidence, he approached *Abre los ojos* with a significant degree of trepidation, primarily because of its scale, risk, bigger budget and international participation. It was a large and much more complex European co-production, involving French and Italian investment, as well as subsidies from Eurimages.[7] Though the lion's share of the finance was shouldered by Sogecine and Las Producciones del Escorpión, the co-pro nature of the project meant that, in return for better distribution deals in foreign markets, certain compromises on international casting might be required

Unsurprisingly, some of the original cast and virtually all of the crew for *Tesis* were rehired for *Abre los ojos*. This allowed the press to compare Amenábar's acting choices, for example, with Almodóvar's repertory-style casting of the 1980s, and talk of the 'chicos' and 'chicas Amenábar' (Amenábar's boys and girls) (see *Cambio 16*, 23 June 1997: 80, and *El Mundo*, 27 December 1997: 10). The casting of Eduardo Noriega as the main male lead, César, was almost inevitable. Amenábar had known him since his third year at University as a drama student from Madrid's main Drama School (Escuela Superior de Arte Dramático or ESAD). Noriega had worked with him and had acted in his short *Luna* (1994) as well as in Mateo Gil's short *Soñé que te mataba* (I Dreamed I Killed You, 1994). He had also played a small, secondary role in the feature *Historias del Kronen* before undertaking Bosco in *Tesis*. And now, given that the figure of the 'posh kid' from *Tesis* was about to reappear in *Abre los ojos*, Noriega seemed the obvious choice. In fact, Amenábar developed the character and wrote the script with Noriega in mind. This virtually guaranteed his continuation in the role. Noriega's reprise of the treacherous 'yuppie' brat may have been seen initially as a simple recycling of the previous character, but this was not the case. The new role was far more demanding, especially at the physical and expressive levels. Apart from the daily grind of three to four hours of make-up at the hands of Colin Arthur, Noriega was asked to convey much of the suffering and paranoia of the 'wrong man' trapped in an existential nightmare from behind a prosthetic mask.[8] Moreover, Noriega's masculine charm and boyish good looks were perfect for the role of the smug narcissist who would get his terrifying and prolonged comeuppance. By destroying his principal assets, his beautiful body and face, the film could mount its critique of appearances, the nature of physical beauty and machismo through a tale of female revenge and male disempowerment.

Alongside Noriega, Amenábar placed Rafael or Fele Martínez, who was another ESAD student and contemporary of Noriega. As noted earlier, Cuerda had not been happy with Amenábar's decision to cast him as Chema in *Tesis*, yet Amenábar saw something of the Chema character in him which, with exhaustive rehearsals, began to take shape. In *Abre los ojos* Amenábar wished to abandon the grungy, misfit look of Chema in favour of a plain, subordinate, male side-kick, who is only 'averagely good looking', lacking in self-confidence and unable to attract women. As a counterpoint to César, Martínez seemed very well cast as Pelayo, the 'nice guy' who, despite his protestations of loyalty, is also happy to see his treacherous best friend humbled (see Perriam 2003: 181–2).

In terms of the two female leads, rather than unknowns Amenábar needed two actresses with experience. He sought to extend the principle of contrasting pairs and create two very attractive but opposed and conflictive images of femininity (Heredero 1997: 113). On the one hand, Sofía represented beauty, charm and warmth, yet she also exuded ordinariness and cleverness for César, as a fantasy love object, the 'girl of his dreams'. She had to seduce him almost instantly by radiating a certain innocent allure and magic, while also binding the spectator into the narrative with her gorgeous looks (Heredero 1997: 113). Amenábar saw in Penélope Cruz this overwhelming power of instant seduction: 'Aquí Penélope Cruz jugaba una función muy importante, porque ella tiene esa magia necesaria para que con muy pocos planos pudiera enamorar a cualquiera' (Rodríguez Marchante 2002: 69–70). (Here Penélope Cruz played a vital role, because she has the necessary magic to make anyone fall in love with her in just a few shots). Morever, given the demands of the script, Amenábar had no qualms in exploiting Cruz's 'to-be-looked-at-ness', including onscreen nudity: 'Tiene como una especie de ángel, tiene gracia, tiene carisma, es una estupenda actriz, y llena la cámara y eso era lo que necesitaba' (Payán 2001: 40) (She has a kind of allure, charm, charisma, she's a great actress, she fills the screen and that is exactly what I was looking for).

By contrast, Núria was another angry, sexy, alienated loner (similar to César). She was also a stalker, unprepared to allow César to discard her without taking revenge. After negotiating with Cuerda, Amenábar chose Najwa Nimri. The choice of the Spanish–Jordanian actress was perhaps slightly odd, given that her previous screen experience was limited to roles in films made by her husband, the young Basque director Daniel Calparsoro. Nimri had specialised in aggressive, edgy parts as a lumpen, androgynous, skinhead junkie (as Alex in *Salto al vacío* (Leap into the Void, 1995), a lesbian thief, manipulative *femme fatale*, with a taste for older women (as Gavi in *Pasajes* (Passageways, 1996) and punk shop assistant/ETA activist trying to escape the movement (as Marrubi in *A ciegas* (Blinded, 1997). She was thus linked on screen with crime, delinquency, grunge and ugliness, the punk lifestyle, alternative sexualities and the Basque cultural underground. However, Amenábar managed to find in her a degree of sensuality, mystery and scary self-confidence which made Nimri seem the perfect counterpoint to the virginal, heterosexual Sofía and the detonator which unleashes César's nightmare. Moreover, these female roles were not complex characters, rather they emerge as one-dimensional archetypes of virtuous virgin and filthy whore, i.e. the clichéd binary of the César's atavistic, macho imagination. Nor were they large parts, even though they have a crucial impact on the fortunes of the main protagonist.

Though the film is set in Madrid, Amenábar was obliged to cast a foreign actor in the role of the 'man on the television', in order to satisfy co-pro arrangements and European marketing. The part of the suave Dr Serge Duvernois, which was a late addition to the script, was played by Gérard Barray (born 1931), a veteran French actor, with an extensive acting career behind him, stretching back to the 1950s. Ordinarily Amenábar would have opposed such international castings, because foreign actors have to be dubbed and this interferes with their credibility and verisimilitude on screen (Payán 2001: 38). In this case Amenábar stood his ground and refused to dub the foreign voices, so that the film does not contain any dubbed voices at all. Moreover, even though his French accent is noticeable, Barray fits the role perfectly and delivers his lines in pristine Spanish.

Leaving aside smaller roles such as the prison guard and the police inspector, the casting of Chete Lera as Antonio, the prison psychiatrist, was widely acclaimed by Spanish critics as inspired. Lera is a veteran Spanish television and screen actor, who was perfectly suited to portraying the unorthodox, bearded, 'shrink without a white coat' figure. He looks and sounds friendly and human, dresses casually and befriends César. He helps unblock the childhood trauma arising from the death of César's parents. He is the symbol of 'happy families' but also the voice of scepticism, historical consciousness and the older generation. He plays the role of a stand-in father figure, even if, in the end, he is revealed as no more than a phantom, a cyber creation who inhabits César's virtual dream.

Narrative comprehension

Talking about the film Amenábar recalls: 'Una de nuestras preocupaciones era la inteligibilidad' (Rodríguez Marchante 2002: 69) (One of our main concerns was understanding). As noted earlier, in terms of its treatment and scripting, *Abre los ojos* went through multiple drafts and countless smaller changes (Sempere 2004: 145), mainly because of persistent problems of structure and spatio-temporal relations which threatened to confuse audience understanding. When Amenábar and Gil laid out in linear fashion the narrative chain of events, they found that they had three films before them, not one. These were divided into three generically separable, nearly self-contained sections comprising a teen romance with a touch of comedy, a suspense thriller and a sci-fi drama. The writers were concerned that this movie triptych might be regarded as three distinct episodes, lacking any narrative coherence or integration (Rodríguez Marchante 2002: 68). Faced with the problem of how to bring them together, it was Mateo Gil who suggested fragmenting the various action lines and combining the three separate parts by means of a series of flashbacks, located at different levels of the main protagonist's psychic reality. This could help unify the narrative and create a more consistent emotional register (of anxiety and paranoia juxtaposed with moments of happiness and stability). On the down side, it could also lead to a rather complex, non-linear and potentially confusing diegesis, giving rise to problems of audience comprehension. By no means a fan of flashbacks and fragmented time schemes, but acknowledging that these might offer a solution to the generic overload, Amenábar reluctantly decided to take the risk. With *Abre los ojos* he knew he was not making a conventional, commercial, mainstream family film or one aimed at children (despite the fact that it was released in late December 1997 and had to compete with American family imports over the Christmas season). He also knew it was going to be a complex and challenging psychological thriller, which would make significant demands on its educated, youth audiences (Rodríguez Marchante 2002: 69–70). And even if the film could not achieve audience engagement at an intellectual level on the issues raised, Amenábar believed he could still 'hook' the spectator emotionally through the film's alluring, dream-like atmospheres (supported by a well-chosen, modern soundtrack) and by the character of Sofía, who dazzles César and who was cast precisely to charm the audience.

In order to compensate for the complexities caused by the flashbacks and the confusions of a hazy time scheme, Amenábar was persuaded to incorporate a form of 'double back-up' into the narrative. On the one hand, this involved introducing the character of the prison psychiatrist Antonio (originally a lawyer). As noted earlier, this was no clichéd man in a white coat, with a mid-European accent, but a far more casual, likeable and believable figure, who could get close to César and help him re-discover why he was in jail. Antonio also repeats the role partly performed by Chema in *Tesis*, acting as a supplementary 'helper/detective', working alongside the main protagonist to clarify the reasons for the murder. And even though he also acts as a surrogate father figure, Amenábar's cruel, final 'twist' is that Antonio, his wife and two daughters are a mere figment of César's imagination, a necessary fiction supplied by L.E. to help stabilise César's tormented psyche.

On the other hand, we have Dr Serge Duvernois, the French-speaking head of L.E. in Madrid and another element of 'redundancy' to help spectator comprehension. In the early stages of scripting, after an interpolated television advertisement for L.E., the character of Duvernois was meant to appear again only at the end of the film as a form of *deus ex machina* (Sempere 2004: 148–9). His task was to explain the situation, to reveal to César (and the audience) the sources of his trauma and the options open to him. Fearful of repeating the sort of mistakes Hitchcock had appeared to make in *Vertigo*, by using a clichéd device to close down an improbable ending, Amenábar (on advice from Cuerda) decided to flesh out the character of Duvernois. This involved giving him several more appearances, distributed evenly across the narrative chain, as a gradual preparation for his authoritative, final 'revelation' on the roof of the Picasso Tower. Hence the sequences on the Pepe Navarro show, in the bar and at the disco, where Duvernois reminds César that his dream and his 'hell' are of his own making. The curious 'twist' as regards Duvernois is that, unlike Antonio, he appears to be real, though he is also able to travel through time and to insert himself into César's virtual dream. Duvernois thus warns César that he is deliberately subverting his own perfect dream by allowing bad memories and desires from his past to come to the surface, and, like Ángela in *Tesis*, is punishing himself.

Amenábar was also concerned with working out the most appropriate form of narration to adopt. Traditionally, in the horror film, fear is created when the line separating spectator and story is blurred or crossed, when the spectator is forced 'inside' the events or action portrayed. Point of view shots help motivate and create this impression by placing the spectator in the position of the characters, i.e. alongside both the pursued and the pursuer. In this connection the last 30 minutes of *Tesis* are a classic (though not totally successful) demonstration of such immersion, which aligns the spectator with Ángela and tries to maintain her and our uncertainty over the identity of the serial killer until the end. Of course, compared to *Tesis*, simply in terms of narrative scale (in spatial and temporal terms), *Abre los ojos* was a much bigger, more convoluted, generic hybrid. As Amenábar had shown already in *Tesis*, to connect the audience with Ángela, he preferred to adopt a mainly subjective, psychological focus, though not from an optical POV standpoint, a shot which he found tiresome, clichéd and clunky (though in *Abre los ojos* it is used sparingly in the interview room with Antonio). He wanted to access and convey as directly as possible the emotions and fears of the main protagonist in the first person, as captured in the famous publicity still for *Tesis*: 'Soy

Ángela y me van a matar' (I'm Ángela and I'm going to be killed). In other words Amenábar was anxious to relay, as convincingly as possible, the reality of César's subjective experience and to foreground the protagonist's identity crisis for the spectator, without any intervening filter. For this reason he did not consider shooting *Abre los ojos* from a third-person perspective, using omniscient narration. He argued that this position tended to overly 'mediate' and editorialise the narrative for the spectator, thereby getting in the way of spectator engagement with the character: As Amenábar asks, '¿Quién de nosotros es Dios para saber lo que nos está pasando o pasará? Todo lo estamos viviendo "sólo" nosotros y parto de ese concepto' (Rodríguez Marchante, 2002: 66) (Who among us is God and can know what happens or will happen to us? I start from the idea that only we are aware of what we are experiencing). This perhaps explains Amenábar's strong preference for point of view shooting, the restriction of vision (of camera, character and spectator), to create the sensation of claustrophobia and the closing down of diegetic space in order to constrain spectator knowledge and understanding. If we, like the characters, know only what we are allowed to see, then the unknown, especially the space offscreen, can be used to generate fear and anxiety. In *Abre los ojos* Amenábar wanted to have the spectator experience exactly what César does: 'Su vida se convierte en un infierno de confusión y el espectador, para bien o para mal, está condenado a seguirle a su mismo nivel' (Rodríguez Marchante 2002: 67) (His life becomes a confusing hell, and the spectator, for better or worse, is forced to follow him at the same level). Of course Amenábar creates this alignment by using not only close-up, interior shots but also exteriors. The famous God's eye, high-angle, crane shot of the Gran Vía, which locates César in a vast, empty, alienating city space, emphasises his vertigo and paranoia. It also suggests a divine vantage point, a superior presence which takes pleasure in the punishment of the young seducer.

Synopsis

The present (perhaps). From a cell in a psychiatric prison in an unidentified location, a 25–year-old César, wearing a prosthetic mask, answers questions from Antonio, a prison psychiatrist. Through flashbacks we learn that the handsome César is extremely successful with women. At his twenty-fifth birthday party, he ignores his latest conquest (Núria) in order to charm Sofía, the stunning guest of his best buddy Pelayo. Smitten with desire, he takes Sofía home but rather than seduce her, he spends an uncharacteristically romantic and 'chaste' night with her. Next morning, convinced he has met the 'girl of his dreams', he unwisely agrees to a lift from the implacable Núria. Jealous, vengeful and high on drugs, she commits suicide by crashing her sports car. César survives but is seriously disfigured and, despite repeated sessions of reconstructive surgery, is transformed into a monster.

Losing Sofía to Pelayo, César gets drunk at a disco and, after being abandoned by his erstwhile buddy, collapses on the pavement in a stupor. When he regains consciousness, things have changed for the better. Sofía says she loves him and the surgeons have now rebuilt his face. Yet he suffers from unpredictable 'déjà vécu' moments. And while making love to Sofía, he imagines she turns into Núria. Recalling Ana in *La cabeza*, so startled is he that he suffocates her with a pillow. In prison Antonio sedates him and helps him trace the source of his trauma. César vaguely remembers a company, called Life Extension. Antonio accompanies him to L.E.'s headquarters in the city. There, they discover that L.E. deals in cryonics and virtual reality, providing rich clients with hibernation services and a new, virtual life story until they are reawakened and remade in the future. Unprepared to continue his simulated existence, created for him by L.E., César opts to put an end to his life in order to escape the VR fantasy, with a return to the real.

Beginnings and endings

As Bordwell and Thompson argue, a film does not simply start, it begins (2004: 80). The opening provides the foundations for what is to come, it inserts the spectator into the image flow and cues the sorts of expectations and reading protocols we will need in order to follow the narrative. With *Abre los ojos* the film opens on a black screen, accompanied on the soundtrack by a female voice, which gradually grows louder, repeating a message (sourced diegetically in a speaking bedside clock): 'Abre los ojos (Open your eyes) ...' We fade up from black to a blurred image of bedclothes, as the ruggedly handsome César wakes up, gets out of bed, pointedly checks his appearance in the bathroom mirror, showers, dresses casually for an appointment, exits his vast, modern apartment and extracts his cool, white VW Beetle from his double garage. As he drives towards the city centre, he is troubled and looks at his watch: there are no people, anywhere. The streets are uncannily empty, the only sound is that of his car engine. This is not the normal, vibrant, bustling Madrid, with its street folk and homeless, with which he is familiar. He reaches the Gran Vía, the city's most famous landmark and thoroughfare and it is totally deserted. Aghast, unbalanced, César runs down the empty street looking in vain for signs of life.[9]

The very same opening sequence replays (almost), only this time César, on getting out of bed, is rather anxious, nervous, irritable, alert to any changes within his private domain. Without completing the sentence, he gently admonishes the brunette in his bed for changing the message on his alarm clock. A friendly gesture? A pointed reminder? Whatever the motive, César regards the new message as an unjustifiable intrusion, an invasion of his privacy and intimacy, made without his approval. He enjoys having sex with women, but not letting them into his life or changing his clock. Like Ángela in *Tesis*, he hates anybody messing with his things, simply because he puts privacy above all else. The slightest infringement of his iron rule, he indicates, 'me toca los huevos' (it pisses me off), as he finally completes downstairs in the garage the sentence he began upstairs. In his car, back in control, all seems well, normal, consonant with what he knows and expects to find. As the extra-diegetic music fades in, César begins another normal day, or so he thinks, since neither he nor the spectator suspects how the next 24 hours will totally transform his existence.

Two male voices fade in over the second waking sequence, from an unidentified, offscreen space. Questioned by Antonio, César talks about his habits and lifestyle, reaffirming the typical narrative of an ordinary, healthy young man, who is no different from anyone else, but who claims he is the victim of an elaborate conspiracy. The second sequence continues, adding detail absent from the first, and offering a seemingly standard, well-motivated, flashback. On his way to pick up his friend, Pelayo, for a game of squash, César drives past a film crew in the street (in reality a second unit, under Mateo Gil). This is a curious, metacinematic motif, in the circumstances (marked again by the use of the term 'splice', later on, in reference to César's dream). There is also a female street mime, with her face painted white, dressed as the tragic Pierrot (a classic stereotype of the *commedia dell'arte*). This makes two, unusual, opening 'dangling causes', waiting to be given narrative functionality. Running late and impatient, César meets Pelayo, who has taken to dieting and whose insistent questioning of the expert seducer indicates his obsessive concern with his lack of success with women: '¿Te la tiraste?' (Did you fuck her?). Pelayo wishes César would disappear so that others might get a chance to pull. While playing squash, and very untypically, César misses a shot. Pelayo jokes that his friend is being punished by God for being too successful with women. César gently rebukes the Almighty: 'Te voy a dar!' (You're for it!), a reference which is soon recycled by Antonio in another voiceover, when he asks César: '¿Crees en Dios?' (Do you believe in God?). And in another 30 minutes of running time, the same transcendental question is chillingly repeated by Núria just before the car crash. Such repetition, in different mouths and contexts, seems to add extra layers of meaning as well as coherence and causality to the narrative.

However, the opening of the film presents events apparently out of order, beginning with a dream or nightmare, followed by a flashback, held together by a linking voiceover. When read in relation to the second, the role of the first waking sequence is clearly that of an attention grabber, an eye opener, a jolt. The eerie, evacuated city centre and the panoramic view of the desolate Gran Vía from the God's eye crane shot are striking, troubling shots, intended for maximum impact. Designed to plunge the spectator into César's nightmare world of uncertainty and disorientation, they provide a little taste of what he has been experiencing in his dreams. But the severity of César's disturbance becomes apparent only when we see how Madrid functions in reality, a vision of which Amenábar provides in the second sequence. Here he emphasises the more specific Spanish meanings of the Gran Vía, that is, not just any old city centre but Madrid's and indeed Spain's most famous, iconic landmark. It is a thoroughfare which exists as such only because it swarms with people, who give it life, including the homeless. It is also exactly where Amenábar himself lives and it symbolises what he calls home. An empty Gran Vía, in this sense, functions as a synecdoche for a city and country drained and devoid of culture and history, representing a 'virtual', postmodern Spain of the spectacle.

As we catch our breath, we start adjusting to what appear to be multiple temporalities: a dream which has no logical narrative positioning or time; a flashback which may correspond to César's 'real' life or to his fake 'virtual' life; a voiceover, which could be a 'present' but who knows? In other words, even as we think we are adjusting to the narrative organisation of the film and getting the hang of where and when we are, the more information we learn tends to undercut our sense of understanding and mastery. Aligned with César and what he knows (initially he appears genuinely not to know why he is in jail, or why he is disfigured and wearing a mask), we share his confusion and disorientation, as we try to disentangle (along with Antonio and César's own personal investigation) the causes of his mental disturbance. Is he really disfigured? Is he dreaming? Are the flashbacks real? Is reality no more than a state of mind?

If the beginning of *Abre los ojos* is designed to disorient and confuse the spectator, the narrative organisation of the film as a whole is less intimidating. In fact, after the unsettling, dream-life prologue of the empty Gran Vía, we find roughly four blocks of narrative time, lasting about 30 minutes each, the first two moving forward in linear fashion. Presented as flashbacks, the first runs from César's second waking sequence up to the suicidal car crash, which is followed by a helpful fade to black. The second block stands as a narrative inversion of the first and covers the period of César's traumatic adjustment to his disfigurement, his meetings with Sofía in the park, discussions with his surgeons and his melancholy encounter with Sofía and Pelayo at the disco, ending with him lying alone and abandoned in the street. Another fade to black. A third section begins with César's rescue and renewed relationship with Sofía, intercut with Antonio's continuing interviews, meetings with doctors, the rebuilding of his face, his murder of Sofía, the police investigation, his first suicide, the appearances of Duvernois in the bar and on television, which trigger César's recall of L.E. and the visit. A fourth and final section finds César, accompanied by Antonio, at the headquarters of LE. Here he recovers a past, retraces vital steps in the signing of his contract and, in light of Duvernois's explanation of his condition, decides he wants to exit the virtual dream and wake up in the real.[10]

In the last section of the film Amenábar recreates for the audience the various stages César went through in drawing up his contract with L.E., including his purchase of Clause 14. This is 'Artificial Perception', a VR dream spliced on to César's memory after death and sold to him as 'signing for paradise'. In a wry dig at the Catholic Church, César says L.E. delivers in reality what priests had been falsely promising for thousands of years: immortality, eternal life. Like César on the squash court, the company has challenged the Almighty and has conquered death! Yet, in his dream life, César believes he has been living a nightmare of random substitutions between Sofía and Núria, of facial scarring which erupts and disappears and a murder charge of which he is convinced of his innocence. The interchangeability of beauty and ugliness (Sofía and Núria) is analogous to César's archaic attitude towards women and suggests he is subconsciously aware of and repelled by his own, disfigured, inner self. Pressed hard by Antonio to remove his mask, a first important moment of self-revelation comes in the men's bathroom. In the mirror, where Antonio sees a perfect face, César sees his own scars and they horrify him. Even if he were whole physically, his inner ugliness would doubtless find a way of manifesting itself. He now begins to realise that he is indeed trapped in a bad dream and wants to wake up, escape the torture, exit the 'montaje' (set up) and open his eyes to the real.

In the final scene on the roof, after the artificial shoot out on the evacuated patio below, Duvernois delivers elements of causality which so far have been missing: he and César met 150 years ago, the night of the disco was chosen for the splice and, on waking, nothing was real. César's memory was wiped and overlaid with the VR dream. César never saw Sofía again, the doctors never fixed his face. César remonstrates that he did not pay to look like a monster, to see Sofía transfigured into Núria and to live a nightmare. Duvernois replies that he paid to be whatever he wanted, that L.E. simply provided the characters and settings, like Antonio, whose wife and two kids are no more real than he is. In short, even though he seems unaware of it, César willed his very own hell. Here the human-centred, existentialist, message championed by Cuerda and taken on board by Amenábar is clearly expressed. Ultimately César cannot blame the company for his 'bad trip'. Whatever memories or subconscious fears and anxieties he had, they came from inside him. They were not imposed externally by his business partners or other enemies, or L.E., nor was there any conspiracy. In other words César is personally responsible for his own demons, actions, inner self and predicament.

The finale sees Duvernois give César two choices: Either he can continue inside the VR dream and L.E. will try to fix the disturbances or he can exit the dream in order to be reborn in the future. It is 2147 'out there', says Duvernois, pointing to an empty Madrid cityscape. Medical science can now rebuild César's face, but to exit the dream César will have to commit suicide again, though, as Duvernois says, dying is a 'mere formality' for him, since he is already dead, having taken his life in 1997. César takes the second option, a second, virtual death and a new life, though he will wake up in the 'real' of mid-twenty-second century America (presumably in Arizona, in the L.E. cryonics storage facility). Before departing, César says a deeply moving goodbye to his virtual family, Sofía, Antonio and Pelayo: a tearful repeat of a childhood trauma when he lost own parents, aged ten. However unreal these characters might be, César treats them as flesh and blood, sealing his VR life with a prolonged kiss for Sofía. He then jumps, falls down the Picasso Tower and the screen fades to black. Then we hear: 'Tranquilo, tranquilo, abre los ojos ...' (Relax, relax, open your eyes), from a warm, reassuring voice which could be that of a nurse, waking César up to his new life in the future. The ending suggests that L.E. and cryonics actually work, that science and technology have indeed triumphed over death. Yet, against a black screen, we are denied any substantive, visible proof, merely an audio interpolation. Is this for real or merely another montage?

Contrasting intertexts

In this section, as noted earlier, I intend to analyse *Abre los ojos* in relation to its principal, acknowledged intertext, Hitchcock's widely cited *Vertigo*. I also wish to explore the possible links between *Abre los ojos* and *The Matrix* (1999), the first of the trilogy and a standard reference point in much recent Anglo-American critical commentary. The fact that the release of *Abre los ojos* in the USA was delayed until April 1999 (coinciding with that of *The Matrix*) created the impression of pre-millennial commonalities. I also propose to locate *Abre los ojos* within the context of Spain's so-called 'X generation' and in relation to the notion of 'yuppie horror'. This is a term used to describe a large number of mainly Hollywood films of the 1980s and early 1990s which deal with catastrophic disruptions to middle-class lifestyles and values and their repercussions.

Yuppie horror

At the beginning of *Abre los ojos* César sums up his lifestyle to Antonio the psychiatrist in terms of three very basic, timeless, animal instincts: 'me gusta comer, dormir y hacer el amor, como todo el mundo' (I like to eat, sleep and make love, like everybody else).[11] He presents himself as just another, normal 25-year-old, whose basic instincts and their satisfaction offer an accurate reflection of his daily life. However, he fails to clarify at this stage how he supports a lifestyle in which he does next to nothing, has lots of sex with no strings and has use of a huge, city-centre designer flat, a house in the suburbs and three cars. Such luxury is possible only for a small minority of privileged, well-off individuals. As a wealthy scion of a family restaurant business, César belongs to Spain's upper-middle classes, a section of Spanish society which Amenábar knows well. The director of *Abre los ojos* describes his own social grouping and its identity thus: 'Mi generación viene marcada ... por el caos y la dejadez. Hemos vivido en casa de nuestros padres, prácticamente, no hemos tenido penurias y hablo desde mi experiencia personal. No tenemos ese gran acontecimiento que haya marcado una generación: el hecho es que somos una equis' (Rodríguez Marchante 2002: 88–9) (My generation is marked ... by turmoil and laziness. We've almost always lived at home, never experienced poverty, and I speak from personal experience. But we haven't lived that crucial event which marked a whole generation; the fact is we're the X generation).[12] By 'X generation' Amenábar refers to his own peers, i.e. those who were far too young to be marked by the Spanish Civil War, the Franco dictatorship or the transition to democracy. These were also the affluent middle-class children who lived through the 1980s and early 1990s, a period of economic growth, followed by slump, unemployment and political scandals. During this time such youngsters tended to live at home and depend on their parents' income for financial support; also, many failed to complete their degrees and experienced high unemployment rates. With increasing numbers of young women also competing in the same tight job market, young men thus saw traditional notions of entitlement, masculine identity and their self-confidence seriously challenged. These factors helped reinforce the phenomenon of 'pasotismo' (apathy, indifference) while also feeding into 'desencanto' or disillusionment with politics (particularly with left-wing parties, such as the PSOE government and its three consecutive terms in office (1982–96), which were plagued by corruption scandals and the backwash of a 'dirty war' against ETA).[13] These were also the depoliticised youngsters who were licensed and encouraged by liberal socialist legislation in the 1980s to experiment with sex, drugs and alcohol while being exposed to the most ubiquitous, rampant forms of exploitative, trash television. As a member of this 'television generation', Amenábar states that 'lo audiovisual es algo innato a nuestra generación: hemos crecido con la televisión y hemos vivido rodeado de imágenes' (Heredero 1997: 96) (the media are something innate to our generation, we've grown up with the television and lived surrounded by images).

Amenábar's first two feature films reveal certain similarities (in terms of the social background of his characters, their aspirations, values and hidden desires, issues of material comfort and attitudes towards sexual promiscuity, drugs, violence etc.) with a subgenre of American horror thrillers of the late 1980s and early 1990s. They also seem to draw upon and recycle aspects of the stylistic and narrative conventions found in films such as *After Hours* (Martin Scorsese, 1985), *Fatal Attraction* (Adrian Lyne, 1987), *Pacific Heights* (John Schlesinger, 1990), *The Hand that Rocks the Cradle* (Curtis Hanson, 1992) and *Single White Female* (Barbet Schroeder, 1992), all of which captured the anxieties and fears of a culture of affluence in an age of recession and deep social upheaval. I refer to what has been called in the USA the 'yuppie horror' of the 1980s and 1990s.[14] In its American context the term 'yuppie' was used to describe a new class of young, urban professionals in the early to mid-1980s who, above and beyond any racial or gender differences, fully embraced the values of asset acquisition, conspicuous consumption, new technologies, making money and the cult of self-interest. This was the 'Me' generation, the 'work hard–play hard' shock troops of a re-energised corporate capitalism, principally concerned with salary, social status, recognition, fame, looks and above all lifestyle. And by way of this horror subgenre, filmmakers (who were also yuppies themselves) began training their cameras on this new, wealthy, but vulnerable cultural phenomenon.

In the Spanish variant of 'yuppie horror', the protagonists are not so much young, thrusting urban professionals who gain their identity and distinction through an exhaustive, corporate 'work ethic' and its lifestyle options (financial success as well as 'burnout'). Rather, we are dealing with the affluent, but lazy, leisure-bound, apathetic, middle classes (predominantly students), who are rather jaded by their market power and consumer choices. Indeed, they are looking for something altogether more risky and challenging, i.e. an escape from the boredom, comfort and anomie of Spanish urban life in the 1990s. In Amenábar's first two films, for example, classic horror conventions are updated, with spatial metaphors of height and depth, ascent and descent, and crossing from one world to another, all reworked and adapted to suit the new, postmodern, urban exteriors and interiors. For example, in *Tesis*, the Faculty building serves as a visual metaphor for a grim, gothic castle of confinement, with its 'aulas' (lecture halls) recast as 'jaulas' (cages), and its stairways and balconies overlooking the internal patio suggestive of vertiginous descent into an under-world of catacombs, riddled by hidden tunnels and secret passage-ways. In *Abre los ojos*, in his opening dream, César exits his luxurious but cold, minimalist, city apartment only to descend into a disori-enting 'other' place, an evacuated, alienating city centre. He is also speaking from an even more chilling location, an unnamed, psychi-atric jail, unaware of why he is there. He suffers a catastrophic spatial shift, experiences a vertiginous fall from mastery and control of a gilded lifestyle to a prison cell. He also feels the sensation of having no firm ground to stand on and the rug being pulled from under him (a motif which will be repeated, verbally and visually, throughout the film). The spectacular car accident, the fall to the pavement after exiting the disco, the cartoons on television showing characters falling from a crumbling precipice, the terror induced by seeing Sofía turn into Núria, all these references suggest not only a paranoid mind in turmoil but also a middle-class fear of instability, of loss of bearings and reference points, of lack of control over one's fate, of a world turned upside-down.

The monster is a manifestly clichéd but still essential icon in the horror lexicon. In yuppie horror, however, there are no burning red eyes or outsize incisors, no supernatural villains. Rather, ever since *Psycho* (1960), the monstrous is a projection of something denied or suppressed in the individual psyche, something hidden inside us. Thus, the monstrous 'other' tends to be the protagonist's other side, a dark 'double'. Monsters are not outside, marauding in the streets, but inside the house, sleeping in the same bed. For example, in Amenábar's short *Himenóptero*, the fixated young cameraman in pursuit of the young actress is arguably a projection of the female director (and by implication of Amenábar himself), anxious to manip-ulate, control and possess, in order to achieve her shot. In *Tesis*, Bosco (Amenábar's Mark Lewis or Norman Bates in the big city) is arguably an incarnation of Ángela's dark side, of what she is terrified of but fascinated by at the same time. In Freudian terms Bosco is Ángela's 'id' let loose, an embodiment of the yuppie mantra that she can have it all if she wants.

In *Abre los ojos* Núria plays a similar role, that of psycho *femme fatale*, a vehicle both for César's considerable sexual appetite and his own death instinct (his own self-annihilation, his desire to contemplate the abyss), which is frighteningly fulfilled. César starts out as a serial womaniser, who wants no ties or distracting responsibilities. Initially Núria seems to fit that template perfectly, as her birthday present to César suggests (a hard fuck in a red dress). According to Hilary Radner, Núria would appear to belong to 'a new generation of *femme fatales*, of psycho femmes, of women who refuse the violence of men' (1999: 248).[15] Núria could also be an iberian cousin of Alex Forrest in *Fatal Attraction* or Catherine Tramell in *Basic Instinct*, i.e. strong, assertive women, in professional jobs (the cost of Núria's outfits and her red Alfa-Romeo sports car, with the white leather interior, suggest a high salary and/or a large private income). Núria is also pro-feminist, someone who will not be denied or messed with. She refuses to be treated like an anonymous whore and will not play by the rules. In an attempt to challenge César's cool indifference, she changes the message on his talking clock, in order to attract his attention. Too self-absorbed, César ticks her off for her violation of his toys. Like Alex Forrest, who bombards Dan with phone calls and leaves him an audiotape, Núria also seeks to subvert César's private world and his masculine sense of power. She wants her revenge, wants to deflate the effortless charm and social control which César exudes. This culminates in her punishing him for his one-night stand/affair with Sofía, even though she knows he has not had sex. If she cannot have him, then no one else can. This is vindictive, violent, drug-induced behaviour, though not necessarily insane; it may simply be symptomatic of a very sick and disturbed 'twenty-something' Spanish yuppie culture.

While César might not be a yuppie in the American mould, where identity and self-worth rest on professional success, his sense of male mastery is predicated on his looks, his physical image. Loss of looks (as shown in *The Picture of Dorian Gray*) comes to haunt, terrorise and finally destroy him. His mistake arises from underestimating Núria, a slip predicated perhaps on his own macho bravado and a lack of insight into Núria's suicidal state of mind. Like the visage of Dorian Gray, handsome and grotesque at the same time, César's rare and angelic external beauty hides other horrors beneath: his narcissism, selfishness, self-absorbtion and cynical betrayal of friendship (for which he is justly criticised by Sofía). So, for César and Núria, the physical revulsion of the monster in classical horror is replaced by a moral or ethical horror at César's serial womanising and Núria's vindictive posessiveness. Both are physically attractive while morally monstrous, as befits the yuppie character template of the 1990s. And with his disfigurement, we see César's true face.

According to the American template, yuppie consciousness and values strongly fetishise appearances and surfaces, valorise conspicuous consumption (large houses and fast cars) and prize materiality far more than the threat of mortality and nothingness. Yet, here, Amenábar inverts the terms of such conventional yuppie wisdom. Rather than the perfection of his possessions, César is concerned by the perfection of his face and lithe masculine body. His vulnerability lies not in his aspiration for material comfort (he has more than enough money from his inheritance and no material needs) but in the fragility of his looks, i.e. his calling card and passport to lifestyle success, his real rather than lucid dream. Unfortunately for César, through Núria, the symbols of the yuppie lifestyle become deadly weapons, the red Alfa (once emblematic of Núria's female self-esteem) is the instrument of her suicide and César's disfigurement and fall to earth.

Where Amenábar seems to coincide with the American film cycle is his focus on the present, on Spain in the late 1990s and what concerns the people of his social milieu, in terms of their personal relations, notions of love, friendship, family, betrayal, responsibility, and how the media portray and shape those values and behaviours. In *Abre los ojos* what appears to disturb Amenábar, however, is the narcissism and self-absorbtion of the post-Me generation. That is, the selfishness of the 'monster inside', a figure which is severely punished for putting self before others. We see this in Núria, in her angst, loneliness, alienation and disconnection from others. Unable to cope with rejection and loss, she fills the void at her core with ever more extreme and bizarre individuated experiences (including drugs), which mask a deep self-loathing and masochism (as in Ángela).

Finally, one of the interesting twists in *Abre los ojos* is to confound the old adage that we are all equal when we are dead, that we cannot take our wealth with us to the grave. The twist is that César's buying power is so considerable that he uses it to extend his own life, in fact to prolong it to eternity, or so it seems. Here, César appears to challenge God's will (as he threatened in the squash game) and, though his journey through his virtual dream is a nightmare, he re-emerges in the real of 2147. It also appears that he has been reanimated, and even rebuilt, thus vindicating the various references in the film to Jules Verne and the positive, forward march of science, technology and medicine, towards a mastery over death and disease. But, as noted earlier, we are given no idea of what state he is in, no information whatsoever on his physical or mental functionality after 150 years in cryostasis. We are thus invited to fill such an enigmatic, open-ended void with our own inferences and anxieties.

Edge of the construct

In *The Matrix* (Andy and Larry Wachowski, 1999), Morpheus (Laurence Fishburne) asks of Neo: 'Have you ever had a dream that you're so sure was real? What if you were unable to wake up from that dream? How would you tell the difference between the dream world and the real world?'

The above questions sound as if they could have (or should have) been uttered by César's simulated psychiatrist Antonio or at the very least by the Madrid head of L.E., the apparently real Dr Serge Duvernois, voice of authority and expert time traveller. Questions about dreams, lucid dreaming, entrapment in a dream turned nightmare and the dualities of reality/perception, reality/dream etc., seem woven into the very fabric of *Abre los ojos*. Since the *Vanilla Sky* (2001) remake, Amenábar's original film has been increasingly retro-fitted by critics into a cycle of 'millennial angst' movies, including *The Matrix*. But to what extent is the film a Spanish take on *The Matrix* and the wave of other virtual reality or 'edge of the construct' films of the 1980s and 1990s, as Joshua Clover calls the micro genre? (2004: 8).

By 'edge of the construct' Clover refers to a key moment in *The Matrix* when, after taking the red pill offered by Morpheus, Neo has revealed to him the fate of humanity (the victory of the machines, the enslavement of the world's population) and the new 'real' as shabby, banal simulacrum. In other words Neo is made aware that what he once thought was infinite reality turns out to be a fake, a limited apparatus, a cascade of green machine language on a screen, which must be translated ad infinitum to generate the false consciousness and VR landscape of the passive human brain. Or, as in *The Truman Show* (Peter Weir, 1998), the edge of the construct is no more than a paper backcloth of a fake horizon, which Truman pierces with the prow of his little boat. The premise of *The Matrix*, like *Dark City* (Alex Proyas, 1998), *The Truman Show* (1998) and *The Thirteenth Floor* (Josef Rusnak, 1999), is that a separate reality is a con, a fake, a hoax or, as César in *Abre los ojos* would say, a 'montaje', an artificial construct, designed to reassure unwary consumers while stealing their money and messing with their minds. Or as deconstructionists of the 1960s such as Derrida, used to argue: 'il n'y a pas de hors-texte' (There is nothing outside the text). That is, there is no material world or tangible social conditions which precede their representation in textual form. Rather, the real is already and only a linguistic, discursive and textual construct, i.e. a sort of matrix. *The Matrix* film posits that there is nothing outside the Code. Humans are trapped as wage slaves in their work cubicles, in corporate towers, where all their needs are met. In this modern version of Lang's dystopian *Metropolis* (1927), *The Matrix* is a homage to the alienated worker or robot, a dehumanised human who is not allowed an imaginary, a dream of a better life, unless of course, he joins the resistance and breaks free of the nightmare of 'false consciousness' in an act of rebellion. Thus Thomas J. Anderson, aka Neo, leads a double life. He is a tech worker by day and a hacker by night, and peddler of illegal, minidisk magic. Nagged by the question 'What is the Matrix?', he is 'selected' for screening as a freecom fighter, by the charismatic and messianic resistance leader Morpheus and is trained to operate as a member of this new elite.

Unlike Neo, César in *Abre los ojos* is no wage slave, nor is he selected for a special task. As his name emblematically suggests, César has no need to work, given his wealth and status. Rather, he is already near the apex of a social elite, who can afford anything they desire. In effect, in the real of 1997, he already 'lives the dream' of a gilded, leisure-based lifestyle. Orphaned aged ten (i.e. in 1982, with the death of his parents), César has inherited their restaurant business and all we know is that he is very rich and very paranoid about his 'socios' (board members), indeed, he shouts at them a great deal, as if overtaken by a childish tantrum. Also César is not chosen by anyone. He himself does the choosing, he sets the rules and boundaries, controls his own space and is master of his own domain and his affections. Or at least, that is how it used to be. For, when the audience enters the film narration, César and his lifestyle are just beginning to implode. He has broken his own iron rule of 'no strings sex' by sleeping twice with the dark, unstoppable Núria. He also lets his desire and machismo overwhelm his common sense by rising to her challenge and accepting a lift from her. Such apparent bravado and stupidity (could it be pangs of conscience?) have devastating consequences and transform him into the Phantom of the Opera (as Antonio wryly observes), with a synthetic mask hiding a terribly disfigured face. So, after the failure of reconstructive surgery and losing Sofía to Pelayo, he commits suicide for the first time, unable to stand the double loss (of face and girl). Before doing so however, he goes for broke and buys the ultimate yuppie lifestyle accessory: immortality. The point is, of course, that César's wealth allows him a get out of jail card. He can afford to purchase from L.E. what is sold to him as 'el paraíso' (paradise), a cryonisation package plus a virtual reality simulation of his own ideal life with Sofía. For César this is a necessary fiction, designed to assuage the pain of his disfigurement and real loss of Sofía. Yet the theory is that César will be unable to tell the difference. His true, painful memories will be wiped, just as L.E. will provide a more than perfect simulacrum of his past via the VR dream.

The Matrix is not, arguably, a film primarily about philosophical or metaphysical issues: reality versus perception, false consciousness, the nature of the real etc. Neither is it really about humankind and its emancipation from oppression in an allegorical political or social frame. At the level of narrative, it is an old-fashioned fantasy about an 'ordinary Joe', a low-grade, tech worker 'drudge' who is chosen and trained as an action hero by a rebel elite and eventually becomes a superhero, a god. This sounds very much like the sort of classic super-hero stories Amenábar himself was so enthralled by when he was seven years old. Rather, as Clover argues persuasively (2004: 23–8), given its notable self-reflexivity, *The Matrix* is more concerned with the power of digital film technology to convey spectacle, via 'bullet time' and the awesome 'Matrix shot': Carrie Anne Moss in kung fu pose, frozen in mid-air, with the camera circling around her. It is also a film which seeks to challenge directly the appeal of the video game market and outdo to the ultimate degree the sensation of 'gamer immersion' in the game world.

Though it certainly engages in spectacle and slick camerawork, *Abre los ojos* is a rather different film, a teen romance spliced on to a psycho-logical thriller (with a Hitchcockian 'wrong man' story line) which segues into a futuristic, sci-fi nightmare. And though it posits a series of levels of perception, according to César's fragmented subjectivity, these are not the typical scenarios of video game action sequences. In structure and narrative the film is closer to the Hitchcockian, paranoid suspense thriller, where the 'wrong man' is trapped in a complex web of conspiracies, which he must try to unravel. Moroever, in terms of diegetic interactivity, César is given only two options by the demonic

Duvernois, i.e. the classic 'return to the real' via a second suicide or the continuation of his 'living death' within the dream/game.

By contrast, where we do find an action thriller whose narrative and style are explicitly underpinned by video gaming motifs and design (plus action scenarios) is in *Nadie concoce a nadie* (Nobody Knows Anybody, 1999), the first feature to be directed by Mateo Gil, Amenábar's close and almost constant collaborator. Here, exploiting the device of a linked series of key Catholic churches targeted for terrorist violence during Holy Week in Seville (echoing the biblical design of Fincher's *Seven*, 1995), Gil transforms the real city centre into a giant grid or video game board. On it he recreates an apocalyptic confrontation between the insane supremacist, terrorist and gamesmaster Sapo (played by Jordi Mollá) and his jaded, 'everyman' lodger, writer Simón, his 'adversario' (adversary), played once again by Eduardo Noriega. If Simón is the innocent victim but also the unwitting hero, destined to save civilisation (akin to Neo in The *Matrix*), Sapo is the deluded, self-appointed, secular hammer of popular religious superstition and false idols, using the tools of science and new technologies (mobiles, CCTV, Web etc.) to destroy the Catholic Church. Traditional religious confrontations between Good and Evil, believers and unbelievers are also updated and overlaid here by a more secular, evenly matched struggle between the Real and the Game. Moreover, part of the film's technophobic agenda is to address collective anxieties about new technologies, the cyber revolution, the networking power of the Web and mobile telephony and the ability of armed groups to mobilise, radicalise, plan and execute major acts of terrorist violence in pursuit of global dominance. Overall, while echoing and prefiguring acts of jihadist terror such as 9/11, Spain's 11M and the UK's 7/7/2005, it is Gil's film (not *Abre los ojos*) which is arguably a rather more explicit amalgamation of the psycho-thriller and the sort of action fantasy contained in *The Matrix*.

Nevertheless, in a sense, César's VR dream life is a kind of individualised, privatised 'matrix', a computer-generated dream world. But it is a consumer purchase entered into freely, via a signed contract. César is no victim of false consciousness, he has simply forgotten the origins of his new digital existence. This, in his case, is a series of electrical signals interpreted by an active (?) brain inside a cryonised body, awaiting resuscitation. Of course, in César's dream world, memories and déjà vu moments bubble up into consciousness from a previous existence, causing confusion over identities, disorientation, anger and trauma (leading to a murder). Is it the technology under-pinning the VR dream which is at fault or is it the return of César's repressed, his basic, primordial, sexual instincts, always associated with Núria and aggressive sex? This is a question left rather vague by Amenábar. What is interesting is that, if in *The Matrix* the real which lies outside the Code is a landscape disfigured by wars, in *Abre los ojos*, the 'real' which haunts César's nightmares is the disfigured landscape of his face, the mutability of his new good looks into scars, and the randomness of the change, over which he has no control.

In *The Matrix* Neo's transformation from humdrum Tom Ander-son into godlike superhero, implies a victory of the resistance over oppression and a break out of the malignant VR 'dream' which enslaves the world. Such messianic pieties find no place in *Abre los ojos*, where César demands to exchange one imperfect VR product for a return to the real, where he seeks the recovery of his looks and lifestyle in a future world. In César's journey back to the 'real' of 2147 there is no struggle to speak of. All he has to do is to commit suicide a second time, a mere formality, says Duvernois, since he is already dead. He then re-awakens in 2147, where medical science can rebuild his face and return his good looks. Though 150 years have passed, César will not age one day.

César appears to be a new consumer of a new digital fantasy (though couched in the analogue film language of the splice), but one who has the choice of exiting that fantasy and benefiting from 'real' scientific advances in the future. In a sense *Abre los ojos* is a cautionary tale about consumer rights in the digital age and about getting more than is bargained for if the deal goes wrong. The film asks us to look closely and carefully at what appears real and what is not, to focus on the notion of 'simulation', i.e. fake realities, reality shows, theme park realities, artificial constructs, to remain aware of where the bounda-ries are, where the edge of the construct lies – in short, to confront the Disneyland question. This arises when real and fake collide, when the 'reality' of Disney's Magic Kingdom seems more real than our own reality. In a sense César buys a Disneyland SIM, a perfect reproduc-tion of an imaginary happy relationship with Sofía, a fantasy, while he awaits in cryostasis to get repaired. Yet, as a protagonist in his own film fiction, César is aware that all is not well, that he gets confused, that irruptions from another existence or level of consciousness are spoiling his SIM and his enjoyment of untold happiness. Just as the spectator leaves the film theatre at the end of the movie, César opts to exit his VR SIM. For both César and the spectator the assumption is that outside the theatre lies the real we are familiar with and that we can tell the difference and see the boundary lines. Yet the anxiety remains that the fake and the SIM might colonise more and more of our consciousness. *Abre los ojos* is thus a film about the fear of the digital revolution, the macabre possibilities of perfect immersion in the simulation. The film asks us to be alert to the status of what we see. The fictional nature of the film we see in the film theatre should help to confirm our grasp of the real, the real outside the cinema. In this sense *Abre los ojos* is also about 'leaving' the film theatre (or failing to), being able to see the join or edge between reality and fantasy, of exiting the performance (of our own role plays) before we need to exit our own lives through more drastic measures such as suicide. The film closes on an apparently comforting tone of voice, encouraging César not to worry and to wake up in 2147. But is this really 2147 or just another simulation? Could there be nothing but repetition and duplication, simply a nightmare of infinite regress, leaving no exit from the Magic Kingdom?

In *The Matrix* (1999) the final battle is played out atop the grand corporate tower, in 2199. The huge business tower is an archaic throw-back to 1999, where people work 168 hours per week and never leave their pods, and where their working week is permanent and unceasing and their salary virtual. In *Abre los ojos*, the finale is also played out atop a 'real' corporate tower (the Torre Picasso), set in Madrid in 2147, headquarters of L.E., symbol of corporate power and Spain's insertion into global business networks. Here César is given the choice of continuing in the dream or walking out of it and returning to a real, though set in the future. César, having had his 'edge of the construct' moment in the offices of L.E. and in the gents' toilet (a repetition of a cruel joke enacted earlier in César's ample bathroom, by Amenábar, Gil and Montero, playing cameos), seems to believe Duvernois, and opts to abandon his VR dream and open his eyes to a new reality through a second suicide. César has had enough of fantasy land, of Disney and simulated lifestyles. His decision recalls that of Cypher in *The Matrix*: the experienced though jaded rebel, who does not even see the code on the screen any more, since he can see through it. He is anxious to drop the freedom fighter persona and get back to the real as he remembers it, to taste the sensuous textures of a piece of steak, feel the real rain on his face and get rich. He sounds like a soul mate for César, desperate to exit the dream of the sunlit park where it never rains.

Vertigo

Apart from staircases, tunnels, mirrors, knives, keys, birds and doppelgängers, to name but a few, one of Hitchcock's most widely used motifs was the act of falling (real, dreamed or imagined), usually shot from a high angle, into a vertiginous abyss. This motif (widely used in *Rear Window, North by Northwest, Psycho* etc.) is central to *Vertigo*. It embodies, as well as representing ex-cop John Ferguson's (aka Scottie) acrophobia (fear of heights), which triggers his vertigo (dizziness, nausea), and which Hitchcock repeatedly and mercilessly exploits. The motif also suggests male powerlessness, loss of control and impotence, as well as a fear of commitment to a love relationship. In *Vertigo* Scottie is the hapless victim of an ingenious hoax created by his treacherous old college buddy and adulterer Gavin Elster. In order to provide cover for the murder of his wife, Madeleine, Elster hires Scottie to spy on this supposedly estranged, frigid, suicidal woman, who is apparently obsessed by another suicide, that of her great-grandmother, Carlotta Valdés, a hundred years earlier. Already traumatised by the death of a police colleague (by falling), as he follows Madeleine (impersonated by Judy), Scottie falls in love with her; but, having failed to stop her committing suicide (or so he thinks), he is plunged into an acute depression, assailed by nightmares, rendered catatonic and briefly institutionalised. On his discharge from hospital, an apparently chance meeting with a certain Judy Barton triggers his attempt to resurrect and remake the figure of Madeleine using Judy as an avatar. Then, just as he shows signs of commitment to his surro-gate love object, he discovers Elster's plot; Judy also falls to her death (surprised by a nun!) from the very same vantage point as Madeleine, thus plunging Scottie into yet another psychological abyss of despair and devastating loss. The irony is that this 'fallen woman' falls for him, literally and figuratively. The lesson of this narratively preposterous and convoluted cautionary tale is that dysfunctional men should beware of projecting their obsessive sexual fantasies on to pliable and vulnerable women and stop abusing them in order to shore up their tormented egos and their need for power, control and stability. At a metacinematic and self-reflexive level, through Scottie, *Vertigo* also comments on Hitchcock's own repeated (and often abusive) acts of 'remaking' and 'refashioning' his female lead actresses in pursuit of his own fantasy ideal of female perfection.

Rather like Bazin, Amenábar is the sort of cinephile who admires and celebrates the craft and skills of classical Hollywood studio pictures and has repeatedly acknowledged his deep admiration for *Vertigo* (Rodríguez Marchante 2002: 82). While co-writing the script he played and replayed the acclaimed Bernard Herrmann score (which helps create the film's vaguely ethereal, surrealist atmosphere) as inspirational background music. He also admits that *Abre los ojos* is a film profoundly indebted to Hitchcock's *Vertigo*, stating 'en *Abre lo ojos* sobre todo había influencias de *Vertigo*' (Payán 2001: 42) (The main influences in *Abre los ojos* were from *Vertigo*). Moreover, *Vertigo* was compulsory viewing for the principal members of his film cast, including Penélope Cruz, who struggled with its exorbitant plotting. Indeed, in the long interview undertaken by Rodríguez Marchante, Amenábar also states: 'es una película que me ha influido y cuya historia me apasiona' (Rodríguez Marchante 2002: 82) (it's a film that has influenced me and whose story fascinates me). He also recognises the indebtedness of *Abre los ojos* to the thriller elements of this Hollywood classic: 'Desde luego es una película muy hitchcockiana' (Heredero 1997: 109) (Of course, it's a very Hitchcockian film).

Also there seems little doubt that, in the early stages of his career, Amenábar's reputation and authorship were boosted, even secured, by his borrowings from and close identification with the master of suspense and his romantic, psychological thrillers. Yet, at the same time, Amenábar feels free to adopt a critical stance: 'No obstante, los clásicos tambien están para desmontarlos y para analizar cómo están hechos' (However, the classics are there to be taken apart and analysed for their modes of construction) (Rodríguez Marchante 2002: 82). Here Amenábar has been quite outspoken regarding what he sees as some of the flaws and problems in Hitchcock's acknowledged masterpiece. For example he regards the beginning of the film, where Hitchcock tries to convey Scottie's growing obsession with Madeleine, as 'muy torpemente llevado' (very clumsily handled) (Heredero 1997: 109). He also thinks that Hitchcock's decision to bring forward to the middle of the film the revelation that Madeleine and Judy are the same person as 'un gran error' (a great mistake) (Heredero 1997: 109), arguing that Hitchcock did so probably because he did not have faith in the scripted film ending and thus sought to downplay it by foregrounding it (Rodríguez Marchante 2002: 81–2). This attitude perhaps reflects Amenábar's own preference for the even more archaic, narrative device of the 'surprise ending' in his films, which Hitchcock disliked intensely. Such advance knowledge helps to create uncertainty over whether Scottie will find out Judy's identity and how well he will cope with the discovery of her deceit. Also Amenábar regards the use of the 'letter of confession', crumpled up and delivered in voiceover by Judy herself as 'un recurso un tanto chapucero' (a rather improvised device) (Rodríguez Marchante 2002: 82), on the grounds that Hitchcock shifts from subjective to omniscient narration, beyond Scottie's own POV. For Amenábar this is a mistake since it breaks the audience identification with Scottie and contravenes 'mi natural rechazo a la narración omnisicente' (Rodríguez Marchante 2002: 82) (my normal rejection of omniscient narration).

At the level of genre, like *Vertigo, Abre los ojos* is something of a hybrid, drawing upon the conventions of the romance, the thriller, but perhaps above all, in the final act, the psychological drama. Moreover, like its progenitor film, *Abre los ojos* represents love and desire as founded upon obsession, image and male fantasy, to the detriment of respect, understanding or companionship towards the female 'other'. The film also contains numerous echoes of and homages to *Vertigo*, direct and indirect. Among the various character echoes, we find the figure of the 'wrong man' (César), charged with murder but who cannot recall the crime. César's emotional, sexual and oedipal cravings are also internally split between the virginal Sofía (Judy) and the self-destructive, *femme fatale* Núria (Madeleine), whose death continues to torment him. Pelayo may even stand for a younger incarnation of Scottie's 'college buddy', represented by Gavin Elster, though the Pelayo character is not shown as manipulative or abusive. The most well-known visual reference is of course the 'green halo' sequence, which repeats the scene in *Vertigo* between Judy and Scottie, where the curtains glow green as Judy emerges transformed as Madeleine. The colour green is also used throughout *Abre los ojos* in clothes, furnishings and portraits (as it is in César's checked shirt and Duvernois's green jumpers). Like Judy, Sofía emerges from the kitchen bathed in green light carrying a glass of water for César, who inhabits Scottie's role. Another obvious Hitchcockian reference is the camera circling César and Sofía as they embrace and kiss for the last time, in a 360–degree pan shot, echoing Scottie and Madeleine. And clearly, the final scene of *Abre los ojos*, on the roof of the Picasso Tower, with the vertical crane shot, recalls the Mission tower of *Vertigo*, where Madeleine/Judy's fall(s) and Scottie's loss are repeated in César's suicidal leap (and recycled in David Fincher's *The Game*, 1997, also inspired by *Vertigo*). As he steps up to jump, César also remarks explicitly that he had quite forgotten his own 'vertigo' (se me olvidó). The motif of repetition is also important here in terms of whether a deadly fall can break the nightmarish circle of repetition and allow both Scottie and César to exit their respective obsessive fantasies and return to 'reality'. Can they move beyond the enclosure of repetition and entrapment in the past to find an opening to a new life, a resurrection, even if it means coping with further loss and solitude? In the case of *Vertigo* repetition seems to lead to failure to exit the nightmare and results in a further dose of trauma and loss for Scottie, even though he survives his experiences, just as Elster successfully escapes from a loveless marriage and evades responsibility for Madeleine's murder. Indeed, both men succeed in manipulating and exploiting women for their own selfish and fantasist ends, without punishment. In *Abre los ojos* the repeated suicide also seems to succeed, as César appears to be reanimated in 2147 and told to open his eyes, even though he is still radically alone in an alien future. In both cases, if such male recuperation is possible, it is done off-camera, out of frame, and left ambiguous. César's reanimation also references Scottie's obsession with refashioning Judy in the dead Madeleine's image as well as tracing the line of desire (tinged with necrofilia) back to the dead Carlotta. Finally, if we ask how Amenábar marks his relationship to *Vertigo* in *Abre los ojos* we could say that he shifts his emphasis from the male compulsion to repeat (to re-create or remake the love object in order to fill an emotional vacuum) to a fear of substitution and transformation (to see the love object usurped by a prior identity), involving a loss of male mastery and control. In this light, as Amenábar explains, 'podría decirse que mi película es una especie de *Vertigo*, pero al revés, teniendo en cuenta que la mía también puede considerarse, en el fondo, como una historia de amor explícitamente romántica' (you could say that my film is a sort of *Vertigo*, but in reverse, keeping in mind that mine can also be seen, fundamentally, as an explicitly romantic love story (Heredero 1997: 109).

Amenábar remade: *Vanilla Sky* (2001)[16]

In the annals of national filmmaking, remarkably few successful Spanish films have attracted any serious commercial interest as raw material for foreign, let alone Hollywood, remaking. Until the mid to late 2000s Amenábar's *Abre los ojos* led the way and, in its day, was the first and only Spanish feature ever to enjoy 'the full Hollywood make-over treatment' (White 2003: 188).[17] Why was this? And why did a relatively obscure Spanish art film, which almost sank without trace in the American market, appeal to the world's biggest and most influential film star of the 1990s? Here several points are worth making. Firstly, let us recall that the executive producer Tom Cruise invited Amenábar himself to remake his own film, an offer which he declined (he had done likewise in response to Jim Sheridan's offer to remake *Tesis* for Hell's Kitchen).[18] Amenábar's second refusal reflected, in part, his nervousness and misgivings about working in the USA. He was concerned, quite understandably, by his unfamiliarity with a very different working environment, but also by his lack of proficiency in English at that time (1998) and above all by the likely difficulties he might face concerning his degree of personal control over the project. He was also heavily influenced by the well-known case of Fernando Trueba who, a few years earlier, had suffered serious and sustained difficulties with the American film unions when trying to shoot his English-language, screwball comedy *Two Much* (1995) in Miami.[19] Moreover, in interview in September 2001, Amenábar admitted that 'estoy bastante alejado de la película y cambiaría muchas cosas' (Rodríguez Marchante 2002: 100) (I feel too distant from the film now and would change a lot of things). Here, reading between the lines, it seems clear that Amenábar was still unhappy with certain key aspects of *Abre los ojos* and perhaps daunted by the prospect of how to fix them. In interview he alluded to issues of poor make-up and problems of narrative comprehension but, above all, to the film's complex and challenging flashback structure, which he had opposed initially as a solution to the problems of narrative integration of the film diegesis.

Secondly, well before Cruise-Wagner Productions bought the remake rights to *Abre los ojos* (thanks to their 'first look' deal on new projects with Paramount), Amenábar was already regarded in Spain by critics, reviewers and audiences as decidedly 'non-Spanish' in his choice of film content and style. Strongly inspired by *The Silence of the Lambs* and cleverly self-reflexive, *Tesis* had broadly adhered to classical Hollywood linear narration, a fairly non-specific *mise-en scène*, strong continuity editing and a comprehensible (double) closure. But probably because of its novel subject matter and dreamy, unsettling flashback structure, as well as its very stylish, glossy, postmodern feel, *Abre los ojos* was widely regarded as a difficult, cryptic, almost unclassifiable 'puzzle' film. This simply reinforced the impression that Amenábar's first two films did not appear organically rooted or 'Spanish' at all, since they lacked strong markers of local cultural identities, settings, customs, language use, exploitation of archetypes etc., which might connect them with earlier national film traditions. And, even taking into account the specificity of the Gran Vía setting for the opening 'waking' sequences, as Amenábar has stated 'llega un momento en que te olvidas que es una historia que se está contando en Madrid porque se podría estar contando en Paris, en Amsterdam o en Nueva York. Es una película que se podría haber rodado perfectamente en otro país' (Payán 2001: 45) (there comes a moment when you forget that this is a story set and narrated in Madrid because it could just as easily be set in Paris, Amsterdam or New York. It's a film that could have been shot perfectly well in another country).

According to Amenábar, the actor-producer Tom Cruise genuinely admired *Abre los ojos* and was attracted to the remake idea, in part, because of the original film's cinematic restraint, its relatively open, uncluttered narrative and its modest, not to say minimalist, character development, which provided ample room and opportunities for reinvention (Rodríguez Marchante 2002: 70). Reviewers have also stressed the fact that Cruise was attracted by the central character of César, who enjoys a charmed lifestyle initially then loses it, then tries to piece it back together but falls deeper into the abyss. This type of narrative arc was strongly reminiscent of Cruise's 'hot shot kid humbled and made wiser' story lines and his roles in *The Firm* (1992), *Rain Man* (1993) and *Jerry McGuire* (1996). Cruise also saw in *Abre los ojos* a cautionary tale about appearances, a metaphor for an acting profession and a gilded lifestyle where, at 39 years old (in 2000/1), looks are everything but do not last for ever. In other words, *Abre los ojos* called attention to Cruise's own mortality and the mutability of his famous good looks, 'shark teeth' grin and athletic body, all essential components of his kinetic screen persona. That is, the film appealed to the actor-producer's vanity and survivability, key themes in his filmography.[20]

Also, if much press and web comment is to be believed, the remake arose quite simply because of Cruise's real-life infatuation with Penélope Cruz. He was reportedly ecstatic after seeing the film and rang Paula Wagner almost immediately, with the intention of buying the remake rights. He appears to have been smitten by a desire to role-play himself, by rehearsing on film a virtual affair, which began during the shooting phase, according to director Crowe (see the DVD Director's Commentary). It soon developed into a real, two-year love affair with his leading lady. This followed his prior flirtation with Renée Zellweger in *Jerry McGuire* and Cruz's dalliances with Matt Damon in *All the Pretty Horses* (1999) and Nicholas Cage in *Captain Corelli's Mandolin*, 2000). Thus, Cruise's haste to secure the remake rights, as well as his invitation to Cruz to reprise the role of Sofía, suggests a great deal more than clever casting choices or homages to the progenitor film. Having failed to persuade Amenábar to direct, Cruise then turned to the former rock music journalist Cameron Crowe, director of soft-centred, snappy romantic comedies *Say Anything* (1989) and *Singles* (1992), his fairy tale, 'rock and roll', quasi-autobiography *Almost Famous* (2000), the romantic comedy *Elizabethtown* (2005) and the extremely successful *Jerry McGuire,* in which Cruise had played the lead. Here, Crowe and Cruise were Oscar-nominated (for Best Original Screenplay and Best Actor), while Cuba Gooding Jr won an Oscar for Best Supporting Actor.

Crowe was a specialist in the field of romantic comedy and all his films had been based on his own, quirky, upbeat, original scripts and relied primarily on clever, rapid-fire dialogue, affectionately drawn characters and, in particular, a sophisticated, modern, 'rock and roll' soundtrack, through which he could homage a previous life and profession and show off his encyclopaedic knowledge of popular music, especially that of the 1970s. However, Crowe was totally untried in the remake sphere, never having undertaken the adaptation of an earlier film or literary property before. Yet, in order to work with Cruise again and perhaps lured by the possibility of repeating the success of *Jerry McGuire,* he took up the challenge and the considerable risk it might pose to his career. Reflecting his music journalism background, Crowe began referring to the task in hand as a process of 'covering' rather than 'remaking', an approach by which, he believed, 'we could honour the original and add some new chords of our own'.[21] And while also wishing to explore more deeply the meanings of love and sex, celebrity and identity, in the new millennium, he also acknowledged the rather 'experimental' nature of the enterprise by seeing the film as 'a perfect kind of Petri dish to explore all this stuff', anxious to engage in a 'cool dialogue with Amenábar's original movie'. [22]

When we compare the films in more detail, we find that Crowe's first foray into the perilous waters of the remake elicits two contrasting responses. On the one hand, he seems determined to make his mark, reaffirm his independence from the European source and stamp his track record and brand identity on to the remake product. He does so explicitly in the opening credits (also repeated in the DVD marketing blurb), trumpeting his ownership of a new film property which has been 'written for the screen and directed by Cameron Crowe', while also acknowledging the screenplay by Amenábar and Mateo Gil. (He also takes a production credit alongside Cruise and Wagner.) On the other hand, as Peter Bradshaw argues, *Vanilla Sky* is a 'very close remake' of its Spanish source, which Crowe approaches with great care as if it were 'some impossibly obscure European source material like a novel or a cave painting or something'.[23] Indeed, while hardly a 'shot for shot' copy (as seen in the case of Gus Van Sant's remake of Hitchcock's *Psycho*), Crowe's 'cover version' is an almost faithful, 'sequence for sequence', repetition of the narrative of the earlier film. But where there was coolness, minimalism and ambiguity in *Abre los ojos*, Crowe seeks to inject greater warmth, sociability and clarity (though Brooks disagrees, 2002). And, for subtitle-averse American audiences, if they did not manage to catch the Amenábar original, *Vanilla Sky* offers a remarkably reliable alternative. At the same time, with a big budget, Crowe was tasked with designing a promotional platform for the talents of a globally recognised megastar (but one who was not appearing in a typical, high-octane, action role, rather something closer to *Rain Man* (1993) or *Magnolia* (1999)). He thus had to negotiate the Scylla and Charybdis of a forging a relationship with the progenitor film text while at the same time trying to manage the demands and expectations of Cruise fans worldwide. In short the project entailed a considerable degree of risk and down side.

In terms of *dramatis personae*, most of Amenábar's principal characters reappear in the Crowe version. But, in a curious instance of postmodern reflexivity and intertextuality, Penélope Cruz reprises the role of Sofía as the 'dream girl' of male fantasy, though the earlier drama student Sofía Cueto of *Abre los ojos* becomes the dancer and dental assistant Sofía Serrano in *Vanilla Sky*. Moreover, Crowe refashions the innocent, 'guileless' Sofía as very sharp-witted, amusing and perceptive, blessed with an extraordinary command of the English language (unlike the real Cruz in 2000). However, problems of diction and fluency in English stretch spectator credibility towards her genius as an amateur philosopher and wit. Yet her warmth, geniality and self-confidence are sufficient to put her dream lover Aames on the spot repeatedly and challenge his smugness with pithy, one-line, observations about his deepest self, such as: 'So this is what's become of rock and roll? A broken guitar behind a glass case on a rich man's wall?'

In the case of the main male lead, Crowe reimagines Amenábar's César as David Aames, a character based on an old school acquaintance, it seems, who 'was a brand name for a life we all wanted'.[24] Unlike the selfish, whinging and deeply unsympathetic 'pijo' César, Aames seems a much more amiable, carefree figure, devoted to his skateboarding, raquetball and modern pop music rather than his corporate business responsibilities. He appears to float blithely through a privileged existence, thanks to his family inheritance, though he is characterised by a certain loneliness and lack of fulfilment. Here Crowe remodels Amenábar's cold, enigmatic, original playboy by significantly softening and humanising his American cousin (while markedly reducing the degree of his facial disfigurement). Moreover, as Crowe points out, Aames's life 'is defined, like so many of us, by pop culture', which the director regards as a structuring matrix for our dreams and desires as well as a common vernacular, which is recognised universally, at least in the West (DVD Director's Commentary). This collective pop consciousness, he argues, is on display in the 'very vivid and psyche-delic dream come true' seen in the Times Square sequence. The hall of mirrors and *mise-en-abyme* evoked here, he reminds us, was also shot 'for real', early on a Sunday morning, as a direct tribute but also as an auteurist response to Amenábar's Gran Vía sequence.[25]

In place of the dark, obsessive, suicidal stalker Núria, Crowe creates a rather different, radiant Julie Gianni (stylishly played by Cameron Diaz), whom noncommittal Aames regards callously as his 'fuck buddy'. She is likeable and sunny, a supplicant rather than a competitor (like 'best friend' Brian, she seeks financial support for her career, as an actress and singer), but also someone who adores Aames deeply and longs for a permanent relationship (though she is reluctant to say so). Unfortunately Aames is so self-absorbed that he fails to register her needs and reads her desire as possessiveness. Also Julie resignifies Aames's troubling appetite for casual, gymnastic sex and the sleazy conventions of the hard-core porn film ('You fucked me four times, you were inside me … I swallowed your cum') into something more meaningful but threatening. For Julie the sexual act has deep moral and symbolic significance. It is tantamount to a sanctified exchange of love, a 'promise' expressed through the body, 'whether you mean it or not'. However, while Aames's amorality, lack of personal commitment and cruel indifference motivate Julie's reaction, her suicidal act of vengeance may appear somewhat abrupt and out of step with her upbeat character.

With a far larger budget than Amenábar, Crowe was able to reshape and even add to the strong cast of supporting players. Amenábar's Pelayo becomes Brian (Jason Lee, a Crowe regular), a struggling young writer, beneficiary of Aames' fortune, but whose role is seriously underwritten. The ever-reliable Kurt Russell plays the affable prison psychiatrist, Dr Curtis McCabe, a 'father figure' role he accepted even before reading the script. Also, the original French head of L.E. in Madrid, Serge Duvernois, is split between technical support (Edmund Ventura, played by Noah Taylor, who doubles as internal narrator) and, back at L.E. base, Rebecca Dearborn (played by Tilda Swinton, a model of camp hyper-efficiency, with echoes of the Scientology profiler). Crowe had enough money left to assign to Aames yet another supportive mentor figure, his loyal lawyer Thomas Tipp (played engagingly by Timothy Spall). The director even manages to visualise Aames's media company board, those scheming 'seven dwarfs' who judge him severely and perhaps seek to steal his majority stock holding by claiming he is insane. And, as if this were not enough, Crowe has Steven Spielberg, as himself, make a fleeting cameo appearance at Aames's birthday party (an auteurist favour Spielberg would extend later to Crowe as a bus passenger in his *Minority Report* (2004)). In short, by displaying on screen Hollywood royalty and a host of courtiers, Crowe indicates his elite connections as well as his auteurist distinction, seeking perhaps to distance if not eclipse the source film.

As regards music, unlike the spare, ethereal soundtrack of the progenitor film, which is a mixture of authored film score by Amenábar himself and interpolated commercial music tracks, in *Vanilla Sky* Crowe and his wife Nancy Wilson select and fashion an elaborate, overdetermining soundscape (with Wilson gaining the screen credit for the music). They mobilise a vast, eclectic selection of numbers which includes two original compositions (from Nancy Wilson and Paul McCartney, who creates the title song), a song from Cameron Diaz (which references her music CD in the film), but mostly extracts from tracks by rock royalty including Bob Dylan, R.E.M., Radiohead, The Beach Boys, Bruce Springsteen, The Rolling Stones, The Monkees, U2 and Peter Gabriel, as well as The Chemical Brothers, Sinéad O'Connor, Looper and many more, even the Icelandic band Sigur Ros, who play over David's final death leap from a vantage point near the World Trade Center towers. However, Crowe's legendary flair with popular music, which is deployed to sustain narrative coherence, flesh out character design and create appropriate mood and atmosphere, rather overwhelms the film narrative. It also shifts the tone and texture of the film away from a dark, challenging psychodrama and critique of yuppie lifestyle, to a 'rom-com' hybrid where an apparently empty, over-glamorised pop culture continues to shape the archetypes of the West's collective unconscious. More broadly, Crowe tends to stuff *Vanilla Sky* with an over-rich mixture of musical, pictorial, filmic and cultural paraphernalia, in order to flesh out Aames's 'rock and roll', 'freewheelin' lifestyle, biography and cultural identity. Yet the massive posters from certain French New Wave filmmakers, including Godard's *Breathless* (1960) and Truffaut's *Jules et Jim* (1961), with its model screen 'love triangle' and car crash symbolism, seem underutilised and rather unmotivated (by character design). The same goes for prints by Rothko, Balthus, Matisse and other artists, as well as the presence of the various guitars, including the busted Gibson SG in the glass case, and homages to Dylan, Björk and John Coltrane, via the hologram. These copious tastes and reference points obviously belong not to Aames but to his creator and animator Crowe, who arguably overburdens his main protagonist with an excessive amount of musical and cultural baggage.

At his thirty-third birthday party Aames addresses his guests framed in front of a massive, stylised colour print of his father's smiling face, which covers one whole wall of his apartment. The implication seems obvious: The young Aames remains trapped and overwhelmed by the pastel-shade ghost of a larger-than-life father figure. But just in case we miss the point, shortly afterwards the uncannily perceptive, latin guest Sofía, whom Aames has only just met, confides: 'You live in the shadow of your father.' In other words, Crowe not only does redesign the anemic César character and give him significant motivational background as a victim of unresolved oedipal difficulties from a bad, authoritarian father. He also reinforces the point continually, deploying multiple motifs and an elaborate network of visual imagery to help support the case (including 'good father' clips from Robert Mulligan's *To Kill a Mockingbird*, 1962, which plays on television in the jail and on the giant screens surrounding Times Square). The motivational background for Aames junior as 'media mogul' *malgré lui* is also amplified by raiding another classic (though sui generis) Hollywood film, *Citizen Kane* (1941), made evident in the 'Citizen dildo' tag. This remains a work which, even nowadays, is considered by scholars and aficionados to be the most important film ever made. Crowe thus hitches his 'cover version' to what was a commercial flop in its day but which has become a critical and institutional icon, masterpiece and undisputed point of reference. It is also a blindingly obvious intertext which Amenábar (who had a strong interest in Welles as a student) appears to have missed altogether in his own version, perhaps deciding it was too clichéd or self-indulgent a comparison to make. In other ways of course, and whether Crowe was aware of it or not, the Kane connection had already touched Amenábar from a different direction earlier in his career, as Spain's 'little Orson' in the mid-1990s, mentioned earlier.

In *Vanilla Sky* Crowe locates the character defects of Aames junior in an unloving and unforgiving father figure. As a result the son is never able to fulfil his father's ambitions for him and is crushed by the weight of paternal success and expectation (which also explain his headaches and fear of heights). Here Anne White argues that this unresolved oedipal trajectory is repeated and replayed in Crowe's own relationship with the Amenábar source text (2003: 194). In short Crowe suffers from his own anxiety of influence as he struggles to maintain his 'cool dialogue' with *Abre los ojos*.[26] As noted earlier, perhaps slightly intimidated by the complexity of its flashback structure, he prefers to leave it alone, focusing his attention more on dialogue, character design and motivation and overall tone and mood. But while paying homage to his Spanish source by respecting the original plotting and film narration, he seeks to foreground his authorship, in ways which seek to diverge from or even outdo the original. In relation to genre, however, this is no easy matter, since he is obliged to confront an unusual combination of paranoid crime drama, erotic thriller à la *Fatal Attraction*, 'love at first sight' romance, a sci-fi last act, reminiscent of the *Twilight Zone*, and an existential parable. In their marketing copy Paramount signal this messy, rather intimidating, hybridity in their tag line: LoveHateDreamsLifeWork-PlayFriendshipSex. Crowe circumvents this problem and its potential confusions by creating a safety net for the spectator through the soundtrack, partly as a refuge for Aames's tortured psyche due to his disfigurement and partly as a demonstration of his wife's (and his) ability to select and play memorable, cool and appropriate rock music for his fans.

As regards the film title, Amenábar's *Abre los ojos* (Open your eyes) evokes its core subject matter through the ocular reference, which suggests to the spectator what the film might have to offer. By contrast

Crowe's title, the rather nebulous, soft and fluffy *Vanilla Sky*, seems an odd choice. Though connected to the film via its pictorial references, including the Monet painting and Aames's skateboard, rather than providing a meaningful hook for the spectator, this enigmatic coinage tends to induce puzzlement and confusion. In fact the title repeats exactly one which he had used earlier as a working title for *Almost Famous* (2000), his semi-autobiographical account of life as a young, *Rolling Stone* reporter. If the 'vanilla sky' of *Almost Famous* referred originally to Crowe's personal musical 'heaven' or 'nirvana' of 1970s American rock and roll, its recycling as a 'cool' brand name for a 1990s yuppie thriller-cum-psychodrama perhaps comes close to being an auteurist indulgence.

Still, Crowe's version is by no means a sensationalist or dumbed-down remake of the source film. In fact Amenábar's almost archetypal study of hollow lifestyles and fake dreams, using relatively undeveloped character templates, cried out for more fleshy, better designed, well-motivated characters. Deriving from his journalistic and music background in MTV, as well as prior filmmaking outings, Crowe displays an anxiety to partially disavow contemporary commercial Hollywood by nostalgically raiding classic film texts, both American and European, as noted earlier. He also wants to show off his knowledge of popular music and film history, his artistic sensibility and auteur credentials, and his own ability to 'riff' on today's saturated film and media intertextual 'array'. Like Amenábar, Crowe seems to acknowledge the unhealthy power of the media, the threat of semiotic overload, the proliferation of visual imagery and how this generates anxieties about appearances, celebrity, looks and ageing. Yet, in the case of his remake, he appears unable to restrain himself, unable to rein in those very impulses and forces his film remake was meant to critique.[27]

Notes

1 It is worth bearing in mind that Amenábar's portrayal of the Life Extension Company is based on a bona-fide, real-life, American, cryonics company called Alcor (based in Phoenix Arizona), whose leaflets and information he used extensively, sometimes verbatim, to create his filmic L.E.

2 The sleepwalking experience, recalled by Amenábar, was in fact incorporated into the script for *Tesis* through Ángela's apparent disposition for somnambulism, though we would not know this, since the relevant sequence was scripted but never shot.

3 This suggests a certain existentialist perspective on Cuerda's part, i.e. an acceptance of the alienation of the individual in a hostile, uncaring universe and a view of human existence as ultimately inexplicable. Also, fate or destiny have nothing to do with the machinations of a super-natural deity; rather, choices are wholly dependent upon the freedom and responsibility of the human subject, who is ultimately responsible for the consequences of his/her actions.

4 Also, rather than divide up the scripting labour according to their usual practice, on *Abre los ojos*, Amenábar and Gil agreed to write counter-intui-tively. In other words Amenábar produced most of the 'romance' scenes while Gil wrote the thriller sections, with both collaborators incorpo-rating material from each other's previous shorts.

5 The press office of Sogecine was in charge of news and background brief-ings regarding the progress of *Abre los ojos*, whose production phase was followed and discussed in minute detail by virtually the whole of the national press. Because Amenábar was now a known director, *Abre los ojos* remains to date the only Spanish-made film ever to fill a cinema in Madrid with over two hundred journalists, all present to collect details of the film's daily shooting schedule (see the piece by Oskar Belategui, in *El Correo Español* (Vizcaya), 12 December 1997, *Sección Fin de Semana* 1).

6 Amenábar's model director in terms of ambiguity and effective metaphorical endings is Stanley Kubrick, whose 2001 *A Space Odyssey* Amenábar admires precisely because of its unclear, speculative, cryptic half-silent ending. Hence his quarrel with Spielberg over a project he took over from Kubrick, *AI* (2000). For Amenábar, Spielberg spoiled the film by being too explicit, and providing too much exposition, because 'cuanto más explícito eres a la hora de mostrar el futuro, más expuesta estás a la metedura de pata' (Rodríguez Marchante 2002: 57) (the more explicit you are when showing the future, the more you risk putting your foot in it).

7 Financial responsibilities for the production were split between Sogecable, Sogecine (Spain, 35 per cent), Las Producciones del Escorpión (Spain, 35 per cent), Les Films Alain Sarde (France, 20 per cent) and Lucky Red (Italy, 10 per cent). The overall budget was between 370 and 410 million pesetas (€2.5 million approximately), though official figures suggest a much lower overall total (see *Academia* (1999), 8–9, indicating a very low budget of 300 million pesetas). Promotion and copies cost a further 110 million pesetas. Moreover, Cuerda had done well to attract some inter-national finance from small, foreign, independent producers, though he failed initially to extract any direct support from Spain's national televi-sion corporation RTVE. However, he did manage to secure funding subsi-dies from ICAA (2.8 million pesetas) and Eurimages (32 million pesetas) as well as 68 million pesetas from Sogepaq in the form of distribution advances. The film was shot between 12 May and 7 July 1997, eight weeks

in all, with 32 days in studio interiors and 19 days spent on location. The latter included Madrid's real and part-derelict prison at Alcalá de Henares, where all the prison interiors were shot, the Faro de Moncloa tower in the city centre (its top floor used as the scenario for César's meetings with his surgeons) and the city's tallest building at the time, the Torre Picasso/ Picasso Tower. *Abre los ojos* was released in Spain on 19 of December 1997, starting in 84 theatres but increasing to 129 after one week, with a running time of 117 minutes. The film achieved an outstanding 170 million pesetas in the first weekend of 1998 and 900 million pesetas in Spain in its first five weeks (*El Periódico de Cataluña*, 29 January 1998, 63) (Perriam gives a lower figure of 700 million pesetas – 2004: 209). And over a 61-week run, the film attracted nearly 1.8 million spectators. It was thus a huge hit domestically. But bizarrely, in its international release, the opening was delayed until April 1999 in the USA, where it only managed 72,976 admissions and paltry box office takings of $370,720, with far fewer seats sold in France (21,195) and the UK (16,370) (imdb.com). In short the film was something of an international box-office flop, not unlike Amenábar's fourth and fifth features.

8 One of the biggest problems when shooting the film was the design and the look of Noriega's make-up. The actor's suffering during the shoot (for which Amenábar is deeply apologetic in his DVD 'Director's Commentary') vividly recalls the sort of agony also suffered by Javier Bardem in relation to his make-up for *Mar adentro*, involving a four-to-five hour make-up marathon per day, plus sores and infections, in order to age him 20 years.

9 At one point Amenábar was tempted to shoot the opening scene using a range of special effects, but he was persuaded not to do so by Cuerda, who still believed it was possible to close down Madrid's busiest avenue for a day and 'do it for real' (Interview). They managed to get the necessary permissions from Madrid City Council and shot the famous scene on 18 August 1996, on a Sunday (Sempere 2000: 91). Unfortunately while the street and pavements were duly cleared for shooting, the balconies were beyond police control. In the relevant sequence, on the right-hand side, mid-frame, there are two individuals on a balcony looking out over the street.

10 Over the last ten to fifteen years, we find a growing scholarly interest in 'complex' film narratives and the narratological, ideological and ludic implications arising from the so-called 'psychological puzzle film', and the 'mind-game' or 'mind fuck' film. See, for example, Jonathan Eig, 'A beautiful mind (fuck): Hollywood structures of identity', *Jump Cut*(2003), 46, at www.ejumpcut.org/archive/jc46.2003/eig.mindfilms/index.html. See also Thomas Elsaesser, 'The mind-game film' in *Puzzle Films: Complex Storytelling in Contemporary Cinema*, Warren Buckland (ed.) (Oxford: Blackwell, 2008), 14–41; and David Bordwell, 'Subjective stories

and network narratives', in *The Way Hollywood Tells It. Story and Style in Modern Movies* (Berkeley and Los Angeles: University of California Press, 2006), 72–103, plus 'Film Futures', in *Poetics of Cinema* (London and New York: Routledge, 2008), 171–87. The debate here seems to focus on whether more recent examples of 'complex' film narratives of the 1990s and 2000s (Nolan's *Memento*, 2000, is perhaps one of the more striking cases) constitute a major shift in narrative cinema, prompting a new and qualitatively different, post-humanist, type of spectator address. Rather than classic protocols of transparency, clarity, closure, illusionism and suspension of disbelief, the new 'complex narratives' appear to emphasise unreliability, instability, synthetic story worlds and entrapment as new forms of visual and cognitive pleasure and openings for spectator agency. Bordwell, however, is of the opinion that there have always been such challenging, experimental forms in Hollywood narrative films and more recent 'complex narratives' are nothing new but rather part of a fruitful, dynamic and very flexible, though updated, set of narrative traditions.

11 César's words echo those of main protagonist Carlos in the novel version of José Angel Mañas's *Historias del Kronen* (1995), where he describes his leisurely, minimal, animalistic lifestyle as consisting of: 'sólo comer, dormir y cagar' (only eat, sleep and shit, 65).

12 Though Amenábar nowhere acknowledges the American source, the term 'X generation' derives from Douglas Coupland's important novel, published in the USA in 1991, *Generation X, Tales for an Accelerated Culture* (New York: St Martin's Press). Here Coupland defines the American 'X-ers' in specific terms as the offspring of the 'baby boomers' (born between 1946 and 1964). By way of rapid global media dissemination, the term has been circulated and recycled in many other countries and contexts, including Spain, where it has been used to identify a certain generational identity among 1990s Spanish youth.

13 See Christopher Ross, *Contemporary Spain. A Handbook* (London and New York: Arnold, 1997, 2nd edn, 2002), 205–9.

14 See Barry Keith Grant, 'Rich and strange: the yuppie horror film', in *Contemporary Hollywood Cinema*, Steve Neale and Murray Smith (eds) (London: Routledge, 1999), 280–93.

15 Hilary Radner, 'New Hollywood's new women. Murder in Mind – Sarah and Margie', in *Contemporary Hollywood Cinema*, Steve Neale and Murray Smith (eds) (London: Routledge, 1999), 247–62.

16 The film title in English, 'Vanilla Sky', refers to a famous Monet painting of 1873, owned by the main character, left to him by his mother. The painting is better known as 'La Seine à Argenteuil'. The 'vanilla sky' in question refers to Monet's seductive colour palette, depicting the warm blues and beiges of a French summer sunset. In Cameron Crowe's adaptation, the term 'vanilla sky' refers to the nickname David Aames

has apparently assigned to the clouds of the Monet original which he reproduces on his skateboard. This mixing of high art with pop culture is meant to suggest the free-wheeling, juvenile, 'rock and roll' lifestyle of the 30–something Aames. The term also suggests, as Crowe indicates, 'a feeling, a state of mind, a dream life that may or may not actually exist'. See Cameron Crowe, '"So lonely I could cry". How Elvis inspired my new movie *Vanilla Sky*', *The Guardian* (11 January 2002), at www.guardian. co.uk/film/2002/jan/11/artsfeatures2/.

17 Leaving aside the rumoured but never realised Hollywood remake with Jane Fonda of Almodóvar's *Mujeres al borde de un ataque de nervios* (Women on the Verge of a Nervous Breakdown, 1988) and the film's more recent repetitions by Almodóvar himself in *Los abrazos rotos* (Broken Embraces, 2009) and on Broadway as a musical (2010), since 2001–2 a trickle of Spanish candidates for foreign remake has begun to emerge. These include the highly successful musical comedy *El otro lado de la cama* (The Other Side of the Bed, Emilio Martínez Lázaro, 2002), remade in French by Ivan Calbérac in 2005 with the title, *On va s'aimer* (2006), and also optioned by Italian television and film producer Cattleya (20 per cent owned by Univeral) and by the Mexican director Antonio Serrano. A Spanish sequel, *Los dos lados de la cama* (Both Sides of the Bed) appeared in 2005, also directed by Martínez Lázaro. Since then, we find a blossoming franchise based around the mega-successful *Rec* (Jaume Balagueró and Paco Plaza, 2007), poorly remade by John Erick Dowdle as *Quarantine* in 2008 and now awaiting two sequels, *Rec Genesis* and *Rec Apocalipsis*, produced by the Barcelona-based horror specialist Filmax. We also find *Cronocrímenes* (Nacho Vigalondo, 2008, remade as *Timecrimes* by Magnolia Productions) and *El orfanato* (Juan Antonio Bayona, 2007), optioned by its original executive producer Guillermo del Toro. Also the remake rights to Pablo Berger's sweet period comedy concerning the porn industry under Franco, *Torremolinos 73* (2003), have been bought by the Chinese company Shenzen Golden Coast Film (founded 1994), directed, scripted and produced by the company's creative source Ah gan or Agan. What all these products have in common is that they draw upon the resources of the genre film, including the comedy, musical, but most notably the psychological thriller as well as horror and sci-fi. The latter types, in many respects, characterise Amenábar's first three features, which have arguably played a key role in cementing the fortunes of the Spanish-sourced foreign and Hollywood remake.

18 Jim Sheridan and Arthur Lappin, who created the Hell's Kitchen Production Company in 1993, based in Dublin, appeared keen to snap up *Tesis* initially as a remake property. However, nothing ever came of their initial interest, confirmed in March 2009 by the author via email.

19 Trueba took a large Spanish team to the USA to make *Two Much*, forgetting that it helps to be American when working in Hollywood. As a result

he suffered a production nightmare. Also, when talking about working in Hollywood, Amenábar always cites the Trueba case, not only in terms of labour relations or the difficulties of making a successful comedy. He also refers to foreign audience tastes and Trueba's misjudgement over the presumed international appeal of an old-fashioned, unmodernised, mainstream comedy formula ('screwball') in the USA and European markets. Paradoxically, the film did remarkably good business in Spain: see Jordan and Morgan-Tamosunas 1998: 72–3, Rodríguez Marchante 2002: 53 and 79 and Payán 2001: 184.

20 We should also keep in mind that during the remake negotiations in 1998 Cruise and his then wife, Nicole Kidman were still working on Kubrick's *Eyes Wide Shut* (1999), a project begun in 1995 and dogged by multiple delays and reshoots. Here Cruise plays an upper-middle class doctor, Bill Harford, whose marital and mental stability are shattered when his wife Alice (Kidman) reveals an overwhelming (though no longer active) sexual fantasy for another man. Bill embarks on a bizarre, underworld odyssey of jealousy and revenge (is it real or a dream?), consisting of casual, anonymous sexual encounters, culminating in a bizarre, high society, 20-minute orgy scene, containing much vigorous simulated coupling (which had to be toned down by CGI in order to avoid an NC 17 rating in America). The film deals with issues of sexual fidelity, the lure of chance encounters, temptations and retreats, but above all with the fissile nature of masculine identity in the face of female sexual fantasies, within a stale and unhappy marriage. The film suggests that corrosive suspicion and jealousy, arising from a fear of betrayal, can drive people to madness, undermine family, married life, trust, commitment and the care of children and more broadly dehumanise society. The title 'Eyes Wide Shut' (which evokes Bill's wilful blindness and self-deception in his marriage) also functions as a useful corollary to 'Open your eyes' (Amenábar's injunction to César, his audiences and himself to beware the lure of seductive surface appearances).

21 See Cameron Crowe, '"So lonely I could cry". How Elvis inspired my new movie *Vanilla Sky*', *The Guardian* (11 January 2002), at www.guardian. co.uk/film/2002/jan/11/artsfeatures2/. Accessed 20 September 2009.

22 Crowe cited in Constantine Verevis, *Film Remakes* (Edinburgh: Edinburgh University Press, 2006), 133.

23 Peter Bradshaw, 'Vanilla Sky', *The Guardian* (25 January 2002), at www. guardian.co.uk/film/2002/jan/25/culture.reviews/. Accessed 22 September 2009.

24 See Cameron Crowe, '"So lonely I could cry". How Elvis inspired my new movie *Vanilla Sky*', *The Guardian* (11 January 2002), at www.guardian. co.uk/film/2002/jan/11/artsfeatures2/. Accessed 20 September 2009.

25 Ibid.

26 Apart from the pieces by Anne White (2003) and Paul Julian Smith

(2004), the phenomenon of the 'indie' remake of *Abre los ojos* has been studied by Daniel Herbert (2006). Here Herbert deals briefly with recent remake theory, while drawing attention to simplistic binaries between national and transnational forces, which he seeks to explore and critique. He regards *Abre los ojos* as a type of film which belongs to a pan-European cinema, engaged in mitigating and contesting the transnational hegemony of Hollywood (2006: 30).

27. After *Vanilla Sky*, which more than covered its budget but attracted very mixed reviews, Cameron Crowe's filmmaking career stalled badly. Four years later he released *Elizabethtown* (2005), a return to more familiar 'rom-com' territory. A 'hot shot' sports footwear designer, played by Orlando Bloom, abandons a suicide attempt (his new shoe is a monumental and costly failure) in order to return home and bury his father and meets the 'girl of his dreams' on the plane, in the shape of a stewardess called Claire (Kirsten Dunst). She helps him overcome his family grief and his company's losses, a trifling $1 billion. The film was shown at the Toronto Film festival in September 2009, at a baggy 138 minutes. It was received badly by buyers, fans, critics and wider audiences and cut down to 120 minutes, but emerged disjointed, lacking in focus and coherence and lop-sided. That is, the secondary and subplot material seemed to stifle the pace and drive of the main romance. *Elizabethtown* was a flop. Crowe, who believed the film could be a return ticket to form and another, more enticing 'rockogram' to all his fans who hated *Vanilla Sky*, has not made a commercial feature since. However, he is developing an adaptation of a memoir by Benjamin Mee, *We Bought a Zoo* (backed by Fox), scheduled for release in December 2011, possibly starring Matt Damon and Scarlett Johansson. Given his lack of success with the film remake and with no experience of adapting a written source, is he about to repeat himself? Crowe could well be entering the nightmare of a downward spiral in his fortunes, possibly marked for eternity by the curse of *Vanilla Sky*. In 2008 Crowe separated from his wife Nancy Wilson (of the rock band Heart) after 22 years of marriage, owing to 'irreconcilable differences'.

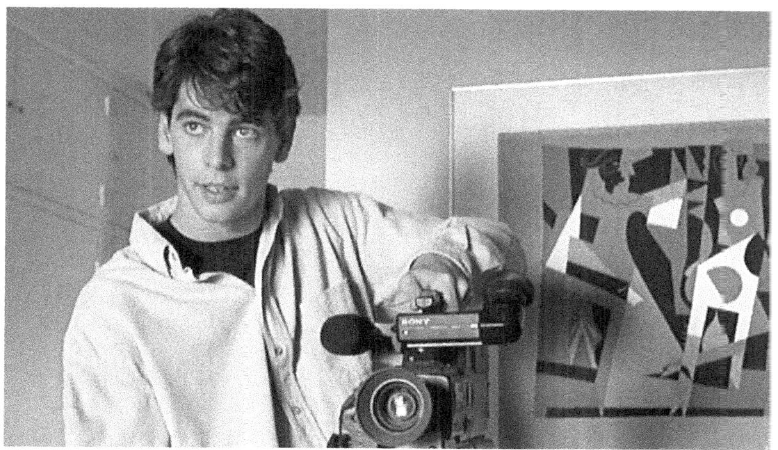

1   Bosco (Eduardo Noriega) prepares to film Ángela (Ana Torrent) in her bedroom in *Tesis*

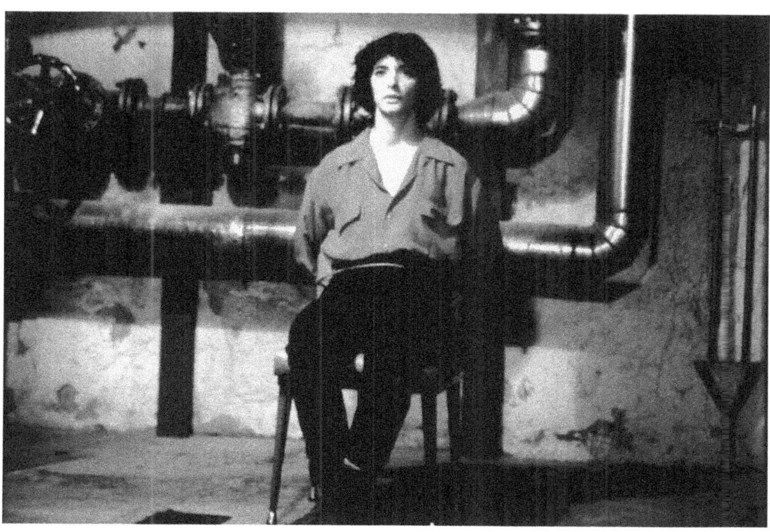

2   Ángela (Ana Torrent) prepares herself for a violent and bloody death in *Tesis*

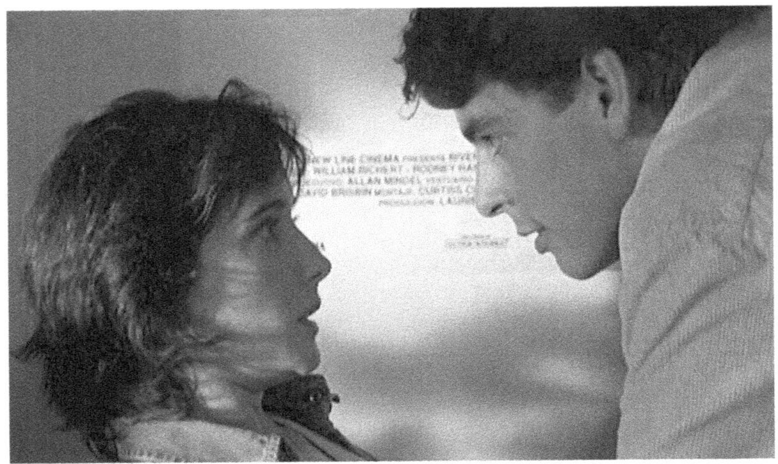

3   Bosco (Eduardo Noriega) is about to fulfil Ángela's darkest fantasy in *Tesis*

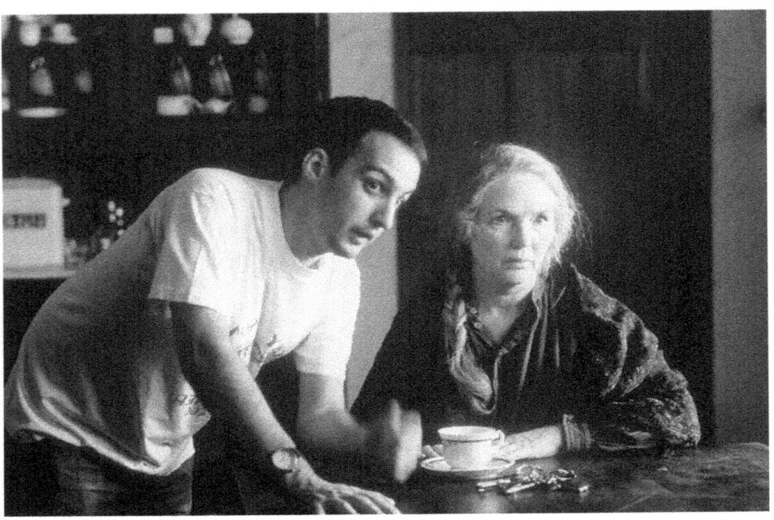

4   Amenábar offers advice to Mrs Mills (Fionnula Flanagan) during the shooting of *The Others*

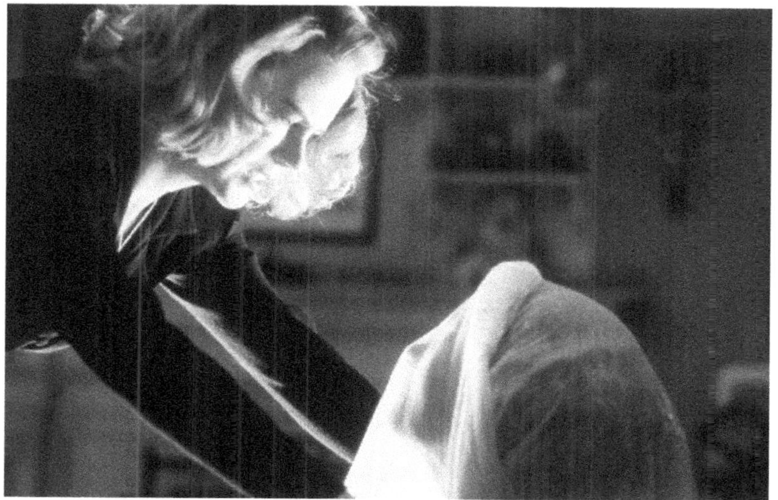

5 Grace (Nicole Kidman) gazes on her daughter transformed into an old hag (Renée Ascherson) in *The Others*.

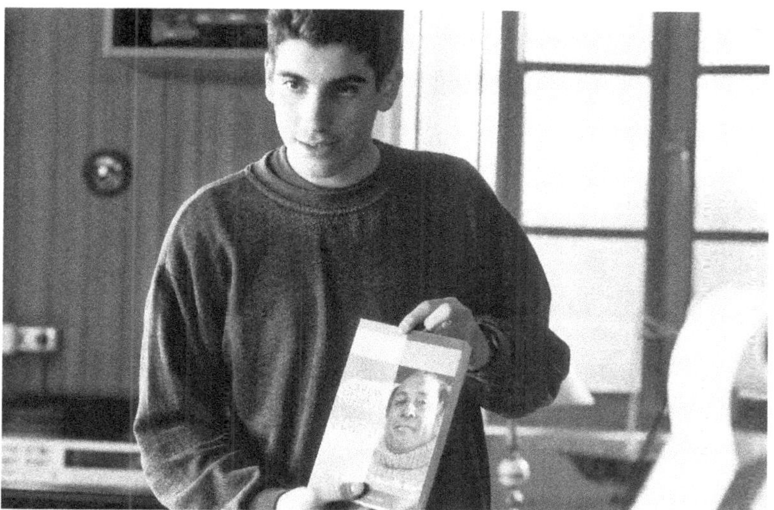

6 Javi (Tamar Novas) proudly picks up Ramón's first published book in *Mar adentro*

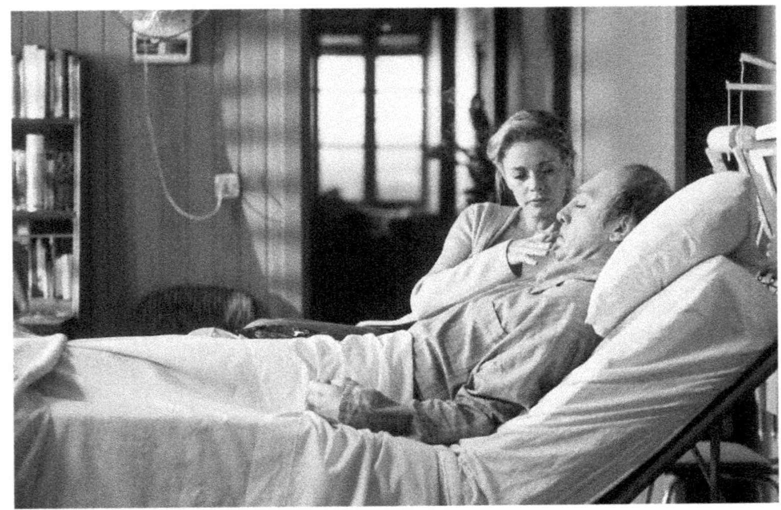

7   Julia (Belén Rueda) helps Ramón (Javier Bardem) enjoy a cigarette in *Mar adentro*

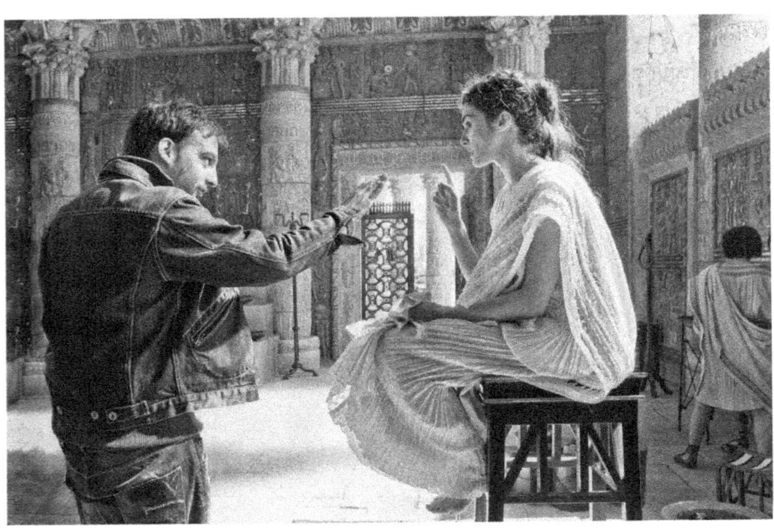

8   Amenábar directs Rachel Weisz in the opening scene of *Ágora*

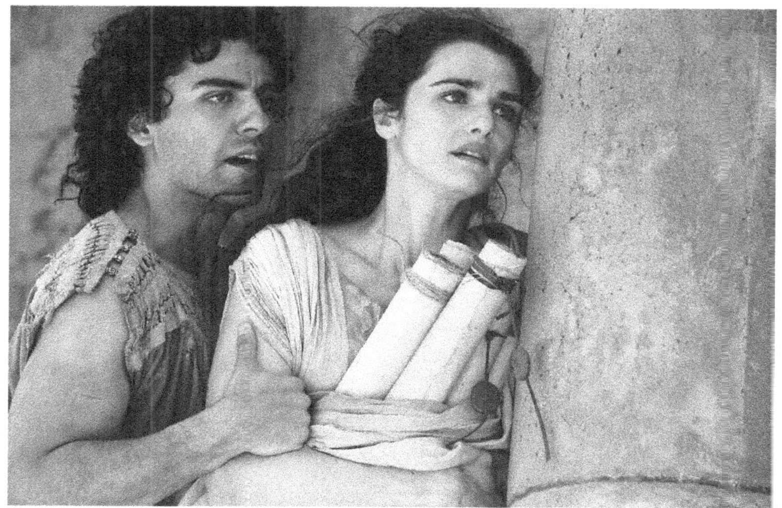

9   Orestes (Oscar Isaac) protects Hypatia (Rachel Weisz) during the Christian attack on the Great Library in *Ágora*

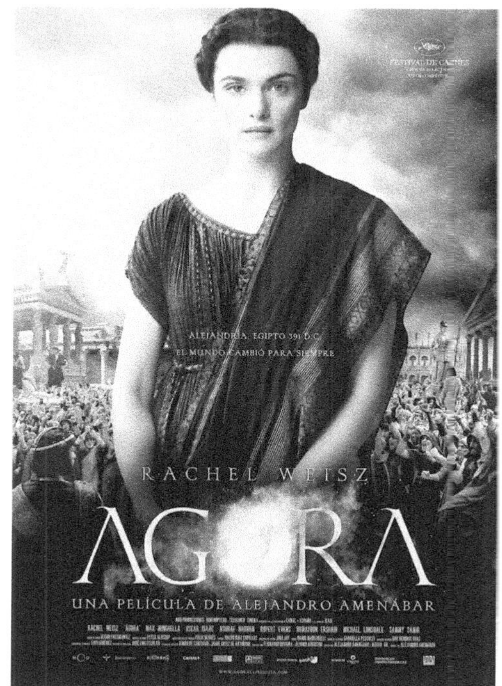

10   Publicity poster showing Rachel Weisz in *Ágora*

5

Clean, quiet, scary movies:
The Others

The Others began as a small-scale, art film project for the European market. The intended setting was Chile, Amenábar's birthplace. The ambition was to explore the repressions of his childhood, especially the impact of religious dogma on family life and the education of children. Over time, however, the film was transformed into the most expensive, biggest-grossing, box-office hit in Spanish film history, as well as an enormous critical and commercial success internationally. Originally written in Spanish and entitled *La casa* (The House), the idea caught the interest of some of the most powerful producers in independent Hollywood, including Bob and Harvey Weinstein of Miramax and Tom Cruise of Cruise/Wagner Productions. The script was given an 'Anglo-Saxon' makeover, redrafted into English and sent out to a number of potential American co-producers for consideration. But it was the Cruise-Miramax offer which was finally accepted. Never before had a Spanish director and his local producers (José Luis Cuerda for Las Producciones del Escorpión and Fernando Bovaira for Sogecine) been involved in such an ambitious, transatlantic, English-language film of this type and on such a scale. And not since Almodóvar's Oscar-nominated *Mujeres al borde de un ataque de nervios* (Women on the Verge of a Nervous Breakdown, 1988) has there been such a globally successful, Spanish film product, financed, produced and directed in Spain, while benefiting from large-scale, world wide, Hollywood distribution, marketing and promotion.

For Amenábar the original impulse to write *La casa* arose in early 1998 during the marketing campaign for *Abre los ojos*. Panicked by the complexity of his second film and fearing the worst from the national box-office and his fans, he began developing an idea with a much simpler, more restrained, linear narrative. It would seek to avoid the spatio-temporal *mise-en-abyme* of *Abre los ojos* and take its generic cues from a rather different source of inspiration, i.e the classical Hollywood horror films he had seen as an adolescent and student, including British gothic romance. He wanted to lock away a handful of characters in a single location and create tension with as few elements as possible, that is to say 'hacer una película casi minimalista' (Rodríguez Marchante 2002: 107) (to make an almost minimalist film). At around the same time he also made a trip with his brother Ricardo to see his relations in Chile. This was where the idea of the single-parent family in peril, alone in a large, claustrophobic, isolated country house began to take shape (Rodríguez Marchante 2002: 108). This was later followed by more detailed research into American and British 1940s and 1950s crime mystery, thriller and horror movies as well as a detailed analysis of Peter Medak's *The Changeling* (1980), Amenábar's benchmark, quiet moody horror film of all time. It was not long before a draft script emerged, one which also drew upon his childhood readings of the adventure and mystery stories of Enid Blyton and Agatha Christie as well as the classic ghost tale of Henry James, *The Turn of the Screw* (1898). Amenábar's narrative revolved around a single mother, two children and a household dominated by religion. It thus signified a return to his own childhood fears and insecurities, mixing his unconventional family life with the repressions of schooling, which so far he had not explored in his films (Rodríguez Marchante 2002: 109) As he stated in interview, 'Esta película es una vuelta a los miedos que han acompañado mi niñez' (Payán 2001: 49) (This film is a return to the fears of my childhood). As a film project *La casa* presented significant stylistic challenges, given Amenábar's ambition to avoid the clichés of contemporary mainstream, CGI-dominated horror in order to make a far more subtle, intelligent, period film, inspired by classical Hollywood style. He was also fascinated by the children's illness, photosensitivty, as a motivational and narrative device and as 'una metáfora y denuncia de ciertos sistemas de educación represiva' ('*Los otros*'. *El Libro* 2001: 220) (a metaphor and critique of certain types of repressive education). When his first transatlantic co-pro deal was finally agreed, as Amenábar indicates in the Spanish version of the film script, 'los otros' were very definitely seen as his American co-producers.[1] He and his team had embarked upon a quite unique French–Spanish–American project which he describes as 'un viaje completamente nuevo, yo diría que insólito para el cine español' ('*Los otros'. El Libro* 2001: 7) (a totally new journey, I'd say unprecedented in Spanish filmmaking).

In this chapter I propose to consider briefly the issue of deal making between the Spanish and American co-pro partners, a matter which arguably deserves far more attention and analysis, given the importance of this event in Spanish film history. This is followed by a summary of key aspects of the co-production process, including Amenábar's relationships with his star Nicole Kidman and her husband Tom Crusie, who was also Executive Producer. I then look at aspects of performance and film technique, including *mise-en-scène* and sound, particularly Amenábar's score for the film. And after a brief comment on narrative and the 'surprise ending', I look at the film in relation to some of its main intertexts (mentioned above) and also as a product which benefits from the late-1990s counter-trend in DIY, minimalist 'quiet horror'. The chapter ends with a reflection on the possible meanings and implications of *The Others*, in relation to Amenábar's continuing dialogue with Catholic doctrine and literalist belief systems.

The deal

The production history of *The Others* really begins with the Sundance Film Festival of 15–25 January 1998, where *Abre los ojos* (1997) was showcased in the World Cinema section. As mentioned earlier, the film was well received by critics. It was also noticed and very highly regarded by Paula Wagner, co-producer with Tom Cruise of Cruise/ Wagner Productions, who recommended that her business partner should view it immediately. After doing so, Cruise moved quickly to secure the remake rights to the film and later hired Cameron Crowe to write the script and direct what became *Vanilla Sky* (2001). Indeed, Cruise was so gobsmacked by Amenábar's second film that he was anxious to know what else he had written. At that time, Amenábar had in development the script of *La casa* (*The House*) in Spanish, the foundation for *The Others*. In other words, with Tom Cruise as linchpin, the remake deal concerning *Abre los ojos* became the spring-board to *The Others*.

Amenábar's Spanish co-producers, Bovaira and Cuerda, had already discussed with him the script of *La casa* and had agreed in principle to develop the project into a film. However, they were unsure whether it would work as a production spoken in Spanish. For Cuerda there were simply too few 'latin' elements in the story line, given its provisional setting within a European immigrant family and community based in the south of Chile (Ubeda-Portugués 2001: 268). The interest shown by Cruise/Wagner Productions helped strengthen this view and thus encouraged the idea of the 'Anglo-Saxon' makeover (with new locations, anglicised names, adjustments to the religious references etc.). *La casa* was duly rewritten and refashioned into an English-language script for Hollywood. However, Cuerda was deeply sceptical that anything positive would emerge from the adventure. But, a few days after receipt of the script in January 1999, a Miramax executive was swiftly dispatched to Sogecine's headquarters in Madrid's Gran Vía to negotiate the distribution rights of the film for all English-speaking and Latin American countries (Ubeda-Portugués 2001: 268).

Miramax was by now a major producer in a very large USA domestic market (with some 35,000 screens nationwide and nearly 300 million inhabitants) and a powerful independent distributor in many foreign markets across the world. The company also moved well over $1 billion per year in film projects (production and distribution) and had a striking commercial track record, having successfully promoted major Oscar-winning, independent films such as *The Piano* (Jane Campion, 1994), *The English Patient* (Anthony Minghella, 1996), *La vita e bella* (Life is Sweet, Roberto Benigni, 1998) and *Shakespeare in Love* (John Madden, 1998). In the end Bovaira and Cuerda decided to deal with Cruise and Miramax, partly because of their track record (including Oscar successes) and global marketing ambitions but also because Amenábar insisted he wished to work in Spain, thus giving him greater creative control and a less stressful shooting schedule (Ubeda-Portugués 2001: 269). At the same time Tom Cruise would act as Executive Producer, implicating Cruise/Wagner Productions in the co-pro deal in a support capacity as external advisers, since Cruise did not put up any of the finance. And while Miramax and Dimension Films took care of distribution, marketing and promotion, the production budget of $17 million would be covered wholly by Sogecine, with Bovaira overseeing the venture in Spain (imdb.com). Towards the end of 1999, at an important lunch at the Tribeca Grill, New York, Bovaira and Amenábar, the Weinstein brothers and Tom Cruise, plus late arrival Nicole Kidman, hurriedly thrashed out the final details of the deal which would launch *The Others*, including the key matter of casting the leading role of Grace.[2] What is clear is that neither Bovaira nor Cuerda, as Spanish co-producers, could fully comprehend the motives or the remarkable degree of interest shown in a small European project by their globally powerful American 'others': 'Sin Miramax, habríamos hecho una película pequeña, europea', argues Bovaira, 'Con ellos, multiplicamos la ambición del proyecto ... Era extraordinario que quisiesen implicarse en un proyecto común con la cinematografía española, que desconocían por completo. Era como un choque de civilizaciones' (Roig 2001: 36) (Without Miramax, we would have made a small, European film. Working with them, we significantly increased the scope of the project ... It was amazing that they wanted to do a co-production with the Spanish film industry, which they didn't know at all. It was like a clash of civilisations).

Production

In the Spring of 2000 Amenábar began to assemble his production team, rehiring some of the crew he had worked with before (e.g. Ricardo Goldstein on sound) as well as several new specialists such as Sonia Grande (Costume Design), Nacho Ruiz Capillas (Editing), Félix Bergés (Visual Effects) and Benjamín Fernández (Production Design) who had just finished work on *Gladiator* (Ridley Scott, 2000). Also, after extensive location searches of Jersey and the UK, it was Associate Producer Eduardo Chapero-Jackson who finally discovered the Palacio de los Hornillos, at Las Fraguas, near Santander, which would serve as the main house for all the exterior shots. Built by an English architect at the beginning of the twentieth century, it was owned by the Marqués del Viso and the Marquesa de Santa Cruz, who were still resident. However, it was decided that most of the interiors would be reconstructed and shot on the main set at El Alamo Studios, Madrid. As for the cast, despite disputes with Miramax over the casting of some of the secondary roles, Amenábar resisted concerted pressures to 'americanise' the smaller parts and retained a strong degree control over the project.[3] The only serious unknown for Amenábar was Nicole Kidman. She was rapidly becoming a global star, a household name, and would clearly benefit the marketing and promotion of the film. She had also agreed to do the part of Grace for a sum well below her usual fee. But, even though she had played Rae Ingram in Philip Noyce's psychological thriller *Dead Calm* (1989) twelve years before (in a role where she evolves from the fragile, traumatised victim of Billy Zane to a Ripley-like monster slayer), she had little or no track record in playing horror (Payán 2001: 50).

The shoot for *The Others* was originally scheduled for 12 weeks from the end of October 1999 through to February 2000. Unfortunately for Amenábar, the start of his production was dependent on the progress of another film, Baz Lurhmann's *Moulin Rouge*, starring Kidman as the voluptuous Parisian courtesan Satine. Here, various accidents on set sustained by Kidman (broken rib, bruised knee, twisted ankle) led to extremely long delays in finishing the picture, which included periods of convalescence in the USA as well as holidays. This meant that *The Others* suffered a massive delay of nearly nine months and did not start shooting interiors until the end of June 2000. Kidman arrived in Madrid on 15 July, with her children, burdened by a limp and at the mercy of a mob of the world's paparazzi. The latter were a constant pressure and serious irritation. They had also disrupted Tom Cruise's low-key arrival at Madrid airport on 24 July, as he flew in to help launch the film at a tumultuous press conference. Indeed, their antics almost caused Kidman and Cruise to consider abandoning Madrid and Spain altogether. For his part Amenábar had used the intervening nine months wisely, meticulously revising the script with the writer-translator Walter Leonard and rehearsing the other roles, especially the scenes involving the children. The long delay also gave him time to double-check his shooting schedule for his first ever English-language film, improve his own command of English and even write the scores for Cuerda's *La lengua de las mariposas* (Butterfly Tongue, 1999) and Mateo Gil's *Nadie conoce a nadie* (Nobody Knows Anybody, 1999).

Apart from the delays, the generally mechanical and laborious process of shooting the film did not get off to a good start, largely because of the peculiarities of Hollywood stardom. After her experience of working with Kubrick on *Eyes Wide Shut* (1999) and his improvisational techniques of character building, Kidman was used to repeating a scene countless times. On *The Others* she expected similar largesse, demanding multiple retakes and a significant degree of control over the development of the character of Grace. Alarm bells began to sound at El Alamo. Articulating the disquiet of the mainly Spanish production team (whose members were used to working on small-scale projects within limited budgets), Cuerda expressed his concerns regarding 'gente de Hollywood': 'La gente de Hollywood se empeña en establecer relaciones de poder. Tiene poder y lo usar. Y yo eso lo llevo fatal. Cuando quieren algo hay que hacerlo, porque si no, hay crisis' (Roig 2001: 40) (Hollywood people insist on imposing power relations. They have power and they use it. This is something I can't stand. When they want something, they have to have it, if not, there's a crisis). Cuerda even believed that Nicole was faking her limp simply in order to undermine the production: 'Cojea para jodernos' (Roig 2001: 40) (She's limping just to fuck us up') he claimed.[4] Shooting at El Alamo resumed, though another lengthy delay in September 2000 allowed Amenábar to pre-edit approximately 80 minutes of interior scenes. This rough edit was also viewed, minutely analysed and commented on by Tom Cruise (from his rented family villa in Madrid) who, if he had a problem, now tended to call Bovaira rather than Amenábar.[5] This was not all. If anything, the shooting phase of *The Others* was straightforward compared to the stresses of editing the film as well as taking account of the results of screen tests in the USA and London, a practice totally unknown in Spain at that time.[6]

An international blockbuster

The Others was released in the USA on 10 August 2001, almost a month before its scheduled European opening. In America, in its first four weeks, the film did excellent business, grossing $57.9 million (source: boxofficemojo.com). And, in terms of generating momentum and sustainability in a crowded market, it did so thanks to its 'plot-twist-at-the-end' formula and a strong 'must see' attitude among spectators created via word of mouth. As an independent, low-key late-summer, horror movie, *The Others* remained at number four in terms of box-office receipts, across the USA, for nearly nine weeks. While not as spectacular as *The Sixth Sense*, *The Others'* $96.5 million gross domestic receipts were extremely good compared to its $17 million budget. It also earned $113.5 million in foreign income (imdb.com). And perhaps thanks to rather than despite the impending divorce between Cruise and Kidman, which had been rumbling in the background from January 2001, *The Others* emerged as a world-wide success, an indie blockbuster. Never before had a Spanish film achieved such a degree of foreign penetration across world markets.[7] Of course, in another sense, the August release of *The Others* in the USA was a godsend. On 11 September 2001 the world's attention was diverted by an event of such magnitude that all film releases would temporarily pale into insignificance. If *The Others* had been released after that date, its commercial career might well have taken a very different turn. Paradoxically, following the Islamist terrorist attack on the Twin Towers in New York, box-office for the film in the USA experienced a second bounce, as American audiences sought quiet, intimate, family-oriented ghost tales rather than action and violence (Roig 2001: 42).

The Others also received overwhelmingly positive, praiseworthy notices all across the world. This confirmed that the film spoke to international audiences in a clear accessible language, offering a ghost story which was intelligent and lacking in gore or effects, and which spectators felt confident to recommend to others by word of mouth. Moreover, and despite the many changes it experienced, the film script provided a solid and attractive foundation and a set of characters who were ably filled by strong performances. Though arguably clichéd, the subgenre and the story line were not weighed down by national referents. Also, the look and address of the film, i.e. very stylish, arty, classical, quiet and 'old-fashioned', struck a chord with mainstream audiences, tired of banal, repetitious contemporary horror, overwhelmed by booming, intrusive soundtracks (Roig 2001: 42). For Amenábar, while the film had been a frustrating and stressful learning experience (given delays, a demanding diva and a relentless executive producer, Cruise), it was also a major triumph. Indeed Cuerda was awestruck by his young protégé's ability to deal with the many pressures of the shoot and praised Amenábar's remarkable success in the American market, aged only 29 (Ubeda-Portugués 2001: 268).

Synopsis

Set on the island of Jersey, near the French coast, in 1945, just as the war is ending, the main action in *The Others* takes place in a vast Victorian mansion, in its own equally extensive grounds. The Germans have recently withdrawn, after five years of occupation. The story concerns the relationships between lone parent Grace Stewart (Nicole Kidman) and her two children Anne (Alakina Mann) and Nicholas (James Bentley). Grace's husband Charles (Christopher Eccleston) went off to fight in the war over a year and half ago and has not yet returned. A week ago, without explanation and without even collecting their clothes or wages, Grace's servants also left. This single-parent family thus live alone in their gloomy, isolated house, submerged in almost permanent darkness, with no electricity, phone, car or radio. The windows and heavy curtains are always drawn, each door of the fifty rooms must be locked before the next one is opened and, because Grace has a history of mental illness and suffers severe migraines, she requires total silence. However, the ostensible reason for such enforced enclosure is that Grace's children suffer from a rare skin disease (Xeroderma pigmentosum or 'photosenstivity') and cannot be exposed to anything stronger than candlelight for fear of blisters, asphyxia and ultimately death.

Grace tutors her children at home and, as an extremely devout Catholic, obliges them to learn their prayers and long passages from the Bible and know by rote the various doctrinal punishments for children who tell lies. The rebellious Anne teases her younger brother with tales of ghosts, even claiming that she talks to 'the others' in the house, for which she gets into serious trouble with her mother. The film opens with the unannounced arrival of a trio of strangers, who claim to be familiar with the house. Grace assumes they are new servants responding to an advertisement for domestic help (an advertisement which she never actually posted). Bertha Mills (Fionnula Flanagan) is the nanny/housekeeper and reasonably talkative, assisted by the rather enigmatic Edmund Tuttle (Eric Sykes), the gardener/ handyman, and a young girl, Lydia (Elaine Cassidy), the maid, who is mute. After the servants are hired and begin to settle in, strange things begin to happen: doors are left open and unlocked, curtains are inexplicably opened, the piano plays by itself, footsteps are heard in empty rooms, the chandelier swings back and forth etc. At first Grace blames the servants, but Anne insists that the disturbances are due to ghosts, including a little boy called Victor and an eyeless old woman. Grace determines to walk to the village to fetch a priest in order to bless her ghost-infested house, but in the mist bumps into her shell-shocked husband Charles (returning from the war), who stays briefly but mysteriously leaves soon after. Gradually, as the disturbances increase, Grace is forced to contemplate a supernatural explanation for such strange events and, in the process, to confront dark, troubling secrets in her own past.

Narrative

Amenábar describes *The Others* as 'mi película menos efectista ... y a la vez más clara...donde más me he contenido ... mi película más lograda' (Rodríguez Marchante 2002: 107) (my least effects-laden film ... and at the same time, my clearest ... where I've been most restrained ... my best-made film). Compared to *Abre los ojos*, *The Others* is a relatively straightforward, linear ghost story. It does not indulge in major spatio-temporal shifts via flashbacks or in spectacular imagery. Nor is it an action film, with a clear narrative arc and set of turning points. Rather, it is a film of tones, moods and atmospheres, where the 'double' opening (the motherly voiceover Genesis story juxtaposed with Grace's blood-curdling scream) immediately establishes the film's rules of engagement by addressing the audience as confused and fearful child. On receipt of the initial edit of the film, the American distributors Miramax were seriously concerned by the apparent imbalance between substance and style and, as noted earlier, the lack of narrative pacing. *The Others* was seen as very well made, with excellent acting performances overall, but with too few plot elements, which lacked focus and purpose and might well squander audience empathy towards the main characters. Moreover, for the Americans, the scares were not strong enough (until the surround sound was applied) and there were not nearly enough of them, though Amenábar was tempted to leave in, for example, the moment when Nicholas wets himself (based on real-life experience, it seems – Interview). Unfortunately, in order to speed up narrative tempo, this and other such sequences were cut.

As in his previous two films, the narrative of *The Others* is organised according to the principles of delay and the strict rationing of plot information. The story arc explores a double or mutual 'haunting' (between Grace's family and the new owners of the house) via a series of encounters (through voices, visions, sounds, the presence of Victor, doors, windows, curtains, the piano, the eyeless old woman etc.), culminating in the séance scene. The film was fully story boarded by Sergio Rozas ('*Los otros.*' *El Libro*, 2001: 236), yet, as noted above, it is not an action film, where strict pre-planning is essential. Indeed, when shooting *The Others*, unlike his previous films, Amenábar was far more amenable to script changes, to exploring new options and giving the actors room to improvise and rewrite their parts, especially Kidman. With Amenábar persuaded to 'go with the flow' on set, far more so than before, the rushes corresponded less and less to what was originally planned. Unlike the 'iron scripts' and tight organisation of *Tesis* and *Abre los ojos*, in *The Others* we find a rather a more diffuse, psychological thriller, where the chain of narrative cause and effect leads to a psychological rather than an action climax. In a sense the action climax in *The Others* has already happened, offscreen.

before we enter the narrative (when Grace murders her children with a pillow and then shoots herself). What we actually see, in effect, is the clash and gradual blurring of the boundaries of two competing worlds (the living and the dead), which climaxes in the séance scene. This is followed by a resolution in which Grace finally is obliged to come to terms with her guilty secrets by revealing the truth about her actions, taking responsibility and renouncing her infantile adherence to Catholic doctrine.

Like all good ghost stories, *The Others* is littered with queries, clues, dangling causes, and enigmas, designed to tease and stimulate. What has Grace done? Who is she? What was her upbringing like? When did she marry? Why did her parents leave the island in 1940? Why no contact since then? Why did Charles go off to war, with the Germans in control of the island, leaving a young, single mother to fend for herself, with two sick children? Why did the original servants abandon the house? Where did the new trio come from and why, especially since they did not know that help was required? Why is Lydia mute? Why has Father Lebrun not come to visit? These are all questions which we as well as Grace have to wrestle with, throughout the film, but, by severely restricting the flow of narrative information, Amenábar aligns the spectator with Grace, as she undertakes her own journey towards a form of spiritual catharsis. As in *Tesis* and *Abre los ojos*, the narrative of *The Others* consists of an investigation into the 'intruders' or 'the others' and raises the problem of definition of which is which. We also find a love story, but one centred upon a mother's suffocating, destructive love for her children, underpinned by guilt, a guilt also shared by her husband, whose character and relationship to his wife are left tantalisingly vague (Rodríguez Marchante 2002: 110).

The narrative is also predicated on the device of the 'surprise ending' and the final revelation of Grace's terrible secret. In test screenings this was the unexpected element which so engaged and enthralled audiences in the USA, who made the connection with the ending of *The Sixth Sense*. Amenábar's task was clear: 'Mi obsesión era que el espectador no se imaginara que ella estaba muerta' (Rodríguez Marchante 2002: 110) (I was obsessed with making sure that the spectator didn't realise she was dead). The fact is that Amenábar's parsimonious, sneaky delivery of narrative information and the distribution of relevant clues and signs are so subtle and unobtrusive that, on a first viewing, very few spectators are able to work out that Grace, her children and the servants are already dead. Hence the considerable level of business from second-time viewers. Even more appealing and counter-intuitive is the idea that the dead are somehow being haunted by the living, that the Marlish family who have bought the gloomy mansion post-invasion, and have hired a medium to contact the real ghosts, are themselves viewed as supernatural intruders. Such an inventive reversal at a narrative level plays a major role in destabilising the false binary thinking which characterises Grace's brittle Catholic beliefs; it also undercuts traditional narrative conventions in gothic horror, such as the triumph of good over evil, which Amenábar was so keen to upend.

Mise-en-scène

As with any ghost story or gothic horror movie where the 'house' plays a pivotal role not only as a setting but also as a protagonist, symbol and metaphor, the visual credibility and coherence of the set design, lighting, costume, props, overall look and its photographic capture (interiors and exteriors) become crucial. This was a job for an accomplished production designer, a role not widely exploited in Spanish cinema at all but a key requirement for a project seeking to create and deliver a high-quality Hollywood look and mood. With *The Others* it was Bovaira who initially made contact with Benjamín Fernández as a possible candidate for 'director artístico' (production designer), while he was finishing off *Gladiator* in Morocco. Paradoxically, Fernández was very well known in Hollywood, but virtually unknown in Spain. The dates coincided and he was hired. Fernández made some preliminary drawings based on a video he had seen of the location house, at Torrelavega, near Santander. However, these were initially rejected by Amenábar as too clean, warm and cosy. The director wished to give the house a far more chilly, dusty, gloomy 'feel', since the script indicated that it was almost empty, very dirty, overgrown, had already been abandoned and was quickly becoming derelict. Their costume designer Sonia Grande also set to work researching 1940s English fashions, under strict instructions to avoid cliché and gothic horror convention in favour of strong verisimilitude. She also had to overcome the problem of how to dress the three servants, struck down by tuberculosis in 1891, but who return to the house in mid-1945. Grande experimented with muted greens and greys for the children, patrician purple for Grace and browns and blacks for the servants. She also had to create a 'used look' for the costumes which would blend in successfully with the subdued tones of house and reflect Grace's repressions and the pasty, sick, ghostly appearance of the children, without giving away their true condition, which is revealed at the end of the film.

Given the MacGuffin of 'photosensitivity', as well as Grace's terrible migraines, the rationale for the spooky, deathly, enclosed settings is strong and the predominance in the film of interior shots and sequences is thus convincingly motivated. This allowed Amenábar to create a very closed, claustrophobic atmosphere, one which exudes entrapment and hysteria. The feeling of imprisonment is augmented by the dark corridors, blacked out by heavy curtains, dimly lit by candles and old lamps, with the corners left almost pitch black and room spaces virtually swallowed by darkness. However, Amenábar is careful not to let such a sinister atmosphere fall into cliché or excess, or alienate the spectator. Like Grace, the viewer searches for answers to the haunting, and is invited to investigate the dark corners and look behind creaky doors.

As a metaphor, prior to the haunting, the house suggests a fortress which protects terrible family secrets but also a vessel which keeps out the daylight, as a ship must keep out the water. In short Grace and her family inhabit a kind of ghost ship, a *Mary Celeste*, set adrift and shrouded in a very thick, wall-like, wet fog, suggestive of an eerie, otherworldly, supernatural realm, as seen from a child's point of view. Such requirements are well served by the set design and costume departments, but, in order to work successfully, they demand an extremely complex and challenging form of 'low light' filmmaking, which combines realism with the imagined fears, scares and terrors of children's mystery stories. And here the cinematographer Javier Aguiresarrobe arguably breaks with classic lighting conventions of Hollywood horror and seeks to create: 'un concreto tipo de tenebrismo, natural, creíble, verosímil' ('*Los otros.*' *El Libro*, 2001: 213–15) (a specific form of darkness, natural, believable, credible). Aguirresarrobe seems to draw upon the classical colour palette of the Dutch Masters, such as Bosch and Rembrandt, but also on the atmospheres of classic 1940s mystery and melodrama, such as Thorold Dickinson's *Gaslight* (1940) and Hitchcock's *Rebecca* (1940), while also creating a tonal and stylistic tribute to the child world of Erice's *El espiritu de la colmena* (The Spirit of the Beehive, 1973). And, apart from a cloak of digital fog (one of Tom Cruise's major concerns), remarkably, Amenábar hardly relies at all on special effects for any of the thrills and scares. Rather, he exploits character reaction shots, the expressiveness of the eyes and faces responding to events, trying to show that what is suggested offscreen is far scarier and suggestive than what is actually seen.

Soundtrack

In order to sustain the verisimilitude of spooky visuals, convention demands that these be supported by a spooky soundtrack. In this regard, and as is well known as one of his trademarks, Amenábar tends to work against the Hollywood grain, avoiding big scores and deafening sound effects in favour of all-round minimalism. Indeed his basic proposition on screen horror is that the most effective way of creating the fear factor and scaring the audience is through the use of silence, appropriately counterbalanced by the sparing use of small sound effects. This also applies to the use of the music track where for Amenábar, the lack or denial of musical accompaniment (and the anxiety this induces) is often a much better way of fostering audience engagement and of scaring them. *The Others* is an extremely quiet, intimate film, pervaded by silence, spoken in whispers, but shredded by the occasional scream and bang. In this respect the opening of the film is exemplary, in the way Amenábar juxtaposes the poised, cloying 'Listen with Mother' voiceover delivered by Grace (which encompasses her children and the theatre audience in the same, infantilising mode of address) with her blood-curdling, hysterical scream, as she emerges from a nightmare. As a film opening and mood setter this is highly effective, counterposing an idyllic vision of harmonious 'happy families' with a Catholic mother in turmoil, harbouring a guilty secret. In this sense Amenábar goes for less not more, he prefers ominous footsteps, muffled music, panicked breathing, anguished screams to loud bangs or explosive bass effects. However, as noted earlier, following test screenings in the USA, he was persuaded (by his American executive producers) to punctuate and enhance the scare factor of the heavy, slamming doors, echoing floorboards and moving furniture with a strong dash of Dolby digital, surround sound.

As regards Amenábar's 40-minute score for *The Others*, and contrary to convention, this was mostly prepared during the long months of pre-production delay, then refined and tested during the shooting period rather than being created afterwards. In fact, during rehearsals with the children, Amenábar played them various phrases and riffs on a tape machine (prepared by him on his office keyboard) in order to get them into the mood on set. Overall, Amenábar wanted a 'música pequeña' (small-scale musical score) for a big but very intimate film. However, it would be based mainly on a series of single instruments (as in the score for *La lengua de las mariposas*) rather than on a dominant, full, symphonic sound. He was looking for something haunting and elegant for his three basic themes: the credit sequence, the communion sequence and the theme of the dead. His themes are dominated by woodwind, strings, chimes and percussion, as well as some ghostly vocals which weave in and out of the mix. The score is functional, expressive of melancholy and pain, but relatively anonymous, i.e. safe, perhaps lacking any clear stylistic qualities that might set it apart from the work of other genre film composers. And though Amenábar has an encyclopaedic knowledge of horror film music and knows all the classic phrases and motifs, he is extremely good at disguising clichéd phrasing and instrumentation. In keeping with the subdued tone and mood of a classic, 1940s-style horror thriller, his soundtrack is definitely small, understated and minimalist and largely avoids clichéd sounds. It also manages to spice up its minimal background atmosphere with the occasional burst of orchestral fright. Yet there is no clear title theme, and no single instrument which carries the burden of the score, even though Amenábar occasionally uses heavy strings to prolong and extend the horror of a scene. Small, safe, slow and not very exciting, the score is nonetheless perfectly suited to adding credible atmosphere to a creepy, 'classically inspired' horror film. And, unlike much mainstream horror, the score does not beat the spectator into early submission with decibel-driven sound effects or heavy metal, rock tracks.

Performance

The divorce between Tom Cruise and Nicole Kidman after nearly eleven years of marriage dominated Hollywood gossip columns in late 2001 and early 2002, with Kidman becoming the most photographed woman in show business. Yet, on a professional level, 2001 was an important year for her, with Golden Globe nominations for *The Others* and *Moulin Rouge* and a Golden Globe Best Actress award for her performance in *Moulin Rouge* (Baz Luhrmann 2001). Much to Amenábar's chagrin, Kidman did not achieve an Oscar nomination for *The Others*, but she did so for *The Hours* the following year (2002) and won the award.

In *The Others*, as the cold, neurotic, religious fanatic, abandoned by her husband and housekeeping staff, Nicole Kidman appears convincingly panicky and unhinged as Grace, as she runs from one room to another, trapped in the repeating hell of her own bizarre house rules (echoing those of Amenábar's childhood). Amenábar keeps her, like us, in the dark until the final scene, as she confronts a supernatural invasion she can no longer ignore. On the whole her performance as Grace in *The Others* was widely praised by critics, who regarded it as a return to decent form after a poor showing in *Eyes Wide Shut* (1999) and an over-heated, over-theatricalised performance in *Moulin Rouge*. While some critics preferred the glamorous, energetic, sexy Kidman of Lurhmann's pastiche, others were happier with the more understated, sexually repressed, guilt-ridden, tormented Grace, though the character was sometimes seen as unsympathetic, not easy to identify with or care about. However, to a large extent, *The Others* helped re-establish Kidman as a serious, classy and controlled screen actress, able to negotiate the line between her brittle, hysterical, control freak side and a softer, warmer, more convincingly maternal side.[8]

It may have been Kidman's film, but the supporting players and performances were by and large seen as excellent, credible and engaging; even Eric Sykes as Mr Tuttle played the role almost straight.[9] Also, Tuttle's amusing habit of endorsing Mrs Mills's opinions by enigmatically repeating her words indicates the housekeeper's eerie power and control over the household, knowing far more than she says. She acts as the perfect nanny, until the servants' secret is revealed. And Fionnula Flanagan's Mrs Mills was Kidman's perfect nemesis. She was the dutiful servant, with the soft, warm eyes, but at the same time extremely creepy and unnerving behind her grandmotherly demeanour. Her quiet, low-key performance, her teasing voice, knowing looks, her ability to comfort the children and her total control of proceedings suggest vast untapped reserves of expressivity. Overall, Flanagan was very convincing as the head housekeeper (with strong echoes of Mrs Danvers in Hitchcock's *Rebecca* (1940), Miss Cooper in Laughton's *Night of the Hunter* (1955) and Mrs Grose in Clayton's *The Innocents* (1961)). At times she even threatened to upstage Kidman, as in the well-judged kitchen scenes with the children.

Despite dire predictions, the two children also performed extremely well, with Alakina Mann receiving outstanding notices. This may have been an embarrassment for those Miramax executives who wished to remove her from the production before principal photography began. Alakina Mann fully inhabits the role of a wilful, knowing and rebellious eight year-old Anne while Nicholas comes over well as her terrified, trusting, 'scaredy cat' brother. Both roles are conveyed with great ease and credibility. Indeed, Anne's teasing and bickering with whingeing, 'cowardy custard' Nicholas bear all the hallmarks of authentic sibling rivalry (doubtless inspired by the young Amenábar and his older brother Ricardo). She is also far more self-confident, aggressive, mature and contemptuous of both grown-ups and children and is the one who finally decides to abandon the house to find her father. Alakina Mann gives a cheeky, steely performance, and shows genuine confusion at the antics of her mother on 'the day that mommy went mad'. The children are not cute or brattish. Rather they behave credibly, in line with a 1940s household and strict Catholic family discipline. And though thoroughly rehearsed, Amenábar managed to coax outstanding performances from them, by allowing them to act and to improvise. Perhaps the only big disappointment in the film was the way Christopher Eccleston was wasted as Charles. He is given little to do but acknowledge the children, get into bed, brood and then abandon the house once again. Yet this truncated presence and performance had to do more with editing decisions than with Eccleston's acknowledged quality as an actor.

Many critics, as well as Amenábar himself, have remarked on the statuesque bearing of Kidman's Grace and her porcelain facial beauty, reminiscent of Grace Kelly in Hitchcock's *Dial M for Murder* and *Rear Window*. Obviously the name Grace is no coincidence but an echo of Hitchcock's fetishised ice blond, and an anglicised version of the original character name in Spanish, Graciela. But, while Cruise and Amenábar have consistently spoken of Kidman's performance in glowing, effusive terms, Kidman herself has been far less complimentary about her own efforts.[10]

Intertextuality

In terms of his own filmmaking, Amenábar has frequently indicated that he has invented nothing new; rather, his aim is to innovate by reworking, defamiliarising and 'turning the screw' another notch or two on what already exists (Sempere 2000: 37). *The Others* is no exception. Indeed his English language debut has a very familiar, classical, 'old-fashioned' and resolutely counter-dominant feel to it. As well as children's bedtime stories, the film brings to mind the Victorian gothic novel and oral storytelling, 'performed' fireside tales and the Christmas ghost story, featuring prim, repressed mothers, strange rebellious children and untrustworthy domestics. Such stereotypes are brought out of cold storage, locked away inside a haunted mansion and made to suffer. Also the fact that Amenábar chooses to reinvigorate the supernatural ghost story with a period tale of a haunted house (one of the most overused conventions in the horror lexicon) is intriguing. It indicates once again a curiously nonchalant attitude towards risk just as it reaffirms his longstanding dissatisfaction with much classical and modern film horror (not nearly scary enough and far too loud).

In terms of its generic lineage, style and look, as noted earlier, *The Others* strongly recalls British and American mystery thrillers and melodramas of the 1940s and 1950s (Rodríguez Marchante 2002: 121–2). It is also strongly inspired by the tones, atmospheres and settings found, for example, in Thorold Dickinson's British thriller *Gaslight* (1940) as well as Hitchcock's *Rebecca* (1940), with its gloomy equivalent of Manderley. Moreover, Grace's hysteria seems as if it might have been borrowed from Ingrid Bergman's Oscar-winning performance as Paula in Cukor's Hollywood remake of *Gaslight* (1944) while her look and hair (including blonde wig, to mark her Englishness) seem lifted straight from the 'woman in jeopardy' figure, incarnated by Grace Kelly (for example, as Lisa in *Rear Window* or Margot in *Dial M for Murder*). Amenábar comments that, on set, Kidman looked so like Kelly that 'Era como si el fantasma de Hitchcock flotara en el ambiente' (Rodríguez Marchante 2002: 114) (It was as if Hitchcock's ghost was floating in the air). Like his mentor in suspense, Amenábar is also a fan of cameos, and does not let us down in *The Others*. He appears in a photograph with colleagues Mateo Gil and Carlos Montero, laid out three on a bed, contained in the 'Book of the Dead'. (One of his neighbours makes an appearance in another photograph.) Also, as an intertextual joke, Amenábar superimposes Eduardo Noriega's face on to a pre-Raphaelite painting of 1855, *The Wounded Cavalier* by W. Shakespeare Burton, which is meant to scare Grace and echo her husband's absence and military background. Amenábar also makes a classic reference-cum-homage at the beginning of *The Others*, where Grace's voiceover recalls the prophetic opening to Charles Laughton's *Night of the Hunter* (1955), where Lilian Gish warns the children to beware of devious priests and hucksters (Rodríguez Marchante 2002: 121). Of course, not all of Amenábar's quotes or allusions are Anglo-American. An important Spanish reference point for *The Others* is undoubtedly Victor Erice's acclaimed *El espiritu de la colmena* (The Spirit of the Beehive, 1973), not only in its sound textures, colour palette and lighting scheme but in its intimate, whispered performances by the two children. These include the eerie invocation 'Soy Ana' uttered by a five-year-old Ana Torrent at the end of the film (which was homaged by the very same Torrent as an adult in *Tesis* (1996) and recycled by the aptly named Anne in *The Others*: 'My name is Anne and I'm walking. I'm walking and my name is Anne').[11]

In this section the main film intertexts which concern me are those which Amenábar has consistently and explicitly claimed as key sources for his film. These are Jack Clayton's *The Innocents* (1961) and Peter Medak's *The Changeling* (1980). I also include a brief note on M. Knight Shyamalan's *The Sixth Sense* (1999).

The Innocents (1961)

In various interviews Amenábar has clearly linked *The Others* to English gothic fiction, the haunted house tale and in particular to Henry James's celebrated ghost story *The Turn of the Screw* (1898) (see Rodríguez Marchante 2002: 77 and 109; 'Los otros', El Libro, 2001: 225). [12] In the context of a debate on national cinema and the 'Spanishness' or otherwise of *The Others*, Núria Triana-Toribio has also made similar connections. As well as the influence of Hitchcock and the overlap in roles between the governess and Grace, she emphasises the 'film's large debts' (2003: 163) to Jack Clayton's *The Innocents*, the first and perhaps the most acclaimed, big-screen version of the James novella to date.[13] Hitherto Amenábar himself has been somewhat coy regarding what he might have borrowed or reworked from this Jamesian tradition. In the following brief account my purpose is to explore Triana-Toribio's claim a little further, suggesting various possible areas of similarity, coincidence and overlap with Clayton's film but also differences and contrasts. The main areas will include *mise-en-scène*, characterisation, key scenes and titles.

Before any detailed analysis we need to take into account the fact that the original screenplay for *The Innocents* was written by Willliam Archibald and based on his stage play of the same name.[14] Also it seems clear that Clayton himself was very keen to keep open his viewers' interpretative options and retain as far as possible the ambiguities and uncertainties both of the earlier play and of the novella. So, at the very least, his film could be read as a tale of a haunting with real ghosts as well as a study in psychological projection and sublimation. It is also worth bearing in mind that, while retaining Archibald's original title, his four core characters, the opening eerie song, the game of hide and seek and Miles's poetic invocation of Quint, Clayton frequently returns to the James novella for material. Also, as well as heavily editing the children's dialogue (a ponderous feature of Archibald's screenplay), Clayton seeks to inject greater pace, dynamism and unease into his story, incorporating many more moments of tension and release, spooky silences and the play of looks and double meanings. He also augments the level of erotic suggestibility, which Archibald had all but excised.

In terms of *mise-en-scène*, Clayton consciously tries to avoid Hammer-style cliché and shlock as well as Hollywood studio gothic. He sets his version of the James tale in the 1860s–70s (the novella is set in 1850). Also he deliberately upends viewer expectations by sending the impressionable governess, Miss Giddens, on a journey not to a dark, old, crumbling gothic mansion but to a Bly House depicted as a fairy palace, a shimmering, overwhelming scene of light and decaying refinement, decorated with marble statues on pedestals, countless roses, animals, birds (white doves) and reptiles. Such conspicuous opulence and faded natural beauty echo Kane's Xanadu, a source which Clayton himself greatly admired for its *mise-en-scène*, cinematography and Toland's staging and shooting in depth (a technique occasionally used in the film by the Oscar-winning cinematographer Freddie Francis). The sumptuous Victorian sets, costumes and decor for *The Innocents* are supported by a very elaborate but subtle sound palette (Flora's eerie opening song and Miles's recitation/invocation of Quint, as well as numerous animal and bird sounds), mainly designed to foreshadow and underline supernatural presences and visitations. Clayton also exploits a far more varied set of performance spaces (to overcome the limitations and claustrophobia of the Archibald stage play) and, apart from the drawing room, corridors and bedroom interiors, uses the garden, drive, greenhouse, terrace, lake and the battlement-style roof of Bly House.

Though his story is set in a very different period and location (in mid-1945, in a remote, post-occupation Jersey), like Clayton, Amenábar rejects old-style Hollywood, gothic cliché but also excess stylisation. He opts instead for a controlled, heavily restrained naturalism in his decor, costume and look etc., emphasising the dusty, sparsely furnished, evacuated spaces, stairs and corridors of his English-style mansion, gradually falling apart. Also like Clayton, Amenábar uses a variety of acting areas, predominantly interiors, such as the drawing room, breakfast room, kitchen, study, attic, landing and music room, but also the garden, shed, lake (built for the purpose) and drive. Yet, in total contrast to the luminous Bly House (and Clayton's decision to shoot a ghost story mainly in daylight), Amenábar plays it safe. His nameless, Victorian gothic-style house of pain is steeped in deep shadows on the inside and mostly fogbound on the outside, with daylight presented as a mortal threat, and darkness as a protective screen. Here Amenábar reworks familiar, clichéd gothic binaries, but within a credible, realist framework, successfully achieving the sensations of isolation and 'otherworldliness' exuded by his large house.

In terms of character selection and development, we find a number of striking similarities between the films. In *The Innocents* Clayton relies on the four main characters used exclusively in Archibald's play, i.e. Miss Giddens the Governess, the two orphaned children (older brother Miles, younger sister Flora) and the housekeeper, Mrs Grose. Crucially, following the credit sequence, Clayton adds an opening scene taken from the novella in which the charismatic, unnamed, absent uncle (a cameo impressively played by Michael Redgrave) interviews Giddens for the job of governess and triggers her romantic infatuation with him. The uncle's presence is strongly felt throughout the film among the core characters (in Giddens's ripe dialogue and its double-entendres, in Miles's frequent jibes against uncaring guardians and feeling cast aside, and especially in uncomplimentary references to the master's appetite for young women, uttered by Mrs Grose). The absent uncle and his womanising habits are duplicated internally in the ghosts of Quint and Jessel (the former valet and governess), who in life were shameless lovers and whose mission in death is to reoccupy the house and repossess the children. Some of these character templates and Clayton's emphasis on rebellious, abandoned children, whose behaviour is dictated by a mistrust of absent parents or guardians, figure strongly in *The Others*. Here the role of the governess (and home tutor) is taken up by Grace, the strict, abandoned mother and fanatical Catholic disciplinarian. Increasingly challenged in her beliefs and suspicious of Anne (as Giddens is of Miles and his eerie adult demeanour and behaviour), Grace resolves to confront and punish her daughter, while denying her account of the 'intruders' (even though she knows it to be truthful). If Giddens is a stand-in mother figure who projects her sexual repressions on to the Bly children (she kisses Miles on the mouth like a lover), Grace is another neurotic mother who (contrary to her own teachings about the denial of Christ) denies her children knowledge of their father's fate in war, her loveless marriage and indeed their own deaths.

As for the children, Clayton's over-precocious, weird and rather too cute Flora (Pamela Franklin) and Miles (Martin Stephens) become Amenábar's far more credible and watchable Anne (Alakina Mann) and Nicholas (James Bentley), only this time as older sister and younger brother. Though slightly younger than Miles, Anne is just as tough, angry and sceptical of adults and like Flora (who wants to know from Miss Giddens where God will take her young soul if she dies) is also determined to ask Grace awkward questions about the afterlife. To complete the quartet, we have the new housekeeper, the wonderfully enigmatic Mrs Mills. Mills bears a striking similarity in age, look and temperament to the friendly, down-to-earth Mrs Grose. She also seems just as self-confident as her counterpart, spookily familiar with the house, while providing an effective foil to Grace's arrogant, patrician attitude towards the servant class and outsiders. Yet Mills is unable (or not allowed) to offer Grace the confidence and intimacy seen early on between Giddens and Grose, who alerts the governess to the troubling, sadomasochistic relationship between Quint and Jessel. She also hints that the children's bad behaviour and Miles's expulsion from school may have something to do with their witnessing the servants *in flagrante* during the daytime. In *The Others* this Jamesian concern with child abuse projected through the Victorian fear of sexuality as a source of evil is less emphatic. Yet Clayton's absent uncle is arguably reintroduced by Amenábar as the war victim Charles, Grace's traumatised, alienated husband. Though very different, both men coincide as absent guardians of children (Charles returns to say a guilty goodbye to his offspring, while the uncle in *The Innocents* refuses to visit at all). Also, as we learn from Grace, Charles abandons his family not merely out of patriotism or the warrior spirit but also because he wants to leave her (motivated perhaps by sexual incompatibilities, exacerbated by Grace's frigidity). Both males thus appear unprepared to shoulder family responsibilities, preferring the lure of seduction, hunting or making war to the more mundane tasks of protecting and raising their wards or families.

As for the supernatural *dramatis personae*, and following Archibald,

Clayton presents the ghosts of Quint and Jessel both as subjective visions of Giddens's imagination and as tangible, objective presences in their own right. He marks Giddens's encounters by always preceding a spectral sighting with a close-up, reaction shot, to signal that it is her POV and emotional turmoil (her repressed sexual desire for the uncle) which are producing the vision. At other times Clayton emphasises the corporeality of the ghosts, using an omniscient, objective camera shot to include haunter and haunted (as in the study scene where Giddens discovers Jessel's real teardrop on a slate and occupies her seating position or the final sequence inside the circle of statues, where Miles, Giddens and the ghost of Quint all appear in shot at the same time). Also, in *The Innocents*, it is Giddens who sees the ghosts, as if contact with the supernatural seemed to be the preserve only of adults. The children appear not to see them; they resent and indeed defy Giddens's increasingly obsessive concern to categorise them as possessed beings, though Miles and Flora both claim to have psychic powers and can sense each other's thoughts and movements. In *The Others* Amenábar recycles but broadly inverts this arrangement, conferring on one of the children the power of clairvoyance. He makes Grace blind (though not deaf) to the presence of the 'intruders' in the house, while he allows Mrs Mills to see and Anne to communicate with the Marlish family and their son Victor. Indeed Anne appears to be psychic and converses quite happily with Victor, whilst the adults in the Marlish family are obliged to hire a medium in order to make contact with the Stewarts.

The Others seems also to contain versions of several key scenes borrowed from *The Innocents*. These include the school room sequence (where Giddens's Latin lesson is replaced by Grace's 'fire and brimstone' Bible stories and the threats of children's limbo), the house search, the attic sequence (where Giddens's discovery of the music box and a cracked miniature photograph of Quint are echoed by Grace's exposure to old photographs and the Book of the Dead) and the final 'pietà' sequence in the garden between Giddens and Miles, which is relocated to the stair landing in *The Others*. There are also possible parallels with *The Innocents* in Amenábar's stylish prologue, and not only with the common fade-up from black screen. In his unconventional opening (having abandoned the idea of an extended flashback originating at Miles's funeral), Clayton juxtaposes two strongly contrasting scenes, which turn out to be an 'after' followed by a 'before'. On the one hand, during the credits, we see a traumatised Giddens, in close-up, in profile, and in semi-darkness screen left (with credits emerging screen right), rubbing her hands as if praying fervently for forgiveness, declaring in whispers her intention to 'save' the children, not to 'destroy' them. Giddens's demonstration of contrition and remorse is accompanied by Flora's spooky 'O Willow Waley' song, a lament for a dead lover, which connects her to Quint and Jessel and functions as a repeated, spectral leitmotif (via music box, piano and humming) throughout the film. Imagery and sound during this credit sequence (shorn of its normal Fox logo and fanfare) thus grab the viewer's attention and raise multiple questions concerning the identity and motivations of the character in shot, her gestures and words, her state of mind, the function of the song, what has happened and the scene's relation to the narrative. This sequence is then directly followed by the interview scene between the uncle and the impressionable Vicar's youngest daughter, showing a very different, beaming, almost adoring Giddens, flattered and seduced by the uncle.

It is just conceivable that Amenábar might have borrowed Clayton's idea of this structurally contrastive, two-scene prologue, but in reverse. Amenábar gives us a 'fictional' followed by a 'real' snapshot of Grace's domestic life. He opens with Grace's bedtime story, involving the voiceover parallel between the Genesis story and her fantasy of domestic bliss and 'happy families', which is gradually undercut by the illustrations we see from the children's books. In the next scene Grace awakes from a nightmare with a piercing scream, effectively contradicting the earlier 'happy families' scenario. Also Grace's scream might well be an echo of Giddens, at the end of *The Innocents* who acknowledges her guilt as she screams out the name of 'Miles', as he dies of a heart attack in her arms.

As regards film technique, much of the success and effectiveness of *The Innocents* as an atmospheric gothic tale are due to the work of Freddie Francis, whose reputation and expertise were based on the acknowledged quality of his black-and-white cinematography (awarded an Oscar for *Sons and Lovers*, 1960). The tone for the whole film is set by the opening sequence, where Giddens is praying, with her face in semi-darkness, illuminated by candlelight (a powerful, indeed inspirational, image and motif recycled by Amenábar and widely used by his distributors to market *The Others*). Francis also captures Bly House in a very striking, painterly way using cinemascope (a format initially of interest to Amenábar), yet he manages to do so by putting objects in the frame which create vertical lines and break up scope's strong horizontal orientation. Also Francis's camera placement and angles are crucial in capturing the ghosts, usually done with a wide shot, with blurred focus (Quint on the battlements, Jessel in the lake and the schoolroom), prefaced by Giddens's reaction shot. For example, while Francis uses the close-up on Deborah Kerr in the opening scene and helps reveal and magnify her extreme emotional distress, he also shoots the ghosts in wide-angle, with the focus slightly hazy or blurred. As noted earlier, rather than exploit shot-reverse shot for dialogue, Francis shoots in depth, with two characters in different planes (one foreground, one in the background) emphasising distance, alienation, lack of contact or communication. *The Innocents* is one of the very few ghost stories shot in daylight (using extremely powerful arc lights) and where the ghosts are real. In order to inject tension through changes of tempo and atmosphere, Clayton exploits moments of silence as well as whispers and furtive looks through camera angles as well as dialogue inflections (Sinyard 2000: 85). Perhaps the most admired technical aspect of *The Innocents* is its widespread use of the slow dissolve, seen in the shot where Giddens's reflection in the window transforms into Quint's leering face or after Miles's recitation, as Giddens and Grose discuss the children, we see Flora's 'innocent' face, which slowly fades from view.

Finally, Amenábar's title. The film title directly recalls the title of an American television adaptation of the James novella made in 1957, screened live, written by Michael Dyne and starring Sarah Churchill (imdb.com), which Amenábar is unlikely to have known or seen. However, as Frayling suggests in his excellent DVD critical commentary on *The Innocents*, the title *The Others* might well have been inspired by a dialogue line, towards the end of the film, between Giddens and Miles. Here, responding to Miles's remark that, with the servants having been sent home, they will have the house to themselves, Giddens replies: 'there are still the others', by which she means not only the spirits of Quint and Jessel but also those of Flora and that of the absent uncle, still of great interest to Giddens – in other words, the others 'inside us'. Amenábar's title thus maintains and pays homage to the rich ambiguities of the notion of the 'innocents', which Clayton retained from Archibald's play. Both titles are resonant, multi-accented and deeply ambiguous, and in Amenábar's case a perfect complement to a work described by his producer, José Luis Cuerda, as 'a little gem' (Ubeda-Portugués 2001: 280).

The Changeling (1980)[15]

With the successful release of *Halloween* (John Carpenter, 1978) and *Friday the Thirteenth* (Sean Cunningham, 1980), the 'have sex and die' slasher craze quickly grew in popularity among teen audiences. By contrast, at the turn of the 1980s, the subgenre of the classical, haunted house story and its more sedate, psychological thrills seemed rather remote, outmoded and destined for the television movie and cable. And while very effective, a ¢7 million, prize-winning, Canadian commercial feature like *The Changeling* appealed largely to older audiences; its cast were in their forties and at the time it was made it seemed decidedly 'old-fashioned'. There were other haunted house films made at the same time, such as *The Amityville Horror* (Stuart Rosenberg, 1979), which relied on its supposed authenticity and of course Kubrick's *The Shining* (1980), which completely broke the mould of the subgenre. Two years later a 'ghost story' film such as *Poltergeist* (Tobe Hooper, 1982) revamped old formats, adding modern effects and gory scares to the haunted house tale, now relocated in middle-class suburbia, on new housing developments built on top of Indian burial grounds.

Nowadays it may seem slow and rather tame, but for Amenábar Peter Medak's *The Changeling* ranks as the quintessential, scary, benchmark 'quiet ghost story'. Eschewing special effects, blood, gore and violence (except for the hallucinatory flashback of the death of police inspector De Witt in a car crash and some spectacular fire scenes). Medak focuses on creating atmosphere and mood, trying to 'wring mystery and suspense from every shot' (DVD Director's Commentary). He does so by literally haunting the viewer, by prising open gaps in the imagination, using a gradual accumulation of simple, clichéd but effective motifs and devices: a single piano key sounding, a door opening by itself, running water taps, a stained-glass window blowing out, loud rhythmic banging, a vision of the drowned boy and the bizarre coincidence that a piece of music composed by Russell one morning is identical to the tune played on a music box, found in the attic room, at the top of the vertiginous staircase. Taking his cues from Hitchcock, including *Rope* (1948) and *Vertigo* (1958), Medak ably visualises and supports these small, supernatural 'signs' with his camera, using an array of classic and modern techniques. Working in wide-screen (and using lenses which often give his interiors a wrap-around effect), he combines odd, off-centre framings with spooky long-range, low-angle shots. He also uses sweeping, floating tracking shots, which glide into and through the downstairs rooms (and on the outside of the house) to suggest suspense, anticipation and ghostly presence. He uses the extreme close-up (Russell is woken up crying, at 6 am, by the banging noises upstairs); he also stages in-depth and mixes occasional bits of choppy editing with the slow zoom and long take, to fully engage the attention of the viewer on character (e.g. the scene where Russell is minutely analysing the tape recording of the séance). The séance scene itself is arguably a technical tour de force, where Medak alternates head shots and much subjective camera with strong, quickly cut-in reaction shots to the psychic medium, to her translator and to the speaking tube on the table. The sequence ends with the attic door closing by itself, as if the child ghost had attended the séance and then returned to his room. This closure is preceded by a very rapid ascending steadicam shot up the stairs (this kit was cutting-edge technology in 1979). Medak also adds a couple of hair-raising, 'spectacle' shots, firstly Russell looking down the well (dug below a haunted bedroom) and then back up again. Overall, Medak's (and John Coquillon's) camerawork, framing, positioning and movement offer a full compendium and primer on how to shoot a ghost story. It is no wonder that Amenábar deeply admires this film, since it so cleverly engages viewer anticipation and dread through an accumulation of little shocks, enigmas and scares, which effectively reinforce each other. These also include such memorable devices as the red rubber ball, which belonged to Russell's daughter Kathy, which bounces down the stairs inexplicably and which always returns; the mini-wheelchair at the top of the stairs which moves by itself and, most notably, the bathroom, attic and séance scenes, from which Amenábar clearly borrows in terms of cinematography, production design and performance aspects.

At the same time, in significant ways, Medak also updates the classic ghost story formula by dispensing with the 'good versus evil' binary for a more secular tale of greed, political corruption and cover-up, unrequited justice, child murder and terrible family secrets. He also creates an old villain (Senator Carmichael, played by the acclaimed veteran Melvyn Douglas) who is punished for his life long deception (with a heart attack) but who is not wholly unsympathetic (thus reminiscent of Grace). Moreover, Medak proposes a new angle on the ghost story. It is that the presence and actions of Joseph's ghost are not malevolent or subversive; rather they are melancholy and bitter, driven by a desire to avenge the parricide in a quest for justice. Joseph works through the traumatised, alienated, grieving but receptive Russell, who becomes the conduit and instrument of retribution on behalf of the dead boy. His increasingly frantic and heated confrontations with Senator Carmichael also function as a means of settling other accounts. This is not only in terms of showing the senator's identity to be based on a lie. It also has to do with Russell's own impotence and despair at being unable to prevent the wholly meaningless death of his own family (marked by his own entrapment in the phone booth in the opening scene).

In the long interview which accompanies the Spanish version of the film script, Amenábar has described *The Others* as drawing heavily on aspects of the same story as *The Changeling* but 'al revés' (2001: 225), i.e., the other way round, a phrase he also uses when comparing *Abre los ojos* to Hitchcock's *Vertigo* (1958). In other words, Amenábar switches or reverses the perspective and tells his story from the point of view of the ghosts, the child murder victims and the *dramatis personae* involved. I suspect he uses the case history and back story of *The Changeling* as a template for the 'front story' of *The Others*, that is, the aftermath of Grace's double infanticide and suicide. Of course, unlike Medak's film, where Joseph's drowning is represented, in *The Others* the murder of the children and Grace's suicide are not explicitly visualised for the viewer in order to secure the twist ending, though 'the day mommy went mad' is partially restaged in Grace's confrontation with the eyeless 'old woman'.

In *The Others* we find numerous links with various aspects of *The Changeling*. Firstly, the gloomy old mansion (the vast grounds, the long drive, isolated house, big music room, the attic room as seat of the crime of infanticide). Secondly, the arrival of new owners, both with a musical connection. John Russell and his family are reimagined as Mr Marlish, a professional concert pianist, his wife and the young Victor, a male version of Russell's daughter Kathy perhaps. Thirdly, Russell is inquisitive and not intimidated by the signs of the haunting, as is Mr Marlish who, in the séance scene in *The Others*, shows great interest in and empathy towards the house ghosts and has tried to contact them. By contrast, Grace shows fierce hostility towards what she calls the 'intruders' and retreats into her mental bunker, shielded by her literalist Catholic faith. Fourthly, Amenábar borrows the name of Russell's handyman – Mr Tuttle – as a homage to Medak and reassigns the name to the gardner (wonderfully played by Eric Sykes). Fifthly, the séance scene (which is placed half-way through

The Changeling and triggers Russell's and Claire's investigation) is borrowed extensively by Amenábar, in its staging and shooting, even down to the way in which the medium communicates with the ghost via automatic writing, which is then translated or decoded by her husband. Sixthly, the early scene in which Russell wakes up, troubled by a dream, haunted by his loss, he cries and looks at his watch; all of this sequence may have been borrowed and recycled in *The Others*, even the use of the extreme close-up in both cases. Grace's scream is also a detail which strongly echoes Miss Giddens's final scene in *The Innocents*. Seventhly, where Russell is open and anxious to reconnect with the world of the dead after the death of his family, Grace is in a state of denial over her matricide and relies on Catholic doctrinal mumbo- jumbo to dismiss the signs of the supernatural (this echoes Carmichael's own denial, as someone who has profited from infanticide and is the beneficiary of the real Joseph's murder).

The Sixth Sense (1999)

Because of its surprise ending and 'big revelation', *The Others* has been widely compared by critics to Shyamalan's *The Sixth Sense*. Indeed, the charge was made that *The Others* was very much a clone of this film, though disguised by its period setting. And, as noted earlier, both Amenábar and his producers were seriously worried about the similarities between the two films, though contracts had been signed and work had already begun on *The Others* by the time *The Sixth Sense* was released in August 1999. For different reasons Amenábar's American distributors Miramax were far less concerned. Indeed, it is arguable that Miramax were seeking to exploit the success of *The Sixth Sense* and say to audiences that, if they liked Shyamalan's film, they would find Amenábar's just as creepy, but also powerful and engaging. They were also anxious to capture some of the success of the earlier film by emulating Buena Vista's release dates and marketing campaign. It so happens that both films were released in August in the USA (*The Others* in August 2001) and, with little hype or advertising, both achieved impressive word of mouth and repeat business from second timers. Moreover, Amenábar's film could be seen to capitalise on the anti-Hollywood, 'clean ghost story' public image of *The Sixth Sense*, reinforcing the trend for classic, old-fashioned, scary movies. These were the ones which avoided excess, overloaded effects and CGI in favour of classic horror conventions: haunted mansions, dark, dusty, abandoned rooms, candles and lamps, old wooden floors, whispered prayers, children singing and crying and no violence, sex, nudity or bad language. In commercial terms it appears that *The Others* did nothing but benefit from the comparison with *The Sixth Sense*.[16]

On closer comparison at a textual level, we find that both films are ghost stories, both exploit the 'single mother' as woman in peril, struggling to cope with the pressures and responsibilities of caring for sick, damaged, unruly children. Both feature absent husbands (as motivation for irregular behaviour and maternal guilt and depression) and prominent child roles (played by Haley Joel Osmont, Alakina Mann and James Bentley), whose maladies and distress are also symptomatic of family breakdown. But where Lynn Sear, in *The Sixth Sense*, feels powerless and incapable of helping her son Cole (thus cueing Dr Malcolm Crowe's role (Bruce Willis) as stand-in father figure and mentor, who sees in his relationship with Cole an opportunity for redemption, following his failure to help a former patient, Vincent), Grace combines the maternal roles of comforter and carer with the patriarchal duties of disciplinarian, teacher, investigator and head of household, supported by a trio of servants. Also, given her erratic behaviour and bouts of 'madness', she is also partly constructed as an oppressive, hysterical, 'monstrous' single mother figure, whose behaviour often contradicts her self-image as loving matriarch and causes distress and pain. In both films single mothers are in trouble and are represented as struggling to maintain family stability and the psychological well-being of their children.

Both films also deal with the relationships between the world of the living and that of the dead and how to negotiate their porous boundaries; both contain characters who are not aware they are dead (Malcolm and Grace, plus her children) and whom the audience believes to be alive. Both adopt a slow, deliberate pace and quiet mood and both are clean movies though *The Others* has rather more humour in it (Tuttle's enigmatic, knowing repetitions of Mrs Mills's remarks, Anne's questions to her mother, Nicholas's complaints about never going anywhere). Also both could work equally well as black-and-white films. Yet, while *The Sixth Sense* has a contemporary setting (in which Lynn is a single mother who works to maintain her family), *The Others* is set in mid-1940s Jersey, at the end of the German occupation. Since her marriage Grace has never been expected to run the household, until her parents leave the island in 1940, before the German invasion, and her husband decides unexpectedly to depart for the front some time in 1944, leaving his family to face the German invaders alone. There are also references to the 1880s (when the three servants whom we see first start to work in the house). These historical markers, the period setting and the resulting generic debt to 1940s, classical Hollywood thriller or melodrama arguably help to differentiate the two films. They also differ in that while Malcolm (as professional psychologist and male authority figure) helps Cole understand his gift of clairvoyance as something positive rather than 'freaky', Charles's bizarre and fleeting 'return home' fails to unify the family or overcome Grace's resentment or his children's despair at being abandoned a second time. In other words, in Charles's case, paternal intervention totally fails to restore domestic stability or any semblance of family reassurance. This suggests that Amenábar blames the breakdown of his dysfunctional family not so much on a lack of parental love or devotion towards children as on the lack of parenting skills. He arguably creates characters who are ill-fitted for married life together and (like Grace) infantilised and traumatised by her own religious upbringing and indoctrination in the home, which she is fated to repeat with her own children. Also both films exploit the device of the sneaky, surprise ending. Such a device may be derivative, but, in terms of generic recycling, it could be argued that Amenábar's unexpected ending exemplifies the successful cloning of a clever device, which still delivers strong audience pleasure. Whether the use of the device has become too familiar to be effective, prompting audiences to refer back to Shyamalan, and whether it destabilises a climactic ending, which loses impact through repetition, is probably a matter of opinion and taste.

Transcendental questions

In *Abre los ojos* just before Núria tries to murder César by crashing her car, she asks him how he defines happiness and whether he believes in God. Tired and hung over, César is unable or unsure of how to deal with such 'cuestiones trascendentales' and their evident sadism, which he fails to spot. Grace, by contrast, especially in front of the children, appears to have an answer for everything, a solid, coherent theology and a watertight set of beliefs, which admit no doubt or error. But, as Amenábar reminds us, her mind is very much like the gloomy mansion she inhabits. The house, cut off from the rest of the island and surrounded by a thick fog and closed to the light, is beyond human time and space and a perfect setting for limbo and purgatory. Moreover, the darkness is an obvious metaphor for Grace's mind and her guilt. As Amenábar puts it: 'La oscuridad reinante no es otra cosa que las fuertes creencias religiosas a las que Grace se aferra y de algún modo dan sentido a su vida pero … le están impidiendo descubrir la verdad, lo que en realidad es y lo que ha hecho' (Rodríguez Marchante 2002: 130) (The all-enveloping darkness is nothing but the strong religious convictions which Grace hangs on to and in a way give meaning to her life but … they prevent her from discovering the truth of what she is and what she has done).

Grace's strict religiosity is at times a strength but also a fatal weakness, since she insists on interpreting the supernatural phenomena which appear to besiege the house through a dogmatic, literalist theology, based on traditional, Old Testament, Catholic doctrine. Also she cannot or will not understand Mrs Mills's warning that 'sometimes the world of the dead gets mixed up with the world of the living'. Grace also refuses to see the darkness of the house as more than a lack of light, indeed as a symbol of her own emotional and spiritual imprisonment, which she has imposed upon herself and the children, through her maternal guilt and the denial of her acts and their consequences. Religious doctrine thus provides her with an alibi for her act of violence. If enlightenment, literally and figuratively, requires seeing things from a different perspective, then Grace actively shuns such openness, and is too afraid and too proud to admit her crime Only when she finally confronts 'the others' in her home and sees herself as 'other' (i.e. dead) and thus the real 'intruder', will she experience the emotional and psychological release and catharsis she desperately needs. Grace's (and the spectator's) trajectory in the film as Amenábar suggests, is thus akin to a journey towards the light, i.e an epiphany involving new forms of self-knowledge and new types of thinking which emerge literally from the 'haunting' and figuratively from the dense fog and inner gloom which grips the house and gradually corrode Grace's doctrinal defences.

The Others can thus be seen as an allegory of Catholic obscurantism, where traditional dogma is assailed by ghosts, ghosts which, in reality, happen to be 'real people' trying to make contact and who seek understanding and a rationale, a calling to account for the abuse of children. Collective, organised religion is thus being tested by its ability to confront, explain and control the supernatural. Grace's archaic belief system is unable to protect her family from being haunted by the living. For Amenábar, her beliefs in good and evil, purgatory, limbo and an afterlife etc. are little more than superstitions and fairy stories. Here he seems to affirm a salutary scepticism not as intolerance or shortsightedness but as a way of evaluating the claims of Grace's religious certainties. Amenábar is no respecter of religion. And he is quite happy to submit its claims to the same scrutiny given to any other idea or argument. Though he does not have a scientific or mathematical background, he seems to be temperamentally inclined towards the scientific method, i.e. of exploring and subjecting ideas and claims to rigorous analysis based on objective evidence and retesting the reliability of that evidence (as we see amply demonstrated by Hypatia in *Ágora*). He is certainly impatient with belief systems which seek to ring-fence certain ideas as sacred or holy, i.e. untouchable, beyond criticism or mockery, and thus off-limits to rational exploration, investigation and critique.

From another perspective *The Others* is also surprisingly autobiographical, a film which taps into all those childhood fears about ghosts, spirits, death and the afterlife that terrified Amenábar as a young boy. The sort of rigid Catholicism taught by Grace and made fun of by Anne and Nicholas is also very close to the sort of crude dogma Amenábar was taught at school in the 1980s and which 40 years previously, under the Franco dictatorship, would have been accepted as absolute truth. Amenábar is obviously aware that things have changed radically and that Spain is nowadays a multi-faith, non-confessional state. Yet his critique of a traditional, authoritarian Catholicism (which in *Ágora* is compared to militant Islam) runs much deeper and has implications for his view of more virulent, literalist, belief systems and their legal codes (such as 'sharia') in the modern day, especially following events such as 9/11, the 11 March attacks in Madrid 2004 and the 7/7 attacks in London in 2005.

To both believers and non-believers *The Others* also raises difficult theological questions such as what separates the living from the dead, what awaits us after death, is there an afterlife, and if so, what form will it take? The idea of an afterlife, for people who wish to believe in something, is immensely attractive, but to maintain such beliefs as true, in the face of evidence to the contrary, is perhaps puzzling. Religion can be exploited as a machine for creating beliefs which lead to great acts of humanity but also to acts of monstrous intolerance and barbarism. *The Others* suggests that to impose religion, especially on children, who are unable to comprehend and are too inexperienced to judge for themselves, is fundamentally wrong and tantamount to child abuse. Children are vulnerable to indoctrination (as Grace was) and, if they fail to question such superstitions, they remain in a state of perpetual infancy (just like Grace). Thankfully, in *The Others*, the children refuse to be taken in by Grace's threats of punishment and eternal damnation. Indeed first Anne and then Nicholas finally escape the house through the window and strike out on their own, echoing Amenábar's own biography and that of his brother Ricardo. Amenábar seems to suggest that, in parenting children, it is more moral to do good for its own sake than out of fear or hatred of the 'other'.

Finally, *The Others* is also a meditation on the genre film, a 'turn of the screw' on a gothic-style ghost story, which seeks to entertain and engage the audience. But this is done not so much by commercial concessions, through its shocks and scares ratio (there are arguably not enough), as through a very stylish, but restrained form of realist drama. This relies mainly on its evocation of moods, atmospheres, glances, dialogues and silences, exchanged mainly between strong female characters. In this regard, if we strip away the supernatural, ghost story material, we find we are in the realm of the family melodrama and the theme of death. Here the film develops Amenábar's fascination with the story line of the young mother with two children, abandoned by her husband, who goes mad and kills her children before committing suicide. If *Tesis* and *Abre los ojos* explore the hysterical side of damaged masculinity, *The Others* probes the dark side of the fragmented family, the terrible impact of fear, loss and abandonment on a vulnerable young mother, the nature of motherly love and how it can kill, the role of Catholic teaching as an alibi for guilt, denial and oppression, but also the transition of Grace and the children towards a new understanding and a certain redemption and catharsis through confession and self-questioning (Rodríguez Marchante 2002: 113). This is Amenábar at work in Almodóvarian territory, but offering a strong dose of realism rather than parody, titillation, cinematic self-reflexivity or melodramatic excess. And, once embarked on her journey of self-discovery, Grace begins as a villain but ends up as (perhaps an unlikely) defender of her family or so it seems. This is an unusual trajectory which in earlier versions of the script was far less clear-cut and which changed radically during shooting, thanks to the dialogue between Kidman's star power (coloured by her own marriage break-up and concern for her adopted children, Isabel and Conor) and Amenábar's notably more amenable, more relaxed and receptive authorship.[17]

Notes

1 In his article 'Horror of allegory: *The Others* and its contexts', Ernesto R. Acevedo-Muñoz opens by asserting that *The Others* was Amenábar's 'first international co-production' (2008: 202). This is not strictly correct. *The Others* was Amenábar's first transatlantic co-pro, spoken in English, involving Cruise/Wagner Productions as well as the American distributor Miramax. His first international (i.e. European) co-pro was *Abre los ojos* (1997), which included French and Italian backers among its investors (Les Films Alain Sarde and Lucky Red), as well as Las Producciones del Escorpion and Sogecine/Sogetel.

2 As noted earlier, on the Spanish side, Amenábar insisted on shooting the film in Spain, with a Spanish crew and on having approval over the final cut of the film (a standard requirement for a European filmmaker, according to Bovaira). This was agreed in principle (Roig 2001: 38). For their part Miramax demanded the right of approval over the casting of the role of Grace. Various names were mentioned including Julianne Moore, Jodie Foster and Juliette Binoche, though Amenábar's first choice was Emily Watson. Also very interested was Nicole Kidman who arrived late, in person, at the Tribeca to pitch for the role (though she had lost her voice). It appears that Amenábar, known for his *sang-froid* and unfazed by stardom, told Kidman in his halting English: 'you are in consideration' for the part. This might have sounded like something of a rebuff to a Hollywood star, but, on checking with Bovaira, Amenábar revised his English to a grammatically correct 'under consideration'. Over coffee and communicating with Kidman by written notes, Amenábar became intrigued and charmed by Kidman's statuesque face and her penetrating gaze, so much so that he was persuaded to cast her as Grace (see Ubeda-Portugués 2001: 269). This arrangement also suited Tom Cruise who, with Miramax, saw Oscar potential in *The Others* as well as a means of sweetening his own impending divorce settlement. As Bovaira confirms, 'la película era un vehículo impresionante para la actriz que la protagonisase' (Roig 2001: 36) (the film was an amazing vehicle for whoever was the lead actress). On Miramax see also, Alisa Perren (2001).

3 For example Miramax wanted performers such as Judi Dench or Kathy Bates for Mrs Mills, Jonny Depp for Charles and Gregory Peck for Mr Tuttle. Miramax were also unhappy with Alakina Mann in the part of Anne, who had decided to become a vegetarian just before filming and was listless, lacking in energy and, allegedly, not delivering an adequate performance in rehearsal. Amenábar stood firm and was unwilling to make any late casting changes. Thankfully, his common sense, impressive coolness, diplomatic skills and keen intuition prevailed and, in line with his usual practice (i.e. casting virtual unknowns such as Fionnula Flanagan, Chris Eccleston, Alakina Mann, James Bentley, Eric Sykes,

Keith Allen etc.), he achieved a striking degree of verisimilitude and credibility in the supporting performances.

4 Another serious concern was Manoj Knight Shyamalan's *The Sixth Sense*, which was released in the USA on 6 August 1999, with a story line, characters and a final twist which seemed uncannily reminiscent cf *The Others*. Bovaira discovered that *The Sixth Sense* had had a small, initial release in the USA via Buena Vista Distribution (beginning in less than a hundred cinemas – but rising to 2,160 – and an equally modest release in Thailand, Taiwan, Hong Kong and Singapore in August and September) which calmed his fears a little, 'Pero la verdad es que nos preocupamos y mucho' (Roig 2001: 39) (But the truth is that we were worried, really worried).

5 As regards the editing, the main problem for the American producers was what they saw as the slow, rather leaden pace of the film. Cruise, who appears to have personally micro-managed the re-editing for Miramax, knew the film frame by frame and kept detailed notes of the changes required to make the narrative flow more easily and quickly. It also appears that he guided Amenábar personally, with copious notes, in the five major re-edits of the film that were finally demanded by Miramax.

6 As for the screen tests, done in London and Los Angeles and often using the title *The Darkness*, the tests revealed that audiences were confused by the confession scene between Grace and Charles. This contained a sequence in which they appear to have sex. Even for liberal West Coast American audiences, the use of sexual relations seemed out of place, poorly motivated, not in keeping with the tone of the scene, and was subsequently cut. The tests also confirmed American worries over pacing, lack of screen shocks and, above all, Amenábar's apparent over-use of silence. This was later mitigated by his producers, with the addition of Dolby Stereo to the (too) few scary moments.

7 The promotional campaign for the film emphasised the 'Anglo-American' side of the project as a major selling point, i.e. the glamorous star image of Nicole Kidman and the involvement in the project of her husband and megastar Tom Cruise as executive producer, while virtually ignoring the name, image and profile of the director (see Triana-Toribio 2003: 152–3). In short, unlike a Spanish auteur product, usually pre-sold on the name of the director, *The Others* was marketed as a Hollywood film, relying predominantly on star imagery (and an effective USA trailer campaign) which, despite his strong national visbility, Amenábar's meagre, international, auteurist profile still lacked. Indeed, concerning the US trailer, Rodríguez Ortega observes in his essay that *The Others* 'relies heavily on Nicole Kidman's star persona, to the point that the name of the Spanish director is not even mentioned' (2008: 55). My reading of Kidman's key role in the distribution and promotion of *The Others*, especially in the USA, and Amenábar's virtual invisibility in the marketing campaign

(confirmed by Rodríguez Ortega and echoed by Triana-Toribio), is at variance with Acevedo-Muñoz, who seems to argue the opposite case (though with no corroborative data), in favour of director Amenábar as prime mover. He claims that 'Amenábar's *Los otros* built upon the director's prestige as a young, energetic, and original director for marketing the Nicole Kidman vehicle' (2008: 202). I maintain that the opposite is true, that is, it was Kidman's star power not Amenábar's directorial prestige, energy or originality which was primarily responsible for promoting and selling the film successfully.

8   For example see the coverage and reviews in the Spanish film magazine *Fotogramas* (September 2001), 15, 43 and 100–5. Also, Hilario J. Rodríguez, 'Los vivos y los muertos', *Dirigido por*, 304 (September 2001), 38–41. Also, see the following web reviews: Amparo Arrospide, 'Reflexión sobre la película de Alejandro Amenábar' at ElDigoras.com; Tonia Palleja, 'Crítica', in www.labutaca.net/films/4/losotros, and Renée Rodríguez, 'Amenábar scares with silence', HispanicMagazine.com (September 2001).

9   The name Tuttle is an uncharacteristically blatant lift of Amenábar's from Medak's *The Changeling* (1979). The name refers to the handyman who looks after Professor John Russell's huge, rented mansion and keeps the central heating and ancient pipework in order.

10 'I hated myself in *The Others*. Absolutely hated it.' 'I was so ill. I was nauseous for ages and was so upset I went to bed.' 'I'm surprised at its success. I thought I was making this strange, atmospheric little thriller with dark undertones' (imdb.com *The Others*, News Articles for 3 and 31 October 2001 and 5 November 2001).

11 It is worth noting that Acevedo-Muñoz reads *The Others*, not so much as a transnational production for global audiences, where signs of national identity are significantly played down, but more as an exemplar of 'national cinema'. Building upon the film's Spanish referents and classic genre conventions, he argues that *The Others* is strongly determined by the 'weight of Spanish political and cultural history' which, nevertheless, allows for an allegorical reading (2008: 202). He also suggests that Amenábar reshapes 'an essentially Spanish narrative' into something more universal, and even the film's very lack of specificity is symptomatic of its 'national context' (2008: 202). He also talks about the 'nationalist concerns' of younger, contemporary Spanish directors, including Amenábar, without being specific (2008: 202). In short, in his desire to 'nationalise' *The Others*, Acevedo-Muñoz arguably overstates Amenábar's location in a post-Franco critical discourse which emphasises the enduring and inescapable impact of the Civil War and Francoism on both historical and filmic memory (using already canonised local or national film referents such as Erice's *El espiritu de la colmena* and Saura's *Cría Cuervos* (Raise Ravens, 1975). He also ignores Amenábar's own emphatic

internationalism or what he calls his 'vocation universelle' (see the interview with Berthier 2007: 222) and the more concrete contexts of production and reception in which the film was actually made, marketed and released, as a transnational, Hollywood co-pro. Moreover, Acevedo-Muñoz's definition of 'national cinema' (2008: 212) is drawn from some very early work done by Andrew Higson (first published in *Screen* in 1989), since when Higson has radically revised his position in favour of transnationalism, border crossings and cultural hybridity. See Higson (2000).

12   Henry James's *The Turn of the Screw* (1898) is probably the most famous Victorian ghost story. Based on an idea given him by the Archbishop of Canterbury (Edward White Benson) in 1895, James's tale was transcribed by his amanuensis (W. Jardine) two years later and in 1898 first serialised in *Colliers Weekly* (New York). The tale is framed by an unnamed narrator and a found manuscript, written by a former governess now dead. It recounts the story of a 20-year-old vicar's daughter hired by a charismatic gentleman living in London to work as a governess in a country house and take care of his niece and nephew (Flora and Miles), in whom he shows not the slightest interest. Despite his selfish, uncaring attitude, Miss Giddens is immediately infatuated by the suave masculine charm of this family benefactor. Soon after she begins her duties, Miles arrives home after being expelled from boarding school. Troubled by the implications of the headmaster's letter, Miss Giddens (she is given no first name) gradually becomes convinced that her predecessor (Mary Jessel) and her Irish lover at Bly House (Peter Quint), both of whom died in unusual circumstances, are using the children to continue an unnatural, evil relationship beyond the grave. Ultimately Giddens's attempt to counteract the perceived threat (of demonic possession?) has unforeseen consequences, leading to Flora's derangement and Miles's death by heart attack. The novella challenges the reader to decide if Giddens is a trustworthy, reliable witness or a neurotic with a fevered imagination, who projects on to the children her sexual infatuation with the absent uncle. Is the novella therefore a projection story rather than a ghost story? The tale has long been a fertile source of critical dispute and interpretation and has survived thanks to its many areas of ambiguity and uncertainty. It has also given rise to a wealth of retellings and adaptations for the stage, radio, television, opera and ballet, not only in English but in many other languages, including two modern Spanish filmed versions: *Otra vuelta de tuerca* (Another Turn of the Screw, Eloy de la Iglesia, 1985) and an English-language television movie, made by RTVE (Spanish state television), *Presence of Mind* (*El celo*, Antoni Aloy, 1999).

13   Clayton was offered *The Innocents* and a $1 million budget by Twentieth Century Fox on condition that he cast Deborah Kerr as Miss Giddens, the governess. In terms of her age Kerr bore little resemblance to James'

20-year-old 'young, untried, nervous woman' of the novella. Yet this was not a serious problem, given the fact that much older actresses, in 1950s adaptations, had played the role successfully, including Beatrice Straight and Flora Robson on stage and Ingrid Bergman in Frankenheimer's live television adaptation of *The Turn of the Screw* (1959) (imdb.com). Also, as Frayling reminds us (on his DVD commentary, 2006), Kerr had played the Victorian English teacher/governess in *The King and I* (Walter Lang, 1956) and was already a big Hollywood star, and her role as Miss Giddens was a major acting challenge for her, running strongly against character type and prior film roles. In Amenábar's case it appears that Tom Cruise's involvement in *The Others* as Executive Producer was also predicated on Nicole Kidman being cast in the role of Grace.

14 Archibald's two-act play was first staged in New York in 1950 and in London two years later. Following a successful off-Broadway run in 1959, the play was bought by Twentieth Century Fox. Archibald was soon commissioned to write a first version of the screenplay, retaining the ambiguous title of his earlier play as well as its basic structure, the four main characters (governess, two children and housekeeper) and a respect for female Hollywood screen stereotypes. Despite studio approval, Clayton was unhappy with the static, theatrical nature of Archibald's version, its single location (the drawing room), its leaden pace and the lack of any visual equivalent for James's ornate, nuanced, overripe prose. A number of other writers were thus called upon to inject spatial variety, narrative pace and more suggestibility into the dialogue. These included John Mortimer (who spent three weeks polishing the Victorian tone of the lines and wrote an extra scene involving the uncle, which was never used) as well as Truman Capote, who had already worked with Clayton on earlier projects, including *Beat the Devil* (John Huston, 1953). Capote virtually rewrote the entire screenplay, mainly contributing ideas and motifs to suggest the moral corruption and decay of Bly House. He also managed to find a visual analogue for James's rich, suggestive prose by portraying Bly House as a luminous, beautiful though decadent mansion, overtaken by a rampant, threatening Nature (encapsulated in the famous, erotically charged shot of the beetle emerging from the painted mouth of the broken, stone cherub, which so disconcerts Giddens). In this way Capote reimagined Bly House, not as a Hammer-like, cinematic cliché (as in seen in the very first of the Hammer horror series, *The Curse of Frankenstein*, Terence Fisher, 1957) but as a steamy, stifling, Southern Gothic hot house (see Sinyard, 2000: 91).

15 *The Changeling* concerns an accomplished composer, academic and classical pianist called John Russell (George C. Scott), who loses his wife and daughter in a freak car accident in upstate New York. In order to escape the past and deal with his loss, grief and visions of his daughter, he takes up a teaching position in Seattle and rents Chessman House,

a vast historical mansion. Shortly after moving in, he is made aware of a presence in the house and discovers an attic room, with several toys, note books, music box and miniature wheelchair. Incorrectly assuming that the haunting is of a small girl, he later finds out that the child ghost was a crippled boy called Joseph, who was murdered by being drowned in the bath by his father over 70 years earlier. Accompanied by estate agent Claire Norman (Trish Van de Vere), Russell tries to free the child from torment (and in the process overcome his own family loss and guilt) by confronting the powerful and wealthy Senator Joseph Carmichael (Melvyn Douglas, the 'changeling' of the film title) with his own morbid family history.

16 According to imdb.com, *The Sixth Sense* (whose initial cost is estimated at $55 million) achieved a worldwide, box-office gross of $672,805,292 (roughly 12 times its budget). This is a quite remarkable result for a small, independent, American movie. However, in comparative terms, if we divide budget costs of $17–20 million into gross worldwide takings of approximately $210 million, *The Others* did nearly as well though over a slightly shorter release period.

17 The motives for Grace's appalling crime are not wholly clear. They appear to be as follows. Her abandonment by her own parents, then later by her husband, leaves her traumatised and trapped, left alone to care for her sick children. Loneliness, depression, anger, migraines and a history of mental illness take their toll, as she increasingly retreats into religion to give her life some semblance of stability and meaning. However, the unexpected departure of her servants is the final straw. Here she reaches her moment of supreme 'impotence' and total entrapment; she quarrels with the children, who misbehave, and then she snaps. Infanticide and then her own suicide function as a release, a safety valve, a form of emancipation from despair. Following the haunting and her children's dissidence, Grace finally admits her crime and demonstrates that, in the face of overwhelming evidence, even the most fervent, fanatical believers can change, have doubts and admit their errors, even in death. Here, apart from creating absorbing screen drama, Amenábar manages to construct and then dismantle certain assumptions about family, good and bad parenting, and social stereotypes. That is, he appears to critique the rigours of single motherhood as a viable family model, if not properly supported by another committed parent, male or female. His scorn is heaped mainly on the enigmatic, 'absent father figure', Charles, which suggests to me a personal gesture towards his own family circumstances. He also tries to soften and humanise old horror clichés by developing believable characters and radically alters the hackneyed 'triumph of good over evil' ending with Grace's journey towards secularism, through the final acknowledgement of her own death and her enduring love for her children.

6

Fighting to die: *Mar adentro*

Amenábar has never seriously thought of himself as a political filmmaker, in the manner of a Costa Gavras or a Ken Loach. Indeed, in the 1990s, he tended to avoid the label whenever journalists or academics posed the question (Interview). Among university friends and colleagues he was always regarded as something of a 'facha' (right-wing, conservative), largely because he was rather shy, often noncommittal and unprepared to jump on the latest, left-wing, political bandwagon. And though he admires directors such as Loach, more for his style than for his ideas, he is not wholly convinced that the cinema is the best medium through which to engage with serious political or social issues: 'Lo que pasa es que el cine político me da miedo porque el cine siempre lleva implícito la manipulación ... El cine es magia ... evasión ... entretenimiento' (Generelo 2004: 76) (The fact is that political cinema scares me because cinema always implies manipulation ... Cinema is magic ... escape...entertainment). If Amenábar shows a keen awareness of the manipulative nature of cinema, his reluctance to make overtly political films or pronouncements has not stopped him taking a principled stand. As he says, 'Cuando hago películas, mi posición es la reflexiva, no la reivindicativa. Nunca me planteé hacer una película sobre la eutanasia para hacer reivindicaciones' (When I make films, I take a reflective not an activist position. I never saw making a film about euthanasia as a way of making demands). 'Pero, evidentemente, te tienes que posicionar. Y sí, estoy a favor' (But, of course, you have to take a stand. And yes, I'm in favour) (see Rocío García, 'Triple Apuesta', *El País Semanal*, no. 1479 (2005)). Indeed, as argued elsewhere in this book, Amenábar's ability to combine sound commercial filmmaking practice with intelligent reflections on certain social issues have helped to underpin his professional success thus far. However, with *Mar adentro* (The Sea Inside), his fourth feature film, he deals not with conventional social or political issues such as unemployment, social deprivation, domestic violence, immigration or ETA terror but with a deeply controversial ethical issue of much wider resonance: euthanasia and the legalisation of assisted dying, as exemplified by the real case of the Spanish quadriplegic Ramón Sampedro.

Sampedro spent many years trying to persuade the Spanish judicial system to de-criminalise assisted dying so that his own GP could offer him a way out of a 'living death', without being imprisoned. The protracted legal action failed so he persuaded a team of friends to take other measures so that he could achieve his right to 'die with dignity'. Like many thousands of Spaniards, Amenábar and his co-scriptwriter Mateo Gil were deeply moved by the Sampedro case, even shocked and angered by the apparent rough justice he appeared to suffer in the Spanish courts.[1] They were also struck by his highly effective media campaign and the fact that he left a video testimony of his own death, filmed on a camcorder. In *Tesis* Amenábar had speculated on the limits of screen violence and whether snuff movies might one day become mainstream fare as media spectacle. In *Mar adentro* he revisits the same terrain of 'death as spectacle', but this time in the context of ethical questions about an individual's 'right to die', as well as his 'end of life' choices and the control he has over them. The film also asks how a filmmaker, so emphatically at the service of audience pleasure, can craft a responsible though commercially appealing 'euthanasia movie'.

Mar adentro, strictly speaking, means 'out to sea' or 'on the high seas'. However, in English, 'The Sea Inside' is just about admissible as poetic licence, given that Ramón was a merchant seaman, who carried the sea inside him and dreamed of returning to the sea. Of course, apart from travel and sexual congress, the motif of the sea relates to Sampedro's past and his tragically unfulfilled life as a seaman, as well as his accident (he wished he had been left to die in the water) and his final days spent overlooking the sea at Boiro, before committing suicide. The title also hints at his narcissism and guilt at having made a reckless dive into a waterless hole, to impress a pretty girl in the cove below. This momentary forgetfulness of his knowledge of the tides (on a dangerous stretch of beach) had devastating consequences which radically transformed his existence thereafter.

In this chapter, given that Amenábar's screen version of the Sampedro story is unavoidably selective and redramatised for the big screen,

I begin by supplying as far as possible a straightforward, non-partisan account of Sampedro's life and death. I proceed by looking at the development of the film project and the role of Gené Gordó (who organised legal and media support for the actual Sampedro campaign) in providing Amenábar with a suitable dramatic focus. I then consider various generic issues which modulate Amenábar's version of the story. I also explore key aspects of casting and performance, a crucial area in a film whose real-life case was still sub judice when it was made. I then compare Amenábar's big-screen version with a Spanish television movie version made three years earlier, which seems to have been forgotten. And, after analysing certain features of narrative technique and film style, finally I explore briefly several aspects of the media construction and reception of Amenábar's pro-euthanasia film, by looking at the arguments for the opposition via a specific case study.

Ramón Sampedro: some factual details[2]

Born in 1943, in Xuño, A Coruña, Galicia, Ramón Sampedro Cameán began working as a ship's mechanic aged 19. As a young man he charmed and seduced women in ports all over the world, including Rotterdam, New York, Rio de Janeiro and Maracaibo. In 1968, aged 25, back home on leave and relaxing at As Furnhas beach, he was on the point of getting married but worried about making a formal commitment and losing his freedom. Perhaps distracted by a pretty girl on the beach, he dived into the sea when the tide was turning. There was not enough water to break his fall. He struck his head on the sea floor and broke his neck, leaving him completely paralysed from the neck down. After being cared for initially by his mother (and told by doctors that he had a few years to live at most), when she died, he was taken to his brother's farmhouse at Porto de Son where he (and his father) were cared for by his older brother and sister-in-law on a meagre pension and the produce from the family garden.

Over time, as a quadriplegic, with an active brain but lacking a functioning body, as well as plotting and fantasising his escape from entrapment, Sampedro cultivated his mind and intellect. He read widely (Camus, Wilde, Flaubert, Swift, Neruda), he wrote letters and verse and even designed a writing easel and a mouth pen. He listened to music (he loved opera, especially Wagner) and the radio, but disliked football. He also invented other gadgets, such as a device to enable him to answer the telephone with his mouth. He was helped to publish a book of letters and poems entitled *Cartas desde el infierno* (Letters from Hell, 1996/2004) and posthumously a book of poetry *Cando eu caia* (When I Fell, 1998/2004). However, he gradually realised that he could not bear an existence as a cultured mind in a broken and useless body. He hated his body and the indignity of being so totally dependent on his family for all his needs (from ablutions to spectacles, teeth to toenails), regarding those around him as physical and psychological slaves. He could have starved himself to death, but refused to put his family through such trauma. He also tried for many years to persuade his local GP (Carlos Peón Fernández) to administer an assisted death. The doctor was sympathetic, but understandably concerned about the consequences, since assisting suicide was illegal in Spain and punishable by up to six years' imprisonment.

Incredibly Sampedro existed in this strange mind-body 'limbo' for over 24 years, until in 1992 he turned for help to the Associación para el Derecho a Morir Dignamente (DMD or Association for the Right to a Dignified Death), based in Barcelona, administered by Gené Gordó and represented in Spain's Senate by Professor Salvador Paniker, one of the country's leading moral philosophers. With support from DMD, between 1992 and 1997, he mounted an elaborate legal and media campaign for the right to die and to decriminalise assisted suicide in Spain, so that others would not be prosecuted if they helped him on his way. He was the first Spaniard ever to petition the national courts on this issue. The case even reached Spain's Supreme Court but was rejected. He then appealed to the European Commission on Human Rights in Strasbourg, where his petition also failed. He even thought of travelling to the Netherlands to die but logistically this would have been extremely complicated and very costly.

By late 1997, helped by his female companion Ramona Maneiro (nicknamed 'Moncha'), and still determined to die (but unable to do it himself), Sampedro was moved out of his brother's house to a rented flat in Boiro, a village some 15 miles away. And following his own ingenious plan (worked out over many years, involving eleven other helpers, each of whom was given a separate task to put the plan into effect, so that no one could be accused of murder), he finally committed suicide in the early morning of 12 January 1998. He did so by drinking a glass of diluted potassium cyanide through a straw, in the flat in Boiro. His final act was filmed on a camcorder, which recorded the whole of his painful and prolonged death scene, offering proof that his suicide was not coerced and that he, and no one else, controlled his final moments. His address to camera, which Amenábar re-creates in part, was a personal testament as well as a fierce polemic against Spain's main institutions, the Church, the Law and the State. In particular he accused Spain's legal establishment, notably its judges, of sequestering his body and showing a callous indifference and lack of sensitivity to his desire to escape a 'humillante esclavitud' (humiliating slavery).

Following Ramón's death, at some stage a copy of the videotape found its way to Salvador Paniker, of DMD. A brief extract was first shown on Spanish television on 4 March 1998, via Antena 3, on its 9 pm news, but without the permission of the family and minus the terrible agony suffered by Ramón. Antena 3 defended its decision to run the controversial footage given its 'indudable importancia social' (*El Mundo*, 6 March 1998), despite ferocious attacks from Ramón's family, television viewers' associations and Spain's Catholic Church. Also, shortly afterwards, in an effort to decriminalise assisted suicide and protect the friends who had helped him, many thousands of Spaniards signed a national DMD petition declaring that they too were responsible for his death. Finally, in January 2005, on a chat show on Tele 5, his surviving companion, Ramona Maneiro, revealed on air that it was she who had prepared his lethal draught and who had switched on the video camera. She was brought before magistrates in Ribeiro, Galicia, in March 2005, but was absolved of any responsibility for his death. By this time the prosecution case against the Sampedro 'eleven' had expired (on 17 March 2005).[3]

Developing the project

It was during the marketing phase of *Abre los ojos* in early 1998 that Amenábar, like the rest of the Spanish population, saw the video images on national television news of Sampedro's final moments. At the time Amenábar was casting around for new film ideas, for something far smaller, less complex and more manageable than his second film had been. He was very struck by the quiet determination, lucidity and coolness with which Sampedro pleaded for his own death, by someone who 'hablara tan bien y pareciera tan erudito en un ambiente rural' (Anon., 'El film más spielbergiano ...', 10 December 2005) (spoke so well and seemed so educated, coming from a country background). A television report showed Sampedro's family circle in context, in rural Galicia, focusing on his room and his window, which resembled a movie screen. In 1998 Amenábar also read the book Sampedro had written with his mouth (*Cartas desde el inferno*, 1996) and felt strangely energised and uplifted by the intellectual case being made by a quadriplegic for an assisted death. He was particularly impressed by Sampedro's matter-of-fact atheism, his argument that after death there is nothing, no heaven, hell, other side or spirit world; we simply return to the nothingness from which we come. He also admired Sampedro's dissidence and stubbornness, his rebellious streak and his courage to grapple with an extremely prickly and sensitive issue which Spanish society preferred to avoid dealing with. However, in 1998, no decision was made to take the topic forward as a viable film project since Amenábar could see no way of dramatising a story which, for him, was so challenging and fascinating but with so little audience appeal.

By mid-2001, however, the situation had changed. Amenábar was completely exhausted by the re-editing and marketing of *The Others* (a project which in all took over three years to complete) and disillusioned by his experience of Hollywood. This had involved a punishing post-production schedule as well as a stressful period lending support to Nicole Kidman during the promotional phase of the film (during which her marriage to Tom Cruise finally broke up). Also, after the massive, international, commercial and critical success of *The Others*, Amenábar was now in a position to take up almost any film project he liked. But by early- to mid-2002, he seems to have lost interest in doing another thriller. And according to the DVD documentary 'Un viaje Mar adentro' (*Mar adentro* DVD, Extras, Disc 2, 2005), he indicates that, though he remained a great admirer of Hollywood filmmaking, there was a risk of being blinded by its generic and commercial priorities to issues and realities closer to home.[4] In other words, he was now emotionally and filmically ready to move on, to detach himself from the Hitchcockian thriller, in favour of stories rooted in Spain, which nonetheless had a potentially universal resonance.

In mid-2002 Amenábar proposed a film version of the Sampedro story to Fernando Bovaira, head of production at Sogecine, in collaboration with his own, newly created production company Himenóptero.[5] Sogecine had financed *Abre los ojos* and *The Others* and regarded Amenábar as a rising star director, after just three films, as well as an international, bankable talent. However, even allowing for the mega-success of *The Others* , producer Bovaira was initially deeply sceptical about the viability of the idea, when first approached by Amenábar: 'La primera reacción fue de shock' (http://clubcultura.com/clubcine/clubcineastas/amenabar) (My first reaction was one of shock) . Indeed, Bovaira could not see a film in it and wanted Amenábar to avoid the lure of a potential 'vanity project', after the enormous success of *Los otros*. He was concerned not only about the deeply depressing subject matter but also by the complications of making a film based on a real, factual case, with legal proceedings still pending, where family members were still alive and would need to be consulted and give permission to tell the story. However, so apparently boundless was Amenábar's enthusiasm for the idea that, in order to overcome such obstacles, he had even thought of taking the production abroad, perhaps to an English-speaking country such as Ireland. Despite these caveats, and after further discussion, Sogecine finally decided to support the project and there began a more intensive exploration of the Sampedro case. It was during this research phase that Amenábar found an angle which would help him dramatise the story. This was provided by the real-life co-ordinator of the pressure group DMD and Sampedro's lawyer, Gené Gordó. She provided Amenábar and Bovaira with much factual information as well as unprecedented access to details of Sampedro's private life and world, especially his love life, his family circumstances and his sardonic sense of humour. Also, a major feature film signed by Spain's most successful young director would undoubtedly reignite the controversy over the Sampedro case, thus providing DMD with significant public relations, reruitment and campaigning opportunities.

Amenábar had never been attracted to the legal side of the Sampedro case or his spats with the Catholic Church. And, though he knew he would have to deal with them somehow, he ruled out any detailed chronological account right from the start. He was also acutely aware that audiences would quickly lose interest with an 'issue' film about assisted dying. And, in any event, he assumed that the legalisation of euthanasia might well be resolved in Spain sooner rather than later and thus make the film look obsolete and too tied to its local context. He thus opted to dramatise the 'untold' story of Ramón Sampedro, the personal, private, human, family side as well as his 'universo femenino' (female universe), i.e. the many women who, over the years, had contacted him, visited him and fallen in love with him. This approach would, he hoped, mitigate the problem of audience alienation by the subject matter, bearing in mind Amenábar's aim of reaching as many spectators as possible: 'yo busco la conexión con el mayor número de espectadores posible' ('El film más spielbergian ...') (I seek to engage with the greatest number of spectators as possible) Amenábar also emphasised that, though he sought to render a truthful account through a respect for the facts, naturalistic decor and performances, his aim was not to make a documentary: 'Es una historia basada en hechos reales pero no es un documental y nunca he querido ceñirme estrictamente a la realidad sino que interviniera la ficción' (http://clubcultura/com/clubcineastas/amenabar) (It's a story based on real facts but it is not a documentary and I have never wished to fully reflect reality, rather to allow fiction to play a role). The challenge facing him would be how to make the audience engage with Sampedro's gloomy obsession with death, i.e. how to provide a credible and realistic account while dealing in fictionalised, film drama, including moments of fantasy and dream. The script, begun in September 2002 and written jointly by Amenábar and Mateo Gil, took eight months to complete and went through many redraftings.[6]

Genre

Despite the risk involved in making a 'euthanasia movie', Amenábar was confident that he had found the right approach, genre and register in which to cast the Sampedro story: 'Of course we had to be careful because we were dealing with real people and real events, but I always felt that melodrama should be the genre and humour should be part of it because Ramón Sampedro had a good sense of humour and he always tried to talk about death in a very ironic way' (Linekin 2004).

Amenábar defines melodrama as a set of film conventions and devices which are combined in order to 'provocar la lágrima' (cause a tear or make us weep, DVD Disc 2 documentary 'El viaje Mar adentro'). He acknowledges that melodrama may have had disreputable origins as bad or low art and an over-indebtedness to emotion and sentimentality, but this is of little concern to him. Nor does it imply the abandonment of his legendary restraint and control over the story or its embedding in the real. Rather, to convey the story, Amenábar saw his main challenge as getting the spectator to leave the theatre 'con una especie de euforia contenida, de lágrima combinada con sonrisa' (Rocío García, 'Triple Apuesta', 2005) (with a kind of contained euphoria, tearful but smiling). And if this meant fulfilling the viewer's expectation of being manipulated emotionally, then so be it. Unlike the very few critics who thought the film was unduly exploitative (e.g. Sergi Sánchez in *La Razón*, Quim Casas in *Dirigido por*, Vicky Wilson in *Sight and Sound*), in *Mar adentro* Amenábar seeks restraint while giving value to the 'lágrima' (tear/emotion) as a form of audience connectivity with the anti-hero, his suffering and the difficult issues he embodies. In this sense, *Mar adentro* is another generic hybrid. In part, it is a bio-pic, a selective, fictionalised version of the life and very controversial death of a famous quadriplegic. It is also, in part, an 'issue film', involving Sampedro's legal quest for the right to a 'dignified death' and his conflictive relations with the courts, judiciary and the Catholic Church. But it is predominantly a 'weepie', which relies heavily on its operatic and ethnic-instrument-inflected soundtrack but also includes elements of comedy and farce, black humour and social realism, while focusing on the ordinary, domestic context of Sampedro's family relations and love life.

As melodrama, *Mar adentro* offers a reversal of more conventional gendered, patriarchal relations in that the victim upon whom attention is principally focused is not female but male. Ramón is a severely damaged, emasculated male, wholly dependent on his family for all his care. Of course his physical incapacity and dependency also signify a radical form of disempowerment and phallic loss, thereby rendering him a 'captive' in his own body, trapped in the home and thus figuratively 'feminised' and infantilised. Indeed the television images of Ramón, displayed semi-nude in bed as shrivelled, vulnerable adult/child, also work as spectacle to provoke audience sympathy for his plight but also public indignation at the quadriplegic's atrophied body. As Fouz-Hernández and Martínez-Expósito argue, the 'fleshiness' of such imagery heightens our discomfort and helps contribute to the 'destabilisation of dominant images of the male body in the cinema' (2007: 103). Yet, at the same time and even though he remonstrates about their subservience, the filmic Ramón is made the centre of family attention. Though his living space is limited, his room constitutes a reasonably stable, orderly little kingdom where, like an ascetic, mini-Buddha, he enjoys a constant stream of visits, letters and phone calls from friends, well-wishers and DMD organisers. (Arguably, the film does not seriously capture or transmit the sensation of claustrophobia, suffering and utter tedium experienced by someone who entitled his book *Letters from Hell*.) Also, what Ramón cannot bear is his impotence, not only his total physical dependency on others but also his phallic loss, the impossibility of satisfying his male sexual desire by conventional means, knowing this will never change. Here we have a set of very powerful ingredients for a 'male weepie', a story of masculinity in acute crisis. The male victim is also at odds with some of his close family, given his immovable goal of achieving an assisted suicide in the face of family opposition. This is anathema to their traditional, working-class values and, for his brother, an affront to his affections after 30 years of self-sacrifice, hardship and the loss of his own career as a seaman. Yet, apart from a few scenes involving José, Amenábar chooses not to emphasise moments of family confrontation and balances José's opposition to assisted suicide with Manuela's motherly indulgence of Ramón. Rather he focuses on Sampedro's relations with the main female quartet (Julia, Rosa, Manuela and Gené), all of whom respond positively and differently to his humour and seductive charm while three of whom compete for his love, i.e. Manuela, Rosa and Julia. They also appear to project some of their own female desires and fantasies, anxieties and fears on to him in stories of impossible romance. As Amenábar presents him, Sampedro is a man in bed surrounded by unfulfilled women, i.e. a powerful, male sexual fantasy. They provide Ramón with opportunities for seduction, companionship and his search for a trusted helper, while he functions for them as a sounding board, therapist, agony aunt and source of wisdom, humour and comfort.

For example, in Sampedro's coolness and determination to die, the Catalan lawyer figure Julia (a compendium of several real women) finds an answer to her own paralysing fear of death and its aftermath. Despite being married, this motivates her to join Ramón in a suicide pact, though later she changes her mind and returns to her husband (decisions which are not clearly dramatised). Rosa, by contrast, falls in love and believes she can stabilise her own chaotic life as a single mother with two children and give it purpose and meaning by reigniting in Ramón the will to live. Yet the reverse happens. On the rebound from his tryst with Julia, Ramón persuades Rosa to renounce her own desire and co-ordinate and facilitate his death wish as an act of love. She accepts, even though she suffers a major affective loss, which elicits a mix of audience emotions (sorrow and pity as well as our admiration for her stoicism). Manuela, the sister-in-law, seems perfectly conditioned to her role as Ramón's nurse, carer and mother substitute, even though he considers her a slave. But it is he and not her husband who gives her life a purpose, the loss of which is deeply traumatic (as evidenced in the emotional departure scene, when Manuela gradually loses control, begins to cry and rushes back into the house to hide her despair). Even Gené, who marries Marc and begins a family, is strongly connected to Sampedro, not only in a professional capacity but also emotionally because she is personally committed to fulfilling his desires and his right to exercise control over his own body. With the birth of her baby (not chronologically accurate in the film), Amenábar offers a compensatory counterpoint for the devastating impact of Ramón's death and his loss to everyone. Overall, through their relations with Sampedro, these women appear to gain strength, purpose, understanding and a new sense of self. Yet, in the end, their female identities and desires are manipulated by and subordinated to the wishes of the male. Their love for Ramón emerges as various forms of female masochism and self-sacrifice, echoing classical, clichéd properties of the 'female weepie'. Indeed it is the women in the film who are called upon to suffer loss and to 'let go', while they grant Ramón his wish to depart this world. Wittingly or not, they appear to reinforce a story of male dominance, of masculine control, of conditional love and affection, underpinned by a consistent pattern of male non-commitment.

Though not a clearly defined generic category, the term 'issue film' perhaps overstates what we find in *Mar adentro*, given that Amenábar treads extremely lightly over this terrain. He tries to avoid a didactic or overly sentimental tone on assisted suicide, though he brings forward the 'issue' almost immediately the film begins, when Julia (our screen proxy) asks the question: '¿Por qué morir, Ramón?' (Why seek death, Ramón?). Here (with Julia gazing on sympathetically, given her own degenerative, motor neurone disease), Sampedro states his case concisely and eloquently, with a smile, in a very cool, matter-of-fact manner, as someone who has set it out many times before. Sampedro's accident denies him tactile experience. Immobilised, he cannot shake Julia's hand, much less touch or caress her; he regards the few feet which separate them as an unbridgeable 'abyss'. His solution: to end his life.

Also, in the film's main courtroom sequence in A Coruña (for which Sampedro leaves his house for the first time in years in the unmodernised wheelchair, in order to read out a prepared statement), Hollywood convention would normally demand that the heroic quadriplegic inject dramatic and rhetorical 'uplift' into the scene by giving his speech, perhaps cued by a strong symphonic score and emphatic courtroom applause. Yet, in reality, the judge denied Sampedro the right to read out his statement in open court. Though Marc speaks on Ramón's behalf, as his advocate, Amenábar resists a golden opportunity here for tearful court melodrama, this time sticking to historical fact. Yet, in the film overall, the legal angle is strongly truncated and played down, and indeed in other places, for scriptwriters Amenábar and Gil, historical accuracy gives way to significant creative licence.

For example, the one scene where a reasonably cool, thoughtful treatment of euthanasia might have been staged is transformed generically into silent comedy and rhetorical slapstick. Padre Francisco comes to speak to Ramón but Francisco's ultra-modern, mouth-operated, wheelchair will not fit the narrow staircase and Sampedro refuses to be carried below. The bad-tempered slanging match which follows takes on the air of a Buster Keaton or Laurel and Hardy short, as the exhausted, but comically mobile young novice shuttles up and down the staircase carrying overheated messages between the two immobile antagonists, who represent diametrically opposed positions.[7] Yet, through spatial, lighting and camera arrangements, we are left in no doubt about where the film stands. Of course, the point in the film where Amenábar is obliged by history and the real case to present the 'issue' in a serious manner is in his almost faithful rendering of Ramón's final moments. This is a poignant, harrowing and accurate sequence, in which Amenábar makes the audience suffer as we watch Bardem/Sampedro drink the poison and then start to die in front of us. But though the beginning of Ramón's piece to camera is accurately reproduced, Amenábar cuts away from the sequence after about three or four minutes, with a dissolve to Gené and her new baby on the beach (compensatory symbol of freedom and rebirth, also echoing the sea and Ramón as sailor and world traveller etc.).[8]

As regards the bio-pic, and as in Spielberg's *Schindler's List* (1993) or Lynch's *The Straight Story* (1998), Amenábar's *Mar adentro* offers us a careful selection and recreation of episodes in Sampedro's life, staged through actors' performances. Of course the legal and religious aspects of the Sampedro story were extremely well known to Spanish film audiences. And as noted above, Amenábar was unable to avoid such elements and was obliged to reference them in his narrative somehow. But what is surprising is just how much of the real Sampedro story is elided and left out of the film. For example Amenábar severely limits his account of Sampedro's life to the last two years or so, which is counterpointed by the moment of the accident in 1968 (the inert body floating in the water acts as a recurring motif). Strangely, the intervening years (1968–92/3) are missing, creating a narrative black hole which is left virtually unreferenced. Amenábar also takes a large number of real people (family, visitors, lovers, legal, religious etc.) and boils them down to a more manageable group of composite figures. For example, Julia, the sophisticated Catalan lawyer (played by Belén Rueda), is a hybrid of several women who helped Ramón with his legal campaign. Padre Francisco, the paraplegic Jesuit priest with whom Ramón trades insults, laced with black humour, is also a composite. By contrast, Rosa, the local factory worker and Ramón's close companion at his death (played by Lola Dueñas), is based partially on the real-life figure of Ramona Maneiro. The same goes for Gené (played by Clara Segura), who gives us Gené Gordó of DMD. Meanwhile, Javi (played by Tamar Novas), Ramón's nephew and fantasy male offspring, is pure invention, based very loosely on a number of different children. At the same time, in Amenábar's version of Sampedro's life, a vast amount of important background is missing: There is no reference to what followed Ramón's accident, no real information on his mother, father or brother at the time nor on Sampedro's relations with them. However, we do learn that Ramón rejected the request from his 'novia' (fiancée) to marry her, given his distressed attitude towards his quadriplegia. Yet, there is no reference to the nature of his spinal fracture, the options open to him, his early medical treatment and the availability of state support and nursing care, nor how his attitudes were shaped towards rehabilitation, care and his rejection of the wheelchair (a symbol of degraded mobility, which clashed with Sampedro's 'all or nothing' view of his condition). Also, quite bizarrely, there is no reference at all to Ramón's GP or to any representative of the medical or caring professions who might have had dealings with him. A further enigma in Amenábar's account has to do with why and indeed when Ramón definitively took to his bed and decided, purely of his own volition, that, rather than try and adapt to his new circumstances, he would contrive his own suicide.

Yet there is no doubting where Amenábar (and Gil) stand on the Sampedro case. Unlike earlier films, with more open endings, where the spectator was left to deliberate on an issue without much guidance, prompting or ideological direction, Amenábar seems keen to defend Sampedro's radical posture and support the case for euthanasia formally and thematically. He also seeks to present Sampedro as a heroic campaigner and freedom fighter, even though the campaign began somewhat belatedly, 24 years after the accident. (The struggle is acknowledged in the plaque dedicated to Ramón on As Furnhas beach, with the words: 'Defensor da vida e a morte digna' (Champion of life and dignity in death). Amenábar also appeals overwhelmingly to the heart rather than the head, connecting character and spectator through visual, verbal and sonic stimuli, to a whole series of dramatic atmospheres and sensations, most of which his hero had been denied 'Ese mundo de sensaciones, contando la historia de alguien que no podía tener sensaciones físicas, me pareció muy interesante' (*Cinemanía* 2004: 9) (That world of sensations, telling the story of someone who could not enjoy physical sensations, seemed very interesting to me). This is particularly true of the film score and its deployment of inserted popular operatic tracks (e.g. 'Nessun dorma')[9] as well as ethnic music, written and played by the gaitero (Galician piper) Carlos Nuñez, who was responsible for the opening and closing 'celebration of life' musical sequences. *Mar adentro* thus emerges as a something of a demonstration piece, a risky and challenging venture, perhaps even a vanity piece, designed to show that Amenábar could create effective melodrama, spiced up with Sampedro's wit and detached worldview. The film tries very hard to celebrate life and Sampedro's inspirational effect on others while providing a legitimation of his own (in reality unswerving) quest for death. Such a feat would not have been possible without the immense and remarkably nuanced performance of Javier Bardem.

Casting and performance

One of the major issues which confronted Amenábar and his producer Fernando Bovaira on *Mar adentro* was how to engage and then sustain audience attention for a thematically sombre and extremely challenging, two-hour film. Perhaps the key decision, on which spectator investment in the movie and commercial success would depend, would be the casting of Ramón Sampedro. For Bovaira, Sampedro was a very complex, introspective, self-deprecating, but hugely charismatic, witty and sensual character, whom the audience had to identify deeply with, care about and if possible come to admire. For Amenábar, committed to an overall tone which had to be 'absolutamente realista', the challenge was how to create a credible Ramón, i.e. find an actor capable of giving a wholly convincing, naturalistic, yet hypnotically seductive performance. Finding someone who could solidly anchor the story in the filmic 'real' was also crucial to Amenábar's other aim: the need to juxtapose, enlarge and 'oxigenar' (oxygenate) a film about immobility with a series of temporal and spatial 'breaks'. These would involve much physical movement and shifts of location as well as dream, fantasy and flashback sequences.They would also be subtly stylised using elements of lighting, cinematography and especially soundtrack.

Javier Bardem was not Amenábar's first choice for Sampedro, partly because of his age (he was 33 in 2003, being asked to play a 55-year-old quadriplegic). He also had a reputation as a quintessentially physical actor, admired for his bodily movement and strong kinetic presence on screen. In fact Amenábar looked at a wide range of older Spanish actors first of all, but none of them appeared capable of inhabiting the role or carrying the film. As for Bardem, Amenábar observes:

> I wasn't sure about casting Javier at all. I hesitated for the obvious reason that if the ageing didn't work, it would distract the audience. I wanted to be able to close my eyes and know that the person speaking was in his fifties. And with Javier I did. Of course, the make-up is good but in fact, age is conveyed through a subtle delivery of energy. (Garnett 2005: 31)

Despite his reservations, Bovaira persuaded Amenábar to offer the role to Bardem. He was Spain's best male actor, with a strong international profile and star image already, having been Oscar-nominated for his role in Julian Schnabel's *Before Night Falls* (2000). As the sick poet Reinaldo Arenas, Bardem already had experience of representing male disability and death by suicide as well as embodying a known and controversial literary figure, who held Fidel Castro uniquely responsible for his untimely demise in 1980, aged 47. Such features seemed well suited to the Sampedro story and also recalled the central role in *The Others* of Nicole Kidman, who had shouldered the main acting and promotional burden of the film two years earlier. Bardem, for his part, hesitated. He was extremely doubtful about accepting the role, for a number of reasons: His age (and how to age 20 years convincingly), his physicality and the way he works with his body, his prior roles (stereotyped very early on as a macho playboy), the language problem (Bardem knew no Galician), the creation of a credible voice with which to deliver and inflect his lines, how to appear real and natural as a bedridden quadriplegic and also the considerable risk involved if the performance did not work. Bardem recalls:

> I read the script and loved it, but I spent a month thinking about it. Because it is one thing to want to do something as a challenge, but in fact you can only take on something if you feel it is a logical step, if you know you will make sense of it. I didn't know if I could do the part until Jo Allen, the make up artist, came on board. I owe 50% of my perfor- mance to her. Because once I had my make-up on, all I had to do was to fill what she created with veracity. (Garnett 2005: 31)

Javier Bardem, a former national rugby player, with a broken nose, began his career in feature films in Bigas Luna's *Jamón, jamón* (1992) and *Huevos de oro* (Golden balls, 1993) as a parodic, oversexed, macho poseur, hired lover and thuggish entrepreneur. However, since then he has largely shaken off this macho stereotype and shown great versatility in roles associated with young and older versions of dis-em- powered and damaged masculinity – as Lisardo the drug pusher in Armendáriz's *Días contados* (Countdown, 1994), the disabled policeman/basketball star in Almodóvar's *Carne trémula* (Live Flesh, 1997), the AIDS victim Reinaldo Arenas in Julian Schnabel's *Before Night Falls* (2000), the introverted male lead in John Malkovich's *The Dancer Upstairs* (2002) and the overweight, unemployed shipworker Santa in *Los lunes al sol* (Mondays in the Sun, Fernando León de Aranoa, 2002). Moroever, in *Carne trémula*, Bardem had already had experi- ence of playing a paraplegic, though nothing comparable to the shriv- elled, bedridden Sampedro or to the demands of this screen role.[10] In fact, Bardem would have to find expressivity and performance from the neck up, mainly through the gaze, facial gestures (his smile) and in the tone and cadence of the voice in his dialogue. Such limitations were totally new territory for Bardem and for the viewer. Rather than gaze admiringly at the beautiful Bardem body and how it moves, the spectator would be encouraged to listen and to reflect on Ramón's words, delivered with his gentle sarcasm and humour.

Bardem finally accepted the role in early summer 2003, and began researching his subject, not only by reading Ramón's books and talking to people who knew him but also by spending time at the Hospital Nacional de Paraplégicos (National Hospital for Paraplegics) in Toledo in July 2003. Here he talked to doctors and saw at first hand how severely disabled people actually moved and talked. Luckily Bardem was in sympathy with Sampedro's wish to die and admired his tough, unwavering resolve to seek an exit from an unbearable existence. This helped him present his version of the character at the main, full-script, read-through in early September 2003 in Madrid. It also prepared him for the exhaustion and tedium of the five hours of make-up time per day and the ten to twelve hours on set, six days a week, for three months. As well as these pressures, Bardem suffered skin infections, cramps, and the massive bodily stress of being trussed up like a Christmas turkey every working day.[11]

Having secured Bardem for the role of Sampedro, Bovaira then hired an experienced casting director (Luis San Narciso) to help select the other main and secondary roles in the film. Narciso's overriding criterion was naturalism, linguistic and cultural as well as role-oriented. Hence the casting of Francesc Garrido as Marc and Clara Segura as Gené, both Catalans and both of whom would make an important contribution to the film's sense of national inclusivity, by using Catalan in their dialogue, when appropriate. Also crucial in this regard was the casting of Sampedro's family, which had to be wholly credible and convincing though not necessarily an accurate representation in every detail. Amenábar wanted unknown actors, able to work in Galician if need be, in order facilitate verisimilitude and spectator identification. The casting of Joan Dalmau (as Joaquín, Ramón's father), Tamar Novas (as Ramón's nephew Javi), Celso Bugallo (as Ramón's brother José) and Mabel Rivera (as Manuela, his sister-in- law) proved to be very apt choices. In fact Amenábar was quite overcome by the degree of realism and naturalness of their performances (Interview). As for the two main female leads, Julia and Rosa, the choice of Lola Dueñas for Rosa was uncontroversial. Dueñas had worked very successfully with Almodóvar as the nurse in *Hable con ella* (Talk to Her, 2004). She was an excellent actress and, for *Mar adentro*, researched her role well. She even interviewed the real-life Ramona Maneiro and incorporated into her performance various tics and gestures such as facial expressions and a distinctive walk used by 'Moncha'.

The only real difficulty arose when Amenábar considered Belén Rueda for the role of Julia. Bovaira opposed the choice, on the grounds that Rueda was first and foremost a television actress and had no experience of filmmaking. She was also too closely identified with her role in the hit national television series *Los Serrano* (The Serrano Family) (starring opposite the veteran actor Antonio Resines, as his wife and, thus, far too well known nationally to provide a credible screen persona for Julia). Bovaira also feared that to cast Rueda might be a step too far, that she might be unable to make the transition to the film set and thus be in danger of playing Julia as a television

character. Amenábar disagreed, arguing that he liked her on television and in her two screen tests, which showed her ability to play
a dramatic character and hold her ground alongside Bardem. And,
echoing his experience with Nicole Kidman, Amenábar needed her
considerable 'aguante' (stamina), that is her ability to do a number
of takes, at the same level of emotional intensity, and still keep the
engine running. He also admired her realism, her ordinariness, her
warm, sympathetic gaze towards Sampedro and her ability to turn
on the tears, in short, her emotional connectivity through the eyes
and ears. Moreover, he was keen to offer her an opportunity to work
in a different environment and challenge industrial stereotypes. For
Amenábar, 'Belén ... resuelve perfectamente las escenas cotidianas ...
además me apetecía ver una cara nueva ... en el cine español' (Belén
... delivers perfectly the daily life scenes ... besides I wanted to see a
new face in Spanish cinema).[12]

Condenado a vivir (2001/2004)

One of the more intriguing aspects of the media controversy
surrounding *Mar adentro* (which included accusations of plagiarism)
is the fact that the Sampedro story had already been told in a Spanish
television version, made in 2001.[13] The 80-minute television movie
was produced by Euro Ficción S.L. and Costa Oeste Producciones
S.A. for a consortium of Spanish regional television companies: Canal
Sur, Tele Madrid, Televisión Autonómica Valencia, Televisión Galicia
(TVG) and Euskal Telebista/Televisión Vasca. The production was
scripted by Javier Maqua and directed by the veteran 1970s producer-
director Roberto Bodegas.[14] Puzzlingly, following its completion, the
tele film appears to be have been screened only once, by TVG, in
2001, with other stakeholder channels shelving it. It was not heard of
again until late 2004 when, to coincide with the commercial release
of *Mar adentro*, Tele Madrid, Canal Sur and other channels resurrected it, presenting it as if it were a quasi-documentary about Ramón
Sampedro rather than a fictitious account. In fact the Bodegas version
begins with a very clear health warning, aware of the sub judice status
of the case, describing itself thus: 'Esta película está basada en la vida
de Ramón Sampedro. Los nombres de los demás personajes han
sido modificados para preservar su identidad. Asimismo, las situa-
ciones han sido adaptadas para la ficción con fines dramáticos' (www.
minutodigital.com/noticias/condenado.htm) (This film is based on

the life of Ramón Sampedro. The names of the other characters have been changed to preserve identities. At the same time, situations have been fictionalised for dramatic purposes.)

In interview Amenábar claims that he heard about *Condenado a vivir* (Condemned to Live) only after finishing *Mar adentro*. But given the coincidence in approach to his own version of the Sampedro story, one which stresses selectivity and a degree of fictional licence over historical or documentary veracity, one wonders whether he or his producer Bovaira took the Bodegas movie into account and, if so, how far. Given their usual thoroughness and minute attention to detail in the research phase for *Mar adentro*, it seems highly unlikely that they were unaware of this earlier version at the time of making the film.

Comparing briefly both versions, the most obvious difference is that while Amenábar's big screen treatment enjoyed a €10 million budget from Sogecine and correspondingly high production values, the Bodegas television movie was made on a shoestring and it shows. And while Amenábar takes his film title from one of Sampedro's erotic love poems 'Mar adentro', Bodegas recycles a dialogue phrase used by the Catalan lawyer figure, here named Pilar, who accuses Ramón's family of having 'condemned him to live'. Hence the tele film title 'Condenado a vivir'. Moreover, because Sampedro's brother José refuses to help him secure a dignified death, the lawyer argues that his family have 'kidnapped' him in order to prolong his suffering. Here we find a markedly stronger ethical edge and conflictual tone to the relationship between the lawyer and Sampedro's family as well as her very personal commitment to the defence of her client's individual rights.

In terms of narrative construction and development, budget differences again have a significant impact on story design, look and sound. Unlike *Mar adentro*, which alternates temporally between 1996–98 and Sampedro's accident in 1968, *Condenado a vivir* starts in 1992, with a letter from Sampedro (played by the mature Galician actor Ernesto Chao) sent to DMD in Barcelona asking for help to die, until his suicide in 1998. Also, unlike *Mar adentro*, the television version boasts no flashback material or dream sequences, no CGI to reduce Sampedro's postrate body or recreate backdrops, no use of windows, frames, screens etc. to suggest metacinematic commentary, no interpolated music tracks etc. In other words we find a much plainer, far more linear, straightforward diegesis, lacking the visual tricks and luxury excess of the Amenábar version. However, though segmented chronologically by intertitles (giving time and place, e.g. Xuño 1992, Xuño 1994 etc.) and thus appearing to be historically accurate, the tele film remains highly elliptical, even though it deals in some detail with Sampedro's legal campaign in the first 30 minutes. Here Ramón receives two working visits from the head of DMD, in this version named Núria, accompanied by her partner Marc. Sampedro also meets the Catalan lawyer, Pilar, already on crutches, who, as part of her campaign to promote and publicise his case, arranges an inter-view with Televisión Galicia. Sampedro succeeds in seducing both women, with his affable temperament, irony, jokes, his smile, his penetrating gaze and his often quite explicit erotic verse (as Núria finds out in a poem he writes with his mouth and sends her by post). After 30 minutes the legal angle recedes in order to introduce Ramón's third and most developed love relationship, that of the real-life Ramona Maneiro figure, here renamed Carmen (and played by a very effective María Bouzas). After seeing the semi-naked Ramón interviewed on television and being deeply moved by his plight, Carmen dedicates a record to him on a pirate radio show she jointly presents with her friend Rosa (a screen name uncannily recycled by Amenábar for his version of Ramona Maneiro). She then arranges to visit him, accompanied by Rosa initially. Gradually, Carmen gets closer to Sampedro (visits him far more often, begins to shave him and prepare his food), in a relationship which emphasises Ramón's role as a good listener as well as a skilled talker. Carmen's increased presence in the house deeply upsets Ramón's sister-in-law and carer, here named Rosalía, who feels threatened by the 'other woman'. This conflict of female desire is bisected narratively by a 'set piece' scene in A Coruña, where (having been prevented from speaking inside the courthouse), Sampedro reads his personal manifesto to the authori-ties on the pavement outside. It is a document signed by hundreds of Spanish artists and intellectuals demanding the right of personal control for Sampedro over the timing and manner of his own death.

In terms of characterisation, Sampedro's brother and his wife (here called Carlos and Rosalía) do the best they can with roles which are seriously underdeveloped and which emerge as very flat, repetitive and one-dimensional. Sampedro's father hardly figures at all. Núria (the Gené Gordó figure) is already with Marc by the time she meets Sampedro and by 1996 has had her baby. Curiously none of the Catalans speaks any Catalan throughout the whole of the film. This linguistic lapse also applies to the Sampedro household, where not a word of Galician is spoken, even by Ramón's niece Remedios (a role played by Javi in Amenábar's version). Crucially and reflecting his importance in the real Sampedro story, Bodegas's scriptwriter includes a major role for Sampedro's family doctor, who helps him die. Also Ramón himself speaks poignantly and at some length about his mother (hardly mentioned in *Mar adentro*), including details such as her fainting and collapsing on the stairs – with a crippled Ramón unable to assist – and dying of a broken heart. Here, Amenábar appears to recycle and incorporate this fainting episode into the character of Julia. Perhaps the major narrative difference in *Condenado a vivir* is that, in the second half, Bodegas foregrounds Sampedro's intimate love story with Carmen (Rosa in *Mar adentro*) while marginalising his relationship with lawyer Pilar. Is it therefore pure coincidence that, in *Mar adentro* Amenábar does the exact opposite? That is, he reverses the character pattern and gives priority to Ramón's love affair with the Catalan lawyer Julia.[15]

If Amenábar (as well as Bovaira and Gil) did know of the Bodegas version during the pre-production phase, I suggest that their strategy in designing *Mar adentro* might have been informed by the following considerations. On the one hand, it seems perfectly admissible that their script should occupy and exploit some of the narrative and character terrain ignored or left undeveloped by Bodegas. For example, this might explain Amenábar's strong focus on the figure of Julia in preference to Rosa, as Sampedro's main love interest (in reality it was the other way round). Also Amenábar saw golden opportunities to incorporate and extend the Catholic Church and Jesuit priest angle as well as exploit and emphasise the use of the different national languages, which are inexplicably absent from the Bodegas version. On the other hand, Amenábar and Gil seem to have ignored some of the medium-size roles given prominence in the Bodegas version, such as the crucial narrative figure of Ramón's GP, bizarrely absent from Amenábar's version.

Overall, taking into account its budget, *Condenado a vivir* is a worthy but dull attempt at telling the Sampedro story, though it contains strong and engaging performances from the two main leads Ernesto Chao (who played Ramón and won a TVG acting prize for his performance) and María Bouzas (Carmen). Yet, owing to a deficient script, many of the smaller roles lack realism and credibility, since they are saddled with unimaginative, weary dialogue. Also the film lacks any pace, tension, energy, dynamism or drama, which might explain its presentation in 2004 as a 'drama doc' or documentary. The music soundtrack by Jesús Yanes, which incorporates a theme tune and is given an 'ethnic feel' by the use of Galician bagpipes, is often laboured and over-intrusive. And while Bodegas emphasises Sampedro's interest in poetry, especially Neruda, Amenábar focuses on his taste for opera, which opens up crucial soundtrack opportunities (such as the use of Wagner and Puccini's 'Nessun Dorma'). All in all, the Bodegas film illustrates rather graphically some of Amenábar's own concerns regarding clunky filmmaking (or 'cine ortopédico'), i.e. predictable, flat and done by numbers (Sempere 2004: 68–9).[16]

Narrative and film technique: jumping out of the window

'This is a story of a man who can hardly move. Even more, he doesn't want to get out of his room', Amenábar says of Ramón Sampedro's inherently uncinematic lifestyle, lying in bed in the care of his brother's family. 'When we were writing, every day Mateo and I just said, 'How are we going to get out of the room today without the audience really noticing?' Then, when we researched the real Ramón and we met the people around him, we found a way to spread out to different characters' lives. And the importance of windows. Every time we could, we just jumped out the window somehow' (Linekin 2004).

As noted earlier, given that 60–70 per cent of the film takes place in one room (amusingly dubbed the Panic Room, by the crew), Amenábar, Gil and producer Bovaira were obsessed with avoiding the sensation of claustrophobia and entrapment for fear of alienating and losing the audience. Hence the need to take regular breaks from the oppressive interiors, to 'oxigenar el relato' (make the story breathe) or as Amenábar also puts it: jump out of the window.

Amenábar establishes the narrative and spectatorial importance of escape by opening the film with a powerfully metacinematic prologue which uses windows as film and mind screens. Not only does the sequence introduce the main character and his recourse to daydreams, it also manages to subtly insert the spectator within the frame as Sampedro's companion in the dream action, while at the same time referring back to Amenábar's previous films, including *Tesis* and *Abre los ojos*. Fading up from a black screen and accompanied by Carlos Nuñez's sprightly galician pipes, the unseen Gené reads extracts from one of Ramón's relaxation manuals (he is about to meet

Julia, the lawyer, for the first time, and is nervous): 'Tranquilo ... Estás más que tranquilo ... Ahora imagina una pantalla, una pantalla de cine que se despliega y se abre ante ti ... Crea en ella el lugar que prefieras. Una playa por ejemplo' (Relax, you feel really relaxed ... Now, imagine a screen, a film screen which opens out in front of you ... Put into it whatever setting you prefer. A beach, for example).

As Gené speaks in voiceover, and within the black screen, we see a white screen gradually unfolding, flooding with light, fading up to a 'paradise island' and beach scene (actually filmed in the Seychelles) where Sampedro takes an imaginary walk, now able to feel multiple sensations ordinarily denied to him (from the water, the heat of the sun and the texture of the sand). With the daydream over, we re-enter his room, where the mind/film screen is replaced by his own room window on the world, overlooking the countryside, where a storm is brewing.

Like the beginning of *Abre los ojos*, the opening sequence is impressive and very cinematic. It is also a clever, multi-accented, summarising 'tour de force'. It interlaces Sampedro's daydreaming activity (qua cinema) with his ability to enter and construct other worlds. We also see the function and importance of his window as a 'view' of his native Galicia and a prompt to memory, including the motifs of the journey, rural life and the sea. The window is also an analogue of a film screen or frame upon which Ramón can insert or paint his own fantasies, and where these can be realised. In short, we witness a classical metaphor for the cinema as a form of dream activity (a motif captured beautifully, for example, in Victor Fleming's version of *The Wizard of Oz* (1939), whose main storytelling device is also the dream). Sonically, the sequence also connects with the ending of *Abre los ojos*, recycling the words used by the nurse to reawake César: 'Tranquilo, tranquilo, abre los ojos', where César escapes from his virtual nightmare after committing suicide a second time. The window also foreshadows other thematic links: firstly, with Sampedro's voyeurism (reminiscent of the photographer L.B. Jeffries in Hitchcock's *Rear Window*, who uses a zoom lens to spy on his neighbours) and, secondly, with the climax of *Mar adentro*, where death is figured as a new (metaphorical) life for Sampedro and given literal form in Gené's new baby. And, as an echo of Amenábar's signs of authorship, the sequence also recalls the opening of *Tesis* in that, like the severed body on the rail track, the spectator (like Ángela) is initially denied any visual sighting of Ramón (the body in the bed) and has access to him only through his voice (sonic foregrounding), as he flirts and jokes with Gené, his (visible) campaign manager, thus establishing very promptly one of his key character traits. All in all, Amenábar offers us a very stylish, subtle and evocative opening (also reminiscent of the opening to Tornatore's *Cinema Paradiso*, 1989). It is one which fully immerses the spectator in the *mise-en-scène*, as a friend or visitor to the as yet invisible and enigmatic Sampedro, while setting up a technical and thematic agenda, and summarising Amenábar's film work into the bargain.

As regards the film narrative, for Spanish audiences (though not for international publics) the outcome of Sampedro's campaign was already very well known. Narrative action lines are thus few and rather slight, characterised by major ellipses and largely replaced by the intimacy of character interaction and various set pieces. Amenábar thus opts for a very light touch narrative thread in the background (i.e. Sampedro's failed attempts to get legal approval for his assisted suicide). The focus is thus mainly on his family and private life, plus the several 'set pieces' woven into the diegesis (e.g. the main court scene in A Coruña, the 'debate' with the Jesuit priest, leading up to the climax represented by the video-captured 'death scene'). There are also a number of montage sequences for exposition and information delivery, such as an early background sequence on Rosa or the use of still photos by Julia (photographed in close-up) to build up Ramón's earlier life. However, by alternating present and past through flashbacks, dreams and numerous montage sequences, as well as repeating motifs (such as the accident itself), Amenábar manages to 'jump cut of the window' quite successfully as well as convey a degree of (though not enough) narrative and character information. This approach also allows him a number of non-narrative breaks in the temporal flow via the use of flashback for fantasy and symbolic purposes (the opening paradise island sequence; the accident scene, as a recurring motif of that limbo area between life and death; the vertigo-inducing flying sequence down to the beach, at varying speeds, accompanied by the 'Nessun dorma' track, which resolves into the signature crane shot of the two lovers on the beach, a shot already used in the accident sequence). However, as Sempere has suggested, in order to slim down the running time there are a number of scenes included by Amenábar which could have been usefully excised on narrative grounds (the finishing and printing of Ramón's book; the scenes between Marc and Gené developing their relationship in Barcelona;

some of the non-dialogue moments between Julia and her husband Germán, 2004: 37–8).

The film is also punctuated by two major narrative set pieces in the diegetic present, sequences which Amenábar is almost obliged to deal with since they form key features of the 'real' Sampedro case, but which are condensations or 'pinceladas' (brushstrokes) of a much more protracted, real historical process: the court hearing in A Coruña and the visit of the Jesuit priest to persuade Ramón to give up his fight for assisted suicide. Sampedro's visit to A Coruña, in his hated wheelchair, provides Amenábar with an opportunity not only to remind the spectator of his long struggle with the law but also to 'jump out of the window' again by getting him out of the house, recycling the motif of travel (repeated in his final journey to Boiro to die) and highlighting his radical detachment from his wider surroundings. Indeed, as he travels inside the minivan (paid for by the ONCE, i.e. Spain's National Organisation for the Blind), and via a montage sequence, Sampedro is shown as a lonely spectator of scenes of daily life in his rural Galicia, abstracted, cut off by the windows of the van, never able to interact with his environment (which includes the two dogs vigorously copulating, an ironic reminder of Sampedro's phallic impotence). Later, with Rosa, the walk in the park extends this 'oxygenating' moment while allowing Sampedro to discuss his suicide plans. As for the 'debate' with the Catholic Church, the sequence condenses a number of visits the real Sampedro actually received from two priests. While the arguments are ostensibly serious and rhetorically bad-tempered, the overall tone is deliberately light-hearted and even comic, thus offering a further 'breathing space' to the spectator. Here, some commentators have been quite hostile to the way Amenábar seems to dumb down the anti-euthanasia case by caricaturing the priest as a ranting demagogue, while refusing to open up Ramón's anti-clericalism to more incisive questioning (see, for example, the review by Vicky Wilson 2005).

Also, in order to generate a much more expansive 'feel' to a film thematically concerned with confinement and immobility, in geographical terms, Amenábar juxtaposes and alternates spatially between Galicia and Barcelona. This allows the film to explore a set of economic, industrial and cultural binary contrasts between the rural/ urban, poor/rich, backward/developed Spain, city-metropolis/'pueblo' etc. This interplay (and Julia's several trips to Galicia by plane) empha-sise the journey motif, Sampedro's previous life as world traveller and Amenábar's concern to let the spectator breathe. It also offers an excessively rosy, optimistic view of Spain as a country that is increasingly interconnected politically, culturally and linguistically.[17]

In *Mar adentro* film technique is rather more on display here than in previous films. These devices range from the use of fade-ups/downs from black to punctuate time and spatial shifts to the vertigo-inducing flying sequence down to the beach (done by helicopter camera) and include the trademark zenith, crane and circling hand-held camera shots, as well as new underwater shots, which capture Ramón, post-accident, in limbo between life and death. While Amenábar still observes his golden rule of 'contención' (restraint) in order to anchor the film in a realistic setting, his aim here is to create a feeling of intimacy and to place the spectator as close as possible to the characters, without triggering claustrophobia. This is done partly by way of very clever dialogue, peppered with Sampedro's typical dry wit and black humour (on the subject of smoking, for example). It is also achieved by Amenábar's decision to use a Super 35mm, wide-screen format, which provides a 2.35:1 aspect ratio. Wide-screen formats have been available since the 1950s, usually used in genres which emphasise spectacle, such as westerns, musicals and historical epics. Yet Amenábar finds great value in this format for dealing with far more private, intimate subjects, especially in setting up varied horizontal compositions, with significant foreground and background detail.[18]

Also, far more so than before, and in the manner of Giuseppe Tornatore and Steven Soderberg, Amenábar uses a number of clever, non-dialogue, transitional montage sequences linked via dissolves. They allow him to 'layer up' several story lines at once, provide character exposition and summarise traits (e.g. Rosa at work, out shopping, indoors, watching television etc., prior to visiting Sampedro). Also Rosa in the radio studio is linked with Ramón, listening to the radio, via her dedication track 'Negra sombra' (Black Shadow). This is also overheard by Gené talking to Ramón on the phone from Barcelona. The same networking and summarising technique is used again to compare and contrast Rosa and her relations with men in Boiro with Gené and Marc in a classy Barcelona restaurant. This is held together and bridged by inserted music tracks (again recycling 'Nessun dorma' and 'Negra sombra'). In fact, the use of music to raise the emotional pitch in order to bind various lives together in different places again suggests a desire for inclusivity and for Spain as one nation. There are also moments where Amenábar cleverly switches the source of his sound and changes the positioning and identification between spectator and character. For example Julia records Sampedro's account of the accident on her tape recorder, but, rather than hearing the account as Ramón delivers it, we are allowed to hear it only later, alongside Julia in her room, as the tape plays over images of the accident. We thus accompany her and engage with her reaction to the story. Meanwhile, Sampedro becomes his own listener, hears his own words played back to him, in a strange role reversal, as listener not subject. Such changes echo similar scenes of 'sound sourcing' games from *Tesis*.

Overall, Amenábar tries to keep the viewer permanently engaged and busy by use of elaborate but not overly intrusive film techniques and by numerous performance cues, looks, gestures and silences, non-dialogue moments as well as retaining many improvised acting moments, possibly indicative of a certain lack of confidence in the narration to hold the viewer's attention. Also, as noted earlier, the film narrative, which shows Sampedro's life as remarkably full of visits, calls, letters, preparations, debates, writing, reading etc., arguably falsifies much of the experience of the real Sampedro as a victim of the crushing boredom and maddening torment of his immobility.

Distribution, promotion, reception

In July 2004 Fine Line Features ('indie' subsidiary of New Line Cinema, which was later folded into Time Warner) struck a deal with Amenábar's Spanish distributor Sogepaq to market *Mar adentro* in all English language speaking areas, including the USA and the UK. According to Marian Koltai-Levine, charged with promoting the film (see DVD Extras documentary, 'La aventura americana'), Fine Line paid $6 million to secure the distribution rights, one of the largest sums ever paid by an American distributor for an independent, foreign-language film. Fine Line had already in 2000/1 distributed Julian Schnabel's *Before Night Falls*, for which Bardem was Oscar-nominated, as noted earlier. Evidently, with a well-known trans-national star like Bardem fronting *Mar adentro* and likely to form the core of their marketing strategy, Fine Line believed they had another winner on their hands, despite probable market aversion to the film's gloomy 'right to die' theme.

The American première and the promotional campaign for *Mar adentro* (December 2004) were preceded by the film's launch in September 2004 in Spain and then later in the rest of Europe. Amenábar's film was selected to represent Spain at the Venice Film Festival (1–11 September), with a national première scheduled for 3 September. With the backing of Sogecine and Sogepaq (production and distribution arms of Sogetel), *Mar adentro* enjoyed a sophisticated and very effective nationwide marketing campaign, in which the parent company PRISA deployed all of its many media assets to publicise and hype the film. Before the première, for example, the weekly magazine of *El País* (*El País Semanal*, 22 August 2004) was fronted by a large publicity still of Bardem as a bedridden Sampedro, and inside by an eight-page spread containing a flattering profile of Sampedro by Manuel Rivas (a well-known Galician writer) and a very respectful interview with Bardem and Amenábar together, by Suso del Toro. PRISA's promotional campaign was probably modelled on the marketing template for *The Others* in 2001, Spain's most commercially successful film of all time. But, in the case of Amenábar's far less commercial 'euthanasia movie', PRISA (via Sogecine and its marketing department) went into overdrive. Almost without exception, the première of *Mar adentro* in Madrid, sponsored by Canal Plus and the Kinepolis cinema chain, was front page news in the all the main national daily papers, including *El Mundo, ABC, La Vanguardia, El Periódico, La Razón* and *El País*. In the case of *El País*, the paper did not only, however, contain an eight-page spread, including a review and interview with Amenábar. It also carried on its front page the now famous and widely reproduced picture of Amenábar, Bardem and Rueda standing alongside Spain's socialist Prime Minister, José Luis Rodríguez Zapatero, his wife, a clutch of ministers and other invited guests. If the picture suggested firm support for the Spanish film industry by the head of government, it also seemed to align the PSOE with the pro-euthanasia sentiment of the film, not to mention Amenábar's own 'outing' several days before.

In Spain the critical reception of *Mar adentro*, in the newspapers and specialist magazines, as well as on the radio and television, was extraordinarily positive and enthusiastic, with very few dissenting voices. In *El País*, Diego Galán dubbed it: 'Hermosa, excepcional, inteligente, arriesgada' (Beautiful, exceptional, intelligent, risky); in *ABC*, Rodríguez Marchante said it was 'Magnífica, vital. llena de un hirviente sentido del humor' (Magnificent, full of life and a keen sense of humour); Carlos Boyero in *El Mundo* claimed: 'Todo es magistral ... Bardem está más allá del elogio pero Belén Rueda y los secundarios también' (It is masterful ... Bardem is beyond praise, like Belén Rueda and the supporting actors). However, Sergi Sánchez in *La Razón* and Mirito Torreiro in *Fotogramas* raised questions about the film's manipulation of spectator sentiments (see Sempere 2004: 54–7). Only Quim Casas in *Dirigido por* (September 2004: 24–5) appeared uneasy about the comparison Amenábar draws between Julia's final decision to go on living (of doubtful value) and Ramón's to die (justified).

In Spain *Mar adentro* opened in 275 cinemas and over the following 12 months attracted two million spectators and made €20 million at the box-office. In the rest of Europe, by contrast, while it collected industry awards at the Venice Film festival (Best International Film, A Grand Jury Prize for Amenábar, the Copa Volpi prize for Best Actor for Javier Bardem) and the European Film Awards (Best Actor and Best Director), commercial success eluded it. With distribution restricted to the UK, Italy and the Netherlands (source: imdb.com), it made a mere €1.5 million. Such signs were not good omens. In the USA the film also struggled very hard to find an audience. Under Koltai-Levine, and having spent so much money on acquiring the rights, the strategy at Fine Line was to bypass television advertising altogether in favour of spending money on travel, publicity, press and pre-release screenings and cultivating word of mouth. This involved Amenábar and Bardem, who became the public, marketing face of *Mar adentro* (always pictured as the young, virile sailor, never the old Ramón) in an exhausting round of radio, television, phone and one-to-one press interviews, plus a number of screenings followed by question and answer sessions. Their involvement in the campaign lasted nearly five months, with Amenábar's participation dogged by his still halting English and various misunderstandings and confusions, largely because he was still an unknown in the USA.[19]

Also, following a high-risk strategy, Fine Line planned the release of *Mar adentro* in the USA for the month of December 2004. In terms of the sheer number and volume of film releases jockeying for position in the American market, December was arguably the worst possible month of all to launch. And bizarrely, compared to the campaign waged by Miramax for *The Others* in September 2001, Fine Line had placed the film in only 23 film theatres, in a mere seven states, clearly anticipating a very difficult, 'slow burn', commercial career for the film. Moreover, the promotional campaign stressed the sentimental, romantic, melodramatic aspects of the film, selling it as a 'weepie' while trying to play down the more challenging legal and ethical aspects of an 'assisted suicide' film. According to Bovaira, who flew out to New York to support the film's release and marketing campaign in mid-December, one of the most crucial tasks for the successful distribution of the film was to achieve nominations and prizes in the run-up to the Oscars, where *Mar adentro* was Spain's official entry for Best Foreign Film. Bovaira made it clear that in order for a film to achieve even minimal visibility in the USA (where only 1 per cent of movies are non-English-language and where the market is so congested), a film needed as many 'avales' (endorsements) as possible, especially Academy Award nominations. Such signs of recognition, even if they did not result in prizes, still linked a film with a powerful global brand name, instantly recognisable all over the world as a mark of quality and peer recognition. For Bovaira the key selling point of *Mar adentro* was its 'intensidad emocional' (emotional intensity); it was a film which 'desde lo local, trata un tema absoluta-mente universal, que puede ser entendido en todo el mundo' (from a local perspective, deals with an absolutely universal theme, which can be understood across the whole world) (see 'La aventura americana', DVD, Disc 2, 2005).

Thankfully the film gained two nominations for the Golden Globes (Best Actor and Best Film) and two for the Oscars (Best Film and Best Make-up). This compensated greatly for a disastrous commercial opening in mid-December, when the film was simply incapable of attracting an audience. Fine Line put this down to market satura-tion and several uncomplimentary reviews (which criticised the film's excess of sentimentality). As a result *Mar adentro* was quickly withdrawn from the theatres with a view to relaunching in February/March 2005 following the Oscars, while reorienting the marketing campaign towards the film awards, which would, in theory, help support box-office. The Spanish embassy in Los Angeles and even Paula Wagner rallied round to support the film. Remarkably, *Mar adentro* went on to win the American Critics' Prize for Best Film as well as the Golden Globe award for Best Film (Bardem was pipped by Leonardo di Caprio in *Aviator*, for Best Actor). Such critical recognition, as well as The Spirit Prize, prior to Oscar night, helped *Mar adentro* win the Oscar for Best Foreign Film of 2004, against strong competi-tion (including the French entry *Les Choristes* (The Choir Boys). To win such peer recognition, critical acclaim and global visibility aged only 32 was a remarkable achievement for Amenábar, despite the fact that, outside of Spain, *Mar adentro* was a commercial flop.[20] Interestingly, of far more personal significance for Amenábar than the Oscar was the letter of congratulation he received from his idol Steven Spielberg, whom he had met on the set of *Minority Report* a year earlier. To receive an Oscar was a mark of professional recognition. But to receive the imprimatur of Spielberg himself was a personal triumph, a sign that he had really passed his degree as a film director.

The other *Mar adentro*

The attendance of Spain's Prime Minister, José Luis Rodríguez Zapatero and his wife Sonsoles Espinosa, as well as six of his ministers, at the première of *Mar adentro* in early September 2004 had unintended consequences. This strong governmental presence was regarded as provocative, not only by their political rivals but also by citizens' platforms such as Hazteoir.org and numerous organisations for the disabled. Indeed Zapatero's support for the film triggered a wave of protest across the country, since it gave the impression that the PSOE government was endorsing a work which celebrated assisted suicide and 'la muerte digna' (dignified death) while ignoring the overwhelming majority of Spain's disabled people and devaluing their struggle for a dignified life. According to Miguel Ascenzo, a rehabilitation specialist in spinal injuries at the hospital in Toledo where Bardem had done research on disability, the film offered a rather one-sided view of the problem, since among paraplegics the number of suicides was very small. Also the film ignored the possibilities that Sampedro might have had open to him regarding rehabilitation and the development of 'una red social de ayuda' (a social support network), which would have provided him with treatment and motivation to regain some mobility. Gustavo Almela, disabled, historian and specialist in accident prevention also argues: 'El caso Sampedro nos perjudicó gravemente ... por una cuestion importante: la desproporcionada difusión mediática que se le dio originó ... que se asociara el término tetraplégico a una person que se quiere suicidar' (The Sampedro case seriously hurt us in one important respect: the disproportionate media attention given to the case ... helped link the term paraplegic to someone who ... wants to commit suicide) (see www.Hazteoir.org/node/279/). María del Mar Cogollos, psychologist, disabled since 1987 and President of the Asociación para el Estudio de la Lesión Medular Espinal (Association for the Study of Spinal

Injuries), was unhappy with 'la historia de un anti-héroe, que no llegó a asumir su realidad ni su condición' (the story of an anti-hero who could not come to terms with his reality or condition) (see www. aciprensa.com). She also believed that 'el caso Sampedro es excepcional y que las personas tetraplégicas no queremos suicidarnos sino que queremos vivir ... con el apoyo psicológico y social necesario para vivir dignamente' (hazteoir.org/node/279/) (the Sampedro case is exceptional, disabled people like us do not want to commit suicide but to live with the psychological and social support necessary to live with dignity). By contrast, in interview, Gené Gordó (Sampedro's lawyer) claimed that 70 per cent of Spaniards were already in favour of euthanasia and that with Amenábar's film 'probablemente el debate se ha ganado. Es un canto a las libertades humanas y un grito de sentido común' (the debate has probably been won. [The film] is a hymn to human freedom and a cry for common sense) (elmundo.es/encuentros/invitados/2004,'10/12135/i).

On the tenth anniversary of Ramón Sampedro's death by assisted suicide (12 January 2008), many friends, well-wishers, local councillors and DMD officials from Spain and across the world gathered at the place on As Furnhas beach where Sampedro initially suffered his tragic accident. They met to recall and honour the public campaign he had championed in life, which had significantly accelerated DMD membership, which now has offices worldwide. Among the many speakers Antonio Batista, regional secretary for DMD in Galicia, acknowledged that in terms of achieving the decriminalisation of euthanasia in Spain: 'no ha habido ningún avance en lo legal' (there has been no progress on the legal front). Support in parliament in 2007 from the PSOE Minister of Health, Bernat Soria, for 'una muerte digna' (a dignified death) had been lukewarm and the proposal from Izquierda Unida (United Left Party) to decriminalise medical intervention failed to attract sufficient votes to make any further progress (see www.adn.es/20080112_1268/4). However, if Spain's centre-left politicians seemed reluctant to press a very thorny issue (there being few votes or electoral advantage to be gained), Batista noted that, since the release of Amenábar's film in 2004, public opinion in Spain had moved significantly towards accepting the 'normalización' (normalisation) of euthanasia. And here, as Ascenzo, Almela and Cogollos – mentioned above – confirm, *Mar adentro* played a crucial, mediating role in consolidating public perceptions and understanding of very complex medical, ethical and moral issues. Moreover, as Gordó and

Batista indicate, it helped shift an already receptive and widespread public mood, even more strongly towards the euthanasia option, even though the Sampedro case was fought primarily to win the legal right to assisted suicide.

If *Mar adentro* helped promote the euthanasia cause in Spain and boosted the credibility of lobby groups, such as DMD, it also created a backlash of critical, alternative and opposed positions and voices, religious and non-religious, who disagreed with some or all of a very well-organised, progressive, centre-left discourse which, until recently, dominated the ideological terrain of end of life choices. Among these voices is that of Javier Romañach Cabrero, teacher, information technology specialist, atheist (like Sampedro) and founding Coordinator of the Foro de Vida Independiente (Forum for an Independent Life, se www.forovidaindependiente.org/node/28). This is a loose, Web-based network and pressure group for the disabled (set up in 2001 and now numbering thousands of members) which fights for human dignity, equality of opportunities and autonomous living (i.e. overcoming dependence on one's family) as well as lobbying state support for better pensions, subsidies, access to public buildings, mobility, transport, housing, jobs etc.[21]

In November 2004 Romañach wrote a very long, closely argued and polemical essay called 'Los errores sutiles del caso Ramón Sampedro'.[22] Published in early 2005, it dealt with what he calls 'la losa mediática generada alrededor de Ramón Sampedro' (the media tombstone [i.e. the one-sided media coverage] generated around Ramón Sampedro). It also includes an impressive analysis of *Mar adentro*, from the perspective of a disability activist unhappy at the media appropriation of the film. This deserves a brief comment here since, as another key social intervention, it has had a significant impact on the debates around disability and euthanasia in Spain, hitherto dominated by the DMD-backed 'dignified death' position.[23] It also contains a detailed critique of Amenábar's film, based on what Romañach calls a series of 'errores sutiles' (subtle mistakes) which he claims serve to mislead the public by simplifying and often ignoring the facts. I propose to outline briefly the bare bones of this critique (17 pages in all), leaving it up to the reader to engage further with Romañach's impressive essay, if so desired, on Amenábar's film and Sampedro's other writings.

Romañach is a strong admirer of Amenábar's work as a whole and considers *Mar adentro* as a technically brilliant 'versión personal' (personal treatment) of the Sampedro story, depicted with the director's customary 'sensibilidad y maestría' (sensitivity and mastery). However, for Romañach, the film concentrates on describing a life rather than exploring Sampedro's arguments and thoughts in any depth. It also takes sides and makes no attempt to hide its admiration for Sampedro's crusade against the law, Church and State. Romañach points to a series of important slippages and omissions which might give rise to confusion and misreading.

Firstly, the elision, mentioned earlier, between the concepts of 'assisted suicide' and 'euthanasia'. These terms are found in the dialogue at the beginning of the film and then later. However, for Romañach, Amenábar arguably fails to distinguish clearly between them since euthanasia is usually understood as the deliberate termination of life (by act or omission), on compassionate grounds, of someone who is terminally ill, usually in a medical context. The concept would not normally apply to cases such as Sampedro, who was reasonably healthy and not terminally ill. The impression is given that the terms are more or less equivalent, which is incorrect.[24]

Secondly, Romañach notes a further factual slippage between Ramón's quadriplegia (paralysis in his four main limbs, legs and arms/hands) and Julia's irreversible degenerative disease. For the spectator these conditions are presented as similar and such similarity helps to secure approval for the (male) choice of death as the best option to recover Sampedro's lost dignity. Yet he was not terminally ill, unlike the fictional Julia.

Thirdly, also, quite subtly says Romañach, Amenábar proposes two different kinds of 'end of life' choices in terms of Ramón's apparently courageous decision to opt for suicide, while Julia is portrayed as lacking such 'valor' (courage) since she decides to return to her husband and continue living. For Romañach, Amenábar presents two very different and contrasting evaluations of these solutions, in which Ramón's 'brave' suicide is shown favourably. And, compared to Julia's worsening condition (her vegetative state, due to Parkinson's disease), which is presented as the 'wrong' choice, Ramón's choice of suicide is shown to have no down side or negative consequences.

Fourthly, Romañach is deeply puzzled by the 'absoluto vacío' (huge gap or hole) in the film of the twenty-odd years between Ramón's accident (1968) and his decision to fight his case in the Spanish courts (starting in 1992). As I noted earlier in this chapter, it seems strange that there is there nothing of interest or relevance in Ramón's life worth exploring during these 24 years.

Fifthly and finally, Romañach calls attention to the way in which the case against Sampedro's 'death with dignity' is presented in the film. Leaving aside the rather muted objections from family members such as Ramón's father and brother, the main burden of the case 'for life' is carried by the Jesuit priest, who is also severely disabled, but mobile and able to work. Yet Padre Francisco, as noted earlier, is arguably caricatured as a ranting, raving, mystical cleric, bereft of coherent argument, unlike Ramón, whose equally demagogic defence of individual freedoms clearly wins the moral high ground in the unequal rhetorical battle.

For Romañach the above points suggest that, though Amenábar feigns neutrality, he cleverly leads the spectator towards a predetermined position, favourable to Sampedro's struggle and supportive of assisted suicide. The film is thus one which has 'mucho más mensaje del que parece a primera vista' (far more message than it seems at first sight), and one which seems designed to ensure that the spectator leaves the cinema with a 'visión unica, dirigida e inconsciente' (a single, calculated and implicit vision).

The other Sampedro

As a young, working-class ship's mechanic, Ramón Sampedro revelled in the life of the merchant seaman and travelled the world. He also took advantage of his good looks, success with women, freedom and lack of responsibilities. After his accident in 1968, all this changed. His self-identity as a rather vain, cocky though charismatic charmer lay in tatters. He seems never to have overcome the shock of his physical paralysis and the damage done to his fine body, where much of his self-esteem was invested. From being a traveller, a go-getter and a man of action, he became overnight a mere brain, a functioning consciousness, as if frozen inside a body that was no longer his. Though the chronology and psychological motivation remain unclear, Ramón reacted angrily to his very serious (though not totally catastrophic) loss of mobility. Firstly, he refused to marry his 'novia' (fiancée), even though she wished to go ahead; he then refused rehabilitation, nursing care and therapy; he also rejected the wheelchair and refused to leave his room or get out of bed. In the final days he also rejected his family when he left for the flat in Boiro in order to die, a move arranged for him by Ramona Maneiro and her sister. Though some of these crucial moments and decisions are referenced in *Mar adentro*, but not quite in context, they show a consistent desire for isolation, withdrawal and a rejection of the world, in short, a continuing trauma at his severe loss.

To add to his despair and suffering, following the accident, it seems his doctors told him that he would probably die anyway within a few years; resentment, anger, self-pity and a death wish might appear logical responses to such apparent hopelessness. However, the doctors were seriously mistaken. Sampedro survived not only the first few years but many more, in fact nearly thirty. The realisation that he was not destined to die might well have deepened Ramón's depression and augmented his panic over his new reality as a 'live head' on a broken body. Unfortunately, in *Mar adentro*, we learn little or nothing of this early period spent with his parents, his interaction with the medical profession nor how he coped mentally with his new condition. We know that, after leaving home, he adapted to his new environment in his brother's house in small ways (making little gadgets such as the mouth pen), but he never accepted his paralysis. He loathed his fractured body, felt as if he were entombed in a corpse and saw no value in a life which, for him, was so degraded in quality. Yet, as Romañach informs us, even in the 1970s, many Spaniards with similar spinal breaks at the seventh vertebra were able to regain some degree of functionality with treatment, rehabilitation and physiotherapy. By contrast Sampedro was never prepared to settle for only a percentage of his former mobility. He refused on principle to make any effort whatsoever. For him it was 'all or nothing', an understandable reaction but arguably a youthful, immature, maximalist attitude, consistent with other decisions noted above. He escaped his mental anguish through voracious reading and listening to music, thus developing new skills and sensitivities as a poet, writer and celebrity. He also attracted many women, some of whom fell in love with him. But, as Mateo Gil suggests, once he had achieved his aim of seduction, he rejected his partner, not only because of the pain and anxieties of impossible love (Amenábar and Gil 2004: 9–10). In later years, with his brother's family still refusing to help him commit suicide, Sampedro searched not for a lover or life companion but for an apprentice or assistant, someone who would help him arrange his own death.

Like his powers of seduction, Sampedro's quest for death was arguably his way of coping with and resisting his suffering. It gave his diminished existence a semblance of structure, purpose, meaning and a goal, through which he could feel motivated and in control, 'alive' and 'free'. It provided a taste, however meagre and unsatisfactory, of a male mastery which he had lost. However, the process of scheming, plotting and realising one's death wish is very difficult to accept as a noble, heroic pursuit or an admirable achievement. Indeed, even to regard Sampedro's quest as an affirmation of human freedom might be seen by some as too perverse to be acceptable. This may well be a form of human struggle which shows singleminded determination and strength but it is difficult to present it as an act worthy of emulation. Yet, while it failed to change the law in Spain, Sampedro's assisted suicide and his controversial recorded testament helped transform the public debate over euthanasia, as well as giving DMD a much-enlarged propaganda platform in favour of the 'right to die'. Acutely aware of the power of the television image (following the enormous impact of his appearance on Galician television as the iconic 'helplesss child in a nappy'), through Ramona Maneiro and other friends, Sampedro planned the camera and recording set up and wrote the text for his very own 'martyrdom video'. Conceived with media dissemination in mind, his accusatory testament berated the Spanish authorities for their indifference to his suffering and for having 'embargoed' his body for 30 years. Now it was his moment to fight back, take control of his own body and assert his freedom of choice: a dignified death by assisted suicide, which he had been denied for so long. Paradoxically, in self-negation and suicide (which was neither peaceful nor pain-free), Sampedro found a purpose and a meaning which he never found in his life or in those around him and which made him a national celebrity, though, in my view, not a hero. In life Ramón Sampedro emerges as a complex, contradictory, difficult yet charismatic and endearing character, but also far more enigmatic, dark and conflicted than the wry, avuncular sage we find presented to us in *Mar adentro*. Amenábar tells us only part of this fascinating story and, rather than biography, gives us something approaching hagiography and myth making, seen from the perspective of the 'light' as he puts it (DVD Extras Director's commentary), a metaphor he also uses in relation to *The Others* and *Ágora*. Unfortunately, Amenábar deliberately keeps us in the dark about the other Sampedro(s). His screen version was no doubt conditioned by family sensitivities and script approval, legal issues and debts of gratitude to DMD. Hence, the apologia for euthanasia and the one-sided presentation of Sampedro as a national hero and towering martyr for his cause. But, in the name of rationalism and secularism, which Amenábar has always strenuously defended, why ignore other important facts? Why treat those 24 missing years as something akin to a 'no go area'? Why did Ramón decide to launch his legal campaign only in the early 1990s? Why was Amenábar strangely reluctant to shine a more probing light on these and other dark corners?

Notes

1 This partly explains their strongly supportive attitude towards his quest for death, which is represented in terms of a personal struggle and a defence of individual human rights. See *Mar adentro, Guión cinematográfico de Alejandro Amenábar y Mateo Gil*, Versión de rodaje (Madrid: Ocho y Medio, Colección Espiral, 2004), 7 (henceforth, *Guión*).

2 For my account of Sampedro's life and death I have relied partly on his own published testimony in *Cartas desde el infierno* (1996) as well as on interview material with Amenábar himself, the DMD website (http://personal2.redestb.es/admd/dmdengli.htm) and other oppositional web sources, as well as Spanish national press coverage, including *El País, El Mundo* and *La Vanguardia*.

3 Maneiro's television confession triggered a bitter confrontation between pro-life and pro-choice advocates in Spain, dividing political parties, the Church and the national media along strongly sectarian lines. It also prompted the socialist Minister of Health, Elena Salgado, to accuse Spain's Catholic Church of stoking up public anxiety about the government's alleged intention of 'regularising' euthanasia. Such controversy also coincided with the international promotional campaign behind *Mar adentro*, leading up to the Golden Globes (16 January 2005) and the Oscars (27 February 2005), where Amenábar won Best Foreign Film in both cases. See www.anarosa.telecinco.es/dn_18.htm; www.forumlibertas.com; El Pais.es/sociedad/. See also Ramona Maneiro's account of her personal relationship with Sampedro (ghosted by Xabier de Blanco), *Querido Ramón. Un testimonio de amor*, Temas de Hoy (Madrid: Planeta, 2005).

4 Amenábar was deeply affected by the worsening condition of a very close personal friend who had followed his career, Sonsoles Peña, 35 years old, who was dying of cancer. Her illness functioned as a distressing (counter) point of reference for him during the preparation and production phases of *Mar adentro*. Both talked at length about dying, death and the afterlife. Sonsoles Peña died in 2004. In 2005 Amenábar said of her: ' Ella luchó muchísimo hasta el final, todo lo contrario que Ramón Sampedro. Me dio tiempo a decirle que le dedicaría la película' (She fought till the end, the opposite of Ramón Sampedro. This gave me time to tell her that I

would dedicate the film to her (see Rocío García, 'Triple Apuesta', *El País Semanal*, 1479, at http://maradentro.splinder.com/2005). *Mar adentro* is indeed fondly dedicated to her memory.

5 The name Himenóptero is taken from the second of Amenábar's shorts, of the same name (1992). The production company was set up in 2002–3, once Amenábar had fulfilled his obligations to make three films for José Luis Cuerda and Las Producciones del Escorpión. Alongside the mighty Sogecine, his company was the main Spanish co-producer on *Mar adentro*. So far Himenóptero has supported three further filmmaking projects: a 14–minute short by Oskar Santos, called *El soñador* (The Dreamer, 2005), a period piece concerned with the strange case of a young Spanish nobleman who can sleep up to three days at a time; a full-length feature, the mystery thriller *El mal ajeno* (For the Good of Others, released 2010), again directed by Oskar Santos, his first feature, and starring the Amenábar protégés Eduardo Noriega and Belén Rueda – and of course, Amenábar's own fifth feature *Ágora* (2009).

6 The 'El Viaje Mar adentro' documentary suggests that Amenábar had rather more control over script development than Gil and that his decisions over the balance of content and film structure prevailed. After completion of the script, meetings were set up with the family and also with Ramona Maneiro, to discuss approval and any changes. Amenábar claims their reactions were largely positive (Interview). However, there were some scenes where the fictional Sampedro's behaviour (for example, when he cries out for Manuela in a panic, apparently regretting his obsessive death wish) was deemed uncharacteristic of the real Ramón, who apparently never wavered in his purpose.

7 The paraplegic cleric, Padre Francisco, is a compendium of two real figures: Javier Gafo, a non-disabled Jesuit priest, who wrote an account of his several visits to talk to Ramón in a volume entitled *Eutanasia y ayuda al suicidio* (Bilbao: Desclée de Brouwer, 1999). A specialist in bio-ethics, Gafo died shortly after Sampedro. The other real visitor was Luis de Moya, a disabled priest and Opus Dei member, who saw Ramón in June 1997. It is this visit which Amenábar recreates, or rather caricatures, when the priest tries to persuade Sampedro to drop his campaign for assisted suicide. The problem of negotiating the stairs with a wheelchair in Sampedro's house is also true, as is the use of an intermediary, a novice priest, who carried the messages. His name is Marius Clavell and he claims, contrary to Amenábar's version, that the encounter between Moya and Sampedro was cheerful and respectful (see Marius Clavell, 'A propósito de *Mar adentro*', *La Vanguardia* (19 February 2005, reproduced at www.condignidad.org/Actor-Mar-adentro.html).

8 In reality Sampedro did not enjoy a 'good death'. Rather, after swallowing the poison, he suffered terrible convulsions and a nasty, prolonged and painful death of over 20 minutes. See *El Periódico de Cataluña*

(1 March 1998, 1; see also http://www.elpais.com/articulo/sociedad/ heredera/ Sampedro/envia/ONU/video/muerte/angustiosa/tetraplejicc/ elpepisoc/20030122elpepisoc_2/Tes/.

9 'Nessun dorma' (None Shall Sleep) is an aria taken from the final act cf Puccini's opera *Turandot*. It is performed by Calaf, Il principe ignoto (The unknown prince), who falls in love at first sight with the exquisice but distant Princess Turandot. Calaf faces a life or death test: any man who wishes to wed Turandot must first answer her three riddles. If he fails, he will be beheaded. In the film the aria is sung by the tenor José Manuel Zapata.

10 Almodóvar's treatment of David's disability is a visual feast of positive images, a powerful spectacle in which his partially disabled body achieves huge sporting success, maintains a monstrous sexual appetite (post-phallic via oral sex) but also underpins his commitment to marriage (see Fouz-Hernández and Martínez-Expósito 2007: 108). Such an excessive, self-confident representation of masculinity is light years away from the emasculated, immobile, shrivelled Sampedro, whose body (through lack of any physical exercise) had badly degraded and atrophied over the years. Indeed, in preparing the character of Ramón, Amenábar had to disguise Bardem's impressive physicality, partly through the design of the bed and Bardem's arched posture (achieved with a harness which forced him to pull in his shoulders) and partly through film magic, i.e. the use of digital effects to reduce the size of Bardem's muscular shoulders, arms and legs, as seen in the long shot of Ramón in bed, almost nude, except for a skimpy towel covering his groin, transforming him into a helpless baby in a nappy; see also, Paula Ponga (2004).

11 Bardem's experience recalls the equally exhausting make-up and acting schedule of Eduardo Noriega on *Abre los ojos*. Also his suffering did not stop there since the first scene of *Mar adentro* that Amenábar shot was arguably the hardest and most emotionally draining of the whole film: Ramón's tearful departure from Xuño to the flat in Boiro by the ONCE-sponsored mini-van.

12 Rueda has successfully developed her screen acting career with impressive performances as Laura in *El orfanato* (The Orphanage, Juan Antonio Bayona, 2007) and Pilar Durán in *Savage Grace* (Tom Kalin, 2007). She also played opposite Eduardo Noriega as Isabel in *El mal ajeno* (For the Good of Others, Oskar Santos, 2009), as Julia/Sara in a Guillermo del Toro production, the thriller *Los ojos de Julia* (Julia's eyes, Guillem Morales, 2010); she starred as the Princesa de Eboli in a lavish television version of the same name (150 minutes, Antena 3, 2010) and plays Silvia's mother in Montxo Armendáriz's study of child abuse *No tengas miedo* (Don't Be Afraid, 2011). It is also worth noting that, over the course of his four film features, Amenábar's approach to his actors, their preparation and their performances have evolved radically; indeed, it has

shown a complete transformation. On *Mar adentro*, he was no longer the nervous, obsessive, autocratic taskmaster of *Tesis*, blinded by his own narrow vision of a performance he was determined to impose on his actors (see Fele Martínez's amusing comments on the DVD Extras for *Tesis* on Amenábar's 'teoría del espejo', theory of the mirror). On his fourth film he was far more at ease and relaxed: " I'm more open, I talk to the actors but I don't tell them exactly what I want them to do' (Balfour 2005). In fact, in order to achieve the sort of naturalistic performances that were required for *Mar adentro*, rather than 'drill and kill' in rehearsal, he encouraged his cast to improvise, invent, stumble over and overlap their lines if need be, work out their own moves and gestures, as long as it helped secure naturalness and audience engagement: 'La intención, la mayor proximidad al espectador. Y para ello ... la libertad de los actores ... [que] añadieron cosas para que aquello fuese lo más natural posible' (The intention was to get as close as possible to the spectator. To achieve it ... I gave the actors their head ... they added things so that everything was as natural as possible' (Anon., 'El film más spielbergiano ...', 10 December 2005).

13 Roberto Bodegas, *Condenado a vivir (La historia de Ramón Sampedro)* (Barcelona: DVD Spain General Distributions, 2004: www.dvdspain.net). Accusations of plagiarism have tended to appear mainly in the form of weblogs in Spanish (usually anonymous). See for example: http://foros. elaleph.com/viewtopic.php?p=3656014; http://blogs.periodistadigital. com/ cinedigital.php/2005/12/30/p7392; www.filmaffinity.com/es/ reviews/1/936995.html.

14 Javier Maqua is a film director and scriptwriter, as is Roberto Bodegas, who was also a key figure in the 'tercera vía' (third way) subtrend in Spanish social comedies of the early 1970s. See Jordan and Morgan-Tamosunas 1998: 66–8.

15 However, for Amenábar, the decision to develop and expand Ramón's relationship with the female Catalan lawyer (rather than with Rosa/ Ramona Maneiro) was extremely problematic, given that in real life she was a married woman. In the theatrical release of the film little material remains of the complex subplot involving Julia and her husband Germán, because it was drastically cut during editing, since audiences in test screenings lost interest during these moments. This explains the almost total lack of motivational material preparing Julia's decision to withdraw from her suicide pact with Ramón. This significant lacuna creates narrative confusion. Also Julia's decision to go on living and to return to her husband leads to all manner of motivational complications, given that the spectator is not privy to their conversations and has to assume that some sort of reconciliation has taken place.

16 Amenábar's *Mar adentro* and Bodegas's *Condenado a vivir* arguably deserve a far more elaborate and detailed comparison than can be given here,

especially in terms of their portrayals of the main *dramatis personae* and their approach to the ethical issues around 'dignified death', as well as their respective media: television movie and feature film. The same could also be said of John Badham's *Whose Life Is It Anyway?* (1981), another 'right to die' movie, starring Richard Dreyfus and John Cassavetes, based on a very successful television play and stage hit and used in Amenábar's research phase.

17 Unfortunately, in light of the pro-secessionist Catalan Statute (approved 20 July 2006) and government support for even greater political autonomy in the Basque Country (including the shameful legalisation of ETA/Bildu and its entry into Basque political institutions after the May elections of 2011), the PSOE is likely to achieve its goal of the balkanisation, i.e. dismemberment, of the Spanish state. One also wonders where the pressure came from to legalise, institutionalise and indeed bankroll a wholly unrepentant terrorist organisation like ETA and its political front Bildu/Sortu until 2015. Was this part of a 'road map' to conflict resolution, culminating in a form of 'pay-back' (agreed much earlier) by the Zapatero government for services rendered in March 2004?

18 Very often, when using wide screen, a director will draw audience attention to only one part of the screen, usually off-centre, or may use it to create multiple points of visual interest (as in the accident scene, where a close-up of the young Ramón's face, side-on, is carefully framed against the rocks, beach, cove and the pretty girl, reclining below).

19 On the DVD documentary 'La aventura americana', referring to his USA promotional tour, Amenábar was puzzled to be bracketed in 2004/5 as the author of a 'radical' film such as *Mar adentro*. Feeling rather intimidated and misunderstood, he summed up his annoyance by saying: 'Este año soy rojo, maricón y pro-eutanasia' (This year I'm seen as a communist, a queer and pro-euthanasia).

20 In its opening weekend in Spain, *Mar adentro* took €2 million from 275 screens and nearly €20 million (twice the budget) by August of 2005, a reasonably good performance. However, elsewhere in Europe and in the USA, the situation was very different. In the UK, for example, the film began on 73 screens, but by February 2005 had grossed only £89 507. In the USA it started on 23 screens (taking a derisory $55,681) but by 2 January 2005, the film was playing in only five theatres. Even after the Oscar 'bounce' (which saw the film find a release on 99 screens by early March 2005), this fell away to 15 screens by 15 May. The total overall box-office take in the USA was $2 million approximately. In Italy, by April 2005, this had reached €708,000 box-office, in the Netherlands €362,000, but in the UK a static £89,507. From January through to May 2005 the film was also released in France, Poland, Argentina, Sweden, Germany and Australia, but it was by no means a commercial success anywhere. Moreover, despite the Oscar, the many prizes and much critical

acclaim, Fine Line were arguably facing a financial loss of between $5 and $10 million. However good, the challenge of making a commercial film based on a quadriplegic fighting for the 'right to die' is arguably insurmountable and probably explains such dismal box-office.

21 Romañach came to public prominence, via radio and television, following the release of *Mar adentro* and his appearance on the prime time TV2 chat show *Las Cerezas* (The Cherry Trees), presented by Julia Otero, in March 2005. Three lengthy clips of this long interview are available on YouTube.

22 Romañach's article can be found at any of the following web sites: www.cuentayrazon.org/revista/pdf/135/Num135_009.pdf; http://www.muertedigna.org/textos/euta109.html; http://www.bioeticaweb.com/content/view/ 1272/833/lang,es/;http://www.fluvium.org/textos/cultura/cul209.htm.

23 For example see the website of the journalist and writer Kiko Rosique at www.kikorosique.com, for his articles: 'Reflujo mar adentro' (21 March 2005) and ' A despecho del señor feudal'(5 September 2004); also, see Jerónimo José Martín, 'Una sentimental apología de la eutanasia' at http://aramo.wordpress/com/2007/12/06/mar-adentro/. See also www.magdabandera.com/archives/000460.html.

24 See the paper by David Rodríguez-Arias (2006), where he makes useful distinctions between these concepts.

7

The rage of unreason: *Ágora*

Amenábar's fifth feature film took all of four years to complete, from initial research and scripting (2005–6), casting, pre-production, shoot and post-production (2007–9) to its first showing at the Cannes Film Festival on 17 May 2009. It was by far the most ambitious and challenging of his career as well as a totally unprecedented project in the history of Spanish filmmaking. This was partly because of its budget, enormous even by the much higher standards in the rest of Europe, though it required considerable extra investment in distribution and exhibition. It was also very demanding because of its sheer scale, complexity and long location shoot (15 weeks at the Fort Ricasoli site on the island of Malta, where Wolfgang Petersen's *Troy* (2003) was partly shot and where Ridley Scott built his part-replica of the Colosseum for *Gladiator*). It was also Amenábar's second production spoken in English, after *The Others*, but on a totally different scale, with a large international cast, as well as between seven hundred and a thousand extras and supported by several hundred local craftsmen who built the sets. In generic terms, for the director and his producer, the film also represented a radical break with previous productions. But in other ways it was a continuation of certain key concerns, technically, thematically and ideologically, particularly with regard to Amenábar's on-going critique of Catholicism, this time framed as a more contemporary clash between the culture and values of science and reason and those of religious fundamentalisms.

Who would have thought that after the whispered intimacies and claustrophobic interiors of *The Others* and *Mar adentro*, Amenábar would turn towards the historical epic? This cinematic form has traditionally demanded large-scale sets, eye-popping vistas, authentic period detail, wide-screen action, major battle sequences and above all epic storytelling through memorable, heroic characters. Though a fan since childhood, Amenábar had absolutely no practical experience of this genre and was risking his reputation as Spain's most versatile and innovative young filmmaker by venturing yet again into totally uncharted territory. Moreover, how would he and Fernando Bovaira, his producer, raise the kind of budget to make such a film? Who in Spain would dare to back such a risky, outlandish project, even one undertaken by the country's most celebrated Oscar winner? As things turned out, apart from Malta's changeable weather and minor problems on set, Amenábar claims the principal photography phase for *Ágora* (17 March–27 June 2008) went remarkably smoothly: 'Esta ha sido mi película mas ambiciosa pero también la que mejor he llevado durante el rodaje. Ha sido sobre todo un viaje de exploración al pasado' (This has been my most ambitious film but also the one I've managed best during the shoot. Above all, it has been a voyage of exploration to the past).[1]

In this final chapter I describe the origins of *Ágora*, including some background on the historical underpinnings of its subject matter and its modern inspiration in the work of a world-famous planetary scientist. I also consider in more detail the production, distribution and exhibition phases, given the film's unprecedented scale and cost and the serious difficulties it faced in finding a distributor for the American market. I also explore *Ágora*'s relationship to genre, to the historical epic tradition in filmmaking and argue that in many ways it presents itself as a 'counter-epic', in its subject matter, scripting, narrative outline, character design and film style, while still observing some classic epic features. I also compare the film briefly to other examples of mainstream Hollywood epic filmmaking, in particular to Ridley Scott's *Gladiator* (2000) and Wolfgang Petersen's *Troy* (2003). I also suggest that weaknesses in scripting and character design compromise spectator engagement and thus weaken the film's appeal to mainstream audiences. In terms of thematics and ideological positioning, whilst Amenábar's critique of religious fundamentalisms and the use of violence is welcome and timely, it is somewhat attenuated by a fanciful, reimagined ending, which mixes defeat for the Hellenic enlightenment with the slave Davus' rejection of religious fanaticism.

Martians and Romans

As indicated in an earlier chapter, since he was a student Amenábar
has always been concerned by the social and moral implications
arising from scientific discovery and advances in modern technology.
This can be seen in *Tesis* in its preoccupation with the 'media effects'
of trash television on the unguarded television spectator; it is also
evident in *Abre los ojos*, given César's familiarity with the internet,
his curiosity about cryogenics and the L.E. company and the film's
passing critique of Catholic dogma as superstitious nonsense, whose
promises concerning the afterlife are portrayed as a sham. Strange
as it may seem to us, and very late in the day, Amenábar developed
a profound, indeed obsessive interest in astronomy. This appears
to have had its beginnings while shooting the prologue section of
Mar adentro, in the Seychelles in 2003–4. During this period he
did a considerable amount of star-gazing and thinking about other
civilisations beyond the confines of the Earth. Then in mid-2005,
after returning from Japan and the promotional campaign for *Mar
adentro*, he took a holiday with friends in and around Ibiza. On the
outward journey by ferry to the island, he resumed his star-gazing
activities. This time he focused on the Milky Way, the experience of
which had an enormous impact upon him. In his introductory notes
to the beautifully illustrated, coffee table 'book of the film', Fernando
Bovaira describes this episode as a kind of 'vértigo cósmico'.[2]

Just as he had done with Eduardo Noriega before shooting *Abre
los ojos*, Amenábar also engaged his holiday companions in sessions
of speculation and 'what if' scenarios concerning the existence of
intelligent life beyond Earth. He was surprised by their reactions and
somewhat deflated by their cynicism towards the possible existence of
different alien life forms, given the sheer size of the universe and the
potential number of life-sustaining planets. As it happens, Amenábar
seems to be convinced of the possibility of alien life throughout
the universe. It was these informal, desultory conversations about
martians which appear to have been the crucible for *Ágora*. Shortly
after the holiday, so elated and energised was he that he managed
to inspire Mateo Gil and Fernando Bovaira with his enthusiasm for
astronomy. He then proposed a film project to them based on a historical survey of the world's great astronomers and scientists, beginning
with Albert Einstein and working backwards towards classical times.

In other words, well before it took the form of a historical epic,
Ágora began rather oddly as a potted history of more than two

thousand years of astronomical and scientific discovery, motivated by the proposition that, apart from the great names, there were serious advances in scientific enquiry well before Copernicus, Galileo, Kepler, Newton and Einstein. At least, this is what I deduce from a section of the long and revealing interview with him recorded by Professor Nancy Berthier, conducted in January 2006 and published in 2007 in French, as the coda to a volume of essays on Amenábar's filmmaking (see bibliography). Two-thirds of the way through this conversation, Amenábar disparages his ten wasted years of religious schooling (between the ages of four and 14) and comments on the sort of inspirational subjects which he had been denied. The latter comprised histories of astronomy and philosophy, particularly those of classical and late antiquity, including topics such as the importance of the circle, symmetry and the speed of light, culminating in relativity and the archetypal scientific genius himself, Albert Einstein (Berthier 2007: 210). Amenábar suggested to Berthier that it might be possible to put together (on film) a survey of astronomy 'dans les dernières 2000 ou 2500 années et je crois que ça peut etre passionant' (Berthier 2007: 210) (in the last 2000–2500 years, and I think it could be really exciting). What also lies behind *Ágora* is arguably a nagging resentment at being cheated of a liberal-humanist, science-oriented education, when, in reality, what Amenábar was forced to swallow as gospel at school was 'Le mythe, c'était Jésus, les saints et les miracles' (Berthier 2007: 210) (Myths, including Jesus, the saints and the miracles. This perhaps explains the rather heavy didactic vein in the film and the director's ambition to instil in the spectator of today the sort of fascination for science which he himself was denied at school, and which he somehow managed to rediscover by researching and making *Ágora*. In the Berthier interview it seems clear that the specific filmic form he would have adopted for this project, had it gone ahead, would have been the documentary, where 'on y fait toujours passer une vision personnelle' (Berthier 2007: 207) (where one can still convey a personal viewpoint). Overall, regarding the origins of the film, as Amenábar reminds us: 'Un amigo dice que empecé haciendo una película de marcianos y acabé rodando una de romanos. *Ágora* tiene en los planos lejanos el punto de vista de un marciano mirando por un telescopio' (A friend told me that I began making a film about Martians and ended up shooting one about Romans. In the long shots, *Ágora* adopts the point of view of a Martian looking through a telescope).[3]

Cosmos

'If I could travel back into time, this is the place I would visit, the Library of Alexandria, at its height, two thousand years ago. Here, in an important sense, began the intellectual adventure which has led us into space. All the knowledge of the ancient world was once within these marble walls ... There was also a great woman, her name was Hypatia, she was a mathematician and astronomer, the last light of the library, whose martyrdom was bound up with the destruction of this place, seven centuries after it was founded' (Carl Sagan, *Cosmos: A Personal Voyage*, voiceover commentary, episode 1, 1980).[4]

The main source of Amenábar's fascination for astronomy and the study of extra-terrestrial life is undoubtedly the figure of Carl Sagan, the planetary scientist and former director of NASA's SETI programme (Search for Extra-Terrestrial Intelligence) in the 1970s and 1980s.[5] Of course, Sagan is known principally for his astonishingly popular and influential television series *Cosmos*, released at the beginning of the 1980s which dazzled and captivated millions of people across the world, most of whom also bought the book of the series.

Who can forget the beautifully slow, lilting, deep-toned, delivery of Sagan's commentary in the PBS TV television series which perhaps more than any other popularisation of astronomy and the scientific method defined television science programmes in the 1980s? Sold to over sixty countries, the series was seen by well over five hundred million people. Sagan (born 1932, died 1996) also triggered a massive, global interest, even a passion, for the study of the stars, in a period still shaped by the Cold War and the gradual unravelling of the Soviet empire. His book of the series, *Cosmos* (1980, reissued in 2002, by Random House), sold more copies than any other English-language science book in the history of the genre up to that point, over two million. This figure was exceeded a few years later only by the astonishing ten million copies sold worldwide of Stephen Hawking's book *A Brief History of Time* (1988), which is the current benchmark for publishers in this sector of the market.[6]

When Amenábar's proposed documentary history of astronomy proved impractical, he searched for other ways of dramatising the same concerns. His extensive research and background reading in the field of classical science provided him with a promising alternative. Having managed to convey his anxieties about the notions of the 'good death' (euthanasia) and individual 'freedom of choice' through the figure of Ramón Sampedro in *Mar adentro*, he found another very powerful symbol of science, rationality and secular martyrdom in the almost forgotten figure of Hypatia of Alexandria. Carl Sagan had introduced Hypatia in the first episode of his *Cosmos* series and had examined her life and ideas in more detail in the final episode, number 13. Amenábar clearly had in mind Sagan's supreme example as a persuasive populariser and communicator when he said in interview: 'además tengo un afán por comunicarme y traducir las lecciones de Sagan a un film, como quise hacer con los poemas de Ramón Sampedro' (besides, I have an ambition to communicate and translate Sagan's lessons into a film, just as I sought to do with Ramón Sampedro's poems).[7]

Alongside his impeccable credentials as a world-class planetary scientist and with well over three hundred papers to his credit, Sagan's version of the history of science in classical antiquity is both elegant and extremely persuasive. In *Cosmos*, in both the book and television series, his view of Hypatia, while flawless in relation to scientific matters, was arguably somewhat speculative in certain historical areas. This was perhaps understandable given the threatening Cold War context of the early 1980s, where Sagan mobilised the figure and the fate of Hypatia as an allegory of intellectual and global destruction. Noting the awesome beauty of the planet, and the fragility of human life and civilisation, via space-based satellite images, Sagan warned of just how easily this priceless earthly treasure could succumb to the uncontrollable forces of rage, ignorance and irrationality. Sagan regarded Hypatia as the culmination of Hellenic scientific rationalism, indeed she was cast as the 'last scientist' in a world of growing dogma, intolerance and violence; in his view, her murder, perpetrated by religious fanatics, transformed her into a martyr for science. This martyrdom thesis was not new rather it followed a tradition which can be traced back to Edward Gibbon's monumental, eighteenth-century study, originally published in six volumes, *The History of the Decline and Fall of the Roman Empire* (1776–89). Here Gibbon argued that Hypatia's violent death was a symbol of how early Christianity was the prime source and likely cause of the downfall of classical learning and ancient civilisation. And, like Sagan, Gibbon also wove together as almost co-terminous the murder of Hypatia and the destruction of the Great Library of Alexandria, by another Christian militia. These events, if creatively intertwined, provide the basis for a powerful parable which suggests a quasi-apocalyptic outcome when we allow religious dogma and its fanatical adherents to challenge and usurp the power of reason.[8]

In historical terms, however, neither the above martyrdom thesis nor the destruction of the Great Library of Alexandria are supported by solid, empirical evidence. In fact, in Amenábar's book of the film, mentioned above, the accompanying text concedes that, by the time Hypatia was alive, the Great Library no longer existed, having been partially (perhaps accidentally) destroyed by fire by Julius Caesar's soldiers in 48 BC (Amenábar et al. 2009: 108 and 114). The library also suffered a long history of decline and degradation, so that by AD 350–60, when Hypatia was probably born, virtually nothing was left standing above ground (though Sagan does mention some linked underground cellars and store rooms in the first television episode of *Cosmos*). However, in his book (and more importantly in the feature film), Amenábar draws our attention to another library, one which Gibbon also happens to mention in his account. This is the library of the Serapeum, the main pagan temple in Alexandria dedicated to the worship of the ancient Egyptian god Serapis. However, it seems that few classical accounts which deal with the sacking and burning of the Serapeum appear to mention the existence of books or a library housed in the temple.[9] Also, if we consider the chronological record, as rendered in Amenábar's film, the library is ransacked and destroyed by the Christian mob before Hypatia is murdered, but in Sagan's television account these two events are in fact temporally reversed. Indeed, in his film, Amenábar is reluctant to clarify these points of historical fact, preferring to conflate the two libraries into one. This helps him perpetuate not only the mythic story of the destruction of the Great Library by religious fanatics: the loss of this symbol of classical learning is revived in *Ágora* as the smaller, 'daughter' library, housed in the Serapeum (a library which may or may not have existed). Amenábar also recycles a further conceit, advocated by Gibbon that Christian fundamentalism was the direct causal agent behind a catastrophic, epochal shift to the intellectual Dark Ages, following Hypatia's gruesome death. But who was Hypatia?

The myth of Hypatia

With *Mar adentro*, his first serious attempt at the bio-pic, Amenábar had at his disposal a wealth of background material and personal information, with which to fashion a reasonably coherent narrative and a series of convincing performances, based on authentic, real-life people. These materials comprised both primary and secondary sources, including books and writings from Ramón Sampedro himself, his own suicide video and several television appearances, as well as accounts from surviving family members and relatives, lawyers, lover, friends etc., not to mention a television movie made by TVG (Televisión de Galicia), all of which helped to inform and shape Amenábar's filmic treatment. Moreover, through television and radio news coverage, Spanish audiences were already well aware of most of the details of this very high profile, controversial case, and thus in a position to evaluate more soberly the fictional portrait of an already established media 'celebrity'. As for his previous trilogy of horror features, these were primarily genre films, a mix of thriller, sci-fi and period ghost story, i.e. works of the imagination, which did not require any special scholarly expertise or acknowledgement of known facts.

In the case of *Ágora* the situation was completely different. Our (and Amenábar's) access to the life and times of Hypatia of Alexandria have been shaped by a significant fictional legacy in poetry, plays, essays and historical novels. The problem is that remarkably little is actually known about Hypatia herself. Literature, fantasy, wishful thinking and political agendas have flooded in to fill the vacuum in the historical record. Also, until recently, there were very few reliable scholarly treatments or biographical accounts of her life and works, such as that of Maria Dzielska, the Polish author of a major biography of Hypatia, first published in 1995.[10] Moreover, we have no idea what she looked like since there are no surviving portraits of her which might provide an approximate likeness. Widely repeated claims for her great beauty, modesty and virginity are therefore difficult to corroborate (Raphael's famous portrait of 1509, for example, is pure invention). Also we have no idea when she was born. Her birth date is often given as AD 370, but more reliable scholarly accounts, such as Dzielska's, suggest AD 350–55. This would make her 60–65 when she was murdered in March 415. Also on the key matter of her death, Dzielska's thesis is that Hypatia was certainly murdered by Christian fanatics, but not primarily for her scientific or pagan beliefs. Rather, her terribly cruel and ritualised assassination (bludgeoned and flayed with broken roof tiles, with her body dismembered and burnt) was the result of her being falsely accused of sorcery by Cyril, the Coptic (i.e. Egyptian) Christian Bishop of Alexandria (Dzielska 1995: 105).

Hypatia was an aristocrat, born into the highest echelons of the academic and cultural elites of Alexandria. She was also the only daughter of Theon, a philosopher and mathematician, the last director of the city's acclaimed Museion (Museum). She was taught the basics of maths, geometry and philosophy by her father and quickly became his closest collaborator as well as his editor. She also developed a reputation in her own right as an acclaimed scholar and teacher, even setting up and running her own school. Hypatia was also an inventor, who helped invent the hydrometer and perhaps with her father developed or refined the astrolabe. Sadly, she has left no primary writings of her own and what we do know of her scholarship, in her own time, is derived from a few surviving classical sources, which comment on her life and career in fourth- and fifth-century Alexandria.[11]

Following Hellenic scholarly traditions, Hypatia's writings largely took the form of commentaries on other, older works of Greek mathematics, conics and astronomy.[12] Unfortunately, none of these has survived. As a teacher Hypatia would have taught in the Greek language; but rather than meet her students in a school or library (such as in the Serapeum, as depicted in *Ágora*) she most likely taught at home. Such was her ability and dedication, it seems, that her school attracted elite students from across the whole of the Eastern Roman empire. Among her pupils were Synesius, who became the Christian Bishop of Ptolemais in Cyrene. His 159 letters constitute a crucial source of information for the little that is known about Hypatia.[13] In the film Orestes is also shown as a pupil, but this was not the case and appears to be dramatic licence on Amenábar's part, though, later, he did become the Roman Prefect of Alexandria and one of Hypatia's closest friends. She was also inspired by the ideas of Plato and Plotinus, hence the so-called 'neo-platonism' of her worldview, which represented a revival of Plato's ideas on essential, pre-existing 'forms', and a commitment to reason, seen as able to reveal order in the universe.[14] So it is historically inaccurate and perhaps even a distortion to regard Hypatia as a pioneering atheist or secularist given her 'neo-platonist', monotheistic outlook. The question arises if Hypatia was so widely admired and revered in Alexandrian intellectual circles, even among cultured and learned Christians (such as her documented admirer Synesius), why was she murdered?

The answer seems to lie not so much in her alleged paganism or secularism, her dedication to rational thought or her beliefs in the scientific method of questioning and testing evidence. This is what

Amenábar's film would have us believe. Rather, it probably lies in the context of the period in which she lived, one of extremely volatile, violent and sectarian politics between Church and State as well as power struggles between opposed Christian factions in the city of Alexandria. This was a period in which increasingly powerful Christian bishops jostled and challenged their co-religionists as well as their civilian rivals for supreme power and control of the city.

Dzielska covers this process, noting a campaign of intimidation and violence against paganism (a mix of Graeco-Hellenic and Egyptian beliefs) strongly supported and encouraged by the Christian Bishop Theophilus of Alexandria (and approved by Emperor Theodosius). This anti-pagan tide led to the destruction and burning of the Serapeum in 391. After the death of Theophilus, in 412, power was passed directly to his young nephew Cyril, who sought to extend the influence of his office and ideology into civil society by encroaching on the powers of the new Civil Governor or Prefect, Orestes (Dzielska 1995: 75–82). Driven by the principle of 'purity' of the faith and what appears to be an increasingly sectarian, expansionist agenda, Cyril initiated pogroms against the Jews and their temples. Governor Orestes complained to Rome about these violent disturbances and sought permission to repress such bad behaviour, but failed to gain imperial support.

Dzielska confirms that the historical Hypatia was a close friend and ally of Orestes and, like him, committed to the maintenance of the old, Roman-based, civil order. Sadly, she seems to have been caught up in a vicious turf war between two opposed factions. Her influence over Orestes and the civil authorities was seen by her Christian enemies not only as dangerous but also as a serious obstacle to any political accommodation between Bishop Cyril and the Prefect. As a result, to weaken and eventually eliminate her, Cyril launched a campaign of slander and intimidation against Hypatia, accusing her of witchcraft and sorcery (Dzielska 1995: 105). Also it is worth noting that Orestes was badly injured during a bout of mob violence, perpetrated by fanatical Nitrian monks, loyal to Cyril. Orestes' soldiers arrested the stone-throwing monk (called Ammonius in the film, but Hierax elsewhere); the culprit died later under torture. Unable to retaliate directly against the Civil Governor, because of his increased security, the above-mentioned grouping of radical monks, led by a certain Peter the 'reader' (and perhaps with the connivance of Bishop Cyril, though this is not fully authenticated), found a softer target in Hypatia, on whom to wreak their revenge for the loss of their tortured comrade. Her death thus appears to be a 'tit for tat', revenge killing, perhaps not unusual for the times. The point is, however, that Hypatia was probably murdered not simply for her ideas, learning and scientific knowledge (which may or may not have threatened the radical Christian worldview). Her death, in March 415, appears to have been motivated by misogyny and deep political tensions, enmities and power struggles between Bishop Cyril and the Prefect Orestes. In other words her murder had less to do with being a martyr for learning or science; rather she was the unfortunate, innocent, female victim and scapegoat for male political and religious rivalries. In the end Orestes fled Alexandria shortly after. Meanwhile, Cyril, who was an academic and scholar and lived another 30 years, became a greatly admired figure in the history of the early Christian Church and, as Sagan pointedly reminds us, was finally canonised as a saint (a sarcastic footnote which Amenábar recycles in his final intertitle).

Ágora: caught between boom and bust

Spain is the fifth largest economy in Europe. Between 2000 and 2007 approximately, low and negative interest rates among the 16 'euro zone' member countries were translated into a regional economic boom of epic proportions. Benefiting from these seven years of plenty, Spain's larger public and private media companies saw their profits rocket, mainly owing to the impact of rising advertising revenues. As a result of this bonanza, the 5 per cent of yearly turnover, which public and private television operators were obliged by law to invest in film production, also rose significantly. This meant that the state operator TVE (Televisión Española), as well as private companies such as Telecinco, Antena 3 and Prisa-owned Sogecable spent overall between €130 and €150 milllion per year on filmmaking for television and theatrical release.[15] Among their film-related activities, public and private television companies became engaged mainly in the purchase of screening rights for films and co-pro deals with local 'independent producers' as well as international partners. With average film budgets in Spain costing between €2 to €2.5 million, these television 'majors' were also well enough capitalised to be able to invest much larger sums in riskier but more profitable ventures.[16] Interviewed in mid-2009, Ghislain Barrois, CEO of Telecinco Cinema, reiterated that the company's main aim was to 'recoup the investment. We're not an NGO and we don't produce films out of the goodness of our hearts'. The enormous success of Telecinco as film financier and producer in the last decade, according to Barrois, was simply 'because we never lose sight of economic performance', making films 'that combine impeccable technical and artistic brilliance with unmistakeable popular appeal'.[17] In 2007, according to Barrois, Telecinco had a problem: they had accumulated 'a huge, colossal budget, but we had no [film] projects'; and it is 'strong projects', as Barrois calls them, on which the company has depended for its filmmaking success. He also regarded Amenábar's *Ágora* as a prime example of a 'strong project', which in its time was a response to the company's problem of excess revenues, for which it sought viable projects in which to invest.

During the first decade of the new millennium, one of the most attractive and potentially lucrative subgenres for Spain's bigger television companies was the historical film and the period drama, often made for small-screen as well as theatrical release. For example, Antena 3 invested €10 million into the €14 million budget assigned to *Los Borgia* (Antonio Hernández, 2006). Telecinco also supplied €23 of the €28 million spend on the blockbuster period action/adventure *Alatriste* (Agustín Díaz Yanes, 2006). It also provided €13 million of the €18 million budget for the acclaimed *El laberinto del Fauno* (Pan's Labyrinth, Guillermo del Toro, 2007). Of course, the policy of using much bigger budgets to seek better returns on investments was no guarantee of success. For example, though Part One of Steven Soderberg's 'Che Guevara' bio-pic, *Che: El Argentino* (2008), made €6.8 million in Spain, this two-part international co-production (Spain, France, USA), financed by Telecinco (with a €30 million budget for the two films) flopped internationally, and earned a mere $5 million in America (source imdb.com). By contrast, *Los Borgia*, *El laberinto del Fauno* and *Alatriste* all came close to recouping their costs and in the case of del Toro's Civil War, gothic fantasy-realist hybrid, made significant profits (against a €14 million budget, the film achieved a €55 million worldwide take – source: boxofficemojo.com). In short, before Amenábar's *Ágora* came on the scene, television companies like Telecinco were already operating according to the principles of the 'high risk–high profit', blockbuster business model. From 2008 of course, the situation changed radically, when the American sub-prime property scandal and the banking crisis (starting in September with Lehman Bros) undermined business confidence worldwide; the impact of the global recession totally transformed the economic and financial environment in which the television companies operated as film producers.

It is against this background, specifically the more benign economic conditions of 2006–7, that we need to locate the green-lighting of Amenábar's *Ágora* by Telecinco Cinema in 2007. The fact is that Fernando Bovaira appeared at the right time in the right place, in search of finance for a hugely ambitious, large-scale, 'peplum' project. Telecinco had the funds and saw promising commercial potential as well as artistic seriousness and quality in Amenábar's toga epic. Needless to say, had Bovaira, tried to raise such big-budget finance in 2008 or after, the attempt would almost certainly have failed. Of course the effects of the 'bust' which followed the worldwide 'boom' had enormous repercussions on the commercial prospects and screen career of *Ágora*, which I outline shortly. But first we need to understand just how the most expensive film in Spanish film history came to be made.

During the latter half of 2007 negotiations were well under way between NBC Universal and Telecinco Cinema, the two dominant co-pro partners involved initially in the financing of the film. Reliable figures are difficult to access for reasons of business secrecy, but we know that NBC Universal was the bigger investor of the two players, probably prepared to finance 50–60 per cent of the budget, with Telecinco Cinema likely to provide the rest. Also it is worth recalling that in 1998/9 Universal Pictures, alongside Dream Works SKG, had part-financed and shared the risk on the very film which resurrected the historical (Roman) epic as a viable commercial proposition, by backing *Gladiator* (Ridley Scott, 2000). However, in the case of *Ágora*, there appear to have been significant differences of opinion between the two co-pro partners, over issues of risk sharing, on both sides. Again, details and figures are unfortunately very sketchy here, for reasons mentioned above. In essence Telecinco Cinema became increasingly unhappy with the way in which NBC Universal sought to hedge its own degree of exposure by loading costs and additional risk on to the Spanish junior partner. At the same time, and recalling his very stressful experience with Hollywood in 2000–1 when shooting his first English-spoken, international co-pro *The Others*, Amenábar was understandably concerned at the prospect of having to concede a significant degree of personal control and oversight in many key creative areas. These would probably have included script revisions choice of acting talent, crew appointments, production design equipment (including CGI), studio space, overseas locations and aspects of post-production. In the end, rather than commit to a costly and problematic Hollywood co-pro, Telecinco Cinema decided to 'go it alone' and provide the lion's share of the budget itself, while placing financial and creative control fully in Spanish hands. This decision to 'renationalise' the project, in effect, was probably taken in August–September 2007, after Amenábar and Bovaira had pitched the film in person to Paulo Vasile, CEO of the parent company Telecinco España (a branch of the Italian media and entertainment combine Mediaset, owned by Silvio Berlusconi).

In his presentation to Vasile it seems that Bovaira provided Telecinco Cinema with a series of projections and financial assumptions: on the basis of vaguely comparable, big-budget, domestic releases in the Spanish market (such as Díaz Yanes's *Alatriste* in 2006), Bovaira estimated domestic box-office returns for *Ágora* at €15 million, while suggesting that foreign earnings could reach upwards of $100 million (with the example of *The Others* clearly in mind). This would leave the producers with around €30 million of profit to share between them. Of course, to ensure that such estimates were convertible into real numbers, it would be absolutely essential to sell and market the product successfully in the USA and guarantee a wide-ranging release of between one and two thousand screens, at least.[18]

Following its withdrawal from the NBC Universal deal,[19] the financial options facing Telecinco and its film division could be set out as follows. The company could in theory spend €50 million of its own money on ten to twenty small budget, local projects of between €2 and €3 million each. However, this would be tantamount to commercial hara-kiri, since at least 90 per cent of such products would make no money at all domestically, either in the theatres or in ancillary markets and only one, possibly two, might cover costs or realise a profit. The more attractive and sensible alternative would be to invest in a high-cost, high-risk, but potentially high-return 'super producción', where – if all went to plan, as outlined above – Telecinco and its partners might just recoup their costs and make a tidy profit. In the end, as principal investor, Vasile plumped for the more high-risk, though more rational, option. And if the down side of this decision for Amenábar and Bovaira was a significantly reduced budget (re-set at €50 million), the up side was that creative control remained largely in the hands of the director.

In the end *Ágora* was financed not through an international co-pro deal but by four Spanish production companies, including one television 'major'. These were Amenábar's own production platform, Himenóptero, as well as the new Mod Producciones, created by Fernando Bovaira (who also produced *Abre los ojos*, *The Others* and *Mar adentro*), Telecinco Cinema (formerly Estudios Picasso) led by Ghislain Barrois and administered by Alvaro Agustín and Jaime Ortiz Artiñano, and finally Canal Plus España, which is part of the PRISA group. The official, €50 million budget for *Ágora* was split four ways, as follows. The main investor was Telecinco Cinema, which provided 88 per cent of the finance (€44 million); the remaining 12 per cent was covered by the other three small companies, with Canal Plus España/Sogecable investing a modest €2 to €3 million and the other two partners (Amenábar and Bovaira) each adding a similar amount. However, it is worth pointing out that the declared working budget of €50 million was significantly below the hugely ambitious sum initially envisaged by Amenábar and Bovaira for *Ágora*. Though not officially disclosed, this was at least €70 million, if not rather more, probably nearer €80 million (Interview 2010; also confirmed by Amenábar himself in the DVD Director's Commentary). And while relatively modest by Hollywood standards, for a big-budget, 'sword and sandals' historical epic, made in Europe, such an amount would have been totally unprecedented. Moreover, had the negotiations among the initial players involved in the project prospered (i.e. between Bovaira, NBC Universal and Telecinco Cinema), Amenábar might well have ended up making the most expensive international co-pro in European film history (way above the $50.3 million for *Asterix and Obelisk. Mission Cleopatra* (Alain Chabat, 2002), France's most expensive and successful blockbuster to date (source: boxofficemojo.com).

Ágoraphobia: reception and the elusive US distributor

As suggested above, if Telecinco was going to recoup its investment in *Ágora* (i.e. including the so-called 'negative' investment involved in making the actual film, plus a major financial outlay on prints, publicity and marketing in Spain), then the film would need to yield between €100 and €150 million worldwide. Such a return would depend crucially on a successful, large-scale release in the American market and many other foreign territories, as well as good business in ancillary markets (where most Hollywood films tend to cover most of their costs and make profits). An obvious precedent for this kind of release can be found in the distribution/exhibition schedule which Miramax helped orchestrate in 2001 for Amenábar's *The Others*, which enjoyed such enormous critical and commercial success worldwide. This is almost certainly the precedent Bovaira would have used to convince Telecinco of *Ágora*'s commercial potential, while keeping very quiet about the dismal failure of *Mar adentro* to make any headway whatsoever in the American market. Had Telecinco Cinema looked more closely at this negative commercial example, Barrois might have hesitated before investing in another challenging 'quality' project, costing five times more, with doubtful commercial prospects abroad.

In reality, the key stumbling block for the production was the quest for a distributor prepared to sell *Ágora* in the USA. The search was difficult, indeed so fraught, that finding a backer was finally put into the hands of a sales agent, Cinetic Media. The process began in late 2008, when Telecinco executives attended the AFM sales convention (American Film Market), in November, where they conducted exploratory enquiries concerning a US release for the film (Interview 2010). A mere two months after the collapse of Lehman Bros, the general climate among American buyers was one of deepening caution and retrenchment, driven by much lower distribution budgets and a 'flight' from foreign, independent pictures. This attitude was especially prevalent towards a high brow, expensive, European, historical epic, such as *Ágora*, which was regarded uniformly as a definite 'hard sell' in the US market, save perhaps for certain niche art cinemas and small, specialist circuits (Interview 2010). Any hope of a large-scale commercial release in the USA seemed unlikely, even then.

Reception at Cannes

Rather than follow the lead of *The Others* and open at Venice in September, *Ágora* made its first public appearance at the Cannes Film Festival on Sunday 17 May 2009. Cannes was the world's most famous and influential film showcase, where *Ágora*'s producers needed to make a major impact on buyers and critics. Needless to say, already aware of the film's lack of appeal in the American market, Amenábar, Bovaira and Telecinco were under serious pressure to demonstrate festival momentum and success. *Ágora* was shown twice at Cannes, once for the press in the morning and again in the evening for a public audience. And though formally part of the official programme, the film was not in competition for the legendary Palme D'Or (unlike Almodóvar's *Los abrazos rotos* (Broken Embraces, 2009) and Isabel Coixet's *Mapa de los sonidos de Tokio* (Map of the Sounds of Tokyo, 2009)). The version of the film supplied by Amenábar was long, comprising a rough cut of approximately 2 hours 21 minutes, which had been hurriedly prepared and still required some editing and polishing. Amenábar was also supported by a small team of key figures connected with the picture, including his producer Bovaira and a sprinkling of the younger actors such as Rachel Weisz, Max Minghella and Oscar Isaac. Perhaps most importantly, the chief executive of Telecinco, Paulo Vasile, also appeared in person, doubly aware of the need to promote Spain's most expensive film as vigorously as possible. In interview, playing up the commercial value of Amenábar's auteurist credentials and his apparent ability to transform genre pictures into works of art, Vasile stated: 'de los autores de cine actuales, Amenábar es un director capaz de hacer todas sus películas diferentes y que todas ellas se hayan convertido en obras de arte en sus respectivos géneros' (among current filmmakers, Amenábar manages to make a different film every time, with all of them becoming works of art in their respective genres). For his own part Amenábar was genuinely grateful to Vasile for backing the film as the main investor and thereby guaranteeing his directorial freedom, focusing on 'el hecho de que Telecinco asumiera la financiación unilateralmente … lo que me ha dado el grado de libertad necesario para poder realizar esta película' (the fact that Telecinco took on the financing of the film by itself … gave me the degree of freedom I needed to make this picture).[20]

In broad terms public reactions to the two Sunday screenings of *Ágora* (from the buyers, press critics and more general audiences) were very positive, with the film evoking generous applause and even a short standing ovation. However, early critical notices were decidedly more mixed. While most critics praised *Ágora*'s superlative production values (in terms of sets, decor, costumes, historical detail, modest and well-integrated CGI, Rachel Weisz's performance etc.) and its daring attitude towards a very controversial subject, they also broadly agreed that the final results were not quite equal to Amenábar's powerful ambition. More specifically, a number of critics were rather concerned by the density of the subject matter, the overlong running time, the excessive didacticism of the script, the lack of emotional and dramatic tension from the film narrative and the critique of religious intolerance and fanaticism, which seemed unduly focused upon Christian violence and sectarianism.

Among Spanish critics, in a filmed report from Cannes, shot by his editor Borja Hermoso on his mobile phone, immediately after the morning screening, the principal film critic of *El País*, Carlos Boyero, summed up his first impressions. While he needed more time to digest and reflect upon the picture, he declared that 'Amenábar se ha arriesgado como siempre ... y se ha metido en un follón importante' (as ever Amenábar has taken a risk ... and got himself into hot water). Despite its many positive features, Boyero observed that 'no es una película que me conmueve ... hay cosas que me fallan ... los actores me fallan ... me molesta el uso de la música continuo', adding 'no es esa obra maestra que yo esperaba' (it is not a film which moves me ... some things do not work ... the actors do not come across well ... I don't like the continuous soundtrack ... it is not the masterpiece I was expecting).[21] In his much longer written review, Boyero stated: 'estoy deseando que me atrape la emoción pero ésta no llega. No consigo meterme dentro de una historia con tantas cosas admirables, condición indispensable que exijo al gran cine' (I am still waiting to be swept away by emotion, but it doesn't happen. I cannot seem to immerse myself in a story which has so many admirable qualities, something which is a prerequisite for great cinema).[22] In similar territory, Luis Martínez, special correspondent in Cannes for *El Mundo*, complained that, where there should have been drama and tension, the spectator was kept in a permanent state of 'anticlimax'. Moreover, 'Por primera vez en la filmografía de Amenábar, la historia no avanza ... la narrativa está detenida en un extraño empeño por impartir una larga clase de historia de la ciencia ... El resultado es mucha astronomía y poca emoción' (For the first time in Amenábar's filmmaking, the story does not move forward ... the narrative is stalled by a strange insistence on delivering a long class on the history of science ... The result is lots of astronomy but little emotion').[23]

By contrast, in his widely read film blog *ABC* film critic Oti Rodríguez Marchante found greatness and much contemporary relevance in a film which managed successfully to blend the large with the small scale: 'Ágora es un peliculón, en todos los sentidos. Es indescriptible el modo que tiene Amenábar de ajustar lo grande y lo pequeño. Gran película, y tan de hoy que asusta' (*Ágora* is a great film, in all senses. It is beyond words the way in which Amenábar reconciles the large and the small scale. A great picture and so contemporary that it's scary).[24]

Among Anglo-American critics, such as Todd McCarthy at *Variety* and Mike Goodridge at *Screen Daily*, opinions were supportive in many areas but also puzzled and divided in others. While fully acknowledging positive aspects, such as its spectacular visuals, great production values, well-choreographed action scenes and intellectual seriousness, McCarthy was concerned by 'a certain heaviness of style and lack of emotional pulse', which 'could pose problems for mass audience acceptance, at least in the US'.[25] On similar ground Goodridge argued that the film 'ultimately fails to hang together narratively and does not engage on the same grand emotional level as the sword and sandal epics of old – *Quo Vadis? Ben Hur* et al. – which it is clearly trying to re-invent'.[26]

The elusive American distributor

This mixed critical reception following Cannes, while largely positive, failed to raise the profile of *Ágora* as a mainstream, commercial proposition for mass audiences. But this was not the only reason why the film did not appeal to American and foreign distributors. The main drawback for buyers at this stage, I believe, was the excessively high price the producers were demanding, one commensurate with the film's €50 million budget, a strategy which was arguably at odds with economic conditions and audience tastes. Not surprisingly, despite a good festival showing at Cannes, the film failed to attract any viable interest from distributors willing to support a US release. This was a disappointment and major setback and forced Amenábar and Bovaira to calculate how they could recut the film into a more attractive product for American and foreign markets. However, at this stage (mid-2009) there seems to have been no pressure from Telecinco to do so. This initiative came from Amenábar himself, in response to festival feedback and the mixed reviews. The film was recut in the summer of 2009, shortened by excising 15 to 16 minutes of exposition and character background. This surgery was performed in anticipation of a planned screening at the Toronto International Film Festival in early September 2009, where American distributors would be invited once again to consider buying a shorter, smoother, more accessible version. The recut *Ágora*, at 126 minutes, was screened twice at Toronto, in the Gala Presentations section, alongside another 16 films including the Darwin bio-pic *Creation* (John Amiel, 2009), *Io Don Giovanni* (Carlos Saura, 2009) and *The Imaginarium of Dr Parnassus*

(Terry Gilliam, 2009).[27] However, once again, it failed to attract any significant interest from the Americans. As Todd Brown put it in his review, 'the film embraces a blend of high cost and high concept that will make it a very hard sell in the multiplex. Basically, Amenábar's backers are likely to lose their collective shirt on this film'.[28]

Telecinco and the local Spanish distributor for *Ágora*, Hispano Fox Film, were only too aware of the financial perils ahead if a successful American release failed to materialise. They had one more chance to find a US distributor, i.e. the film's domestic release. They had to demonstrate to American buyers that *Ágora* could operate as a strong, commercially viable product in its home market, above all one which appealed to mainstream audiences. If it was successful at home, American distributors might just be persuaded to give the film a second look. In terms of the domestic release, Spaniards were already well primed by a series of trailers, an early teaser trailer shown on the Web in February 2009 and two more in theatres, with the website for *Ágora* fully updated in August 2009 (www.agoralapelicula.com). In fact Telecinco and Fox embarked on the biggest and most expensive film promotional campaign ever undertaken in Spain, a marketing 'blitzkrieg', far outstripping the very successful advertising package behind *Alatriste* in 2006.[29] They deployed their considerable media assets to create mass public interest and anticipation in a national film 'event', while repeating the marketing model they had used with *Alatriste*. This time, for example, they introduced a 'countdown' device begun on Telecinco two weeks before the première, plus a logo of the lighthouse of Alexandria in a corner of the television screen. The campaign culminated in a gargantuan pre-release screening on 6 October at the Kinepolis multiplex in Madrid, where over four thousand specially invited guests (including a cohort of PSOE politicians) were able to watch the film simultaneously on nine screens.

Released in Spain on Friday 9 October, with a massive 476 copies, in its first four days *Ágora* attracted €7 million at the box-office, the best opening weekend in 2009, even outstripping Hollywood fare such as *Up* (2009) and *Ice Age: Dawn of the Dinosaurs* (which made €5.3 million).[30] Within four weeks the film had grossed €16.7 millions and by mid-January 2010 nearly €21 million, attracting 3.38 million spectators (source: mcu.es). It was also well received critically, with 13 Goya nominations and 7 awards; these were mainly in the technical categories but also included that of Best Original Script. Overall, *Ágora*'s domestic release was a major success financially, though this was achieved only by orchestrating a massive media campaign in order to create public awareness for the film. Yet box-office figures were still not as good as those for *The Others*, though significantly higher than Bovaira's projected take of €15 millions, indicated earlier. What is not clear at this stage is the precise cost of the colossal marketing campaign behind the film, but it is likely to have been well in excess of the €2 million spent on marketing *Alatriste* in 2006. However, despite excellent box-office in Spain, foreign buyers still appeared hesitant to pick up *Ágora*, even though serious enquiries had been received from Fox and Sony.[31] Uncannily, the film seemed to be repeating the same release profile as *Alatriste* which, after a very successful national campaign (earning over €16 million), virtually disappeared without trace in the rest of the world, even in Latin America. An American buyer thus remained elusive, that is, until 17 November 2009, when the small independent US distributor Newmarket agreed to handle *Ágora* in the USA.

Newmarket (founded 1994) specialised in selling US and foreign, independent titles, such as *Memento* (2002), *Donnie Darko* (1999), *The Prestige* (2006) and most notably Mel Gibson's phenomenally successful *The Passion of the Christ* (2004). However, its acquisition of *Ágora* also coincided with the takeover of the company by EMG (Exclusive Media Group), a complicating factor which at the time did not appear to bode well for *Ágora*'s campaign in the American market. In fact, after its purchase in November 2009 (for an undisclosed figure), the film had to wait until 28 May 2010 for its US release. This was a worrying sign. Indeed, little or no investment appears to have been made in promoting the film by Newmarket, though it is difficult to judge the release campaign without more concrete data. Compared to its Spanish premiere, in the USA *Ágora* was given a distinctly low-key, indeed minimalist opening in New York and Los Angeles, on a mere four screens, even though in relative terms, the results after one week were a respectable $41,326 on its first weekend (source: boxofficemojo.com). Over a 12–week campaign (June–August 2010), the film played in 17 theatres, though most weekends it was running in only four to five locales. As of 21 October 2010, *Ágora* had grossed $619,423 (source: boxofficemojo.com), some €468,190. This was not exactly a catastrophic result but, for a €50–€60 million epic, it came pretty close. Until the situation becomes clearer, we need to assume that Newmarket found it so difficult to sell *Ágora* in the USA that it decided to cut its losses, spend virtually nothing on promotion and honour its contract with a 'micro' release in niche, art house locales. In terms of its release in foreign territories, *Ágora* was scheduled to be seen in over twenty countries (e.g. France, Portugal, Lebanon, Kuwait, Russia, Slovenia, Hungary, Singapore, Poland, UK, Germany, Italy, but in Latin America, only in Argentina). Apart from Italy and France, however, where it earned nearly €3 million and €2 million respectively, provisional box-office figures were very disappointing (see imdb.com). Such poor returns also bring seriously into question Amenábar's much vaunted status as a commercially successful, art film director, given that for only one out of his five features (*The Others*) has strong domestic box-office has been matched by strong foreign earnings.

The historical epic

Since its beginnings, cinema has been fascinated by large-scale art works which seek to recreate the past, as seen in Méliès's *Pygmalion et Galatée* (1898) and *Cléopatre* (1899), *Samson et Delilah* (Ferdinand Zecca, 1902), the very first Italian antiquarian epic feature *Gli ultimi giorni di Pompeii* (*The Last Days of Pompei*, Arturo Ambrosio, 1908), and its imitators such as *Quo Vadis?* (Enrico Guazzoni, 1912) and *Cabiria* (Giovanni Pastrone, 1914). But it was arguably Cecil B. DeMille who, inspired by the Italian examples, established the conventions of the film epic as a popular and profitable cinematic spectacle in *Judith of Bethulia* (1913), *Birth of a Nation* (1915), *Intolerance* (1916) and later *Cleopatra* (1934) etc. DeMille also set the standards for the genre, mixing light titillation with serious, edifying stories and cautionary tales, presented on a grand scale. In the 1950s and 1960s, in response to the studios' loss of their exhibition outlets and falling audiences, the film epic became a staple of Hollywood production schedules, including DeMille's *Samson and Delilah* (1949) and *The Ten Commandments* (1956), William Wyler's *Ben Hur* (1959), Kubrick's *Spartacus* (1960), Joseph L. Manckiewicz's *Cleopatra* (1963), David Lean's *Lawrence of Arabia* (1963) and Anthony Mann's *The Fall of the Roman Empire* (1964).

Owing mainly to cost overruns and a saturated market, the film epic disappeared in the late 1960s and 1970s to be replaced by the disaster movie, such as *The Poseidon Adventure* (1971) and *The Towering Inferno* (1975), plus television mini-series such as *Roots* and *Shogun*. Yet it was still visible in the epic dimensions of the *Star Wars* franchise and of course Spielberg's *Jaws* (1975), both pioneers of the action blockbuster, yet the genre faltered again after the failure of Cimino's epic western *Heaven's Gate* (1980). In the 1990s it was revived in Kevin Costner's independently produced *Dances with Wolves* (1990), Steven Spielberg's *Schindler's List* (1993), Mel Gibson's *Braveheart* (1995) and James Cameron's *Titanic* (1997), one of the most commercially successful films of all time. Then, following the unexpected success of Spielberg's *Saving Private Ryan* (1998), American studios began briefly to make historical epics in a more regular fashion, including Ridley Scott's *Gladiator* (2000). Drawing on elements of the 'Roman' epic of the 1950s and 1960s, *Gladiator* helped inspire such films as *Troy* (2003), *Alexander* (2004), *The Passion of the Christ* (2004), *King Arthur* (2004) and *Kingdom of Heaven* (2005). And though the latter did not appear to generate sufficient returns to justify sustained investment, the shelf-life of the film epic may have been prolonged by the astonishing success of James Cameron's *Avatar* (2009). But what do we mean by historical epic?

Derek Elley argues that 'The chief feature of the historical epic is not imitation but *reinterpretation*. It is those works which have carefully respected the legacy received from other art forms, and adapted and built upon it in a thoroughly filmic way, which are the true historical epics of the cinema' (1984: 1).[32] Steve Neale sees film 'epic' as a term strongly rooted in the 1950s, which combined two broad trends: historical films with ancient world settings and large-scale productions of all kinds which exploited lavish production values, new technologies and new modes of distribution to differentiate them from other productions and from television (2000: 85).[33] Perhaps the most useful and appropriate definition for our purposes is that of Babington amd Evans, who emphasise in the film epic its subject matter of 'world historical events, the distant myths or more recent turning points of culture' (1993: 4).[34] The 'epic' treatment of such historical milestones requires a canvas of great scale where the use of cinematic style can be deployed to convey the 'grandeur' as well as the 'overwhelming cultural significance' (1993: 4) of such pivotal events. At the same time, while the historical film epic seeks to instil awe and wonder in the spectator, it is also concerned with edification as well as entertainment. It is thus a type of cinema which takes itself extremely seriously as having a viewpoint not only regarding key moments of epochal change in the past but also as a major intervention on the implications of such events for the modern day. Thus, the sort of perspective the film epic adopts on crucial events of the past almost inevitably becomes readable in the present as a form of modern allegory.

Ágora: Synopsis

Ágora is divided into two parts or acts, which explore two specific historical moments or periods in the life and death of Hypatia of Alexandria. In part one, the film is set at the end of the fourth century, in AD 391, when the city of Alexandria and Egypt are still under the control of a waning Roman Empire, but one which has already adopted Christianity as the dominant faith. Emperor Theodosius, ruling from Constantinople, has also outlawed all non-Christian, public worship. In Alexandria, Bishop Theophilus seeks to root out heresy and implant the Christian faith throughout the city. After a credit sequence set in near-Earth orbit, the narrative of *Ágora* begins in interiors, with Hypatia teaching a class of elite students, a mix of pagans and Christians, of different ethnicities, from across the empire. She lectures in a room inside the temple complex of the Serapeum (dedicated to the Egyptian god Serapis) and adjacent to the library (which Amenábar calls the 'daughter library' in the dialogue and which stands in for the 'mother library' or 'Great Library of Alexandria', which no longer exists at this time). In broad terms the first part of the film shuttles between scenes which depict, firstly, Hypatia's teaching, scholarly work and domestic life with her father and their servants or slaves; secondly, a fictional 'love quadrangle' between Hypatia and three of her admirers, i.e. two of her students, Orestes and Synesius, and her personal slave Davus; and thirdly, in the background, a vicious cycle of social and political unrest and inter-faith struggles between a ruling (though dwindling) pagan elite (i.e. worshippers of multiple gods), a rapidly expanding community of poor Christians, led by Bishop Theophilus and his religious police and a significant and sizeable Jewish community. Hypatia consistently speaks out against the frequent riots and armed conflict in the city and tries to prevent external religious divisions from disrupting her classes; she also calls upon her students collectively to unite and act as 'brothers', whatever their differences.

In the face of multiple provocations by rabble-rousing militants (e.g. their arrogant mockery of the pagan gods, Ammonius' fire-walking 'miracle' and the burning of a pagan noble in the agora), the library director Theon approves an act of armed retaliation against the Christians. However, the pagans are taken aback by the extraordinary growth in the Christian population and the ferocity of their fighting. Outnumbered and overwhelmed by the Christian counter-attack, the pagans take refuge behind the enormous gates of the temple/library complex. A siege ensues. It is finally resolved by imperial decree, read out publicly by the Roman Prefect of the city. It pardons the pagans but orders them to abandon the fortress-like area and hand it over to the Christians. The pagans flee. The Christians burst in, topple the great statue of Serapis and destroy the statues of other pagan gods; they also trash and burn the library. Hypatia salvages what she can of the library's priceless contents; she also calls Davus an 'idiot' for not having come to her aid sooner. This outburst upsets and alienates the young slave and propels him to abandon his mistress for a new life of freedom as a Christian and member of the black-clad Parabolani militia (who resemble the Taliban). Intoxicated by the excitement and violence of the incursion, Davus tries to rape Hypatia in her own house, but draws back at the last minute. Ashamed of his behaviour, he offers her his sword and requests punishment by death, but she declines. Showing remarkable control and cool, Hypatia removes Davus' slave collar and sets him free. This double act of forgiveness and liberation will be crucial in Davus' moral and religious trajectory in part two.

Parts one and two are linked by a series of intertitles, which provide information to the viewer. Curiously, Amenábar refuses to be specific about chronology, saying only 'years later'. In fact the second part of the film begins in 412, i.e. 21 years later, with the death and funeral of Bishop Theophilus. During this intervening period, a new political order has emerged in the gradually fragmenting Roman Empire, which has split between West and East. The city of Rome has been sacked for three days during 410 by invading Goths. In Alexandria, after the destruction of the Serapeum, the pagans have lost much of their influence, with many having fled the city or converted to Christianity. The Jewish community remains more or less intact but not for long. Theon has died from a head wound and Hypatia teaches and researches from home. She remains a much-admired citizen of Alexandria, as well as counsellor and adviser to the city council, but refuses to convert. Orestes is now the new Roman Prefect but, like a growing number of key Roman officials, faced with the power of the Christians in the city, is a recent but doubting convert. Synesius, who remains friends and in contact with Orestes, has also risen to become

Christian Bishop of Ptolemais. Hypatia remains on good terms with Orestes. He accompanies her on field trips, defends her independence and has developed a satisfying though platonic friendship with her. As a seasoned Parabolanus, Davus forms part of a Christian brotherhood of ascetic monks who combine charitable work with the strict and violent enforcement of the faith, as dictated by the young and inexperienced Cyril, the new Christian bishop of Alexandria. Having taken over the position from his uncle Theophilus, the ambitious Cyril seeks to extend his political power and influence across the city through further acts of forced conversion and baptism. His ambition is to eliminate rival religions and impose Christianity as the supreme and only faith in Alexandria.

The Parabolani are ordered to stone the Jews in the amphitheatre on the Sabbath (a day on which the latter are forbidden by religious law to retaliate). Soon after, the raid provokes a tit-for-tat backlash in which many Christians are stoned to death, having been lured by the Jews into a trap inside a church, though neither Davus nor Ammonius seems affected. The unusual Jewish retaliation gives Cyril the perfect excuse to storm the Jewish quarter and kill, convert or drive out the Jews from the city, thus maximising the power and reach of the Christian faith. Meanwhile, steeped in astronomy and somewhat oblivious to the political machinations of the Christian leadership, who regard her as a political threat, Hypatia finally discovers that the orbits of the planets are not circular but elliptical, i.e. impure rather than pure. She also learns that, rather than the Earth, it is the sun which stands at the centre of our solar system.

The final obstacle in Cyril's way to supreme spiritual and temporal power in Alexandria is Hypatia, whom he regards as far too influential over the city council and its Prefect, Orestes. Cyril also claims that Hypatia's science is subversive and tantamount to sorcery and witchcraft. He also refuses to meet with Orestes to negotiate a peace but demands that the Prefect attend church where (after switching his Bible reading and claiming it to be the word of God), orders that women should be modest and silent and not teach men (a pointed remark deliberately aimed at Hypatia). He then demands that Orestes should kneel and submit to the power of the holy scriptures. Orestes refuses. This leads to him being stoned by Ammonius. Rescued by his soldiers, Orestes has Ammonius executed. Cyril sees an opportunity here for the forced conversion of Hypatia. Synesius is called in to act as mediator in Hypatia's conversion. Under great political pressure,

Orestes betrays Hypatia and withdraws his support for her, yet she still refuses to convert. Cyril declares publicly that Hypatia is a witch, giving him grounds to move against her, using his religious police, the Parabolani. Davus learns that Hypatia is to be arrested and he tries in vain to warn her. Knowing that she will suffer an excruciating death by stoning, and with her consent, he suffocates her. Informed by Davus that she has fainted, the Parabolani monks stone her inert body. Cyril achieves his ambition. He has eliminated all of his rivals through the manipulation of religious superstition, lies and brute force. A final intertitle tells us that only in the seventeenth century would Johannes Kepler (re-)discover the elliptical paths of planetary motion, first confirmed by Hypatia, following the previously discredited theory of Aristarchus of Samos.

Ágora as historical epic

In interview during the Cannes Film Festival, Amenábar said he regarded *Ágora* as a film which 'no es fácilmente clasificable' (is not easily classifiable); he also indicated: 'Está a medio camino a lo comercial. Pero es muy personal' (It's half way to being commercial but it's also very personal).[35] If *Ágora* is a mixture of very personal auteur cinema but at the same time significantly shaped by commercial pressures, though difficult to classify, then where does it stand in relation to classical and more modern variants of the epic genre?

In some ways *Ágora* respects certain familiar conventions of the genre, having been the product of a long period of research and preparation during which Amenábar reviewed a vast number of classical and more contemporary epic films, a few of which I refer to shortly. The film adopts a two-part or two-act structure, with a break in the middle, filled by an intertitle, which harks back to the classical epic form of the 1950s and the use of an intermission. Also echoing classical style, Amenábar commissioned a three-minute overture from his musical director, Dario Marianelli, which, unfortunately, had to be cut after the screenings at the Cannes Film Festival. And, like *Gladiator*, *Ágora* opens using a now familiar, almost obligatory wailing, ethnic, Enya-like, female voice, to establish a sombre mood. However, at the same time, Amenábar's approach to the film epic is very distinct and personal. This can be seen immediately in his unusual choice of historical setting and subject matter. This is not a conventional Roman epic set in the first or second centuries, when

Christianity was still an outlawed cult and its adherents enslaved and sacrificed in the arenas of the empire for bloodthirsty public entertainment. Rather, it deals with a period very rarely touched upon at all in the Roman epic, i.e. after AD 313, which saw the legalisation of all religious cults by Emperor Constantine and the outbreak of power struggles between factions of a rapidly expanding Christian religion, during the fourth and fifth centuries.

Amenábar also defies expectations not by presenting his Christian believers as meek and mild-mannered victims of Roman oppression; rather, he focuses on a radical, aggressive, numerically thriving Christianity, engaged in a 'holy war' for supremacy, which overwhelms the waning Hellenic (pagan) enlightenment and civilisation of Alexandria. Later, it turns on the Jewish population of the city, attacks and expels them, while imposing an oppressive theocracy through intimidation and violence. This focus on the rise of a warlike Christian fundamentalism in conflict with a 'progressive' though effete paganism is totally new and a challenging departure from traditional epic subject matter. Also new is the choice of principal protagonist, Hypatia, a historically authentic but virtually unknown figure for most audiences, whose story has never until now enjoyed the big-screen treatment. The choice of Hypatia also challenges epic conventions in gender terms, since in most cases, until very recently, the 'peplum' has been dominated by male protagonists and by the exploits of male action heroes (Judah ben Hur, Spartacus, Maximus, Achilles, Alexander etc.). However, though acting as an adviser to Prefect Orestes in part two, Hypatia is far from being a mythic or action-oriented heroine. Rather, she is an intellectual, a philosopher and scientist and in Amenábar's personal rendition primarily an astronomer. She is also portrayed as a secular sage and martyr, i.e. a version of her story which overlaps with Amenábar's hagiographical portrait of Ramón Sampedro. Overall, in its setting, subject matter and challenging thematics, *Ágora* is a powerful statement of intent, showing how a European filmmaker seeks to compete with Hollywood on its own turf, while radically revising some of the basic features of the epic genre.

Also the film title *Ágora* is polysemically rich. While clearly referring to the marketplace, public square and the multi-ethnic and multi-religious student class taught by Hypatia, this intriguing Greek coinage recalls the director's penchant for classical language terms, as seen in the name of his own production company and that of his second short film, both called *Himenóptero*. The use of a Greek term also refers to the 'European' origins of the project and the 'high culture' pedigree of an art film which has a serious point to make. However, rather than follow the Mel Gibson route and foreground linguistic authenticity as a mark of product differentiation, as in *The Passion of the Christ* (2004), Amenábar plays safe and shoots in English rather than in Greek or Latin, anxious to ensure distribution in vital Anglo-American markets. The term 'agora' also has implications regarding the settling and resolution of conflict, with Amenábar emphatically on the side of reason, negotiation and peaceful resolution, as is Hypatia. The 'agora' is also a metaphor for human 'coexistence' and the health of the planet, as well as a banner for its heroine's intellectual and scientific roots, i.e. Graeco-Roman civilisation, which is crushed by religious fanaticism. Here, in exploring Amenábar's version of the historical epic, I propose to consider briefly how his film style compares and contrasts with that of certain recent mainstream epics, such as *Gladiator* and *Troy*. I also wish to look briefly at the scripting and character design of the film. I argue that weaknesses in these areas perhaps prevent the film from engaging the spectator more effectively at the emotional level and thereby weaken the its appeal to wider, mainstream audiences.

Film style

Gladiator was a film which took its cues from the mega-successful *Titanic* (1997) but particularly from *Saving Private Ryan* (1998) and which arguably reignited studio interest in the wartime and Roman epic in the new millennium as viable projects and profitable investments. It is worth acknowledging here the crucial importance of Spielberg's *Saving Private Ryan* as a major turning point in the renaissance of the historical, especially wartime, epic, set both in modern and in historically more remote times (e.g. in *Gladiator*, but also in *Pearl Harbor* (2001), *Enemy at the Gates* (2001), *Captain Corelli's Mandolin* (2001), *Black Hawk Down* (2001), *Windtalkers* (2002), *We Were Soldiers* (2002), as well as more historically distant epics such as the Civil War drama *Ride with the Devil* (Ang Lee, 1999) and Mel Gibson's *The Patriot* (2000). All of these films, to a greater or lesser extent, are inspired by and owe a debt to the innovative, immersive, ultra-vérité filming style of *Saving Private Ryan*. For Ridley Scott, Spielberg's film 'threw down the gauntlet' to directors of epic films, especially in recreating battle sequences (such as the bloody Omaha beach landings); from now on, Scott observed, the epic filmmaker 'had better take people right there and have metal whizzing past their ears'.[36] My proposition is that *Ágora* had to respond to these changes in shooting the historical epic mentioned above, which were quickly adopted by many other studio productions. I believe this explains why Amenábar decided to sell *Ágora* to Telecinco and Universal as a form of spectacle which, while modest in its CGI extensions, created a powerful, credible *mise-en-scène* in technical terms. And it did so by trying to copy a style of vérité camerawork, reminiscent of television news filming, which was strongly immersive, immediate and 'hyperrealistic', as if shot through the director's own eyes, whose camera places the viewer in the thick of the action. As Amenábar states: 'El empeño de todo el equipo era devolverle la vida con un enfoque hiperrealista, conseguir que los espectadores vean, sientan y huelan una civilización remota como si fuera su propia realidad (The aim of the entire team was to bring [the city] back to life using a hyperrealist focus, to ensure that the spectators see, feel and smell a remote civilisation as if it were their own reality).[37]

In terms of production and art design, Amenábar and his technical department heads successfully recreate the city of Alexandria and its key locations (the library, Serapeum, 'agora', city streets etc.) through strong visual spectacle. The viewer is thus able to enjoy the scale as well as the remarkable detail of the image. The film also achieves an almost seamless integration of constructed sets, real live action and digital imagery, as in the wide, panoramic shots of the library, with the lighthouse and port in the background, the bird's eye shots of the city layout and the aerial views of the Nile Delta. Here such 'spectacular realism' renders the spectator conscious of the technical craftsmanship involved, which seeks to elicit the 'wow' factor, while simultaneously helping to transport the viewer back to fourth-century Egypt. The detailed recreations of the streets, buildings, amphitheatre, temple, statues, marketplace, houses, municipal senate (or *curia*) and their detailed Graeco-Roman-Egyptian decoration etc. look very convincing and successfully draw the spectator into the fictional world. Though costume often tends towards the generic and anachronistic (e.g. the colour coding for Christians, Jews and pagans – blue, black and beige – and the use of first- rather than fourth-century Roman soldiers' uniforms and armour), Amenábar seeks further realism through his minute attention to faces and by selecting his extras partly on the basis of their correspondence to the 'Fayoum portraits' or painted panels of mummified Alexandrians of two thousand years ago.[38] Overall,

Ágora compares very well with other contemporary epics, in sealing the gap between film representation and imagined referent. This ground-level realism is complemented by the frequent use of cosmic spectacle, i.e. grand-scale vista shots, viewed from on high, including numerous 'satellite/Google Earth' shots, where the camera pans, arcs and wheels left and right, placing the viewer outside and high above the action. From this Godlike, or 'Martian' vantage point as Amenábar sees it, the viewer is called upon to reflect on events, putting into perspective their importance in relation to the beauty and fragility of the planet, within the context of the cosmos. This cosmic 'perspectivism' so to speak, is totally new to the historical epic and exploits features from, while paying homage to, Carl Sagan's television series *Cosmos* and the 'walk through' visuals used therein.

In his press conference at Cannes in May 2009, while talking about the films he had used as reference points in his research for *Ágora*, Amenábar pointed out: 'Desde luego, esto no quiere ser *Troya*' (Of course this film does not try to be *Troy*). He added that he had no wish to 'convertir la violencia en el centro de la historia (place violence at the centre of the story).[39] Here, I believe, Amenábar is possibly a little harsh on Wolfgang Petersen's admittedly highly abridged but well-structured and handsomely shot adaptation of Homer's *Iliad*. The film includes a wide assortment of battle and combat sequences culminating in the excellently choreographed duel between Achilles and Hector in front of Troy's massive walls. But *Troy* is arguably not overwhelmed by scenes of violence, as Amenábar seems to imply. Rather, war, conquest and death are complemented by many intimate, sombre, quieter scenes where a powerful, impressive cast including Brad Pitt (Achilles), Orlando Bloom (Paris), Eric Bana (Hector , Julie Christie (Thetis), Peter O'Toole (Priam), Brendan Gleeson (Menelaus), Brian Cox (Agamemnon), Sean Bean (Odysseus) and Helen Kruger (Helen) are forced to confront loss, cowardice, rage, guilt, honour, loyalty and the afterlife.[40]

Of course, unlike *Troy*, *Alexander* or *Gladiator*, *Ágora* is not primarily an action picture, though it includes a number of action sequences, which involve crowds surging, street fighting, a good deal of stoning, the destruction of the library etc. but little one-to-one combat and no armies or set-piece battles. Also, unlike its contemporaries, despite its hand-held camerawork, *Ágora* does not adopt the kind of kinetic, 'impact aesthetic' we find in *Gladiator*, i.e. close-in, shaky, hand-held camerawork and faster than normal shutter speeds, which produce a strobic quality in order to evoke the dynamics and stresses of the conflict (as in the long opening sequence of *Gladiator* set in Germania). Indeed, Amenábar deliberately avoids this sort of extended action filming and refuses to immerse the spectator in the characters' disorientation and sense of chaos in battle. As he indicates: 'No he querido mostrar la violencia con tinte épico sino como algo feo y sucio' (I refuse to show violence in epic terms, rather as something ugly and dirty).[41] In fact Amenábar adopts more elegant, indirect and suggestive options to represent panic, destruction and pivotal events such as the flying streamers of the scrolls and the use of inverted framing during the sacking of the Serapeum. In this connection, as in *Tesis*, his approach to representing violence is that of the impressionistic brushstroke, combining a few fleeting seconds of action with numerous cut-aways to higher vantage points, often using his favourite zenith shot. The aim seems to be to foster detachment and reflection rather than immersion and visceral excitement. Also, from on high, using fast motion shots, he prefers to portray those engaged in street violence as ants or cockroaches, drawing an accusatory parallel between those who employ violence (not only Christian militants but also pagans and Jews) and the behaviour of pests or insects. His cinematography and editing are thus mobilised in support of an anti-violence and anti-war agenda.

Scripting and character

As Geoff King has argued, while spectacle is clearly a key ingredient of the epic film, it is not used simply for its own sake. It also functions as a context and a supporting framework for narrative and is used to align audiences with narrative development through character interaction (2002: 342–3). That is, the viewer's 'journey' through the succession of onscreen events depends crucially on a small group of central characters who help articulate events (the what, who, when and why) in clearly explained sequences of cause and effect. Moreover, in the epic film, thematic material tends to be offset and complemented by some form of heterosexual romance. In the case of *Ágora*, however, the ways in which these dimensions are organised diverge significantly from Hollywood convention and present challenges for spectator engagement. These difficulties lie, I suggest, not so much in performance but in the screenplay, particularly in character design and motivation.

As mentioned earlier, numerous reviewers of *Ágora* have remarked on the difficulties for the spectator in becoming emotionally engaged by screen events and characters. In part this has to do with the 16 minutes of character background and exposition cut from the film after the Cannes Film Festival in 2009. It also relates to the choice of subject matter and Amenábar's apparent mission to educate the audience a little in classical astronomy. Though imaginatively and inventively realised, what Cosmo Landesman calls Hypatia's 'difficult to follow astronomical speculations' arguably compromise audience attention, for lack of basic knowledge in the field.[42] Also, Amenábar s frequent use of satellite shots (which suggest that from a cosmic perspective violent politico-religious squabbles in Alexandria are relatively unimportant or innocuous) break audience connection with the dramatic action, as do the frequent cut-aways and zenith shots.

Also, in both principal and supporting characters, there is sometimes a lack of drive, tension and conflict in basic design as well as interaction and pursuit of goals. For example, the 'baddies' of the story, Theophilus, Cyril and Ammonius, are fairly lightly sketched and monotone, i.e. largely one-dimensional, stock constructs, designed (in looks, costume and voice) to represent the irresistible rise and threat of fundamentalist Christianity (read Islam). As for Hypatia, she is highly motivated by an irrepressible desire to decipher the enigmas of gravity, planetary motion and the structure of the universe. Her researches are also organised narratively according to a progressive arc or pattern of development, i.e. from an initial adherence to Ptolemy's geocentrist or earth-centred model, passing through the heliocentrism of Aristarchus of Samos (mid-point in the film) to her discovery of the ellipse as the key form (and alternative to the circle) through which to understand planetary orbits, near the end. However, in the process, though her ideas evolve, Hypatia's geeky, wide-eyed, otherworldly character changes very little. Even after the trauma and destruction of the Serapeum, there is no break, change of direction or collapse of fortunes. Though deeply distraught at the loss of the library, she readjusts to working at home and continues to teach, study and experiment in her sand pit as before. Nor does she age a day or lose her gorgeous looks, even though 21 years pass between the first and second acts (391 and 412).

As for her father, Theon, Michael Lonsdale is well cast and convincing as the ageing and frail mathematician and library director, whose daughter now corrects his calculations. But there is little debate or disagreement over scientific matters and rarely a wrong word between a doting father and dutiful daughter. Indeed Theon approves of Hypatia's humiliation of Orestes (via the 'gift' of her bloodied menstrual towel), defends her fierce independence, her chastity and her decision never to marry (submission to a husband, he believes, would destroy her academic career at a stroke) and celebrates her scholarly dedication to her writing and research. In one of the very few moments of domestic tension, triggered by the discovery of a Christian symbol in Theon's house, Hypatia intervenes verbally to prevent her father from beating Davus. But there is no discussion or extended argument, perhaps out of a daughter's respect for paternal authority. Later, under siege in the temple complex, Theon also blames himself for unleashing the bloody cycle of violence between pagans and Christians, which arguably reinforces the impression of weakness and waning self-confidence within the city's educated, pagan elite.

The script for *Ágora* also reintroduces the 'teen drama/love quadrangle' patterning with which we are familiar from previous Amenábar films. This time Hypatia faces not two but three romantic suitors. These are clever young men but from radically different social strata, a feature which allows Amenábar to graft the theme of class struggle and social difference on to the primary conflict of religious intolerance and fanaticism. The main figures are two of Hypatia's pupils and scions of the wealthy upper classes, Orestes and Synesius, the former an exhibitionist and womaniser (like his father, according to Theon), the latter an introvert and already a prickly Christian, easily provoked into defending the faith from Orestes' dry humour. Both men subsequently fulfil their destinies and achieve key positions in Alexandrian political and religious life, though these transitions are elided and left unexplained. The third pretender is Davus, the ultra-brainy slave, unlike Medoro, his colleague, who is far less gifted and already a Christian. Davus has blossomed intellectually and practically in Hypatia's service. Indeed, without prompting, he has constructed a teaching aid, i.e. a model of Ptolemy's universe, no doubt inspired by his love and admiration for his mistress. Such handiwork functions as a symbol and token of the power of a scientific education and its progenitor Hypatia, while vaguely echoing Ramón Sampedro's skill at making useful gadgets. All three young men suffer desperately from a massive adolescent crush on their beautiful 'lady philosopher'. However, Amenábar concentrates on the stories of only two of them

(Davus and Orestes) who are desperate to gain Hypatia's favour. Here, in Orestes and Davus, we find further echoes of the characters and relationships between Bosco and Chema in *Tesis* and César and Pelayo in *Abre los ojos*.

If Hypatia resembles a Helen of Troy or a classical Joan of Arc with a Ph.D., her obsession with astronomy and her renunciation of more worldly pursuits render her largely detached and remote. According to Dzielska (1995: 89), historically speaking, this image of Hypatia as a quasi-vestal virgin, wedded to science, appears to be fairly accurate, though one source, Damascius' *Life of Isidore*, reproduced in the *Suda*, claims Hypatia was married to the philospher Isidorus.[43] In a sense Amenábar's decision to abandon heterosexual romance for female self-abnegation and devotion to the intellect may appear an inspired one, since it is so unusual in the historical epic and such a strong antidote to the saturated sexualisation, for example, of a series like HBO's *Rome*. However, in dramatic terms, it leaves *Ágora* with a potential black hole, i.e. a narrative zone and a key dimension of character building and screen interaction which are left under-developed, and which are normally crucial in creating viewer identification and alignment to character. Given that so little is known about Hypatia's real private life, Amenábar had ample opportunities available to him to refashion character relationships or invent completely new figures (as he did in the case of Davus). As Hypatia's interpreter, Rachel Weisz was so concerned by the design and limitations placed on Hypatia's scripted character (whom she regarded as a mere 'brain on legs' and thus lacking in appeal for mainstream audiences) that she implored Amenábar to include a sex scene: 'I actually told Alejandro they should shoot a scene where she was looking at the stars and masturbating ... I suggested a PG version, where her hand went out of frame, and you're watching her come, looking at the stars. He wouldn't go for it. I begged him. I wanted to know about that stuff. What's up? What's her sexuality? What's her deviancy?'[44]

Needless to say, Amenábar refused to be deflected. But he reassured his star that the character she was playing, though something of a reclusive, nunlike figure, was deeply in love with the heavens and the life of the mind. And in her performance Weisz evokes this nerdy, euphoric enthusiasm very effectively. Yet, as Landesman points out, there is something missing in Hypatia, which he refers to as 'intimacy'. We certainly admire Hypatia, but *Ágora* does not seem to allow us 'to get to know her and like her'.[45] That is, Amenábar is so anxious for the audience to buy into Hypatia's legendary status as a pagan 'martyr for science' that the script elides or excludes significant intimate detail, which could have been developed to connect and bind audiences to the character.

Much of Hypatia's reputation as a martyr for science rests on the barbaric nature of her death at the hands of Christian monks, determined to vent their religious zeal and hatred of women through the ritualised stoning, dismemberment and burning of her body. The classical sources seem to agree, in broad terms, that this is what happened in March 415. However, given his squeamishness and deep aversion to screen violence as spectacle, Amenábar refuses to engage with such barbaric cruelty, preferring to provide his audiences with a much abridged 'reimagining' of Hypatia's agonising death. He thus rewrites history, determined to 'tell' more than 'show' visually what happened using devices exploited in his previous films. If what emerges is a quite blatant distortion of a famous and terrible martyrdom, it is nonetheless both elegant and inventive. The problem is that it risks confusing the audience, since they may regard what they see on screen as based on a factual historical account. Rather than dramatise her torture, Amenábar has a monk tell Hypatia in detailed terms of the grisly fate which awaits her, thus mixing sadism with Hypatia's sense of apprehension (and, at the same time, repeating a dramatic device used by Bosco at the end of *Tesis*). Also, before she is stoned, Davus gently suffocates her, thus sparing her the terrible pain and suffering of the macho ritual; her relatively painless death also recycles the ending of *Mar adentro* and its controversial eulogy of euthanasia. A final intertitle adds further historical detail of what became of Hypatia's body. All this is done quite economically and effectively, with screen drama and factual exposition held together by the glue of self-referential, intertextuality. But what is the point of Amenábar's ending?

As the critic A.O. Scott argues in his review of *Ágora* in the *New York Times* : 'Films about ideological strife in the past frequently reassure modern audiences with a vision of progress in which ignorance is at least partly vanquished and enlightenment is allowed to prevail.'[46] In keeping with his revisionist designs on the Roman epic, Amenábar seems to do the opposite, ending on an extremely bleak note. At the end of *Ágora* a demographically unstoppable, radical Christianity (i.e. fundamentalist Islam), supported by imperial decrees, finally defeats Western learning, values and science by force, eliminates its ideological rivals and takes power in Alexandria, as supreme religious authority. Like other films by Amenábar, *Ágora* stands as yet another cautionary tale, this time concerned with the dangers of religious intolerance and fanaticism, which create the conditions for extremism, violence, chaos and conquest. This is certainly a timely reminder of such dangers and threats, but since 11 September 2001 most people are probably already aware of these concerns, though perhaps not sufficiently well-informed by their political and religious leaders as to how to tackle them.

Also, what are we to make of Davus' intervention in providing Hypatia with a more humane death? Here the director recasts history in terms of a certain 'progressive', left-wing, social agenda which is strongly aligned with PSOE social policy. As in the case of his pro-feminist rendition of his heroine, Amenábar takes the opportunity of Hypatia's demise to re-advertise his enthusiasm and message in favour of euthanasia and assisted dying as legitimate 'end of life' options, despite being counter-factual. Biography also plays a part here, since in terms of Amenábar's own religious trajectory, from deist to atheist, Davus is arguably his avatar. In relation to religious fanaticism, the figure of Davus shows how even good-natured, imaginative, clever young men are susceptible to religious rhetoric and can be persuaded to commit acts of barbarism in the name of God. Yet Davus also manages to transcend the 'madness' of his rage and unreason through his lingering love for Hypatia and his acknowledgement of her Christlike kindness and forgiveness (for his attempted rape), i.e. qualities which he does not find among his thuggish Parabolani comrades. Hence Amenábar's double ending: on a political level, a crushing defeat for Hellenic (pagan) learning and civilisation by the irrational forces of religous zealotry; on a more personal, intimate level, through Davus, a rejection of religious fanaticism, a 'reawakening' and 'return' to reason and enlightenment inspired not by a religious but by a secular education and grounded in science and philosophy. But in the face of religious intolerance and extremism, acts of violence and global threats of domination and conquest in the real world, are secular reason and logic enough? To paraphrase a resonant dialogue line in *Ágora*, 'Is philosophy really what we need at times like these?'

Notes

1 See Anon., 'Ovación a Amenábar en el esperado estreno de *Ágora*', 17 May 2009 at www.culturaclasica.com/?q=node/2825. Accessed 28 May 2010.

2 Amenábar et al., *Ágora. El viaje al mundo antiguo de Alejandro Amenábar* (Madrid: Libros Cúpula, 2009), 9.

3 See Gregorio Belinchón, 'Entrevista con Alejandro Amenábar *Director de cine* "Empecé haciendo una de marcianos y acabé rodando una de romanos" www.elpais.com/articulo/cultura/Empece/haciendo/marcianos/acabe/rodando/romanos/elpepicul/20091003elpepicul_1/Tes. Accessed 28 May 2010.

4 See www.youtube.com/watch?v=OLlVnKOb4Mk. Accessed 25 May 2010

5 This has now morphed into the SETI institute (see www.seti.org/csc) and the Carl Sagan Centre for the Study of Life in the Universe. It was Sagan who, in his working out of the 'Drake equation', concluded that the probabilities 'concerning the abundance of planets and the origins of life are likely to be high', whilst the 'likelihood of the evolution of intelligence and technological civilisations' was also high (see Sagan's commentary: 'Space topics: search for extraterrestrial intelligence. Is earth-life relevant? A rebuttal' at www.planetary.org/explore/topics/search_for_life/seti/sagan2.html). Accessed 26 May 2010.

6 For a useful overview of the phenomenon of the popularisation of science in the media see Michael B. Shermer, 'Stephen Jay Gould as historian of science and scientific historian, popular scientist and scientific popula-riser', *Social Studies of Science*, 32:4 (August 2002), 489–525, especially 490–1.

7 See note 3 for reference.

8 See Bryan J. Whitfield's 'The beauty of reasoning: a re-examination of Hypatia of Alexandria', in *The Mathematics Educator*, 6:1 (1995), 14–21 at: http://math.coe.uga.edu/tme/issues/vo6n1/4whitfield.pdf. Accessed 26 May 2010.

9 This is the view of Tim O'Neill, classicist, medievalist and self-styled historian of science, whose web blog (Armarium Magnum) offers an informative and stimulating account of Hypatia of Alexandria folded into a commentary which seeks to debunk Amenábar's film. See ' "Ágora" and Hypatia – Hollywood strikes again' at http://armariummagnus.blogspot.com/2009/05/Ágora-and-hypatia-hollywood-strikes.html. See also his update essay, 'Hypatia and Ágora Redux' at http://armariummagnus.blogspot.com/201%5/hypatia-and-Ágora-redux.html. Accessed 27 May 2010

10 In one of the few reliable modern biographies, written in English and published in 1995, the Polish scholar Maria Dzielska indicates this dearth of material in her first chapter on Hypatia. See Maria Dzielska, *Hypatia of Alexandria* (trans F. Lytra) (Cambridge, Mass: Harvard University Press,

1995. See also Michael A.B. Deakin, *Hypatia of Alexandria: Mathemati-cian and Martyr* (Amherst NY: Prometheus Books, 2007).

11 The mathematician Michael Deakin (michael.deakin@sci.monash.edu.au) mentions a small number of key classical sources, originally written in Greek, but now available online, in English. See 'The primary sources for the life and work of Hypatia of Alexandria' by Michael A.B. Deakin, History of Mathematics Paper 63, August 1995, Mathematics Department, Monash University, Clayton 3168, Australia. He includes (1) an entry in the *Suda Lexicon*, (2) a passage in the *Ecclesiastical History of Socrates Scholasticus*, (3) an excerpt from *The Chronicle of John, Coptic Bishop of Nikiu*, (4) q number of letters by Hypatia's pupil, Synesius of Cyrene and (4) four miscellaneous short extracts from other works. See www.polyamory.org/~howard/Hypatia/primary-sources.html. Accessed 28 May 2010.

12 For example it is thought that she collaborated in the writing and revision of her father's edition of Euclid's *Elements*, which in his *Cosmos* series Carl Sagan homaged as still a 'great read'. She might well have helped to edit, or even write, *The Astronomical Canon*, which formed part of her father's 11–part commentary on Ptolemy's *Almagest*; she also produced other commentaries in maths and geometry based on the 13–volume *Arithmetica* of Diophantus of Alexandria, as well as Apollonius' *Conics* and other works by Ptolemy.

13 Translations of Synesius' letters are available on-line at: www.livius.org/su-sz/synesius/synesius_cyrene.html and www.livius.org/su-sz/synesius/synesius_letters.html. Accessed 28 May 2010.

14 Neo-platonism posits a single, transcendent source, an ultimate reality, from which all existence emanates and with which an individual soul can be mystically united and absorbed into 'the One', i.e. God. What we now call Christianity is very much a syncretism or mixture of borrowings from neo-platonism, as well as neo-Pythogoreanism, Greek Gnosticism and the Hebrew religion. For example, Synesius of Cyrene (c. 370–c. 413) was a neo-platonic philosopher, and one who converted to Christianity, but lacked deep personal conviction, it seems. Amenábar's portrayal of Synesius in *Ágora* is, historically speaking, eccentric and inaccurate.

15 This figure does not include rapidly growing levels of taxpayer subsidies disbursed by ICAA, Spain's National Film Institute, which reached nearly €90 million in 2008, source: mcu.es. Accessed 30 May 2010.

16 It is worth pointing out that since 2002/3, in its various divisions, Telecinco had done excellent business, with earnings approaching €1 billion gross overall (Interview). However, the company CEO Paulo Vasile was well known for being violently opposed to spending his domestic revenues on a loss-making activity such as Spanish filmmaking. He was even more at odds with the ruling PSOE government's over-generous support for what he called 'películas inútiles', i.e. poorly made and largely unprofitable

local films. On the whole Spanish filmmaking fails consistently to cover its costs, let alone make profits. The vast majority of the 150–70 local film projects made annually over the last few years depend almost entirely on subsidies of one type or another, provided by the taxpayer or by obligatory spending imposed by government on the television companies.

17   See 'Interview: Ghislain Barrois CEO of Telecinco Cinema: how to make quality films with commercial appeal, out of obligation', at http://cineuropa.org/interview.aspx?lanf=edanddocumentID=111618. Accessed 28 May 2010

18   See Nacho Gay, 'La superproducción de Telecinco en el aire: 'Ágora no encuentra distribuidor en EEUU', at www.elconfidencial.com/ocioytelevi-sion/Ágora-problemas-distribucion-eeuu-20091008.html. Accessed 28 May 2010.

19   Interestingly, NBC Universal did not drop out of the deal altogether. Through Focus Features International it took responsibility for the inter-national distribution of the film, while Hispano Fox Film took care of the domestic release in Spain.

20   See 'Amenábar: *Ágora* iba a recaer en Hollywood y al final fue Telecinco la que la produjo', www. formulatv.com/1,20090517,11398,1.html. Accessed 30 May 2010.

21   See www.elpais.com/videos/cultura/Croissant/Croissette/Ágora/Tengo/sensaciones/bastante/encontradas/elpvidcul/20090517elpepucul_1/Ves/. Accessed 30 May 2010

22   Carlos Boyero, 'Grandioso proyecto con resultado notable', see www.elpais.com/articulo/cultura/Grandioso/proyecto/resultado/notable/elpepicul/20090518elpepicul_7/Tes. Accessed 30 May 2010

23   Luis Martínez, 'Amenábar imparte una clase, larga y premiosa, de "astronomía emocional"', see www.elmundo.es/elmundo/2009/05/17/cultura/1242564962.html. Accessed 30 May 2010.

24   See http://blogs.abc.es/index.php?blog=338andp=4014andmore=1andc=1andtb=1andpb=1). See also Alberto Bermejo, 'Espectáculo y conocimiento', www.elmundo.es/metropoli/2009/10/14/cine/1255541561.html, and Mirito Torreiro, at www.fotogramas.es/Peliculas/Ágora/Critica/% 28offset%29/ Accessed 30 May 2010.

25   Todd McCarthy, 'Ágora', *Variety*, www.variety.com/index.asp?layout=fes tivalsandjump=reviewandreviewid=VE1117940282andcs=1. Accessed 30 May 2010.

26   Mike Goodridge, '*Ágora*', www.screendaily.com/reviews/cannes-reviews-Ágora. Accessed 30 May 2010.

27   TIFF programme publicity sought to underline not only the film's commitment to 'big ideas' of religious intolerance opposed to rational enquiry but also a greater stress on the youthful romance aspect destroyed by sectarian conflict. It framed *Ágora* as a 'rousing historical epic', Weisz's performance rather improbably as a 'smouldering turn', and the film's

love triangle as 'put to the test under the weight of the city's violent social upheaval'. See http://tiff.net/filmsandschedules/films/Ágora. Accessed 30 May 2010.

28 Todd Brown, 10 September 2009, 'TIFF 09: Ágora Review', www.twitch-film.net/reviews/2009/09/ cannes-09–Ágora-review.php. Accessed 30 May 2010.

29 To do so they hired the specialist services of Publiespaña and its Depart-ment of 'Iniciativas Especiales', alongside the marketing agency Mindshare España. The latter sought to bind the South Korean company LG Electronics España into an exclusive deal with Amenábar's film, with both trading on the concept of 'shared values' such as leadership and technological innovation. See http://lgmoviles.wordpress.com/2009/1%7/lg-electronics-parocina-el-estreno-de-Ágora-la-ultima-pelicula-de-alejandro-amenabar/). Accessed 30 May 2010.

30 However, the prize for the best opening weekend ever for a Spanish film must go to Santiago Segura's dumb crime comedy *Torrente 4: Lethal Crisis* (2011), earning €8.2 million (source: mcu.es).

31 See Sharon Swart and Pamela Mcclintock, 'US distribs take fresh look at *Ágora*', at www.variety.com/article/VR1118010234.html?categoryid=1278 andcs=1. Accessed 30 May 2010.

32 Derek Elley, *The Epic Film: Myth and History* (London: Routledge Keegan Paul, 1984).

33 Steve Neale, *Genre and Hollywood* (London: Routledge, 2000).

34 Bruce Babington and Peter William Evans, *Biblical Epics: Sacred Narra-tive in the Hollywood Cinema* (Manchester: Manchester University Press, 1993).

35 EFE, 'Amenábar muestra su "viaje de exploración al pasado"', www.abc.es/hemeroteca/historico-17–05–2009/ab). Accessed 30 May 2010

36 Christopher Noxon, 'The Roman Empire rises again', *Los Angeles Times* (23 April 2000), 5.

37. See Anon., 'Amenábar inicia el lunes el rodaje de "Ágora"', at www.elmundo.es/elmundo/2008/03/13/cultura/1205407686.html Accessed 30 May 2010.

38 See Amenábar et al., *Ágora. El viaje al mundo antiguo de Alejandro Amen-ábar* (Madrid: Libros Cúpula, 2009), 76–9.

39 Borja Hermoso, 'Contra los fundamentalismos', 18 May 2009/, www.elpais.com/articulo/cultura/fundamentalismos. Accessed 30 May 2010.

40 Frederic and Mary Ann Brusat argue that, rather than the 'clangor of war', Petersen has chosen 'to put the main accent on the intimate dramas that cause men to plunge into battle', see http://spiritualityandpractice.com/films/films.php?id=8486. Todd McCarthy suggests that the violence in *Troy* is 'not nearly as bloody or gruesome as that in *Braveheart*' while also remarking that Pitt's Achilles is rather too stylised, fetishised and contemporary in voice and look, which clashes with the rest of a seasoned,

Anglo-spheric cast. See Todd McCarthy, 'Troy', *Variety* at www.variety.
com/review/VE1117923745.html?categoryid=31andcs=1andp=0. Accessed
2 June 2010.

41   See José Arenas, 'Alejandro Amenábar: "No he querido mostrar la violencia
con tinte épico sino como algo feo y sucio"', at www.abc.es/20091004/
espectaculos-cine-querido-mostrar-violencia-tinte-20091004.html.
Accessed 2 June 2010.

42   Cosmo Landesman, '*Ágora*: a more thoughtful ancient-world epic', *The
Sunday Times*, 25 April 2010, at http://entertainment.timesonline.co.uk/
tol/arts_and_entertainment/film/film_reviews/article7103752.ece.
Accessed 2 June 2010.

43   See a translation of the relevant document source at http://cosmopolis/
com/alexandria/hypatia-bio-suda.html. Accessed 3 June 2010.

44   See Tom Shone, 'Rachel Weisz on motherhood, movies and metaphysics',
The Sunday Times, 11 April 2010 at http://entertainment.timesonline.co.
uk/tol/arts_and_entertainment/film/article7091467.ece. Accessed 3 June
2010.

45   See note 42 for full reference.

46   See A.O. Scott, 'Love among the togas and the intolerant', at http://
movies.nytimes.com/201%5/28/movies/28Ágora.html. Accessed 3 June
2010.

Afterword

Over a period of roughly two decades (1991–2011) Amenábar has made a small though hugely influential and impressive group of films, comprising five features and fours shorts. Of course his filmmaking activity also includes a wide range of collaborations as well as several projects as film producer plus support for new and not-so-new creative personnel and other technical specialists. For example, let us recall that he has always championed the making of shorts, as a leading student practitioner himself as well as a collaborator with Mateo Gil, Carlos Montero, Guillermo Fernández etc. He was also heavily involved in Mateo Gil's outstanding *Allanamiento de morada* (Breaking and Entering, 1998) and acted as producer on Oskar Santos' prize-winning short *El soñador* (The Dreamer, 2004), which achieved competition success in film festivals at Sitges and New York (source: imdb.com). Amenábar also played a key role in launching Mateo Gil's feature career, making multiple contributions to his debut film *Nadie conoce a nadie* (Nobody Knows Anybody, 1999). He also helped restart José Luis Cuerda's own faltering career with the very successful *La lengua de las mariposas* (Butterfly's Tongue, 1999). In both cases, he was responsible for the film score. Also, under the rubric of his own company Himenóptero (in collaboration with Fernando Bovaira's Mod Producciones), he also produced *El mal ajeno* (For the Good of Others, 2009), the first main feature of Oskar Santos, his student contemporary from Madrid's Complutense University, who shot the documentary 'Un viaje Mar adentro' (see DVD Extras).

Amenábar has also played a key role in developing the careers of a growing number of fine actors and actresses, notably Nicole Kidman, Javier Bardem, Penélope Cruz, Ana Torrent, Eduardo Noriega, Rafael (Fele) Martínez and Belén Rueda, among many others. And if measured not only by his Oscar success for *Mar adentro* and a cabinet crammed full of international awards but by the degree of recognition and support he has enjoyed in Spain through its National Film Institute (ICAA) and its Film Academy, Amenábar today is by far the nation's most acclaimed and admired filmmaker of all time. Moreover, after joining the Film Academy's Executive Committee in 2006 and lending his support to the controversial Ley de Cine of 2007, he became something of an official ambassador and 'poster boy' for the national industry and the government's film policy. Also, while his films virtually guarantee strong commercial box-office in the home market, they also tend to attract very positive peer recognition. This can be seen in his 36 Goya awards to date, with eight personal 'cabezones' (statuette heads) to his credit. In short Amenábar now occupies a special, indeed privileged, position as a leading creative talent at the apex of the Spanish film industry, though he is not without his critics.[1] He has also reached a stage in his career full of enticing opportunities as well as significant risks. Enjoying enormous national prestige and serious international recognition within the profession, he appears to have a long career ahead of him.

Of course, as mentioned in the introduction to this book, questions of authorship continue to complicate any view of Amenábar as a single, creative individual, sole progenitor of the work usually ascribed to him or source of its meanings. Virtually all of his filmmaking, apart from *The Others*, has been done in close collaboration with his university colleague, student flatmate and best friend, Mateo Gil. Since they met in 1990 Gil has been intimately involved in Amenábar's choice of projects and their development, as well as scripting, casting, shooting and working as his production assistant and/or second unit director. The same applies, of course, to Amenábar's own close involvement in Gil's shorts and his one main feature to date, *Nadie conoce a nadie* (Nobody Knows Anybody, 1999). In effect, despite temporary breaks from each other (in *Luna* and *The Others*), Gil and Amenábar have formed a species of double-act, a writing and filmmaking partnership, in which their filmic obsessions and ambitions as well as aspects of their personal relationships have become inextricably intertwined. Of course each of them has worked on separate projects too. Gil's more recent outings, for example, have included the script for *El método* (The Method, Marcelo Piñeyro, 2005), an 80–minute television movie *Regreso a Moira* (Return to Moira, 2006), for the horror series *Películas para no dormir* (Films to Keep You Awake, Tele5 and Filmax),

a further, Goya-winning short called *Dime que yo* (Tell Me that I ...',
2008) and a version of the allegedly 'unfilmable' novel *Pedro Páramo*
(abandoned by Sogecine in 2008 for financial reasons).[2]

At the same time other key figures have been highly influential in
helping to develop and reshape Amenábar's projects and scripts, such
as producers José Luis Cuerda (on *Tesis* and *Abre los ojos*), Fernando
Bovaira (on *The Others, Mar adentro* and *Ágora*) and more recently
Telecinco's Álvaro Agustín as well as Bovaira (on *Ágora*). In this connection, if Bovaira has occupied the role of an older sibling for Amenábar,
then Cuerda arguably represents the adoptive father figure, in at least
two modes. He has played to perfection the benign university tutor
Amenábar never had as well as the grouchy, but extremely supportive
'padrino' (godfather), who gave the 'boy wonder' his big break (just as
Amenábar has done more recently for Oskar Santos). In other words,
despite his reputation as a 'jack-of-all-trades' or a postmodern version
of Orson Welles, Amenábar's work and career to date have been
successful thanks in no small measure to the contributions of a range
of close friends, collaborators and many other valued specialists.

However, while it is vital to acknowledge the contributions to
his work, for example of production designers such as Benjamin
Fernández (on *The Others*) or Guy Dyas (on *Ágora*) or cinematographers like Burmann or Aguirresarrobe, Amenábar's decisions
on *mise-en-scène* or his choice of lens or framing, in the end, rest on
his own judgement in relation to the task in hand. Moreover, the
consistent display of a certain set of choices or technical repertoire,
even across a fairly modest body of work, suggests that the resulting
style and outlook, however fuzzy, also belong to him. Hence my view
of Amenábar as a still evolving auteur, given his age, the stage he
has reached in his career, his output and style and the increasing
degree of control he manages to exercise over his work. At the level
of Buckland's notion of 'internal authorship', i.e. writing, planning,
shooting, post-production and overall technical and creative mastery,
Amenábar's authorship now seems solidly established. It is characterised by his meticulous research and preparation, his co-written
original scripts, his often unusual, very personal, choice of subject
matter (e.g. the unexpected decision to dramatise the Sampedro case),
his atypical, counter-dominant, approach to genre (as seen in *Ágora*)
and the strong degree of formal and intertextual integration between
his films as well as his personal control over editing, sound and the
film score (until *Ágora*). He is also fully *au fait* with the creative and

technical demands of current filmmaking processes and, given his reputation, can organise finance and distribution for his own and other projects using his production company Himenóptero. Short of owning his own studio and distribution platform, Amenábar now controls both internal (creative) and external (business) aspects of his filmmaking to a very high degree, even though he still lacks the public image, promotional profile, brand identity, marketing savvy and showmanship of an Almodóvar. But to what extent do Amenábar's films display signs of a distinctive style, recurring thematic concerns and a personal attitude or worldview?

In broad terms, at the level of style, unlike some of his colleagues, who have been and continue to be identified with a certain postmodern, trash aesthetic (Almodóvar, de la Iglesia, Segura etc.), Amenábar has deliberately steered clear of this option. Indeed, apart from his first short and in contradistinction to the many parodic, in-joke, comic-horror hybrids, which have been so successfully exploited in Spain, Amenábar draws his inspiration mainly from classical Hollywood and more contemporary Anglo-American, independent sources. He also adds to the mix certain elements from popular and art-inflected Spanish sources (especially Berlanga and Erice), seasoned with a strong dose of black humour. For example, as Andy Willis has observed, the films of Amenábar's horror-thriller trilogy are 'clean', gore-free and 'serious' approaches to the genre, representing a certain 'victory of the serious' in Spanish horror filmmaking for the new millennium (2004: 247–9).

Also, while his style might be strongly Anglo-American, his films seek to exploit, as well as to update and refashion, traditional genre formats. For example, in *Tesis*, while Amenábar uses snuff as a pretext to critique trash television as damaging, exploitative spectacle, he introduces into Spanish filmmaking for the first time the ambiguous figure of the female, student investigator. Here Ángela is someone motivated by a desire less to solve the crime, it seems, than to submit to it, driven by a dark fantasy of becoming a rape and murder victim. Amenábar also gives far more prominence to sound (and thereby authorial control over spectator engagement), not only on the sound-track and via the alternation of sound sourcing (in the battle of the Walkmans). He also foregrounds Ángela's own private consumption of the snuff film at the audio level. This stimulates both her identification with the victim and the (taboo) 'thrill' of aurally re-imagining Vanessa's suffering. Such explorations of perverse female desire as aural pleasure and deeply masochistic fantasy are arguably very uncommon in Spanish horror. Yet, at the same time, Amenábar is not above exploiting the most hoary, old-fashioned, clichéd conventions of Hollywood gothic, as in the blackout in the Faculty tunnels and the use of thunder and lightning just before another blackout in Bosco's bungalow.

Amenábar's knack for imaginative recycling and introducing the unexpected is evidenced not only through his surprise endings but also through his highly restrained, non-parodic, self-conscious modes of narration, accompanied by small, often minimalist soundscapes (as in *The Others*). This recurring aesthetics of discretion is strongly anti-mainstream. It also suggests a view of spectator engagement based not on ironic distantiation and citationality but on a strong degree of realism, immersion, attentiveness, affective investment and empathy towards narrative arc and character interplay. Hence Amenábar's consistent aim of giving primacy to storytelling and narrative momentum over film style, unlike Almodóvar, where this relation-ship tends to be reversed (see D'Lugo 2006: 10–11). Yet, as argued in the chapter on *Tesis*, Amenábar's filmmaking can also be very self-reflexive, catering for audience pleasure through self-conscious, stylistic play and by foregrounding marks of stylistic and narratorial intervention.

Beginning in his shorts and continuing through his features, Amenábar shows a consistent and repeated use of certain basic tech-niques, motifs and figures: the classical three-act screenplay (until *Ágora*, with its two-act structure, linked by intertitles), triangular (and quadrangular) character patterning, the use of sound over black screen as an opening gambit, with a black screen to close. We also find widespread use of offscreen space, plus trademark tracking, circling and zenith shots, repetition and interior duplication of motifs (the mirror and the eye as reflective surfaces, various types of screens, windows, frames and transition points), film and video equipment (video tape, camera or camcorder, playback machines, remotes and CCTV surveillance), telephone, cars (accidents, keys, car models as markers of status), photographs, pillows, regular cameo appearances etc., symmetrical beginnings and endings, ambiguous narrative closures (save perhaps for *Mar adentro*), spare and unobtrusive soundscapes (until the highly operatic *Mar adentro* and heavily symphonic *Ágora*), strong intertextual integration between the main features (e.g. linking the ending of *Abre los ojos* with the beginning of *Mar adentro*, and the end of *Mar adentro* with the end of *Ágora*) and a consistent taste for black humour and jokes, to compensate for the seriousness of the subject matter. Such regular, recycled elements suggest a portfolio of conventions, filming habits and personal tics which indicate a reasonably distinctive, though still evolving, authorial style.

Paradoxically, while Amenábar's films are predominantly character- and dialogue-driven pieces, set mainly in claustrophobic, oppressive interiors, his character creations (and their family contexts) remain relatively spare, thinly drawn and poorly motivated. Within the horror trilogy, for example, characters include predominantly middle-class media undergraduates and their teachers (though Chema is probably lower- or lower-middle-class, like Pelayo), spoilt rich kids and drama students, as well as young war widows or single Catholic mothers, their sick children and strange servants. By and large they come across as enigmatic and cipher-like, lacking in depth, family background, history or roots. In part this may be due to over-ambitious narrative design and slippages between scripting, storyboarding and shooting, giving rise to excess story material and copious editing. But rather flat characters also find their artistic rationale in Amenábar's portrayal of his vacuous, white, middle-class, X generation characters and their detachment, naivety and youthful alienation. They also indicate Amenábar's taste for ambiguity and making the spectator work hard at establishing motivation, thus encouraging narrative engagement.

At the same time Amenábar's films seem predicated on rather naive, adolescent plot lines of 'love at first sight', instant infatuations and 'fatal attractions', where largely inexperienced young characters, often stuck at an infantile level of sexual development, cause themselves no end of trouble. They stumble unawares into relationships which result in a traumatic fall into maturity, by way of a confrontation with a threatening world full of sexual violence, criminality and media manipulation. They suffer psychic fragmentation, abandonment and various forms of catastrophic loss (of looks, body functions, love objects, husbands, identities etc.). Trapped in a repeating 'situation limite', they undergo a painful, life-changing journey at a massive cost to their sense of self. Their catharsis invariably brings with it a renewed awareness of their naivety, defective vision and need for greater clarity, control and far-sightedness.

For example, in *Tesis*, Ángela is attractive though she dresses down; she is not sexually active, has little experience of young men and her sexuality is ambiguous. Her ambition is to escape the strictures of her middle-class family background. Her voyeurism and interest in spying are remarkably potent, as is her appetite for extreme images and her need to achieve a more transcendent, controlling relationship to the visual text of screen violence (akin to Chema's). She is also driven by the thrill of the abyss, by a desire to confront 'real' violence and death. She is therefore fascinated by Bosco's reputation as a womaniser, misogynist and serial murderer. But, as the rather androgynous 'woman in peril', she genuinely becomes aware of female victimisation only when she herself is put in the position of Bosco's seventh snuff victim. However, by finally killing off her 'dream man' (and alter ego), she is in a position to vanquish her voyeurism, masochism and self-loathing. She does so in part by dropping her thesis and the bogus façade of scholarly legitimacy and objectivity this gave to her personal fascination for violence and death. And, by teaming up with Chema in an unlikely friendship, she rejects her class background and vaguely 'comes out', more openly acknowledging her unusual tastes in a horror-gore fan culture but also reminding us of her distinctive, high-culture, literary interests, which include Oscar Wilde's fairy tales (with which Chema is also familiar).

Apart from strong though ambiguously gendered females, Amenábar's films also seem dominated by physically impaired, damaged and emasculated males. These include the headless Alberto and the obsessive, autistic Bosco of Amenábar's early shorts as well as the Bosco of *Tesis*, the disfigured César, the radically immobilised and shrivelled figure of Ramón Sampedro in *Mar adentro* and the effete intellectual elite of Alexandria, represented by Hypatia's father Theon. In one way or another most of these male characters experience various forms of enforced passivity, immobility or entrapment. These are states which are traditionally linked, not to masculine strength but to femininity, female weakness, subordination and lack of freedom. Amenábar's filmmaking, in both shorts and features, thus repeatedly restages the male fascination with and fear of strong, determined, confident women, who induce in men anxiety, impotence and lack. For example, given their voyeurism and taste for hard-core porn and screen violence, in *Tesis*, the erstwhile buddies Chema and Bosco seem deeply disturbed by female desire and sexuality. The latter appear to represent male lack, entrapment and the threat of castration. Amenábar counters this danger by invoking the male fantasy of the serial killer (Bosco) and that of female dismemberment (the snuff scenario in *Tesis*, the ritualised, sadistic slaughter of Hypatia in *Ágora*, which is only partially visualised). By violently re-enacting their loss at the level of female anatomy, young men like Bosco seek to assuage their sexual rage towards women and their likely gender confusion, and to restore their wholeness.

In *Abre los ojos*, through the drama student Sofía, Amenábar also introduces the dangerous world of the theatre and the theatrical, where woman represents masquerade, illusion and duplicity. The film shows how young men fail to recognise the boundary lines between the real and the performance, thus exposing their inability to control female theatricality, resulting in abuse and violence. Also, through Núria, Amenábar reintroduces the bold, threatening, female character from *Luna*, whose aggressive sexuality provokes in César (and in the male spectator) similar retaliatory aggression, seen later in the murder of Sofía/Núria. In *Mar adentro* Ramón is capable of experiencing sexuality but does so only within the context of fantasy, given his total lack of sensations below the neck. Of course, he could devise other methods, as Julia suggests, but he refuses to experiment, unprepared to accept a degraded form of non-phallic, sexual relations. In response he arguably projects his resentments onto the women with whom he falls in love, since they are the only ones who supply him with a whole body. Ramón can then recover his own wholeness symbolically and psychically by seducing and then abandoning his lovers. The process of seduction thus provides a temporary 'buzz', a sensation of vitality and male transcendence (a form of resistance to impotence), but it is not enough to compensate for his condition. In a sense, for Ramón, the wholeness, potency and plenitude of male identity depend on mastering and somehow invalidating or eliminating female identity. In short all these male characters come to realise the awesome costs of their voyeurism, narcissism, egoism, lack of commitment and withholding of solidarity towards others. They are fallen men, males in fragments, symbols of lack and dysfunction, but also resentful and angry towards those with whole bodies, i.e. women.

Few if any of Amenábar's characters are able to cope with or overcome their traumas or accept and adapt to their loss. Ramón flatly refuses the wheelchair and the degraded life of a quadriplegic. And apart from Ángela (who joins a much humbled Chema), all find a remedy in self-annihilation via suicide (Hypatia's 'mercy killing' at the hand of Davus, however, is obviously fanciful and invented but is represented and legitimised as an act of love). But, fearful of death and the afterlife, they retreat into fantasy worlds. They immerse themselves in consolatory fictions provided by old as well as new style religions. Grace exists in a form of spiritual limbo, protected by the bogus certainties of Catholic dogma. César can afford to opt for the far more advanced technology of L.E., whose luxury packages promise eternal happiness in a virtual paradise, under the complete control of the client. Significantly, though he still relies on daydreams and fantasy in order to cope with his condition, Ramón is the only one who accepts the finality of physical death and does not seek an insurance through resurrection, since he is not afraid to die or face an eternity of nothingness. Hypatia is presented (misleadingly) as a rationalist and sceptic (rather than a monotheistic neo-platonist), somehow free of anxieties over her own death and driven by a belief in the emancipatory power of science and reason over nature. And it is this apparently cool, clear-headed, agnostic response to the question of death and the lack of an afterlife which speaks powerfully to Amenábar and perhaps allows him to come to terms with his fears concerning his own mortality.

With so much enforced inactivity in his films, Amenábar's males also offer perfect avatars for the role of the cinema spectator. Characters function as voyeurs and identification figures for audiences who, in their turn, are invited to share and experience the guilty desires exposed on screen. What these reveal are the serious dangers and devastating consequences of compulsive 'looking for pleasure' and especially of immersion and over-investment in the narratives and 'looks' of others. Here, for example, César massively over-subscribes to the narrative of Sofía and her image of bodily perfection, as does Ángela in the 'angelic' look of Bosco. Amenábar's films thus act as cautionary tales for the incautious. They also appear to disrupt classical (Mulveyan) gaze theory by reversing conventional hierarchies and putting males in focus as objects of female voyeuristic interest (Bosco, César, Charles, Ramón etc., though nunlike Hypatia appears to have eyes only for the beauty of the planets and the stars). Such ocular fascination can be seen in Silvia's controlling looks at Bosco and María in *Himenóptero* and in Luna's obsessive, coquettish gaze towards Alberto in *Luna*. An active female gaze also underlies Ángela's masochistic and fetishistic infatuation with Bosco, Núria's sadistic, vampish desire for César, and Rosa's maternal investment in Ramón, whose atrophied, infantilised body also becomes a form of national televisual spectacle, aimed at the empathetic, maternal, female gaze. Here, and in other Amenábar films, we find spaces and positions opening up which do not automatically prioritise an aggressive, sadistic, controlling male gaze. Rather, possession and power over the look can be shared and sometimes belong to female characters, as seen at the end of *Tesis*, where it is the woman who controls the gaze: In the lift, having abandoned the 'reality show' and about to exit the hospital, Ángela casts the final sideways glance towards a disempowered, bruised and submissive Chema (still in his pyjamas).

Finally, Amenábar's filmmaking seems to place considerable emphasis on the perversions of looking and the gaze, psychic fragmentation, ambiguous sexual indentities, body consciousness and the deceptiveness of appearances, as well as death and resurrection. Without wishing to pigeonhole or limit our interpretive options, such concerns show significant thematic affinities with New Queer Cinema. This trend emerged in the late 1980s and early 1990s, across the festival circuits (such as Sundance), as a challenge to fixed gender representations and the binary 'normality' of heterosexuality and homosexuality. According to Aaron this cinema provided an outlet to some of the more marginal voices within the field of non-straight sexual identities.[3] And in films such as *Poison* (Todd Haynes, 1991), *My Own Private Idaho* (Gus Van Sant, 1991), *Swoon* (Tom Kalin, 1992) and *The Living End* (Gregg Araki, 1992), New Queer Cinema seemed unapologetic regarding its subject matter or character flaws. It was keen to challenge the past by recovering queer content and anxious to aestheticise violence and criminal behaviour while defying genre and even death through AIDS (Aaron 2006: 398–400).

As noted earlier, there are no explicitly gay figures in Amenábar's story lines. Yet it remains the case that most of his characters betray unusual, non-conventional, sexual identities. His villains (including Silvia, Luna, Castro, the two Boscos, César, Grace, Ramón and even Hypatia) seem to defy easy definition and assimilation into clear-cut sexual categories. Indeed, through her commitment to 'sofrosine' (prudence and control of the appetites), Hypatia renounces worldly pleasures in favour of science and her study of the heavens; her friendship with Orestes is strictly platonic. Like Silvia and Bosco in *Himenóptero*, Ángela and Chema in *Tesis* emerge as an odd couple, an unlikely partnership between a possibly gay man and a lesbian or bisexual woman. And, as regards Ángela's ambiguous sexuality, we find a significant clue in the poster of her favourite film, *My Own Private Idaho*. This is a road narrative and one of the founding movies

of Queer Cinema. It deals with the lives, dreams and disappoint-
ments of marginal sexualities (two apparently gay buddies, an outlaw
couple, male hustlers) and a journey (Mick and Scott set off to find
the former's lost mother, without success; gay poseur Scott finally
returns to his wealthy family, straight sex and marriage). Van Sant
treats homosexual relations with great frankness as well as tenderness, epitomised perhaps by the final confessional scene around the
campfire. The film is clearly important for Ángela and obviously has
deep personal and perhaps emblematic significance for her creator
and alter ego Amenábar.

Also, as noted in the section on *Luna*, Amenábar seems to acknowledge the linkage between sex and danger, as if the fear of AIDS operates
as a ghostly presence at the centre of that film, just as it hovers in the
background of Van Sant's film. Moreover, Amenábar's main source
for *Tesis* was *The Silence of the Lambs* (Demme, 1991), which focuses
not only on a sexually ambiguous Clarice but also on the queer figure
par excellence, Buffalo Bill, i.e. the wannabe transsexual, who seeks
reincarnation through bodily transformation. We find similar desires
for a change of identity in Ángela and in César, after the car accident
when, before committing suicide, he signs up for cryonisation and
resurrection in 2147. And while Grace is miraculously resurrected after
her suicide, but refuses to acknowledge her status in limbo, Ramón
defies his suffering and 'living death' by finally reasserting control
over his own body and finding liberation in death. These are weighty
issues. I suggest that Amenábar's continuing fascination with them
across his filmmaking career, until he came out in 2004, does not
simply derive from an oppressive childhood Catholicism, which he
rebelled against and rejected. Part of his rejection is arguably linked to
his own sexual identity seeking an outlet or change, possibly deterred
by a fear of AIDS or family disapproval, but echoed in the different
ways his characters cope with, resist or defy death.

If we can point to affinities in Amenábar's filmmaking with New
Queer Cinema, his films also share some commonalities with what
Jeffrey Sconce refers to as 'smart cinema'.[4] That is, a loose, untidy
grouping of mainly contemporary, independent art movies which
reinvest in classical forms of narration and *mise-en-scène* and showcase
youthful disaffection, but where the protagonists do not 'search for
meaning' so much as get 'fucked by fate', which depends primarily
on coincidence and synchronicity. Such films as *Slacker* (Richard
Linklater, 1991), *American Beauty* (Sam Mendes, 1999) and *Donnie*

Darko (Richard Kelly, 2001), explore the alienation arising from Western consumer culture, the anomie of middle-class suburbia, the critique of white middle-class families, ill-suited to provide stable environments for their children and the family seen as a source of emotional and sexual dysfunctionality.

Since the beginning of his career Amenábar has enjoyed a remarkable level of critical and commercial success within Spain. And since the turn of the millennium, on the commercial front, no fewer than three of his feature films have figured consistently in the country's 'top ten' biggest grossing pictures. *The Others* (with 6.4 million admissions and a domestic gross of over €27 million) remains Spain's most commercially successful film of all time. *Mar adentro* enjoyed over four million local admissions and took nearly €20 million at the box-office, while *Ágora* attracted 3.3 million spectators and grossed €21.3 million (source: mcu.es). Apart from a further handful of films which have also broken the €20 million barrier in the domestic market, no other Spanish director has managed to generate such outstanding totals in such a sustained fashion.[5] However, when we consider Amenábar's fortunes in foreign markets, especially the USA, a rather different, far less triumphalist picture emerges.

As seen earlier, in terms of admissions, *Abre los ojos* attracted nearly 1.8 million spectators in Spain, a clear indicator of strong audience interest, stimulated by the Goya success of *Tesis*. However, the film's patchy and delayed international release campaign (at festivals, on television, on video and DVD as well as in theatres) generated low admission levels, with just under 73,000 in the USA, 22,000 in France, 16,000 in the UK and 4,000 in the Netherlands (source: imdb.com), for example. As for box-office in the world's largest market, the USA, we find a rather dismal gross for *Abre los ojos* of just $370,720, over a nine-week campaign, in 34 theatres at its widest point, mid-April to mid-June 1999 (source: boxofficemojo.com). This deeply disappointing outcome perhaps reflects poor distribution, poor dates, a crowded market and the fact that foreign subtitled films in the USA always struggle to find an audience. By contrast, in 2001 *The Others* was a major hit not only in Spain but also worldwide, grossing $113 million in foreign earnings and $96.5 million in the USA, totalling approximately $210 millions (source: mcu.es). This was a tremendous result, even before including ancillary revenues. However, since then, Amenábar has struggled to reproduce anything like the worldwide commercial success generated by his haunted house chiller. Indeed his last two films may have been enormous domestic hits but they have also been massive international flops (reflecting the release profile of Díaz Yanes's *Alatriste*, 2006). *Mar adentro*, budgeted at €10 million and released in over 40 countries since 2004, attracted very poor admissions in most European countries (even in its better markets, including the UK, the Netherlands, Germany, Italy and France). In the USA the film struggled to earn just over $2 million (source: imdb. com). As for *Ágora*, while it did reasonably well in France (grossing €2.3 million) and in Italy (€2.8 million), in the key market which really mattered and for which it was designed to compete strongly, i.e. the USA, it took a meagre $620,000 (€465,000), over a 21-week campaign, playing at its widest in 17 theatres (source: boxoffficemojo. com). This figure also represents a mere 1.6 per cent of its worldwide box-office takings of $38 million (€28.5 million) against a production and marketing budget of well in excess of €100 million. *Ágora* will probably be remembered as Spain's most expensive film ever, but also as its most conspicuous failure internationally.

Moreover, such results not only remind us that the producers of *Ágora* have sustained major losses of some €70–100 million, most of which Telecinco will be required to absorb. They also suggest that, after two glaring commercial failures, Amenábar's film products may no longer be favoured by distributors abroad, and will be seen increasingly as a 'hard sell' in international markets, unable to cover costs or appeal to mainstream filmgoers. If such perceptions are correct, then this is bound to impact negatively on any future financing of an Amenábar-branded project and will alienate foreign investors. Of course, as noted earlier, the economic crisis of 2008–9 totally transformed the market conditions and outlook of foreign distributors towards pictures such as *Ágora*. And in a wider historical context, between Twentieth Century Fox's financial nightmare represented by *Cleopatra* (1963) and the commercially successful *Gladiator* (2000), the sword-and-sandals historical epic fell seriously out of favour with general film-going publics. Ridley Scott's *Gladiator* revived an almost defunct epic tradition and made serious profits (well over $280 million on a $110 million budget, source: imdb.com). Yet, as producers Fernando Bovaira and Álvaro Agustín would have known, since 2000, box-office results have been very mixed for films such as *Hero* (Zhang Yimou, 2002), *Troy* (Wolfgang Petersen, 2004), *King Arthur* (Antoine Fuqua, 2004), *Alexander* (Oliver Stone, 2004), *Kingdom of Heaven* (Ridley Scott, 2005), *300* (Zack Snyder, 2006), *The Last Legion*

(Doug Leffer, 2007) and *10000 BC* (Roland Emmerich, 2008). Apart from *300*, few of these films have covered costs and even fewer have made any profits. In other words *Ágora* was already likely to be the biggest and most dangerous gamble of Amenábar's professional career. Given his commitment to exhaustive research, we can assume that Amenábar studied the background to Oliver Stone's *Alexander*, one of the most exemplary failures of this type of picture since 2000. Budgeted at $155 million, with a running time of 175 minutes and grossing a mere $34 million in the USA (with $133 million in foreign earnings), the film was flayed by most Anglo-American critics, mainly for its over-compressed narrative, linguistic peculiarities, treatment of homosexuality, dryness and lack of audience engagement. As the maverick auteur of such impressive dissections of war and power as *Platoon* (1986), *Wall Street* (1987), *Born on the Fourth of July* (1989), *JFK* (1991) and *Nixon* (1995), not only Stone's reputation but the credibility of his producers, cast and crew were severely damaged. Whether this is the ultimate fate awaiting *Ágora*, only time will tell. What we can suggest is that Amenábar, like Stone, has had to learn a bitter lesson in hubris, one of serious talent and hard graft being unequal to ambition and over-confidence, perhaps even of 'going a genre too far'. But what now? What are Amenábar's options for future projects?

In late 2007 press reports suggested that he had acquired the rights to film the third instalment of Arthur C. Clarke's Space Odyssey series: '2061: Odyssey 3', following Stanley Kubrick and Peter Hyams, who were responsible for the first and second episodes.[6] Tom Hanks, who initially expressed serious interest in producing as well as starring in the third instalment, mysteriously dropped out of the bidding. This left the way open for Amenábar, one of Kubrick's most devoted fans. Of course, whether this project is being prepped for a third journey of interplanetary discovery is another matter altogether. After the debacle of *Mar adentro* and *Ágora* in foreign markets, Amenábar's personal capital and credibility as a successful commercial director beyond Spain have been significantly dented. Moreover, standing in the shadow of Kubrick's iconic *2001 A Space Odyssey* (1969), he will struggle to find willing backers for a major sci-fi epic, which will also require a mega-budget and most likely a change of scriptwriting personnel, if American investors are to be involved.

Other options for Amenábar might well include a documentary feature (for screening on television as well as in film theatres) on astronomy, in line with the concept which predated *Ágora* and which focused on pre-Copernican science in late antiquity. Here, however, I suspect Amenábar might have difficulties in Spain in re-establishing his bona fides among the scientific and astronomical communities as a historically reliable populariser of scientific discovery. For many Spanish astronomers and scientists more widely, his rendition of Hypatia of Alexandria as primarily an astronomer (rather than a philosopher) and as having discovered the ellipse as the key to planetary motion, 1,200 years before Kepler, was a welcome boost and powerful promotional vehicle for science education in Spain and beyond. Unfortunately the portrayal was also totally fanciful, a serious distortion of an admittedly thin historical record, and the 'precursor of Kepler' angle simply false. Whatever credibility Amenábar might have had here as a cheerleader of female scientific achievement has been vitiated somewhat by his historical licence and pro-feminist hagiography; he should probably avoid any landings in this area.

A further option, which he has often referred to, might be a fiction feature inspired by an aspect of the Pinochet military coup in Chile in 1973 or the aftermath of the 'dirty war', events which his family managed to avoid but whose preparations led to their exile in Spain and to a successful filmmaking career for Amenábar. However, he has always been rather reluctant to engage with such nightmares of historical memory directly through his camera. A more contemporary and relevant option, sometimes mentioned by his fans in the blogosphere who agree with his condemnation of ETA violence, is that he should focus his lens on the devastating, home-grown nightmare of the '11M' (11 March 2004). This refers to the terrorist bombings of Madrid's suburban rail system, designed by the planners of the coup to radically alter the outcome of the March 2004 General Elections in favour of the PSOE. However, thousands of Spanish filmmaking personnel depend for their livelihoods on generous state subsidies from the PSOE-led government and an inner core of left-wing actors and artists, including many filmmakers, operate as a praetorian guard and political lobby for Zapatero and the party (as seen in the 2008 elections and their 'Plataforma de Apoyo a Zapatero' or PAZ). It is thus very unlikely that they or Amenábar (also a fellow traveller) would risk bringing into question the government's 'versión oficial' (official version) of those events. I refer to the 'Al Qaeda' cover story whose task it has been to shield the PSOE's breathtaking degree of involvement in the coup.[7] Moreover, thus far, there are no indications (verbal, visual or in the blogosphere) that Amenábar himself might one day examine the '11M', with or without the sort of probing, CNN-style realism he sought to simulate via his camera eye in *Ágora*.

Finally, perhaps in the spirit of a 'back to basics' agenda, I suspect Amenábar will set aside epic and political cinema in favour of a return to his own filmmaking roots, i.e. to the low(ish)-budget, small-scale, international co-pro, horror thriller, and take stock for a while. The signs are that he may do so by either producing or directing the film adaptation of a literary property.[8] In April 2010 he bought the screen rights to *Fin* (The End, El Acantilado, Barcelona, 2009), a best-selling debut novel by a certain David Monteagudo, a Galician who used to work in a cardboard factory in Vilafranca, near Barcelona. Uncannily, the plot line of the novel echoes certain aspects of Mateo Gil's *Nadie conoce a nadie* (1999), not least the apocalyptic revenge narrative of an abused young man, turned megalomaniac: Nine old friends who used to go climbing together as adolescents all agree to meet up 25 years later at a mountain lodge. However, only eight of them show up, i.e. all those who, as a group, once played a terrible trick on the ninth person, nicknamed 'El Profeta', who is missing. Containing elements of the social novel, psychological drama and horror-thriller and recalling Stephen King's *Carrie* (1974 and *Dreamcatcher* (2001) and Cormac MacCarthy's *The Road* (2006, adapted for film by John Hillcoat, 2009), this sounds like promising material for a somewhat humbled Amenábar, perhaps anxious to atone for his earlier Hellenic hubris and reconnect with his fans.

Notes

1 Leaving aside the many skits and parodies now to be found on YouTube, we find a bizarre, graphic riposte, made in comic-book form, written by the film critic Jordi Costa and drawn by Darío Adanti, *Mis problemas con Amenábar* (Madrid: Glénat, 2009). Costa's claim, tinged with envy, is that, far from being a filmmaking prodigy, Amenábar is nothing but a privileged 'pijo' (posh brat). He is 'un buen chico que filma obras maestras' (a nice kid who makes masterpieces), but one who does not deserve his success, whose talent is a mere simulacrum (product of a collective delirium) and whose aim is 'la asfixia de lo dionisiaco' (the stifling of desire). See Anon., 'El crítico Jordi Costa critica duramente a Alejandro Amenábar en su última obra', www.abc.es/20091006/cultura-cine/critico-jordi-costa-critica-200910062226.html.

2 After an 11–year break since *Nadie conoce a nadie* (1999) Gil makes his English-language debut and second feature, with a Spain-France-Bolivia

co-pro, a western called *Blackthorn* (2011). It is billed as a sequel to *Butch Cassidy and the Sundance Kid* (George Roy Hill, 1969). Here Butch (now called James Blackthorn, played by Sam Shepard), long-exiled in Bolivia and anxious for one last glimpse of home, decides to head north. On the way he meets the young villain Ernesto Apodaca (played by Eduardo Noriega); they decide to travel together but not to revive the old bank-robbing duo.

3 See Michele Aaron, 'New queer cinema', in *Contemporary American Cinema*, Linda Ruth Williams and Michael Hammond (eds) (Maidenhead: Open University Press, 2006, 398–409.

4 Jeffrey Sconce, 'Smart cinema', in *Contemporary American Cinema*, Linda Ruth Williams and Michael Hammond (eds)(Maidenhead: Open University Press, 2006, 429–439.

5 Examples of other 'top ten' grossing films include Santiago Segura's *Torrente 2. Misión en Marbella* (Mission in Marbella, 2001, 5.32 million spectators, €22 million box-office) and his *Torrente 3. El protector* (The Bodyguard, 2005, 3.57 million spectators, €18 million); *Torrente 4: Lethal Crisis* attracted 2.5 million specators and made €18 million). Also we have, Juan Antonio Bayona's *El orfanato* (The Orphanage, 2007, 4.42 million admissions, €25 million) and Javier Fesser's *La gran aventura de Mortadelo y Filemón* (Mortadelo and Filemón: The Big Adventure, 2003, 4,985 million spectators and €22.85 million) (source: mcu.es). By contrast and contrary to dominant perceptions, Almodóvar's domestic grosses are relatively modest, as seen in his best performer of the last decade, *Volver* (To Return, 2006), which attracted 1.93 million spectators and overall box-office of €10.24 million. Oscar-winning *Todo sobre mi madre* (All About My Mother, 1999) also did well in Spain with 2.56 million admissions and $9,962 million gross. Compare these numbers with *La mala educación* (Bad Education, 2004), with 1.24 million admissions and €6.1 million gross and the disappointing figures for *Los abrazos rotos* (Broken Embraces, 2009), with only 691,447 spectators and €4,41 million gross (source: mcu.es).

6 See Mary Carmen Rodríguez, 'Lo Nuevo de Alejandro Amenábar , www. lashorasperdidas.com/index.php/2007/12/28/lo-nuevo-de-alejandro-amenabar/.

7 On these matters see the analysis by Casimiro García Abadillo, *La venganza* (Madrid: La Esfera de los libros, 2005) and the rather more technical *Titadyn* (Madrid: La Esfera de los libros, 2009), García Abadillo's follow-up study, co-written with the forensic chemist Antonio Iglesias. The book explores in detail the explosives used in the coup, the role of the Bomb Disposal Squad (TEDAX) and its notorious controller, Juan Jesús Sánchez Manzano. It also confirms that Sánchez Manzano shamelessly lied to the various judicial investigations into the 11M, for which he was later promoted by Rubalcaba, Minister of the Interior. See the very early *El Mundo* coverage

of April–May 2004, such as the remarkably detailed and prescient analyses by Fernando Múgica, for example, 'Los agujeros negros del 11–M. Una versión policial repleta de incongruencias', 23 April 2004, at www.elmundo.es/elmundo/2004/04/19/enespecial/1082356558.html. See also the recording of a 65–minute lecture/QandA, delivered to victims' organisations in Vigo, 2007, by the journalist Luis del Pino at www.youtube.com/watch?v=Nbhgc76x4-sandfeature=related. Also of interest is the 2010 video evidence from the six court-appointed forensic chemists and their findings, which showed that the explosive used in the 11M bombings was in fact Tytadine, not Goma 2 Eco. This totally contradicts the PSOE government's Al Qaeda hypothesis and confirms the long-suspected ETA linkage to the atrocity, consistently claimed by the Aznar government. Demonised as a liar by his socialist opponents, Aznar was right from the very beginning, it seems. See: www.youtube.com/watch?v=VSDF0R9dfoI 'La pericial de explosivos: en el 11M no estalló Goma 2 eco'.

8 The rumour which circulated in Spain at the end of December 2010 that Amenábar was ready to team up once again with Javier Bardem to make a period drama entitled 'Duques' is unconfirmed and looks like a hoax. It appears to have originated from the Fundación Cristina Enea, San Sebastián, where Amenábar was apparently researching the life and work of an allegedly distant relative, the Duque de Mandas, Fermín Lasala y Collado and his wife, Cristina Bruneti de los Cobos (to be played, allegedly, by the Basque actress Bárbara Goenaga). Further press and internet checks carried out in January–February 2011 failed to give any credence to the rumour.

Filmography

Shorts

La cabeza (The Head, 1991) 15 mins
Director: Alejandro Amenábar
Screenplay: Alejandro Amenábar
Camera: Mateo Gil and Alejandro Amenábar
Editing: Alejandro Amenábar
Music: Alejandro Amenábar and Alfredo Alonso
Sound: Alejandro Amenábar
Leading players: Sandra Gil (Ana) and Edmundo Morzwit (Pseudonym for Alejandro Amenábar) (Roberto)
Dubbing actress: Nieves Herranz

Himenóptero (Himenopterus, 1992) 31 minutes
Director: Alejandro Amenábar
Screenplay: Alejandro Amenábar
Camera: Mateo Gil and Alejandro Amenábar
Editing: Alejandro Amenábar
Music: Alejandro Amenábar
Sound: Alejandro Amenábar
Leading players: Raquel Gómez (Silvia), Juana Macías (Mónica), Nieves Herranz (María) and Alejandro Amenábar (Bosco)

Luna

Video version *Luna* (Moon, 1994) 30 minutes
Director: Alejandro Amenábar
Screenplay: Alejandro Amenábar and Mateo Gil
Camera: Mateo Gil and Alejandro Amenábar
Editing: Alejandro Amenábar
Music: Alejandro Amenábar
Sound: Alejandro Amenábar

Leading players: Nieves Herranz (Luna), Eduardo Noriega (Alberto) and Alejandro Amenábar (Waiter)

Film version: *Luna* (1995) 35mm 12 minutes
Director: Alejandro Amenábar
Screenplay: Alejandro Amenábar and Mateo Gil
Camera: Mateo Gil and Alejandro Amenábar
Editing: Alejandro Amenábar
Music: José Sánchez Sanz / Alejandro Amenábar
Sound: Alejandro Amenábar
Leading players: Nieves Herranz (Luna), Eduardo Noriega (Alberto), Joserra Cardiñanos (garage attendant)

Features

Tesis (Thesis, 1996) 125 minutes
Production companies: Las Producciones del Escorpión, Sogepaq
Producer: José Luis Cuerda
Executive Producer: Emiliano Otegui
Director: Alejandro Amenábar
Screenplay: Alejandro Amenábar
Cinematography: Hans Burmann
Music: Alejandro Amenábar and Mariano Marín
Sound: Goldstein and Steinberg
Editing : María Elena Sáenz de Rozas
Production Design: Wolfgang Burmann
Make-up: María Isabel Adánez Almenara
Costume Design: Ana Cuerda
Second Unit Director: Mateo Gil
Special Effects: Reyes Abades
Leading players: Ana Torrent (Ángela Márquez), Fele Martínez (Chema), Eduardo Noriega (Bosco Herranz), Xavier Elorriaga (Jorge Castro), Miguel Picazo (Figueroa), Nieves Herranz (Sena Márquez), Rosa Campillo (Yolanda), Olga Margallo (Vanessa), Francisco Hernández (Ángela's Father) Rosa Ávila (Ángela's Mother) Teresa Castañeda (TV Announcer), José Miguel Caballero (Library Clerk) Joserra Cardiñanos (Police Guard), Julio Vélez (Station Guard), Pilar Ortega (Sales Clerk)

Abre los ojos (Open Your Eyes, 1997) 117 minutes
Production companies: Las Producciones del Escorpión, Sogecine/Sogetel, Les Films Alain Sarde, Lucky Red, Canal Plus España
Director: Alejandro Amenábar
Producers: José Luis Cuerda, Fernando Bovaira
Associate Producers: Ana Amigo, Andrea Occhipinti, Alain Sarde

Production director: Emiliano Otegui
Screenplay: Alejandro Amenábar and Mateo Gil
Cinematography: Hans Burmann
Sound: Goldstein and Steinberg
Music: Alejandro Amenábar and Mariano Marín
Editing: María Elena Saínz de Rozas
Art Direction: Wolfgang Burmann
Set Design: Carola Angulo
Costume design: Concha Solera
Make-up: Paca Almenara
Special Effects Make-up: Colin Arthur
Second Unit Director Mateo Gil
Special Effects: Reyes Abades
Leading Players: Eduardo Noriega (César), Penélope Cruz (Sofía), Chete Lera
    (Antonio), Fele Martínez (Pelayo), Najwa Nimri (Núria), Gérard Barray
    (Duvernois), Jorge de Juan (Assistant L.E.), Miguel Palenzuela (Police
    Inspector), plus Alejandro Amenábar, Mateo Gil and Carlos Montero (Men
    in bathroom)

The Others (2001) 100 minutes
Production companies: Las Producciones del Escorpión, Sogecine, Le Studio
    Canal, Cruise-Wagner Productions, Miramax Films
Producers: José Luis Cuerda, Fernando Bovaira, Sunmin Park
Executive Producers: Bob Weinstein, Harvey Weinstein, Tom Cruise, Paula
    Wagner, Rick Schwartz
Associate Producer: Eduardo Chapero-Jackson
Screenplay: Alejandro Amenábar
Director: Alejandro Amenábar
Music: Alejandro Amenábar and Lucio Godoy
Cinematography: Javier Aguirresarobe
Editing: Alejandro Amenábar, Nacho Ruiz Capillas
Sound: Ricardo Goldstein
Production Design: Benjamín Fernández
Art Direction: Benjamín Fernández
Costume Design: Sonia Grande
Make-up: Ana López Puigcerver
Special Effects: Félix Bergés
Leading players: Nicole Kidman (Grace Stewart), Fionnula Flanagan Bertha
    Mills), Christopher Eccleston (Charles Stewart), Alakina Mann (Anne
    Stewart), James Bentley (Nicholas Stewart), Eric Sykes (Edmund Tuttle),
    Elaine Cassidy (Lydia), Renée Asherson (Old Woman), Alexander Vince
    (Victor Marlish), Keith Allen (Mr Marlish), Michelle Fairley (Mrs Marlish)

Mar adentro (The Sea Inside, 2004) 125 minutes
Production companies: Himenóptero, Sogecine/Sogetel, in co-production with UGC Images (France) and Eyescreen (Italy) and in collaboration with TVE, Canal Plus España, TVG, Filmanova Invest and with the support of Eurimages and ICAA
Producers: Alejandro Amenábar, Fernando Bovaira
Director: Alejandro Amenábar
Screenplay: Alejandro Amenábar and Mateo Gil
Music: Alejandro Amenábar, with Carlos Nuñez
Cinematography: Javier Aguirresarrobe
Production Director: Emiliano Otegui
Casting: Luis San Narciso
Editing: Alejandro Amenábar, Nacho Ruiz Capillas
Art Direction: Benjamín Fernández
Set Design: Benjamín Fernández
Sound: Ricardo Steinberg
Costume: Sonia Grande
Make-up: Ana López Puigcerver, Jo Allen
Special Effects: Raúl Romanillos, Pau Costa
Leading Players: Javier Bardem (Ramón Sampedro), Belén Rueda (Julia), Lola Dueñas (Rosa), Mabel Rivera (Manuela Sampedro), Celso Bugallo (José Sampedro), Clara Segura (Gené Gordó), Joan Dalmau (Joaquín), Alberto Jiménez (Germán), Tamar Novas (Javier Sampedro), Francesc Garrido (Marc), José María Pou (Father Francisco), Alberto Amarilla (Brother Andrés).

Ágora (2009) 126 minutes
Production companies: Mod Producciones, Himenóptero, Telecinco Cinema, in collaboration with Canal Plus España and Cinebiss, with the support of ICAA.
Producers: Alejandro Amenábar, Fernando Bovaira, Álvaro Agustín
Executive Producers: Simón de Santiago, Jaime Ortiz de Artiñano
Director: Alejandro Amenábar
Second Unit Director: Mateo Gil
Screenplay: Alejandro Amenábar and Mateo Gil
Music: Darío Marianelli
Cinematography: Xavi Giménez
Line Producer: José Luis Escolar
Production Management: Carlos Ruiz Boceta
Production Designer: Guy Hendrix Dyas
Set Decoration: Larry Dias
Casting: Jina Jay
Editing: Alejandro Amenábar, Nacho Ruiz Capillas
Supervising Art Director: Frank Walsh

Sound Editor: Glenn Freemantle
Costume Design: Gabriella Pescucci
Make-up Co-ordinator: Marcello Genovese
Visual Effects Supervisor: Felix Bergés
Special Effects Supervisor: Chris Reynolds
Leading Players: Rachel Weisz (Hypatia), Max Minghella (Davus), Oscar Isaac (Orestes), Ashraf Barhom (Ammonius), Michael Lonsdale (Theon), Rupert Evans (Synesius), Sami Samir (Cyril), Manuel Cauchi (Theophilus), Homayoun Ershadi (Aspasius), Richard Durden (Olympius), Oshri Cohen (Medorus), Omar Mostafa (Isidorus)

Bibliography

Books and journal articles

Aaron, Michele (2006), 'New Queer Cinema', in *Contemporary American Cinema*, Linda Ruth Williams and Michael Hammond (eds), Maidenhead: Open University Press, pp. 398–409.

Academia. Revista del cine español: El proceso creativo del último cine español, 26 (Summer 1999).

Acevedo-Muñoz, Ernesto R. (2008), 'Horror of allegory: *The Others* and its contexts', in *Contemporary Spanish Cinema and Genre*, Jay Beck and Vicente Rodríguez Ortega (eds), Manchester: Manchester University Press, 2008, pp. 202–18.

Aguilar, Carlos (coord.) (2005), *Cine fantástico y de terror español 1984–2004*, San Sebastián: Semana de Cine fantástico y de terror español, 1984–2004, Donostia Kultura.

Allen, Richard and Sam Ishi-Gonzales (2004), *Hitchcock. Past and Future*, London and New York: Routledge.

Allinson, Mark (1997), 'Not matadors, not natural born killers: Violence in three films by young Spanish directors', *Bulletin of Hispanic Studies*, 74:1, pp. 315–29.

Allinson, Mark (2001), *A Spanish Labyrinth: The Films of Pedro Almodóvar*, London: I.B. Tauris.

Allinson, Mark (2003), 'Is the auteur dead? The case of Juanma Bajo Ulloa', *International Journal of Iberian Studies*, 15:3, pp. 143–51.

Amago, Samuel (2004), 'Horror and ambivalence in *Tesis*: Alejandro Amenábar's reflections on the postmodern condition', *Revista de Estudios Hispáncos* 38:1, pp. 143–58.

Amenábar, Alejandro (1997/1998), *Tesis (Guión)*, Barcelona: Planeta, Colección Booket.

Amenábar, Alejandro (2001), *Los otros. Una película de Alejandro Amenábar. El libro*, Madrid: Ocho y medio, Libros de Cine, SGAE.

Amenábar, Alejandro and Mateo Gil (2004), *Mar adentro. Guión Cinematográfico de Alejandro Amenábar y Mateo Gil*, Versión de rodaje, Madrid: Ocho y Medio, Colección Espiral.

Amenábar, Alejandro et al. (2009), *Ágora. El viaje al mundo antiguo de Alejandro Amenábar*, Madrid: Libros Cúpula.

Anuario Fotogramas 2003 (2003), Barcelona: Comunicaciones y Publicaciones.

Arroyo, José. (2003), 'La comunidad' (review), *Sight and Sound*, 13:7, pp. 37–38.

Austin, Guy (1996), *Contemporary French Cinema. An Introduction*, Manchester: Manchester University Press.

Babington, Bruce and Peter William Evans (1993), *Biblical Epics: Sacred Narrative in the Hollywood Cinema*, Manchester: Manchester University Press.

Barr, Charles (2002), *Vertigo*, London: BFI Film Classics.

Barroso, Miguel Angel and Gil-Delgado, Fernando (2002), *Cine español en cien películas*, Madrid: Ediciones Jaguar.

Bazin, André (1978), *Orson Welles. A Critical View*, New York: Harper and Row.

Bazin, André, (1985), 'On the *politique des auteurs*', in *Cahiers du cinéma: The 1950s*, Jim Hillier (ed.), Cambridge (MA): Harvard University Press, pp. 248–59.

Berthier, Nancy (ed.) (2007a), *Le cinéma d'Alejandro Amenábar*, Toulouse: Presses Universitaires du Mirail.

Berthier, Nancy (2007b), 'Voir ou ne pas voir: la fonction du hors champ dans *Tesis*', in *Le cinéma d'Alejandro Amenábar*, Nancy Berthier (ed.), Toulouse: Presses Universitaires du Mirail, pp. 43–56.

Besas, Peter (1985), *Behind the Spanish Lens: Spanish Cinema under Fascism and Democracy*, Denver: Arden Press.

Black, Jeremy (2002), 'Realist horror: from execution videos to snuff films' in *Underground USA: Filmmaking Beyond the Hollywood Canon*, Xavier Mendik and Steven J. Schneider (eds), London: Wallflower Press, pp. 63–75.

Borau, José Luis (ed.) (1998), *Diccionario del cine español*, Madrid: Alianza Editorial.

Bordwell, David (1979). 'The art cinema as a mode of film practice', *Film Criticism*, 4:1, pp. 56–64, reprinted in *The European Cinema Reader*, Catherine Fowler (ed.), London and New York: Routledge, 2002, pp. 94–102.

Bordwell, David (1985), *Narration in the Fiction Film*, London: Routledge.

Bordwell, David (1997), *On the History of Film Style*, Cambridge (MA) and London: Harvard University Press.

Bordwell, David (2000), *Planet Hong Kong. Popular Cinema and the Art of Entertainment*, Cambridge (MA) and London: Harvard University Press.

Bordwell, David (2002), 'Intensified continuity. visual style in contemporary American film', *Film Quarterly*, 55:3, pp. 16–28.

Bordwell, David (2006), 'Subjective stories and network narratives' in *The Way Hollywood Tells It. Story and Style in Modern Movies*, Berkeley and Los Angeles: University of California Press, pp. 72–103.

Bordwell, David, Janet Staiger and Kristen Thompson (1985), *The Classical Hollywood Cinema. Film Style and Mode of Production to 1960*, New York: Columbia University Press.

Bordwell, David and Noel Carroll (1996), *Post Theory: Reconstructing Film Studies*, Madison: University of Wisconsin Press.

Bordwell, David and Kristen Thompson (2001), *Film Art*, 6th edn, New York: McGraw Hill.

Bordwell, David and Kristen Thompson (2003), *Film History. An Introduction*, 2nd edn, NewYork: McGraw Hill.

Bordwell, David and KristenThompson (2004), *Film Art. An Introduction*, 7th edn, New York: McGraw Hill.

Bourdieu, Pierre (1984), *Distinction: A Social Critique of the Judgement of Taste*, trans Richard Nice, Cambridge (MA): Harvard University Press.

Brooks, Xan (2002), 'Vanilla Sky' (review), *Sight and Sound* (February), pp. 52–3.

Buckland, Warren (2006), *Directed by Steven Spielberg. Poetics of the Contemporary Hollywood Blockbuster*, New York and London: Continuum.

Buckley, Christine A. (2002) 'Alejandro Amenábar's *Tesis*: art, commerce and renewal in Spanish Cinema', *Post-Script. Essays in Film and the Humanities*, 21:2 (Winter–Spring), pp. 1–15.

Buse, Peter, Núria Triana-Toribio and Andrew Willis (2004), 'Esto no es un juego, es *"Acción Mutante"*: the provocations of Álex de la Iglesia', *Journal of Iberian and Latin American Studies*, 10:1, pp. 9–22.

Caparrós Lera, José María (1999), *Historia crítica del cine español (desde 1897 hasta hoy)*, Barcelona: Ariel.

Caparrós Lera, José María (2004), *El cine del nuevo siglo (2001–2003)*, Madrid: Ediciones Rialp.

Caparrós Lera, José María (2007), *Historia del cine español*, Madrid: TandB Editores.

Casas, Quim (2004), 'Deseando morir', *Dirigido por*, 337 (September), pp. 24–5.

Castro, Antonio (1974), *El cine español en el banquillo*, Valencia`; Fernando Torres.

Chibnall, Steve (2000), *J. Lee Thompson*, Manchester: Manchester University Press.

Christie, Ian and Andrew Moor (eds) (2005), *The Cinema of Michael Powell. International Perspectives on an English Filmmaker*, London: British Film Institute.

Clover, Carol J. (1992), *Men, Women and Chainsaws: Gender in the Modern Horror Film*. London: BFI and Princeton (NJ): Princeton University Press.

Clover, Joshua (2004), *The Matrix*, London: BFI.

Collins, Jim (1993), 'Genericity in the nineties: eclectic irony and the new sincerity', in *Film Theory Goes to the Movies*, Jim Collins, Hilary Radner and Ava Preacher Collins (eds), London: Routledge, pp. 242–63.

Conrich, Ian. (2003), 'Mass media/mass murder: serial killer cinema and the modern violated body', in *Criminal Visions: Media Representations of Crime and Justice*, Paul Mason (ed.), Portland (OR): Willand Publishing, pp. 156–71.

Cook, Pam (1999), 'No fixed address: the women's picture from *Outrage* to *Blue Steel*', in *Contemporary Hollywood Cinema*, Steve Neale and Murray Smith (eds), London and New York: Routledge, pp. 229–46.

Cook, Pam (2007), *The Cinema Book*, 3rd edn, London: BFI.

Corner, John (1996), *The Art of Record: A Critical Introduction to Documentary*, Manchester: Manchester University Press.

Corner, John (1998), *Studying Media: Problems of Theory and Method*, Edinburgh: Edinburgh University Press.

Corner, John (1999), *Critical Ideas in Television Studies*. Oxford: Oxford University Press.

Corrigan, Timothy (1991), *A Cinema Without Walls: Movies and Culture After Vietnam*, New Brunswick (NJ): Rutgers University Press.

Costa, Jordi and Darío Adanti (2009), *Mis problemas con Amenábar*, Madrid: Glénat.

Coupland, Douglas (1991), *Generation X. Tales for an Accelerated Culture*, New York: St Martin's Press.

Creed, Barbara (1996), 'The *Crash* debate: anal wounds, metallic kisses', *Screen*, 39, pp. 175–9.

Cueto, Roberto (coord.) (1998), *Los desarraigados en el cine español*, Gijón: Festival Internacional de Cine de Gijón.

D'Lugo, Marvin (1997), *Guide to the Cinema of Spain*, Westport: Greenwood Press.

D'Lugo, Marvin (2002a), 'Recent Spanish cinema in national and global contexts', *Post-Script. Essays in Film and the Humanities* 21:2 (Winter–Spring), 21: 2, pp. 1–13.

D'Lugo Marvin (2002b), 'The geopolitical aesthetic in recent Spanish cinema', *Post-Script. Essays in Film and the Humanities*, 21:2 Winter–Spring), pp. 14–23.

D'Lugo, Marvin (2006), *Pedro Almodóvar*, Urbana and Chicago: University of Illinois Press.

Davies, Ann (2005), 'Can the contemporary crime thriller be Spanish?', *Studies in European Cinema*, 2:3, pp. 173–83.

Deakin, Michael (2007), *Hypatia of Alexandria, Mathematician and Martyr*, Amherst (NY): Prometheus Books.

Denzin, Norman (1995). *The Cinematic Society. The Voyeur's Gaze*, London: Sage.

Derry, Charles (1988), *The Suspense Thriller. Films in the Shadow of Alfred Hitchcock*, Jefferson (NC): McFarland Press.

Díez Puertas, Emeterio (2002), *El montaje del Franquismo, La política cinematográfica de las fuerzas sublevadas*, Barcelona: Laertes.

Doane, Mary Ann (1982), 'Film and the masquerade: theorising the female spectator', *Screen*, 23 3–4, (September/October), pp. 74–87.

Dzielska, Maria (1995), *Hypatia of Alexandria*, trans F. Lytra, Cambridge (MA): Harvard University Press.

Elley, Derek (1984), *The Epic Film: Myth and History*, London: Routledge & Keegan Paul.

Elsaesser, Thomas (2008), 'The mind-game film' in *Puzzle Films: Complex Storytelling in Contemporary Cinema*, Warren Buckland (ed.), Oxford: Blackwell, pp. 14–41.

Esquirol, Meritxell and Josep Luis Fecé (2001), 'Un freak en el parque de atracciones: Torrente, el brazo tonto de la ley', *Archivos de la Filmoteca*, 39 (October), pp. 27–39.

Evans, Peter William (1996), *Women on the Verge of a Nervous Breakdown*, London: BFI.

Faulkner, Sally (2004a), 'The question of authenticity: Camus's film adaptation of Cela's *La colmena*', *Studies in Hispanic Cinemas*, 1:2, pp. 17–25.

Faulkner, Sally (2004b), *Literary Adaptations in Spanish Cinema*, London: Tamesis.

Forrest, Jennifer and Leonard R. Koos (2002), *Dead Ringers. The Remake in Theory and Practice*, Albany: SUNY Press.

Fouz-Hernández, Santiago (2000), '¿Generación X? Spanish urban youth culture at the end of the century in Mañas/Armendáriz's *Historias del Kronen*', *Romance Studies*, 18:1, pp. 83–98.

Fouz-Hernández, Santiago and Alfredo Martínez-Expósito (2007), *Live Flesh. The Male Body in Contemporary Spanish Cinema*, London: I.B. Tauris.

Freeland, Cynthia A. (1995), 'Realist horror', in *Philosophy and Film*, C.A. Freeland and T.E. Wartenberg (eds), New York: Routledge, pp. 126–42.

Gafo, Javier (1999), *Eutanasia y ayuda al suicidio*, Bilbao, Desclée de Brouwer.

García Abadillo, Casimiro (2005), *La venganza*, Madrid: La Esfera de los libros.

García Abadillo, Casimiro (2009), *Titadyn*, Madrid: La Esfera de los libros.

García Fernández, Emilio C. (1985), *Historia ilustrada del cine español*, Barcelona: Planeta.

García Fernández, Emilio C. (2002), *El cine español entre 1896 y 1939. Historia, industria, filmografía y documentos*, Barcelona: Ariel Cine.

Garnett, Daisy (2005), 'Undercover operative', *Telegraph Magazine*, 25 January, pp. 29–33.

Gascó, Daniel and Mario Vitale (2005), 'Alejandro Amenábar. Los laberintos del demiurgo', in *Cortos pero intensos. Las películas breves de los cineastas españoles*, Pedro Medina and Luis. M. González (eds), 35 Festival de Cine de Alcalá de Henares–Comunidad de Madrid, pp. 30–7.

Generelo, Jesús (2004), ' De Amenábar a Alejandro. La verdad desde dentro', *Zero*, 67 (September), pp. 74–81.

Genette, Gérard (1982), *Palimpsests. Literature in the Second Degree*, Paris. Seuil.

Gledhill, Christine (2000), 'Rethinking genre', *Reinventing Film Studies*, in Christine Gledhill and Linda Williams (eds), London: Arnold, pp. 221–43.

Gómez, María Asunción and Santiago Juan-Navarro (2002), *Alejandro Amenábar*, Paris: Cinéastes, Col. Caméra Incognita.

Gottlieb, Sidney and Christopher Brookehouse (eds) (2002), *Framing Hitchcock, Selected Essays from The Hitchcock Annual*, Detroit (MI): Wayne State University Press.

Grant, Barry Keith (1999), 'Rich and Strange: The yuppie horror film', in *Contemporary Hollywood Cinema*, Steve Neale and Murray Smith (eds), London: Routledge, pp. 280–93.

Grant, Catherine (2000), 'www.auteur.com', *Screen*, 41:1 (Spring), pp 101–8.

Gubern, Román (1981), *La censura. Función política y ordenamiento jurídico bajo el franquismo 1936–1975*, Barcelona: Península.

Gubern, Román (1989), *La imagen pornográfica y otras perversiones ópticas*, Madrid: Akal.

Gubern, Román et al. (1995), *Historia del cine español*, Madrid: Cátedra.

Gunning, Tom (1986/2000), 'The cinema of attractions: early film, its spectator and the avant garde', in *The Film Studies Reader*, Joanne Hollows, Peter Hutchings, Mark Jancovich (eds), London: Arnold, pp. 161–5.

Gubern, Román (2004), *Patologías de la imagen*, Barcelona: Anagrama.

Hayward, Susan (2006), *Cinema Studies. The Key Concepts*, 3rd edn, London: Routledge.

Herbert, Daniel (2006), 'Sky's the limit. Transnationality and identity in *Abre los ojos* and *Vanilla Sky*', *Film Quarterly*, 60:1, pp. 28–38.

Heredero, Carlos F. (1997), *Espejo de miradas: Entrevistas con nuevos directores del cine español de los años noventa*, Madrid: Festival de Cine de Alcalá de Henares.

Heredero, Carlos F. (1999a), 'Cine español. Nueva generación', *Dirigido por* (April), pp. 50–67.

Heredero, Carlos F. (1999b), *20 nuevos directores del cine español*, Madrid: Alianza Editorial.

Heredero, Carlos F. and Antonio Santamarina (2002), *Semillas de futuro: Cine español 1990–2001*, Madrid: Sociedad Estatal España Nuevo Milenio.

Heredero, Carlos F. and José Enrique Monterde (eds) (2003), *Los nuevos cines en España. Ilusiones y desencantos de los años sesenta*, Valencia: Institut Valencià de Cinematografia.

Higson, Andrew (2000), 'The limiting imagination of national cinema' in *Cinema and Nation*, M. Hjort and S. Mackenzie (eds), London: Routledge, pp. 63–73.

Holmes, Diana and Robert Ingram (1998), *François Truffaut*, French Film Directors, Manchester: Manchester University Press.

Hopewell, John (1986), *Out of the Past: Spanish Cinema after Franco*, London: BFI.

Hopewell, John (1989), *El cine español después de Franco*, Madrid: El Arquero.

Horton, Andrew and Stuart Y. McDougal (eds) (1998), *Play It Again Sam. Retakes on Remakes*, Berkeley: University of California Press.

Jordan, Barry (1999), 'Refiguring the past in the post-Franco fiction film: Fernando Trueba's *Belle Epoque*', in *Sound on Vision, Studies in Spanish Cinema*, Special Issue of the *Bulletin of Hispanic Studies*, 76:1, Robin Fiddian and Ian Michael (eds) (Glasgow), pp. 139–56.

Jordan, Barry (2000a), 'How Spanish is it? Spanish cinema and national identity', in *Contemporary Spanish Cultural Studies*, Barry Jordan and Rikki Morgan-Tamosunas (eds), London: Arnold, pp. 68–78.

Jordan, Barry (2000b), 'The Spanish film industry in the 1980s and 1990s', in *Contemporary Spanish Cultural Studies*, Barry Jordan and Rikki Morgan-Tamosunas (eds), London: Arnold, pp. 179–92.

Jordan, Barry (2003a), 'Revisiting the "comedia sexy ibérica": *No desearás al vecino del quinto* (Ramón Fernández, 1971)', *International Journal of Iberian Studies*, 15: 3, pp. 167–86.

Jordan, Barry (2003b), 'Spain's new cinema of the 1990s: Santiago Segura and the Torrente phenomenon', *New Cinemas: Journal of Contemporary Film*, 1:3, pp. 191–207.

Jordan, Barry (2007), 'Review article: Nancy Berthier (ed.), *Le cinéma d'Alejandro Amenábar*', *Studies in Hispanic Cinemas*, 4:3, pp. 199–212.

Jordan, Barry and Mark Allinson (2005), *Spanish Cinema. A Student's Guide*, London: Hodder Arnold.

Jordan, Barry and Rikki Morgan-Tamosunas (1998), *Contemporary Spanish Cinema*, Manchester: Manchester University Press.

Kael, Pauline (1974), *The Citizen Kane Book*, New York: Bantam.

Katz, Steven D. (1991), *Film Directing. Shot by Shot. Visualising from Concept to Screen*, Stoneham (MA): Michael Wiese Productions.

Kawin, Bruce (1992), *How Movies Work*, Berkeley, Los Angeles and London: University of California Press.

Kerekes, David and David Slater (1995), *Killing for Culture: An Illustrated History of the Death Film from Mondo to Snuff*, London: Creation Books.

Kinder, Marsha (1983), 'The children of Franco in the new Spanish cinema', *Quarterly Review of Film Studies*, 8:2, pp. 57–76.

Kinder, Marsha (1987), 'Pleasure and the new Spanish mentality: a conversation with Pedro Almodóvar', *Film Quarterly*, 41:1, pp. 33–44.

Kinder, Marsha (1993), *Blood Cinema. The Reconstruction of National Identity*, Berkeley: University of California Press.

Kinder, Marsha (ed.) (1997), *Refiguring Spain: Cinema / Media / Representation*, Durham (NC) and London: Duke University Press.

King, Geoff (2002), *New Hollywood Cinema. An Introduction*, London: I.B. Tauris.

Lázaro Reboll, Antonio and Andrew Willis (eds), *Spanish Popular Cinema*, Manchester: Manchester University Press.

Leitch, Thomas M. (2003), 'Twelve fallacies in contemporary adaptation theory', *Criticism*, 45:2 (Spring), pp. 149–71.

Leitch, Thomas M. (2006), 'How to steal from Hitchcock', in *After Hitchcock. Influence, Imitation and Intertextuality*, David Boyd and R. Barton Palmer (eds), Austin: University of Texas Press, pp. 251–70.

Lev, Leora (2001), 'Returns of the repressed: memory, oblivion and abjection in Spanish cinema', *Revista de Estudios Hispánicos*, 35, pp. 165–78.

López García, José Luis (2005), *El nuevo cine español de Almodóvar a Amenábar*, Madrid: Notorious Ediciones.

Losilla, Carlos (1989). 'Legislación, industria y escritura' in *Escritos sobre el cine espanol 1973–1987*, J.A. Hurtado and F. Picó (eds), Valencia: Filmoteca de la Generalitat Valenciana, pp. 39–43.

Losilla, Carlos (2005), 'Contra ese cine español. Panorama general al incio de un nuevo siglo', *Archivos de la Filmoteca*, 49 (February), pp. 124–45

Maltby, Richard (1995), *Hollywood Cinema*, Oxford: Blackwell (2nd edn. 2003).

Mañas, José Angel (1994), *Historias del Kronen*, Barcelona: Destino.

Maneiro, Ramona (2005), *Querido Ramón. Un testimonio de amor*, Temas de Hoy, Madrid: Planeta.

Maule, Rosanna (2000), 'Death and reflexivity in Alejandro Amenábar's *Tesis*', *Torre de Papel*, 10:1 (Spring), pp. 1–11.

Mazdon, Lucy (2000), *Encore Hollywood. Remaking French Cinema*, London: BFI.

Mérida de San Román, Pablo (2002), *El cine español Larousse*, Barcelona: Spes Editorial.

Mira, Alberto (ed.) (2005), *The Cinema of Spain and Portugal*, London: Wallflower Press.

Monterde, José Enrique (1993), *Veinte años de cine español (1973–1992). Un cine bajo la paradoja* Barcelona: Paidós.

Monterde. José Enrique (1995) ' El cine de la autarquía (1939–1950)' in *Historia del cine español*, Román Gubern et al., Madrid: Cátedra, pp. 181–238.

Moreiras Menor, Cristina (2002), *Cultura herida: Literatura y cine en la España democrática*. Madrid: Ediciones Libertarias.

Mulvey, Laura (1975), 'Visual pleasure and narrative cinema', *Screen*, 16 3, pp. 6–18, reprinted in Laura Mulvey (1989), *Visual and Other Pleasures*, Houndmills, Basingstoke: Macmillan, pp. 14–28.

Neale, Steve (1993), 'Melo talk: On the meaning and use of the term "melodrama' in the American trade press', *The Velvet Light Trap*, 32 (Fall), pp. 66–89.

Neale, Steve (2000), *Genre and Hollywood*, London: Routledge.

Neale, Steve (2007), 'The suspense thriller', in *The Cinema Book*, 3rd edn. Pam Cook (ed.), London: BFI, pp. 286–7.

Palacio, Manuel and Guido Cortell (1997), '*Tesis*', in *Antología crítica del cine español, 1906–1995. Flor en la sombra*, Julio Pérez-Perucha (ed.), Madrid: Cátedra, pp. 964–6.

Palacios, Jesús (1998), 'Ni rebeldes, ni causa: Los años noventa', in *Los desarraigados en el cine español*, Roberto Cueto (ed.), Gijón: Festival Internacional Cine de Gijón, pp. 113–40.

Payán, Miguel Juan (2001), *El cine español actual*, Madrid: Ediciones JC.

Peláez, J.V. and J.C. Rueda (eds) (2002), *Ver Cine. Los públicos cinematográficos en el siglo XX*, Madrid: Ediciones Rialp.

Pérez Perucha, Julio (1995), 'Narración de un aciago destino (1896–1930)', in R. Gubern et al., *Historia del cine español*, Madrid: Cátedra, pp. 19–121.

Pérez Perucha, Julio (ed.) (1997), *Antología crítica del cine español, 1906–1995. Flor en la sombra*. Madrid: Cátedra.

Perren, Alisa (2001), 'Sex, lies and marketing. Miramax and the development of the quality indie blockbuster', *Film Quarterly*, 55:2, pp. 30–38.

Perriam, Chris (2003), *Stars and Masculinities in Spanish Cinema*, Oxford: Oxford University Press.

Perriam, Chris (2004), 'Alejandro Amenábar's *Abre los ojos* / Open your eyes (1997)', in *Spanish Popular Cinema*, Antonio Lázaro Reboll and Andrew Willis (eds), Manchester: Manchester University Press, pp. 209–21.

Pinedo, Isabel (1996), 'Recreational terror: postmodern elements in the contemporary horror film', *Journal of Film and Video*, 48:1–2, pp. 17–31.

Pinedo, Isabel (1997), *Recreational Terror: Women and the Pleasures of Horror Film Viewing*, Albany: State University of New York.

Powrie, Phil and Keith Reader (2002), *French Cinema: A Student's Guide*, London: Arnold.

Puigdoménech, Jordi (2007), *Treinta años de cine español en democracia (1977–2007)*, Madrid: Ediciones JC.

Quintana, Angel (2005), 'Modelos realistas en un tiempo de emergencia en lo político', *Archivos de la Filmoteca*, 49 (February), pp. 10–31.

Rabalska, Carmen (1999), 'A dark desire for the grotesque', in *Spanish Cinema: Calling the Shots*, Rob Rix and R. Rodríguez-Saona (eds), Leeds: Leeds Iberian Papers, pp. 91–111.

Radner, Hilary (1999), 'New Hollywood's new women. Murder in mind – Sarah and Margie', in *Contemporary Hollywood Cinema*, Steve Neale and Murray Smith (eds), London: Routledge, pp. 247–62.

Rodríguez-Marchante, Oti (2002), *Amenábar. Vocación de intriga*, Madrid: Páginas de Espuma.

Rodríguez-Ortega, Vicente (2008), 'Trailing the Spanish auteur: Almodóvar's, Amenábar's and Álex de la Iglesia's generic routes in the US market', in *Contemporary Spanish Cinema and Genre*, Jay Beck and Vicente Rodríguez-Ortega, Manchester: Manchester University Press, pp. 44–64.

Ross, Christopher (2002), *Contemporary Spain. A Handbook*, 2nd edn, London and New York: Hodder and Stoughton.

Russell, Dominique (2006), 'Sounds like horror: Alejandro Amenábar's thesis on audio-visual violence', *Canadian Journal of Film Studies*, 15:2 (Fall), pp. 81–95.

Rycroft, Charles (1968), *A Critical Dictionary of Psychoanalysis*. London: Penguin.

Sampedro, Ramón (1996/2004), *Cartas desde el infierno*, Madrid: Planeta.

Sampedro, Ramón (1998), *Cando eu caia*, A Coruña: Xerais. Republished in Spanish as *Cuando yo caiga, Poemas de Ramón Sampedro*, Madrid: Ediciones Martínez Roca, 2004.

Sánchez-Navarro, Jordi (2005), *Freaks en acción. Álex de la Iglesia o el cine como fuga*, Madrid: Calamar Ediciones.

Sarris, Andrew (1968), *The American Cinema: Directions and Directors, 1929–1968*, New York: Dutton.

Schneider, Steven J. (2003), 'Murder as art / the art of murder: aestheticising violence in modern cinematic horror', in *Dark Thoughts: Philosophic Reflections on Cinematic Horror*, S. J. Schneider and D. Shaw (eds), Lanham: Scarecrow Press, pp. 174–97.

Sconce, Jeffrey (1993), 'Spectacles of death: identification, reflexivity and contemporary horror', *Film Theory Goes to the Movies*, Jim Collins et al. (eds), London: Routledge, pp. 103–19.

Sconce, Jeffrey (1995), 'Trashing the academy: taste, excess and an emerging politics of cinematic style', *Screen*, 36:4, pp. 371–93.

Sconce, Jeffrey (2006), 'Smart cinema', in *Contemporary American Cinema*, Linda Ruth Williams and Michael Hammond (eds), Maidenhead: Open University Press, pp. 429–39.

Seguin, Jean Claude (1995), *Historia del cine español*, Madrid: Acento.

Sempere, Antonio (2000), *Alejandro Amenábar. Cine en las venas*, Madrid: Ediciones Nuer.

Sempere, Antonio (2004), *Amenábar, Amenábar*, Alicante: Editorial Club Universitario.

Shermer, Michael B. (2002), 'Stephen Jay Gould as historian of science and scientific historian, popular scientist and scientific populariser', *Social Studies of Science*, 32:4 (August), 489–525.

Sinyard, Neil (2000), *Jack Clayton*, British Film Makers, Manchester: Manchester University Press.

Smith, Paul Julian (1993), 'Almodóvar's *Tacones lejanos* (High Heels): *Imitation of Life*', *Donaire*, 1 (September), pp. 44–7.

Smith, Paul Julian (1996), 'Kika: vision machine' in *Vision Machines, Cinema, Literature and Sexuality in Spain and Cuba 1983–93*, London and New York: Verso, pp. 37–55.

Smith, Paul Julian (2000a), *Desire Unlimited. The Cinema of Pedro Almodovar*, 2nd edn, London: Verso.

Smith, Paul Julian (2000b), *The Moderns: Time, Space and Subjectivity in Contemporary Spanish Culture*, Oxford: Oxford University Press.

Smith, Paul Julian (2001), 'The Others', *Sight and Sound*, 11:11, p. 54.

Smith, Paul Julian (2003), *Contemporary Spanish Culture: TV, Fashion, Art and Film*, Cambridge: Polity.

Smith, Paul Julian (2004), 'High Anxiety: *Abre los ojos / Vanilla Sky*', *Journal of Romance Studies*, 4:1 (Spring), pp. 91–102.

Smith, Paul Julian (2006), 'Towards the Spanish youth movie: *Historias del Kronen*', in *Spanish Visual Culture. Cinema, Television, Internet*, Manchester: Manchester University Press, pp. 75–90.

Stam, Robert (2000/2007), *Film Theory. An Introduction*, Oxford: Blackwell.

Stone, Rob (2002), *Spanish Cinema*, London: Longman.

Stone, Rob (2007), *Julio Medem*, Spanish and Latin American Filmmakers, Manchester: Manchester University Press.

Tasker, Yvonne (2002), *The Silence of the Lambs*, London: BFI.

Terassa, Jacques (2007), 'Les écrans noirs d'Alejandro Amenábar: des voix en quête d'images', in *Le cinéma d'Alejandro Amenábar*, Nancy Berthier (ed.), Toulouse: Presses Universitaires du Mirai, pp. 27–42.

Thompson, Kristen (1985), *Exporting Entertainment. America in the World Film Market 1907–1934*, London: BFI.

Thompson, Kristen (1999/2001), *Storytelling in the New Hollywood. Understanding Classical Narrative Technique*, Cambridge (MA) and London: Harvard University Press.

Torreiro, Casimiro (2009). 'Una dictadura liberal (1962–1969)' and 'Del tardofranquismo a la democracia (1969–1982)', in *Historia del cine español, 1995/2009*, 6th edn, Gubern et al., Madrid: Cátedra, pp. 295–340 and pp. 341–97.

Torres, Antonio M. (1994/96), *Diccionario Espasa. Cine español*, 2nd edn, Madrid, Espasa Calpe.

Triana-Toribio, Núria (2000), 'A punk called Pedro: La movida in the films of Pedro Almodóvar', in *Contemporary Spanish Cultural Studies*, Barry Jordan and Rikki Morgan-Tamosunas (eds), London: Arnold, pp. 274–82.

Triana-Toribio, Núria (2003), *Spanish National Cinema*. London: Routledge.

Triana-Toribio, Núria (2004), 'The Spanish popular auteur. Álex de la Iglesia as polemical tool', *New Cinemas: Journal of Contemporary* Film, 2:3, pp. 139–48.

Triana-Toribio, Núria (2008), 'Auteurism and commerce in contemporary Spanish cinema: *directores mediáticos*', *Screen*, 49.3 (Autumn), pp. 259–76.

Truffaut, François (1967), *Hitchcock*, New York: Simon and Shuster.

Tudor, Andrew (1997), 'Why horror? the peculiar pleasures of a popular genre', *Cultural Studies*, 11:3, pp. 443–63.

Tudor, Andrew (2002), 'From paranoia to postmodernism? The horror movie in late modern society', in *Genre and Contemporary Hollywood*, Steve Neale (ed.), London: British Film Institute, pp. 105–15.

Ubeda-Portugués, Alberto (2001), *José Luis Cuerda. Ética de un corredor de fondo*, Madrid: Sociedad de Autores y Editores.

Urdacci, Alfredo (2005), *Días de ruido y furia. La televisión que me tocó vivir*, Barcelona: Random House Mondadori.

Vera, Cecilia (2002), *Cómo hacer cine 2. El día de la bestia, de Álex de la Iglesia*, Madrid: Editorial Fundamentos, Colección Arte.

Vera, Cecilia (2003), *Cómo hacer cine 1. Tesis, de Alejandro Amenábar*, 2nd edn, Madrid: Editorial Fundamentos, Colección Arte.

Vera, Cecilia (2005), *Cómo hacer cine 5. La madre muerta, de Juanma Bajo Ulloa*, Madrid: Editorial Fundamentos, Colección Arte.

Verevis, Constantine (2004), 'Remaking film', *Film Studies*, 4 (Summer), pp. 87–102.

Verevis, Constantine (2006), *Film Remakes*, Edinburgh: Edinburgh University Press.

Vidal, Núria (1988), *El cine de Pedro Almodóvar*, Barcelona: Destino.

Vincendeau, Ginette (ed.) (1995), *Encyclopedia of European Cinema*, London: Routledge.

Wayne, Mike (2002). *The Politics of Contemporary European Cinema: Histories, Borders, Diasporas*. Bristol: Intellect.

White, Anne (2003), 'Seeing double? The remaking of Alejandro Amenábar's *Abre los ojos* as Cameron Crowe's *Vanilla Sky*', *International Journal of Iberian Studies*, 15:3, pp. 187–96.

Whitehead, Mark (2003), *Slasher Movies*, 2nd edn, Herts: Cox and Wyman.

Williams, Linda (1984), 'When the woman looks', in *Re-Visions. Essays in Feminist Film Criticism*, M.A. Doane, P. Mellencamp and L. Williams (eds), Frederick, (MD): The American Film Institute / University Publications of America, pp. 83–99.

Williams, Linda (2005), *The Erotic Thriller in Contemporary Cinema*, Edinburgh: Edinburgh University Press.

Willis, Andrew (2004), 'From the margins to the mainstream: trends in recent Spanish horror cinema', in *Spanish Popular Cinema*, Antonio Lázaro Reboll and Andrew Willis (eds), Manchester: Manchester University Press, pp. 237–49.

Wilson, Vicky (2005), 'The Sea Inside', *Sight and Sound*, 3 (March), pp 72–3.

Wood, Robin (1989/2002), *Hitchcock's Films Revisited*. revised edn, New York: Columbia University Press.

Zatlin, Phyllis (2001), 'You are being watched: metafilmic devices in *Tesis*', *Letras Peninsulares*, 14:2–3 (Fall), pp. 243–54.

Zunzunegui, Santos (2002), *Historias de España: ¿De qué hablamos cuando hablamos de cine español?*, Valencia: Institut Valencià de Cinematografia.

Newspaper and magazine articles

Amenábar, Alejandro, '*Abre los ojos*: Un día cualquiera de rodaje', *El Mundo* (*Sección Cinelandia*) (27 December 1997), p. 10.

'Amenábar sale del closet', *El Mundo* (15 September 2004), p. 38.

'Antonio Castro, Entrevista: el cine español de ahora es absolutamente inútil'. *Interviú* (17 March 1997), pp. 90–1.

Belategui, Oscar, *El Correo Español* (Vizcaya) (12 December 1997), *Sección Fin de Semana*, p. 1.

Bonet Mojica, Lluís. 'Nada ni nadie es lo que parece', *La Vanguardia-Barcelona* (24 December 1997), p. 40.

Bou, Núria and Xavier Pérez, 'La fórmula de l'èxit', *Avui–Barcelona* (21 April 1996), p. 8.

Corral, Amaya, 'Amenábar. La tesis del debutante', *Antena Semanal–Madrid* (21 April 1996), p. 37.

Del Barrio, Ana and Luis Pérez, 'De estudiante a director de cine', *El Mundo, Suplemento* (27 September 1995), pp. 3–4.

Del Teso, Begoña, 'Licenciado, aún no doctor', *El Diario Vasco* (15 April 1996), p. 86.

Del Toro, Suso, 'Entrevista', *El País Semanal* (22 August 2004), pp. 12–14.

'Entrevista con Alejandro Amenábar', *Cinemanía*, 118 (2004), 9.

Fernández Santos, Angel, 'Celuloide en las venas', *El País–Madrid* (21 December 1997), p. 39.

García, Rocío, 'Julio Medem empieza de cero', *El País* (27 June 2008), p. 38.

Gilbey, Ryan, 'That's so Amenábar', *Independent on Sunday* (22 February 2005), p. 13.

Heredero, Carlos F., 'La "Tesis" de Alejandro Amenábar', *Diario 16* (17 February 1996), p. 32

Hermoso, Borja, 'Muertes en directo para una arriesgada ópera prima', *El Mundo* (10 April 1996), p. 81

Leyra, Paloma, 'Alejandro Amenábar', *El Semanal* (18 February 1996), p. 72.

Lamata, Susana López, 'Ahora me miran con ojo crítico', *Cambio 16* (23 June 1997), pp. 80–1.

McCarthy, Todd, '*Ágora*', *Variety* (18 May 2009), p. 15.

'*Mar adentro*: el cine de Amenábar', Suplemento Especial (September 2004), 108, *Cinemanía*, 16 pp.

Noxon, Christopher, 'The Roman Empire rises again', *Los Angeles Times* (23 April 2000), p. 5.

Pita, Elena, 'Entrevista a Alejandro Amenábar', *La Revista de El Mundo*, Madrid (16 February 1997), pp. 15–16.

Polo, Miguel, 'Entrevista a Alejandro Amenábar', *Interviú*, Madrid (17 February, 1997), pp. 43–4.

Ponga, Paula, 'El más listo de la clase: Alejandro Amenábar', *Fotogramas*, 1859 (December 1997), p. 118.

Ponga, Paula, 'Amenábar nos cuenta su película mas íntima', *Fotogramas*, 1931 (September 2004), pp. 80–1.

Rodríguez, Hilario J., 'Los vivos y los muertos', *Dirigido por*, 304 (September 2001), pp. 38–41.

Rodríguez-Marchante, Enrique, 'Tesis: Hay películas que matan', *ABC*, Madrid (13 April 1996), p. 86.

Rubio, Teresa, 'Los Goya reactivan la carrera de la película *Tesis*', *El Periódico* (29 January 1997), p. 57.

Ruiz, Rafael and Gregorio Belinchón, '20 personajes para 20 años de Goyas', *El País Semanal*, 1531 (29 January 2006), p. 47.

Smith, Sean, 'Finding the story inside', *Newsweek* (27 December 2004–3 January 2005), pp. 68–70.

Internet sources

Anon., 'Amenábar inicia el lunes el rodaje de *Ágora*', www.elmundo.es/elmundo/2008/03/13/cultura/1205407686.html. Accesed 30 May 2010.

Anon., 'El film más spielbergiano de Alejandro Amenábar', www. axxon.com.ar/not/142/c-1420040.htm. Accessed 10 December 2005.

Anon., "Amenábar: '*Ágora* iba a recaer en Hollywood y al final fue Telecinco la que la produjo', www. formulatv.com/1,20090517,11398,1.html. Accessed 30 May 2010.

Anon., 'El crítico Jordi Costa critica duramente a Alejandro Amenábar en su última obra', www.abc.es/20091006/cultura-cine/critico-jordi-costa-critica-20091006226.html. Accessed 10 January 2010.

Anon., 'Ovación a Amenábar en el esperado estreno de *Ágora*', 17 May 2009, www.culturaclasica.com/?q=node/2825. Accessed 28 May 2010.

Arenas, José, 'Alejandro Amenábar: 'No he querido mostrar la violencia con tinte épico sino como algo feo y sucio', www.abc.es/20091004/espectaculos-cine-querido-mostrar-violencia-tinte-20091004 html. Accessed 2 June 2010.

Arrospide, Amparo, 'Reflexión sobre la película de Alejandro Amenábar', www.El Digoras.com. Accessed 6 June 2006.

Balfour, Brad (2005), interview with Amenábar in *G 21* magazine, www.g21.net/nystate37.htm Accessed 24 February 2006.

Belinchón, Gregorio, 'Entrevista con Alejandro Amenábar *Director de cine* "Empecé haciendo una de marcianos y acabé rodando una de romanos"', www.elpais.com/articulo/cultura/Empece/haciendo/marcianos/acabe/rodando/romanos/elpepicul/20091003elpepicul_1/Tes. Accessed 28 May 2010.

Bermejo, Alberto, 'Espectáculo y conocimiento', www.elmundo.es/metropoli/2009/10/14/cine/1255541561.html. Accessed 29 May 2010.

Boyero, Carlos, 'Grandioso proyecto con resultado notable', www.elpais.com/articulo/cultura/Grandioso/proyecto/resultado/notable/elpepicu_/20090518elpepicul_7/Tes. Accessed 30 May 2010.

Boyero, Carlos, 'Croissant en la Croisette', at Videogalería,www.elpais.com/multigalerias/Croissant_Croisette/20090514elpepucul_1/Zes. Accessed 30 May 2010.

Bradshaw, Peter, 'Vanilla Sky', *The Guardian*, 25 January 2002, www.guardian.co.uk/film/2002/jan/25/culture.reviews/ Accessed 22 September 2009.

Brown, Todd, 'TIFF 09: *Ágora* Review', twitchfilm.net/reviews/2009/09/cannes-09–Ágora-review.php. Accessed 30 May 2010.

Brusat, Frederic and Mary, http://spiritualityandpractice.com/films/films.php?id=8486. Accessed 30 May 2010.

Clavell, Marius, 'A propósito de *Mar adentro*', *La Vanguardia* (19 February 2005), reproduced at www.condignidad.org/Actor-Mar-adentro.html. Accessed 22.07.08.

Crowe, Cameron, '"So lonely I could cry". How Elvis inspired my new movie *Vanilla Sky*', *The Guardian*, 11 January 2002, www.guardian.co.uk/film/2002/jan/11/artsfeatures2/. Accessed 22 July 2009.

Deakin, Michael A. B. (1995), 'The primary sources for the life and work of Hypatia of Alexandria', History of Mathematics Paper 63, Mathematics Department, Monash University, Clayton 3168, Australia, www.polyamory.org/~howard/Hypatia/primary-sources.html. Accessed 10 July 2010.

Deakin Michael, 'Ockham's Razor', Radio National Transcripts, www.abc.net.au/rn/science/ockham/or030897.htm. Accessed 23 July 2008.

EFE, 'Amenábar muestra su "viaje de exploración al pasado"', www.abc.es/hemeroteca/historico-17–05–2009/ab. Accessed 30 May 2010.

Eig, Jonathan, 'A beautiful mind (fuck): Hollywood structures of identity', *Jump Cut*, 46: 2003, www.ejumpcut.org/archive/jc46.2003/eig.mind films/index.html. Accessed 8 December 2005.

'Evolución del cine español 1996–2003' (2003), source: ICAA: www.mcu.es/cinel. Accessed 9 December 2005.

Forum for an Independent Life, http://es.groups.yahoo.com/group/vidaindependiente/. Accessed 22 July 2008.

Fuchs, Cynthia, Interview with Amenábar, www.popmatters.com/film/interviews/amenabar-alejandro.shtml. Accessed 13 July 2006.

Fuchs, Cynthia, Review of *The Others*, www.popmatters.com/film/reviews/o/others.shtml. Accessed 13 February 2006.

García, Rocío, 'Triple Apuesta', *El País Semanal*, 1479, reproduced at http://maradentro.splinder.com/2005. Accessed 22 July 2008.

Gay, Nacho, 'La superproducción de Telecinco en el aire: '*Ágora*'no encuentra distribuidor en EEUU', www.elconfidencial.com/ocioytelevision/Ágora-problemas-distribucion-eeuu-20091008.html. Accessed 28 May 2010.

Goodridge, Mike, '*Ágora*', www.screendaily.com/reviews/cannes-reveiws-Ágora. Accessed 30 May 2010.

Hermoso, Borja, 'Contra los fundamentalismos' (18 May 2009), www.elpais.com/articulo/cultura/fundamentalismos. Accessed 30 May 2010.

Hills, Matt (2003), 'Whose postmodern horror? Alejandro Amenábar's *Tesis* (1996)', *Kinoeye* 3:5, www.kinoeye.org. Accessed 25 March 2004.

'Interview: Ghislain Barrois CEO of Telecinco Cinema: how to make quality films with commercial appeal, out of obligation', http://cineuropa.org/interview.aspx?lanf=edanddocumentID=111618. Accessed 28 May 2010.

Jackson, Neil (2003), 'The cultural construction of snuff', *Kinoeye*, 3:5 (May), at www.kinoeye.org. Accessed 25 March 2004.

Jerónimo, José Martín, 'Una sentimental apología de la eutanasia', http://aramo.wordpress/com/2007/12/06/mar-adentro/ Accessed 12 July 2008.

La Caze, Marguerite (2003), 'The violence of the spectacle. Alejandro Amenábar's *Tesis* (Thesis, 1996)', *Kinoeye*, 3:5, at www.kinoeye.org. Accessed 25 March 2004.

Landesman, Cosmo, '*Ágora*: a more thoughtful ancient-world epic', *The Sunday Times* (25 April 2010), http://entertainment.timesonline.co.uk/tol/arts_and_entertainment/film/film_reviews/article7103752.ece. Accessed 2 June 2010.

Lev, Leora (2000), '*Tesis* (critical essay)', *Critical Quarterly* 54:1, 34–8, at www.findarticles.com. Accessed 23 March 2004.

Linekin, Kim, Interview with Amenábar at The Toronto Film Festival 2004 www.ffwdweekly.com/Issues/2005/0303/film2.htm. Accessed 11 December 2005,

Múgica, Fernando, 'Los agujeros negros del 11–M. Una versión policial repleta de incongruencias', 23 April 2004, www.elmundo.es/elmundo/2004/04/19/enespecial/1082356558.html. Accessed 10 October 2010.

McCarthy, Todd '*Ágora*', *Variety*, www.variety.com/index.asp?layout=festivals andjump=reviewandreviewid=VE1117940282andcs=1. Accessed 30 May 2010.

McCarthy, Todd, '*Troy*', *Variety*, www.variety.com/review/VE1117923741.html?categoryid=31andcs=1andp=0. Accessed 2 June 2010.

Martínez, Luis 'Amenábar imparte una clase, larga y premiosa, de "astronomía emocional"', www.elmundo.es/elmundo/2009/05/17/cultura/1242564962.html. Accessed 30 May 2010.

O'Neill, Tim, '"*Ágora*" and Hypatia – Hollywood strikes again', http://armariummagnus.blogspot.com/2009/05/Ágora-and-hypatia-hollywood-strikes.html. Accessed 27 May 2010.

O'Neill, Tim, 'Hypatia and *Ágora* Redux', http://armariummagnus.blogspot.com/2010/05/hypatia-and-Ágora-redux.html. Accessed 27 May 2010.

Palleja, Tonia, 'Crítica', in www.labutaca.net/films/4/losotros.html. Accessed 20 May 2010.

Prisa.com: 'Especial *Los otros*', www.elpais.com/especiales/2001/losotros/portada.html. Accessed 22 July 2006.

Rodríguez, Mary Carmen, 'Lo Nuevo de Alejandro Amenábar', www.lashorasperdidas.com/index.php/2007/12/28/lo-nuevo-de-alejandro-amenabar/ Accessed 12 October 2009.

Rodríguez, Renée, 'Amenábar scares with silence', www.HispanicMagazine.com (September 2001) Accessed 22 July 2006.

Rodríguez-Arias, David (2006), 'Eutanasia: propuesta de definición', www.dilemmata.net/. Accessed 13 October 2006.

Rodrígez Ortega, Vicente (2005), '"Snuffing Hollywood": transmedia horror in *Tesis*' in *Senses of Cinema* (2005), www.sensesofcinema.com/contents/05/36/tesis.html. Accessed 10 October 2006.

Roig, Alex M., 'Los secretos de Los otros', *El País Semanal*, 2001, pp. 34–42, www.elpais.com/Especiales/2001/losotros/docs/otros/pdf. Accessed 15 October 2006.

Romañach, Javier (2005), 'Los sutiles errores del caso Sampedro', www.cuentayrazon.org/revista/pdf/135/Num135_009.pdf. Accessed 17 October 2006.

Sagan, Carl, 'Space topics: search for extraterrestrial intelligence. Is earth-life relevant? A rebuttal', www.planetary.org/explore/topics/search_for_life/seti/sagan2.htm. Accessed 26 May 2010.

Carl Sagan, 'Carl Sagan introduces the library at Alexandria', www.youtube.com/watch?v=OLlVnKOb4Mk. Accessed 25 May 2010.

Scott, A.O., 'Love among the togas and the intolerant', http://movies.nytimes.com/2010/05/28/movies/28Ágora.html. Accessed 3 June 2010.

Shone, Tom, 'Rachel Weisz on motherhood, movies and metaphysics', *The Sunday Times*, 11 April 2010, http://entertainment.timesonline.co.uk/tol/arts_and_entertainment/film/article7091467.ece. Accessed 3 June 2010.

Swart, Sharon and Pamela Mcclintock, 'US distribs take fresh look at *Ágora*', www.variety.com/article/VR1118010234.html?categoryid=1278andcs=1. Accessed 30 May 2010.

Torreiro, Mirito, http://www.fotogramas.es/Peliculas/Ágora/Critica/%28offset%29/. Accessed 30 May 2010.

Whitfield, Bryan J., 'The beauty of reasoning: a re-examination of Hypatia of Alexandria', *The Mathematics Educator*, 6:1, pp. 14–21, http://math.coe.uga.edu/tme/issues/vo6n1/4whitfield.pdf.

DVD/YouTube

Roberto Bodegas, *Condenado a vivir (La historia de Ramón Sampedro)* Barcelona: DVD Spain General Distributions, 2004: www.dvdspain.net.

'La pericial de explosivos: en el 11M no estalló Goma 2 eco', www.youtube.com/watch?v=VSDF0R9dfoI Accessed 10 October 2010.

Index

EU authorised representative for GPSR:
Easy Access System Europe, Mustamäe tee 50,
10621 Tallinn, Estonia
gpsr.requests@easproject.com

www.ingramcontent.com/pod-product-compliance
Ingram Content Group UK Ltd.
Pitfield, Milton Keynes, MK11 3LW, UK
UKHW020039170726
7214IPUK00036B/293